# ASIA
# 1992
# YEARBOOK

# In the four worlds of Motorola, one language is spoken.

Fifty years ago, Motorola was the brand name of our car radio.

Today, Motorola is a global electronics company at the leading edge of four technological arenas: communications, components, computing, control. These are the four worlds where electronic miracles will be happening throughout the 1990s, into the next millennium.

In these four arenas, we offer not only the highest quality products and services like semiconductors, computers, space communications, cellular telephones, pagers, two-way radios, data networks and engine controls—we offer our unshakeable belief in one simple, single overriding objective.

Total customer satisfaction.

And because we know our worlds so well, we can offer our customers limitless imagination in each, and incomparable synergy from all.

**Total customer satisfaction.**
That's the language we speak.

Ⓜ **MOTOROLA**

Ⓜ and Motorola are registered trademarks of Motorola, Inc. ©1990 Motorola, Inc.

# CREDIT LYONNAIS THE GREAT EUROPEAN BANK IN ASIA.

 **CREDIT LYONNAIS GROUP**

# FOREWORD
## ASIA YEARBOOK, 32nd EDITION

T*he 1992 Yearbook is the first edition to be published in full colour since the series was launched. The book has also been extensively redesigned by Art Director John Hull, and the type face changed to the slightly larger Palatino font.*

GAVIN GREENWOOD
*Editor*
Hongkong, December 1991.

---

The Asia 1992 Yearbook was written and compiled by:

| | | | | |
|---|---|---|---|---|
| Salamat Ali; | Mark Clifford; | Lily Kan; | John McBeth; | Brian Shaw; |
| Suhaini Aznam; | Sucheta Dalal; | Jonathan Karp; | Hamish McDonald; | Shim Jae Hoon; |
| N. Balakrishnan; | Alan Deans; | Lincoln Kaye; | Stacy Mosher; | Manik de Silva; |
| Julian Baum; | Robert Delfs; | Robert Keith-Reid; | K. Nadarajah; | Kedar Man Singh; |
| Paul Bayfield; | Carl Goldstein; | Chris Kucway; | David Porter; | Rodney Tasker; |
| Philip Bowring; | Paul Handley; | V. G. Kulkarni; | Steve Proctor; | Michael Taylor; |
| Harald Bruning; | Michael Hass; | Ivan Kwong; | Sophie Quinn-Judge; | Rigoberto Tiglao; |
| Adrian Buzo; | Murray Hiebert; | Winnie Law; | Ahmed Rashid; | Doug Tsuruoka; |
| Rowan Callick; | Martin Howell; | Mary Lee; | Jacqueline Rees; | Michael Vatikiotis; |
| Alexander Casella; | Ricky Hui; | Paul Lee; | Louise do Rosario; | Judy Walker; |
| Elizabeth Cheng; | Shada Islam; | Ray Leung; | Anthony Rowley; | Sarah Walls; |
| Tai Ming Cheung; | Colin James; | Gene Linn; | Alan Sanders; | Michael Westlake. |
| Henry Chiu; | Syed Kamaluddin; | Bertil Lintner; | Adam Schwarz; | |
| Ringo Chung; | | Michael Malik; | | |

# CONTENTS

**\*DEFINITIONS:** in the consolidated statistical data for all countries in the region on pages 6-9, definitions adopted for terms used are:

**Consumer price index** — unless otherwise indicated refers to price movements averaged on a nationwide basis; **Debt-service ratio** — repayments and interest on official debt as a percentage of merchandise exports; **Government revenue and expenditure** — budget totals, including both current or operating and capital or development accounts; **Merchandise exports** — includes re-exports of previously imported goods. Exports are fob, imports are cif; **Terms of trade index** — relates unit value of exports to the unit value of import; **Outstanding foreign debt** — excludes undistributed foreign credits; **Balance of payments** — the sum of the current account, capital account and transfers etc. but *excluding* IMF transactions; **Net services receipts** — all current non-merchandise receipts (travel, insurance, interest, dividends, etc.) except transfers *less* payments.

Far Eastern Economic
**REVIEW**

All Rights Reserved. ©
Published under licence by National Fair Ltd a wholly owned subsidiary of Review Publishing Company Ltd. Hongkong, 1992.

**Offices:** Editorial, Executive, Advertising, Accounts & Circulation 181-185 Gloucester Road, Hongkong.
**Postal address:** GPO Box 160, Hongkong.
**Cable:** REVIEW HONGKONG (*Editorial*); REVIEWADS HONGKONG (*Executive, Advertising & Accounts*); REVIEWCIRC HONGKONG (*Circulation*).
**Telex:** 75297 ECWEK HX (*Editorial*); 62497 REVAD HX (*Executive, Accounts & Advertising*); 66452 REVCD HX (*Circulation*).
**Fax:** 8345571 (*Editorial*); 8345987 (*Executive & Accounts*); 8346051 (*Advertising*); 722436 (*Circulation*).
**Telephone:** 8328381 (*Editorial*), 8328300 (*Executive, Advertising, Accounts, Adv. Production & Circulation*).

Printed by Dai Nippon Printing Co. (HK) Ltd,
Tsuen Wan Industrial Centre, 2-5/F., 220-248 Texaco Road,
Tsuen Wan, N.T., Hongkong.

**ISBN 9-627-01047-2**

# Going East.
# Staying Westin.

The Westin Plaza, Singapore,
What better place for your
next meeting?

**THE WESTIN PLAZA**
**Singapore**

**WESTIN**
HOTELS & RESORTS

# REGIONAL PERFORMANCE FIGURES

| | Afghanistan | Australia | Bangladesh | Bhutan | Brunei | Burma | Cambodia | China | Fiji | Hongkong | India | Indonesia | Japan | North Korea | South Korea |
|---|---|---|---|---|---|---|---|---|---|---|---|---|---|---|---|
| **Area** (*'000 km²*) | 652 | 7,682.3 | 148 | 46.5 | 5.8 | 677 | 181 | 9,600 | 18.3 | 1.074 | 3,288 | 1,948 | 377.7 | 122.1 | 99.2 |
| % cultivated | 12 | 2.2 | 59.84 | 8.8 | 0.28 | 20 | 11 | 10 | 15 | 8 | 52 | n.a. | 13.9 | 19 | 21.5 |
| % forest | 2.6 | 5.3 | 13.43 | 68.7 | 85 | 39 | 60 | 13 | 46 | 20.5 | 11.1 | n.a. | 66.4 | 74 | 65.4 |
| % pasture | 0.46 | 3.9 | 4.47 | 1.9 | 1 | 2 | 3 | 33.2 | 3 | nil | 4.3 | n.a. | 1.7 | 1 | 0.1 |
| **Population** | | | | | | | | | | | | | | | |
| Total 1991 (*m*) | 16.6 | 17.5 | 116.6 | 0.7 | 0.3 | 42.1 | 7.1 | 1,151.3 | 0.7 | 5.9 | 859.2 | 181.4 | 123.8 | 21.8 | 43.2 |
| % average annual growth '83-'90 | 2.6 | 0.8 | 2.4 | 2 | 2.5 | 1.9 | 2.2 | 1.4 | 2 | 0.7 | 2 | 1.7 | 0.3 | 1.8 | 0.9 |
| Projected year 2010 (*m*) | 32.7 | 21.7 | 176.6 | 1 | 0.4 | 58.6 | 10 | 1,420.3 | 0.9 | 64 | 1,157.8 | 237.9 | 135.8 | 28.5 | 48.1 |
| Years until population doubles | 27 | 91 | 28 | 35 | 27 | 36 | 32 | 48 | 35 | 99 | 34 | 41 | 210 | 39 | 79 |
| Urban population as % of total | 18 | 85 | 14 | 13 | 59 | 24 | 11 | 26 | 39 | 93 | 27 | 31 | 77 | 64 | 71 |
| Death rate per 1,000 | 22 | 7 | 13 | 19 | 3 | 13 | 16 | 7 | 4 | 5 | 10 | 8 | 7 | 6 | 6 |
| Birth rate per 1,000 | 48 | 15 | 37 | 39 | 29 | 32 | 38 | 21 | 24 | 12 | 31 | 25 | 10 | 24 | 15 |
| Infant mortality per 1,000 | 182 | 7.7 | 120 | 142 | 7 | 95 | 125 | 33 | 21 | 7.4 | 91 | 73 | 4.5 | 30 | 23 |
| % aged under 15 years | 43 | 22 | 44 | 39 | 36 | 38 | 37 | 27 | 37 | 22 | 36 | 37 | 18 | 29 | 27 |
| Life expectancy (*years*) | 41 | 76 | 53 | 47 | 71 | 55 | 49 | 69 | 62 | 77 | 57 | 61 | 79 | 69 | 71 |
| **Students** | | | | | | | | | | | | | | | |
| Primary | 627,880 | 1.76m | 11m | 63,643[26] | 36,983[23] | 5.42m | 919,500[13] | 122.42m | 139,000 | 524,919 | 123m | 29.66m | 9.16m | n.a. | 4.7m |
| Secondary | 281,990 | 1.28m | 3.51m | 4,370[26] | 18,748 | 1.26m | 98,800[13] | 51.05m | 46,000 | 431,381 | 17.2m | 10.09m | 5.19m | n.a. | 4.4m |
| University | 20,881 | 485,075 | 55,813 | 407[26] | 935[24] | 218,848 | 11,500[13] | 2.06m | 2,000 | 35,789 | 2.43m | 1.70m | 2.21m | n.a. | 1.06m |
| **Workforce** | | | | | | | | | | | | | | | |
| Total (*m*) | 7.78 | 7.6 | 36.48 | 0.65 | 0.09 | 15.7 | 3.75 | 567.4 | 260,000 | 2.12 | 314 | 78.01 | 66.1 | 9.6 | 19.3 |
| % in commerce, services | 405,000 | 67.6 | 19.11 | 3.6 | 26.4 | 8.87 | 23 | 13.09 | 40 | 44.7 | 11.2 | 29.82 | 54.1 | n.a. | 46 |
| % in manufacturing | 162,000 | 14.4 | 11.25 | 0.7 | 8.6 | 7.19 | 28 | 17.06 | 23.68 | 24.7 | 18.4 | 10.4 | 23.7 | 39 | 25 |
| % in agriculture, fishing | 287,000 | 5.3 | 54.34 | 93 | 5 | 67.87 | 80.9 | 60.23 | 3 | 0.8[26] | 52.2 | 53.33[11] | 7.2 | 43 | 17 |
| % in construction | 78,000 | 6.6 | 4.18 | n.a. | 33[24] | 1.19 | n.a. | 4.51 | 6.44 | 2.4 | 7.5 | 2.63 | 9.5 | n.a. | 8 |
| % govt., public authorities | 73,200 | 4.6 | 11.12 | 2 | 40 | 7.77 | n.a. | 1.9 | 23 | 6.7 | 6.5 | 2.7 | 3 | 18 | 4 |
| **Social** | | | | | | | | | | | | | | | |
| Persons per hospital bed | 6.4 | n.a. | 3,311 | 1,500 | 260 | 1,597 | 625 | 434.78 | 435 | 229.4 | 1,300 | 1,484 | 64 | n.a. | 313 |
| Persons per doctor | 2.2 | 174 | 5,338 | 9,700 | 1,690 | 3,485 | 2,552[22] | 649.35 | 2,050 | 949.2 | 2,522 | 6,742 | 611 | n.a. | 1,007 |
| Literacy rate (%) | 23.5 | 90 | 29 | 20 | 80.3 | 78.5 | 70 est. | 86 | n.a. | 86 | 52.11 | n.a. | 99.7 | n.a. | 98 |
| TV sets ('000) | n.a. | n.a. | 526 | n.a. | 63 | n.a. | 40 | 168,069 | 55 est. | n.a. | 76,450 | 9,176 | n.a. | n.a. | n.a. |
| Radios ('000) | n.a. | n.a. | 4,190 | 15 | 92 | n.a. | 750 | 266,396 | 450 est. | n.a. | 97,800 | n.a. | n.a. | n.a. | n.a. |
| Telephones ('000) | 33,315[1] | 4,889.1 | 256 | 1.99 | 49 | 73.55 | 5 | 126,910 | 71.77 | 3,106 est. | 5,000 | 2,026 | n.a. | n.a. | n.a. |
| Cars | 74,054[1] | 7.67m | 55,000 | 2,340[6] | 88,997 | n.a. | n.a. | 1.52m | 40,233 | 207,229 | 2.48m | 1.64m | 58.5m | n.a. | 2.41m |
| Trucks and commercial vehicles | n.a. | 2.05m | 56,000 | 1,629 | 13,246 | 106,563 | 7,100 | 3.68m | 27,600 | 118,440 | 3m | 1.74m | 21.5m | n.a. | 1.42m |
| Motorcycles | 5,909 | 304,000 | 205,000 | 2,882[7] | 3,270 | n.a. | n.a. | 4.12m | 4,107 | 17,430 | 10.6m | 8.39m | n.a. | n.a. | 1.47m |
| Length of railways (*km*) | nil | 35,763 | 2,892 | nil | 12 | 4,500 | 648 | 53,378 | 640 | 100.5 | 65,023 | 4,227 | 26,994 | n.a. | 6,456 |
| Length of paved highway (*km*) | n.a. | 38,219 | 7,559 | 2,280 | 1,093[12] | n.a. | 2,000 | 883,464 | 900 | 1,484 | 1.9m | 50,050 | 5,228 | n.a. | 1,550 |
| **Production & Prices** | | | | | | | | | | | | | | | |
| GDP at market prices ('90, US$b) | n.a. | 293 | 22.8 | 0.28 | 3.7 | 7.93 | 1.56[12] | 338.81 | 1.22 | 70 | 220 | 99.61 | 3,123.5 | 21.5 | 239.7 |
| Per capita income ('90, US$) | n.a. | 13,480 | 200 | 185 | 15,200 | 195 | 190[12] | 298.47 | 1,682 | 12,068 | 350 | 560 | 25,273 | 987 | 5,569 |
| GDP in local currency (*b*) 1988 | 127.5 | 339.8 | 597.14 | 3.86 | 5.85 | 47.14 | n.a. | 1,401.82[19] | 1.38 | 434,023 | 2,944 | n.a. | 365,823 | 24.1 | 127,962 |
| 1989 | 118.5 | 371.9 | 659.60 | n.a. | 5.91 | 48.82 | n.a. | 1,591.63[19] | 1.59 | 490,811 | 3,488.9 | 142,020 | 383,093 | 24.4 | 143,001 |
| 1990 | 114.8 | 379.5 | 750.41 | n.a. | 6.44 | 51.54 | n.a. | 17,686.10[19] | 1.81 | 546,058 | 3,949 | 166,630 | 404,655 | 23.4 | 169,701 |
| 1991 (*forecast/estimate*) | 123.8 | n.a. | 846.62 | n.a. | n.a. | n.a. | n.a. | 19,100.99[19] | n.a. | 569,900 | 4,070 | n.a. | 459,600 | 22.1 | 200,000 |
| GDP real growth '90 (%) | 7.2[2] | -0.86 | 6.2 | 9 | 2.7[13] | 5.1 | n.a. | 5.2[19] | 5 | 2.4 | 5.3 | 7.4 | 5.2 | -3.7 | 9 |
| 1991 (*forecast/estimate*) | n.a. | 1.5 | 4 | 3 | n.a. | 4.9 | n.a. | 6[19] | 2 | 4 | 3 | 6.5 | 3.8 | -2.0 | 9 |
| % avg. GDP growth '86-'90 | 7.2 | 3.7[3] | 3.9 | 8.3[8] | n.a. | -1.42 | n.a. | 7.84[19] | 8.9 | 5.3 | 5.9 | | 4.7 | 1 | 10.22 |
| Agriculture as % GDP | 79.86 | 4.1 | 37.6 | 45 | n.a. | 39.3 | 80 | 34.65[19] | 19.6 | 0.29 | 32.1 | 23.45 | 2.6 | n.a. | 7.9 |
| Manufacturing as % GDP | 5.7 | 15.9[4] | 9.9 | 6 | n.a. | 9.0 | n.a. | 45.81[19] | 11.43 | 18.3 | 28.8 | 18.38 | 28.9 | n.a. | 33.5 |
| Gross capital formation as % GDP | n.a. | n.a. | 10.68 | n.a. | n.a. | 14[9] | n.a. | 25.16[19] | n.a. | 26.5 | 23.6 | n.a. | 33.7 | n.a. | 37 |
| Consumer prices (% rise) 1990 | 58 | 5.3 | 9.3 | 10.9 | n.a. | 40 est. | 140 est. | 2.1 | 8.1 | 9.8 | 6.6 | 9.53 | -3 | n.a. | 8.6 |
| 1991 (*forecast/estimate*) | n.a. | 3.75 | 0.5 | n.a. | n.a. | 60 est. | 200 | 4 | 7 | 12 | 13.6 | n.a. | 2.4 | n.a. | 9.6 |
| GDP deflator '90 (% change) | n.a. | 3.0 | 7.1 | n.a. | n.a. | n.a. | n.a. | 3.25[19] | n.a. | 8.4 | 6.7 | n.a. | 2.4 | n.a. | 8.9 |
| Money growth '90 (M2, %) | 15.3 | 6.6[5] | 9.4 | 34.89 | n.a. | 29.6[10] | n.a. | 16.2 | n.a. | 21 | 16.6 | 25 | 11.7 | n.a. | 21.2 |

[1] Inc. trucks  [2] 1986-90  [3] Constant prices  [4] Market prices  [5] M3  [6] 1988 (inc. jeeps)  [7] Inc. scooters  [8] 1983-88  [9] 1985  [10] Money supply (M1, % change)
[11] Inc. forestry  [12] 1988  [13] 1989  [19] GNP  [22] In Phnom Penh, 90,160 in countryside  [23] 1986  [24] 1987  [25] M1+M2  [26] 1990

| | Laos | Macau | Malaysia | Maldives | Mongolia | Nepal | New Zealand | Pakistan | Papua New Guinea | Philippines | Singapore | Sri Lanka | Taiwan | Thailand | Vietnam |
|---|---|---|---|---|---|---|---|---|---|---|---|---|---|---|---|
| **Area ('000 km²)** | 236.8 | 0.017 | 330.4 | 0.298 | 1,565 | 147.18 | 270.5 | 802 | 462.8 | 300 | 0.63 | 65.6 | 36 | 513 | 332 |
| % cultivated | 3 | n.a. | 15 | n.a. | 0.8 | 18 | 1.6 | 20.7 | 3 | 41[26] | 1.9 | 26 | 25 | 50 | 20 |
| % forest | 40 | n.a. | 80 | n.a. | 9 | 36.5 | 26.6 | 0.8 | 80 | 53[13] | 4.5 | 11.2 | 64 | 27 | 31 |
| % pasture | n.a. | nil | 2 | n.a. | 79 | 13.4 | 35.1 | 0.8 | 2 | 1.4[26] | n.a. | 0.3 | n.a. | 8 | 15 |
| **Population** | | | | | | | | | | | | | | | |
| Total 1991 (m) | 4.1 | 0.4 | 18.3 | 0.2 | 2.2 | 19.6 | 3.5 | 117.5 | 3.9 | 62.3 | 2.8 | 17.4 | 20.5 | 57.5 | 67.6 |
| % average annual growth '83-'90 | 2.2 | 1.4 | 2.5 | 3.7 | 2.7 | 2.5 | 0.9 | 3 | 2.3 | 2.6 | 1.3 | 1.5 | 1.1 | 1.75 | 2.3 |
| Projected year 2010 (m) | 6 | 0.5 | 27 | 0.4 | 3.5 | 30.6 | 4 | 195.2 | 5.9 | 85.6 | 3.2 | 21.4 | 23.8 | 70.7 | 92 |
| Years until population doubles | 32 | 51 | 28 | 19 | 25 | 28 | 75 | 23 | 31 | 27 | 55 | 47 | 62 | 40 | 31 |
| Urban population as % of total | 16 | 97 | 35 | 28 | 57 | 7 | 84 | 28 | 19 | 42 | 100 | 22 | 71 | 24 | 20 |
| Death rate per 1,000 | 15 | 3 | 5 | 9 | 8 | 17 | 8 | 13 | 12 | 7 | 5 | 6 | 5 | 7 | 9 |
| Birth rate per 1,000 | 37 | 17 | 29 | 46 | 36 | 42 | 17 | 43 | 34 | 33 | 18 | 21 | 16 | 24 | 32 |
| Infant mortality per 1,000 | 124 | 10 | 29 | 72 | 64 | 112 | 10.6 | 112 | 59 | 54 | 6.6 | 19.4 | 6.2 | 29 | 44 |
| % aged under 15 years | 41 | 22 | 37 | 45 | 44 | 42 | 23 | 45 | 41 | 39 | 23 | 35 | 27 | 34 | 39 |
| Life expectancy (years) | 50 | 77 | 68 | 61 | 65 | 52 | 74 | 57 | 54 | 64 | 75 | 70 | 74 | 65 | 63 |
| **Students** | | | | | | | | | | | | | | | |
| Primary | 495,375[12] | 32,639 | 2.45 | 6,617 | 488,900 | 2.85m | 420,064 | 8.86m | 418,926 | 10.28m | 257,932 | 2.13m[26] | 2.35m | 6.96m | 11m |
| Secondary | 69,226[12] | 16,862 | 1.3 | 3,899 | | 697,100 | 230,996 | 3.51m | 55,690 | 3.9m | 161,029 | 1.85[26] | 1.93m | 2.23m | 662,100 |
| University | 20,093[12] | 2,464 | 60,030 | nil | 13,200 | 87,300 | 150,790 | 649,200 | 7,160 | 1.5m | 55,562 | 29,781 | 462,492 | 848,512 | 114,000 |
| **Workforce** | | | | | | | | | | | | | | | |
| Total (m) | 1.85 | 0.25 | 7.05 | 0.06 | 0.65 | 8.6 | 1,433.5 | 32.81 | 0.19 | 23.56 | 1.52 | 7[26] | 8.42 | 31.8 | 32.8 |
| % in commerce, services | 17.8 | 45.5 | 32.9 | 2 | 20 | 6.5 | 43.8 | 17.4 | 56 | 14.47 | 31.9 | n.a. | 45.5 | 14 | 12.5 |
| % in manufacturing | 1.6 | 35.5 | 19.5 | 15 | 19 | 0.5 | 18.0 | 12.84 | 12 | 10.33 | 27.6 | n.a. | 31.4 | 17 | 11.2 |
| % in agriculture, fishing | 80 | 0.5 | 27.8 | 26 | 29 | 91.1 | 10.6 | 51.15 | 32 | 44.73[11] | 0.1 | 47.8 | 12.85 | 56.5 | 72.3 |
| % in construction | 0.6 | 9 | 6.4 | 6 | 6.5 | 0.3 | 5.5 | 6.38 | 6 | 4.38 | 8.8 | 3 | 8.23 | 6 | 2.7 |
| % govt., public authorities | n.a. | 5.5 | 12.8 | 21 | 23 | 1.6 | 20.6 | n.a. | 22 | 8.18 | 4.6 | 21.4 | 16.78 | 4.5 | 0.78 |
| **Social** | | | | | | | | | | | | | | | |
| Persons per hospital bed | 362 | 423 | 714 | 1,277 | 85 | 4,238 | 127 | 1,535 | 728 | 1,686 | 312 | 340 | 228 | 639 | 294 |
| Persons per doctor | 26,150 | 834 | 385 | 5,330 | 357 | 16.50 | 469 | 2,127 | 11,200 | n.a. | 791 | 1,164 | 913 | 4,523 | 3,031 |
| Literacy rate (%) | 41 | 90 est. | 76 | 95.4[13] | n.a. | 36.4 | n.a. | 26.2 | 32.1 | 83.32 | 90 | 87.2 | 93.2 | 70 | 82 |
| TV sets ('000) | n.a. | n.a. | 1,741 | 6.5 | 132.9 | 200,000 | n.a. | 107.8 | 60 | 3,399 | 575 | 441 | 3,398 | n.a. | n.a. |
| Radios ('000) | 367 | n.a. | 445 | 27.34 | 222.5 | 2,100 | n.a. | n.a. | 62 | 7,388 | 128 | 3,324 | 13,992 | n.a. | n.a. |
| Telephones ('000) | 6.2 | 100 | 1,580 | 7.39 | 62.6 | 78,400 | n.a. | 1,073.5 | 73 | 888 | 1,220 | 108 | 5,893 | 1,400 | 140-150 |
| Cars | 15,000 | 27,639 | 1.49m | 630 | 5,000 | 19,534 | 1.5m | 548,300 | 11,799[12] | 454,554 | 286,756 | 163,779 | 2.32m | 2.2m | n.a. |
| Trucks and commercial vehicles | 2,250 | 3,493 | n.a. | 380 | 27,316 | 17,595 | 307,173 | 228,999 | 29,021[12] | 783,262 | 127,000 | 242,887 | 750,966 | 567,000 | n.a. |
| Motorcycles | n.a. | 17,651 | 2.79m | 3,351 | n.a. | 31,984 | 82,326 | 980,857 | 1,204[12] | 382,426 | 122,525 | 307,392 | 8.46m | 4.8m | n.a. |
| Length of railways (km) | nil | nil | 1,644 | nil | 1,807 | 52 | 3,950 | 8,775 | nil | 539[26] | n.a. | 1,394 | 2,469.5 | 3,755 | 3,220 |
| Length of paved highway (km) | 2,447 | n.a. | 46,890 | nil | 1,200 | 2,981 | 52,370 | 165,032 | 3,344 | 160,560 | 2,882 | 25,979 | 19,997.8 | 45,000 | 13,000 |
| **Production & Prices** | | | | | | | | | | | | | | | |
| GDP at market prices ('90, US$b) | 0.55[12] | 3.7 | 29.32 | 0.09 | 1.93 | 3.15 | 43.6 | 41.49 | 3.2 | 43.86 | 33.74 | 8.01 | 157.01 | 80.4 | 0.06[13] |
| Per capita income ('90, US$) | 156[13] | 8,100 | 2,297 | 641.16 | 522 | 164.8 | 11,370 | 376 | 865 | 672 | 11,245 | 418[26] | 7,332 | 1,413 | 200 est. |
| GDP in local currency (b) 1988 | 19.6 | 21.6 | 66.30 | 0.77 | 10.2 | 168.8 | 64.8 | 675.39 | 3.2 | 803.02 | 48.22 | 222 | 3,496.95 | 1,507 | 9,751 |
| 1989 | 20.5 | 24.7 | 72.08 | 0.84 | 10.6 | 78.2 | 69.8 | 769.75 | 3 | 922.56 | 52.67 | 251.9 | 3,878.55 | 1,776 | 17,414 |
| 1990 | n.a. | 29.6 | 79.16 | 0.97 | n.a. | 88.7 | 70.8 | 862.45 | 3.1 | 1,066.31 | 57.02 | 321.1 | 4,243.06 | 2,051 | 27,117 |
| 1991 (forecast/estimate) | n.a. | n.a. | 85.49 | 1.05 | n.a. | 100.6 | 70.8 | 1,016.73 | 3.4 | 582.56 | 60.72 | 384.1 | 4,709.60 | 2,359 | n.a. |
| GDP real growth '90 (%) | 9.0 | 6.2 | 10 | 15.1 | 4.3[13] | 3.6 | -1.3 | 4.63 | -3.7 | 2.16 | 8.3 | 6.2 | 8.4 | 10 | 2.4 |
| 1991 (forecast/estimate) | 6-7 | n.a. | 8.3 | n.a. | nil | 4.1 | -1.5 | 5.58 | 7.8 | n.a. | 6.5 | 5.2 | 11.55 | 8 | 3.8 |
| % avg. GDP growth '86-'90 | n.a. | 8.1 | 6.7 | n.a. | 5.5 | 4.6 | 0.8 | n.a. | 4.8 | 4.80 | 8 | 3.4 | 8.78 | 9.9 | 4.8 |
| Agriculture as % GDP | 60 | n.a. | 18.7 | 8.9 | 16.1 | 56.4 | 5.7 | 44.9 | 28.4 | 21.15 | 0.3 | 23.3 | 4.22 | 12.4 | 50 |
| Manufacturing as % GDP | 16.1 | 32 est. | 27 | 5.73 | 27.2 | 4.9 | 12.2 | 19.02 | 10 | 25.45 | 29 | 17.4 | 34.14 | 26.1 | 32 |
| Gross capital formation as % GDP | n.a. | 22 | n.a. | 38 | n.a. | 15.8 | 20.7 | 17.35 | 25.3 | 21.66 | 38.5 | 22.5 | 22.18 | 35.5 | n.a. |
| Consumer prices (% rise) 1990 | 18 | 8 | 3.1 | 1.06 | | 9.1 | 4.9 | 6.11 | 7 | 12.64 | 3.4 | 21.3 | 4.13 | 6 | 90 |
| 1991 (forecast/estimate) | 15 | n.a. | 4.5 | 1.21 | 100 | 8.6 | 2.2 | 12.58 | 5.5 | 17-18 | 3 | 14 | 3.52 | 5.2 | 70 |
| GDP deflator '90 (% change) | n.a. | 10.4 | n.a. | n.a. | 2.7 | 9.42 | 2.9 | 9.64 | 4.3 | 13.16 | 3.2 | 20 | 4.1 | +5 | n.a. |
| Money growth '90 (M2, %) | 89 | 25.5 | 12.8 | n.a. | n.a. | 18.6 | 1.3 | 17.9 | 0.3[25] | 18.4 | 20 | 19.1 | 9.9 | 26.7 | 100 |

Sources: 1991 World Population Data Sheet of the population Reference Bureau, Inc. Washington; REVIEW Correspondents.

For definitions, see current yearbook.

# REGIONAL PERFORMANCE FIGURES

| | Afghanistan | Australia | Bangladesh | Bhutan | Brunei | Burma | Cambodia | China | Fiji | Hongkong | India | Indonesia | Japan | North Korea | South Korea |
|---|---|---|---|---|---|---|---|---|---|---|---|---|---|---|---|
| **Public Expenditure** | | | | | | | | | | | | | | | |
| Central govt. expenditure (US$b) | | | | | | | | | | | | | | | |
| 1990 | n.a. | 73.36 | 2.05 | 0.1 | n.a. | 1.7 | n.a. | 65.04 | 0.40 | 11.5 | 59.2 | 13.53 | 536.4 | n.a. | 37 |
| 1991 (budget or estimate) | n.a. | 78.38 | 2.05 | n.a. | n.a. | 1.8 | n.a. | 67.06 | 0.41 | 13.43 | 44.3 | 15.51 | 535.2 | n.a. | 42.4 |
| Defence as % GDP | n.a. | 2.4 | 1.39 | n.a. | n.a. | n.a. | n.a. | 1.64[19] | n.a. | 18.44 | 2.4 | n.a. | 0.95 | 21.5 | 5 |
| Defence as % budget | n.a. | 9.6 | 16.14 | n.a. | n.a. | 31.8 | n.a. | 8.55 | 6.7 | n.a. | 14.4 | 7.63 | 6.2 | n.a. | 25.1 |
| Education as % budget | n.a. | 7.9 | 14.06[26] | 7.08 | n.a. | 18.9 | n.a. | 18.14 | 20 | 17.1 | 1.54 | 5.22 | 7.7 | n.a. | 20.3 |
| Central govt. revenue (US$b) | | | | | | | | | | | | | | | |
| 1990 | n.a. | 74.83 | 2.06 | 0.06 | n.a. | 1.3 | n.a. | 62.16 | 0.36 | 11.5 | 57 | 16.03 | 536.4 | n.a. | 49.7 |
| 1991 (budget estimate) | n.a. | 76.28 | 2.19 | n.a. | n.a. | 1.4 | n.a. | 64.62 | 0.36 | 13.18 | 40.5 | 20.40 | 535.2 | n.a. | 48.0 |
| % personal income tax | n.a. | 51.8 | 3.4 | 2 | n.a. | 16 | nil | n.a. | 39.7 | 25.15 | 3.8 | 20.63 | 43 | n.a. | 17 |
| % company income tax | n.a. | 14.6 | 10.29 | 2 | n.a. | 28 | n.a. | 60.74 | 13 | 47.13 | 6.02 | | 29.8 | n.a. | 12 |
| % customs, excise, sales, VAT | n.a. | 22.9 | 62.18 | 23.65 | n.a. | 24 | n.a. | 5.51 | 40.68 | 5.7 | 54.6 | 34.25 | 15.4 | n.a. | 47 |
| Budget surplus (or deficit) as % GDP | n.a. | 0.5 | 0.6 | 6.97 | n.a. | -15 | n.a. | -0.85 | n.a. | 0.34 | 6.5 | 1.3 | -1.2 | n.a. | 2 |
| **Foreign Trade** | | | | | | | | | | | | | | | |
| Merchandise exports (US$m) | | | | | | | | | | | | | | | |
| 1989 | 236 | 37,948 | 1,300 | 70.8 | 2,172 | 337.38 | 33.72 | 52,538 | 424 | 73.14b | 12,644 | 23,830 | 275,175 | 2,050 | 62,377 |
| 1990 | 269 | 39,995 | 1,486 | 68.02 | n.a. | 542 | 25.74 | 62,091 | 513 | 82.03b | 15,378 | 28,143 | 286,948 | 2,100 | 65,016 |
| 1991 (estimate) | 275 | n.a. | 1,700 | n.a. | n.a. | 638 | 80 | 64,897 | n.a. | 97.53b | 18,079 | n.a. | n.a. | 2,020 | 70,500 |
| % manufactures | n.a. | 21.5 | 84.82 | n.a. | n.a. | n.a. | n.a. | 74.58 | 26 | 61.7 | 72.6 | 42.21 | 80 | n.a. | 94.9 |
| % food and farm products | n.a. | 26.8 | 15.18 | n.a. | n.a. | n.a. | n.a. | 11.45 | 52 | 2.15 | 19.4 | 7.4 | 0.6 | n.a. | 3.8 |
| % metals and minerals | n.a. | 51.6 | n.a. | n.a. | n.a. | n.a. | n.a. | 14.13 | 9 | 0.65 | 5.1 | 28.61 | 17.6 | n.a. | 1.3 |
| Merchandise imports (US$m) | | | | | | | | | | | | | | | |
| 1989 | 681 | 40,469 | 3,375 | 119.93 | 1,390 | 529.7 | 91.52 | 59,140 | 580.6 | 72.15b | 23,849 | 17,374 | 210,847 | 2,600 | 61,465 |
| 1990 | 820 | 38,031 | 3,759 | 101.13 | n.a. | 1,096 | 69.23 | 53,345 | 736.5 | 82.37b | 26,235 | 23,028 | 234,799 | 2,620 | 69,844 |
| 1991 (estimate) | 900 | n.a. | 3,600 | n.a. | n.a. | 1,020 | 180 | 56,499 | n.a. | 101b | 32,000 | n.a. | n.a. | 2,500 | 81,500 |
| % plant, capital equipment | n.a. | 44.5 | 29.86 | n.a. | n.a. | 7.0 | n.a. | 31.58 | n.a. | 14.71 | 26.6 | 43.9 | 14 | n.a. | 36.5 |
| % raw materials and food | 10.4 | 9.8 | 56.45 | n.a. | n.a. | 18 | n.a. | 16.09 | 18.2 | 44.5 | 14 | 36.3 | 13.7 | n.a. | 56.2 |
| % energy | 0.2 | 6.4 | 13.69 | n.a. | n.a. | n.a. | n.a. | 2.38 | 14.3 | 2.26 | 14.5 | 14.71 | 36.2 | n.a. | 9.1 |
| Foreign trade as % GDP | n.a. | 26.6 | 23.01 | n.a. | n.a. | 12 | n.a. | 34.07[19] | n.a. | 232 | 19.3 | n.a. | 36.3 | 21 | 56 |
| % energy imported (net) | n.a. | n.a. | 1.41 | n.a. | n.a. | n.a. | 100 | nil | n.a. | 100 | 40[20] | n.a. | 84 | 10 | 87.9 |
| % food imported (net) | n.a. | n.a. | 1.5 | n.a. | n.a. | n.a. | n.a. | nil | n.a. | 89 | n.a. | n.a. | 32 | n.a. | 3 |
| % trade with Pacific region (excluding US and Japan) | 6.3 | 16.7 | n.a. | n.a. | n.a. | 48 | n.a. | 51.07 | 56 | n.a. | 2.1 | 28.4 | 29.3 | n.a. | 24 |
| % trade with Japan | 17.7 | 23 | n.a. | n.a. | n.a. | 15 | n.a. | 14.38 | 9.3 | 10.89 | 8.79 | 42.55 | 3.5[28] | 10.6 | 22 |
| % trade with US | 0.7 | 17 | n.a. | n.a. | n.a. | 1.3 | nil | 10.63 | 11.3 | 16.05 | 13.8 | 13.1 | 27.4 | nil | 28 |
| Terms of trade index change (%) | | | | | | | | | | | | | | | |
| 1989 | n.a. | -1.6 | -9.0 | n.a. | n.a. | 82.8 | n.a. | 7.4 | n.a. | 1.4 | -5 | n.a. | -4.2 | n.a. | 7.6 |
| 1990 | n.a. | -5.2 | -2.6 | n.a. | n.a. | 68.6 | n.a. | n.a. | n.a. | 1.1 | +2.5 | n.a. | -6.1 | n.a. | -1 |
| 1991 (estimate) | n.a. | n.a. | +1.0 | n.a. | n.a. | n.a. | n.a. | n.a. | n.a. | 1.3 | n.a. | n.a. | n.a. | n.a. | n.a. |
| Number of visitors 1990 | n.a. | 2.2m | n.a. | 1,540 | n.a. | 8,968 | 1,542 | 27.46m | 278,000 | 6.04m | 1.4m | 2.1m | 35m | n.a. | 2.9m |
| Services receipts (US$m) | | | | | | | | | | | | | | | |
| Tourism 1989 | n.a. | 3,542 | 16.9 | 1.95 | n.a. | 4.5 | n.a. | 1,860 | 198.9 | 4,731 | 1,500 | 1,284.4 | 3,143 | n.a. | 3,311 |
| 1990 | n.a. | 3,825 | 20.1 | 1.93 | n.a. | 6.2 | n.a. | 2,218 | 227.79 | 5,032 | 1,300 | 2,105.3 | 3,578 | n.a. | 3,161 |
| Investment 1989 | n.a. | 3,906 | 78.8 | n.a. | n.a. | n.a. | n.a. | 11,479 | n.a. | n.a. | 1,350 | n.a. | 101,785 | n.a. | 1,680 |
| 1990 | n.a. | 3,890 | 66.8 | n.a. | n.a. | n.a. | n.a. | 12,085 | n.a. | n.a. | 2,190 | n.a. | 122,167 | n.a. | 2,445 |
| Transfers 1989 | n.a. | 3,586 | n.a. | 24.74 | n.a. | n.a. | n.a. | 595 | 15.32 | n.a. | 841.9 | n.a. | 18,090 | n.a. | 1,341 |
| 1990 | n.a. | 3,638 | n.a. | 26.72 | n.a. | n.a. | n.a. | 373 | 2.68 | n.a. | 854 | n.a. | 18,099 | n.a. | 1,543 |
| Services payments (US$m) | | | | | | | | | | | | | | | |
| Tourism 1989 | -7.96 | 4,032 | 113.3 | n.a. | n.a. | n.a. | n.a. | 572 | n.a. | 4.16 | n.a. | n.a. | 22,490 | n.a. | 2,356 |
| 1990 | -8.88 | 4,054 | 112.3 | n.a. | n.a. | n.a. | n.a. | n.a. | n.a. | 4.59 | n.a. | n.a. | 24,928 | n.a. | 2,768 |
| Investment 1989 | n.a. | 17,427 | 213.5 | n.a. | n.a. | n.a. | n.a. | 8,866 | n.a. | n.a. | n.a. | n.a. | 78,343 | n.a. | 2,945 |
| 1990 | n.a. | 17,232 | 189.7 | n.a. | n.a. | n.a. | n.a. | 9,426 | n.a. | n.a. | n.a. | n.a. | 98,963 | n.a. | 3,400 |
| Transfers 1989 | n.a. | -1,724 | n.a. | 36.67 | n.a. | n.a. | n.a. | 146 | n.a. | n.a. | n.a. | n.a. | 25,845 | n.a. | 2,619 |
| 1990 | n.a. | -1,721 | n.a. | 33.15 | n.a. | n.a. | n.a. | 99 | n.a. | n.a. | n.a. | n.a. | 27,631 | n.a. | 3,211 |
| Current-account balance (US$m) | | | | | | | | | | | | | | | |
| 1989 | -402.14 | -17,683 | -1,407 | 66.95 | n.a. | n.a. | n.a. | 4,317 | 31.92 | n.a. | -6,240 | n.a. | 57,157 | n.a. | 5,055 |
| 1990 | -518.25 | -12,130 | -1,570 | 40.58 | n.a. | n.a. | n.a. | 8,998 | 7.39 | n.a. | -7,290 | n.a. | 35,761 | n.a. | -2,179 |
| 1991 (forecast) | n.a. | n.a. | -1,270 | n.a. | n.a. | n.a. | n.a. | n.a. | n.a. | n.a. | n.a. | n.a. | n.a. | n.a. | -6,000 |
| Capital-account balance (US$m) | | | | | | | | | | | | | | | |
| 1989 | 79.59 | 11,536 | 1,177 | n.a. | n.a. | n.a. | n.a. | 6,487.29 | 0.67 | n.a. | 6,210 | n.a. | -89,246 | n.a. | -3,363 |
| 1990 | 47.86 | 10,290 | 1,630 | n.a. | n.a. | n.a. | n.a. | 6,952.11 | 61.48 | n.a. | 4,800 | n.a. | -43,586 | n.a. | 548 |
| 1991 (forecast) | n.a. | n.a. | 1,494 | n.a. | n.a. | n.a. | n.a. | n.a. | n.a. | n.a. | n.a. | n.a. | n.a. | n.a. | n.a. |
| Foreign reserves (US$m) | n.a. | 24,047 | 880 | 65.29 | 27,000 | 468.3 | n.a. | 28,594 | 256 | n.a. | 2,320 | 5,028 | 66,888 | n.a. | 14,822 |
| Public foreign debt (US$m) | n.a. | 133,269 | 10,680 | 73.62 | n.a. | 4,104 | n.a. | 42,600 | 243.9 | n.a. | 64,970[21] | n.a. | nil | n.a. | 31,700 |
| Public debt-service ratio (%) | n.a. | n.a. | 19.8 | 9.2 | n.a. | 37.6 | n.a. | 15 | 11.7 | n.a. | 21.3 | n.a. | nil | n.a. | 9 |

[13] 1989  [14] Electricity  [15] Timber & coffee  [16] Tin & gypsum  [17] Excl. petroleum  [18] Exchange reserves of Monetary Authority
[19] GNP  [20] Petroleum only  [21] Total debt, inc. private  [26] 1990  [27] Private transfers only  [28] % trade with China

ASIA 1992 YEARBOOK

| Indicator | Laos | Macau | Malaysia | Maldives | Mongolia | Nepal | New Zealand | Pakistan | Papua New Guinea | Philippines | Singapore | Sri Lanka | Taiwan | Thailand | Vietnam |
|---|---|---|---|---|---|---|---|---|---|---|---|---|---|---|---|
| **Public Expenditure** | | | | | | | | | | | | | | | |
| Central govt. expenditure (US$b) 1990 | 0.22 | 0.686 | 12.56 | 0.07 | 1.24 | 0.67 | 18.4 | 9.58 | 1.07 | 7.29 | 5.35 | 2.49 | 48.89 | 11.9 | 0.68 est. |
| 1991 (budget or estimate) | n.a. | 0.723 | 14 | 0.8 | 0.22 | 0.57 | 16.1 | 10.79 | 1.27 | 7.46 | 6 | 2.81 | 44.42 | 13.8 | n.a. |
| Defence as % GDP | n.a. | 2 | n.a. | 13.03 | n.a. | 1.1 | 1.7 | 6.98 | 1.5 | 2.18 | 5.4 | 4.5 | 5.43 | 2.8 | n.a. |
| Defence as % budget | n.a. | 8.4 | 4.5 | 21.32 | 8.7 | 4.6 | 4.3 | 38.2 | 4 | 10.99 | 38 | 12.5 | 27.9 | 18.9 | n.a. |
| Education as % budget | 5.4 | 7.6 | n.a. | 12.57 | 16 | 8.6 | 15.3 | 5.5 | 16.9 | 16.80 | 20 | 4.5 | 14.9 | 19.5 | 12 |
| Central govt. revenue (US$b) 1990 | 0.22 | 0.750 | 10.05 | 0.06 | 1.21 | 0.32 | 17.1 | 7.52 | 0.99 | 7.29 | 9.72 | 1.76 | 44.23 | 16.1 | 0.7 est. |
| 1991 (budget estimate) | n.a. | 0.695 | 11.01 | 0.05 | 0.18 | 0.25 | 15.1 | 8.56 | 1.06 | 7.64 | 10.5 | 1.86 | 31.63 | 18.7 | n.a. |
| % personal income tax | n.a. | n.a. | 9 | nil | 0.7 | 5 | 46.4 | n.a. | 20.6 | 16.89 | 6.7 | 4.1 | 12.1 | 12.7 | n.a. |
| % company income tax | n.a. | 32 | 13 | nil | 37 | 1.4 | 8.0 | n.a. | 9.6 | 11.01 | n.a. | 6 | 13.4 | 14.3 | n.a. |
| % customs, excise, sales, VAT | 10 | 7.6 | 25.3 | 31.16 | 66 | 57.9 | 8.6 | 4.57 | 29.4 | 57.29 | 8 | 15.1 | 40.12 | 68.9 | n.a. |
| Budget surplus (or deficit) as % GDP | -10.8 | n.a. | 5.1 | 21.37 | n.a. | 11.3 | -2.4 | 5.3 | -2.8 | -2.69 | 2.45 | -9.9 | 3.02 | 5.2 | n.a. |
| **Foreign Trade** | | | | | | | | | | | | | | | |
| Merchandise exports (US$m) 1989 | 97 | 1,649 | 24,924 | 38.05 | 715.43 | 165.4 | 9,369.5 | 4,634 | 1,132 | 7,821 | 51.55b | 1,558.8 | 73,959 | 19,997 | 1,946 |
| 1990 | n.a. | 1,705 | 28,908 | 47.74 | 349.73 | 181 | 9,094.0 | 4,926 | 1,111 | 8,186 | 56.33b | 1,984 | 75,188 | 22,871 | 2,189 |
| 1991 (estimate) | n.a. | n.a. | 33,299 | n.a. | 275 | 238.1 | 9,315.4 | 5,849 | 1,277 | 4,169 | 61b | 2,240.6 | 80,769 | 27,700 | 2,090 |
| % manufactures | 45[14] | 99 | 58.9 | 45.84 | 17.5 | 78.1 | 25.2 | 57 | 5 | 69.72 | 57.2 | 52.2 | 96.17 | 74.7 | 37[13] |
| % food and farm products | 42[15] | 0.7 | 4.1 | 29.07 | 35.7 | 15 | 44.6 | n.a. | 15 | 17.01 | 2.9 | 36.3 | 3.2 | 22.5 | 47.8[13] |
| % metals and minerals | 6[16] | nil | 5.0[17] | 17.47 | 42.8 | n.a. | 9.9 | n.a. | 80 | 8.83 | n.a. | 9[26] | 0.63 | 1.3 | 29[13] |
| Merchandise imports (US$m) 1989 | 230 | 1,458 | 22,535 | 96.90 | 968.52 | 643.4 | 7,167.1 | 7,207 | 1,152 | 10,419 | 57.3b | 2,225.4 | 62,463 | 25,479 | 2,565 |
| 1990 | n.a. | 1,543 | 28,532 | 124.92 | 489.01 | 643.4 | 8,611.7 | 7,411 | 1,050 | 12,206 | 65b | 2,686.1 | 65,776 | 32,858 | 2,595 |
| 1991 (estimate) | n.a. | n.a. | 33,083 | n.a. | 380 | 757.6 | 9,008.6 | 8,325 | 1,060 | 5,942 | 70b | 2,897.8 | 73,178 | 38,800 | 2,463 |
| % plant, capital equipment | n.a. | 11.9 | 37.6 | n.a. | 29.6 | 25.2 | 22.2 | 33 | 36[26] | 25.58 | 44.7 | 17.7 | 17.52 | 38.8 | 36 |
| % raw materials and food | n.a. | 72.6 | 3.6 | 1.87 | 12.5 | n.a. | 12 | 51 | 31[26] | 5.48 | 6 | 67 | 70.44 | 35.3 | n.a. |
| % energy | n.a. | 4.7 | 0.5 | n.a. | 27.3 | 9.83 | 6 | 22 | 10.5[26] | 15.09 | 15.8 | 13.3 | 7.66 | 9.3 | 52 |
| Foreign trade as % GDP | 35 | 87.8 | 1.9 | 51.81 | 46 | 31.6 | 44 | n.a. | 61.4[26] | 46.49 | 360 | 58.3 | 77.18 | 69.9 | n.a. |
| % energy imported (net) | n.a. | 2 | nil | n.a. | n.a. | 9.83 | 27.4 | 27.9 | 55.1[26] | 11.63[26] | 100 | 10 | 93.4 | 60 | n.a. |
| % food imported (net) | n.a. | 4.1 | nil | n.a. | | 9.32 | 13.5 | | 17.4[26] | n.a. | 95 | 2 | 2 | n.a. | n.a. |
| % trade with Pacific region (excluding US and Japan) | n.a. | 44.5 | 36 | n.a. | n.a. | n.a. | 39.3 | 19.03 | nil | 20.81 | 46 | n.a. | 19.83 | 25 | n.a. |
| % trade with Japan | n.a. | 7.1 | 19.3 | 8 | 5 | n.a. | 15.9 | 10.87 | 45 | 18.87 | 8.5 | 18.7 | 19.96 | 25.2 | 25.4 |
| % trade with US | -1 | 21.4 | 17.2 | 24 | nil | n.a. | 15.3 | 11.34 | 11 | 26.78 | 20.4 | 30 | 28.18 | 15.7 | nil |
| Terms of trade index change (%) 1989 | n.a. | 124.8 | -1.5 | -2.5 | n.a. | 13.5 | 6.1 | 89.58 | -16.1 | -7.58 | -3.5 | -5.5 | 5.77 | -3.9 | n.a. |
| 1990 | n.a. | 126.1 | -2.0 | -5.6 | n.a. | 5.53 | 3.2 | 89.73 | -6 | -9.90 | 0.6 | -1.4 | 9.02 | -2.9 | n.a. |
| 1991 (estimate) | n.a. | n.a. | -1.0 | n.a. | n.a. | 25 | 6.4 | 77.95 | n.a. | n.a. | 0.5 | 1.3 | n.a. | +0.2 | n.a. |
| Number of visitors 1990 | 2,621[13] | 5.9m | 7.5m | 195,156 | 236,500 | 254,885 | 1.01m | n.a. | 41,000 | 1.02m | 5.31m | 297,888 | 1.71m | 5.3m | 250,000 |
| Services receipts (US$m) — Tourism 1989 | 0.13 | n.a. | 1,038 | 10.89 | 5 | 107.8 | 983.1 | n.a. | n.a. | 469 | 3.7b | 76.5 | 2,699 | 3,780 | n.a. |
| 1990 | n.a. | n.a. | 1,662 | 13.46 | n.a. | 109.6 | 1,086.9 | n.a. | n.a. | 465 | 4.5b | 120 | 1,741 | 4,336 | n.a. |
| Investment 1989 | n.a. | n.a. | 1,030 | 2.4 | n.a. | 19.8 | 722.3 | n.a. | n.a. | 359 | 4.7b | 58.4 | 6,598 | 651 | n.a. |
| 1990 | n.a. | n.a. | 1,093 | 3 | n.a. | 22.9 | 957.3 | n.a. | n.a. | 393 | 6.1b | 96.8 | 6,878 | 1,089 | n.a. |
| Transfers 1989 | n.a. | n.a. | 206.82 | 19.7 | n.a. | 117.2 | 570.8 | n.a. | 186 | 832 | 0.39b | 543.1[27] | 1,630 | 282 | n.a. |
| 1990 | n.a. | n.a. | 210.49 | 12.8 | n.a. | 106.3 | 1,079.1 | n.a. | 113 | 717 | 0.38b | 568.4[27] | 1,661 | 278 | n.a. |
| Services payments (US$m) — Tourism 1989 | n.a. | n.a. | 1,380 | n.a. | n.a. | 47.5 | 1,294.3 | n.a. | n.a. | 77 | 3.81b | 68.3 | 4,922 | 3,780 | n.a. |
| 1990 | n.a. | n.a. | 1,416 | n.a. | n.a. | 41.9 | 1,302.5 | n.a. | n.a. | 111 | 4.5b | 79.4 | 4,984 | 4,541 | n.a. |
| Investment 1989 | n.a. | n.a. | 2,928 | 11 | n.a. | 5.6 | 2,843.2 | n.a. | n.a. | 2,706 | 4.95b | 217.6 | 2,776 | 2,266 | n.a. |
| 1990 | n.a. | n.a. | 3,139 | 12.8 | n.a. | 11.4 | 2,572.1 | n.a. | n.a. | 2,452 | 6.09b | 245.1 | 2,488 | 2,722 | n.a. |
| Transfers 1989 | n.a. | n.a. | 129.73 | 3 | n.a. | 10.1 | 338.8 | n.a. | n.a. | 2 | 396 | 27.5 | 3,755 | 34 | n.a. |
| 1990 | n.a. | n.a. | 132.94 | 3 | n.a. | 7.4 | 512.4 | n.a. | n.a. | 3 | 386 | 31.4 | 2,396 | 65 | n.a. |
| Current-account balance (US$m) 1989 | -122 | n.a. | -148.26 | 0.3 | n.a. | -249.1 | 470.2 | -1,934 | -312 | -1,456 | 1.66b | -307.1 | 11,384 | -2,526 | -1,100 |
| 1990 | -139.8 | n.a. | -1,736 | 4.2 | n.a. | -272.2 | 1,440.4 | -1,891 | -113 | -2,688 | 2.4b | -241 | 10,866 | -7,283 | -500 |
| 1991 (forecast) | n.a. | n.a. | -1,464 | -12.4 | n.a. | -269.1 | 1,333.1 | -2,113 | n.a. | -606 | 3b | -577.2 | n.a. | -8,000 | -700 |
| Capital-account balance (US$m) 1989 | n.a. | n.a. | -667.16 | -4.5 | n.a. | 252.1 | 759.3 | 1,952 | 210 | 1,518 | -5.33b | 276.1 | -8,231 | 5,970 | -34 |
| 1990 | n.a. | n.a. | -327.55 | -2.7 | n.a. | 365.3 | 1,730.7 | 1,671 | 183 | 1,488 | -9.89b | 403.8 | -10,725 | 8,068 | -7 |
| 1991 (forecast) | n.a. | n.a. | n.a. | -2.4 | n.a. | 175 | 1,844.5 | 1,708 | n.a. | 1,348 | -11b | 471 | n.a. | 11,000 | n.a. |
| Foreign reserves (US$m) | 58 | 557[18] | 9,980 | 24.4 | 33.1 | 453.7 | 3,468.3 | 290 | 281.1 | 1,993.11 | 27.81b | 927 | 72.44 | 18,000 | 114 |
| Public foreign debt (US$m) | 1,260 | n.a. | 15,320 | 69 | 14,585 | 1,070.1 | 16,314.5 | 15,950 | 1,033.5 | 23,457 | 40 | 4,415.5 | 11,213.6 | 11,100 | 14,600 |
| Public debt-service ratio (%) | 15.4 | n.a. | 3.5 | 4.6 | n.a. | 4.5 | 22 | 7.6 | 17.2 | 20.1 | 0.2 | 15.2 | n.a. | 10.6 | 60 |

For definitions, see current yearbook.

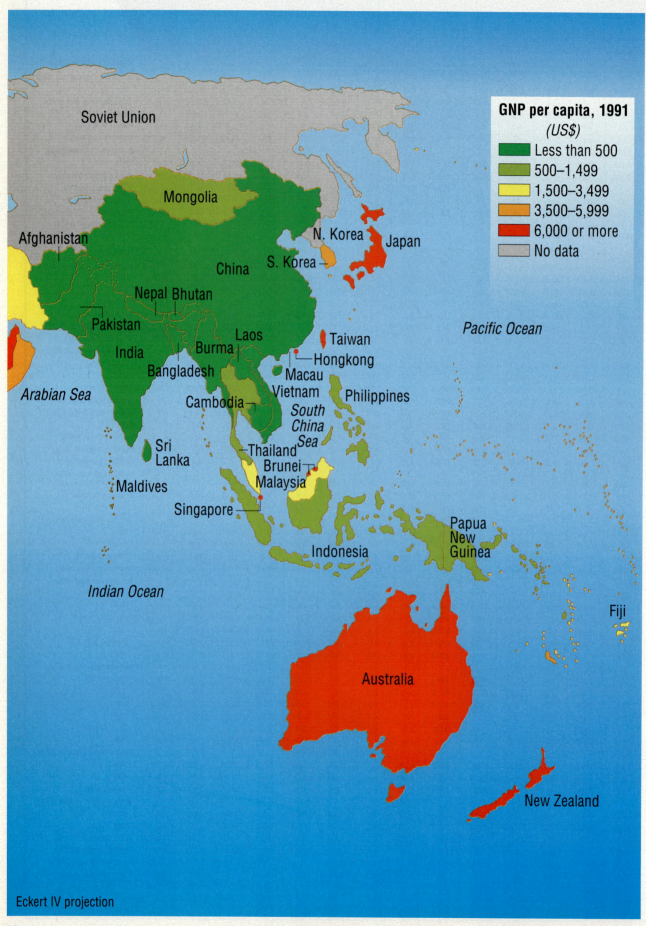

**GNP per capita, 1991**
*(US$)*

- Less than 500
- 500–1,499
- 1,500–3,499
- 3,500–5,999
- 6,000 or more
- No data

Soviet Union

Mongolia

Afghanistan

China

N. Korea

Japan

S. Korea

Nepal Bhutan

Pacific Ocean

Pakistan

India

Burma

Laos

Taiwan

Hongkong

Bangladesh

Macau

Vietnam

Philippines

Arabian Sea

Cambodia

South China Sea

Sri Lanka

Thailand

Brunei

Maldives

Malaysia

Singapore

Indonesia

Papua New Guinea

Indian Ocean

Fiji

Australia

New Zealand

Eckert IV projection

# OVERVIEW

According to the rhetoric of the Gulf War victors, 1991 was the year of the New World Order. US-Soviet detente was the occasion for the imposition by the West, through the medium of the UN, of a degree of order on an unruly Middle East. But for Asia, 1991 was more redolent of the waning of an old order than the creation of a new one.

The year was marked by increasing strains between Asian nations and their traditional allies outside the region. And though it saw the prospect of peace in two local conflicts which had long been nourished by global power plays, it marked the ending of old certainties and the emergence of more complex patterns of power and influence. Symbolically, it was appropriate that the year was also the 50th anniversary of the attack on Pearl Harbour and Japan's attempt to substitute its own East Asian empire for those of the Western colonial powers.

The Gulf War was a watershed. Although most Asian nations backed the liberation of Kuwait with troops, money or rhetoric, there was much resentment in East Asia — notably in Japan and South Korea — over Western demands that they do more to help the war effort.

Equally, though the Gulf War briefly highlighted the utility of US bases in the Philippines, this factor was soon overshadowed by declining US interest in their strategic value. This was fortuitously brought home by an Act of God in June when the eruption of Mt Pinatubo rendered Clark airbase useless. So when the Philippine Senate rejected a new bases agreement in September, it did so in the knowledge that the US no longer had an overwhelming interest in twisting the arms or crossing the palms of the senators.

The US military presence will not vanish from Asia. Guam offers a relatively close alternative to Subic Bay, while bases in Japan and South Korea remain important. In addition, lesser facilities have been agreed with Singapore, and more informally, with other Asean countries. The US has even taken the opportunity of Moscow's decline to strike up a useful naval dialogue with India. Nevertheless, the US military role in the region is slowly waning, and reluctant though many of Japan's people and neighbours may be, Tokyo's presence — especially naval — will continue to grow.

International detente almost brought peace to Cambodia during 1991, and brought it a good deal closer in Afghanistan. But its greatest strategic impact was perhaps in South Korea, as Seoul's wooing of Moscow with offers of aid and trade paid off dramatically. When Soviet President Mikhail Gorbachov met South Korean President Roh Tae Woo in Cheju, he announced a Soviet switch to a "two Korea" policy which so isolated Pyongyang that — following pressure from Peking — the North agreed to drop its "one Korea" policy and apply for UN membership at the same time as the South.

However, the political troubles in the crumbling Soviet Union put in doubt some of the gains of Seoul's northern diplomacy. In addition, overtures to the North, which had been proceeding quite well, appeared to snag on the question of Pyongyang's nuclear ambitions — which while uncertain remain sufficiently alarming to cause serious concern to Tokyo and Washington as well as Seoul.

Seoul and Washington seemed to agree that if Pyongyang's bomb making ambitions were halted, there could be an accord

to withdraw US nuclear weapons based in the South. Although there is still a theoretical military threat from the North, Seoul has become at least as worried about the unpredictability of Pyongyang politics in the face of a likely succession struggle when Kim Il Sung dies.

While Seoul courted Moscow, Tokyo held itself aloof. The result was that Japan failed to commit itself to providing massive aid for the crumbling Soviet economy, and was unable to negotiate the return of its lost islands.

Apart from the Gulf War, the other issue where a fissure appeared between Asia and its trans-Pacific partners were trade blocs. This was summed up in the struggle for ascendancy between two sets of acronyms: Apec (Asia-Pacific Economic Cooperation forum) and EAEG (East Asian Economic Grouping, later transmogrified into the East Asia Economic Caucus [EAEC]). The first embraced a pan-Pacific identity of interest, the latter a narrower, all-Asian grouping that excluded the US, Canada and — depending on definitions — Australasia.

Apec's origins stemmed from an Australian-inspired idea to create a community of interests in the face of the perceived protectionist threat of post-1992 Europe. The EAEG concept, launched by Malaysian Prime Minister Datuk Seri Mahathir

Mohamad in late 1990, was impelled by pan-Asian sentiments and aimed more specifically at the possible threat to Asian interests of the North America Free Trade Area (Nafta).

While few Asian's were worried when Nafta embraced only the US and Canada, the inclusion of low cost, developing Mexico radically altered the equation. Some feared Nafta would extend even further and embrace other Latin American countries, which in turn would acquire a preferential edge in the US market and become a magnet for investment that would otherwise have gone to Asia.

Mahathir's proposal got at best a lukewarm official reception in the region. While Tokyo tried to appear neutral, Seoul — which hosted Apec's 1991 summit — was openly critical, not least from fears that the EAEG/EAEC would be dominated by Japan. Indonesia was also cool to the idea, preferring to seek a balance in its relations with Japan, the US and Europe. The fact was that however much some Asian nations resented the US or feared Nafta, the US remained the primary export market for almost all of them.

Meanwhile, Asia's own attempt at a sub-regional bloc — Asean — made little convincing progress in 1991. At a meeting in Kuala Lumpur during July, members agreed to aim for free trade between themselves within 15 years. But so many exclusions were made even at the beginning — including the entire agricultural sector — that there were serious doubts whether the goal had much practical significance.

For all the talk of Apec, EAEG/EAEC and Asean, the barriers to trade within the Asian region were often more formidable than to trade with other areas. While figures show Northeast Asian countries have increased the share of their trade accounted for by Southeast Asia — as these booming economies suck in consumer durables and capital goods from their more developed neighbours — Southeast Asian trade in the other direction has been nothing like so buoyant.

Nonetheless, the Southeast Asian economies increasingly look northwards for their main sources of capital and industrial investment. In the short term there may even be overinvestment in new manufacturing plants, as world markets stagnate and domestic ones do not expand as fast as hoped. In the medium term, Southeast Asian countries face the problem of a decline in Japanese and Taiwanese investment due to overcapacity, tight money and weak profits. In the longer term, however, the outflow of investment from Northeast Asia should ensure close ties and continuing trade-based development throughout the region.

Another irritant in Asia's relations with the West during 1991 was the latter's emphasis on human rights and democracy. This was most apparent in Sino-US relations, but also caused strains between the EC and Asean in relation both to Asean's attitude towards Burma and the human-rights strings attached to aid.

The extension of Japan's generally benign influence in the region was not matched by advances in its politics at home. Although former prime minister Toshiki Kaifu succeeded in retaining his clean image while many around him became mired in financial scandals that emerged in the wake of the collapse of the stockmarket and land speculation booms, he was unable to survive dissatisfaction within the Liberal Democratic Party (LDP) over his performance and was replaced in late October by Kiichi Miyazawa. While Miyazawa is well known and respected overseas, the nature of LDP politics make it unlikely that he will be able to map a more coherent strategy for guiding Japan's foreign and trade policies.

Domestic politics were relatively quiet in much of Asia during 1991, with the notable exception of the Subcontinent. India suffered another trauma when Congress party leader Rajiv Gandhi was assassinated on 21 May during the country's general election campaign. But the election itself led to a revival of Congress and the stemming of a strong challenge by the Hindu nationalist Bharatiya Janata Party. Further, the new government of Prime Minister P. V. Narasimha Rao proved more decisive than many observers expected.

Under pressure from a foreign-exchange crisis and the need for IMF support, Narasimha Rao and his Finance Minister Manmohan Singh introduced sweeping economic liberalisation measures, including a much less restrictive attitude to foreign investment, the reduction of trade barriers and the promise of long-term reforms of the banking sector and loss-making public enterprises.

Meanwhile, next door in Pakistan, Prime Minister Nawaz Sharif's government was making even more dramatic moves towards liberalising the economy as huge chunks of Pakistan's extensive, and largely inefficient, public-sector industries and financial institutions were put up for whole or partial sale. While it remains to be seen how successful the hastily conceived and politically flavoured programme will be, it was further testimony to the economic changes sweeping through South Asia as it sought to emulate the faster growing countries to the east.

Bangladesh also started to move towards both economic liberalisation and greater fiscal rectitude in the aftermath of Begum Khaleda Zia's Bangladesh National Party victory in the 27 February elections. While the success of the widow of an assassinated former prime minister over Sheikh Hasina Wajed, daughter of Bangladesh's assassinated founding father Sheikh Mujib, was regarded as an electoral upset, the fairly honest and peaceful elections were themselves a victory in a country which had manifestly suffered previous violent changes of power. Nevertheless, the new government faces formidable obstacles in quelling lawlessness and getting the economy moving after years of waste and mismanagement under former president H. M. Ershad, resigned in December 1990 after weeks of anti-government demonstrations. Ershad was sentenced to 10 years imprisonment in June after being convicted of illegal arms possession.

Democracy, however, still remained a dream in neighbouring Burma. The ruling State Law and Order Restoration Council's (SLORC) iron grip on a people who had conclusively rejected them in the May 1990 elections continued to tighten during the year. The award of the Nobel Peace Prize to detained opposition leader Aung Sang Suu Kyi in October also put the SLORC on the defensive. Further, the economic liberalisation policies previously enunciated by the SLORC lost momentum as political exigencies took precedence. Nevertheless, the government continued to profit from timber, gem and other deals with Thai businessmen, which helped pay for the arms it received from China.

Thailand experienced another form of military intervention during the year. The uneasy balance between elected civilian and military forces broke down in late February when a military coup toppled the government of Chatichai Choonhavan, ostensibly because of its pervasive corruption. An interim civilian government installed by the military and headed by a respected bureaucrat Anand Pancharayun made its mark with a clean and efficient administration. However, neither military intervention nor the temporary Anand administration could resolve the underlying problems of Thai politics, where money and personal ambitions remain as powerful ingredients as the interplay of institutionalised civilian and military groups.

Malaysia basked in political stability following Mahathir's National Front coalition election victory in 1990 and another year of rapid economic growth. However, as 1991 ended, Kuala Lumpur faced the prospect of a sharp economic slowdown and political jockeying for the eventual succession to the leadership.

The succession in Singapore, personified by Prime Minister Goh Chok Tong, had a difficult first year despite a buoyant economy. In a general election held on 31 August, the vote for the ruling People's Action Party (PAP) was reduced to 61% from 63% in the 1988 polls, while the opposition presence in parliament rose from a single seat to four MPs. Given the decision of Singapore's founding father Lee Kuan Yew to relinquish his post as prime minister in November 1990, such a slippage in the vote may have seemed unsurprising. But Goh had set a public goal of increasing the PAP share as a vote of confidence in his more liberal attitudes. As a result, he came in for criticism and pressure from harder-line PAP members, including his predecessor.

Lee's retirement from the prime ministership — though not from politics — is unlikely to be emulated in Indonesia. President Suharto made plain his intention to run for another term in 1992. The economy continued to made headway and weather some severe overheating in the financial sector. The country also played a more conspicuous role in Asean and international affairs, though separatist problems in East Timor and Aceh continued to affect its image.

While Indonesia had made a significant contribution to the solution of the Cambodian problem, in the event much of the kudos for October's peace settlement went to the UN Security Council members, notably France. Whether the uneasy agreement between the various Khmer parties will hold remains to be seen, but by the end of 1991 almost all outside parties had an interest in settlement — not least the Thais with their economic interests in Cambodia, and both China and Vietnam, who made their own rapprochement.

China and Vietnam shared common dilemmas: how to maintain the credibility of communist party leadership after the collapse of communism in most other countries, and how to promote relatively liberal, market oriented economic policies without undermining their political authority. While Vietnam brought in some younger leaders and kept itself open to foreign capital as the day when the US embargo would end drew slowly closer, political movement remained glacial.

Peking pursued a generally successful foreign policy, using its Gulf War position to regain ground with the West and by being more helpful on issues relating to the Korean peninsula and Indochina. However, officially enunciated domestic policy appeared to vary widely between economic liberalism and echoes of the Mao era. Although economic growth remains strong in those regions and economic sectors relatively free of central control, state-owned heavy industries continue to be a burden while an inability to bring about fiscal reform threatens to rekindle inflation.

China also took a tough line towards Hongkong. It extracted a visit to Peking from British Prime Minister John Major before it gave its blessing to the colony's new airport — a project that was supposed to be within the domain of the Hongkong Government. It also won an unequal contest with London over interpretations of the Sino-British Joint Declaration on Hongkong, and generally made every effort to undermine attempts to allow Hongkong residents more say in running their own affairs. Despite the overwhelming defeat of pro-China candidates in Hongkong's first direct elections to some Legislative Council seats, Peking maintained unremitting hostility towards local democrats and their aspirations to play a role in government.

Similar examples of Peking's imperious attitude were also evident in threats against pro-independence sentiments in Taiwan. The ruling Kuomintang was equally concerned about this trend, though Taiwan's electorate appeared to take a pragmatic attitude towards the issue. While cautiously continuing to develop economic relations with China, Taiwan had some success in rebuilding its own international links.

China, however, may soon have reason to be more concerned at what is happening in the states along its northern and eastern borders, notably nuclear-armed Russia and mainly Muslim Kazhakstan. Kazhakstan emerged from the wreckage of the Soviet Union during 1991 as a major player in its own right, with a formidable leader in its President Nursultan Nazarbayev. Virtually unthinkable at the start of the year, this seismic shift in Central Asia represents one of the many new complications to have emerged in the region during 1991 as a result of the collapse of the old order. **— PHILIP BOWRING**

# POWER GAME

Desert storms and superpower implosions, as well as volcanic eruptions in the Philippines, shook Asia's strategic environment to its foundations in 1991, leaving defence planners scrambling to respond to the fluid aftermath of these developments. The rapid disintegration of the Soviet Union and the one-sided, US-led victory against Iraq in the Gulf War shattered long-held assumptions defining global and regional strategic balances, as well as how modern wars can be fought in the high-technology era.

Less developed and small countries, who can ill-afford to allot scarce resources to defence, would like to cut their military spending. But they are inhibited from doing so because of a perceived power vacuum left by the Soviet collapse as well as a shrinking US presence in Asia, that could well accelerate in the next few years. And with some of the larger regional states perhaps looking to take advantage of this opportunity to expand their influence, strong pressures remain for states to continue to develop their military capabilities.

The Soviet Union's transformation from a strong unified superpower into a federation of loosely tied republics in the space of a few weeks following August's failed putsch holds far-reaching strategic implications for Asia, in particular for neighbouring countries. Shortly after the coup, the new Soviet Prime Minister Ivan Silayev announced that the 1992 defence budget would be cut by 50% to Rbl 50 billion (US$84.5 billion) — though a significant level of military expenditure is not included in the official budget.

This will mean a much smaller and less centrally controlled Soviet Far Eastern military presence. The Russian Republic, whose authority stretches over much of the Soviet Far Eastern territories, is certain to play a more assertive role in defining foreign and security policies with Asian states. This will include in particular the Northern Territories — or Kurile Islands — dispute with Japan.

When Soviet President Mikhail Gorbachov visited Tokyo in April, he was unable to meet Japanese demands for a return of the four islands. This was a major disappointment to the Japanese, who had hoped for some movement on the issue, especially as they dangled the carrot of substantial financial aid on a positive resolution of the problem. Gorbachov's inability to compromise appeared to be due to pressure from hardliners in his government, in particular military leaders such as now disgraced former Soviet defence minister Gen. Dimitri Yazov — who declared that the Kuriles were too strategically important to be returned to Japan. One of the few gestures Gorbachov made was to announce a token reduction of some 2,000 troops based in the disputed islands. Following the coup, Russian President Boris Yeltsin seems to have softened his position on the islands and appears to be more flexible over a staged return of the Kuriles to Japan.

The main military value of the Kuriles is to provide protection for strategic missile submarines of the Soviet Pacific Fleet deployed in the Sea of Okhotsk, regarded by the Soviets as a sanctuary against US and Japanese naval forces. These submarines are a key element of the Soviet nuclear deterrent force,

Gulf War: shots heard around the world.

but their value even before the August coup appeared to have been downgraded with the signing of the Strategic Arms Reduction Talks treaty between Moscow and Washington in July to cut their nuclear arsenals by up to one-third. Proposals are now being seriously floated by Yeltsin, top military commanders and leaders of other republics for further sweeping nuclear arms cuts of at least 50%.

How far Soviet conventional forces will be pruned has yet to be decided, but as military forces in this region have been spared much of the wrenching reductions and restructuring of Soviet forces in the European theatre, they could be in for substantial cutbacks. Indeed, Far Eastern forces have benefited considerably from the European draw-down following the signing of the Conventional Forces in Europe (CFE) agreement and the continuing withdrawal of Soviet forces from the former Warsaw Pact bloc countries of Eastern Europe. Far Eastern units have received modern weapon systems, including tanks and aircraft, to replace ageing equipment.

Before the coup, regional Soviet military commanders had insisted there would be no further unilateral cutbacks following the completion of a 120,000 troop reduction announced by Gorbachov in December 1988. They wanted to keep in place the 40-odd divisions located in the Far Eastern theatre, which extends from east of the Ural Mountains to the maritime provinces on the Pacific coast. Nearly half these divisions are located in the Far Eastern Military District, which faces both Japan and the eastern sector of the Sino-Soviet border.

The CFE accord had caused concern among Japanese defence planners, as Tokyo considered peace in Europe was being secured at Japan's expense, particularly with the massive transfer of Soviet weapons and war-stocks east of the Urals — including more than 10,000 tanks.

Nevertheless, the continued reduction of Soviet military power places Japan in a difficult position. The dilemma, ironically, arises from the country's dependence on the US security umbrella. During the Cold War, the US-Japan defence relationship was solidly anchored on meeting the Soviet threat. But this consensus appears to be unravelling in the post–Cold War era as US and Japanese assessments of the Soviet military threat increasingly diverge. While the US grows steadily less concerned about the Soviets, the Japanese remain acutely wary and still see them as a potential threat — though publicly they have stopped referring to the Soviets in this context.

Tokyo is, therefore, fearful of being eventually marginalised by the US-Soviet detente, especially as Washington and Moscow are cooperating closely on a growing number of security issues. These range from mutual nuclear and conventional arms reductions, joint efforts to end various regional conflicts and deepening ties between the Soviet and US military establishments. The US is pressing the Japanese to enter into a security dialogue with the Soviets, something Tokyo has so far refused to do.

Perhaps the ultimate irony is that the greatest source of concern for Japanese security planners now is not a possible

Soviet attack, but the threat of Soviet arms-control proposals. The Soviets have suggested numerous initiatives for arms control in the Pacific, primarily focused on reducing naval forces. These have been quickly rejected by the US, who refuse to entertain any suggestions that could undermine their naval supremacy in the region, and by Japan. More difficult for the Japanese to ignore are invitations to observe Soviet military exercises and various other confidence building measures, including naval port visits, especially as the Soviet and US navies are engaging in such a process.

Nonetheless, with the continuing retreat of Soviet military power and the growing security dialogue between Moscow, Washington and its European allies, Tokyo's security planners will have an increasingly difficult time explaining to the Japanese electorate why they remain the only country in the Western alliance yet to come to terms with the end of the Cold War and military confrontation with the Soviets.

These pressures have so far only had a limited impact on Japan's continuing military build-up, with spending in the 1991-95 defence programme being trimmed from an average growth of more than 5% in real terms in the 1980s to a still healthy 3% increase.

The Japanese Defence Agency (JDA) this year asked for a 5.4% increase in defence spending to ¥4.62 trillion (US$33.5 billion) to pay for the purchase of 28 locally built Type 90 tanks, nine warships, 11 F15 fighters, 10 Patriot ground-to-air missile systems and other weapons. There was no request, however, for Boeing E3 air-borne early warning aircraft (Awacs), which the US has been urging the Japanese to buy to help offset the two countries' trade gap. The JDA had included the Awacs in the country's ¥22.75 trillion 1991-95 mid-term defence plan, but disagreements between the Japanese and Boeing over the price of the aircraft appears to have scuttled the deal.

The Japanese are also looking to find new missions for the military to perform, and options being considered include providing greater support to the US and UN in regional conflicts. The belated dispatch of Japanese minesweepers to the Gulf and discussions over the secondment of Japanese troops for UN peace-keeping missions are key developments in this re-orientation. Tokyo is also considering providing greater logistical support for US forces stationed in Japan, in part to help offset the reduction in US military forces in the region over the next decade, which will primarily involve US support rather than combat personnel.

The Chinese are more relaxed about the Soviets militarily, if not politically. Peking has, for example, raised no public concerns over the Soviet redeployment of weapons and material from Europe to east of the Urals, in part not to create tensions that could have disrupted the rapid development in Sino-Soviet military ties before the coup. Peking also wants to acquire advanced Soviet weapons to boost its floundering military modernisation efforts, and has accepted Moscow's assurances that its forces pose no danger to China's security.

While the re-establishment of Sino-Soviet military ties removes a major source of potential friction in Asia, it is of growing concern to some states in the region. Soviet weapons sales to China — including an agreement signed in May for the Chinese purchase of 24 Su27 combat aircraft — are another

area of worry for Japan, Taiwan and other states and could help boost the arms race in Asia. China began taking delivery of a small number of the Su27s in June, which will eventually be deployed either in the country's central or eastern provinces following Moscow's insistence that the aircraft cannot be stationed in northern China facing Soviet forces.

The aftermath of the Soviet coup could, however, slow the pace of future Sino-Soviet military cooperation. Moscow may reassess additional arms sales and cooperation in weapons production, particularly with the decline in influence of the military and defence industrial sectors in Soviet policymaking.

Taiwan has followed China's purchase of the Su27s with concern, and has made efforts to try and acquire more sophisticated combat aircraft to offset the developments on the mainland. There are reports that Taiwan and Israel signed a memorandum of understanding in the middle of the year for 40 Kfir fighters, while Taipei has pushed Washington to sell it more advanced F16 fighters — something the US has declined to do in order to avoid antagonising Peking. Taiwan's efforts to acquire foreign combat aircraft also reflects concerns that the development of its own indigenous defence fighter (IDF) is not going well. In August, an IDF prototype crashed and the aircraft have experienced problems due to an inadequate, under-powered engine.

China is also looking to trim the size of its armed forces, with reports of between 200-500,000 troops being axed, many from the 1 million deployed facing Soviet divisions across the country's northern border. Nonetheless, the Chinese remain wary of long-term Soviet strategic intentions, in particular with the possible ethnic and other types of instability that will stem from the looser structure of power in the post-communist Soviet state.

China has pressed for a symbolic partial demilitarisation of the Sino-Soviet border and for the reduction of Soviet forces in the region to the levels of the early 1960s, before Sino-Soviet tensions escalated into strategic confrontation. At that time, the Soviets only had some 15 divisions in the Far East.

THE STOCK HOUSE

**Soviet coup attempt: Russia awakes.**

Politically, however, the failed coup has sparked fears within China's conservative leadership of possible threats to the country's own internal security. This is likely to see a renewed political clampdown within the People's Liberation Army (PLA) and its internal security arm, the People's Armed Police. Since the Peking crackdown in June 1989, political and conservative military leaders have been particularly concerned over the PLA's political reliability.

An exhaustive politicisation campaign has been waged by hardline political commissars led by Gen. Yang Baibing, director of the PLA General Political Department, to weed out possible dissent in the ranks and reaffirm the army's loyalty to the communist party. In the aftermath of the Gulf War, there was a gradual shift of emphasis away from politicisation to professionalism in PLA priorities, but this could be reversed by the impact of the Soviet coup.

The Gulf War painfully underlined how backward and unprepared the PLA is to fight a modern war. Although PLA planners acknowledged this fact some years ago, lack of funds have prevented them from tackling the problem.

To allow the PLA to begin to modestly upgrade its capability, the government raised defence appropriations this year by 12% to Rmb 32.5 billion (US$6 billion). While the increased funds fall far short of what the PLA requires for a major modernisation programme, it nevertheless signals that the military is again at the top of national priorities.

While China pushed ahead with higher defence budgets, the momentum of India's military build-up eased slightly with a cutback in defence spending as the new Congress-led minority government tried to rein in a spiralling budget deficit. Although the armed forces received a modest 3.8% increase to Rs 183.5 billion (US$7.1 billion), after inflation this represents a real reduction of between 5-6%. As a result, the navy's acquisition of a new aircraft carrier was cancelled.

The financial constraints on India's military will be even more deeply felt following a 20% devaluation of the rupee, which will affect foreign weapons purchases. The scale of future arms imports, which come overwhelmingly from the Soviet Union, was also put in doubt following the Soviet coup. New Delhi relies on Moscow for at least 70% of its equipment, and though Soviet officials emphasised that the upheavals would not affect Indo-Soviet relations, the reality is different.

In recent months, Soviet arms factories have been demanding hard currency for spare parts which the Indian armed forces need to maintain its weapons. But New Delhi's foreign-currency reserves were severely depleted with the sharp rise in the cost of importing oil following Iraq's invasion of Kuwait. Consequently, in August India's Defence Minister Krishna Kumar went to Moscow to negotiate the acquisition of arms and spare parts through the two countries' rupee-rouble barter trade regime.

Nonetheless, India remains committed to a long-term build-up of its defence capabilities, primarily to offset military developments in Pakistan. Indian defence officials announced that the country would begin to mass-produce two locally built missiles for deployment in 1992. These are the Prithvi, a battlefield support missile with a range of 250 km, and the short range anti-aircraft Trishul missile.

Subic Bay: paradise lost.

There are question marks, however, over the viability of two other indigenous weapons projects, the Arjun main battle tank and the Light Combat Aircraft (LCA). Indian defence policymakers are now reassessing the Arjun programme, which after 17 years of development is still plagued by serious problems. In July, the Soviet Union offered its latest combat aircraft, including the multi-role Su37 and the MiG30 fighter, as an alternative to the LCA.

There have been efforts to improve confidence between India and Pakistan, including an agreement not to attack each other's nuclear facilities which came into effect in January, and an arrangement in April to give prior notice on military exercises. Despite these developments, the two countries' relations continue to remain tense, with continuing military clashes along their borders in Kashmir and Punjab.

This growth of the military reach of India, China and Japan is a mounting source of concern to Southeast Asian and other states in the region, in particular in the face of the retreat of Soviet and — to a lesser extent — US military power from the area. The almost complete withdrawal of Soviet warships and aircraft from Cam Ranh Bay in Vietnam, as well as an abrupt cutback in Soviet military assistance to Vietnam and Cambodia, have removed the Soviet Union from the military calcula-

tions of Asean countries.

The rapidly changing international environment is pushing Asean states to reconsider security ties among themselves and with external powers. In July at the Asean post-ministerial conference in Kuala Lumpur, Japan's Foreign Minister Taro Nakayama suggested the establishment of a framework for discussing regional security issues between Asean and major powers. The Asean response was predictably cautious, with officials talking broadly of the need to improve security by enhancing confidence through economic cooperation and other non-military measures.

At the working military level, Asean countries continued to forge closer ties — though deep-rooted suspicions and tensions remain not far from the surface. Although Singapore and Indonesia signed an agreement in early August to jointly develop an air-combat range in eastern Sumatra, a week later Singaporean officials expressed concern at the first-ever joint field exercise held between the Indonesian and Malaysian armed forces in southern Johor, close to Singapore.

Asean states continued their efforts to build up their military capabilities. Malaysia announced in June that it would allocate nearly M$6 billion (US$2.15 billion) for defence expenditure in the country's sixth national development plan over the next 10 years. This represents more than a 230% increase over defence spending for the previous plan. Most of the funds are intended to go towards purchasing weapons from Britain, including the acquisition of 28 Hawk fighter aircraft costing US$740 million, two missile corvettes, construction of several major bases and the possible purchase of submarines.

Malaysia also announced plans to form a rapid deployment force of around 10-15,000 troops to be operational by 1993. This reflects growing concern in Kuala Lumpur over the possibility of conflict in the Spratly Islands during the next few years. Malaysia, China, Vietnam, the Philippines and Taiwan claim sovereignty over some or all of the archipelago. Malaysia began building an airstrip on one of the three Spratly atolls that it claims, partly to strengthen its defences on them and also ostensibly to develop tourist facilities. With this emphasis on a more technologically sophisticated and mobile organisation, the armed forces will trim back its numbers from 120,000 to around 100,000 personnel.

Other Asean states also raised their defence spending in the past year to meet new weapons purchases. Thailand increased its 1991 defence budget by 13.5% to Baht 68.73 billion (US$2.75 billion), representing nearly 15% of the country's national expenditure. Despite this hefty increase, Thai military commanders maintain there are insufficient funds to purchase new weapons systems, and have pushed for a special extra-budgetary account to cover additional arms buys.

These funds would be used to finance the acquisition of a 7,800-dwt German-built helicopter carrier, due to be delivered in late 1994; an additional squadron of F16 fighters; Italian-Brazilian AMX ground-attack aircraft and 30 A7E Corsair II strike aircraft for the Thai navy from the US Government. But with the declining land threat from Vietnam and Cambodia, the Thai army announced it would cut back its purchase of surplus US M60 tanks from 300 to 100 tanks.

Other Asean and Southeast Asian countries are also planning to expand their inventories. In August, the Philippines announced it would buy five F16 fighters to boost the air force's ageing front-line fleet of fighters, and will take delivery of 10 OV-10 counter-insurgency aircraft.

The Indonesian air force is also negotiating to buy several dozen Hawk fighter/trainer aircraft, to complement 20 of the same aircraft it bought from Britain in the early 1980s. Although no deal has yet been signed, discussions are believed to be at an advanced stage, with the Indonesian aerospace industry looking to locally produce the Hawk. Besides Indonesia and Malaysia, Brunei last year signed a memorandum of understanding to purchase Hawks, and the Philippines and Thailand have expressed interest in the aircraft.

Burma is also stepping up its weapons purchases, primarily looking to China for assistance. The Burmese armed forces are acquiring a dozen F7 fighters, six Hainan-class patrol boats, around 100 light and medium tanks, substantial numbers of armoured personnel carriers, anti-aircraft guns and large amounts of munitions. In addition, Yugoslavia and Poland have both supplied military equipment to Burma, including G4 Super Galeb strike aircraft and transport helicopters.

The momentum towards increased Asean security cooperation looks likely to accelerate with the decision by the Philippines' Senate on 16 September to reject a treaty extending US rights to the use of Subic Bay naval base, primarily because they considered US compensation as inadequate. Manila now seems set to allow the US three years to withdraw its naval forces from Subic.

The Senate decision marks a turning point in US-Philippine relations as well as for the geo-strategic landscape of Southeast Asia, where a permanent US military presence has been taken almost for granted for the past century. Although the bases have irked Philippine and other Southeast Asian nationalists from time to time, defence planners have seen the US presence as a key component in ensuring the region's security. Senior Southeast Asian policy-makers say that the pullout of

**Korean peninsula: watch and wait.**

the US from the Philippines could see other powers, in particular China, become more assertive in the region.

Even before the rejection of the Subic Bay agreement, Washington had decided to abandon Clark airbase, the second major US military facility in the Philippines, after the sudden eruption of Mt Pinatubo in mid-June covered Clark, Subic and surrounding areas in thick layers of ash and lava. The economic, military and other costs to the Philippines from the withdrawal of US assistance if the bases are closed down appear to be high. The country would lose more than US$200 million annually in direct US compensation for the bases over the next 10 years, a reduction in US military aid to the armed forces and the possibility — according to some senior Philippines military officials — of another coup or a boost to the flagging fortunes of the communist-led insurgency movement.

The US is now studying options to relocate its military units, which are primarily naval forces, from the Philippines to other parts of Asia. It appears certain that this presence will be dispersed from Singapore and Japan to the US dependent territory of Guam rather than in one single location as with Subic. Some of these facilities will provide temporary staging facilities rather than permanent basing rights. Singapore, for example, has allowed US aircraft and warships to use its military

facilities on a routine but non-permanent basis.

To what extent Washington will continue to maintain a sizeable military presence in Asia with the end of the Cold War will depend on the domestic debate over the future direction of US defence policy.

Although the Pentagon has already drawn up plans to reduce its military presence in Asia by 10-12%, or around 15,000 personnel, by 1992 this could be speeded up and expanded if more budget cuts materialise. US President George Bush, however, says the US role to guard against regional conflicts requires a continued strong and global US military presence.

The collapse of communism around the world has only tentatively begun to be felt on the Korean peninsula. North Korea's refusal to allow international inspection of its nuclear facilities at Yongbyon has prompted growing regional concerns, in particular from South Korea, Japan and the US, that Pyongyang is within a few years of acquiring the capability to produce a crude nuclear bomb.

Seoul's concern over the Yongbyon facilities was shown when South Korea's Defence Minister Lee Jong Koo remarked that South might have to launch a commando raid if the North did not open Yongbyon to international inspection. However, Bush's announcement in late September that the US would remove its nuclear weapons based in South Korea may be met by Pyongyang's agreement to international inspection.

In addition to Pyongyang's suspected nuclear activities, regional states are also worried about North Korea's missile developments — not least after South Korean defence officials reported the North was developing a new missile, the Rodong-1, with an 800-km range that could reach Japan.

Nonetheless, with Moscow and Peking increasingly unwilling to provide military and other assistance to Pyongyang, South Korean defence planners have begun to consider a time when the North Korean threat and the US–South Korean military alliance no longer define their strategic perceptions.

Visible evidence of this more relaxed security posture is a slowdown in the growth of South Korea's defence budget. Although defence appropriations in 1991 were 10% more than for 1990, after readjustment for inflation this was a decline in real terms of between 2-5%, the first cut in defence spending in recent years. While the decrease was relatively small, its impact is significant because defence planning has rested on the assumption of a steadily growing allocation of resources. Consequently, military chiefs are having to reassess procurement and organisational priorities.

Among indications of reduced South Korean concerns over the threat from the North includes a reduction in the size of the annual "Team Spirit" military exercises between the South Korean and US armed forces. Next year's exercises will involve 100,000 troops, against the 200,000 deployed in 1991.

The most publicised example of this reassessment in South Korea's defence priorities was the decision by Seoul in March to reverse an order for the acquisition of 120 US-built F/A18 combat aircraft and instead buy, as well as license produce, 120 cheaper F16s. The reversal was primarily based on cost, as the price tag for the F/A18 project had jumped from an original US$5 billion to US$6.5 billion by 1991 while the F16s are estimated to cost US$5.3 billion over the next five years.

# Does your corporate bank open doors or knock on them ?

## LTCB opens doors to a world of financial possibilities.

We know what's going on — in your industry and ours. Our influential, independent position in global finance makes us a prime source of information as well as funding for your ventures.

Money isn't everything...especially in finance. Sometimes you need a door-opener, too.

 **LTCB**

## The Long-Term Credit Bank of Japan, Limited

Tokyo, London, Paris, Brussels, Frankfurt, Zurich, Milan, Madrid, Bahrain,
New York, Chicago, Los Angeles, Greenwich, Philadelphia, Toronto,
Atlanta, Dallas, Mexico City, São Paulo, Rio de Janeiro,
Hong Kong, Singapore, Beijing, Shanghai, Guangzou, Seoul, Bangkok,
Kuala Lumpur, Jakarta, Sydney, Melbourne

# POPULATION

Complacency is taking root in the struggle to keep the world's population under control. As developing countries follow the developed in reducing fertility rates, there is a growing belief that the problem is being solved. Women in developing countries now each produce an average of 3.9 children compared with 6.1 some 30 years ago — a trend greatly helped by developments in East Asia, where the family size has been reduced from 6.1 to 2.7. South Asia, where the baby boom is more serious, has also made progress by reducing the average number of children per woman to 4.7.

However, there is a tendency to overlook the fact that the world population is still growing as more women are reaching marriageable age. On the best information available, the UN estimates world population currently at 5.4 billion, that it will take just 10 years to reach 6.4 billion, by 2025 it will top 8.5 and will then double to more than 10 billion within the next 100 years. The UN estimates world population will not level off until it has topped 11.6 billion.

The UN sees Asia's population rising from its present 3.1 billion to 4.9 billion in 2025. This represents a growth rate of 1.8%, the average increase for the world as a whole, and means that the number of potential parents doubles every 39 years. Most of the increase will be in South Asia, where the population will leap from 1.2 to 2.1 billion and overtake the population of East Asia, currently home to 20% of the world's total population. South Asia will also see the largest population growth in numerical terms of any region in the world.

Within East Asia, the birth rate in Japan has dropped below replacement level with an average family size of fewer than two children, a point China will probably reach before the end of this century.

What has caused concern over the population explosion to ease is that the growth rate has fallen in every five-year period since 1965-70, when the world's population was expanding at 2.04% a year. However, as absolute population growth lags well behind falls in the percentage growth rate, the time it takes for the world population to grow by an extra billion contracts. From 3 to 4 billion took 15 years between 1960-75, to 5 billion took almost 13 years, to 6 billion took 12 years, and reaching 7 billion will probably also take 12 years. Only then will the gap start to grow again, with 8 billion reached in 2024.

The problem is that 94 out of every 100 children are born in the developing world, where pressures on land and resources are widespread.

While the World Bank says the gap between rich and poor nations, at least in terms of infant mortality and life expectancy, has narrowed more quickly due to the spread of medical technology, improved sanitation, better nutrition and education, it also points out that living standards in some countries have actually fallen over the past 30 years.

The UN estimates that 75% of poor people in the developing world live in ecologically fragile zones, with some 580 million people subsisting in absolute poverty on marginal or fragile land. In this respect, Asia is the worst affected. While 24 billion tonnes of topsoil are lost around the world each year, 44% of Asia's arable land is affected by moderate or severe soil erosion. This compares with 40% in Africa, 31% in Western Europe and 30% in the US.

Explosive urban growth, partly as a result of mass migration from land too poor to sustain increasing population, means many countries have doubled their urban population in 10 years. In Asia, while the population as a whole is growing by 1.8% a year, the annual growth of the urban population is 4.2%. The spread of urban growth is roughly equal throughout the region.

The UN says: "Apart from the escalating need for city services, housing, water and sanitation, governments are presented with the formidable task of supplying food for urban populations. In 1969, developing countries imported 20 million tonnes of cereals. By 1983 that had tripled and by the end of the century it is projected to be 112 million tonnes."

It is the imbalance of population growth that is the primary cause for concern. While some countries, such as China and Thailand, have experienced a sharp decline in reproduction — in China's case through a strict government policy, but elsewhere as a result of increased personal choice — over-population shows signs of becoming a catastrophe in some parts of the world.

William Brass, emeritus professor of medical demography at the University of London, cites Bangladesh as being in "a desperate situation, with rapid population growth and few signs that it will come under control in the near future." With 115 million people, Bangladesh already ranks ninth in the population league table, though there are more than 50 countries with a greater area of habitable land.

What makes the example of Bangladesh particularly worrying is that the country has made considerable progress in reducing its rate of population increase. The birthrate has

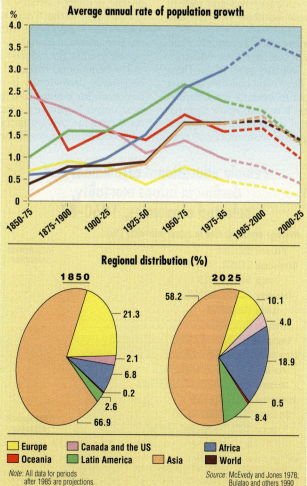

## Population change by region, 1850-2025

**Average annual rate of population growth**

Regional distribution (%)

1850
- 21.3
- 2.1
- 6.8
- 0.2
- 2.6
- 66.9

2025
- 58.2
- 10.1
- 4.0
- 18.9
- 0.5
- 8.4

Europe
Oceania
Canada and the US
Latin America
Africa
Asia
World

*Note*: All data for periods after 1985 are projections.

*Source*: McEvedy and Jones 1978; Bulatao and others 1990

**Educated females: key to child survival.**

fallen from 48 per 1,000 in 1971 to 38 per 1,000 at present. While only 5% of couples used contraception 15 years ago, the figure has risen to 33% and should reach 50% by 2000. These figures can be put into context by a comparison with Thailand, where the proportion of married women using contraception has risen from 15% in 1970 to 70% at present, and where the fertility rate has been halved in 20 years.

The International Planned Parenthood Federation (IPPF), the world's second-largest voluntary organisation, eschews coercion in persuading couples to use contraceptives and instead emphasises that fewer babies mean healthier children and healthier mothers.

IPPF spokeswoman Frances Perrow says: "For family planning to become part of people's lives you have to demonstrate that it is in their interests to use it. In many parts of the Third World women think they need to have eight children because four will die and they will need four to work the land. Family planning officers have to show that if women space their babies further, allowing each longer at the breast to get a good start in life, their survival rate improves dramatically. A two-year gap between children can cut the infant mortality rate by a third."

The World Bank has called for more government spending on family planning projects to help children survive infancy. "A 20% rise in the proportion of villages with a family planning clinic would reduce infant mortality by more than 4% in India," the bank reports.

Nutrition obviously also plays a large part in raising life expectancy. A World Bank study shows that improvements in nutrition account for four-tenths of the decline in mortality rates, with nearly all the effect concentrated on infant mortality rates.

However, the bank also found a correlation between female levels of education and a decline in infant mortality.

Pakistan, Bangladesh and India, where the average number of years of schooling for girls is comparatively low, have reduced infant mortality rates by less than 2% a year — in Bangladesh's case by only 1% a year. Indonesia, which stands in the median range, has achieved a 2.5% reduction in infant mortality, while Hongkong, Singapore, South Korea and Malaysia — which have better records in educating girls — have been reducing infant mortality by 4% a year. Japan, where girls stay in school longer than in any other Asian country, has seen the decline in infant mortality run at more than 6% a year.

According to the World Bank: "An extra year of education for women is associated with a drop of 2 percentage points in the rate of infant mortality. Household-level studies have reported even larger reductions of 5-10 percentage points."

The bank found that cutting infant mortality rates does not necessarily dramatically increase the population, since better education for women also cuts fertility rates. Countries with near universal primary education for boys, but where enrolment rates for girls lag far behind, have twice the infant mortality and fertility rates of countries with a smaller gender gap.

"Failing to raise women's level of education closer to men's detracts from the social benefits of raising men's," the bank said.

While the decline in death rates from about 30 per thousand in 1945 to about 10 per thousand now has outweighed the decline in fertility rates, the bank said: "Urbanisation and economic growth in developing countries both tend to reduce population growth. They make caring for children more difficult or more expensive; they encourage parents to spend more on educating each child than on supporting a bigger family. In India, farm households in higher-growth areas which were exposed to the new technologies of the green revolution had fewer children and gave them significantly more

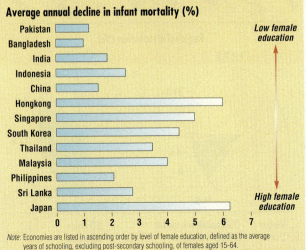

**Female educational attainment and decline in infant mortality, selected economies, 1960-87**

Average annual decline in infant mortality (%)

*Low female education*

| | |
|---|---|
| Pakistan | |
| Bangladesh | |
| India | |
| Indonesia | |
| China | |
| Hongkong | |
| Singapore | |
| South Korea | |
| Thailand | |
| Malaysia | |
| Philippines | |
| Sri Lanka | |
| Japan | |

0  1  2  3  4  5  6  7

*High female education*

Note: Economies are listed in ascending order by level of female education, defined as the average years of schooling, excluding post-secondary schooling, of females aged 15-64.

Source: World Bank data

schooling than did those in other areas."

The bank continued: "But income control is neither necessary nor sufficient to control population. Family planning programmes can work. The implementation of these programmes has contributed significantly to the decline of fertility in low-income countries such as Indonesia and Sri Lanka. Thailand has successfully reduced its population growth rate from 3.1% in the 1960s to 1.9% in the 1980s and the total fertility rate declined from 6.3 children in 1965 to 2.5 in 1989."

Despite progress in reducing population growth and in producing more food, the world has been consuming more grain than it has produced since 1987. UN and US figures show a prolonged "grasshopper" phase of overconsuming rice and cereals — so-called after the fable in which the grasshopper eats through the summer and makes no provision for winter. The grain mountains that towered over agricultural markets and international politics have been eroded to foothills. Part of the reason has been drought and crop failures in the US, Africa, China and the Soviet Union that saw the world consume in two years 152 million tonnes more grain than it produced, an amount equivalent to half the US' annual production.

Some agronomists and conservationists see these figures as an early warning of greater trouble to come. They say the extraordinary acceleration in food production from the 1960s to the 1980s, fed by technical advances, is tapering off. This is an ominous signal for Asia, where many countries were at the forefront of progress during the boom years.

The green revolution in the 1960s and 1970s was possible because of high-yielding hybrid varieties of wheat and maize, dwarf varieties of rice and the introduction of chemical fertilisers and pesticides. India doubled its average yield of wheat within a few years after the introduction of these improvements, while in China — where rural reforms provided added flexibility in farming practices — new grain varieties and farming techniques made it possible to support 22% of the world's population on 7% of its arable land.

Lester Brown of the Worldwatch Institute in Washington, however, cautions that the surpluses of the early 1980s will come to be seen as borrowed production based on over-farming and over-irrigating, both ecologically destructive in the long term. "If you subtract production based on unsustainable use of land and water, there is a built-in deficiency in world food production even in a good year," Brown says.

A sideline to the population debate — and a warning of what could happen in other Asian countries if growth is curbed too suddenly — is provided by China. Until the late 1950s the population structure was pyramid shaped, with a broad base of young people supporting progressively fewer older people. China was then a "paediatric" country with far more children than adults.

This began to change during the enforced collectivisation of the Great Leap Forward in the late 1950s and early 1960s, and is now manifested in a shortage of men and women in their early 30s. The decline in the birthrate since enforced birth controls were introduced in the 1970s has been even more dramatic, and has resulted in a large number of young adults in their early 20s with a diminishing number of teenagers and children in each subsequent year. The real problems will emerge as these groups have to support their elders as they reach retirement age.

"Demographic ageing is a phenomenon often disregarded in the long list of difficulties facing the Third World," the UN notes. "However, it will become one of the major economic and social problems as an ineluctable demographic change takes place in countries that are hardly prepared to cope with it because it is completely new."

# REFUGEES

A number of factors have combined to reduce the pressures that create refugees throughout Asia, and the trend appears to signal a general decline among those who are seeking to escape instability and persecution. However, economic pressures — both existing and potential — are likely to remain a force that will drive some to seek a better future beyond their own country's borders.

By mid-1991, the total number of boat people arrivals from Vietnam in the Asean region stood at 768, against 19,935 by mid-1990. During the first six months of 1991 voluntary repatriation to Vietnam from Asean members reached some 3,000, or about four times the arrival rate.

The available evidence indicates this massive drop in arrivals can be credited to a combination of improved socio-economic conditions in Vietnam, expansion of legal departures through the Orderly Departure Programme and the success of the UN High Commissioner for Refugees' (UNHCR) information campaign. This campaign sought to warn potential boat people of the dangers of illegal departure and of the need to be recognised as a refugee as a prerequisite for resettlement from first asylum camps.

However, while the movement of boat people from southern Vietnam to the Asean region appears to have virtually ended, the exodus from central and northern Vietnam to Hongkong during the first half of 1991 (12,929) quadrupled against the same period in 1990 (2,993), though it remained some 40% below the level of 1989 (22,975).

As no new developments occurred inside Vietnam in terms of human rights that would justify an increased rate of departure, the causes for the renewed exodus to Hongkong resulted from a number of other factors. These include the ease and safety of access, low departure cost — some US$50 from northern Vietnam — and increased economic hardship in the traditionally depressed centre of the country following Vietnam's switch to a market economy and a corresponding cut in state subsidies.

A compounding factor was misinformation from abroad, notably the rumour that boat people would be resettled or given work in Kuwait. In addition, Hongkong's policy of giving US$30 a month for one year to those who agreed to voluntary repatriation from the colony — a total of 9,352 by the end of August — and Vietnam's agreement not to prosecute those who left illegally, might actually have encouraged departures of people from depressed areas who felt they had nothing to lose by leaving.

By mid-1991, Hongkong had to bear the brunt of some 60% of the region's entire boat

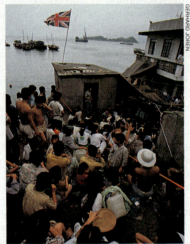

**Boat people: coming and going.**

people population — 57,590 against Asean's 53,200 — and at a cost of some US$100 million borne mainly by local taxpayers. Given that some 80% of the total are not expected to meet refugee status criteria and would therefore have to return to Vietnam, it was increasingly obvious that the cost of maintaining non-refugees in camps greatly exceeds the expense caused by recognised refugees.

While the minuscule arrival rate in the Asean region clearly reduced the urgency for action by the countries concerned, Hongkong's share of the caseload and the continued high — albeit reduced — arrival rate put the colony under pressure to establish an acceptable repatriation mechanism with Hanoi for the non-refugees in parallel to the voluntary repatriation process. In late September, Hanoi signalled that it was prepared to accept the return of its nationals held in Hongkong camps who had been designated "illegal immigrants" by the colonial authorities. Following Vietnam's apparent change of position, the attitude of the US Government towards the "involuntary repatriation" of migrants seeking refuge in Hongkong now remains the main stumbling block in emptying the colony's camps.

The fate of Khmer refugees in Thailand continues to hinge on the negotiations to find a solution to the Cambodian conflict. Except for some 14,600 refugees in the UNHCR-run Khao I Dang camp, the remaining 340,000 displaced Khmers are in six sites on the Thai side of the Thai-Cambodian border under the aegis of the UN Border Relief Organisation.

These people were initially on the Cambodian side of the border and were driven into Thailand during the 1984 Vietnamese offensive. Each camp has a Khmer administration tied to one of the three resistance factions. Although individual residents of the camps are not generally part of a faction, it is estimated that the Khmer People's National Liberation Front administration includes some 200,000 refugees, Prince Norodom Sihanouk's resistance faction another 60,000 and the Khmer Rouge a further 65,000 or so.

Contingency repatriation plans by UNHCR include four staging areas from which refugees will be processed for return. What role the factions will play in the repatriation process is unclear, and is likely to remain so pending a comprehensive peace settlement.

Contrary to the handling of the Vietnamese boat people, screening Lao asylum seekers arriving in Thailand for refugee status — and the mandatory repatriation of those who fail to meet the criteria — has

## Refugees in Asia

**Arrivals in Hongkong**
*No. of people*

| | 1989 | 1990 | 1991 (Jan.-June) |
|---|---|---|---|

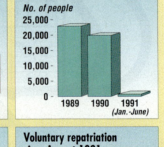

**Arrivals in Asean**
*No. of people*

| | 1989 | 1990 | 1991 (Jan.-June) |
|---|---|---|---|

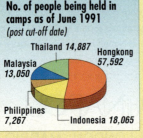

**No. of people being held in camps as of June 1991**
*(post cut-off date)*

Thailand 14,887
Hongkong 57,592
Malaysia 13,050
Philippines 7,267
Indonesia 18,065

**Voluntary repatriation since August 1991**

| | No. of people |
|---|---|
| Hongkong | 9,352 |
| Thailand | 1,606 |
| Indonesia | 1,434 |
| Malaysia | 381 |
| Philippines | 145 |
| **Total** | **13,156** |

*Source: UNHCR*

failed to arouse much international interest or concern. Screening started in July 1985, and since 1986 the Lao Government has accepted the return — whether voluntary or mandatory — of all those screened out.

In practice, all returnees are treated by Vientiane as volunteers and the UNHCR-monitored programme has been uncontroversial. With new arrivals having virtually ceased, the present number of Lao refugees in Thailand stands at some 55,500. Of this total, 7,500 are lowland Lao and 48,000 are mainly Hmong hill tribes people. Due to their association with the US during the Vietnam War, the Hmong pose a special problem and for many years did not fit either resettlement or repatriation schemes.

The evolving situation in Laos has recently opened new avenues for solutions, and contacts have been established between the Lao Government, Thai authorities, Hmong leaders and UNHCR for a possible repatriation of the group with appropriate guarantees.

After Indochina, Afghanistan has been the other largest source of refugees in Asia. There are officially some 3 million Afghan refugees in Pakistan and another 2 million in Iran. However, some sources question the accuracy of these figures, arguing that they include traditional migrants as well as people who have become integrated in their country of asylum.

Since the Soviet Union withdrew its forces from Afghanistan in early 1989, more than 300,000 refugees have been repatriated — half from Iran and half from Pakistan — and a similar number are expected to return this year. However, the extension of the contested areas as each party seeks to acquire more territory ahead of possible negotiations, coupled with disagreements among the Afghan resistance groups, has thwarted any larger-scale organised repatriation.

What impact the present upheaval in the Soviet Union will have on the level of Moscow's aid to Kabul — estimated at US$250 million a month — is unknown, but no major changes are expected in the refugee situation until a clarification of the internal Afghan political and military equation.

Refugees in Asia are, for the most part, the by-product of regional conflicts fought either with direct superpower involvement or by superpower proxies. As the level of superpower confrontation decreases, regional conflicts will either be solved through negotiations or will fade in intensity and scope. This, in turn, should lead to a reduction in the region's refugee population, and while Asia's diasporas might not come to an immediate end, their nature will change.

For example, Vietnam's switch towards a market economy has created economic shifts that have a serious negative impact on poorer areas of the country, and will continue to do so until conditions stabilise. Such conditions will almost certainly produce population movement, though in the absence of persecution not refugees under the rubric of UN definition.

Generally improved relations have already brought about the beginning of a normalisation of ties between China and Vietnam. The ultimate result should be a Cambodian peace settlement that would include a solution to the Khmer refugee problem.

The fragmentation of power in Afghanistan, on the other hand, may result in a less clear solution. However, given the Soviet Union's likely further disengagement from Afghanistan, it is doubtful that Western nations will continue to support Afghan refugees in camps in Pakistan and Iran, particularly if the conflict becomes one of primarily tribal confrontation.

The overall trend towards conflict resolution is a clear indicator that — with variables — many of Asia's pressing refugee issues are on the way to being brought to a conclusion. However, whether the result will permit an eventual minority of genuine refugees to continue to seek asylum is uncertain. □

# DEVELOPMENT BANKS AND AID

As commercial bank lending to the poorer countries contracted dramatically through the 1980s, development banks came to play an increasingly important role as sources of finance. But official grants and foreign direct investment could not, and cannot, compensate fully for the drying up of funds, and there has been a decline in the flow of net resources.

Three factors stand out as being of particular importance to Asia: its relatively disadvantaged status within the World Bank given the proportion of the world's poor who live in the region; the major and growing importance of Japan as an alternative source of finance for Asian development; and the inability of the Asian Development Bank (ADB) to compensate for the capital shortfalls.

As a result of these factors, the World Bank is seeking to co-opt Japan into playing a wider role in the development process in Asia, especially in poorer areas. This could change the nature of Asian economic development over the next decade.

Asia has become the "step-child" of international development, according to Attila Karaosmanoglu, until recently vice-president for Asia at the World Bank and now one of three managing directors in the office of the bank's new president Lewis Preston. Karaosmanoglu would like Japan to act as foster parent to Asian development, shifting its emphasis from the rather narrow economic focus of its traditional official development assistance (ODA) policies to embrace broader social objectives.

The World Bank wants Tokyo to help India and other South Asian countries to adopt the Japanese system of education, which Karaosmanoglu sees as having contributed greatly to Japan's post-war economic success. It also wants Japan to codify its industrial and technological policies to provide a kind of development manual for less-developed Asian countries.

Malaysian Prime Minister Datuk Seri Mahathir Mohamad, in particular among Asian leaders, has been a vocal critic of Western models of economic development. Mahathir's "Look East" stance is reflected in his request that Japan lead a proposed East Asian Economic Grouping.

The question is how far the World Bank can promote free-market economics in Asia without offending other philosophies of development. So far, the debate appears to be going the way of the champions of free markets, though there is a growing debate over what kind of economic model is most appropriate in less-developed economies, and over what degree of state intervention is needed to prime the pump of economic activity.

World Bank officials recently found themselves at odds with Tokyo over the issue of subsidised credits, which were part of the Japanese way towards post-war growth. Tokyo has for now conceded the bank's point that directed credits and soft "policy loans" can distort the overall allocation of resources within an economy. But the onus of proving that the economies of poorer nations can take off in a largely intervention-free environment still lies with the World Bank's advocates of "market-friendly" development.

It remains to be seen to what extent Japanese development philosophies can be synthesised with those of the bank and the IMF. The former is pushing ahead with its aim of getting Japan intellectually involved in the development process beyond the realm of its financial contributions, which nowadays are commensurate with its status as the second-largest shareholder in the World Bank behind the US.

On environmental issues — as evidenced in the launching of Japan's US$5.5 million "green aid" plan for Thailand — the World Bank already claims some success. The plan, which is designed to tackle industrial pollution, is along the lines recommended to Tokyo by the bank. Officials hope there will be further opportunities to match the World Bank's global environment facility with Japanese money and expertise.

But wider cooperation could prove to be a more elusive goal. Whereas the multilateral lenders increasingly make their loans conditional upon structural economic reform, Japan as a bilateral donor tends to favour the financing of infrastructural development rather than macro- or micro-economic adjustments. The Japanese aid philosophy also stresses "self-help" by advancing funds on relatively hard terms.

Development specialists argue over whether the so-called Asian economic miracle — or, more precisely, the East Asian miracle — was achieved through letting markets operate freely, or through enlightened government intervention. World Bank officials, however, are more oriented towards specific issues. Asia receives 30-40% of World Bank loans each year and the cumulative Asian loan portfolio (on a commitment rather than disbursement basis) totals more than US$50 billion. The region accounts for about two thirds of the developing world's population.

In recent years, it has been proportionately disadvantaged in comparison with less-populous regions, such as Africa, and could find its position further eroded by the almost universal concern with offering aid to the stricken economies of the Soviet Union and Eastern Europe. Ironically, the World Bank has never needed less to worry about its bottom line. For several years now it has earned more than US$1 billion net, thereby strengthening an already healthy balance sheet.

World Bank officials, meanwhile, point to the emergence of "macro-economic strains" in India and China, together with the weak economic performance over the past decade of Bangladesh, Laos, Burma, Nepal, Papua New Guinea, the Philip-

## Long-term financial flows to low- and middle-income economies, 1981-90

| US$ billion | 1981 | 1982 | 1983 | 1984 | 1985 | 1986 | 1987 | 1988 | 1989 | 1990* |
|---|---|---|---|---|---|---|---|---|---|---|
| Long-term aggregate net resource flows | 99.9 | 88.4 | 68.2 | 61.9 | 56.6 | 51.2 | 46.1 | 60.9 | 63.3 | 71.0 |
| Official development finance | 33.7 | 33.8 | 31.6 | 34.0 | 31.8 | 33.6 | 32.2 | 36.2 | 36.6 | 46.9 |
| Official grants | 11.4 | 10.4 | 9.9 | 11.4 | 13.2 | 14.0 | 14.9 | 18.0 | 18.6 | 19.5 |
| Net official lending | 22.3 | 23.4 | 21.7 | 22.6 | 18.6 | 19.6 | 17.3 | 18.3 | 18.0 | 27.4 |
| Bilateral | 12.9 | 11.9 | 10.6 | 10.3 | 6.4 | 6.3 | 4.9 | 6.8 | 6.1 | 10.4 |
| Multilateral | 9.4 | 11.5 | 11.0 | 12.4 | 12.2 | 13.3 | 12.4 | 11.5 | 11.9 | 16.9 |
| Net private loans | 53.3 | 43.6 | 28.1 | 19.6 | 14.3 | 8.1 | 0.7 | 5.5 | 4.3 | 2.3 |
| Commercial banks | 44.0 | 30.9 | 19.8 | 14.6 | 4.7 | 2.4 | -1.1 | 0.7 | 3.0 | n.a. |
| Bonds | 1.3 | 4.8 | 1.0 | 0.3 | 5.0 | 1.3 | 0.2 | 2.2 | 0.3 | n.a. |
| Others | 8.0 | 7.8 | 7.4 | 4.7 | 4.5 | 4.4 | 1.6 | 2.6 | 1.0 | n.a. |
| Foreign direct investment | 12.9 | 11.1 | 8.5 | 8.4 | 10.5 | 9.5 | 13.2 | 19.1 | 22.4† | 21.8 |
| Long-term aggregate net transfers# | 45.7 | 27.4 | 10.5 | -0.9 | -7.4 | -10.0 | -16.8 | -9.5 | -1.0 | 9.3 |

n.a.=Not available
*Preliminary
†Estimate
#Long-term aggregate net resource flows minus interest payments and reinvested and remitted profits

*Source*: World Bank

pines, Vietnam and the Pacific Islands.

"We believe that if Asia is to resume its impressive performance of growth with equity, it needs to launch a second wave of reforms, make more determined efforts for poverty reduction and population control and initiate a concerted programme for an environment-friendly development strategy," Karaosmanoglu says.

Ideas will be just as important as finance for promoting development, he says. "There is a need to look at medium- and long-term issues in Asia [such as education, poverty elimination and the environment] more than anyone is doing at present."

It is at this point that enhanced cooperation with Japan is supposed to enter the picture. Financial cooperation is already well established: Japan has co-financed World Bank–assisted projects to the tune of US$12.5 billion since 1970, but the bank is now anxious to draw Japan deeper into the development process. Not that the institution is short of prescriptions for developing countries. A good deal of its recent lending has taken the form of so-called structural adjustment loans, rather than straight project or programme credit, especially in Africa and Latin America.

Less than 10% of the World Bank's Asian lending takes this form, a tribute in part to the generally sound economic policies being pursued by the region's governments. This may prove to be a blessing if, as is speculated, the bank's new president seeks to restrict adjustment-type lending in favour of a more conventional financing role.

Asia's record of loan disbursement and implementation is also relatively good, according to World Bank senior economist Vinod Thomas. The region has the capacity to absorb more bank lending than is on offer, he notes. But the bank is up against two constraints. Its loans cannot exceed 20% of total external borrowing by a country, and loans to any one country must not exceed 10% of the institution's own capital.

The World Bank's two main operating arms — the International Bank for Reconstruction and Development and the International Development Association — disbursed US$29.4 billion to Asia in 1987-91. Although in nominal terms this was larger than for any other region, Asia lagged significantly on a per-capita basis. Latin America, for instance, with an aggregate population nowhere near those of China and India alone, received gross disbursements of nearly US$23 billion over the four-year period.

There appears little chance at present that the Manila-based ADB can take up the slack. The annual meeting of the ADB's governors in Vancouver in April concluded without a decision on the amount of new funds to be committed by donors to the Asian Development Fund (ADF), the bank's arm for dispensing soft loans to the region's poorest countries. The meeting also failed to resolve whether to resume lending to China and to grant India access to ADF funds.

The last ADF replenishment in 1986 — the so-called ADF 5 — totalled US$3.6 billion and has been extended to five years

instead of the originally intended four. At the current pace of lending, ADF 5, which is running largely on repayments from past loans and gains from currency realignments, will be totally depleted by the second quarter of 1992.

In 1990, new commitments by the ADF totalled US$1.5 billion, up just 9% over the previous year and far short of the hopes of would-be recipients. The ADB's regular loans rose 10% in 1990 to US$2.5 billion.

The ADB is shifting away from its traditional role as a lender to public-sector projects in favour of advancing credit to engineer economic and environmental reforms in its client countries. Asia's poorest nations, therefore, are having to implement sensitive economic reform programmes with declining financial backing from institutions such as the ADB.

With the ADB and the World Bank putting increased emphasis on lending linked to structural reform, borrowing countries can no longer expect almost automatic funding for infrastructural developments unless they agree to policy reforms prescribed by the development banks.

Countries that do not wish to swallow such medicine cannot turn to commercial banks to supply them with no-strings financing, and the international capital markets are open only to a few, relatively successful economies, such as Asia's four newly industrialised countries and Thailand and Malaysia.

Asian countries, therefore, are likely to look to Japan with its still booming external surplus for more aid in the future. Japan does not emphasise economic restructuring in its bilateral aid programmes in the same way as the multilateral institutions. But its ODA is much more heavily oriented towards loans and less towards grants than that of other bilateral donors. And Japanese loans are usually on less easy terms than those offered by the World Bank or the ADB.

Japan's global impact on foreign aid may not be as great as many imagined when it temporarily overtook the US as the world's largest provider of ODA in 1989. This was largely due to exchange-rate shifts and other technical factors. By the following year, the US had assumed the top slot again.

But Japan's economic influence in the Asian region is growing, not only through the provision of aid but also through its direct investment in manufacturing. Foreign direct investment has been a major compensation for the contraction in commercial bank lending to developing countries, and Japan has become the largest investor in Asia in terms of annual flows if not in terms of total investment stock.

Thus, through aid and direct investment, Japan's economic influence in Asia could in time overshadow that of Western bilateral donors and the multilateral institutions, which are more preoccupied with other regions of the world. Such trends are likely to be reinforced by an increasing concentration by Japanese commercial banks on lending to Asia and by the increasing use of Japan's capital markets by Asian borrowers.  □

## Net transfers to Asia

| US$ million | China | | India | | Indonesia | | Total for the region | |
|---|---|---|---|---|---|---|---|---|
| Fiscal years | '91 | '87-'91 | '91 | '87-'91 | '91 | '87-'91 | '91 | '87-'91 |
| World Bank commitments | 1,579 | 6,635 | 2,049 | 12,804 | 1,638 | 7,344 | 7,491 | 36,128 |
| Gross disbursements | 1,114 | 4,853 | 1,901 | 9,996 | 1,259 | 6,549 | 5,828 | 29,419 |
| Repayments | 236 | 477 | 595 | 2,202 | 605 | 2,294 | 2,665 | 12,677 |
| Net disbursements | 878 | 4,376 | 1,306 | 7,794 | 653 | 4,255 | 3,164 | 16,742 |
| Interest and charges | 236 | 818 | 742 | 2,886 | 786 | 3,199 | 2,693 | 11,889 |
| Net transfer | 642 | 3,558 | 564 | 4,928 | -133 | 1,056 | 470 | 4,853 |

Source: World Bank Annual Report 1991

Asia's poor: more aid needed.

# Behind some of the world's best cars you will find some of the best ideas.

*Geamatics, AEG's breakthrough in systems automation for better quality, improved safety and environmental acceptability.*

1481 E

The demands put on today's automobiles are increasing with each passing day. Better quality, improved safety and environmental issues are among the major challenges. Together with the highest standard in reliability.

In achieving this goal, AEG's best ideas are the result of setting the highest standards in process expertise and uncompromising performance of its products. With Geamatics, AEG's breakthrough in automation systems for products, systems and customer solutions. Flexibility and continuity guarantee the security of your investment, especially if the expansion is undertaken gradually. The advantage to the automotive industry: Systems, such as those needed in production management technology, surface technology, material handling and testing systems as well as in building automation, all come from one source. With programmable logic controllers from Modicon, the core element of Geamatics.

Because today only those who take a holistic, integrated approach in thought as well as action will also be able to improve even the best automobiles in the future.

**Future needs Ge▲matics.**

*AEG. Member of the Daimler-Benz-Group.*

# TRADE

Efforts to secure a new Uruguay Round trade liberalisation package following the collapse of the "final" ministerial session in Brussels in December 1990 dominated the world trade agenda throughout 1991. There were hopes that the much-sought global trade accord would be ready by the end of the year. However, analysts predicted that given the complexity of the issues under discussion and the lack of progress on the key problem of world farm reform, the Uruguay Round would be extended into early 1992.

Disillusionment with the multilateral trading system led a number of Asian nations, spearheaded by Malaysia, to consider the creation of a regional trade bloc to be known as the East Asian Economic Group. In addition, the US and Canada began talks with Mexico on the establishment of a North American Free Trade Agreement (Nafta). As 1992 drew nearer, the EC came even closer to the elimination of its internal trade barriers and the creation of a single European market.

The formation of the regional trade blocs fuelled concern that the global, non-discriminatory trading system enshrined in the Gatt may be slowly dying. Several international trade experts argued, however, that if the emerging blocs cooperated with each other and agreed to abide by Gatt rules, the multilateral trading system would be reinforced rather than weakened.

An evaluation of regional trade arrangements drawn up by the UN Conference on Trade and Development (Unctad) stressed that such moves could help rationalise production and promote growth. However, Unctad also warned that such blocs cannot replace a properly functioning multilateral trading system and developing countries risked being marginalised as the world broke up into trading segments.

Despite such concerns, the Gulf War at the start of 1991 — coupled with general disillusionment with the negotiating tactics of the US and EC — prevented an early resumption of the stalled trade round. Later, as negotiators began to tackle the complex issues of farm reform, the extension of the multi-fibre agreement (MFA) and the need for a new services accord, they were distracted by political and economic turmoil in the Soviet Union and Eastern Europe.

Efforts to breathe new life into the Uruguay Round took place against a sombre backdrop as world economic growth, hit by the financial fallout from the Gulf crisis, faltered for the third successive year and international trade slowed. Figures published by the IMF, however, held out some hope for 1992. The IMF forecast that world economic growth would accelerate to close to 3% after dropping to about 1% in 1991.

The global rebound would be paced by a recovery in the US where the economy would expand by about 3%, the IMF said. Growth in Japan would slow to slightly under 4% in 1992 from just over 4% in 1991, while recovery in the Middle East would also help stimulate world economic growth, it added.

Most analysts agreed that the developing economies of Asia, Eastern Europe and Africa would need much more time to recover from the impact of the Gulf War. The Asian Development Bank (ADB) stressed that the Gulf crisis had cost its developing member countries more than US$1.2 billion in lost exports and foregone foreign-exchange remittances from migrant workers.

Asia was also hard hit by higher oil prices, except for oil exporting nations like Malaysia and Indonesia. The IMF confirmed that growth in Asian developing economies slipped to 5% in 1991, from 5.2% in 1990 and 5.5% in 1989. The ADB confirmed, however, that Southeast Asia continued to record growth rates ranging between 6.5% and 8.5%.

Hurt by the economic slump, world merchandise trade growth fell in volume terms from 7% in 1989 to 5% in 1990 with a further modest slowdown in 1991. Experts at the Gatt secretariat in Geneva said the depreciation of the dollar triggered a 13% increase in the value of world trade in goods to a new record level of US$3.5 trillion. Trade in services — including transportation, tourism, telecommunications and banking — rose 12% in 1990 to approximately US$770 billion.

Asia's leading exporters of manufactures — notably Hongkong, Singapore, Thailand and Malaysia — recorded average export and import volume growth rates of 7.5 % and 11.5% respectively, well above the world average. Not surprisingly, given their high stake in world trade, Asian countries were particularly disappointed at the collapse of the Uruguay Round at the end of 1990.

The ministerial meeting in Brussels held from 3-7 December 1990 faltered and then broke down over the thorny problem of agricultural reform. The farm dispute prevented negotiators from reaching agreement on the 14 other issues on the agenda, including the future of the world textiles trade — an issue of special importance of Asian nations. Questions such as anti-dumping policy, tropical goods, tariffs and negotiations on a new services agreement were also put on ice.

Gatt director-general Arthur Dunkel managed to get the negotiations back on track in late February. But uncertainty about whether the US Congress would renew the "fast track" trade procedure — under which Congress has to accept or reject any deal negotiated as a package, without amendments — cast a pall over all proceedings in Geneva for the first half of the year. Congress finally extended the administration's fast track authority for two years at the end of May.

Meanwhile, Dunkel attempted to inject new life into the round by streamlining procedures so that the 15 negotiating groups set up in Brussels were reduced to seven. He warned repeatedly that participants would have to show more political will if they hoped to finish the round by the end of 1990. In response, ministers attending an annual meeting of the OECD in Paris declared that the round was "the highest economic priority on the international economic agenda." A similar verbal commitment was made by Western leaders at the economic summit held in London in July.

While Western leaders gave their full political support to the Gatt negotiations, discussions in Geneva continued to mark time. Frustrated negotiators admitted that the round had run into a "credibility gap" as governments, preoccupied by events in the Soviet Union and Eastern Europe, lost interest in the core issues of international trade.

However, one of those issues — the future of the MFA — demanded and, in the end, received top priority. Asian nations had made it clear from the start of the round in 1986 that they were particularly interested in phasing out the 30-year-old agreement and securing a liberalisation of world textile and clothing trade. In Brussels at the end of 1990, negotiators came tantalisingly close to a deal under which MFA restrictions would have been gradually removed over a transitional period of eight to 10 years. But, the collapse of the ministerial talks also blocked an accord on textiles.

For the first half of 1991, textile exporters and importers focused on both the long-term phasing out of the MFA and, with the MFA scheduled to expire on 31 July, on the short-term problem of renewing the agreement for an interim period while the Uruguay Round negotiations continued. Asian exporters demanded that the renewed MFA should incorporate certain improvements in their access to markets and that importing nations should agree to a moratorium on new restrictions during the interim period.

Under a last-minute deal hammered out in Geneva, MFA signatories agreed to a 17-month extension of the agreement from July 1991 to end-December 1992. Importing countries agreed to restrain protectionism through "rollback and standstill" measures, but refused demands for a complete moratorium on restrictions. The EC and the US insisted that since the MFA was only being "rolled over," they would also carry out a "neutral extension" of their bilateral agreements with textile suppliers. Despite these warnings, several Asian countries said they would try and obtain better quotas and growth rates for their exports to the EC and the US.

Hopes that the EC may finally be embarking on the kind of reform of its common agricultural policy (CAP) demanded by both the US and the other 14 so-called Cairns Group exporting nations began to emerge by mid-1991. After months of heated debate, the European Commission finally came up with proposals for radical changes in the CAP involving a 35% cut in cereal prices over the next three years and plans to compensate farmers for lost revenue through direct income support. The EC argued that the plan would help to cut its notorious food surpluses — and reduce the massive export subsidies that distort world trade.

**MFA: Asia loses out again.**

Other farm exporting nations were predictably sceptical about the EC plan, but admitted that the community appeared to be tackling its CAP problems with unprecedented seriousness. The impact of the proposals on the Uruguay Round was not clear by the end of 1991, but EC negotiators were confident that CAP reform would help create a "climate of confidence" in the Gatt talks.

Inside the EC, however, the commission's proposals came under fierce attack from French farmers, who were also worried by the EC's clear political commitment to increase imports of East European farm products. But OECD statistics showing that the major industrialised countries spent US$300 billion during 1990 alone subsidising agriculture provided the European Commission with the ammunition it needed to press ahead with its demands for CAP reform. Following French suggestions, the EC agreed that the bulk of its increased food imports from Hungary, Poland and other East European states would be dispatched as food aid to the Soviet Union.

While the EC held up the agricultural discussions within the round, negotiations on a first-ever services agreement were slowed by US demands that maritime transport be excluded from the future international pact. Washington refused to have its domestic shipping laws made subject to an international services agreement that would impose a multilateral dispute settlement system.

Despite the stalemate in the Uruguay Round, however, Gatt experts noted that at least eight Asian nations, ranging from Bangladesh and Pakistan to South Korea and Japan, had taken the lead over the past four years in liberalising imports by either reducing tariffs, eliminating restrictive quotas or removing non-tariff barriers. The EC's efforts to remove import barriers had been "modest," Gatt said.

Bilateral trade skirmishes between Washington, Brussels and Tokyo continued in 1991. The EC and the US squabbled over EC subsidies for the Airbus and in the corn gluten and oilseed sectors. But, it was Japan that came in for the fiercest bilateral trade attacks from both the EC and the US. A CIA-funded study depicting Japan as an adversary bent on dominating the world economy highlighted the deepening unease in economic relations between Washington and Tokyo.

French Prime Minister Edith Cresson helped sour the already difficult relations between the EC and Japan with her anti-Japanese rhetoric. In a series of widely publicised interviews, Cresson criticised Japanese working habits and denounced the Japanese market as "hermetically sealed." She also managed to delay the signing of an EC-Japan "political declaration" in The Hague in July. But the deal, finally signed by then prime minister Toshiki Kaifu and Netherlands Premier Ruud Lubbers, promised to add a new political and diplomatic dimension to EC-Japan relations.

Despite the words of goodwill, however, the EC and Japan clashed more than once during the year over Brussels' planned treatment of Japanese car exports after the creation of the European single market at the end of 1992. Under a "transitional arrangement" worked out in July with Tokyo, the EC agreed to limit Japan's share of the EC car market to about 2.4 million vehicles, or just under 16% of all cars sold in the EC by 1999. Despite Japanese protests, the EC said this would include both direct exports from Japan and production by Japanese factories based in Europe.

Several Japanese carmakers insisted, however, that there was no agreement on including EC-produced cars in the overall deal. Yutaka Kume, chief executive of Nissan Motor and president of the Japan Automobile Manufacturers' Association, said Japanese carmakers would decide how many cars were produced in Europe without EC interference.

After four years of tense relations, the EC and South Korea hammered out an accord on protecting intellectual property which officials said would help normalise trade links between Seoul and Brussels. Under the terms of the past, South Korea promised not to discriminate against EC firms in granting patent protection in the pharmaceutical and other key sectors.

The EC also promised to revitalise its trade links with Asean following three days of ministerial talks in Luxembourg during May. Ministers from both sides agreed to renegotiate their 10-year-old cooperation agreement, but Asean representatives warned that they would fiercely resist EC attempts to introduce human-rights criteria into their dialogue with the Southeast Asian grouping.

While trade relations with much of Asia look destined to remain uneasy, the EC moved slowly but surely towards expanding its economic links with members of the European Free Trade Area (Efta) and the emerging democracies of Eastern Europe. At the same time, after considerable internal debate and French demands for protection from competing farm products, the EC agreed to widen its "association" links with Hungary, Poland and Czechoslovakia.

Despite the promise of wider economic relations, a number of Efta and East European states made it clear that they were determined to apply for full EC membership. Sweden and Austria applied formally in 1991 but others, including Norway, Finland, Hungary and Poland, were expected to make membership requests soon. ☐

# ASIAN MARKETS

## Finance

**Australia** The Australian currency remained comparatively stable during the year, trading within a 77-80 US cent range, a tight 4% variation that had not been seen since the currency floated in 1983.

The movement for most of the year had been up, despite a continued easing in monetary policy that saw the central bank cut official interest rates three times in line with a trend that began in January 1990 when rates stood at 18%.

By the end of October cash rates were set at 9.5%, though the trades union movement continued to call for them to be eased still further in order to stimulate employment. Unemployment topped 10% late in the year, and is expected to remain at these high levels for the immediate future. While the sharp decline in nominal interest rates could be expected to cut the floor under the value of the currency, it remained strong because real interest rates have deliberately been kept high.

Australia's self-induced recession — brought about by the tight monetary conditions of 1988-89 and exacerbated by worldwide economic slowdown — led to a sharp decline in inflation. The federal government's own forecasts of 4% or so for the 1991-92 year have already been overtaken, and the figures seem likely to come close to 2%.

The government now wants to ensure this hard-won reduction in the inflation rate can be locked in for the medium term. Part of its strategy is to keep real interest rates high in an effort to control any rebound in demand as economic conditions improve. The official line remains that real rates of 5-6% for the short term are necessary to break Australia's traditional boom-bust economic cycle. It is unlikely, therefore, that the local dollar will weaken against its US counterpart until the government alters its policy.

There are some clear signs that this policy is working. Economic forecaster Syntec, for example, has produced figures to show evidence of a healthy recovery based on the steadily improving current-account deficit and the merchandise account — despite continuing weakness in commodity prices.

Syntec also maintained local businesses are learning to compete effectively in the export markets to offset the sharp fall in opportunities at home. The country is now exporting more than it imports and is starting to repay its huge foreign borrowings at a time when global interest rates are falling — factors that could fuel a sharp rise in the local dollar.

While there have been no signs that real interest rates will fall to counter such an eventuality, the government has allowed the central bank to intervene in the market to cap the dollar at around the 80 US cent level. While these moves led the local dollar to slip below 79 US cents during the third quarter, a further drop in official rates will be necessary before it can be expected to fall any lower.

**Thailand** Sharp shifts between the US dollar, deutschemark and yen dominated the baht's movements in most of 1991.

Nevertheless, the baht held its rough alignment with the dollar through the mechanism of the Bank of Thailand's (BOT, the central bank) currency basket.

Although some analysts saw a lessening of the dollar's weighting in the BOT basket, central bankers say the makeup remained unchanged. That would mean the dollar still kept a roughly 85% share of the basket, the analysts said. Nevertheless, the dollar anchor has diminished somewhat due to the easing of foreign-exchange controls, which began in 1990 and were almost complete in 1991. The Gulf War brought sharp shifts in international currency movements, but the central bank proved able to limit their effects on the baht.

The baht traded in a 2.5% shift range against the dollar, though by October it was 1.6% lower than at the end of 1990. It traded in a 6% range against the yen, but swung 18% between its high and low against the deutschemark.

The dollar's overall firmness against the baht was related to BOT's attempts to cool the economy by maintaining tight liquidity, which left Thailand's prime lending rate at 16% over the year's first three quarters. By comparison, offshore interest rates were soft because of Washington's attempts to kick-start the US economy and the 4% gap between the two encouraged heavy overseas borrowing by Thai companies.

Thai banks, the conduits for most of the overseas loans due to an exemption on withholding tax on interest paid on such loans, saw their net foreign liabilities rise to US$2.6 billion by July compared to US$724 million a year earlier.

The incoming money made it difficult for BOT to gear down the economy, which had been expanding at a double-digit pace until 1991. Imports continued to grow at a high rate compared to exports, leaving the country with an expected current-account deficit over 8% of GDP for 1991.

The combination of a large current-account deficit and an economy spurred by continued capital inflow, helped weaken the baht. The situation provoked concern in the second quarter among outside economists and currency traders that the baht would have to be devalued. But BOT officials made a convincing argument to keep it in its trading range by pointing out that imports were still production-oriented, manufactured exports were growing at 28% and inflation was under control. By the fourth quarter, with the economy clearly slowing, devaluation fears faded.

**Hongkong** Apart from a brief period early in the year, the Hongkong dollar surged above the peg that links it to the US currency at a rate of HK$7.80 to US$1. After hovering in a HK$7.79-7.78 range for the first five months of the year, it strengthened further to HK$7.76-7.74.

A short, anomalous interval divided these two periods when the Hongkong Government inadvertently demonstrated what happens under a fixed rate system if one of the currencies offers a significantly higher rate of interest than the other. At the end of May, a political decision was made by Hongkong's

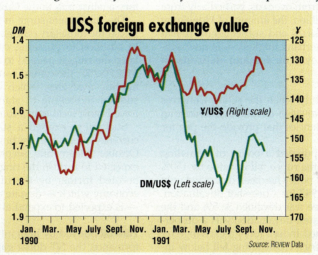

**US$ foreign exchange value**

¥/US$ (Right scale)

DM/US$ (Left scale)

Jan. Mar. May July Sept. Nov. | Jan. Mar. May July Sept. Nov.
1990 | 1991

Source: REVIEW Data

Governor Sir David Wilson that the administration must be seen to be fighting inflation, which had reached 13.9% during the previous month. The result was that the Hongkong Association of Banks — the cartel which fixes the colony's retail interest rates — was directed to raise interest rates by a full percentage point, despite the fact that interbank markets in both the US and Hongkong were anticipating interest-rate cuts.

The Hongkong dollar responded immediately as speculative money — including cash from China — pushed the currency as high as HK$7.724. This level, if sustained, would have undermined the credibility of the government's often stated determination to retain the peg under any circumstances. Inevitably, this attempt to execute an independent monetary policy was short-lived, and the government brought local rates back into line with US rates within six weeks.

The Hongkong dollar also firmed against the yen in the first half of the year, rising from a low of HK$6.099 to ¥100 in February to a peak of HK$5.466 in June — again reflecting the government's attempt to pursue a high interest-rate policy. One result of this strengthening was indicated in the colony's massive surge in Japanese imports. By the second half of the year, however, the currency slowly but persistently weakened again to HK$5.981 in late October.

The year was also marked by the rising volume of Hongkong dollars repatriated from overseas, particularly from China. At more than HK$68 billion, the amount of Hongkong dollars held by overseas banks — and subsequently re-lent back to the colony through interbank markets — is now substantially larger than the level of demand deposits in Hongkong's banking system.

**India** The rupee tumbled in July when the ruling Congress coalition opted for a hefty two-stage devaluation averaging 20% against the basket of currencies that provide the peg for the local unit.

The government has long pursued a policy of "crawling devaluation," which has seen the rupee fall in value by 150% in the past 10 years alone. This policy has been discarded only twice since independence in 1947 for a one-shot devaluation, the first in 1966 when the rupee was devalued 36.5% and the second in July this year. The latest devaluation was a desperate move. The Gulf War drained India's foreign-exchange reserves so badly that the country's credit rating fell below investment grade. There were fears of a debt default and withdrawal of short-term loans and non-resident Indian deposits — which, attracted by high interest rates, total more than Rs 200 billion (US$7.75 billion).

With foreign-exchange reserves down to US$1.2 billion, barely adequate to meet 15 days of import, the new government had to act fast to restore confidence and devalued the rupee. This appears to have worked, at least for the short term, as the rupee has since held firm against the US dollar. According to S. Venkitaramanan, governor of the country's central bank, this is because most of India's foreign trade is dollar denominated. However, the rupee has slid significantly against other major currencies. Inclusive of the impact of devaluation, the rupee fell by 23.9% against sterling, 32.3% against the deutschemark, 27.33% against the yen and 22.6% against the US dollar during the July-September period.

Surging inflation of over 15% has, however, eroded the benefits of devaluation from 20% to 14%. Foreign-exchange dealers said the government had accepted the possibility of a further downward adjustment of 10% against the basket of currencies. Despite government denials, a further devaluation seems inevitable following the announcement in July that the rupee would be made freely convertible within three years. In order to move towards this goal, the rupee will have to be pegged more realistically against major foreign currencies.

**Malaysia** The ringgit's mostly bearish performance throughout the year was an unavoidable by-product of Malaysia's low interest rates and weak balance-of-payments position. Despite repeated interventions by the central bank, the local unit hit a 26-year low against the US dollar on 3 July, closing at M$2.795 to US$1.

The current-account deficit, which reached M$4.7 billion in 1990, is expected to deepen this year. This, combined with strong commercial demand for US dollars and low returns on domestic interest rates, exerted downward pressure on the currency. The ringgit's weakness is also aggravating the problem of "imported" inflation, as the country steps up purchases of foreign machinery and luxury goods in line with its most prodigious economic expansion since the 1970s. Large-scale capital outflows from Malaysia are also escalating as businessmen convert their ringgit-denominated profits into other currencies in order to take advantage of higher overseas interest rates.

The central bank checked further erosions in the ringgit's value as the year drew on, in marked contrast to the start of the year when the local unit experienced a brief period of strength against the US dollar. It ended January at M$2.70 to US$1, after opening the month at M$2.7005. But any initial advantages evaporated after US-led forces scored a swift victory against Iraq in the Gulf War.

The subsequent surge in the US dollar and other currencies forced the monetary officials to adopt a more cautious position. In addition to pursuing currency interventions designed to keep the ringgit pegged to a rough trading range of between M$2.70-2.77, the central bank also introduced tough inflation-fighting measures, which were capped on 16 August by a sudden tightening of statutory reserve requirements that forced most local banks to raise their base lending rates.

Such steps exerted a stabilising effect on the Malaysian currency, which was trading at around M$2.7482 at the end of October. Meanwhile, scepticism over the US economy was expected to furnish the ringgit with more short-term support, boosted further by the underlying strength of Malaysia's economy which — despite an anticipated slowdown this year — is expected to expand at 7-7.5% until the mid-1990s.

**Taiwan** Buoyed by high interest rates and a strong trade performance, the NT dollar gained modestly during most of the year. The stronger currency helped the government finance infrastructure development projects and kept financial liberalisation policies on track.

Unlike 1990, when speculators were betting on a depreciation of the local currency, the year saw some speculation in the opposite direction. The central bank was caught at mid-year in a contradiction between its policies of keeping interest rates high and the exchange rate within a narrow limit.

Although Taiwan's trade surplus contracted, its overall export performance rebounded and reversed much of the pessimism of a year earlier. The favourable trade balance, combined with the central bank's policy of keeping local interest rates well above those in Japan and the US, brought strong pressure on the local dollar to appreciate. From a high of NT$27.50 to US$1 in March to October's NT$26.40, the local currency appreciated some 4% against the US dollar.

Although political tensions late in the year threatened to drive the currency lower, analysts said central bank intervention stabilised the unit and kept it from sliding. An announcement on 24 October that the central bank would reopen the forward exchange market sent the local dollar to an 18-month high of NT$26.375 to US$1.

The local dollar appreciated even more strongly against the deutschemark and yen, both actively traded on the Taipei interbank offering market. The local interbank market reached a record one-day peak volume of US$2.1 billion in February, while daily transactions were averaging more than US$1 billion by September. Currencies traded had expanded from US, Japanese and German units to include eight other Asian and European currencies.

High interest rates and a strong currency also helped reduce outward capital flows — which had reached an excessive level in 1990 — during the year. In an attempt to keep the money at home, the Ministry of Finance equalised the limits for annual foreign-exchange remittances in April, raising the inbound limit from US$2 million to US$3 million and reducing the outbound limit from US$5 million to US$3 million.

Critics of the central bank's policies pointed to excessive growth in the money supply which exceeded the bank's target during most of the year and reached a two-year high in August of nearly 18%. At mid-year, the central bank sold large amounts of NT dollars to reduce appreciation pressures. Bankers said interest rates would have to fall further if central bank intervention continued as the money market could not absorb such large amounts of cash.

## New Zealand

The big puzzle in the New Zealand financial markets was the local dollar's continued defiance of gravity. Despite a huge plunge in interest rates, even compared with foreign rates, the dollar moved very little. At the time of the abortive Soviet coup in August the NZ dollar showed its strength by being one of the currencies into which investors fled.

It dropped from a monthly average of 58.4 on the trade weighted index in January to 58 in September, with long stints in between above 59. Comparable figures for the rate against the US dollar were NZ$1 to 59.5 US cents in January and 58.2 US cents in September, and at NZ$1 to ¥79.70 in January and ¥78.40 in September.

However, these rates remained 8-10% above the levels most exporters regarded as desirable — an argument that carried considerable weight as prices for agricultural products, still around 50% of New Zealand's exports, fell and the balance of payments remained heavily in deficit.

Nevertheless, the resilience of the NZ dollar was to some extent illusory. With the second-lowest inflation rate in the OECD by mid-year and better promised in the second half, the real exchange rate was falling faster than the nominal rate. Although some analysts continued to expect a substantial fall at some point, most reckoned the local dollar would continue to hold its own unless there is a dramatic reversal of government policy.

## Pakistan

The rupee's par value is adjusted by Pakistan's central bank against a managed float of currencies comprising of, among others, US dollars, yen, Saudi riyals, French francs, deutschemarks, lira and sterling. The dollar's relative weight reflects Pakistan's close economic ties with the US in terms of loans, defence purchases and bilateral trade. Pakistan is also heavily dependent on foreign loans to meet its import bill and support its balance of payments.

The rupee has depreciated 55% against the US dollar, 46% against sterling, 72.7% against the deutschemark and 75% against the yen between January 1982 and June 1990. It has fallen an average of 9% a year over the past decade, according to local merchant bank figures.

Although the rupee held reasonably steady against hard currencies in 1990, aside from a few brief rallies it resumed its slide in 1991. Its depreciation against the yen, dollar and riyal in that order was sharply noticeable, though it remained almost static against the deutschemark and sterling. The sharp decline against the dollar began on 27 December 1990, when it fell from Rs 21.85 to US$1 Rs 22.18 in the spot market. This

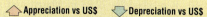

# How they performed against the US dollar in 1991
## (End of 1990=100)

△ Appreciation vs US$     ▽ Depreciation vs US$

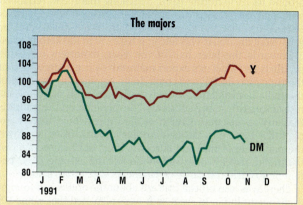

The majors

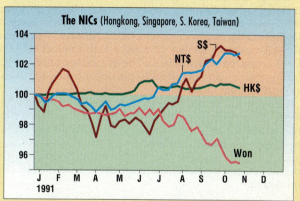

The NICs (Hongkong, Singapore, S. Korea, Taiwan)

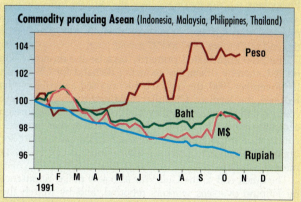

Commodity producing Asean (Indonesia, Malaysia, Philippines, Thailand)

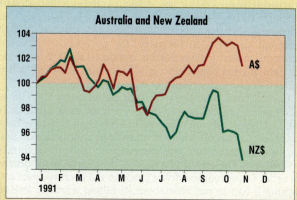

Australia and New Zealand

was in sharp contrast to a loss of only 0.55% in dollar value terms since July 1990, when oil prices began rising and Pakistan's economy was battered by the adverse effects of the Gulf crisis.

By the end of February, the rupee spot rate had fallen to Rs 22.12 to US$1. It reached Rs 22.88 in March and slipped to around Rs 23.50 during April, indicating that it had remained artificially overvalued during the Gulf crisis. It was too weak to keep up with the post-war strength of the dollar, and by early May the dollar was fetching Rs 25.50 in the kerb market.

Towards the later half of the year, exporters of textile products — Pakistan's export mainstay — began arguing that the rupee would have to come down significantly because of the Indian devaluation. However, there was strong domestic resistance against any substantial devaluation on the grounds that any abrupt depreciation of the rupee would merely expand the trade gap through costlier imports. Bringing down the par value of the local currency to its old balance against the Indian rupee would simply double the existing US$2 billion or so current balance-of-payments gap, critics said.

There was also official concern about the outflow of foreign exchange to India. In August, it was calculated that while US dollars purchased through foreign-exchange bearer certificate from the banks at Rs 25.05 to US$1, plus a bank commission of Rs 2 per dollar, were worth Rs 27.05 in Pakistan — against a Rs 24.53 spot rate — they attracted a kerb value of Rs 37 to US$1 across the border in India. The money smuggled out not only earned a premium of Rs 10 per dollar but also financed smuggling from India.

One solution would be to increase interest on foreign-currency deposits, however the central bank has regulated interest rate at a 0.25% above the London interbank rate on the basis that the banks could not earn enough on deposits to justify a higher rate. The rate of interest in Pakistan on the dollar, yen and deutschemark was about 7% and about 13% on sterling.

## Philippines

For the first time since the country officially went on a floating-rate exchange system in the 1960s, the peso appreciated through most of the year, rising from P28 to US$1 at the end of October 1990 to P27 a year later.

The peso appreciated primarily because the economy contracted, thereby drastically reducing demand for US dollars. In November 1990, the central bank imposed a regulation that reduced the level of US-dollar holdings commercial banks could retain above which they had to dispose to the foreign-exchange market. However, this market softened as industries cut back on imports in reaction to an additional import levy imposed to generate revenues after efforts to enact new tax measures collapsed.

The quick end to the Gulf War also saw dollar remittances by Filipino overseas workers rebound, and by March they reached their pre-crisis levels. Adding to the supply of dollars in the financial system were the commercial banks' improved efficiency in attracting remittances previously coursed through informal channels. In February, the government imposed economic austerity measures that convinced the IMF to extend its "seal of good housekeeping." This in turn unlocked stalled foreign loan disbursements totalling US$700 million.

Central bank officials have since claimed that the P28 to US$1 rate set in 25 October 1990, which the bank unofficially pegged through its interventions in the foreign-exchange market, had "overshot" mainly because of its miscalculation that such an exchange rate was necessary to discourage further speculation. The miscalculation cost the central bank dearly. In order to prevent the dollar's rate in the country from collapsing it had to purchase about P1 billion worth of foreign exchange from the banks. This was one major reason for the

money supply's expansion beyond programme targets, which in turn added to inflationary pressures.

The central bank's purchases of foreign exchange, together with the inflow of previously stalled foreign loans, served to dramatically increase the country's gross foreign-exchange reserves to their highest ever level at US$3.6 billion. These reserves now largely underpin the country's financial system, as they give the central bank sufficient resources to prevent speculation on the US dollar when the exchange rate reverses itself with increased import demand.

The peso's appreciation marked a watershed in the Manila foreign-exchange market by substantially weakening the usual speculative forces that had previously prevented the local currency's exchange rate from smoothly seeking its international value. The most credible forecast is that, barring a balance-of-payments crisis, the peso will depreciate to only the P28 to US$1 levels in 1992.

## Indonesia

As in recent years, Indonesia's target in 1991 was to allow the rupiah to depreciate by approximately 5%. The real effective exchange rate of the rupiah depreciated by about 7% in the 12 months to January 1991, but the rate was expected to slow slightly throughout the year.

Bank Indonesia (BI), the central bank, measures the rupiah against a basket of currencies, of which the US dollar is the most important. BI sets an "indication rate" for the rupiah each morning and, after surveying market sentiment, fixes a rate at the end of the day.

Trading in the rupiah by foreign-exchange dealers has increased in the past two years, a consequence of BI's decision to permit market forces to play a greater role in determining the currency's value. However, BI is unlikely to move much further towards a free floating system for the rupiah, as one of its aims is to keep the local unit at a level which makes Indonesia's non-oil exports competitive with exports from other Asian nations.

In the first quarter of the year, fears of a major devaluation led bankers to buy US dollars, which caused a decrease in reserves held by BI. To discourage speculation against the rupiah, in late February Finance Minister Johannes Sumarlin ordered state-owned banks to use Rps 8 trillion (US$4.2 billion) of deposits held by state-owned enterprises to buy short-term BI securities called SBI's.

The central bank then returned all but Rps 400 billion of this amount back into circulation by buying from banks a money-market instrument called SBPUs. The manoeuvre, referred to as the "Sumarlin shock," sapped liquidity out of the system, effectively ended speculation and gave the government more tools with which to effect monetary policy.

Indonesia's monetary officials are generally given high marks for their prudent handling of exchange and interest-rate policy. But these officials are, to some extent, handicapped by having few instruments at their disposal. The reserve requirement for banks was lowered in October 1988 from 15% to 2%, a level which makes the requirement ineffective as a policy tool.

It is also difficult for BI to use open-market transactions to effect policy, principally because the markets for government securities are thinly traded and heavily weighted towards short-maturity instruments. The Sumarlin shock, by putting more central bank paper into circulation, eases monetary policy implementation. In August, BI announced it would issue more longer-maturity securities.

A reduction of BI-subsidised credit programmes, however, helped push up interest rates from below 20% in 1990 to 25-30% for most of 1991. High rates induced many Indonesian corporations to borrow offshore and place loan proceeds on deposit in Indonesia. While one effect was to strengthen the

# THE MORE THE QUESTIONS ???
# THE FEWER THE ANSWERS

COGEMA SERVICES

Options increase. Questions accumulate. Optimum fuel management for your nuclear reactors calls for more numerous and complex strategies.
Whatever your question, the Cogema group helps to provide an answer. Cogema, the major nuclear fuel cycle group, is the only company with expertise in the whole nuclear fuel cycle. Our know-how draws upon more than forty-five years of experience.
Whatever your question, the Cogema group is your closest adviser. Uranium mining and conversion, enrichment, fuel assembly fabrication, reprocessing, transportation, spent fuel conditioning, storage, engineering, consulting, each Cogema group product and service meets your requirements for quality and competitive advantage.
Whatever your question, the Cogema group supports your strategy. Cogema experts contribute to the efficiency of your power generation system. In each step of the nuclear fuel cycle, our industrial commitment means reliable products, flexible services and long-term security of supply.
Whatever your question, the Cogema group is committed to you. Today and tomorrow.

COGEMA: THE MAJOR NUCLEAR FUEL CYCLE GROUP.
2, rue Paul Dautier. 78140 Vélizy-Villacoublay. France. Phone: 33 (1) 39 46 96 41. Fax: 33 (1) 34 65 09 21.

rupiah, another was to increase Indonesian risk to exchange-rate fluctuations.

In July, members of the Association of Private Banks agreed to lower deposit rates, but implementation of this plan has been patchy. The main reason is Indonesia's huge demand for capital, a result of massive private investment in recent years and a large-scale government programme to upgrade infrastructure. The only effective way to bring down interest rates is for the government to loosen the reins on monetary growth, a step it is unlikely to take in the near term given continuing fears of inflationary pressures. Inflation rose 9.5% in 1990, up from 6.1% in 1989, and was running at an annual pace of 11.1% through August.

**Singapore** At the end of October the local dollar was trading at S$1.69 to US$1, almost the same as the S$1.7050 it was trading at in October 1990. However, during the middle of the year the local unit hit levels as low as 1.79 due to the strong US dollar and intervention by the monetary authorities to ensure it did not appreciate too rapidly.

The local currency is actively managed by the central bank, the Monetary Authority of Singapore (MAS), in order to maintain a low enough level to keep the country's exports competitive while also maintaining a high enough level to ensure imported inflation is kept at manageable levels.

The MAS is helped in this through rigid rules it enforces on banks to prevent them "internationalising" the currency. The rules forbid banks from trading in the currency except to meet normal trading commitments and bars them from speculating with the Singapore dollar. The banks are also not allowed to fund loans in Singapore dollars for overseas investments or for third-country transactions.

This leaves the MAS as the dominant player in the Singapore dollar, allowing it to control the currency's movements as it wishes. When some foreign banks broke the rules against speculation in 1985 by aggressively shorting the local currency against the US dollar, the MAS engineered a massive short squeeze which caused the offending institutions heavy losses. Since then, banks have not sought to interfere in the MAS setting the target for the local currency.

While the MAS' guidelines for managing the local dollar are not publicised, analysts believe it employs a basket of currencies drawn from Singapore's major trading partners which it lets the local unit broadly track. As Singapore's main trading partners are, in order of importance, the US, the EC and Japan, the currency is presumed to mainly follow the US dollar, albeit in a narrower band. It appears to do this by trailing the US unit, not weakening as much as the US dollar during trough periods and not strengthening as much during peaks.

As the Singapore economy started showing signs of slowing since the second half of the year — GDP growth for the entire year is expected to be only about 6.5% compared with 8.3% for 1990 — the MAS was faced with the task of easing interest rates to stimulate the local economy. However, it also had to maintain the currency at reasonably strong levels in order to contain consumer-price inflation, which was running at 4% in July — high by Singapore's standards.

Although lower interest rates normally lead to a lower currency, since the Singapore dollar is more than 100% backed by external reserves — and is generally thought to be undervalued — the MAS was able to effectively carry out its "low interest, strong currency" policy.

**Bangladesh** Between July and September, the Bangladesh currency depreciated by about 5% to around Taka 37.33 to US$1 while gaining marginally against other convertible currencies. This compares with a 1% decline in its value against the US dollar between September 1990 and July 1991. Following India's sweeping devaluation in July, the taka gained nearly 24% against the rupee between June 1990 and July 1991. India is Bangladesh's leading trading partner.

Because of a substantial downward adjustment by Bangladesh's other important trading partners, Pakistan and Nepal, the taka has appreciated against both. However, it does not appear to have affected its trading patterns yet, though the recessionary trend has been reflected in overall foreign trade.

Since 1983, Dhaka's exchange-rate management has been based on a trade-weighted basket of currencies, with the US dollar acting as the intervening currency. The taka's rate against other currencies is determined by the daily New York currency market cross rate.

The government has effectively transferred the country's foreign trade transactions from the official to the secondary market, where importers have to pay a premium over the official rate. For the past two or three years, virtually all exports and non-aid financed imports have been transacted through the secondary market.

As the level of the foreign-exchange trading increased, the government tried to narrow the gap between the official and secondary market. While the differential rate was about 15% in 1984-85 and 6.5% in 1987-88, it was maintained at around 2% between 1989-91. Central bank authorities are keen to maintain a unified rate and are anxious to ensure that the two rates do not vary widely.

The blackmarket or "open market" rate, as it is generally referred to in Bangladesh, has been steadily maintained at 5-6% above the official rate over the past year — a relatively low margin in the region.

**South Korea** Battered by a record trade deficit and a second year of 10% inflation, the won continued its slide with no sign that it is approaching bottom. Policymakers have apparently decided that continuing devaluation is the easiest way to cope with the country's economic problems, and unless South Korea's trade situation changes dramatically the won is likely to continue falling throughout 1992. Indeed, business leaders have called for a Won 800 to US$1 level from its present Won 750 rate, and dealers say that level is likely to be breached some time in 1992.

It is hard to make a case for the won strengthening against

any major currency. The won/yen rate, which is critical for South Korea's export competitiveness, may test its historical low of Won 6 to ¥1 in 1992, assuming the country's balance of payments remain weak and inflation continues to run around 10%. South Korea is expected to rack up a second consecutive year of trade deficits with Japan in 1991.

South Korea's foreign-exchange market remained hampered by strict government regulations, designed to prevent speculative transactions, and the tight liquidity at many local companies. Nevertheless, the government took a cautious step towards liberalisation on 1 September, when it widened the daily foreign-exchange trading limits from 0.4% to 0.6% of the previous day's average rate. This followed a slight easing of the country's onerous documentation requirements on 1 July. Proof of an underlying commercial transaction is required for most foreign-exchange deals.

The Ministry of Finance (MoF) has also said it will revise the foreign-exchange control act to further liberalise currency trading. A key feature of the revision, scheduled to take effect on 1 September 1992, will be the adoption of a negative system of foreign-exchange transactions. All transactions are currently prohibited unless the law specifically allows them. The negative system will, in principle, liberalise all transactions except those specifically prohibited. The MoF hopes this reform will remove some of the many ambiguities in South Korea's foreign-exchange market.

**Japan** With global capital flows moving in favour of the US dollar during much of 1991, the yen lost ground to the US unit, though it enjoyed relative strength against an uncertainty-plagued deutschemark. In 1992 the yen is likely to make headway against the dollar and a number of other major currencies, with the possible exception of the deutschemark.

In theory, the yen should have performed much better than it did relative to the dollar during the year. With short-term Japanese interest rates moving somewhat above 7.5% by the middle of the year and consumer-price inflation being contained at 3.5% — giving a real interest rate of 4% — differentials favoured the yen.

But non-economic factors helped override the US real rate of interest slipping around 1.5% as the Federal Reserve progressively eased its monetary stance. In the wake of the Gulf War and the disintegration of the Soviet Union, sentiment rather than economic fundamentals favoured the US dollar.

Towards the end of the year, however, the yen began to gain strength against the dollar and other key currencies, despite Japanese official and market rates of interest trending lower. One reason for this was the perception that the crises in both the Gulf and the Soviet Union had passed. This permitted portfolio capital flows to again follow economic fundamentals rather than to seek safe havens.

The sluggish response of the US economy to stimulative measures also suggested that further cuts in US interest rates were due — eroding prospects for a closing of the real interest-rate gap between the US and Japan.

From around July onward, Japan was experiencing the unusual phenomenon of a growing surplus on its current account and a new inflow on long-term capital account. This partly reflected the withdrawal of Japanese investors from overseas bond markets — a shift favouring yen appreciation. Yet another bull factor for the yen is that Japanese inflation is perceived to be under better control than that elsewhere.

The one threat to the yen in 1992 appears to come not from the US dollar but from the deutschemark. Germany is perceived now to be getting on top of its reunification problems, and while this would lead to a decline in German interest rates, it would also bolster confidence in the economy and the deutschemark. □

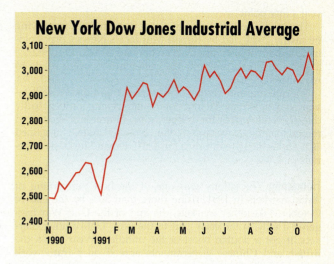

**New York Dow Jones Industrial Average**

## Investment

**Australia** Falling interest rates and a strong currency helped the Australian stockmarket turn in its best performance in recent times during the year. The inexorable rise from its January low point led the All Ordinaries stock indicator to break through a two-year down trend, and set the scene for further gains in 1992.

A positive factor was that investors were prepared to overlook many negative influences. Among the bear points were depressed commodity prices; the worst batch of profit results in more than a decade; forecasts of continuing weak business conditions; and a strong challenge to the leadership of the Prime Minister Bob Hawke's government.

The reason investors ignored the gloom came back to fundamentals, not least that shares began to look like a good bet as interest rates continued their slide. Overseas sentiment helped buoy the optimism. While the Australian sharemarket is nowhere near regaining the peak levels of 1987, the fact that new records were achieved in New York and London were pyschologically important. This was demonstrated when many front-line stocks reached new highs.

The biggest gains, however, were made by the large industrial concerns. Share prices in this sector rose collectively by more than 40% from their January lows, compared with gains of 35% by the market as a whole. Many individual industry groupings also shone, but few more so than banking and media stocks.

The rush for quality banking shares was remarkable because of the continuing high levels of bad and doubtful debts — a product of the recession — and the impact it had on profits. However, demand was so strong that even huge share issues by National Australia Bank, ANZ Banking Group and Commonwealth Bank of Australia, were readily taken up. Bank shares gained 50% from the

Australia

year's low point.

The media sector turned in a star performance, improving by nearly 200%, led by Rupert Murdoch's News Corp. holding company which rose from an opening of A$3.19 (US$2.50) a share to break through A$13 after moves were made to refinance the group.

The mining and resources sector — traditionally well favoured by international investors — fared comparatively badly due to weak prices for copper, zinc, aluminium, gold and mineral sands. Nevertheless, the resources index still gained 30% and is likely to improve further if demand for basic materials pick up.

**Hongkong** The colony was one of the best performing of Asian markets in 1991, rising more than 30% by the end of October. Like other markets, the end of the Gulf War triggered a rally in the early part of the year. Unlike other markets, it got a double boost in the middle of year when the British and Chinese governments agreed on a framework under which Hongkong could go ahead with massive infrastructural projects. The second boost followed the US decision to renew China's most-favoured nation status, at least for 1991.

The result was that in July the Hang Seng Index surged past its 1987 high and through the 4,000 barrier. However, the index's gains were made on sluggish trading volumes, leading several international brokerages — mainly US securities firms — to axe their Hongkong equity operations.

The year also saw a record number of new listings on the bourse, primarily from construction companies seeking to raise capital before bidding on infrastructure related projects, and industrial companies wanting to expand their production capacity in China.

As well as the record number of new listings, the bourse had its fair share of major transactions. Hopewell Holdings' HK$5.5-5.8 billion (US$709-748 million) one-for-one rights issue in June caused some slight gagging, though the long-expected deal was eventually taken up. But the debut of Citic Pacific — 49% ultimately held by China through a state-owned corporation and a ministry — was greeted with great enthusiasm, particularly after it led a consortium that bought a local company for HK$6.9 billion.

Another major feature of the year was the rise to unquestioned pre-eminence of Cheung Kong's Li Ka-shing. Li's proliferation of minority interests in Hongkong counters gave some observers the impression that there was no one else worth watching in the local market.

Technically, however, the market remained underdeveloped, with bans remaining on short-selling and the futures exchange still hampered by the more than HK$1 billion defaults which attended the 1987 stockmarket crash. Moreover, market regulators remained acutely sensitive throughout the year. The Securities and Futures Commission (SFC) demanded the Stock Exchange Council be reformed to better reflect the market's structure and the interests of all the bourse's users. Attempts at negotiated compromises between the SFC and the exchange were repeatedly rebuffed by smaller Chinese brokers, leaving the door open for the SFC to compel the exchange to reform.

**India** The year opened to a crash in equity values, as a speculative bubble built up during the Gulf crisis burst when the government imposed fresh levies to meet higher import costs. Almost all the country's 19 stock exchanges remained closed for a time and the Bombay Stock Exchange (BSE), which accounts for 65% of the market turnover, shut its doors for over two weeks.

The BSE Sensitive Index (Sensex) of 30 scrips fell below 1,000 points from an 9 October 1990 peak of 1,603 points and around Rs 400 million (US$15.5 million) in equity value was wiped out from the Rs 1.1 billion peak.

However, by the end of January all stock exchanges had reopened for trading, heavily supported by financial institutions and bank-sponsored mutual funds. The index went up 7% in just two trading sessions before 1 February.

The rally continued through February, aided by the end of the Gulf War, as Indian investors continued to ignore the country's economic and political problems. The Sensex was up 14% to 1,179.3 by the end of February. The fall of Chandra Shekar's minority government caused the bulls to pause, particularly when the government swapped 20 tonnes of confiscated gold with a Swiss bank, giving the country the first real indication of the seriousness of the foreign-exchange crises.

India's stockmarkets witnessed an unusual degree of speculation this year as huge amounts "black" money found its way to the secondary markets and large investors pledged their long-term holdings with foreign banks and used the funds to

play the bourses. Brokers also reported large amounts of funds from political parties being invested through a few market operators.

The mutual fund concept also gained momentum as small investors found them a better alternative to bank deposits. Brokers said some operators have been pushing up share prices and then unloading them on mutual funds at peak levels by exerting pressure through political connections.

Given this situation, the ground-breaking budget and industrial policy, coupled with the trade policy announced in July that unshackled industry and raised the limit for foreign investment and an amnesty offered to black-money hoarders, was the kind of news the market needed to fuel a further bull run.

The stock exchanges had a 12-week rally from end-July in which all the negative fundamentals — notably soaring inflation, the current-account deficit and the adverse corporate results that are likely in the second half of 1991 — were ignored. Trading volumes reached Rs 2.5 billion a day while the Sensex reached a record high of 1,912.51 in September. However, the rally fizzled later that month and stock indices slid slowly lower. The rise in prices over each two-week cycle no longer matched the cost of carrying over trades, and operators were

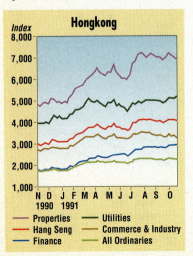

# Our future is looking to us

Chemistry improves our way of life – everywhere and in everything. Drawing its resources from the air, water and ground, it has to find a way to use these precious resources without upsetting nature's equilibrium.

One of the greatest challenges facing our World. A permanent challenge for chemists developing new products for our future. For Atochem it is a commitment.

**ATO**
**ATOCHEM**
elf aquitaine

*THE KEY TO THE CHALLENGE*

forced to liquidate their bull positions.

On 1 October the government announced an amnesty scheme whereby money can be brought in through non-resident Indians as gifts to resident Indians with no questions asked. This resulted in a lot of unaccounted money leaving the capital market — and indeed the country — illegally in order that may be brought back legally.

**Indonesia** Mirroring the broader economy, the Jakarta Stock Exchange (JSE) struggled during the year after 18 months of explosive growth. The JSE composite index opened 1991 at 409 and fell steadily throughout the year.

The most obvious cause was high deposit rates offered by banks which drained liquidity out of the JSE. In addition, brokers identified an outdated trading and settlement system, lax regulation and unreliable financial statements from listed companies as other factors contributing to the market slowdown. After averaging a daily turnover of US$10-20 million for much of 1990, turnover fell to US$5-10 million for most of 1991. Market capitalisation, based on listed shares, is about US$7-8 billion.

Marzuki Usman, the head of the market watchdog agency, Bapepam, said in July that the JSE would be turned over to private owners before the end of 1991. However, a debate over the proper number of shareholders for a privatised exchange has delayed progress on this front.

There are 281 brokers licensed to trade stocks on the JSE, against only 139 listed stocks as of October. For many of the smaller brokers, competition has pushed down commission levels to well below 1%. One foreign broker estimated that the top 20 brokerages account for 75% of market turnover, leaving the remainder to be fought over by some 260 brokers.

The larger brokerage houses and many Finance Ministry officials favour a limited number of shareholders in a privatised exchange with an entry price of Rps 200-300 million (US$101,500-152,500) each. Small brokerage houses, however, say all existing brokers should be entitled to become shareholders in the bourse.

The issue is important because the level of the market's start-up capital will determine how fast the JSE can upgrade its facilities. In September, US consulting firm Price Waterhouse submitted a study of the JSE to Bapepam that recommended the exchange invest in a fully automated trading and settlement system in order to make local brokers "internationally competitive."

Apart from outdated equipment, the JSE is also labouring under a crisis of confidence. Many firms that went public in 1990 produced earnings results well below what was projected just before their initial public offer.

Several proposed regulatory changes may help improve interest in the market. Bills forwarded to parliament in mid-year would allow foreigners to buy shares in bank stocks — currently the only scrip off-limits to overseas investors — and would encourage insurance and pension funds to invest more in the equity market. In addition, another bill would allow a tax exemption for flow-through investment vehicles like mutual funds and venture-capital firms. In August, the parliament gave preliminary approval to these bills, and they were expected to be passed into law by the end of the year.

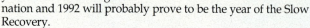

**Japan** If 1990 was the year of the Great Crash on the Tokyo stockmarket, 1991 is best classified as the year of the Great Stagnation and 1992 will probably prove to be the year of the Slow Recovery.

Measured on the Nikkei-225 stock average, the market fell by nearly one half — from close to 40,000 to just above 20,000 — during 1990 before recovering to around 24,000 by the year end. Early 1991 saw a false dawn as the Nikkei edged back up to 27,000, only to slide back to a 22,000-23,000 trading range late in the year.

Interest rates hold the key to much — though not all — of the market's performance. After being pushed resolutely upward under Bank of Japan guidance during 1990, the official discount rate held firm at 6% until July when signs of incipient weakness in the economy allowed the rate to be edged downward by half a point. Market interest rates were also trending downward towards the end of the year.

This took some of the selling pressure out of the stockmarket, but a wave of financial scandals involving leading Japanese brokers and banks administered a hard blow to sentiment. Foreign as well as domestic investors took fright and withdrew funds from the market.

The basic problem is that Tokyo stocks are still far from cheap, by international standards at least. With the market at around 23,000 by October, stocks were still on average selling at around 35 times net earnings and yielding little more than 0.5% annually. Fundamentals may not influence Tokyo stock prices to the same extent as elsewhere as some 75% of all shareholdings are accounted for by inter-company ownership. Such holdings are not normally traded and therefore only the so-called free float of shares are subject to normal investment criteria.

But the Tokyo market is as liquidity-driven as much as any other and towards the end of the year the shortage of corporate, institutional and individual liquidity was becoming more marked. Corporations ran down their big cash balances substantially during 1991 in order to finance major capital-investment programmes, while banks and insurance companies — both major stockmarket investors in the past — also found their funds dwindling under the impact of an official tight-money policy.

Investment trusts, another major player in the Tokyo stockmarket, also suffered big redemptions in the wake of the market crash and because of the adverse impact which various financial scandals had on sentiment.

Corporations and financial institutions are expected to redeem a large proportion of the *tokkin* managed funds they hold with Japanese stockbrokers and trust banks early in 1992. This is expected to exert further downward pressure on stock prices.

On top of all this, corporate earnings in Japan are projected

# Focussing on the future – Düsseldorf.

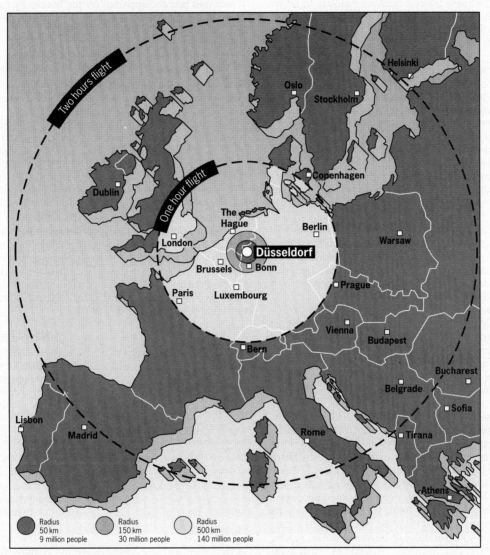

Radius 50 km — 9 million people
Radius 150 km — 30 million people
Radius 500 km — 140 million people

In Europe the borders are changing. Düsseldorf, the international center for trade and services, is situated in the heart of Europe and offers excellent links to the European market. Within a day´s truck journey 140 million people can be reached, more than 40% of all the inhabitants of the European Community. There are already more than 4000 companies from all over the world located in Düsseldorf, among them about 360 from Japan, more than 50 from Korea and over 50 from Taiwan, R.O.C. They all contribute to making Düsseldorf one of the leading locations for Asian business in Europe. Düsseldorf – make it your location in the European Single Market.

Nice to see you!

City of Düsseldorf
Office for City Promotion
and Economic Development
Mr. Hans von Schaper
Mühlenstraße 29
D-4000 Düsseldorf 1
Federal Republic of Germany
Fax: 211/8 99-47 76

**EUROPE, GERMANY, DÜSSELDORF.**

to decline by around 10% on average during the financial year to April 1992.

The best the Tokyo stockmarket would seem to hope for — at least during the early part of 1992 — is to hold its ground or possibly even advance slightly to around 25,000-26,000 as official and market rates of interest are pushed lower in line with falling economic activity.

But given that Japanese interest rates are unlikely to return to their low levels of the late 1980s in the foreseeable future, and that the liquidity bubble has finally burst, no major bull market is in sight.

**Malaysia** Share prices began to recover lost ground even before US-led coalition forces stormed into Kuwait early in 1991. But the bullish upturn did not last beyond mid-year: by October, the Kuala Lumpur Composite Index (KLCI) had slipped below the 530-level, little improved from its 501.23 opening level on 2 January.

Brokers blamed a variety of causes for the market's uninspired performance. Some said the Kuala Lumpur Stock Exchange (KLSE) was suffering from a dearth of fresh incentives after such stalwarts as the construction sector and counters linked to the ruling party failed to deliver their accustomed punch.

Access to liquidity was also a problem in the face of small but telling increments in Malaysia's relatively low interest rates and a tighter government stance towards monetary policy. Analysts further noted that rights issues had siphoned off over M$9 billion (US$3.29 billion) from the market over the past two-and-a-half years.

In addition, foreign fund managers lost their taste for the market after the Malaysian currency dipped sharply against the US dollar in early July and eroded the value of their ringgit-denominated securities.

The apparent downturn in the last months of the year capped a trading year which was rocked by unexpected events. A swift end to the Gulf War in February sparked a three-month bull run which peaked on 29 May, when the KLCI closed at a record high of 635.02. Despite its short duration the rally posed a welcome change from December 1990, when scores of companies suspended rights issues and other financing measures in the face of a general slump in share prices and lack of investor confidence.

Numbers of blue-chips also charged to record highs in the run-up. Telekom Malaysia, the privatised national telephone monopoly, breached M$12 per share by mid-year from its M$5 initial listing price in late 1990. But Telekom's performance, as well as those of other government-linked stocks, owed as much to market interventions by state-run investment companies as they did to the fundamentals of the companies concerned. This led some foreign fund managers to question whether Malaysia's politically driven market was worth the risk.

Local shares also took a dive in mid-August, when news of the abortive coup in the Soviet Union combined with an unexpected tightening of

statutory reserve requirements by Malaysia's central bank to trigger a temporary market rout. The KLCI lost 3.3% of its value on 15 August — plunging 18.66 points to close at 550.92 — though prices rebounded after investors adjusted to the reserve changes and on news that the Soviet putsch had collapsed.

But the rebound did little to counter bearish sentiment which had become apparent on the bourse by the final quarter. While bulls argued the market had merely entered a consolidation phase, the outlook remains cloudy and many institutions and punters are sidelined.

The knocks taken by investors failed to dampen participation in the Kuala Lumpur market. A total of 299 companies were listed on the exchange as of 2 August, and could swell to about 340 by the end of the year. This compares with 285 at the end of 1990.

The market value of all shares listed on the KLSE reached M$167 billion as of 31 July, compared with M$131.7 billion as of 31 December 1990. The aggregate capitalisation of the KLSE's Second Board also passed the M$1 billion mark in June, kindling hopes that secondary stocks in Kuala Lumpur will soon be able to outperform their rivals in other regional bourses.

There were encouraging signs throughout the year that the KLSE was improving the depth and sophistication of its services. Exchange officials are gradually phasing in a M$30 million central depositary system which is expected to be fully operational by 1993. The government is also expected to launch a new Securities and Exchange Commission by early 1992, which will substantially strengthen its oversight of the securities market.

**New Zealand** The year's big event on the New Zealand market was the transfer of the Top 40 index from Barclays Bank to the stock exchange, thereby ending a 30-year tradition. Otherwise a flat performance, reflecting the economy, signalled a dismal time for investors and brokers.

The new Stock Exchange Top 40 index started at the same time as the worldwide float of 31% of Telecom Corp.'s shares at around NZ$484 million (US$275 million), one third on the New Zealand exchange. New Zealand purchases of foreign-issued stock raised the total local holding to NZ$773 million. The new listing provided a welcome addition to what had become an extremely narrow market, with only eight to 10 listed stocks big enough to warrant international attention.

That there was money looking for equities was evident in other successful issues by Corporate Investments, Fletcher Challenge and, though it came towards the end and encountered the beginnings of indigestion, Carter Holt Harvey. Institutions started the year underweighted in shares, though foreign funds continued to maintain — and in some cases increase — their presence on hopes of eventual gains from the new government's tough budgetary and anti-inflation policies. One important new foreign source was Singapore, which

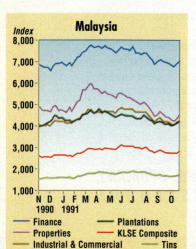

took 5% of Brierley Investments.

The market accordingly crawled out of its opening trough of 1,142 on 15 January, a six-year low even if inflation were discounted. However, after peaking at 1,580 on 7 May, the index jammed in the 1,400 range. Further rises in 1992 will depend on real evidence of the better profits corporates have been saying will come on the back of growth.

Another reason for the market's sluggish tone was continuing private investor wariness, bred by years toward, cavalier treatment towards minority shareholders and the absence of legal redress. The government's declaration that it intends to introduce new securities legislation may help restore private investor interest in the market.

The market was also challenged by bonds, which was where the serious money was made on the New Zealand markets during the year. Bonds gave total returns (yield and capital gain) in the year to August of around 21%, or just over 12% in US dollar terms. The monthly average interest rate for the benchmark five-year government bonds dropped from 12.2% in January to 9.3% in September and were trading around 8.6% in early October.

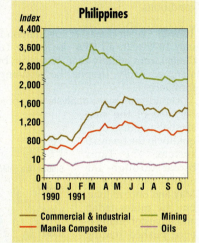

**Philippines**

Index

Commercial & industrial — Mining
Manila Composite — Oils

## Philippines

In the first half of the year the stockmarket turned in the best performance among Asia's bourses with a 63% gain, in US dollar terms, followed by Taiwan with a 29% gain. The rise resulted from the government's efforts to start putting the country's economic affairs in order in December 1990, and the negligible effects of the Gulf War.

Once the coalition forces began their assault on Iraq, the Manila Composite Index embarked on a near continuous climb from its 600-point level in January to over the 1,000-point barrier by April. The market appeared to be consolidating for another surge in May, and several companies rushed to finalise requirements for listing their stocks as the index touched 1,200 points by June. They were led by Ayala Land Corp., property flagship of the Ayala group of companies, whose P1.5 billion (US$55.5 million) offering was the bourse's largest capitalised scrip.

However, the eruption of Mt Pinatubo on 17 June unnerved the market. Ayala Land's 5 July listing could not be called off, with disastrous results for the company. Ayala Land's price began to continually slip to its October 1990 level of P18.50, mirroring the index's steep fall towards the 900-point level. The adverse psychological impact of the volcano's eruption was exacerbated by clear indications that the imposition of a 9% import levy and the government's tight monetary policy had pushed the economy into recession.

Another period of market uncertainty developed over Manila's handling of the US military bases agreement. Pro-bases proponents, led by President Corazon Aquino's administration, pushed the scenario of an economic crisis if a new bases treaty was not ratified by the Senate. The 16 September vote went against any extension of the treaty, but once it became clear that the country could survive, the stockmarket reacted with new-found optimism and the index gradually, if erratically, rose.

By mid-October it had recrossed the 1,000-level, and at least 20 enterprises — including Manila Electric Co., Philippine National Bank, Philippine Airlines and National Steel Corp. — made plans to list their stocks in the market. These firms could change the face of the local stockmarket, which has only about 40 firms that are viewed by analysts as serious investments.

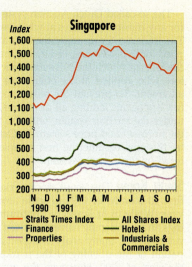

**Singapore**

Index

Straits Times Index — All Shares Index
Finance — Hotels
Properties — Industrials & Commercials

## Singapore

The Gulf War cast its pall over the local stockmarket at the start of the year, but once Iraq's military defeat seemed assured in late January prices and volumes began to soar to reach record levels over the first quarter.

But the hangover soon set in, and volumes and prices started to ease during the second half of the second quarter. By late October, prices and volumes had fallen to just a quarter of what they were at the beginning of the year. In the third quarter ending September, the key Straits Times Industrial index was trading at 1,360.63, compared with 1,489.89 at the end of second quarter and 1,154.48 at the end of 1990 when the world waited for the Gulf War to begin.

During August's attempted coup in the Soviet Union, the Singapore market fell by 5.8%, or more than most other world bourses, and for most of the third quarter failed to mount a convincing rally. More worrying than the downturn was the fact that there was probably more bad news to come as the local economy weakened, though it was still expected to post a 6.5% growth rate in 1991 against 1990's 8.3%. Nevertheless, buyers remained hesitant on the assumption that a convincing economic recovery will not happen until 1993.

The corporate scene was also quiet, with few major takeovers or even takeover bids. The tail-end of 1990's United Industrial Corp.'s (UIC) takeover of Singapore Land, however, continued to be played out during the year. Oei Hong Leong had to resign as UIC's chief executive after revealing the company had to make provisions for losses in property investments in Japan. He sold most of his stake in UIC to Indonesian tycoon Liem Swee Leong.

The sparkle even went out of Singapore's traditionally frenetic Initial Public Offering market. An offer from stockbrokers Kay Hian–James Capel was undersubscribed, raising only 20% of the amount needed after coming to market during the Gulf crisis. Even Scotts Holdings, which was offered in early August, was oversubscribed by only 1.3 times. It also fell below the offer price of S$1.25 (73 US cents) only on its debut, and had not managed to rise above that level by mid-October.

Apart from the poor market sentiment, the central bank, the Monetary Authority of Singapore — which also regulates the securities markets — became concerned with the destabilising effect huge oversubscription rates have had on interbank and other interest rates. In a single two-week span, interbank rates switchbacked through a 2-60% range. Apart from prosecuting individuals putting in multiple applications under different names, the authorities also introduced a new system to eliminate oversubscription altogether.

The so-called Dutch Auction system allows investors to bid for any number of shares at whatever price they consider fair. The underwriter arranges the bids and number of shares applied for in descending order, and the offer price of the issue is the level at which the full subscription rate is achieved. Investors who applied at the offer price and above get their full allotment. To prevent the remote possibility of a single or a few applicants landing all the shares, only a portion is offered under the auction system, with the remainder offered under the normal fixed price system. In October, Singapore Computer Systems became the first company to be successfully offered under the new system.

**South Korea** The Seoul stockmarket see-sawed during the first 10 months of 1991 to settle around where it started the year. While tight liquidity, continuing weak corporate earnings and a widening current-account deficit helped keep share prices down, many analysts expect a late-year rally in anticipation of the opening of the market to foreign investors at the start of 1992. However, the guidelines for allowing foreign investment are, as expected, restrictive. Foreign investors are allowed to hold a maximum of 10% of any company's shares — with lower limits for some strategic industries — and no individual investor may hold more than 3% of any company's shares.

Nevertheless, the long-awaited opening was about the only good news in a market that remained depressed for the third consecutive year. Since topping the 1,000-point level in April 1989, the market has fallen as South Korea's economy weakened and the supply of new stock overwhelmed investor demand.

For the second year, the Seoul Composite index briefly dipped below the 600-level before rebounding. Except for a flurry of activity in June and July, trading volume remained weak.

Many securities houses managed to eke out a profit in fiscal 1990 largely by some creative bookkeeping which allowed them to ignore losses for their own account, but virtually all the 25 more established securities houses showed heavy losses during the first half of fiscal 1991. Increased competition made matters tougher. The number of domestic brokers increased to 31 from 25 during the year, as the government successfully encouraged five short-term finance firms to convert to banks or securities companies. The Ministry of Finance (MoF) also allowed the state-owned Korea Development Bank to set up a securities affiliate. The move is part of the MoF's efforts to erode the influence of the country's short-term finance companies, which were originally set up to pull money out of the kerb market and into organised financial institutions.

The MoF also allowed four foreign securities firms — Baring Securites, Citicorp Scrimgeour Vickers, Merrill Lynch and Jardine Fleming — to set up branches in Seoul. The ministry had rejected Japan's so-called Big Four — Daiwa, Nikko, Nomura and Yamaichi — and W. I. Carr in the first round

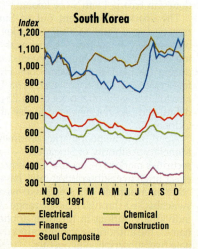

**Index**

**South Korea**

1990 1991

— Electrical    — Chemical
— Finance       — Construction
— Seoul Composite

of applications. Foreign brokers will have to invest Won 10-20 billion (US$13.3-26.6 million) in capital in South Korea, a requirement that many saw as excessive, while membership to the Korea Stock Exchange will cost extra.

Eight South Korean securities companies — Daewoo, Daishin, Lucky, Hyundai, Dongsuh, Coryo, Ssangyong and Tongyang — were also granted permission by Seoul to open branches in London, where they will invest a total of £60 million (US$102 million).

The market for overseas equity-linked issues — mainly convertible bonds — was its most active ever, as the MoF allowed companies to take advantage of the opportunity to issue abroad before the stockmarket opened to direct investment. The government also finally managed to float the Korea Asia Fund, a US$100 million closed-end mutual fund whose launch was repeatedly postponed because of weak market conditions.

**Taiwan** The stockmarket's reputation for volatility continued into 1991 with an 85% rise in the Taiwan Weighted index (Taiex) from January-June. However, by late in the year it had slumped badly, despite the economy's strong overall performance.

At mid-year, many analysts were predicting sustained rallies because of the substantial amounts of liquidity in the financial system. The Taiex broke through the 6,000-level twice in May and once in June, but the rallies faded and investor indifference pushed trading volumes to record lows by the third quarter.

Analysts said the central bank's high interest-rate policy drew investors' attention away from the bourse. The prime rate remained above 9% at

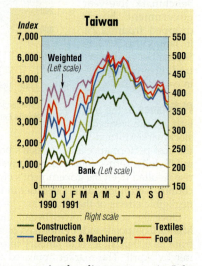

**Index**

**Taiwan**

Weighted (Left scale)

Bank (Left scale)

1990 1991

Right scale

— Construction        — Textiles
— Electronics & Machinery  — Food

most banks, despite three cuts in the discount rate in July and September. By September, the bond and money markets were for the first time more active than the stockmarket as investors sought safer, longer-term investments at attractive yields.

Earlier in the year the market was unsettled by government investigations of suspected tax evasion by securities and listed companies. One big player was indicted in June for evading 1989 taxes, while the communications minister was forced to resign over an insider trading scandal involving his immediate family.

The market's weakness made it sensitive to foreign and domestic political news. The Taiex dropped 9.4% in the two days after the abortive Moscow coup attempt in August, one of the sharpest falls of any world market. In October, the market fell more than 10% after the leading local opposition party announced its support for Taiwan's independence.

Major structural developments included the introduction of foreign institutional investors and the liberalisation of margin lending. By October, the Securities and Exchange Commission had approved a total of US$700 million in capital investments from overseas. Most was destined for the stock and bond markets, with the largest share (US$250 million) invested from

Hongkong-based institutions and the remainder from Japan (US$175 million), Britain (US$120 million), the US (US$100 million) and Ireland (US$50 million).

The volume of foreign investment was relatively small, but finance officials expected its net effect would be to stabilise a market where more than 90% of the daily turnover represents transactions by individual stockholders.

Despite strong earnings, financials were generally weak as investors watched the licensing and capitalisation of 15 new private banks due to open for business in early 1992. The central government also began selling its minority stake in the big three commercial banks, though the provincial government remains unwilling to privatise its majority shares. Overall, the government's privatisation programme for more than two dozen state-run companies has seen little progress.

There were 17 new listings on the exchange by the end of the third quarter, bringing to 225 the total number of listings for 215 companies.

**Thailand** The Securities Exchange of Thailand (SET) found itself stretched for a number of reasons during the year as rapid expansion forced major adjustments in the trading system, the legal and administrative framework and in investor attitudes after four years of bullish growth.

The market again grew sharply, with the number of quoted companies climbing to 260 by October against 214 at the end of 1990. Capitalisation grew to Baht 765 billion (US$30 billion) at the end of October from Baht 604.5 billion a year earlier. New issues to be added to the SET before the end of the year were expected to raise market capitalisation well past Baht 800 billion.

However, this probably represents a final burst as rapid economic growth catches up with the country. By mid-year, credit had tightened and market capital calls and initial offerings had sapped investor stamina and assets. Listed companies started turning in sharp downturns in earnings, and a small — but growing — number began recording losses. With expansion and operating costs eating up margins, few were expected to improve significantly by the turn of the year.

This drove many foreign institutions from the market, though most were counting on returning in 1992. In their absence, local players could not support the market. Major banks hit the market heavily early in the year, and by July it became apparent to underwriters of prospective blue-chip listing Thai Airways International that the market would not support their efforts to raise capital. While the state airline was listed, it took no action to expand its capital base or distribute shares to the public.

Tanayong and Bangkok Land, a pair of new property counters owned by the Kanjanapas family, raised over Baht 10 billion from investors and together accounted for 11-12% of market capitalisation. However, this helped give the market a total direct property bias of more than 20% just as the property market itself was heading into a slump and possibly worse. By mid-year, property counters had shown themselves unable to get close to earnings forecasts and most analysts expected bad news.

The market's attraction to overseas institutional investors also waned as even blue-chips turned in sagging earnings reports, while reverberations from the 23 February military coup continued to signal political uncertainty. These tremors affected the market just as it transformed its dealing operations. In May, the overcrowded floor was replaced by fully computerised trading. Brokers and punters adapted to the new system with few problems.

As the market grew, new challenges for regulatory officials emerged — notably the asset-swap method employed by

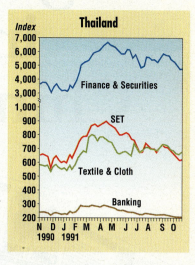

Tanayong. The government quickly finalised a draft bill to set up institutional and fundamental rules for dealing with the market in the future. Informally known as the SEC (Securities Exchange Commission) bill, it creates a major new independent and potentially powerful body to supervise capital markets and related institutions in the future. Some analysts felt the establishment of the SEC would create another tier between market operation and political interference, and result in better enforcement of exchange rules.

The establishment of new listing procedures and takeover rules was linked to this development. The listing procedure compels companies to provide more information to the SET and public prior to offer-ing their shares. The takeover rules demand public disclosure of an accumulation of more than 5% of a firm's shares by an investor, and requires that a general offer for the counter be made if an investor acquires more than 25% of its stock. ☐

# A guaranteed way to improve your China trade balance.

The CHINA TRADE REPORT shows you how to take advantage of the billions of opportunities China offers . . . as well as to avoid potentially adverse developments.

The CHINA TRADE REPORT, published monthly by the Review Publishing Company, is acknowledged by leading business executives to be the most informative, most up-to-date newsletter of its kind.

The CHINA TRADE REPORT covers all the issues related to doing business with China, whether you are trading or investing. Plus it reports on a broad range of industries such as agriculture, textiles, electronics, transport, banking and more.

The CHINA TRADE REPORT also publishes all the vital statistics on the Chinese economy. It is essential reading for anyone who watches China.

We are so sure you will find the CHINA TRADE REPORT indispensable, we offer you our money-back guarantee for any undelivered issues of your subscription should you ever become dissatisfied.

## A confidential monthly newsletter. Exclusive to subscribers.

# COMMODITIES

An experiment in Malaysia intended to test whether robots can tap rubber trees and replace increasingly scarce and expensive workers offers an extreme example of the problems facing one of the region's main commodity producers. If the machines prove viable, they would offer a technical solution to the problems inherent with a diminishing pool of cheap labour, without having to rely on the politically and socially sensitive expedient of importing foreign workers.

However, Malaysia is likely to remain an exception rather than the rule for many years as its regional competitors — principally Indonesia and Thailand at present, but no doubt Indochina and Burma in the future — have ample supplies of cheap labour and huge areas that remain unplanted or unmined.

Equally, while the robots may still come too late for Malaysia to save the country's once-vital rubber industry, the process that threatens it may also offer a salvation for other commodities through a combination of mechanisation and downstream industries that add value to primary produce. And while manufacturing and the robust domestic growth rates of the more buoyant Asian economies tend to overshadow the contribution made by the plantation and mining sectors, it is worth recalling that Malaysia

**Malaysian rubber: running out of labour.**

— one of the more diversified regional economies — earned M$21 billion (US$7.63 billion) from commodity exports in 1990, or 28% of its total export earnings.

In addition to whatever internal factors that may affect production, external events and technological advances can either boost or wreck entire commodity-based industries — the rapid demise of the tin industry offers an obvious example of the latter. During the past year, however, three major factors influenced the world's commodity producers — the continuing recession among some of the leading industrialised countries, the anxieties that attended the Gulf crisis and fears over the future of the Soviet Union.

While the quick defeat of Iraq spared the world economy a possible steep downturn, an expected strong recovery in the US failed to materialise. The result was sagging demand for industrial commodities such as rubber and non-ferrous metals. Combined with an oversupply of some commodities, such as sugar, this produced another lacklustre year for commodities in general. However, some commodities, including rice and palm oil, rebounded from low 1990 prices.

Turmoil in the Soviet Union, a major exporter of some commodities — notably metals — and an importer of others —

particularly grain — introduced volatility into the market. The price of nickel, for example, jumped 2.5% when the August coup attempt seemed to threaten supplies, only to fall when Soviet President Mikhail Gorbachov returned to Moscow. With the Soviet Union's economy falling apart, the country's need for imported grain and oilseeds hung over world markets, alternately boosting prices when it appeared that Western governments and banks would provide credit for purchases and driving them down when it appeared they would not.

However, 1992 might be a slightly better year for commodities. Prices and demand may rebound slightly due to a stronger US economy and the needs of the Soviet Union, while encouraging political trends in Asia may boost commodity trading in the region. Former enemies China and Taiwan began barter trade in grain in 1991, while peace in Cambodia could mark its — and by extension Vietnam's — reintegration into the Asian economy.

**Grain** The world grain trade will probably surge in the 1991-92 crop year as production declines, according to the US Department of Agriculture (USDA). Output will drop 7% to 550 million tonnes, largely due to US dry weather and government programmes to reduce planting. Trade is set to rise 12%, mainly on increased demand in the Soviet Union and China.

Production of rice, which Asia dominates in both output and consumption, is expected to drop 2% in 1991-92 to 345.8 million tonnes of milled rice, while trade in calendar 1992 rises 2.4% to 12.9 million tonnes. Grain producers in China and the Philippines escaped the worst short-term consequences of natural disasters during the year, but still face uncertain prospects. China lost 20-30 million tonnes of grain when summer floods hit 18 provinces destroying 5.23 million ha of crops. But

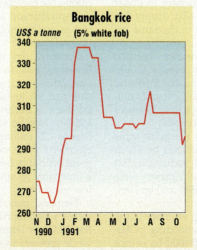

**Bangkok rice**
US$ a tonne    (5% white fob)

serious damage was limited to Anhui and Jiangsu provinces, and prospects were good for bumper summer grain harvests in Shandong, Hebei, Sichuan, Yunnan and Guizhou provinces.

More importantly, these losses will not prevent China from posting its fourth consecutive strong harvest. The government forecasts the 1991 grain crop would reach 425 million tonnes, down 10 million tonnes from 1990, but still one of the highest totals it has ever recorded. Nevertheless, the US Government expects flood losses to boost Chinese wheat imports 40% for the 1991-92 crop year to 13.5 million tonnes. The losses caused wheat output to drop 4% in 1991-92 to 94 million tonnes, and flood waters destroyed 4 million tonnes of wheat that had been stored in the open.

While Chinese officials assert the flood damage is temporary, long-term problems loom. Agricultural Minister Liu Zhongyi declared China must consistently invest in water conservancy and other aspects of agriculture. The trend, he said, has been to invest after bad crop years and ignore potential problems after good harvests.

The USDA said in August that Chinese purchasing had been "brisk," and the Chinese were still negotiating to buy wheat. "China has already bought 4.3 million tonnes from the US, 1.5 million from the EC, reportedly 1.3 million from Canada and more than 300,000 from Argentina," the USDA reported.

But US grain industry officials note that any cut in China's most-favoured nation (MFN) trade status might bring US sales to China to a halt. They recall that China did not buy US wheat between 1983-87 due to a textile trade dispute. President George Bush successfully resisted calls to abolish MFN for the time being, but may face even more determined demands in 1992.

In the Philippines, the June eruption of the Mt Pinatubo volcano caused almost no damage to standing rice because harvesting was nearly complete for the dry-season crop. A thick covering of ash will render only about 20,000 ha out of the country's total of 3.6 million ha under rice cultivation unplantable for the wet-season crop from July to December.

A more pressing problem in the month after the first eruption was a drought in northern Luzon that damaged rice and corn crops. The Philippine Government said 234,000 tonnes of corn in the area were lost, but added corn imports would not be needed because stocks were sufficient.

The Philippines did resume rice imports in March with a 63,000-tonne purchase from the US. The US sale, subsidised under Washington's PL 480 aid programme, provoked accusations of unfair trade practices from Thailand. Long-term credit provided by the US lowered the price to a net fob price of US$157 a tonne, compared with the comparable Thai quote of US$239. A senior Thai official also charged that the US aimed to take over some of the country's Middle East rice market through subsidised sales. In recent years Thailand had sold 1.3 million tonnes of rice a year to the Middle East.

The Thai Government again lost a large amount of money during the year in an effort to prop up rice prices. The loss came when it sold 280,000 tonnes of low- and medium-quality rice to exporters after buying early in the year. Overall, however, production was expected to rebound from the poor 1990-91 crop by 16% to 13.2 million tonnes, according to the USDA, which expected Thai 1992 rice exports to increase 7% to 4.5 million tonnes, partly due to tighter US supplies.

Thailand also faced less competition from Vietnam, which has rapidly increased its exports in the past few years. But a poor crop in northern Vietnam caused the country to divert supplies for domestic use. Exports in January-May dropped to 250,000 tonnes compared to 1 million tonnes in the same period in 1990.

Indonesia remains generally self-sufficient in rice after two record harvests, though the USDA said the country would probably import 600,000 tonnes of the grain in late 1991 and early 1992. Output in 1991-92 is expected to fall 1% to 29 million tonnes, and could slide further if indications that the major planting season for 1992 may be late prove accurate.

Japan has encountered sagging demand for rice at the same time it lowered the price it pays to local producers by 1% in 1991. The government had planned a 2-3% reduction, but protests by farmers caused it to compromise. Farmers were already squeezed by a 12.2% reduction since 1987 and by slack demand and higher production costs.

Cambodia's tentative entry as a developing member of the Asian economy was inauspicious. Disastrous flooding in August and September destroyed more than 100,000 ha of rice crops, raising the need for international relief efforts for the chronically food-short nation.

Asian imports of corn, mainly from the US, may level off as demand for feedgrain slumps. One factor is liberalisation of meat imports, especially in Japan, which reduced the growth in the use of feedgrains by local meat producers. US corn sales to Taiwan may also suffer from competition from China after the two countries reportedly entered into their first barter deal, under which Taiwan sent rice to China in exchange for corn.

**Rubber** Production of natural rubber, once a pillar of the Southeast Asian economy, is in danger of collapse. Prices for Malaysian benchmark grade Ribbed Smoked Sheet One have steadily dropped from M$3.10 (US$1.12) a kg in 1988 to an average of M$2.33 in 1990 and about M$2.25 for much of 1991. The International Natural Rubber Organisation (Inro) can sustain prices at about that level by buying rubber when it falls below a target price. But that is not enough, given rising labour costs.

Malaysia, Thailand and Indonesia produce about 70% of the world's natural rubber, but Malaysian Primary Industries Minister Lim Keng Yaik warned during the year that low prices threaten long-term production by the three rapidly industrialising countries.

The crisis resulted in a meeting of the Association of Natural Rubber Producing Countries (ANPRC) in June, the first at the ministerial level for 15 years. ANPRC — comprising Malaysia, Indonesia, Thailand, India, Papua New Guinea, Singapore and Sri Lanka — urged industrialised nations not to impose tariff and non-tariff barriers to rubber imports. It also vowed to improve productivity, and Malaysia began experimenting with latex-collecting robots, which it hopes can eventually be produced for around M$30 each and be attached to all of the country's 500 million or so rubber trees.

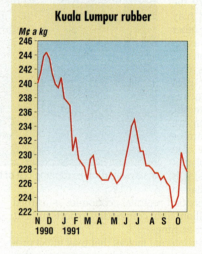

**Kuala Lumpur rubber**

M¢ a kg

N D J F M A M J J A S O
1990  1991

A more important and difficult task will be for ANPRC to ensure a healthy balance of supply and demand by setting quotas for members and ensuring they adhere to them. If not, over-production and price-cutting might doom Inro efforts, just as similar problems led to the collapse of arrangements for tin and cocoa.

For now, dry weather in Malaysia and Indonesia and reduced tapping in Malaysia have helped reduce supplies and stockpiles during the past two years. Malaysian output dropped 9% to 1.29 million tonnes in 1990, while Indonesian production declined some 5% to almost the same level. An industry source said Indonesian production might sink further to 1.23 million tonnes in 1991, mainly because of fuel and electricity price increases set by the government. A government official in Jakarta also said output might not increase for a long time as smallholders lacked the capital to replace old, low-yield trees.

Thailand may now take over Malaysia's position as the world's leading rubber producer. Thai output grew rapidly in the 1980s as large areas were opened to rubber production, while growers took advantage of significantly cheaper labour than Malaysia. Production in Thailand reached 1.275 million tonnes in 1990, just 16,000 tonnes below Malaysia.

**Oilseeds** Production and exports of palm oil and palm kernels should continue to rise in 1992, with Malaysia and Indonesia — respectively the world's first and second largest producers that together account for 78% of total palm-oil output — reaping most of the benefit.

Malaysia's 1991-92 output is expected to rise 8% to 6.6 million tonnes as yields recover from a decline in 1990-91, according to the USDA. Indonesia's 1991-92 output is forecast to reach 2.7 million tonnes, also a gain of 8%, due to increased area, maturing trees and good weather. Malaysian palm-kernel output should rise 9% in 1991-92 to 2 million tonnes, making up 56% of the world's production.

The price for current delivery of palm oil on the Kuala Lumpur market rose to M$796 per tonne in late September compared with M$674 a year earlier as large stocks held in 1990 declined. Exports rose, partly on increased demand from China due to revived economic growth, and Malaysia's exports of palm oil gained 14.4% in 1990 to 5.93 million tonnes. The country's exports to China soared 63% to 798,000 tonnes as China overtook Pakistan as Malaysia's principal customer. China's huge market provides room for further growth, but there are doubts that the country has enough foreign exchange to fund increasing purchases.

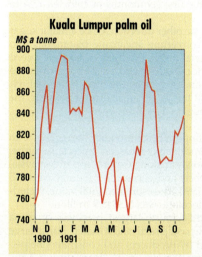

**Kuala Lumpur palm oil**
M$ a tonne

Long-term prospects, however, are cloudy as the price for crude palm oil (CPO) has plunged from US$584 a tonne in 1980 to US$275 in 1990 while labour costs have risen steadily. One answer is to lower production costs while developing downstream industries that can use CPO as feedstock. Malaysia, which already has an overcapacity in CPO refining, plans to move further downstream.

FPG Oleochemicals, a Proctor and Gamble joint venture, announced during the year that it would expand planned output of its proposed methyl ester plant in Malaysia from 50,000 tonnes a year to 150,000 tonnes. The output will be used as feedstock for detergent-grade alcohol in plants in Malaysia and Europe. Japanese toiletries company Kao is another firm that invested in oleochemicals in Malaysia. Palm Oil Research Institute of Malaysia increased its research and development budget 6% last year to M$36 million, and launched a research project with China's Xian Oils and Fats Research Institute.

Ridwan Dereinda, director of Indonesia's Agribusiness Studies and Development Centre, also sees production of CPO-based detergents and soap as holding promise. He noted that Indonesians now use only 0.3 kg of detergent a year per capita, compared with 29.1 kg in the US. The importance of the growing Asian market was reflected in the US$4 million investment by Indonesian state plantation companies in a CPO refinery in Shandong, China.

Indonesia also pressed ahead with a project to end soybean imports by 1994 — the country imported 700,000 tonnes of soybeans in 1990. The plan calls for soybean production on the country's abundant peat fields, but has run into problems because the peat lacks minerals and is highly acid. One possible solution is to use equally abundant volcanic ash as a fertiliser.

The Philippines' coconut exports face a short-term problem due to a cyclical downturn in production after two years of strong growth. Low rainfall and a powerful typhoon in November 1990 also curtailed production. Mt Pinatubo's eruption, however, caused little damage because of the distance of most growing areas from the volcano.

The USDA predicts Philippine copra output will drop 10% in 1991-92 to 2 million tonnes, which would still give the Philippines 42% of total world production. Here, again, development of oleochemical production could provide long-term stimulus for oilseed producers. The Philippine Department of Science and Technology is hoping to make cocodiesel, a 50-50 mix of diesel and coconut oils, commercially viable while methyl ester produced from coconut oil might be used in diesel-fuel substitutes and sucrose development.

**Metals** Low prices and slack demand due to weakness in the world economy hurt metals producers and exporters in Asia. Prices fluctuated sharply on events in the Soviet Union, but gains were not stable enough to provide fundamental relief.

Tin once again proved to be the most troubled sector. Massive stockpiles, 44,300 tonnes at the end of 1990, drove prices down 29% in 1990 to an average of M$16.45 a kg. The price then plunged below M$15 for much of 1991. The Department of Mines in Malaysia, long the world's top producer, estimated 1991 output would be 23,000 tonnes, 20% below 1990's post-war low. The number of mines in operation at the end of June 1991 was 111, compared with 141 in 1990 and 847 in 1980. And low prices will probably drive even more mines out of business, particularly since most remaining mines are relatively high-cost gravel pump operations.

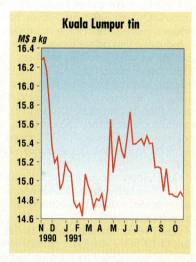

**Kuala Lumpur tin**
M$ a kg

Indonesian tin producers also suffered. State firm PT Tambang Timah, which produced 21,000 tonnes of the country's 27,000-tonne output in 1990, replaced all but one of its directors and planned to shed half its 24,000-strong workforce to stem its losses. The company's production costs were about US$6,000 a tonne last year, compared with tin prices of about US$5,000. The firm hoped the restructuring would lower costs to US$4,700 a tonne.

Depressed copper prices put a damper on one of the Philippines' biggest money earners. Export revenue in the first six months of 1991 fell 10% to US$257 million. In the same period, production of copper concentrates dropped 17% to 311,597 dry tonnes. Atlas Consolidated Mining, the Philippines largest copper miner, suspended development of a copper deposit in Cebu in August due to low prices.

There was some good news on non-ferrous metals. In August, Nonoc Mining and Industrial Corp. received the financing and government approval it needed to reopen its nickel mine and refining plant on Nonoc Island near northeast Mindanao. The giant operation had been closed since

Nonoc's parent company, Marinduque Mining and Industrial Corp., went bankrupt in 1984. The plant could earn US$300-400 million a year, based on current nickel prices.

Indonesia also stands to reap a windfall from a new agreement with a huge mining concern. Freeport Indonesia Inc. reached a tentative agreement on a new contract with the government allowing the firm to exploit a vast tract of land in Irian Jaya for 50 years. The focus of development will be Grasberg Mountain, with its estimated 396 million tonnes of ore reserves. The reserves have an average grade of 1.54% copper, 2.03 g of gold a tonne and 3.40 g of silver a tonne. Capacity of the mill near the site will be expanded from 31,700 tonnes a day in 1990 to 57,000 tonnes in 1992.

Events in the Soviet Union, a major gold exporter, whipsawed gold prices. Rumours that the Soviets were selling large quantities of the metal to prop up their faltering economy undercut prices, while other reports that the Soviet's stocks were much lower than presumed buoyed the market. Overall, such oscillations had little lasting effect as prices continued to remain depressed.

Indonesia was one of the countries hit by lower gold prices. Exports of gold bars and jewellery plunged 36% in 1990 to 13.5 tonnes. Illegal miners accounted for all the decline, though, as production by registered firms rose 67% to 11.7 tonnes. The government expected these firms to produce more than 13 tonnes of gold in 1991. The increase was forecast to come from the Freeport mine, which expected to raise gold output 2.4 tonnes to 7.1 tonnes. But the average price fell 5.7% to US$364.93 per ounce in the first six months of 1991.

Gold production at Philippine mines dropped 14% in the first half of last year to 12.2 tonnes, worth US$134 million. A larger amount, though, is exported illegally, according to government estimates.

China overcame widespread floods to boost gold production 11.3% in the first eight months of the year. All gold mines that had been closed by flooding had reopened by September, the government said. The Eighth Five-Year Plan adopted for 1991-95 allocates Rmb 7-8 billion (US$1.3-1.5 million) in investment for the gold industry to finance a 40% increase in production capacity over the previous plan.

**Sugar** World sugar prices continued to fall as production for 1991-92 exceeded consumption by more than 1.9 million tonnes, according to the USDA. This is bad news for sugar exporters in the region, including Thailand, Australia and the Philippines.

The USDA expects Thai exports for 1991-92 to equal the previous year's strong 2.6 million tonnes. Australia's 1991-92 crop should increase to 3.69 million tonnes, reflecting better weather and expanded acreage. Exports may also rise after declining 10% in 1990-91 to an estimated 2.7 million tonnes. The Philippines' 1991-92 crop is forecast to gain 7% to 1.9 million tonnes as planting area and recovery rates increase.

The only ready market for high-priced Philippine sugar is the US, where the government subsidises imports from the Philippines under a special programme. The US transferred 48,000 tonnes of the Philippines' quota to South Africa last year after that country officially abandoned its apartheid policy. But industry sources said that amount can be put to

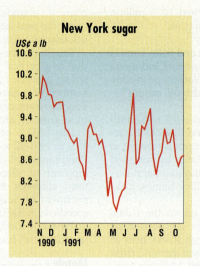

good use on the domestic market to replace 35,000 tonnes lost in the Mt Pinatubo eruption and thereby hold down local price increases. Exports for 1991-92 may be about 300,000 tonnes.

Thailand is debating whether to liberalise its heavily controlled and subsidised sugar industry. Deputy Industry Minister Veera Susangkarakarn has said increased free market competition would improve efficiency.

Asia's sugar importers, meanwhile, will gain from lower prices. Japan's purchases for 1990-91 are expected to rise 8% to 1.85 million tonnes due to increased consumption and decreased local production. The same factors should push Indonesian imports in 1991-92 to 351,000 tonnes, up 17%, according to the USDA.

China floods missed the country's primary sugar producing areas in the south, northeast and northwest. The government — which seems intent on encouraging the industry — increased procurement prices and helped spur a 3% increase in the record 1990-91 level to 6.8 million tonnes in 1991-92. Imports in the first six months of 1991 fell 13% to 521,223 tonnes.

Taiwan is moving in the other direction. Once a major sugar exporter, it is steadily converting sugarcane plantations into industrial and recreational areas. Production fell to a record low of 409,000 tonnes for 1990-91, and was tipped to fall to between 300-350,000 tonnes a year by the turn of the century. Taiwan imported 50,000 tonnes of sugar during the year, the first time it has ever bought sugar from overseas.

**Cocoa** Cocoa, another important commodity struggling with low prices and overproduction, faces an uncertain future. It is the third-largest money-making export crop in Malaysia, after oil palm and rubber, and earned the country M$448.5 million exports during 1990. The estimated total value, including cocoa butter and chocolate, was M$848.9 million.

Malaysia is the world's fourth-largest producer of cocoa beans after the Ivory Coast, Brazil and Ghana. But a large overhang of stocks held by producers and consumers helped push prices to their lowest point in 16 years during May, though prices rose later in the year partly on expectations of poor harvests in Brazil and West Africa. However, over-production may again force prices down.

Indonesia wants to increase its market share from about 3% in 1990 to 12% in 2000. Malaysia plans to introduce new planting practices that would double cocoa bean production in the next four years from about 260,000 tonnes in 1990. Producing countries can be expected to get around low prices for cocoa beans by increasingly processing them into cocoa butter or powder and confectionaries. The amount of cocoa beans processed in Malaysia rose from 7,000 tonnes in 1980 to about almost 86,000 tonnes in 1990. □

# SUCCESS IN THE AIR. SUCCESS IN SPACE. OUR NAME SAYS IT ALL. AEROSPATIALE.

AIRBUS

AIRBUS accounts for 30% of the world civil aviation market. In a range extending from the twin engine medium haul to the four engine long haul aircraft, 1760 AIRBUS have already been sold throughout the world. The 330 AIRBUS sold to Asia-Pacific airlines and 430 to airlines in the USA clearly demonstrate its huge commercial success.

AEROSPATIALE ploughs back more than 35% of its turnover into research and development. This percentage, the world's highest, firmly places AEROSPATIALE at the very heart of all major European aerospace projects. From the outset, its history has been marked by a series of international successes that are the fruit of true cooperation - as demonstrated by ARIANE with 50% of the launch vehicle market, and ATR's 25% market share in com-

muter aircraft. 70% of AEROSPATIALE's turnover is realised in programmes which involve cooperation of one sort or another - with 20% of these in Asia.

Within the context of a partnership built upon free exchange of information, methodology, technology and human expertise, Taiwan has a significant role to play in the ATR cargo programme, as well as in the local assembly of the highly successful Ecureuil light helicopter programme.

AEROSPATIALE, driving force in the European aerospace industry, will tomorrow be spearheading the partnership aimed at developing a new supersonic aircraft - and thereby add to the legend it has already created for itself in the skies.

## aerospatiale

AEROSPATIALE Representative Office Hong Kong Hutchinson House Rooms 2104/5 Harcourt Road Hong Kong Tel: 5257274 Fax: 8106042

# ENERGY

Convulsions in the world oil industry due to the Gulf crisis caused only marginal lasting effects in Asia. The jump in crude oil prices to more than US$40 a barrel after Iraq's invasion of Kuwait in August 1990 was too short-lived to alter the economies of either importers or exporters, as prices soon edged back to the US$20 level.

The war and disruption of oil supplies from Iraq and Kuwait did, however, reinforce realisation of the need to diversify sources and accelerated the process of increasing investment in oil and gas exploration. The impact of this recognition varied, particularly for Asia's exporters.

Indonesia — with its proven potential, varied geological structures and government experience in dealing with foreign oil companies — benefited most among the Southeast Asian producers from the rise in exploration interest. Indonesia signed a record 22 production sharing contracts in the year to September, compared with 19 for all 1990 and 10 in 1989.

The agreement signed by PT Petronusa during the year marked the first time an Indonesian oil company had signed a production sharing contract, and indicated the growth of local technical and financial sophistication.

The 22 contracts require oil companies to spend a total of at least US$150 million on exploration activity. Oil firms spent almost US$2.3 billion exploring in Indonesia in 1991, or more than 80% more than 1990, according to a report produced by the US Embassy in Jakarta. Oil companies planned to shoot 63,000 km of seismic surveys and sink 199 exploration wells during the year. "Never has the interest in Indonesia been greater, at least in terms of foreign companies seeking new exploration areas," the report said. Production capacity reached 1.7 million barrels per day (bpd) during 1991, against 1.46 million bpd of crude oil and condensate in 1990.

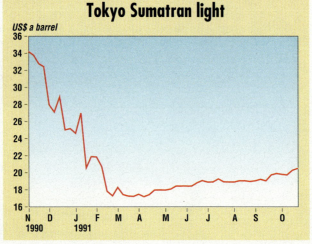

**Tokyo Sumatran light**

US$ a barrel

While only 36 of Indonesia's 60 known basins have been explored so far, the US report cautioned that "future exploration will be more difficult, as 55% of the basins' areas — largely those less explored — are in water at a depth of over 200 m."

As a result of higher prices due to the Gulf crisis, oil and gas revenue for the 1990-91 fiscal year rose by more than 78% over the original government forecast to Rps 19.18 trillion (US$9.71 billion). The government expected oil and gas revenues to shrink 15.5% from that inflated level for the fiscal year ending in April 1992 to Rps 16.27 trillion, still comfortably above the original estimate of Rps 15 trillion.

Malaysia, with its spare capacity and unfettered by Opec quotas because — unlike Indonesia — it is not a member, was able to take advantage of rising oil prices early in the Gulf crisis, raising output from 595,000 bpd before the war to 630,000 bpd in 1991.

However, with most of its promising exploration areas already contracted out or surveyed, Malaysia could not share in the resurgence of interest in searching for new hyrdocarbon

reserves. Nevertheless, the government expects the industry to spend M$17 billion (US$6.18 billion) on exploration between 1991-93, with 129 wells expected to be drilled. Most new contracts will have to be for deep-sea blocks.

Malaysia also increased natural gas output of to an estimated 8.06 million tonnes, a rise of 20%. It expects natural gas to provide more than 51% of the energy for the country's power generation by 1995. The government has already spent M$2.6 billion on the Peninsular Gas Utilisation Project, which includes a pipeline from northeastern Trengganu state to Singapore, gas processing plants and a gas terminal. The project, undertaken by national oil company Petronas and Esso Production Malaysia Inc., will provide gas for a burgeoning petrochemical industry, including a trioxide plant and an ethane-based plant in Trengganu.

China is Asia's leading oil producer, has the largest potential oil fields and faces the greatest problems. As domestic demand is expected to rise about 5% a year, production stagnates. Output rose only 0.46% in 1990 to 2.84 million bpd after a 0.45% increase in 1989. While output for the first seven months of 1991 increased more than 1.6% over the same period a year earlier, exports continue to fall from a high of 30.03 million tonnes in 1985 to 23.99 million tonnes in 1990.

A recent report by the East-West Center in Hawaii asserted that "from a net exporter of over 600,000 bpd of crude and products as recently as 1985, China may well be on its way to becoming a net importer on the same scale by 2000. Oil exports still gross for China an average of US$3 billion per year in hard currency, but by 2000 payments for imports may reach US$12 billion to US$14 billion, consuming some 10% to 15% of total export earnings."

In part, China's oil industry is the victim of the country's success, as GDP growth of 5-6% a year boosts domestic demand. Some factors, however, are beyond China's limited technical abilities. Production is slipping in ageing fields in eastern China, while promising basins in the northwest are remote and have difficult geological structures. Nevertheless, the barriers keeping China from coping with these challenges are essentially of the government's own making. Inefficient state-run firms cost China tens of billions of renminbi each year that could be invested in oil exploration, while foreign oil firms remain uneasy about the political and legal risks of investing in the country.

Perhaps most importantly, however, has been China's refusal to allow foreign companies to participate in the onshore oil industry. The main reasons are ideological and stem from a desire to keep "bourgeois liberalism" at arm's length while demonstrating that the socialist system can develop the fields independently.

Reality started to set in during 1991. China signed an agreement in April calling for the Japan National Oil Corp. to provide money and personnel for seismic tests in the Tarim Basin, the most promising area in the northwest. In May,

Prime Minister Li Peng acknowledged for the first time that foreign investment and technology would be needed to develop the Tarim Basin. But these moves stopped short of allowing foreign firms to participate in risk exploration in the costly development of exploration, production and distribution of oil in the remote area. "The Chinese leadership doesn't understand the urgency of the problem. They don't realise how fast they must get incremental production on line," one foreign industry analyst said.

The picture is brighter offshore, partly because officials in China National Offshore Oil Corp. (CNOOC) are more attuned to international practices. Offshore production was expected to reach 2 million tonnes last year, about double the 1990 total, and is well on the way to fulfilling CNOOC's goal of 8 million tonnes in 1995.

But the scale is much too small to make up for declines in the East China fields and meet increasing domestic demand. In addition, foreign interest is falling as oil firms conclude it is unlikely they will find large fields. The number of contracts signed dropped from 10 in 1989 to five in 1990, and most of the agreements did not involve drilling.

Thailand's consumption of petroleum products rose 9.7% in the first half of 1991 to 525,600 bpd. Domestic sources supply only about 30% of the total, or some 157,100 bpd of oil equivalent — most of it in the form of natural gas.

However, some relief from Thailand's high petroleum bill may be in sight after 17 contracts for oil exploration were signed during 1991. The agreements oblige companies, including Texaco and Royal Dutch/Shell, to spend US$150 million in the next three years to carry out more than 40,000 km of seismic surveys and drill 28 exploratory wells.

Thailand's cooperation with Vietnam also offers hope for the development of offshore natural gas resources. Hanoi agreed in principle in September to give Thailand access to fields off Vietnam's southern coast. Thai Deputy Industry Minister Vira Susangkaradan said the Big Bear field could produce 300-500 million ft³ of gas per day and give Thailand a source of energy for 30 years. Hanoi has also suggested that Bangkok study the possibility of developing the White Tiger gas field, currently a joint Vietnamese-Soviet exploration area.

**Exploration: poised to take off.**

**Consumption: driven by rising demand.**

The Philippines is undergoing a modest, but badly needed, increase in exploration. Higher oil prices during the Gulf crisis strained the country's struggling economy and stretched the fragile social fabric, as riots followed government announcements of higher retail fuel prices in the controlled market. Imports account for almost all the country's 220,000 bpd consumption, while production dropped from a high of 8.5 million barrels in 1979 to 2 million in 1989 because of political instability and economic problems.

But with Southeast Asia's most attractive contract conditions for foreign companies, the 12 Filipino and foreign oil-drilling companies are thought by some analysts to be on the verge of potentially useful discoveries. Three foreign and one local consortium are due to drill two offshore wells each in the last quarter of 1991 through the first half of 1992.

Taiwan, with its strong economy, was much better able to withstand higher oil prices. Its import bill soared 35% in 1990 to US$4.1 billion, despite a 3% drop in fuel oil and liquefied petroleum gas imports. State-run China Petroleum Corp. ranged as far afield as Ecuador and the Soviet Union to negotiate oil-exploration deals and reduce its dependence on the Middle East.

Cambodia's efforts to enter the regional economy may make it a new producer. In late 1991 the country signed its first oil exploration contract in decades, and France's Compagnie Europeene des Petroles and Britain's Enterprise Oil will jointly explore 5,000 km² off Kompong Som province.

Another result of the Gulf crisis was the increased interest in coal, which is seen as a more stable fuel for the region's booming economies. Industry analysts forecast coal consumption among Asean members will soar from 19 million tonnes a year in 1990 to 85 million tonnes in 2000.

The biggest beneficiaries in Asia would be coal exporters China and Indonesia. China forecast its coal exports would rise 11% in 1991 to 20 million tonnes. Indirect exports to Taiwan reached 500,000 tonnes in 1990 and could surge if Taipei authorises direct exports, as many observers expect.

Indonesia projects a 21% jump in production to 13.5 million tonnes in 1991, with a further increase to 29 million tonnes by 1995. Indonesian coal exports were expected to grow by over 20% during 1991 to more than 6 million tonnes. □

# FISHING

Environmental issues have become increasingly prominent in both the North and South Pacific fisheries, with indications during the year that the concern initially focused on the driftnetting of albacore could spread to other tuna fisheries and other fishing techniques.

The Wellington Convention outlawing driftnetting — a technique based on using 30-60-km-long nets favoured mainly by the Japanese and Taiwanese fishing industry — and prohibiting port access or other assistance to driftnetters, came into force in the South Pacific in May. However, the driftnetters had already virtually disappeared from the region, down from a peak of 130-180 vessels in 1988-89 to reportedly less than a dozen Taiwanese driftnetters in the 1990-91 season.

Japan, Taiwan and South Korea still use small-mesh driftnets in the North Pacific, notably in the squid fisheries, but are under increasing pressure there too. A UN global ban on driftnets is planned for July 1992, and the US was expected strongly to support it at a UN debate in late 1991.

In October 1990, the US Senate banned the use of large-scale driftnets in its extended economic zone (EEZ) and by US fishing fleets anywhere in the world. A US Government report released in June 1991 found driftnetting was severely affecting its West Coast marine resources, killing 41 million sea creatures other than squid in 1990. Public concern particularly over dolphin deaths led the US Senate in August to approve mandatory trade sanctions against countries involved in driftnetting. Shortly afterwards, however, the law was ruled in violation of the Gatt.

Ridding the South Pacific of driftnetters has proved easier than persuading Japan, Taiwan and South Korea to accept a management regime for the once endangered albacore stocks. South Pacific fisheries experts are still concerned that past driftnetting of juvenile albacore could affect population of adult albacore on which the longline fishery depends. Negotiations were continuing, with both sides due to meet again in Fiji at the end of the year.

With a haul of 30,000 tonnes in 1990, the high-quality albacore catch represents only a fraction of the total Western Pacific tuna fishery. At 1.2 million tonnes a year, the fishery — covering the Southwest Pacific, Indonesia and the Philippines — is the world's largest. The bulk is made up of skipjack (785,000 tonnes) and

yellowfin (340,000 tonnes). The fishery has doubled in size in a decade, largely due to the expansion of purse-seining, which now accounts for 660,000 tonnes of the total catch. Between 1985 and 1990 the purse-seining fleet doubled, and while skipjack is not in danger, yellowfin may be.

Pacific Island countries are now collaborating through the Forum Fisheries Agency (FFA), the principal body behind the South Pacific anti-driftnetting campaign, to develop a mechanism to control further purse-seining expansion.

FFA director Philipp Muller, the Western Samoan technocrat who brought the FFA to international prominence, left the post this year and will be replaced by former Solomon Islands prime minister Sir Peter Kenilorea. Under Muller's leadership, the FFA in 1982 set regionally agreed conditions for access by foreign fishing vessels, including registration, and in 1986 negotiated the first South Pacific multilateral fishing agreement with the US. Revised access conditions came into effect during the year amid concern over increased reports of non-compliance, and discussions began with the US on arrangements once the present treaty expires in 1993.

The major concerns in the South China fishery are similar to those in the South Pacific: in July a Food and Agriculture Organisation committee listed them as overfishing, inadequate assessment of stocks, poor statistics, conflicts between subsectors, destructive fishing practices and habitat destruction, post-harvest losses, rising costs, the need for value-added products and aquaculture development.

Competition for stocks is evident in many places. Thailand, Vietnam and Malaysia became involved in a "fishing war" after the countries declared overlapping EEZs in the Gulf of Thailand. Hundreds of fishermen from the three countries were arrested, boats were impounded or destroyed, while numerous gun battles between rival fishing trawlers or patrol boats seeking to enforce territorial sovereignty were reported.

Shrimp prices in Japan slumped again during the year, badly affecting export-farming operations in countries such as Thailand and the Philippines, where the industry is worth over US$200 million. However, Philippine exports of carrageenan — a seaweed derivative — received a boost when the US Department of Agriculture classified it as a safe food additive.

| Marine catch | | |
|---|---|---|
| Fish, crustaceans, molluscs | '000 tonnes | |
| | 1988 | 1989 |
| 1 Soviet Union | 11,350 | 11,300 |
| 2 China | 10,350 | 11,200 |
| 3 Japan | 11,950 | 11,150 |
| 4 US | 5,950 | 5,750 |
| 5 India | 3,150 | 3,600 |
| 6 South Korea | 2,750 | 2,850 |
| 7 Thailand | 2,800 | 2,800 |
| 8 Indonesia | 2,700 | 2,700 |
| 9 Philippines | 2,000 | 2,100 |
| 10 North Korea | 1,700 | 1,700 |
| 11 Vietnam | 850 | 850 |
| 12 Bangladesh | 850 | 850 |
| 13 Burma | 700 | 700 |
| 14 Malaysia | 600 | 600 |
| 15 New Zealand | 500 | 500 |
| 16 Pakistan | 450 | 450 |
| 17 Hongkong | 250 | 250 |
| 18 Sri Lanka | 200 | 200 |
| 19 Australia | 200 | 200 |
| 20 Maldives | 70 | 70 |
| 21 Cambodia | 70 | 70 |
| 22 Fiji | 30 | 30 |

Source: UN

**Tuna: Western Pacific catch doubled in a decade.**

GERHARD JÖREN

# HOT DOGS

# IN HANOI?

When they can make a good hot dog in Hanoi, you'll read about it in the All-Asia Guide. Seasoned travellers know even small details can assume immense importance when travelling in remote or unfamiliar territory. *The Far Eastern Economic Review's* All-Asia Guide has established itself as the most authoritative and detailed guide to the region. This just published, completely revised edition covers literally every country in Asia, including for the first time Soviet Asia and Siberia. Written by experts who really know each country, it not only reveals the best about them, but points out shortcomings and how to avoid them. A mine of up-to-the-minute information, featuring in-depth histories of each country... invaluable for understanding Asia's diversity of people and cultures.

## Shipping

The message for most of 1991 was that freight rates would have to rise. A rash of bulk-carrier sinkings from 1990 onwards propelled the quest for greater quality in ship-design and building, crew competence and loading and un-loading techniques was one factor behind higher costs. Others included the US Oil Pollution Act — which added to the drive for quality and therefore costs — higher insurance rates and a fall in shipyard capacity that reduced the supply of new vessels and pushed up the price of those being built.

Not that the situation was all bad for ship-owners — at least in the bulk trades. While the liner companies continued to cut each others' throats with low rates in the trans-Pacific container trades because of excess capacity, the bulkers found reasonable and steady rates for most of 1991, though a long-expected downturn seemed to have arrived in the third quarter.

Demand for most heavy commodities either went flat or started to fall, with the effects of the Gulf War's trade cut-off still evident and the world's economic recession still biting. But shipyard congestion brought both a slow supply of new vessels and slow repair times, while the sinkings also added to the shortage of capacity and helped keep rates firm despite weakening demand. And there were real hopes of even better times in 1992 and beyond.

Political events and natural disasters seemed likely to bene-fit the grain, coal and oil trades in particular. A shortage of labour in the Soviet Union following the political turmoil there, for example, meant that about a third of the 1991 grain harvest had rotted in the fields, according to some analysts. And as there were difficulties in obtaining payments from Soviet or-ganisations, grain shipments would have to be financed from other sources, which in turn would mean good market condi-tions for bulk shipments in 1992-93.

Similar cases have been made about the potential for grain shipments to China following disastrous floods that inundated croplands during 1991, and to the Philippines after the erup-tion of the Mt Pinatubo volcano covered arable land with ash in mid-1991.

The lifting of the US trade embargo on South Africa seemed likely to benefit the coal and oil trades, though the expansion of coal export capacity in South Africa — as well as re-estab-lishing markets — might make this a longer-term prospect. Relaxing the UN trade embargo against Iraq would mean a resumption of oil shipments — but against that, other Opec members might not cut their exports to offset Iraq's re-entry into the market, so rates might fall sharply.

Shipbuilding also looks set to pick up, despite the high prices that partly reflect a shortage of equipment suppliers who turned to other types of manufacturing during the ship-ping slump and contraction of yard capacity in the mid-1980s.

Brokers have estimated the world's tanker fleet could be

reduced by up to a third because of new anti-pollution measures imposed by the International Maritime Organisation, a UN specialist body. These would make the economics of retrofitting older tankers problematic — and in any case, the market for life-extensions of tankers is constrained by shipyard capacity. Added to the pressure on yards already full with orders for double-bottom and double-hull tankers because of the new US law, the result was likely to be that demand would far outstrip yard capacity.

Frank Chao, president of Hongkong's Wah Kwong shipping company, has pointed out that with Japan having about 90,000 shipyard workers and producing close to 40% of the world's new ships, the prospects for China were tremendous. Labour costs for China's 450,000 shipyard workers were low by international standards, while their exposure to foreign standards coupled with a steady stream of engineers graduating from the country's universities could see China becoming the world's largest shipbuilding nation over the next 25 years, Chao believes.

Wah Kwong already uses Chinese yards for tank-cleaning and minor repairs, and — depending on how well these tasks are carried out — plans to send its ships there for more advanced work. If Wah Kwong's experiment is successful, other foreign shipping companies are likely to follow its example. China could also benefit from an expected rise in scrap prices following Taiwan's exit from this market.

Demand at shipyards was not only strong for tankers. There are indications that self-discharging bulkers are the wave of the future, with the size of the world's fleet of these vessels doubling over the next few years. These have proved popular in Southeast Asia, where short-haul ships of 9-12,000 dwt can speed up feeder trips by using their own gear to load and unload instead of using often inadequate port facilities.

One unusual order during 1991 came from China, whose China Ocean Steamship Co. (Cosco) booked two 3,490-dwt, 20-ft equivalent unit (teu) container ships to be built by China Shipbuilding Corp. in Taiwan. Six other ships were being sought from German yards, and it was believed that the shortage of shipyard capacity had led Cosco to overcome political difficulties in its bid to obtain a fleet of large container ships. The order was placed through Hongkong-based Ken Wa Shipping, which runs Cosco and China Merchants Steam Navigation ships on European routes.

The drive for greater quality in all aspects of shipping was highlighted by the resolution of a political battle between ship management companies in April. Eight Asian-based companies were among 35 founder-members of the International Ship Managers Association (Isma), a group whose aim is "to drive a wedge between poor quality and good quality shipping."

Isma's Asian members comprise one company in Bombay, four in Hongkong and three in Singapore, with other members scattered across Europe and the US. The group has set up a code of conduct to establish norms for ship managers in crew standards, financial reporting to owners and charterers, safety and business ethics. Adherence to the code will be monitored by any one of four major ship classification societies.

Isma grew from moves in 1989 by the world's largest ship management companies, known as the Group of Five, to establish a code of practice. Smaller companies saw the moves

A *Reputation* for speed, reliability, and efficiency.

A global transportation network.

Dedicated to Quality Service

as an attempt to form an exclusive club with a sanctimonious approach to worldwide problems, and succeeded in forcing Isma to be open to all companies willing to adopt its code of practice.

The vast majority of ship managers were already conforming to Isma standards as a matter of sensible business practice. The "pirate" image of some companies had brought deep suspicion upon the whole industry from insurers, and membership of Isma could be regarded as a useful mark of respectability and a good marketing tool.

Further emphasis on quality management of crews and ships came with two conferences — one in Oslo during June and the other in Hongkong during October — which were set up specifically to look at the causes of accidents involving 30 large bulk-carriers since the start of 1990. The list of ships included 18 sinkings, many without trace, and involved the deaths of more than 300 mostly Filipino and Indian seafarers.

The recent losses formed part of 70 bulk-carrier losses over the past 15 years, about 60% of them ships of more than 100,000 dwt and about 75% of them involving the carriage of high-density ores. Four of them had been loaded in the West Australian port of Dampier, and fingers were initially pointed at high-speed loading rates used there and at the other ports from which the ships had sailed.

At the Hongkong conference, representatives from an ore company pointed out that the ships had been loaded in accordance with load plans prepared by the ships' officers and as instructed by the ships' masters. They also said that Dampier loading crews had on occasion refused to load various ships because of visible structural damage — the ships had been forced to undertake repairs and be properly inspected before loading was permitted.

Although debate on the issue has often been characterised by arguments between ship-designers, builders, classification societies, owners, managers, insurers and stevedoring concerns over responsibility for the casualties, by the time of the Hongkong conference there seemed to be general agreement that no one sector of the shipping industry was entirely at fault and that collective action was needed.

**Bulk carriers: heavy losses.**

Structural failure remains the root cause of the problem: in one case, in which only the master was saved, the ship took only seven seconds to sink. In the recent losses, the ships had an average age of 18 years, and ship surveyors pointed to well-known areas of potential cracking on ships' side-frames — caused by uneven stresses from pressure of the cargo inside against water pressure outside. If these cracks spread to the side plating, the inevitable result is flooding of a hold, leading in turn to extra stresses on the hull and its possible or even probable break-up.

The finger-pointing was the result of horror-stories told about bulkers by all sectors of the industry. The use of high-tensile steel to provide thinner plating in ships was brought about by designers seeking to save structural weight through the use of computer-aided design techniques.

But this steel corrodes at the same rate as mild steel, and thus loses critical strength faster. Inspections were difficult to

perform in cavernous, badly lit holds at port calls without delaying ships, whose crews were under pressure from owners and charterers to stick to schedules.

Insurers had been under pressure to obtain business virtually at any low rate in a market with too much capacity, and so had taken on business which should have been rejected or at least deferred for inspection. Loaders were under pressure to be quick, and their bulldozers and 25-tonne grabs were capable of severely damaging ships' frames and other internal structures unless carefully handled.

Crews have been cut to the minimum to save costs, and therefore have little time to perform proper inspections en route or to undertake much routine maintenance. Crews are known to have ignored builders' loading plans, thus overstressing ships through uneven loading. They are also known to try to keep up speed in heavy weather, putting extra loads on an already heavily stressed and perhaps poorly loaded structure.

The ships themselves were, in effect, found to have been built to standards which have not withstood the transition from tradition — which included adding a large safety factor as insurance — to modern design and technology. The rules have now been changed to strengthen hulls in newbuildings.

The point apparently now taken to heart is that these accidents were avoidable, and that had they been aircraft there would have been a huge public outcry instead of the apparent indifference which has characterised the losses. The intention is that safety must be enhanced by the industry policing itself — because otherwise governments may take the matter out of the industry's hands.

Swire subsidiary China Navigation Co. ordered bulkers built to the new, stronger specifications after looking at the possibility of buying a second-hand bulker — which was later among the more recent losses. It ordered three 162,500-dwt vessels from a Belfast yard at around US$61 million each.

Asian crews were involved because of the practice of "flagging out" ships by developed countries to avoid the expense of hiring their own nationals. And development of a consistent and higher standard of crew training is a major concern of Isma, among other bodies. Even Asian countries, however, are now finding they have manpower problems — mainly due to the declining number of those who want to work at sea rather than expense.

South Korea has decided to allow up to 10,000 seafarers to be hired from China and Southeast Asia to serve as crew on South Korean ships. They will boost the country's total crew pool by a third, and the move is seen as part of a general relaxation of regulations for the South Korean shipping industry as a whole, with all restrictions perhaps being removed by 1995.

Apart from safety and quality assurance within their own ranks, Asian shipping companies were also watching the uncertain steps being taken towards a single market in Europe after the end of 1992.

While the philosophy of a single European market is broadly welcomed, the methodology of its implementation is still unstated. Harmonisation of customs regulations, for example, would be a boon to Asian shippers and shipping lines, as would wage equalisation across the EC and Eastern Europe, which would hand Asian shipyards an automatic cost advantage. Some also feel that major hubs such as Marseilles could act as the major European distribution centres for Asian cargoes, obviating the need to take part-cargoes around to northern European ports.

However, others — either concerned about being locked out of post-1992 EC or simply pursuing a business opportunity, have elected to invest in Europe. Hongkong International Terminals (HIT), for example, arguing that growth in the colony is now limited for the foreseeable future, has followed in Orient Overseas Container Line's footsteps in buying into Felxistowe in Britain. With this foothold in Europe, HIT is now believed to be looking at other port or terminal opportunities in Germany.

Port developments proceeded apace elsewhere during the year. In March, Cosco and China Merchant Holdings joined HIT and Modern Terminals Ltd to develop a HK$7 billion (US$897 million) container terminal on reclaimed land in Hongkong's harbour. The first of four berths on this, Terminal 8, is due to open in August 1993. Its predecessor, T7, started operating two years ahead of schedule in November 1990.

In Singapore, marginally ahead of Hongkong as the world's top container port, work was nearing completion at the new Brani Terminal, with one of its two berths due to open early in 1992. This US$640 million project is Singapore's third container terminal, and port officials are planning to be able to handle 36 million teu a year by 2030, up from 1991's 5.2 million — which will rise to 10 million in 1994, when all of Brani's nine berths will be open to complement the 14 at the other two terminals.

The year also marked the passing of one of the world's greatest modern shipping men, Sir Yue-kong Pao, who died on 23 September aged 72. Pao built up Hongkong-based Worldwide Shipping into the world's largest independent tanker-owner, and was one of the few to read the signs when soaring oil prices during the mid-1970s slashed demand. He responded by gutting his fleet, which enabled Worldwide to survive the ensuing slump with the result that the company continues to retain its position as one of the world's largest tanker-owners. ☐

# Aviation

**S**urvival was the name of the game for 1991, with very little cheer evident even among Asia's airlines — where results and traffic were relatively high compared with most of the rest of the world. Orders for new aircraft slowed to a relative trickle, with engine-manufacturers engaging in their own bloodbath in attempts to gain market share.

The almost eight-month Gulf crisis provided a convenient scapegoat for the world's airline industry, most of which had been experiencing declines in traffic since late 1989 as the first whispers of economic recession began to intrude into financial results. In truth, the Gulf situation merely accelerated and then magnified the airlines' woes.

Jet fuel doubled in price for a relatively short time during 1990 and early 1991 as speculators entered the crude-oil market to rip out huge profits. While there was indeed a temporary shortage, with the time needed for refineries to change production fractions after the loss of Kuwaiti and Iraqi capacity, this was short-lived. The price collapsed with the start of fighting in mid-January, and it is not expected to be a major factor except for inflation rises in the foreseeable future.

The overall effect of the traffic drop was, in line with expec-

Falling traffic: waiting for the upturn.

tations, worst for US-based airlines already financially weakened by their soft domestic market. Even among the strongest, declining traffic forced sharp changes in previous plans for global expansion. In Europe, the effects have been less obviously dramatic but are still causing concern. British Airways parked Lockheed TriStars and brand-new Boeing 767s because of falls in traffic, Air Europe collapsed and various carriers asked for government help to stay in business until the market recovers.

Predictions that Asian carriers — backed by higher economic growth rates in the region as a whole as well as their generally higher profitability — would suffer less proved correct, though perhaps not to the extent expected.

While intra-regional travel was forecast to be a major cushion against drops in trans-Pacific and Asia-Europe traffic, to the consternation of several airlines Japan's outbound traffic fell away sharply during the crisis. Recovery, though it is happening, is slower than had been hoped.

But as a Boeing forecaster commented at the end of the Gulf War: "You can't base forecasts for the next several years on events over the past six weeks." Partly by default, because of the huge backlog of orders for new aircraft, airlines have been forced to adopt nine to 10 year planning views instead of the more usual three to four years.

There were some postponements of orders — largely by Middle Eastern carriers — and the production slots opened by these have been snapped up by other airlines. But some re-equipment and expansion decisions were delayed for several months, in some cases — notably Japan Airlines (JAL) and Hongkong's Cathay Pacific Airways — with announcements still pending late into the year. There was also one startling switch: Singapore Airlines dropped five firm orders and 15 options for McDonnell Douglas MD11s in favour of Airbus A340s because of problems with the MD11's lower-than-predicted range.

On the safety front, the crash of an Austrian-based Lauda Air Boeing 767-300 in Thailand about 20 minutes after taking off from Bangkok led to moves which are expected to bring new thinking to the design of engine thrust-reversers, used to slow the aircraft on the ground. After the crash in May, in which all 223 people aboard died, examination of the wreckage found that one engine's reverser had been deployed in flight.

Initial suspicions centred on the possibility that a bomb had been placed aboard, and widespread looting of the wreckage by local people as well as wild statements made by Thai officials did nothing to clarify the investigation. Eventually, the bomb theory came to nothing, as did another theory that a small consignment of lithium batteries might have started a fire which interfered with the aircraft's electronic engine controls.

Boeing initially issued a statement that deployment of a thrust-reverser in flight was tested during the 767's certification — several different safety systems would have to be inoperative for this to happen, and in any case, even if it did somehow happen then the engine would automatically cut back to idle power. There was also a device which would re-stow the reverser automatically.

But Boeing and accident investigators later found that if a hydraulic seal disintegrated, a piece of the seal could jam open

**Lauda Air crash: assumptions shattered.**

a valve and the system would then deploy the reverser, in line with comments made by the Lauda Air pilots recorded on the aircraft's cockpit voice-recorder. The flight data-recorder was too badly damaged for information to be recovered.

Worse, it was then found that the inflight testing of a deployed reverser had been performed at low speed and low altitude, with the engine concerned at idle thrust. A test in a simulator proved that, at the Lauda Air 767's speed, altitude and power-settings the pilots would have had only three seconds after the reverser deployed before the aircraft became uncontrollable — not enough time for the engine to be cut back to idle thrust.

While the evidence was only circumstantial — the Lauda Air valves implicated were not recovered from the Thai jungle despite several searches — the reverser theory led to a swift move to lock out the reverser systems on similar 767s worldwide, with some 757s also involved, while extra safety systems were added. Only seven aircraft — from Royal Brunei Airlines, Shanghai Airlines and Air China — in Asia were involved. An Air China 767 was later damaged when it overran a runway at Stockholm and — despite having landed a long way down the runway — it arguably could have stopped earlier had its reversers been usable.

Four-engined aircraft were exempted from extra safety actions on the grounds that their aerodynamics were sufficiently different as to maintain control — thus avoiding problems for the 747-400. Airbus aircraft were also exempted because their reverser systems operate differently.

But the legal and certification implications are enormous, the thinking now being that reversers must be treated with the same caution in design as basic flight controls. Modifications of some kind to almost every aircraft now in service are virtually inevitable, with the costs involved ultimately to be borne by passengers in the form of increased fares.

Another significant event involved a Singapore Airlines (SIA) shuttle flight from Kuala Lumpur to Singapore's Changi airport on 26 March. Four Pakistani men hijacked the flight, which had a total of 129 people aboard, and after landing demanded the release of various people jailed in Pakistan. Early next morning the Airbus A310 was stormed by Singaporean commandos, who killed all four hijackers. All the passengers were unhurt — the only injuries were to two stewards who had been thrown out of the aircraft by the hijackers during the night to reinforce their demands.

SIA found itself embroiled in a major row with Canada in 1991, with Canada giving a year's notice of termination of the Singapore-Canada air-service agreement shortly after SIA had launched a service from Singapore to Toronto via Vienna and Amsterdam. Air Canada had previously stopped serving Singapore via Europe, and was worried by its loss of traffic to SIA on the trans-Atlantic portion of the route.

In July, China finally gave its approval for Hongkong's planned new airport after guarantees were given regarding the amount of reserves to be left intact when China resumes sovereignty over the colony in 1997. The decision cleared the way for an avalanche of contracts to be let, most of which were expected to be in place by early 1992.

Other significant events included:

JAL's profit for the half-year to 30 September 1991 plunged 91% to ¥2.7 billion (US$20.7 million). Both JAL and All Nippon Airways (ANA) were hit by a national edict that overseas holiday travel was unseemly while the Gulf War was going on.

In the year to 31 March 1991, ANA's number of passengers carried rose only 17% because of the Gulf crisis, against a forecast of 30%. In December 1990, ANA announced firm orders and options worth US$5.8 billion for 25 of Boeing's planned 777 twin-engined airliner and 10 four-engined Airbus Industrie A340 long-range jets. ANA, bolstered by its domestic route network, made a net profit of ¥11.9 billion for the six months to 30 September 1991.

Korean Air expects its international load factor to rise only half a percentage point to 73.1% for 1991, and forecasts a drop of 3.8 points to 70% on its domestic routes. Rival Asiana Airlines, a subsidiary of South Korea's Kumho transport group, began flying to Japan and Hongkong after two years of domestic services. It has plans for routes to Taipei and Bangkok in the region, and is looking at the US and Europe for late 1991 after it takes delivery of two 747-400s on firm order.

Taiwan's China Airlines (CAL) announced a plan for partial privatisation in 1993, hoping to raise up to US$128 million, though no details were available. It made a record profit of US$152.8 million for 1990, up 17% over the 1989 figure. Officials said the profit would have been even higher but for the Gulf crisis, based on a huge increase in passengers flying to Hongkong en route to China and an increase in overseas travel by Taiwan residents generally as the NT dollar has appreciated against the US dollar.

CAL will also benefit from its majority ownership of a new airline, Mandarin Airlines, set up to fly to Australia from mid-October and to other countries which have denied CAL landing rights because of political problems with Peking. The only cloud on the horizon is competition from Eva Airlines, owned by the giant Evergreen shipping company, which started operating in July on overseas routes.

In Hongkong, Cathay reported a 9.8% fall in profits for calendar 1990 to US$384 million. In mid-year Cathay announced the conversion of three options outstanding for 747-400s into firm orders, and postponed its decision on a fourth — 10 were due to be in service by the end of 1991, with nine more on firm order and 12 options. Also, Cathay has firm orders for 10 Airbus A330s with options for a further 14.

Cathay was expected to make a decision on up to 30 other aircraft — possibly Boeing 777s, larger versions of the A330 or the long-range A340 — late in the year. The decision was being complicated by slower than expected traffic growth and by a parallel decision — for A320s or Boeing 757s — expected from associate company Dragonair.

Cathay opened a new route from Hongkong direct to Johannesburg in South Africa in August, and expected to start twice-weekly services to Hanoi and Ho Chi Minh City in Vietnam in December.

Philippine Airlines (PAL) was inching closer to privatisation, with British Airways among foreign carriers said to be interested in buying at least part of it. A group of PAL pilots offered to buy the airline for US$357 million late in 1990, intending to sell off 40% to an unnamed foreign buyer and some of the rest to PAL employees and the public. But the government said that the airline would be sold by public bidding. PAL declared a profit of US$14.4 million for the six months to 31 March.

Thai Airways International was exempted from a government-imposed debt ceiling, that had seriously hampered its expansion in the past, following a military coup in March. The airline announced a profit for 1989-90 of Baht 6.754 billion (US$263 million), its second highest since its creation in 1960, with Baht 2-3 billion forecast for the 1990-91 year. In June, Thai announced orders for six Boeing 777s worth US$900 million, plus options on a further six.

Malaysia Airlines, under attack from government officials who want it to hive off its present loss-making domestic services to another carrier, ordered six more 747-400s and took options on a further six. It already had two firm orders and one option.

SIA placed a further firm order for six 747-400s in March 1991. SIA's results for the year to 31 March included a 23.9% drop in net consolidated group profit over the previous year to US$516 million. While continuing to take a long-term view of the market, as demonstrated by its March orders, SIA was also strenuously trying to control rises in costs. Even so, its half-year pre-tax profit to 30 September 1991 fell 7% to S$634.5 million (US$374 million).

Indonesia's Garuda ordered three more MD11s, bringing its total commitments for the type to 10, including one option. The first was due for delivery in 1991, though delays in production and shortfalls in payload and range were expected to push this date back. It also ordered 12 Fokker 100 short-haul jets with deliveries to start in 1993, as well as nine Airbus A330s for regional services with deliveries commencing in 1996-97. Early in 1991, it agreed to lease six A300-600s from Australia's Ansett Worldwide Aviation Services.

Australia's government-owned Qantas announced in early April 1991 that it might have to dismiss up to 5,000 of its 20,000 or so staff to cut losses. It was predicting an operating loss of US$234 million for the year to 30 June, which would be offset by the sale of nine of its older 747s. It was negotiating to buy 7.5% of Air New Zealand (ANZ) held by American Airlines (AA) — Qantas already holds 19.9% of ANZ, and wants to have 35% eventually.

Efforts to prepare Qantas for partial privatisation are being hampered by its own financial problems as well as those of

foreign airlines seen as potential buyers, as a direct result of traffic and revenue lost during the Gulf crisis. Its ANZ shareholding became the centre of controversy because of guarantees on share values it gave to its partners in the consortium — New Zealand's Brierley Investments, AA and JAL — which bought ANZ from the New Zealand Government in 1988.

Domestic carrier Australian Airlines is also a target of Qantas' purchasing ambitions. Qantas says it needs to buy a chunk of the government-owned carrier, which is also intended to be sold, to give it a "feed" from domestic routes on to its international services. Australian Airlines announced an after-tax profit of A$66 million (US$52.7 million) for the year to 30 June, a strong turnaround from the previous year's A$13.7 million loss.

Australian start-up domestic carrier Compass Airlines, using Airbus A300s and pricing seats at a little below those on Australian and Ansett, has managed to gain enough market share to survive and grow without — so far — creating a mutually destructive fare war. Spawned by Australia's liberalisation of domestic routes, Compass has been able to skim the cream from heavily travelled trunk routes, effectively protecting itself from retaliation by "umbrella-pricing" and by limiting its ambitions to a relatively few routes.

On the Subcontinent, Air India announcd a record net profit of US$31.2 million to 31 March, having previously said it expected to end its 1990-91 year with a loss of more than US$50 million, compared with a profit of US$38.8 million in the year to 31 March 1990. The Gulf crisis was blamed for the expected loss, because Gulf routes accounted for about 24% of Air In-

**Rising confidence: high hopes for new airlines.**

dia's revenue and 38% of its profits. Before flights to the Gulf region had to be scaled back, the airline had expected a profit of US$17 million for 1990-91. The record profit was attributed to "prudent financial management."

Largely domestic carrier Indian Airlines said it expected to make a loss of US$47.2 million in the year to 31 March 1991, and forecast a loss for the current year as well. Its 1990-91 problems stemmed from the grounding of its Airbus A320 fleet for several months after a crash in February 1990 — since found to have been caused by pilot error. The adverse impact of the Gulf crisis was blamed for its poor results continuing.

Ailing domestic Indian carrier Vayudoot, with debts estimated at US$20.5 million, was in danger of closure, according to government officials. An alternative being considered was privatisation of the government-owned carrier, which was set up in 1981 to link smaller cities. □

# VOLVO DRIVERS DESERVE TO BE CAGED

There is only one safe place to put our drivers. It's in a cage.

Not just an ordinary cage. But a cage designed to absorb the impact of collisions where they most hurt.

On the side.

Because that's where you are most likely to suffer serious injuries in an accident. One in every five accidents happen on the side.

That is why at Volvo we have developed SIPS, our Side Impact Protection System.

SIPS really is a major breakthrough in automotive safety.

SIPS absorbs the violent energy of a side collision and disperses the impact energy around the passengers.

In the diagram, you can see how the reinforced floor, roof, door sills and pillars redirect the force of the impact.

SIPS literally puts a protective cage between you and danger. Yet you won't for a moment feel caged.

Not in the new Volvo 960.

With the combined features of the new

3-litre, 24 valve, six-cylinder engine and the newly developed 4-speed gearbox that's electronically controlled, together they provide a unique driveline concept.

Performance that's a pleasure to drive.

Inside the 960 is pure luxury with electronically adjustable front seats with memory, climate control and leather seats and more.

But most importantly, it comes standard with SIPS. Your safety cage.

Test drive the new Volvo 960 for yourself. It's a cage you can really live with.

## VOLVO

# ASIA/PACIFIC

## Asean

The end of the Cold War and the virtual collapse of communism in Europe provoked a crisis of identity for Asean in the course of 1991. Deliberations at the 1990 Asean foreign ministers' meeting in Jakarta had focused on the need for the association to come to terms and adapt to a rapidly changing world. However, by the next meeting in Kuala Lumpur in July 1991 there was still no agreement on what could be done to consolidate regional cooperation.

The sheer pace of global change has made a deep impact on Asean. Events in the Gulf, Eastern Europe and the Soviet Union have upset the traditionally close relationship Asean has maintained with the Western powers. The emergence of the US as the single superpower, and the EC's increasing size and economic potential have put Asean on the defensive.

At one extreme there are those within Asean who regard the association in danger of being rendered irrelevant by the emergence of new groupings in Asia, such as the Asia Pacific Economic Cooperation initiative first suggested by Australia. "If Asean remains the way it is, it's not going anywhere," a senior Indonesian foreign ministry official remarked in May. Others are more sanguine, believing that rapid changes on the global scene will have a cathartic effect, prompting more effective regional cooperation.

There is general agreement that the way to proceed is towards greater economic cooperation between member states. The prospect of strong economic blocs in Europe and North America has generated considerable concern in the region. Fears of protectionism prompted Malaysia to suggest adoption by Asean of its East Asia Economic Group (EAEG) concept.

Debate over EAEG dominated Asean affairs for much of the year. Singapore was quick to endorse the idea, while Indonesia expressed reservations. Thailand, demonstrating a new interest in Asean affairs after the fall of the Chatichai Choonhavan government in February 1991, dusted off an old proposal for the creation of a free-trade area in Asean.

**Foreign ties: Western pressure on human rights, Burma.**

Asean officials were unable to reach agreement on any of these proposals in time for their annual foreign ministers' meeting at the end of July. Instead, the issue was held over for further discussion at senior official level, and for eventual perusal by the six Asean heads of government who will meet at the fourth Asean summit in Singapore in January 1992.

External affairs continued to preoccupy Asean officials in the non-economic field. The prospects of a Cambodian settlement improved in the course of the year, but regional optimism was tempered by an awareness that the peace process Asean has helped guide was gradually being taken out of their hands. China's rapprochement with Vietnam was seen as the catalyst for agreement among the warring Cambodian factions, and there were fears that an eventual settlement could fall short of the comprehensive framework sought by Asean.

Meanwhile, Asean signalled the enlargement of its circle of external dialogue partners by conferring such status on South Korea and inviting the Soviet and Chinese foreign ministers to the Asean foreign ministers' meeting in Kuala Lumpur as "observers." Asean's current dialogue partners — the US, EC, Japan, Australia, New Zealand and Canada — continued to press for more discussion of regional security.

Asean officials were reluctant to oblige, however, citing their collective neutralist philosophy and aversion for multilateral defence arrangements. In the face of a Japanese proposal for enhanced dialogue on security matters, Asean declared that security was already a fundamental aspect of their deliberations and there was no need for a separate forum to discuss such issues.

Japan emerged for the first time as a major player in the dialogue sessions at the Kuala Lumpur meeting. This confirmed Asean feelings that Tokyo would seek to play a more political role in the region. By the end of the year, Japan's declared intention to send a military contingent to Cambodia to help oversee an eventual settlement appeared to confirm the trend.

A move by the EC to introduce a human-rights clause into a new economic cooperation agreement to be concluded bilaterally with Asean further compounded the association's uncertainty and suspicion about the "new world order." EC-Asean relations were shaken after a ministerial meeting in Luxembourg in May where the issue was hotly debated.

Asean is strongly opposed to conditions being attached to trade and aid from the EC, which it regards as an imposition on its own definition of human rights. "Asean is of the view that the development of human rights cannot be at the same pace as those in . . . the West," Singapore's Foreign Minister Wong Kan Seng said.

A compromise of sorts was fashioned at the ministerial meeting in Kuala Lumpur. The EC indicated that the precise wording of the new agreement would not amount to conditionality, though EC officials in Brussels insist that a clause on human rights and the environment will be inserted into new trade and aid agreements.

Asean closed ranks on another related issue after the US urged the association to exert pressure on the regime in Burma. But Asean members are united in their resolve not to intervene in the domestic affairs of neighbouring states, preferring to adopt instead a policy of "constructive engagement."

Attention is now focusing on the forthcoming Asean summit in Singapore. Yet despite the apparent desire to strengthen intra-Asean cooperation, analysts doubt whether anything more than an intention to study proposals further will emerge at the meeting. While an economic treaty is a remote possibility, there is broad agreement on taking steps towards establishing a free-trade area.

Many analysts now see Asean in a state of flux. Apart from preoccupation with what shape it should take as a more integrated economic unit, the association will also have to address the issue of how much larger its membership should become in the wake of a peace settlement in Cambodia and the normalisation of relations with Laos and Vietnam. □

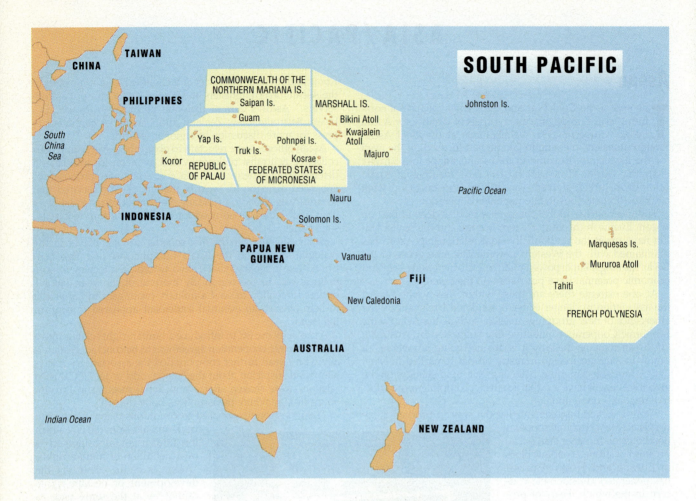

**SOUTH PACIFIC**

# South Pacific

After a decade marked by headlines proclaiming "problems in paradise" — notably, two military coups, a secessionist war and a violent independence struggle — the South Pacific began the 1990s in contrastingly unobtrusive fashion.

If the 22nd South Pacific Forum (SPF) was any guide, the end of the century in what US President George Bush termed "the aquatic continent" is likely to be marked by greater regional stability, concentration on the bread-and-butter issues of trade and economic development and continued wrestling with the conundrum of how to achieve growth without wrecking the environment.

This year's forum summit, hosted by one of the SPF's newest members, the Federated States of Micronesia, was described by one observer as "relatively calm and uncontroversial."

Fiji's Prime Minister Ratu Sir Kamisese Mara, a founding member of the forum who had briefly fallen from favour as a result of his role in Fiji's military coups, was honoured at his last SPF meeting by being made spokesman. Australia's Prime Minister Bob Hawke, Mara's principal antagonist in 1990, stayed away. Hawke had been criticised by many forum countries for his support for US plans to incinerate chemical weapons on Johnston Island.

Economic prospects and trade dominated the forum discussions. Leaders agreed there was a key role for regional action, emphasised the need to develop private-sector activity and reduce dependence on foreign aid. They also repeated previously expressed environmental concerns about global warming and French nuclear testing.

The SPF has achieved remarkable diplomatic success on environmental issues in recent years, given that it represents — apart from Australia and New Zealand — just 5 million people scattered across a vast ocean. The campaign to stamp out driftnets, used principally by Japan and Taiwan, has been an unqualified success, with both countries agreeing to stop driftnet fishing in the South Pacific.

In October 1990, after the forum expressed strong opposition to the use of the Johnston Atoll Chemical Agent Disposal System (JACADS) for the disposal of weapon stocks from Germany, Bush held an unprecedented meeting in Hawaii with the island leaders. They were assured that JACADS would be dismantled once stocks on Johnston and in the forum region had been destroyed.

The SPF intends to continue its high profile on environmental issues, and plans to send a high-level delegation to the UN Conference on Environment and Development in Brazil in 1992. It also stressed the urgency of an international convention on climate change, charging industrial countries with the primary responsibility for reducing so-called greenhouse gas emissions. Environmentalists claim such emissions could cause global warming which, in turn, could lead to rising sea levels that would swamp and destroy some Pacific island countries.

One perennial environmental issue on which the forum has made no headway is nuclear testing, which continues to strain relations between the South Pacific nations and the nuclear powers.

Although island leaders had raised the issue with Bush during the Hawaii meeting in late 1990, the US president gave no undertaking that Washington would ratify the SPF's South

Pacific Nuclear Free Zone Treaty. He also refused to put pressure on Paris to halt its nuclear weapon testing programme at Mururoa Atoll in French Polynesia.

The issue was further highlighted when Greenpeace announced that water samples gathered in December 1990 near Mururoa Atoll contained radioactive caesium 134 and cobalt 60. Five activists were arrested during the visit — the first since French Government agents blew up Greenpeace's Rainbow Warrior ship in New Zealand in 1985, killing a member of the crew.

Four months later, then French prime minister Michel Rocard crowned three years' efforts to restore relations with the region with a visit to New Zealand, during which he apologised for the Rainbow Warrior affair while defending French testing. A week after Rocard left New Zealand, and shortly before he resigned as prime minister and was replaced by Edith Cresson, France detonated its first warhead of the season. In June, French President Francois Mitterrand's government decorated one of the special forces' officers responsible for the attack on the Rainbow Warrior — an action Wellington described as "frankly disgusting."

The SPF's successes with environmental issues have not been mirrored in the region's trade and economic development. As a recent World Bank report noted, the South Pacific is more aid-dependent than any other part of the developing world. Papua New Guinea aside, regional World Bank members averaged just 0.6% annual growth in the 1980s.

These issues were taken up in Fiji during February at the first Pacific Island Countries–Donors Meeting. In July, the SPF summit identified private-sector development, improved strategic planning and better links with the outside world as the key solutions to its economic problems.

In the interests of economic growth, the forum summit also moved cautiously towards a two-China policy. Only four SPF states — Tonga, Nauru, Tuvalu and the Solomon Islands — have diplomatic relations with Taiwan, but their concern that their trading partner be included in the dialogue process carried the day. The forum agreed "in principle that a separate dialogue meeting should be held with Taiwan." The US, Canada, Japan, China, the EC, France and Britain are already involved in the Post-Forum Dialogue, which was instituted in 1989.

The forum also discussed the French Pacific territory of New Caledonia, a source of concern to the island states since a violent struggle over independence erupted in 1984.

Diplomatic negotiations with France resulted in the SPF sending a mission to the territory in mid-1991 to monitor progress under the 10-year peace plan, intended to precede a planned referendum on independence in 1998. The forum hopes to send annual missions to New Caledonia to monitor economic and political developments.

Despite the peace plan's aim to foster economic development in the interior of New Caledonia, economic activity remained largely focused in the capital, Noumea, where two thirds of the population live. On the political front, tensions within the independence movement, which has been deeply divided since the 1989 assassination of its leader, Jean-Marie Tjibaou, were exacerbated after local pro-French leader Jacques Lafleur formally called for a consensus solution between the two sides before the 1998 referendum.

In French Polynesia, France's other large Pacific territory, elections in March resulted in the return to power of conservative leader Gaston Flosse in an alliance with Emile Vernaudon, who sits nationally as a member of Mitterrand's Presidential Majority.

Following the polls, Flosse suffered two major defeats. In June, a planned US$95 million Japanese golf and hotel project on Moorea Island was roundly rejected by local residents. In

July, unions blockaded roads leading into the capital, Papeete, in protest over a package of increased indirect taxes, designed to reduce the territory's massive deficit. The unions wanted income tax introduced instead. The police smashed the road blocks, but the tax package was abandoned after France promised additional subsidies. By September, the Flosse/ Vernaudon alliance had broken up, and Flosse joined forces with the party of Papeete's Mayor Jean Juventin.

Meanwhile, in Vanuatu the year marked the end of an era with the ousting of prime minister Walter Lini, the "Father of Independence." Lini, whose 11-year reign was ended by a vote of no-confidence following a bitter struggle within his Vanua'aku Pati, was the last of the island leaders who took their countries to independence in the 1970s and 1980s to have remained continuously in power. Donald Kalpokas, whom Lini endorsed as his eventual successor in February only to sack him as foreign minister in June, became the new prime minister.

Lini's ousting followed months of political turmoil in Vanuatu, during which Lini — in poor health since a stroke in 1987 — sacked seven ministers, demoted others and dismissed numerous staff. Following the leadership challenge, he tried to have parliament dissolved. Despite echoes of a similar leadership challenge in 1988, Vanuatu emerged from the crisis with its democratic institutions strengthened and its media freer.

Dumped by his own party, Lini formed the National United Party, and announced plans to contest the general elections due in December 1991.

There were signs in other Pacific countries of greater political maturity and gradual strengthening of democratic processes. All Western Samoans over 21 are now entitled to vote — though they can still only vote for chiefs. The April elections were the first held under universal suffrage, which was introduced by Tofilau Eti Alesana's ruling Human Rights Protection Party. The government was returned with a comfortable majority.

In nearby Tonga, pro-democracy campaigner Akilisi Poheva triggered a political scandal through a court action launched in 1989 over the government's sales of Tongan passports to foreigners, notably Hongkong Chinese. Sales over the past nine years have netted more than HK$200 million (US$25.6 million). While most were Tongan Protected Persons' passports, which conferred no nationality or right of abode, in March the government was forced to admit that it had also sold 426 ordinary passports — one beneficiary was former Philippines' first lady Imelda Marcos — and had to rush through special legislation retrospectively legalising the sales. Several thousand Tongans took to the streets in protest, and Poheva warned that the writing was on the wall for Tonga's powerful monarchy.

In the Solomon Islands, tension continued with Papua New Guinea over the secessionist movement in neighbouring Bougainville. In March, former Solomon's prime minister Ezekel Alebua called on his government to recognise the breakaway province as an independent state. In August, Papua New Guinea delivered a second formal protest note over the free movement of the rebels into the Solomon Islands, which are separated from Bougainville by a few kilometres of sea but joined by close ethnic and cultural links.

The Federated States of Micronesia and the Republic of the Marshall Islands were formally admitted to the UN in September. Both became independent in 1986, but the UN only terminated the US-administered trusteeship of which they were a part in 1990 after the US gave an assurance it had no plans to develop military facilities in the region, and the Soviet Union accordingly dropped its opposition to the termination. □

# Asian and Pacific Organisations

The UN Transitional Authority for Cambodia (Untac) joined the list of Asian and Pacific international organisations on 31 October after being approved at the reconvened Paris Conference on Cambodia. Untac will supervise the demobilisation of 70% of the armed forces of the four factions that have been at war since the Vietnamese army drove the Khmer Rouge out of Cambodia in 1979, assist the repatriation of some 300,000 Cambodians who took refuge in camps along the Thai border and prepare the country for elections.

In his enthusiasm to return Cambodia to normalcy, Prince Norodom Sihanouk also applied to resume his country's membership in the Mekong Committee, which suspended projects in the country nearly 20 years ago. The annual Thailand-China Joint Commission meeting agreed in late November 1990 to set up a committee to undertake feasibility studies on China's participation in the Lower Mekong Basin Development Project as the prospects for a solution to the Cambodian problem improved. With the formation of Untac, it appeared certain that China would become a full member in the Mekong Committee, which sets policy for the technical work of the project.

A non-governmental economic organisation also moved to recognise the new realities of the region. The Pacific Economic Cooperation Council (Pecc), formed in 1980 by academic, business and government representatives, admitted Chile, Hongkong, Mexico and Peru to membership at its mid-1991 conference. The Soviet Union became a Pecc member at the end of the year.

In another move, the Asean Inter-Parliamentary Organisation (AIPO) — which is not affiliated to any of Asean's various organs — agreed to establish a permanent secretariat in Jakarta. The AIPO issues political communiques each year, and in some respects serves as a rival to Asean.

Security concerns took on a new dimension during 1991, with the likely closure of US bases in the Philippines over the next three years and the Soviet Union's pledge to complete the withdrawal of its forces from Vietnam in 1992.

More parochial security concerns, however, continued to influence regional relations. Kuala Lumpur and Bangkok, for example, agreed to upgrade their respective representation in the Malaysia-Thai Joint Commission to bring together ministerial-level officials on security matters. This development was partly in response to the growing number of Thai fishing boats being detained in Malaysia's territorial waters.

Broader security concerns were raised at a series of meetings, starting with a week-long conference on North Pacific security issues held in Canada during April and attended by representatives from, China, Japan, the two Koreas, the Soviet Union, the US and Canada. Following the Asean post-ministerial meeting in July, Japan — in a move that surprised US diplomats and analysts — suggested a review of security issues, a call later echoed by Australia.

Another security arrangement, largely otiose since the mid-1980s, also looked though it might be revived. Anzus, a defence treaty that linked Australia, New Zealand and the US was effectively suspended by Washington in 1986 after Wellington's decision to refuse US ships to dock at the country's ports unless they declared they carried no nuclear weapons. The present New Zealand Government, which favours improving ties with the US, has restored at least some military and intelligence links with Washington — partly by through its modest contribution to the Gulf War. In addition, President George Bush's initiative to remove certain types of nuclear weapons from warships is also likely to end the original cause of contention between the two former military allies.

On the economic front, central bank governors of the Southeast Asian Central Bank Group — after 25 or so years of annual meetings — produced the Asia-Pacific Central Bank Group. In February, the Bank of Japan governor hosted the new group's first meeting which brought together the heads of the central banks of Australia, Indonesia, Malaysia, New Zealand, the Philippines, Singapore, South Korea and Thailand. China is to be invited to the group's second meeting.

Among private banks, the 107-member Asian Bankers Association (ABA), of which 93 banks are from the Asia-Pacific region, launched a system that will enable members to share credit information. ABA also agreed to increase exchanges between management and to establish training programmes and joint studies.

In West Asia, the Economic Cooperation Organisation (ECO), which links Iran, Pakistan and Turkey, agreed to a 10% reduction in tariffs to their US$62 billion annual trade. In addition, ECO decided to launch an investment bank to promote joint ventures, with the three countries' central banks providing capital and administrators, and also agreed to study investment and trade opportunities in Soviet Central Asia.

The summit of the South Asian Association for Regional Cooperation (Saarc) finally got under way in late November 1990 in the Maldives after a one-year postponement. Apart from calling for Iraq's unconditional withdrawal from Kuwait and aid to offset the impact of the Gulf crisis on Saarc countries through higher oil prices and decreased guestworker remittances, the summit leaders signed a convention on cooperation in fighting drug abuse and trafficking. Differences, however, remained over bilateral disputes and trade.

Among technical bodies, the Southeast Asian Ministers of Education Organisation (Seameo) opened the regional centre for Vocational and Technical Education (Voctech) in Brunei — the eighth facility created under Seameo auspices and the first regional organisation to be based in Brunei. Germany became the fifth Seameo associate member in 1990, and Laos resumed participation in Seameo's Tropical Medicine and Public Health Project during 1991. Although Laos joined Seameo almost from its inception, Vientiane refused to participate after Vietnam withdrew from the organisation in 1980 and while Seameo continued to recognise Pol Pot's defunct regime instead of the Phnom Penh government.

Asia's oldest regional organisation, the Asian Productivity Organisation, celebrated its 30th anniversary with a conference in Bangkok on the theme "Better Quality of Work Life Through Productivity," with sessions on equitable sharing of productivity gains, corporate culture and human resource development strategies.

During 1991 the Indian Agricultural Statistics Research Institute in New Delhi sponsored a seminar on food crop estimation techniques for the Afro-Asian Rural Reconstruction Organisation.

The Southeast Asian Fisheries Development Centre now has departments in Malaysia, the Philippines, Singapore and Thailand. During most of 1991, the Aquaculture Department's main facility on Panay in the Philippines was still rebuilding at its Tigbauan main station after a typhoon devastated one side of the island in November 1990.

In the South Pacific, the South Pacific Forum's (SPF) principal economic agreement, the South Pacific Regional Trade and Economic Cooperation Agreement (Sparteca) failed to make much progress. Australia's decision to impose quota limits on garments from Fiji nullified most of the benefits of Sparteca for Suva, the largest trading country among the South Pacific island nations. Nevertheless, Australia agreed to abolish quotas on cloth, footwear and textiles from March 1992, three years earlier than originally planned.

In an attempt to start the process towards an eventual common market, the three Melanesian countries of Papua New Guinea, the Solomon Islands and Vanuatu agreed to mutual tariff reductions of 10% at their annual summit meeting before the SPF. However, little further momentum was gained at the SPF's annual summit in Pohnpei.

The South Pacific Trade Commission (SPTC) received permission from SPF member countries to provide advisory services to foster increased trade between Australia and French territories in the Pacific. Private-sector executives from French Polynesia and New Caledonia, in turn, attended an SPTC training course in Australia in February.

Several SPF subsidiary bodies were active during the year. The South Pacific Regional Shipping Council (SPRSC), composed of the region's shipping ministers, accepted the offer from Canada's International Centre for Ocean Development to implement portions of the South Pacific Maritime Development Plan with a C$500,000 (US$645,000) donation. The projects include port safety seminars, boat-building and repair facilities study, regional marine training scheme planning, regional marine legal services and training for ship surveyors.

The SPRSC admitted Niue and the Marshall Islands as new members of the Pacific Forum Line (PFL), the shipping ministers' major project. PFL services were extended to Brisbane, Australia, in 1990, though because private-sector competitors continue to take most of the profits in the region the PFL expects three years of losses until its routes become rationalised. After Australia and New Zealand announced their unwillingness to subsidise feeder service from Fiji to Majuro via Tuvalu and Kiribati beyond 1993 due to mounting losses, the PFL turned to Japan for support. Although Tokyo offered to supply a container ship to Kiribati, PFL wanted a container/breakbulk vessel to conform to Kiribati's lack of containerised facilities and negotiations subsequently broke down.

The South Pacific Applied Geoscience Commission continued its hydrocarbon potential assessment in Tonga, Solomon Islands and Vanuatu. Ocean thermal energy conversion, ocean wave energy and gold exploration were considered as future projects. A UN Development Programme expert, however, noted that the region lacked the infrastructure to support and maintain such projects, and instead recommended an energy conservation programme.

In 1990 the South Pacific Regional Environment Protection Treaty obtained the minimum number of signatures to go into effect, though regional interest is little in evidence. Four South Pacific countries have not signed the document and five others have failed to ratify the treaty. France was able to sign because the treaty excludes nuclear testing from its scope. Johnston Island, where the US stores nuclear and chemical waste, is excluded from the geographic scope of the treaty.

In 1991 the South Pacific Regional Environmental Programme (SPREP), which implements the treaty, began its second full year of operation as an independent inter-governmental organisation — provisionally based in Noumea. Western Samoa lobbied to host the permanent headquarters, which operates with contributions of about US$250,000 from member countries and international aid donations of three times that amount. SPREP's work programme identified climatic change and rising sea levels, coastal management, energy conservation, environmental impact assessment and marine and other forms of pollution as its priority projects.

The South Pacific Commission (SPC) remained under the shadow of the SPF. When New Caledonia's southern provincial government decided in mid-1990 to develop the site at Anse Vata, Noumea, on which the dilapidated 45-year-old SPC headquarters stands, French Polynesia put in a bid for a new headquarters if there were to be a change of venue. The French Government — seeking to keep the SPC in New Caledonia — offered another site in Noumea, but SPC member countries

pressured Paris to construct a new building on the present site. France and New Caledonia, however, offered to defray only one third of the US$30 million the new building's cost, the rest to be borne by the other countries in the region.

Meanwhile, SPC member countries agreed to increase assessments in 1991 by 10%, though Britain — in an unprecedented move — agreed to raise its contribution by only 6%. In addition, the US remained in arrears for the second consecutive year. Tuvalu, whose income is derived from investments, felt unable to pay in 1991 due to its sharp fall in income due to the worldwide recession. Japan, which has observer status, reiterated its desire to become a full member of SPC and Chile, another observer, was also invited to join. As a result of these considerations, the SPC headquarters site selection question was deferred for consideration until 1992.

At the end of 1990, Bush — in an attempt to assist a Republican senatorial candidate in Hawaii — hastily arranged a meeting with the heads of state from 11 Pacific island nations. Although he failed to persuade Hawaiian voters and the candidate lost, Bush did offer to extend the US–South Pacific Regional Fisheries Treaty with a provision outlawing the driftnet method of fishing. He also pledged to establish an Asian-Pacific growth fund in the US' Overseas Price Investment Corp., and proposed an annual Joint Commercial Commission (JCC) meeting to promote trade with the island nations by identifying commercial opportunities within the region.

Although island nations applauded the JCC proposal, details still have to be worked out. The US proposed the commission be based in Honolulu, which the Pacific leaders accepted until a funding formula for the new organisation is worked out. After such an interim period, they hoped the JCC headquarters could move to an island nation.                □

## Asian and Pacific Organisations

| | |
|---|---|
| Aarro | Afro-Asian Rural Reconstruction Organisation |
| ABA | Asian Bankers Association |
| ACS | Asean Committee in Seoul |
| ACU | Asian Clearing Union |
| AIPO | Asean Inter-Parliamentary Organisation |
| AJIV | Asean Joint Industrial Venture |
| Anzus | Security Treaty between Australia, New Zealand, and the US |
| Apec | Asia Pacific Economic Cooperation initiative |
| APO | Asian Productivity Organisation |
| Apsa | Asean Petroleum Security Arrangement |
| Apta | Asean Preferential Trading Arrangements |
| ATPC | Association of Tin Producing Countries |
| Certa | Closer Economic Cooperation Relations Treaty Agreement |
| EAEG | East Asia Economic Grouping |
| EC | European Community |
| ECO | Economic Cooperation Organisation |
| FFA | Forum Fisheries Agency |
| Inro | International Natural Rubber Organisation |
| Itto | International Tropical Timber Organisation |
| JCC | Joint Commercial Commission |
| Mop | Margin of preference |
| Nafta | North American Free Trade Association |
| Pecc | Pacific Economic Cooperation Council |
| PFL | Pacific Forum Line |
| PIC | Pacific Islands Conference |
| PIDP | Pacific Islands Development Programme |
| Saarc | South Asian Association for Regional Cooperation |
| Seacen | Southeast Asian Central Bank Group |
| Seafdec | Southeast Asian Fisheries Development Centre |
| Seameo | Southeast Asian Ministers of Education Organisation |
| Seato | Southeast Asia Treaty Organisation |
| Sopac | South Pacific Applied Geoscience Commission |
| Sparteca | South Pacific Regional Trade and Economic Cooperation Agreement |
| SPC | South Pacific Commission |
| SPF | South Pacific Forum |
| SPREP | South Pacific Regional Environmental Programme |
| SPRSC | South Pacific Regional Shipping Council |
| SPTC | South Pacific Trade Commission |
| Tropmed | Tropical Medicine and Public Health Project |
| UNDP | UN Development Programme |
| Untac | UN Transitional Authority for Cambodia |

# AFGHANISTAN

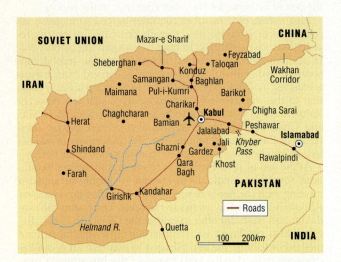

Map labels: SOVIET UNION, CHINA, Mazar-e Sharif, Feyzabad, Sheberghan, Taloqan, Konduz, Wakhan Corridor, Samangan, Baghlan, Barikot, Maimana, Pul-i-Kumri, Charikar, Kabul, Chighar Sarai, Chaghcharan, Bamian, Jalalabad, Peshawar, Herat, Jali, Khyber Pass, Islamabad, Ghazni, Gardez, Rawalpindi, Qara Bagh, Khost, PAKISTAN, Shindand, Girishk, Kandahar, Farah, Helmand R., Quetta, INDIA, IRAN

— Roads

0  100  200km

Serving as a buffer between the British and Russian empires, Afghanistan spent much of the 19th century being either wooed or menaced by the two dominant regional powers. Concern over Russian influence led Britain into two wars with Afghanistan. The first, between 1839-42, saw British forces routed while the second, between 1878-80, led to the emergence of modern Afghanistan. Under King Abd ar-Rahman the country assumed its present borders, while his son and successor Habibullah introduced social reforms that encouraged the development of a modern nationalist movement. Habibullah was assassinated in 1919 and succeeded by his son Amanullah, who proclaimed Afghanistan independent the same year. Following a short, indecisive war with Britain, the two countries signed the Treaty of Rawalpindi which restored the peace and led to Britain recognising Afghan independence. Between 1919-29 Amanullah, influenced by events in Soviet Russia, tried to modernise the country but ran into opposition from conservatives. Gen. Mohammed Nadir Shah ousted him and pursued conservative policies until he was assassinated in 1933. He was succeeded by his son Zahir Shah, who ruled until July 1973 when Gen. Mohammed Daud seized power, proclaimed Afghanistan a republic and installed himself as president. In April 1978, a revolutionary military council under Col Abdul Qadir ousted Daud and the Democratic Republic of Afghanistan — headed by communist leader Noor Mohammed Taraki — was proclaimed. Hafizullah Amin, a vice-premier in the Taraki government, seized power in September 1979 but was ousted by Babrak Karmal. In December 1979, the Soviet Union sent its forces into Afghanistan to support the regime against anti-communist guerillas. Soviet appointee Maj.-Gen. Mohammad Najibullah replaced Karmal as communist party secretary-general in May 1986, and in October 1987 was elected president of the Revolutionary Council and the party presidium. Soviet forces withdrew in February 1989, but the war continued as numerous rebel factions, backed by the US, Pakistan and some Middle Eastern countries, maintained their efforts to topple the government.

# Politics/Social Affairs

The political and military stalemate in the 13-year-old Afghan civil war continued in 1991. Both the Kabul regime and the mujahideen guerillas made small military gains in the field, but came no nearer to a dialogue despite a number of peace efforts. However, the abortive coup attempt in Moscow during August brought about a new agreement between the US and the Soviet Union on Afghanistan, raising hopes of an eventual settlement.

Meanwhile, the Gulf War heightened the tensions in the faction-ridden Afghan Interim Government (AIG), formed by the mujahideen in Peshawar under Pakistani auspices in 1989, and brought it to the verge of collapse.

The Afghan military continued to carry out a holding operation throughout the year, rarely going on the offensive and using massive airpower and Scud missiles to keep the mujahideen at bay. Pakistan attempted to heal the growing rifts within the mujahideen and restore their morale by backing some field commanders to attack Khost, some 25 km from the Pakistan-Afghanistan border, in March. The last serious attempt to capture this strategic garrison — birthplace of some of the regime's top generals — was in the winter of 1987-88.

The attack involved some 12,000 guerillas, including the most important commanders, and was supported by Pakistani artillery based on the border. The government retaliated with high-altitude bombing and Scud missile attacks. Nevertheless, Khost fell on 31 March following 17 days of intense fighting, in which an estimated 800 fighters were killed.

The victory was followed by intense friction between fundamentalist leader Gulbuddin Hekmatyar's Hizbe Islamic group, which demanded the bulk of the booty, and other commanders and parties. The 23-man mujahideen *Shura*, or council of commanders, attempted to form a new administration, but it quickly fell apart.

On 30 April, Pakistan's Afghan Cell held a crucial meeting at which President Ghulam Ishaq Khan took the lead in persuading Pakistan's military powerbrokers to use the Khost victory to support the UN peacemaking efforts. At the same time, in a move to maintain pressure on the Afghan Government, Pakistan's intelligence services encouraged the mujahideen to step up pressure against Gardez, another key garrison town in northeastern Afghanistan, and Kandahar in the south. But the Kandahar siege was lifted in July after heavy fighting between two mujahideen fundamentalist parties, Hizbe Islami and Jamaat-e-Islami. Pressure against Gardez also petered out.

Meanwhile, in June the Afghan army launched a massive operation in Logar province. Mujahideen camps and arms dumps of the Hizbe Islami were attacked, hundreds of rebels were killed and huge quantities of arms captured.

For President Mohammad Najibullah, 1991 required a delicate balancing act to retain the loyalty of the Khalq and his own Parcham factions of the ruling Watan Party, formerly known as the People's Democratic Party of Afghanistan. Senior Khalqi army officers were sent off to the provinces and repeatedly moved around the country in an effort to prevent them consolidating a grip on any one region.

In preparation for an eventual peace settlement, the Watan Party attempted — with some success — to democratise itself under a new generation of officials seeking to distance themselves from the Stalinist ideology of the past and reform the party from within.

However, while the president backed the party's democratic wing, he was opposed by a strong hardline faction of Pashtun nationalists who rejected offering too many concessions to the mujahideen and Pakistan. This faction also opposes a greater role for the minority ethnic Afghan groups and seeks a greater Pashtunistan — which would include Pashtun areas of Pakistan. The real struggle in Watan is between hardline Pashtuns and non-Pashtun groupings allied with moderate Pashtuns. This serious ethnic cleavage is also now the main issue dividing the mujahideen.

Najibullah: balancing act.

The Pashtuns, who make up an estimated 40% of the Afghan population — and the majority of Pakistan's North-West Frontier Province — have always dominated the minority Tajiks, Uzbeks, Hazaras, Baluch and Turkomen peoples. But the war has given the minorities a new sense of identity and increasing influence in provinces where they are a majority. Further, some of the most prominent mujahideen field commanders and Afghan army officers are non-Pashtuns. As a result, relations between the Pashtuns and the Tajiks, who dominate northern Afghanistan, have become extremely tense.

In July, Soltan Ali Keshtmand, a Shia from the Parcham faction, resigned as prime minister and Najibullah brought more non-party people into the cabinet. Nevertheless, the mujahideen failed to respond to Najibullah's statements that he was willing to hold elections, talk to anyone from the opposition, turn Afghanistan into a non-aligned nation, disband the Afghan army and announce a ceasefire.

Another Parcham leader, Babrak Karmal, who was brought to power by Soviet support in 1978 and subsequently ousted, returned to Kabul and a clique of pro-Soviet hardline Parchamis opposed to Najibullah gravitated around him. However, Karmal received a severe setback after the failed August coup in Moscow, which left Afghanistan's future even more uncertain.

For several weeks, the lack of signals from Moscow of its future policy towards Afghanistan led to massive price rises, and many in the capital tried to move money out of the country and stocked up on black market food and petrol. Mujahideen outside Kabul also began to rocket the city and the airport after a lull of several months.

However, the mujahideen failed to unite and take advantage of the opportunity. On 30 August, Maulvi Jamilur Rehman, head of the pro-Saudi Ahle Hadith party, was assassinated on the Pakistan-Afghanistan border and his supporters blamed Hekmatyar's group. These acute divisions among the mujahideen only increased the already prevalent tension between the moderates and the fundamentalists.

But hopes for a political settlement increased after the US and the Soviet Union agreed on 13 September to cut arms supplies to both warring factions in Afghanistan from 1 January 1992, prompting a number of peace proposals from Najibullah.

As the year drew to a close, political changes in Moscow led to growing uncertainty in Kabul as to the longevity of the regime. It was clear that Najibullah was prepared to step down from office if he was given an honourable exit and was convinced his departure would not create a power vacuum which could lead to anarchy and fragment the country even further. However, the bitterly divided Pakistan-based mujahideen continued to vacillate, rejecting his proposals without offering any of their own.

After prolonged disputes, the mujahideen finally cobbled together delegations to visit the UN General Assembly and Moscow in late September to hold direct talks with Soviet officials. But these and other diplomatic efforts were sabotaged by attacks on Gardez and Jalalabad in September and October by the Pakistan-backed fundamentalist mujahideen, and hopes for a peaceful settlement remained in limbo.

Afghan officials said that there were many people the mujahideen could talk to outside the Watan Party. Two thirds of the Afghan cabinet, including the new Prime Minister Fazal Haq Khaliqyar, are non-party politicians with relatively clean records. There are two new opposition groups in Kabul, who both favour the return of ex-king Zahir Shah and have publicly demanded Najibullah's resignation.

The National Salvation Front, made up of old political figures from the Zahir Shah era in the 1960s, would like to see the UN put together a committee of neutral Afghans to initiate the intra-Afghan dialogue. The Movement for Unity, Democracy and Freedom, made up of younger intellectuals — some of whom have ties with Watan — are demanding direct talks with the mujahideen.

The existence of such groups in Kabul demonstrates how far Najibullah has had to open up the political system because of internal pressures, and these groups could be an effective bridge between Watan and the mujahideen. Some Kabul officials believe the Watan Party could survive by striking a broad deal with moderate mujahideen, which would isolate fundamentalist radicals like Hekmatyar.

But a UN-sponsored agreement among all the interested regional countries cannot guarantee peace in Afghanistan. Many observers fear that the deep ethnic divide, the secularism of Watan and the Islamic zeal of the mujahideen will prove irreconcilable. They believe the huge quantities of arms and ammunition in the country, the power of local guerilla commanders and the physical damage wrought by the long war, will ensure that warlordism continues indefinitely and that Afghanistan will split along ethnic lines. ☐

# Foreign Relations

Despite a series of diplomatic initiatives during 1991, there was still no clear-cut resolution in sight for the Afghan civil war. While hopes for a political settlement were raised after the US and the Soviet Union agreed in September to cut arms supplies to Kabul and the rebel mujahideen from 1 January 1992, prompting President Najibullah to renew his offers of peace proposals to the mujahideen, problems remained in securing the agreement of the various interested parties inside and outside the country. By year-end, the situation on the ground looked more uncertain than ever.

In December 1990, hopes for an Afghan peace settlement were high ahead of a meeting between US Secretary of State James Baker and then Soviet foreign minister Eduard Shevardnadze. However, reports that Moscow and the US would agree to "negative symmetry," or the cessation of weapons supplies to both sides in the Afghan war, did not materialise. Shevardnadze belatedly insisted that the US guarantee a ceasefire and that Pakistan and Saudi Arabia also end arms shipments to the mujahideen. There were also disagreements over when negative symmetry should start and the format of an interim government in Kabul.

Immediately afterwards, Shevardnadze resigned in the first public indication that Soviet President Mikhail Gorbachov was increasingly coming under the sway of the hardliners in the Soviet military. The appointment of Gen. Boris Gromov, an Afghan War veteran and hawkish Najibullah supporter, as deputy interior minister further confirmed this view.

Moscow then announced in January 1991 that Afghanistan would receive Rbl 400 million (US$714 million) in aid for 1991. Of this, Rbl 280 million would be grant aid, compared to Rbl 120 million grant aid given in 1990. This pledge by Moscow did not include figures for the stepped-up aid the Afghan regime received in food, fuel and consumer items in separate deals with the Soviet Central Asian republics. Moscow's increased aid dismayed US and Pakistani officials, as it demonstrated the Soviet military had no intention of striking a peace deal in the near future.

There were also increasing signs in Moscow that the army, fearful of Islamic fundamentalism creeping into the five Asian republics from Afghanistan, saw the continuation of the Najibullah regime as the only bulwark for long-term Soviet security. Soviet generals clearly believed that the loss of interest in the US Congress on the Afghan issue, divisions within the mujahideen and the Gulf War would force Washington to gradually drop its aid to the mujahideen. Waning US interest in Afghanistan gave Najibullah breathing space in which he intensified efforts for secret diplomatic overtures to the moderate mujahideen leaders based in Pakistan.

The changing mood in the US was emphasised by the state department's 1990 Report on Human Rights in Afghanistan, which made a dramatic shift from Washington's decade-long outright condemnation of the Kabul regime. The report stated "that human rights in regime-controlled areas improved in 1990 . . . while resistance groups have attacked, tortured, killed or imprisoned persons opposed to their programmes."

The report also accused the government's intelligence apparatus of torture and other atrocities, and said the lack of political rights, freedom of speech and assembly and the denial of fair trials to its political opponents remained the hallmark of the regime. However, it stated that in many areas the regime had improved on its past performance.

Significantly, the toughest criticism in the report was reserved for the fundamentalist mujahideen group Hizbe Islami, led by Gulbuddin Hekmatyar, which was accused of carrying out political killings in Pakistan, kidnapping its opponents and other abuses.

The deep divisions within the mujahideen widened further as a result of the Gulf War, and brought the Afghan Interim Government (AIG) — formed in Peshawar under Pakistani auspices in 1989 — to the verge of collapse. While some 300 Afghan mujahideen from two moderate parties arrived in Saudi Arabia to help the Western-led alliance against Iraq, five of the other seven Pakistan-based parties supported Iraq and condemned the presence of US troops in Saudi Arabia. Hekmatyar and Abdul Rasul Sayaf, who leads the pro-Saudi Wahabbi party Ittehad-e-Islami, were in the forefront of condemning the Saudis. The Saudis, who had been the principal financial backers of the fundamentalist parties, saw their influence within the mujahideen greatly reduced.

Pakistan attempted to heal the growing rifts within the mujahideen and restore their morale by backing the eventually successful attack which in March brought the strategic town of Khost under rebel control. The Pakistani involvement prompted complaints from Afghan Foreign Minister Abdul Wakil to the UN, accusing Pakistan of using troops and its heavy artillery to shell Khost. Islamabad denied the charges, but Pakistani military officials hoped that if Khost fell the Pakistan Government would recognise the AIG, which could then set up its interim capital in Khost and demand recognition from the US.

After mujahideen disunity in the wake of their victory prevented this happening, Pakistan began an intense diplomatic effort to convince the Soviets and the Kabul regime that it was serious about peace negotiations. This "talk and fight strategy" adopted by Pakistan and the mujahideen encouraged the UN secretary-general's special representative for Afghanistan, Benon Sevan, to intensify his long-running shuttle diplomacy between the five involved countries — Pakistan, Saudi Arabia, Iran, the US and the Soviet Union — to create an international consensus on ending the war. In April, he told the REVIEW that there was a unique opportunity after Khost and the Gulf War to accelerate diplomatic efforts towards achieving an international disengagement from Afghanistan and to allow the Afghans to decide their own future.

The Khost victory also encouraged the US Congress to pay up the second tranche of the US$250 million committed in covert military aid to the guerillas for 1991. The US had so far withheld US$125 million because of the mujahideen disunity and lack of military successes.

On 21 May, UN Secretary-General Perez de Cuellar for the first time set out the parameters of a comprehensive peace settlement in Afghanistan. De Cuellar said that the elements of a settlement, which the UN was working on, must include: a ceasefire in the war between the mujahideen and the Kabul regime; a cessation of arms supplies by all countries involved in the conflict; the end to all outside interference and the right of all Afghans to choose their own government. A transitional broad-based government with appropriate powers and authority would arrange for elections, which the UN also offered to help organise.

Sevan had already got broad agreement on all these points from Pakistan, Afghanistan, Iran, Saudi Arabia, the US and the Soviet Union and the moderate mujahideen leaders. However, the statement made no mention of the future role of Najibullah, and the fundamentalist mujahideen condemned the UN plan for not demanding that he step down.

The mujahideen for a time increased their pressure on Gardez and Kandahar, but this petered out in July. By now the AIG had split irrevocably. Yunus Khalis, who headed his own faction of the Hizbe Islami, formally left the AIG and the deep US and Saudi aid cuts during the Gulf War led to large-scale redundancies among the staff of AIG ministries set up in Peshawar.

In July, two separate peace efforts were mounted by Switzerland and Sudan. Officials from both countries visited Islamabad, Kabul and Peshawar to talk to the mujahideen and Najibullah, but failed to achieve any progress.

More substantial negotiations were held in two rounds of tripartite talks in July and August between Pakistan, Iran and mujahideen leaders based in Iran and Pakistan. But the fundamentalist parties in Peshawar still refused to participate in these talks. Iran and Pakistan attempted to bring the faction-ridden mujahideen groups onto a common platform in order to take the UN peace process forward. Criticism from Kabul and the international community stressed that even if Najibullah were to step down as demanded by the mujahideen, there was no alternative mujahideen united group that could take power in Kabul.

Encouraged by these talks, the Soviet Union responded positively when it sent Nikolai Kozyrev, a senior Soviet diplomat, for talks to Islamabad on 11 August. In his two days in the Pakistani capital he also met some mujahideen leaders, which signalled the highest level of negotiations between the Soviets

Mujahideen: foreign interest wanes.

and the guerillas for nearly three years. On his return to Moscow, Kozyrev issued a statement praising Pakistan's attempts to follow the spirit of the UN peace proposal.

All negotiations, however, were thrown off track by the August coup attempt in Moscow. While fundamentalist mujahideen welcomed the coup attempt, moderate leaders were pleased when President Mikhail Gorbachov returned to power. The reaction in Kabul was much more severe. Russian President Boris Yeltsin had long been urging a cut-off in Soviet aid to Najibullah. With the influence of the Soviet military — which has insisted on continuing food and arms supplies to Kabul — much diminished, Yeltsin was expected to have a freer hand to push for a settlement.

In Kabul, where many thought that Soviet aid may be immediately cut off, Afghan Prime Minister Fazil Haq Khaliqyar urgently requested that India supply a promised 50,000 tonnes of grain. He also called on the Soviet Union to ship 200,000 tonnes of grain to see the government through the winter months. Najibullah appealed personally to Yeltsin to continue Soviet support, and told the Afghan parliament that mujahideen leaders were free to come to Kabul and hold talks.

It was not until 13 September that the first indication of Moscow's changed policy towards Afghanistan emerged,

when the US and the Soviet Union issued a joint statement calling for an end to arms supplies to both sides in the war from 1 January 1992. Both promised not to increase supplies to the belligerents during the intervening period, and appealed to other countries — notably Pakistan and Saudi Arabia — to do the same. The UN secretary-general, Pakistan, Iran, Saudi Arabia and Afghanistan welcomed the accord, but panic increased in Kabul as to how long the Najibullah regime could survive without Soviet aid.

He hastily sent delegations to the Soviet Central Asian republics asking for supplies through separate treaty arrangements. The republics have always viewed Najibullah's survival as crucial if they are to block a mujahideen victory in Kabul that could spread Islamic fundamentalism to their region.

Some diplomats saw the 1 January deadline as representing a Soviet concession to the republics to give them time to adjust to the accord, and a US concession to allow Pakistan and Saudi Arabia to back the guerillas for a final push against Kabul. Saudi and Pakistani officials said they could not contemplate having to deal with Najibullah were he still in power in January.

During this period the UN secretary-general visited both Iran and Saudi Arabia, where he held intensive talks on Afghanistan and issued a warning that any assault on Kabul at this stage would seriously jeopardise the peace process.

After prolonged disputes, mujahideen delegations visited both the UN General Assembly and Moscow in late September to hold direct talks with Soviet officials. Soviet Foreign Minister Boris Pankin suggested that while the presidency of Afghanistan could be given to the mujahideen, Khaliqyar should remain prime minister. These proposals were partially accepted by Sighbatullah Mujadedi, the president of the AIG and the leading moderate mujahideen figure. A major political obstacle to a settlement has been the reluctance by Pakistan and the mujahideen to open an intra-Afghan dialogue with the Kabul regime, as called for in the May UN peace plan.

But Pakistan's Inter Services Intelligence (ISI) agency backed the fundamentalist mujahideen for another major offensive against Gardez, which began on 20 September. Diplomatic efforts received another setback when fundamentalist guerillas renewed their attacks on Jalalabad on 12 October. The Kabul regime responded by bombing guerilla positions and the next day, under pressure from the ISI and the fundamentalists, Mujadedi backtracked on his commitment in New York and rejected Khaliqyar's offer of a meeting in Geneva in November. The same day, the Soviet ambassador in Kabul, Boris Pastoukhov, issued a statement that said Moscow would continue to back Najibullah and denied suggesting he be replaced by a mujahideen candidate.

Meanwhile, the plight of Afghan refugees worsened as donor countries cut aid and fundamentalist guerilla groups continued a bombing campaign against Western aid agency offices in Peshawar. By the end of the year a number of private Western charities had left Peshawar. These threats became so severe by September that all UN aid bodies and the International Committee of the Red Cross suspended their activities in the Afghan countryside, though they continued to maintain a strong presence in Kabul and a few other cities. □

# Economy/Infrastructure

The Afghan Government, with an economy virtually destroyed by 13 years of war and tight state controls, took dramatic steps to survive by deregulating food and fuel supplies and offering incentives to the private sector to ensure supplies. Disruption in the Soviet Union, which provides Afghanistan with most of its economic aid, has also severely affected the country's ability to feed itself.

Fearing further cuts of aid because of the US-Soviet accord in September to end arms supplies to Kabul by January 1992, President Najibullah has put his weight behind a large-scale deregulation programme. The ruling Watan Party, which once practised hardline Stalinist state control over the economy, has now lifted the state monopoly over the import of food and fuel, allowing private entrepreneurs to take it over.

Afghanistan's traditional private-sector members, many of whom had either fled abroad or become full-time narcotics or arms smugglers, have taken immediate advantage of this opportunity and rapidly secured enough supplies to ensure the regime will have enough food and fuel to last through the harsh Afghan winter.

By October, Afghan traders had signed deals with Germany, France, Hungary and the Soviet Union for some 500,000 tonnes of wheat, which will arrive via Central Asia. They also made four separate deals with Soviet oil companies for the supply of 186,000 tonnes of petroleum products. The traders said they could guarantee oil supplies through the winter with the oil, paid for in US dollars and sweetened with "gifts" for Soviet oil executives. Afghanistan is entirely dependent on the Soviet Union for petrol, diesel and kerosene for cooking and heating.

Afghanistan now relies on foreign sources for virtually all its food. Some 300 trucks loaded with wheat, sugar, rice and ghee, cross unpaved mountain roads each day from Pakistan's Pashtun tribal area to feed Kabul and cities in eastern Afghanistan. Southern Afghanistan and Kandahar are supplied through the Pakistani city of Quetta, while western Afghanistan is fed through Iran and the Soviet city of Torgundi, north of Herat.

Northern Afghanistan is almost entirely provisioned from the Soviet Union. Much of this trade is technically smuggling, though few Afghans differentiate between legitimate and illegal trade.

The Afghan economy is in a critical state. Production has declined, as has government revenue, while the money supply and the budget deficit is increasing. In 1978, the year of the Marxist coup in Kabul, exports earned around US$210 million while remittances from Afghan workers fetched around US$125 million. During 1990-91, exports are not expected to touch US$60 million, while workers' remittances will earn only another US$40 million.

Exports of dried and fresh fruit have fallen from US$45 million in 1978 to just US$3 million in 1990-91 and wool from US$18 million to just US$1.5 million. Agricultural produc-

Reconstruction: the long road to recovery.

tion and manufacturing has been wiped out in many areas because of the war, which has also led to some 5 million Afghans out of a 1978 population of 18 million to flee the country.

At the same time, imports have jumped dramatically. In 1977, imports were valued at US$420 million. They reached US$681 million in 1989 and will climb to US$820 million in 1991. Due to technical problems, Afghanistan has been unable to supply the Soviet Union with gas from its northern gas fields for the past two years. These had earned the country some US$300 million a year during the past decade.

The plight of the economy can be judged by the fact that wider economic statistics are unavailable or wildly contradictory, with different ministries producing different figures. While the State Bank estimated inflation at around 58%, others said it was more like 80% and expected to rise even further during the winter.

The dramatic slide of the afghani, the national currency, is also fuelling inflation as the government prints notes in an effort to soak up the US dollars in the market. In the first week of October, US$1 fetched Afs 1,100 in Kabul's unofficial money market — acknowledged even by the government as the country's major source of foreign exchange. Currency dealers said they can supply about US$100,000 a week, but fear that the local currency could climb to Afs 1,500 to US$1 within the next six months unless there is a peace settlement.

Hard currencies come largely from the narcotics trade, the sale of weapons by both the government and the mujahideen and goods smuggled from Pakistan and the Soviet Union. Since Pakistan deregulated foreign currency this year, there has also been a huge influx of dollars into Kabul brought over by Pashtun currency dealers based in Peshawar.

Legal sources of hard currency stem from transit commissions earned by the government for goods coming to Kabul and then returning to Pakistan, exports, dollars exchanged by some 200 foreign diplomats and aid workers in Kabul, as well as money earned during the Gulf War when Afghanistan granted overflight rights to US transport aircraft.

With the monthly salary of a doctor or civil servant at just Afs 5,000, the purchasing power of even the middle class has been dramatically reduced. However, some 75,000 civil servants' and 150,000 soldiers' families receive cheap flour, sugar and rice under a government ration scheme. However, in October the government was five months behind in distributing ration coupons because of a slow-down in direct food aid from the Soviet Union.

A new Economic Consultative Council to encourage the private sector has been set up, headed by Fareed Zaref, a former deputy foreign minister. Officials on the council say they want to remove all obstacles for the private sector by passing new laws which will prevent the army from seizing anything it needs, provide government transport so that food and fuel can reach Kabul along the Salang highway from Tirmiz, and allow the market to set prices rather than the government. A series of new laws intended to encourage the currency changers to form private banks are also planned. □

# AUSTRALIA

Australia was declared a British colony on 26 January 1788 when a party of 1,030 settlers, of whom 736 were convicts, landed in New South Wales. Britain remained the dominant focus in Australian social and political life until the Pacific War broke out in 1941, when the threat of Japanese encroachment forced the country to look increasingly towards the US for its defence. The first two decades of the post-war era were marked by a foreign policy that sought to support the regional aims of both London and Washington, notably in defence. Australian forces participated in the Korean War, the Malayan Emergency, Indonesia's "Confrontation" against Malaysia and in support of the US in Vietnam. While the latter war seriously divided the nation, it had little long-term impact on Canberra's view that the US remained the country's principal patron. Britain's accession to the EC in the early 1970s largely completed this process, and Australia now sees itself as part of the Asia-Pacific region while maintaining strong links with the industrialised West and Japan. Australian domestic and foreign policies underwent further dramatic changes in 1973-74 as the new socialist administration of Gough Whitlam attempted to give the country a more independent stance. The subsequent toppling of Whitlam's Labor government and the Liberal–National Country Party coalition's victory in a snap general election in the mid-1970s politically traumatised the country. The coalition won the 1977 and 1980 general elections, but were ousted by the Australian Labor Party, headed by Bob Hawke, in 1983. Hawke's government has won every election since, though it is expected to face a strong challenge in the next polls from the Liberal-National coalition. The Commonwealth of Australia, a member of the Commonwealth, is divided into six states: New South Wales, Victoria, Queensland, Western Australia, South Australia and Tasmania, plus the Northern Territory, and is governed under a federal system from Canberra in the Australian Capital Territory. Australia also administers several small Indian and Pacific Ocean islands.

## Politics/Social Affairs

The battle over who will lead the Australian Labor Party at the next federal election dominated national politics throughout 1991.

Speculation about when Deputy Prime Minister and Treasurer Paul Keating would make his run for Prime Minister Bob Hawke's job arose intermittently throughout 1990, and began in earnest soon after the Gulf War ended. Keating has never hidden his desire to take over from Hawke, and in May dropped a political bombshell when he told a journalist that he and Hawke had agreed a deal on the leadership in November 1989, before two witnesses, just prior to the 1990 general elections.

The deal was made at the prime minister's official residence in Sydney and became known as the "Kirribilli House deal." According to Keating, it was agreed that if he dropped public discussion of the leadership, Hawke would hand over the reins of office after the 1990 election.

The two witnesses were Australian Confederation of Trade Unions boss Bill Kelty — very much a Keating man — and Hawke's friend and international transport tycoon Sir Peter Abeles. Neither Hawke, Kelty nor Abeles attempted to deny Keating's version. But Hawke had apparently already changed his mind when he promised voters during the election campaign that if elected he would see out a full term of office.

The revelations, on top of a series of scandals involving state Labor governments, angered many Australians who regard the prime ministership as an elected position which should not be the subject of backroom deals. The whole incident further tarnished the ailing Labor Party's image and eventually provoked an official leadership challenge by Keating in early June.

The 110 members of Labor's federal caucus, comprising all party members of both houses of parliament, were subjected to intense lobbying by supporters of both men. Queensland Labor members were threatened with loss of party pre-selection if they did not support Hawke, which proved his salvation. He retained the leadership by 66 votes to 44.

Keating resigned as party deputy leader and treasurer and moved to the backbench, promising not to launch another leadership challenge — though his supporters have said there will be another bid.

Labor's political problems in Canberra were played out against revelations of financial mismanagement by Labor governments in three states — Victoria, South Australia and

Western Australia. Commissions of enquiry in the three states exposed inept government dealings and, in Western Australia, dubious relations between government ministers and some suspect business cronies, served to keep the issues before the public for most of the year.

The evidence in Western Australia was the most sensational and, for Labor, the most dangerous, as federal politicians such as Hawke and Keating were linked to the surrounding publicity — if not the substance — of "WA Inc," as the scandal was dubbed.

Former Western Australian premier Brian Burke, who had recently been appointed ambassador to Ireland and the Vatican, emerged from the early days of Commission hearings unable to explain how he had used thousands of dollars of party funds to buy stamps which he had put into his personal collection, or how millions of dollars of taxpayers money had been lost on deals with failed entrepreneurs such as Laurie Connell and Alan Bond.

In South Australia, Labor Premier and Treasurer John Bannon had long been regarded as an impeccable leader. But in February, Bannon had to announce an A$1 billion (US$1.25 billion) rescue package for the South Australian State Bank. It later emerged that for months he had ignored reports that the bank's affairs were in bad shape.

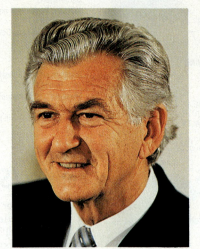

Hawke: tarnished image.

The government of Victoria, once the heartland of Australian wealth, is bankrupt. Under former Labor premier John Cain, A$3 billion of taxpayers money disappeared as government financial institutions, including the State Bank of Victoria and its investment arm, Tricontinental, collapsed.

In the island state of Tasmania, minority Labor Premier Michael Field has broken ranks with the five Green Independents who put him in office. His Liberal predecessor, opposition leader Robin Gray, has had to appear before an enquiry investigating alleged attempts by a Tasmanian newspaper proprietor to bribe a Labor MP to change sides in an attempt to keep the Gray Liberal government in office.

Only in Queensland, where Labor leader Wayne Goss is still relatively new — having taken office from the discredited National Party at the end of 1990 — is there any sense of political success in Australia.

The general disaffection with politics is not only directed at Labor. In New South Wales, elections at the end of May showed voters were not prepared to turn unquestioningly to the opposition in an effort to find competent politicians. Heading the only non-Labor state government, Liberal Premier Nick Greiner's confidence of sweeping back to power on Labor scandals across the country proved over-optimistic. Instead, the Greiner administration had to rely on a motley collection of four independents to govern with a paper-thin majority.

Liberal opposition leaders in the beleaguered Labor-governed states have failed to exhibit any political charisma and are largely expected to win office only by default — if indeed they do — at the next state elections.

At the federal level, Liberal leader John Hewson is still finding his feet. Hewson had been in parliament only one term when he was made party leader after distinguishing himself as an economics spokesman on the hustings for the Liberals during the 1990s federal elections.

The big question mark over Hewson, however, is whether he can sell a goods and services tax to the electorate he pledged to introduce should he become prime minister. Although most economists agree on its merits, Labor never ran the electoral risk of putting it on the agenda.

The Liberals' junior coalition partner, the rural-based National Party, is almost a spent force in Australian politics, with its old formidable base in Queensland still reeling from an enquiry which exposed the corruption endemic in that state under former National leader Sir Joh Bjelke Petersen.

Meanwhile, Australia's minor party, the Democrats, formed in the late 1970s by former Liberal minister Don Chipp "to keep the bastards honest," has had its own set-back. The Democrats have held the balance of power in the federal upper house, the Senate, for several years and been the party on the high moral ground. But in mid-1991, a leadership battle among Democrat senators, with allegations that then leader Janet Powell's sexual relationship with another senator interfered with her political judgment, showed the Democrats could be as dirty fighters as any other party.

The bleak political background gives little heart to Australians facing a continuing decline in their standard of living and rising unemployment. Unemployment has hovered at around 10-11% during the year, a shattering experience for a nation for whom full employment has always been a cardinal principle. And along with unemployment, more than 13% of Australians are now classified as living below the poverty line.

The economic situation has given rise to rare agreement among diverse groups in one area about which Australians traditionally disagree — the level of the country's immigration intake. This year, the Labor government reduced immigration by 12% — or 15,000 people — bringing the predicted total of immigrants to 110,000. This represents a substantial cut on the years when it was customary to aim for intakes of from 160,000-180,000 new migrants.

Government officials, as well as the opposition and the trade unions, are now calling for that intake to be halved. They argue that the serious deterioration in the economy means Australia simply cannot absorb more than 50,000-60,000 immigrants a year, if that, and implicitly reject the previous majority view that migrants were a stimulus to the economy. However, perhaps a more telling indicator is that immigration applications for Australia dropped by 15% in 1991. ☐

# Foreign Relations

Australia despatched a small naval contingent to the Gulf to join the UN-sponsored international blockade against Iraq after President Saddam Hussein annexed neighbouring Kuwait.

Prime Minister Bob Hawke responded immediately when US President George Bush called for allies, and in doing so became the first Labor prime minister to commit Australians to war. Hawke made the commitment without consulting his cabinet, an act that brought him some criticism, especially from within his own party. However, most people supported Hawke's move and, given the short duration of the conflict and because there were no Australian casualties, that support held.

Some critics expressed concern that Australia's Gulf commitment would be seen as a departure from the Asia-Pacific regional security focus the government has sought to promote. Foreign Minister Gareth Evans denied this when he told delegates at an international conference in February that while Australia's primary focus remained the region, "we will be ready to contribute beyond the region when it is appropriate, in our interests and within our capabilities to do so."

Evans argued the criticism demonstrated a lack of awareness of the efforts Canberra was making in the region on arms control, the South Pacific nuclear weapons free zone, Cambodia and through the Australian initiative which resulted in the Asia Pacific Economic Cooperation (Apec) process.

In the aftermath of the Gulf War, and despite the easing of superpower rivalry between the Soviet Union and the US, Australia re-affirmed its desire for a strong US presence in the Asia-Pacific region.

"Strategically, the situation in our region is much more fluid and complex than that in the Europe–North Atlantic theatre, where the benefits of the passing of the Cold War have been most dramatic," Evans said.

He continued: "Asia is a diverse and non-homogeneous region, with little sense of common cultural identity. There are many different issues of contention and many different 'fronts,' unlike Europe where there has been an overwhelming East-West confrontation. And despite the prospect, and indeed the reality, of superpower cooperation in our region, each of those fronts has its own background of conflict and its own dynamic of confrontation, independent, at least to a degree, of the changing pattern of superpower relations."

According to Evans, the Gulf War confirmed "the wholly desirable trend" — seen also in Cambodia, Afghanistan and Namibia — of cooperation between the major powers under the auspices of the UN in resolving regional conflicts. "The Asia-Pacific region will benefit from these developments and in the case of Cambodia has already started to do so," he said.

Australia has a perhaps inflated belief that her own contributions led the way to the establishment of Cambodia's Supreme National Council (SNC) during the year as an effective negotiating forum for a peaceful unified government. In July, Australia became the first country to announce diplomatic links with and appoint an ambassador to the SNC, while at the same time resuming direct aid to Cambodia.

Australia also expressed satisfaction with the continuing momentum of Apec, Canberra's other particular regional interest. Evans told the Asean post-ministerial conference in Kuala Lumpur in July that "from Australia's perspective the most important policy issue for Apec to be pressing is non-discriminatory regional trade liberalisation. If Apec is to be an effective vehicle for enhanced regional economic cooperation, it has to be able to deliver progress on a number of fronts, but trade policy is central."

Relations with Indonesia continued to improve during the year, with the Australian Broadcasting Corp. (ABC) being given permission to re-open its office in Jakarta, closed by the Indonesian Government 11 years ago when ABC journalists were banned from the country.

In a more cautious move, Australia lifted the remaining economic and political restrictions on relations with China that had been imposed following the crackdown in June 1989. China also allowed an Australian human-rights delegation to visit the country — the first permitted to do so. Its members felt the main achievement was to have the issue recognised in China as one the international community was concerned

about.

The three Chinese economic entities — China, Hongkong and Taiwan — are increasingly important to Australia, accounting for 8% of Australian trade during the year. Hongkong remained Australia's eighth-largest source of foreign investment, while Taiwan became Australia's sixth-largest export market. Australia remains committed to the view that reunification of Taiwan with China is a domestic matter and tries not to get caught up in rivalries between the two, not always successfully.

Negotiations to set up a direct air service between Australia and Taiwan became a case in point. Both Taipei and Peking sought to exact all possible political mileage from the deal, even arguing over the wording of a disclaimer on visas issued in Taiwan for entry to Australia. By the end of the year it looked as if the matter had been settled and the air service is expected to start in 1992.

With the approach of the 50th anniversary of the outbreak of the Pacific War, some ambivalence returned to Australia's attitude towards Japan. Australian leaders continued to take the view of their predecessors that Japan should play a wider role in world affairs, noting that Australia would accept Japan's armed forces contributing to UN peacekeeping duties in Cambodia or the Gulf. Nevertheless, Australians across the political and occupational spectrum remain cautious about Japan, and speak openly of unease over such issues as the censoring and re-writing of Japanese school text books that give a distorted account of Japan's role in World War II.

Regardless of these lingering suspicions, Japan remains Australia's major trading partner, and Canberra has consistently urged that Tokyo play a leadership role in the Uruguay Round of Gatt trade negotiations — in particular by being prepared to make some significant gestures in the liberalisation of access to her own markets.

**Gulf War: all at sea with GHB.**

Australia has also looked to Japan for strong support of the Apec process, and the two countries are now linked by the vexed multi-function polis project — a Japanese-initiated concept of a new high-technology leisure and industrial centre billed as a "city of the 21st century" to be situated near Adelaide in South Australia. The project has been greeted with varying degrees of cynicism and euphoria by nationals of both countries.

A lesser headache in the region during the year was the rising intensity of Malaysian Prime Minister Datuk Seri Mahathir Mohamad's hostility towards Australia. Differences in national attitudes on human-rights issues, capital punishment and the logging of rainforests all provoked the Malaysian prime minister. However, Mahathir took particular offence at an ABC television series set in an unnamed Asian country which he felt insulted Malaysia. Canberra had no responsibility for the fictional series — or for what many viewers in Australia felt was its appalling quality — but in an effort to soothe relations between the two countries, Evans apologised to the Malaysians for the production while pointing out that "Australian governments cannot tell anyone in the media how to behave."

Relations with the US, apart from the Gulf War, were soured by complaints from Australian wheat farmers that they were losing markets to the US Export Enhancement Programme

(EEP) — under which Washington heavily subsidises US wheat exports. The US argument is that it is trying to enforce a reform of the EC's agricultural policies and is not targeting traditional Australian markets.

After the Gulf War, which hurt Australia's Middle East exports, Bush said "all possible care will be taken to avoid disruption of traditional markets where Australia, as a non-subsidising exporter, has significant interests. This includes the Middle East."

But within weeks of the statement being made, the US announced a 300,000-tonne EEP wheat initiative to Yemen, which forced down prices in a vital Australian market.

The Australian Government has long sought to separate trade and security issues in its relations with the US, but the country's rural lobby — which has traditionally been unquestioning in its faith in the US alliance — is now for the first time suggesting that the US military facilities in Australia should be used as a bargaining chip in the trade battles.

# Economy/Infrastructure

The Australian economy, which was in bad shape by the end of 1990, moved further into recession throughout 1991. The labour market deteriorated more rapidly than had been predicted the previous year, business investment continued to decline, farm incomes failed to pick up, there was a sharp decline in terms of trade and business consumer confidence remained weak.

While inflation fell to 3.4%, the lowest it has been for many years, this largely reflected falling demand. Any benefits for average Australians were barely noticeable, as the nation continued to pay a heavy price for the 1980s investment boom when over-gearing of assets, reckless overseas borrowing and irresponsible property speculation were greeted by Prime Minister Bob Hawke's Labor Government as the hallmarks of success.

Australia's overseas debt rose from A$13.5 billion (US$10.75 billion at late-1991 exchange rates) in 1980 to A$155 billion within 10 years. In the August 1991 federal budget, treasury officials sought to put the best light on the situation by noting that "even though the terms of trade were weaker, there was a significant improvement in the current account in 1990-91."

They continued: "Subdued domestic demand contributed by reducing the demand for imports and allowing the switching of some domestic production to exports. The very strong net export performance meant that domestic production did not fall so sharply as demand. It also produced a merchandise trade surplus of A$2.5 billion, our first merchandise trade surplus since 1987-88. While the current account improved overall, it still remained large relative to output under the weight of the continuing cost of servicing the stock of debt."

Australia has traditionally been a capital importer with a significant current-account deficit. However, what marked the 1980s excesses was not only the size of the resulting deficit, but the degree to which it had been financed through borrowings rather than equity. Net equity accounted for 75% of net external liabilities in 1980-81 and net external debt was equal to around 6% of GDP. By 1991, the net external debt accounted for 75% of net external liabilities and represented more than 35% of GDP.

Treasury figures also revealed that terms of trade fell by 5.2% through 1990-91. This fall reduced the purchasing power of national income by around 1%, which the treasury said made a substantial contribution to the continuing economic downturn. Severe falls in farm export prices, especially for wheat and wool, accounted for most of the decline in terms of trade. Non-farm commodity export prices changed little and, despite the lowering of the exchange rate, import prices grew slowly.

Australian wheat farmers had a particularly bad year. Wheat prices slumped by about one third due to record world harvests. Australia also became caught in the crossfire between the US and EC subsidy wars, which drove down prices in its traditional markets while vital Middle Eastern markets were lost because of the Gulf War.

Wool prices had fallen in 1990, when the Labor government reduced the reserve price for wool from A$8.70 to A$7.00 per kg. The government then abandoned the reserve price scheme, which had offered growers a level of protection against hard times, as Australia suffered from continuing low levels of demand for wool and a huge accumulation of wool stocks. Prices then fell dramatically in February 1991 from about A$7.00 per kg to A$4.30. Prices rose slowly to A$5.70 by the middle of the year, but the industry — which has long served as an indicator of national confidence — suffered one of its most serious setbacks ever.

Overall, farm product prices fell by 26% during the year and farm export prices by 15%. Along with rising costs, the falling prices meant a massive drop in farm income of around 80%. The treasury points out that though the Australian farm sector is only around 3% of GDP, the extent of the decline was far more severe than anticipated and contributed substantially to the nation's poor economic performance.

Business fixed investment fell from A$33 billion in 1990 to A$29 billion in 1991, a fall of 10.9%. The drop was in keeping with a continuing decline from the artificially high levels of the mid-1980s. Investment in non-residential construction fell 14.5% on the previous year, reflecting declining business profitability and the continuing effects of the high interest rates of the preceding two years.

Investment in housing also declined through the year, slipping just over 11% from A$11.6 billion to A$10.3 billion. Although home interest rates and house prices fell during the period, fewer people could afford to buy homes as real household income fell and unemployment, or the risk of it, grew.

In its 1991 budget, the government admitted the seriousness of the crisis of confidence in the country. "Business and consumer confidence fell sharply in Australia over the course of 1989 and remained at historically low levels through 1990 and early 1991. The extent of decline . . . was greater than in previous downturns in the 1980s and . . . low levels of confidence were recorded for longer."

Asset prices — for equities, houses and offices — fell for the first time in more than 10 years. In conjunction with high debt levels, this resulted in reduced incentives to invest, reduced net wealth, weakened company balance sheets and increased insolvency. Prices for shares fell by 12% and for commercial property by 20%, which made it hard for many businesses to refinance debts. The resulting businesses failures meant further falls in investment and increased unemployment.

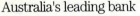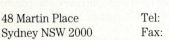

Unlike previous Australian recessions, excessive wage growth was not a factor in the downturn in employment. The government's agreement with the trade union movement, the so-called Accord, in which excessive wage demands are held back in return for tax concessions, played some part in keeping the lid on wages. However, the government's wages policy received a set-back in April, when the Australian Industrial Relations Commission refused to endorse the 1991 Accord plan for a transition to a more decentralised and flexible wage-fixing system.

**Agriculture: trouble in the country.**

The commission came down in favour of strengthening the country's centralised wage fixing system, and effectively rejected the argument that moves towards enterprise-based wage negotiations were essential for increasing employment prospects and investment.

The government's efforts in March to boost industry's confidence with a major policy statement also soon ran into trouble. The government continued its line that reduced protection of some major industries would promote competition in the domestic market and said that general tariffs would be phased down to 5% by 1996. Tariffs on passenger motor vehicles and components would be reduced to 15% by 2000 and tariffs on textiles, clothing and footwear would be phased down to a maximum of 25% over the same period.

The drive to remove tariffs remained popular until the end of 1991, when near panic set in among the trade union umbrella body, the Australian Council of Trade Unions, and some senior government ministers. These critics called for a more interventionist approach, and predicted chaos if the country's manufacturing sector was exposed to the rationalist policies that gave financial institutions such a free rein during the 1980s.

Tensions on industrial policy were also reflected in the government's haste to embrace so-called new federalism, a programme initiated by Canberra bureaucrats to secure much-needed infrastructural reform through a series of fundamental changes in state-federal relations.

Arguments over central vs state powers are as old and as

bitter in Australia as are the battles over free trade vs protection. In the late 1960s, the federal government began to pursue a centralist approach, which intensified in the early 1970s when the then Labor government headed by Gough Whitlam expanded its responsibilities in such areas as social welfare, education, health and environmental protection.

In 1991, in an effort to create a single national market and increase national efficiency in transport policy, the Hawke government began serious negotiations with Australia's six states and two territories to return some responsibilities in welfare, education and other areas as a trade-off for the states agreeing to much-needed micro-economic reform.

However, sensational failures in financial management by the Labor-ruled states during the 1980s, and the examples of corruption in the conservative states during the same decade, have made public interest groups hostile to the very idea of increasing state responsibilities. For political reasons, therefore, reform is far from guaranteed.

The government has also made efforts to reform the troubled waterfront and shipping industries, committing A$154 million to redundancy and retraining packages for dock workers during the year. The government is aiming at fundamental changes in employment practices on the over-manned waterfronts and improved efficiency of port authorities.

By the end of the year, treasury officials and some analysts believed the downturn in the economy had run its course and that activity would pick up by the second half of 1992. The expected recovery would be driven by an upturn in the housing sector, modest growth in private consumption and the non-farm stock cycle, according to this view.

A modest fall in interest rates during the year gave credence to this scenario for some observers, but others were not so sanguine. The business sector stepped up a massive campaign towards the end of the year to remove disincentives to investment in large development projects, such as mines and pulp mills, and to provide a more direct incentive to invest through depreciation provisions. □

# Data

**Major agriculture** (1991 provisional): Wheat, 15.40 million tonnes (14.21 million); wool, 846,524 tonnes (842,489); sugarcane, 24.60 million tonnes (26.94 million); meat (1990-91p), 2.71 million tonnes (2.62 million).

**Oil and natural gas** (1988-89): Crude oil (incl. condensate), 28,427 mega litres (31,297); natural gas, 15,264 giga litres (14,751).

**Mining** (1988-89): Coal, 149.12 million tonnes (136.42 million); lignite, 48.66 million tonnes (44.28 million); iron ore, 97.62 million tonnes (102.2 million); nickel, 63,100 tonnes (72,231); uranium concentrate, 4,216 tonnes (3,556).

**Major imports** (1990-91): Automatic data processing machines, parts and accessories, A$3.1 billion (A$3.21 billion); petroleum oil products, A$2.91 billion (A$2.29 billion); aircraft and aerospace equipment, A$2.72 billion (A$2.3 billion); passenger motor vehicles, A$2.22 billion (same); paper products, A$1.15 billion (A$1.3 billion).

**Major exports** (1990-91): Coal, A$6.39 billion (A$5.82 billion); gold (non-monetary), A$3.7 billion (A$2.84 billion); petroleum products, A$3.21 billion (A$2 billion); meat, A$2.97 billion (A$2.67 billion); alumina, A$2.73 billion (same); wool, A$2.72 billion (A$4.05 billion); iron ore concentrates and agglomerates (excl. iron pyrites), A$2.56 billion (A$2.2 billion); aluminium, A$2.14 billion (A$2.3 billion); wheat, A$1.78 billion (A$2.56 billion).

**Tourism** (1990): Arrivals, 2.215 million (2.08 million); departures, 2.17 million (1.99 million).

**Major banks:** Reserve Bank of Australia, GPO Box 3947, Sydney, NSW 2001, tel. (02) 234-9333, tlx 20106; Commonwealth Bank of Australia, GPO Box 2719, Sydney, NSW 2001, tel. (02) 227-7111, tlx 120345; Westpac Banking Corp., GPO Box 1, Sydney, NSW 2001, tel. (02) 226-3311, tlx 20122; Australia and New Zealand Banking Group, GPO Box 537E,

Melbourne, Vic 3001, tel. (03) 658-2955, tlx 139920; National Australia Bank, GPO Box 84A, Melbourne, Vic 3001, tel. (03) 641 3500, tlx 30241.

**Government ministries:** Treasury, Parkes Place, Canberra, ACT 2600, tel. (062) 632-111, tlx 62010, 62372, fax (062) 732-614; Foreign Affairs and Trade, Administration Building, Parkes Place, Canberra, ACT 2600, tel. (062) 619-111, tlx 62007, fax (062) 733-577; Industry, Technology & Commerce, 51 Allara Street, Canberra, ACT 2600, tel. (062) 761-000, tlx 62654, fax (062) 276-111; Primary Industry and Energy, Blackall Street, Barton, Canberra, ACT 2600, tel. (062) 723-933, tlx 62188, fax (062) 725-161; Transport and Communications, Myuna Complex, Northbourne Avenue, Canberra, ACT 2600, tel. (062) 747-111, tlx 62018, fax (062) 572-505.

**Public holidays** (1992): 1 Jan. (New Year's Day), 27 Jan. (Australia Day), 16 Mar. (Canberra Day), 17-20 Apr. (Easter weekend), 25 Apr. (Anzac Day), 8 June (Queen's Birthday), 5 Oct. (Labour Day), 25 Dec. (Christmas Day), 26 Dec. (Boxing Day).

**Tax:** Income tax is progressive, starting at 21% at A$5,250 a year, rising to 47% for earnings about A$50,000 a year. In addition a 1.25% levy on taxable income is charged to fund the universal medical insurance scheme.

**Currency:** Australian dollar (100 cents). Conversion Oct. 1991, A$1.27 = US$1 (1990, A$1.20).

**Weather:** Temperate in the south, with hot and sunny summers Dec.-Mar. and cool, wet winters June-Aug. Tropical in the north, marked by a hot and humid wet season Nov.-Apr. and a hot dry season May-Oct. Most of Australia receives 3,000 hours of sunlight annually. Sydney has an average 1,215 mm of rain a year.

# BANGLADESH

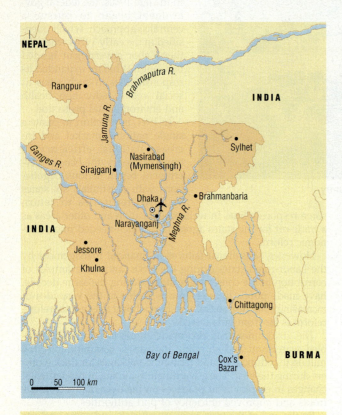

NEPAL

Rangpur •

Brahmaputra R.

Jamuna R.

INDIA

Ganges R.

Sirajganj •

Nasirabad (Mymensingh) •

• Sylhet

INDIA

Dhaka ⊙✈

• Brahmanbaria

Narayanganj •

Meghna R.

Jessore •

Khulna •

• Chittagong

Bay of Bengal

Cox's Bazar

BURMA

0  50  100 km

**Head of State**
Abdur Rahman Biswas.
**Prime Minister (Head of Government and Defence, Establishment and Cabinet Division)**
Begum Khaleda Zia;
**Law and Justice**
Mirza Ghulam Hafz;
**Agriculture, Irrigation and Water Development**
Majedul Huq;
**Foreign Affairs**
A. S. M. Mustafizur Rahman;
**Finance**
M. Saifur Rahman;
**Local Government and Rural Development**
Abdus Salam Talukdar;
**Communications**
Oli Ahmed;
**Commerce**
M. K. Anwar;
**Post, Telephone and Telecommunications**
M. Keramat Ali;
**Industries**
Shamsul Islam Khan;

**Health and Family Welfare**
Chowdhury Kamal Ibne Yusuf;
**Social Welfare and Women's Affairs**
Tariqul Islam;
**Energy and Mineral Resources**
Khandkar Mosharraf Hossain;
**Works**
Rafiqul Islam Meah;
**Food**
Mohammad Shamsul Islam;
**Labour and Manpower**
Abdul Mannan Bhuiyan;
**Home Affairs**
Abdul Matin Chowdhury;
**Education**
Jamiruddin Sircar;
**Information**
Nazmul Huda;
**Environment and Forestry**
Abdullah Al Noman;
**Planning**
A. Z. M. Zahiruddin Khan;
**Attorney-General**
Aminul Huq;
**Chief Justice**
Shahabuddin Ahmed.

# Politics/Social Affairs

President H. M. Ershad was forced to resign on 4 December 1990 after a few weeks of what initially appeared to be ritualistic agitation by an alliance of opposition parties. The opposition campaign — based around calls for general strikes and demands for Ershad's resignation — began in November 1990 and rapidly proved uncontrollable by the administration. Chief Justice Shahabuddin Ahmed assumed the post of acting president on 6 December.

The swift and ignominious end of a powerful president who, after capturing power in a bloodless coup in March 1982 ruled the country with impunity, would have been unthinkable even a week before Ershad actually resigned. He had thrived by dividing the opposition and through making deals with most of the country's myriad political parties. Significantly, the only important party he or his followers apparently failed to come to terms with was the Bangladesh Nationalist Party (BNP), whose leader Begum Khaleda Zia would have nothing to do with Ershad or his administration.

Nevertheless, the BNP's refusal to compromise with Ershad's government was never likely in itself to have dislodged the former president. What really made the difference was the formation of the All Party Student Unity (APSU) by the student wings of various political parties. The BNP's student wing, Jtiyatabadi Chatra Dal, or Nationalist Student Organisation, emerged the most powerful in Dhaka and beyond and assumed the APSU leadership. This development forced the leaders of the BNP and the eight-strong alliance led by the Awami League (AL) to close ranks and fight the regime as a united front. All efforts to divide the APSU failed, and its popular support rapidly strengthened, with even government employees joining the movement.

This development left the army — Ershad's main powerbase — with two choices: either support him through repression or remain neutral. The majority, led by the new army chief of staff Lieut-Gen. Nuruddin Khan, opted for the second choice. Without the army's support, Ershad's regime collapsed.

Although Ershad did bring a semblance of political stability, introduced a number of economic and administrative reforms

In December 1970, East Pakistan's Awami League leader Sheikh Mujibur Rahman gained a huge majority during an election and, over the protests of West Pakistan, stuck to his demand of regional autonomy. After talks between Mujib and President Yahya Khan broke down, on 25 March 1971 the Pakistan army took control. India joined the war in early December and Bangladesh became independent. A new constitution was framed to establish Westminster-style parliamentary democracy and Mujib swept back to power in March 1973. His government was toppled in a military coup on 15 August 1975, Mujib was assassinated and Khandker Mustaque Ahmed became president. Following a series of coups, in November 1975 A. M. Sayem was appointed president, though the new army chief, Maj.-Gen. Ziaur Rahman, was the de facto ruler and took over the presidency in April 1977. Zia was assassinated by rebel army officers on 30 May 1981. Vice-President Abdus Sattar was formally elected president on 15 November 1981, but was toppled by a bloodless coup led by army chief of staff Lieut-Gen. H. M. Ershad on 24 March 1982. Ershad took over the presidency from S. M. Ahsanuddin Chowdhury on 11 December 1983. He held elections on 7 May 1986 in which his Jatiya Party won a majority. He resigned from the army on 31 August and was elected president on 15 October 1986. Ershad was himself deposed in December 1990 following anti-government protests, and was subsequently tried and convicted of a number of offences and jailed. Khaleda Zia became prime minister after a general election in February 1991. In September, Bangladesh's constitution was amended to return the country to its Westminster-style form of governance, ending 16 years of executive presidential rule.

and championed the interests of the private sector during his nine years of rule, his policies could not be properly implemented largely due to cronyism and corruption. Further, he tampered with the country's democratic system to prolong his stay in power, treated Bangladesh as his personal fiefdom and allowed his cronies to terrorise their opponents by misusing state power.

Ahmed formed a caretaker, neutral government as the country's acting president and held parliamentary elections on 27 February 1991. Observers from a number of countries including Britain, the US, Australia, France, Canada, India, Pakistan and Nepal were present during the polls and declared them to be generally free and fair.

Ershad, who was arrested on charges or corruption and misuse of state power, and Khaleda each contested five constituencies and won them all, while the AL's Sheikh Hasina lost two of the three seats she contested. Under local laws, a candidate can contest up to five seats but can only retain one in the event of victory.

Ershad contested from his home district of Rangpur while Khaleda tested her popularity from two in Dhaka, one each from Feni, Chittagong and Bogra. Hasina lost both seats in Dhaka to relatively unknown BNP candidates.

The BNP with 140 seats in the 330-seat parliament emerged as the largest party followed by AL with 84, signalling the voters' approval of Khaleda's stand against the Ershad regime. In addition to the 300 popularly elected seats, the parliament has 30 seats reserved for women and chosen by the elected MPs. BNP managed to get 28 of the women seats by entering into an arrangement with the rightwing Jamaat-e-Islami, conceding the other two to them.

However, Hasina attempted to block the formation of the cabinet by Khaleda. She told Ahmed that if he appointed Khaleda as prime minister, her party would launch a mass agitation. Hasina's contention was that the acting president would lose his neutrality since he would become part of the BNP government. The BNP retaliated by threatening to launch its own mass movement to counter the AL's challenge. However, Ahmed rejected Hasina's plea and held that the formation of a council of ministers would not affect his neutrality. In March, Khaleda became Bangladesh's first woman prime minister.

By-elections for 11 seats — four each vacated by Khaleda and Ershad, one each by the AL's Tofael Ahmed and Abdur Razzak and another caused by the death of an AL leader — held on 11 September further strengthened the BNP's position. BNP won five, including all four vacated by Khaleda and the one vacated by Tofael Ahmed. Hasina, who had earlier accused the neutral administration of "subtly rigging" the February parliamentary polls, lost no time in accusing the BNP government of "widespread violence and rigging" the by-elections as well. With 170 members in the house, BNP now has an absolute majority.

However, the AL now controls 90 seats — including five from the Bangladesh Krishak Sramik Awami League, an AL splinter group which rejoined the party — and represents a formidable challenge to the BNP. That it has yet proved to be a more serious opponent rests largely on the inconsistency of Hasina's public utterances, which have embarrassed many AL supporters. As the daughter of the late president Sheikh Mjuibur Rahman, the country's founding father, Hasina enjoys an advantage over other party leaders. However, her strategy

Khaleda: strong popular support.

in dealing with her opponents means she is likely in time to face a tough challenge from younger aspirants for leadership.

Ershad's Jatiya Party (JP) with 35 seats is the third largest in parliament while the rightwing Jamaat is the fourth with 20. While a host of corruption and other charges are pending against Ershad's followers, many of them remain in influential national positions and still command a significant amount of power and money — a factor that explains the JP's performance in the September by-elections.

Meanwhile, a 15 September referendum on a constitutional amendment bill adopted by parliament in August to switch from the present presidential form of government to a Westminster-style parliamentary system returned a 84% "yes" vote. On 19 September, Ahmed signed a bill that made the prime minister executive head of government and the president titular head of state. Ahmed himself stood down as acting president in October as Abdur Rahman Biswas took over the post.

While Khaleda's restraint and moderation during the election campaign built on her already firm support, her performance during the aftermath of a major cyclone that hit Bangladesh on 30 April further consolidated her political position. Khaleda was credited with handling the crisis well, helped by the fortuitous proximity of a US naval task force steaming home from the Gulf War, which proved a crucial factor in limiting the extent of the disaster. Hasina's virulent criticism of the BNP government for accepting US aid, by contrast, lost the AL leader much political support. ☐

# Foreign Relations

D espite changes in the administration, the basic tenet of the country's foreign policy — to remain active both in bilateral and international forums — remained unchanged. However, Dhaka's policy of seeking a balance in its relations between the two superpowers was jolted by the disintegration of the Soviet Union. The new government responded by paying more attention to Moscow in an apparent bid to show a discreet trend towards independence in its foreign policy.

Bangladesh has long garnered sympathy from most of the international community for its variety of problems. Dhaka's helplessness in the face of regular natural calamities that can wreck much of whatever progress may have been made in agriculture or the nascent industrial sector, invariably produces material support in addition to continuing aid programmes.

As the most populous of the least developed countries (LDC), Bangladesh has sought a leadership role among the group of poorest nations through its reasonably well trained bureaucracy and network of embassies. This role was manifested during the second meeting of the LDCs in Paris in late 1990, where a substantial new "programme of action" was adopted.

The Paris meeting tried to establish that aid donors should set aside 0.2% of their GNP for the LDCs, up from 0.15% agreed to by donors at the first Paris meeting in 1981. However, this was not accepted by the US and Japan on the grounds that since the earlier target of 0.15% of the GNP was not achieved by many countries, a still higher target was impractical. It was finally agreed that those countries that failed to meet the earlier target would try to do so during the next decade, and those who had succeeded should try to improve on their previous performance. This was considered a major success for the LDCs.

The success of the Paris meeting will need further follow up, particularly in the light of the rapidly changing global situation. The aid climate now looks increasingly uncertain, and Bangladesh will seek to focus on the issue in the 46th session of the UN General Assembly meeting. LDC delegation leaders attending the UN session will informally meet in New York to map out the group's new programme for obtaining the developed nations continuing support.

Current thinking about revising the criteria for being on the list of LDCs has already caused some controversy. The main issue worrying Dhaka is the population criteria for determining whether a country can be described as a LDC. One suggestion is that countries with a population in excess of 75 million cannot be a member of the group, which would lose Bangladesh its LDC status if adopted.

Soon after taking over power, Prime Minister Begum Khaleda Zia adopted a low-key policy to deal with the Middle East, China, the Soviet Union and India. Her first overseas visit was to Saudi Arabia, the United Arab Emirates (UAE) and Kuwait. She held discussions with the rulers of all three countries, which employ a large number of Bangladeshi workers, who assured her that more would be recruited. Khaleda also visited China, which has had good relations with Bangladesh for many years.

Foreign Minister Mustafizur Rahman, who accompanied the

# Economy/Infrastructure

Prime Minister Khaleda Zia's new government has been cautiously trying to redeem its electoral pledges and improve the nation's shattered economy. This task has been made harder by the political agitation that toppled former president H. M. Ershad's regime in December 1990, Bangladesh's worst recorded cyclone in April 1991, heavy rains in June and severe flooding in early September that inundated about 40% of the country.

While the full impact of the September floods has yet to be assessed, a substantial portion of the country's standing cash crops appear to have been damaged. The government launched an emergency programme to help farmers retrieve whatever is left and to quickly prepare the land for a quick crop after the flood waters receded.

In addition to these domestic travails, the Gulf War also severely damaged the economy. About 65,000 Bangladeshi workers employed in Kuwait and Iraq had to be repatriated following the Iraqi invasion of Kuwait at great expense to the government. In addition, workers' remittances declined during the crisis, exports slowed and the cost of imports rose in line with higher oil prices.

The drop in imports hit government revenues through a shortfall in customs duties, which account for a major portion of the country's earnings. Unsurprisingly, economic growth

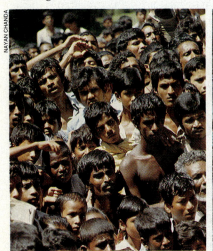

**Employment: hoping for jobs abroad as traditional industries are hit by falling exports.**

prime minister on her Middle East and China trips, also made an official trip to Moscow in July. In quick succession, he travelled to Iran, the UAE and India. The Teheran visit was intended to correct Dhaka's somewhat pro-Iraqi stance in the past few years.

Although Rahman's trip to New Delhi turned out to be little more than a goodwill visit, it helped focus attention on outstanding disputes between the two countries. Influential sections of the Indian press welcomed the "positive attitude" demonstrated by Khaleda's government to resolve the issues, and urged New Delhi to fulfil its pledge to hand over the Teen Bigha Corridor that links Bangladeshi enclaves within India to Dhaka.

Pakistan also sought to reach a working relationship with the new government in Dhaka. However, Pakistan quietly requested Bangladesh not to press for an early solution to contentious issues like the repatriation of "stranded Pakistanis" and non-Bengali migrants from India who had opted for Pakistan in 1971, or sharing assets remaining from before the country split from Pakistan in 1971.  □

during the 1990-91 financial year declined to 3.5% from an earlier estimated growth of 4.2%. The current 1991-92 year's GDP, set at 5.7%, may not be achieved if the impact of September's floods cannot be quickly absorbed.

In another blow, the country's Fourth Five-Year Plan (July 1990–June 1995) initiated by Ershad's ousted government has not been formally approved by the World Bank. The bank has insisted that Bangladesh adopt a rolling three-year investment plan and coordinate its action programme with aid donors in line with agreed investment priorities.

The plan's annual growth target has been set at 5% compared to the previous plan's 5.4% — and actual achievement of 3.8%. However, the plan's new strategy is to bring in the country's poor and the informal sector of the economy within the planning process. This reflects the recognition of the inherent resilience of the poor and the informal sector, which helped the country recover from a seemingly endless series of natural calamities.

However, some analysts are sceptical and argue that any attempt by the government to control or guide the informal sector's development efforts may rob it of its intrinsic strength.

Finance and Planning Minister Saifur Rahman, who had previously held the post under a Bangladesh Nationalist Party administration in 1980-81, in presenting his budget questioned the government's excessive control. Rahman said "unnecessary and excessive governmental control distorts the economy, which prevents the citizens from using their spontaneous creativity, generates inefficiency and creates opportunities for dishonest appropriation of rent by those who are involved in management of the economy and the state. Therefore, unnecessary governmental control over the economy should be dispensed with."

Since assuming power in March, the new government has tried to reduce the country's dependence on foreign assistance by introducing a series of fiscal measures aimed at increasing the contribution drawn from domestic resources. During 1989-90, foreign assistance accounted for 99% of the budget's annual development plan (ADP), reduced to 96% by the former regime in 1990-91. However, the new government managed to improve the domestic resource contribution to 12.6% of the ADP for 1990-91 and to 14% for the current fiscal year of a still higher ADP allocation. Rahman said the government intended to raise the proportion of domestic resources to finance the ADP to 35% by 1995 and to over 50% by the turn of the century.

Dependence on foreign assistance for implementing the ADP stemmed from rising current-account expenditures. For example, between 1983-84 and 1989-90, annual growth of revenue earnings averaged 14% while that of current-account expenditures was 18%. The Ershad regime, which felt constantly threatened by mounting popular agitation, sought to buy support by raising the wages of civil servants and the military. Further, in order to keep the army — his main support base — content, Ershad also routinely increased the defence budget.

Broad money supply and credit during 1990-91 increased less than that was forecast. It was also estimated that net credit to the government would increase by 11.57% and by 10.74% to the public sector during the year. Instead, credit to the government contracted by 22% and credit to the public sector expanded by only 3%, largely as a result of a policy intended to restrain revenue expenditures. Credit to the private sector rose by only 6.74% compared to an expected growth of 12.26%.

In an effort to reverse the recessionary trend following the contraction of the broad money supply and credit — especially in the private sector — a number of corrective steps were taken in early April. Commercial banks reserve ratio was reduced from 10% to 8% and statutory liquidity ratio from 25% to 23%. Measures were taken to encourage imports and the banks were permitted to fix — based on bank-client relationship — the margin for imports of industrial raw materials, while the margin requirements for consumer goods' imports were reduced.

In order to encourage more foreign and local investment

**Natural disasters: an unending cycle.**

in the private sector, the government also announced a new industrial policy (NIP) on 29 July with generous tax incentives and other matching inducements. It has pledged to remove the distinctions between local and foreign investors and reduce the state's role in the economy. Specific measures include steps to encourage new businesses, provide tax exemptions to exporters and allow foreign investors 100% ownership of ventures anywhere in the country.

Announcing the NIP, Industries Minister Shamsul Islam Khan said the government's aim was to give "full operational freedom to the private sector." Khan has also acknowledged that industrial policies initiated in 1982 and 1986 had failed to attract sufficient local or foreign investment, and said efforts would be made to learn from past mistakes. The NIP followed financial liberalisation measures that removed various foreign-exchange controls from 1 July. Among other things, these measures allowed foreign companies to repatriate profits without government approval and both foreigners and non-resident Bangladeshis to buy shares on the Dhaka Stock Exchange.

The sectors that will remain exclusively under government control include: arms, ammunition and defence equipment; security printing, such as currency-note printing and minting coinage; tree planting and felling in reserved forest areas; air and rail transport; power generation and transmission, except for supplies produced by large industrial users for their own consumption; telecommunications. Even in communications, private-sector participation would be encouraged in parallel with public services in rural areas and, subject to government approval, in specialised areas such as cellular phones and paging equipment. □

## Data

**Major industries** (1990-91): Jutegoods, 309,200 tonnes* (529,000); textile yarn, 1.9 million bales* (2.8 million); fabrics, 41 million m* (88.7 million); paper and newsprint, 90,000 tonnes (97,000); food products, 39,683 tonnes (59,359); sugar, 240,000 tonnes (184,000); fertiliser (urea and tsp), 1.5 million tonnes (1.61 million); iron and steel, 125,180 tonnes* (179,000); cement, 315,000 tonnes (337,000); diesel engines, 4,000 (1,172); assembled colour TVs, 65,000 sets (70,000); assembled vehicles, 1,200 units (2,388).
*First 8 months 1991.

**Major agriculture** (1990-91): Foodgrains, 19.23 million tonnes (18.7 million); tea, 43.34 million kg (42.12 million); potatoes, 2.18 million tonnes (1.58 million); pulses, 457,000 tonnes (521,000); tobacco, 40,000 tonnes (38,000); fisheries, 893,000 tonnes (847,000); raw jute, 4.7 million bales (4.64 million).

**Major imports** (1990-91): Plant and capital equipment, US$1.13 billion (US$275 million); raw materials and food, US$2.1 billion (US$2.14 billion); petroleum, US$514.6 million (US$337.5 million).

**Major exports** (1990-91): Manufactured goods, US$1.21 billion (US$1.20 billion); food and agriculture, US$225.5 million (US$324 million).

**Tourism and transport:** International and domestic airlines, Biman Bangladesh Airlines, Air India, Indian Airlines, British Airways, Druk Air, Emirates, Gulf Air, Kuwait Airways, Nepal Airlines, Pakistan International; railway network, extensive coach and waterborne transport network; car hire available.

**Finance:** Total 23 banks, incl. 7 local private banks, 6 foreign banks, 3 joint-venture, 4 public-sector specialised development banks; 3 private-sector and 1 public-sector finance companies; 2 public-sector, 13 private-sector and 1 foreign private insurance companies; stock exchange in Dhaka with 132 listed companies. Banks, government and commercial offices are closed on Fridays.

**Currency:** Taka (100 pousha). Taka 37.33 = US$1 (official rate), semi-official secondary market rate, Taka 38.34 = US$1. Conversation as at mid-Oct. 1991.

# BHUTAN

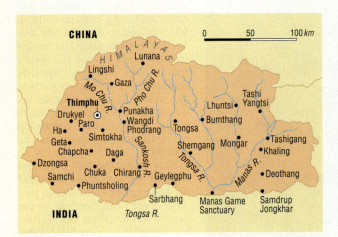

**Head of State and Head of Government**
King Jigme Singye Wangchuck.
**Representative of His Majesty in the Ministry of Finance**
HRH Ashi Sonam Chhoden Wangchuck;
**Minister of Finance**
Lyonpo Dorji Tshering;
**Representative of His Majesty in the Ministry of Agriculture**
HRH Ashi Dechan Wangmo Wangchuck Dorji;
**Minister of Home Affairs**
Lyonpo Dago Tshering;
**Minister of Foreign Affairs**
Lyonpo Dawa Tsering;
**Representative of His Majesty in the Ministry of Communications**
HRH Ashi Dechan Wangmo Wangchuck Dorji;

**Minister of Communications and Minister of Social Services**
Lyonpo Dr T. Tobgyal;
**Minister of Trade and Industries**
Lyonpo Om Pradhan;
**Minister of Planning**
Lyonpo Chenkyab Dorji;
**Special Commission on Customs and Traditions Chairman**
vacant;
**Speaker of the National Assembly**
Dasho Pasang Dorji;
**Chief Justice**
Dasho Sonam Tobgye;
**Chief Operations Officer of Royal Bhutan Army**
Lieut- Gen. Lam Dorji.

Modern Bhutan draws its roots from an autonomous polity that emerged in the country's western region during the 17th century. This regime was characterised by a dual system of spiritual and temporal rulers — styled Je Khenpo and Desi respectively — which continued until the 1907 election of Sir Ugyen Wangchuck as Bhutan's first hereditary king. Relations with British India were for many years typified by border disputes and annexations of Bhutanese territory by the Raj. King Ugyen Wangchuck's emergence came against a backdrop of mounting concern over the Chinese Government's claims to much of the Himalayan littoral. China occupied Lhasa and much of Tibet in 1910 and also laid claim to Nepal, Sikkim and Bhutan. Fears of Chinese encroachment solidified Anglo-Bhutanese ties, which in turn led to the 1910 Treaty of Punakha. Under the treaty, British India agreed not to interfere in the internal affairs of Bhutan, while the kingdom agreed to be guided by advice from New Delhi in regard to its external relations. Similar provisions were included in the 1949 Indo-Bhutan Treaty, and New Delhi remains the country's principal benefactor. King Ugyen Wangchuck was succeeded by his son Jigme Wangchuck in 1926, who ruled until 1952. His son Jigme Dorji Wangchuck held the throne until his death in 1972 to be succeeded by his son, the present King Jigme Singye Wangchuck, in the same year. Bhutan was admitted to the UN in 1971, and has since received extensive assistance from the world body and other public and private sources. During the 1980s, the king implemented a series of educational and language measures to strengthen the nation's identity. In 1989, a policy known as Driglam Namza was launched that called on all Bhutanese to wear national dress in public, reduced the number of foreign visitors allowed into the country, halted television broadcasts from India and issued work permits to non-nationals. Despite the apparent acceptance of these measures by Bhutanese of Nepalese extraction living in the southern region of the country, during 1990-91 disaffected members of this group left for India or Nepal, claiming the government's policies to be "undemocratic." Some have since become involved in a campaign of terrorism and intimidation to establish a "Gorkha" homeland in Bhutan, and have raided isolated Bhutanese communities from across the adjoining Indian border in an effort to drive out their inhabitants.

# Politics/Social Affairs

The government has had two major preoccupations in 1991. The first has been to strengthen the security of the state against continuing forays into the country by members of the banned Bhutan People's Party (BPP), and the second was to implement the 1992-97 Seventh Plan despite attempts by militants to destroy the infrastructure of development in the south.

Many of the militants are advocates of a "Greater Nepal," asserting the right of Nepalese to political sovereignty over neighbouring territories they live in. Some adhere to the notion of "Gorkaland," an entity that would include parts of India, Bhutan and Nepal. Tied up in both these notions is the demand that immigrants from Nepal should have the freedom to express their Hindu culture, especially in southern districts of Bhutan, where their numbers may exceed those of native Bhutanese.

None of this is unacceptable to the Bhutan Government. King Jigme Singye Wangchuck has consistently stated that legal immigrants from Nepal have an honourable place in Bhutanese affairs, but they must be loyal to a sovereign and unified state of Bhutan and they must adhere to Bhutanese customs.

Some of the militants — collectively called anti-nationals — are undoubtedly Bhutanese citizens. But they also include many who lost their right of domicile when the 1985 Citizenship Act, which declared 1958 as the cut-off point for citizenship by domicile in Bhutan, was rigorously enforced.

Frequent attacks on the rural population occurred in the south during the year, particularly in Samchi district but also around Sarbhang and Samdrup Jongkhar. The raiders normally comprise armed groups of between six to 15 uniformed youths, and usually took place at night on isolated rural households. The attackers allegedly frequently commit rape, steal cash and hoarded gold and silver and beat or threaten those thought to support government policies. The money buys food for those living in encampments on the Indian side, as well as arms, which are easily purchased in northeastern India.

There have also been more daring daylight operations involving between 20 to 50 armed men, and several vehicles have been burned, hijacked or destroyed by electrically detonated land-mines. More than 168 Bhutanese nationals — almost all ethnic Nepalese — have been kidnapped since September 1990 and taken across the border. Several were executed after being tortured.

Several thousand Nepalese squatters have fled to Nepal, notably the eastern Jhapa district — some because they were unable to prove a right of domicile and others because of tension between immigrants and ethnic Bhutanese. Although many of them still claim the right to Bhutan citizenship, some Bhutanese feel that they lost it by leaving the country.

By September, some 10,000 Bhutanese volunteers of military age had undergone eight weeks of basic training in three eastern region militia camps. Several hundred others had received similar training at Bhutan army camps. The 5,000-strong regular army's size was augmented by more than one third, and the Royal Bodyguard and police were also able to accept additional trained men.

Against the backdrop of the militant's campaign, the king's travels to the affected areas and his request for information and opinions from the people living there led to reports in the Indian and Nepalese press accusing him of drumming up anti-Nepalese sentiment. However, King Jigme has stressed in his statements that while lawlessness must be addressed, legal immigrants from Nepal have an important and constructive role to play in Bhutanese affairs.

By September 1991, the king had extended amnesty to more than 800 suspected militants arrested by the security forces. He pointed out that such acts of clemency were not a sign of weakness or lack of resolve on the part of the government, but evidence of its restraint and understanding in dealing with the anti-national movement. He has also expressed the hope "that better sense would prevail and that the anti-nationals would discontinue their acts of violence and terrorism." Many of the activists are former students who dropped out from secondary schools, and a few have already returned to their families.

Officials argue that the government has made significant efforts to accommodate the Nepalese-origin community, particularly by allocating disproportionately large funds for the development of health and educational facilities in the south where Nepalese immigrants have mainly settled. Bhutanese of Nepalese extraction have also risen to important places in the civil service.

King Jigme: seeking unity.

But they also point out that such treatment is predicated on the acceptance of Bhutanese ways by the newcomers. The militants, on the other hand, are fighting for the establishment of a Greater Nepal or a Gorkaland and it is difficult to see how the recent attempts by the government could reach a compromise.

As one village leader from Haa told a public meeting attended by the king: "If they are not happy to live in our country despite such generosity and [welfare grants] from the government, they should leave quietly. But if they, who came in as guests, intend to take over as hosts and turn out the owners of the house, we the people of Haa will fight for our rightful heritage and drive them out of the country."

The risks involved in the attempts to have an "equal opportunity" civil service were underlined in May when Bhim Subba, the Director-General of Power and R. B. Basnet, the managing director of the State Trading Corp. of Bhutan, along with eight other more junior government officials, fled to Kathmandu. Subba had been promoted to director of power despite the reservations among some, who felt that southern Bhutanese were being treated more favourably than their experience and numbers warranted.

His further promotion to director-general was announced in late April, even though his younger brother is a senior and active member of the anti-national group. The timing of the flight seems to have been directly related to the start of an audit of his department by Bhutanese and Indian experts. Initial analysis indicated fraud to the tune of millions of ngultrum, Bhutan's currency, with evidence pointing to the direct involvement of the senior defectors. These apparent examples of trust betrayed have brought almost all ethnic Nepalese under a cloud.

Much of the debate now turns on the speed and direction of change. King Jigme is strongly committed to the politics of development, including political change, and says the precise form of government — and even the future of the monarchy — is not the major concern. However, it is not clear that all those in high places share his commitment.

For example, Home Minister Dasho Dago Tshering told village representatives and officials in Samchi that surveys had revealed large illegal land holdings in the district, involving both nationals and non-nationals encroaching on forest land and converting government land to cash-crop use. The "easy possibility" of acquiring land "prompted the influx of many outsiders into the country," the minister said, and added that the encroachment was "also part of a deliberate attempt to increase the demographic strength of the Nepalese population." In fact, many non-nationals were originally brought into the country as cheap labour to work these holdings.

While he said the government has instructed that no punishment should be applied towards current illegal holdings, henceforth the laws and regulations will "have to be strictly implemented" in all districts. It was time, he said, for the people "to decide clearly what they should do for their own welfare and that of their district and country."

A number of measures have also been taken to strengthen the sense of national identity. For example, all teachers and new graduates must now take a formal oath of allegiance before commencing their careers while judicial proceedings are in future to be documented in *dzongkha* — the vernacular national language — instead of in the classical text *choekay*. The practical effect should be to make proceedings more accessible to plaintiffs, and for case history to become more relevant as a guide for consistency of decisions.

In addition, new identity cards have been prepared, new rules concerning the import of labour now apply and surveys of existing — and often conflicting — land claims are proceeding. Land surveys and stricter application of the laws should facilitate a stronger documentary basis for claims to citizenship.

The establishment of *gewog yargye tshogpas*, or block development committees, in all Bhutan's 192 *gewogs* was formally instituted on 15 July. Made up of popularly elected representatives, the committees are intended to allow for greater village-level participation in the decision-making process.

The actual strength of the committees will be determined by the size and population of the *gewogs*, but in general each will be made up of five to 13 members. Elections to the committees is to be "based on individual merit and qualification." The members will, in turn, elect representatives to the *dzongkhag yargye tshogchung*, or district development committees. □

# Foreign Relations

Bhutan's foreign affairs during 1991 were, as ever, dominated by its ties with India. Although links with New Delhi was strengthened over a range of political and economic issues, the assassination of Rajiv Gandhi in May left Bhutan deeply shocked. King Jigme attended Gandhi's funeral and as a mark of affection and respect, a seven-day period of national mourning was declared in Bhutan.

At the beginning of September, the king made a four-day visit to New Delhi to meet India's new leadership. The two sides discussed economic and security issues, and also signed a civil aviation agreement.

Earlier, in a February visit West Bengal's Chief Minister Jyoti Basu reiterated an assurance first made in 1990 that he would not permit his state to be used for any agitation against Bhutan. He also said the state's border police would be augmented to curb terrorist activities.

Trade arrangements continued with Nepal and Bangladesh, though with difficulty because of the lawless border situation. There were only limited opportunities to advance Bhutan's interests with other South Asian Association for Regional Cooperation (Saarc) member-states, though Bhutan continued to participate in meetings of experts and officials in the region.

Bangladesh's fifth resident ambassador to Bhutan, Muazzem Ali, presented his credentials on 18 February. Following the disastrous cyclones in April, the king personally contributed US$100,000 to Bangladesh's prime minister's fund, and a convoy of trucks took 180 tonnes of rice and wheat and 60 tonnes of cement as a bilateral grant for the cyclone victims.

Notable visitors included Thailand's Crown Prince Maha Vajiralongkorn in late June and Saarc chairman President Maumoon Abdul Gayoom of the Maldives, who came in mid-August.

# Economy/Infrastructure

The Royal Monetary Authority effected a 19% devaluation of the ngultrum in early July — from an average Nu 20.75 to US$1 at the end of June to Nu 25.45 — following similar action by India. The move reflected the long-standing peg between the two currencies.

Inflation was fuelled by rising prices of imports from India and escalating wages in the private sector. The rate of inflation rose to 12% by August 1991, from 9.4% in December 1990. The burden of security measures in the south also saw extensive cost-cutting by all government departments for the 1990-91, and particularly the 1991-92, budgets.

In August, an IMF–World Bank mission proposed structural reform measures affecting public enterprises, industries, trade, taxes, the financial sector, the labour market and foreign investment. The mission highlighted the "sharp and continued weakening in the balance of payments with India and the associated loss in Indian rupee reserves," and the need to achieve growth targets without further aggravating macroeconomic imbalances. Bap Kesang, managing director of the Royal Monetary Authority, said most of the recommendations had already been considered by the government and would be implemented during the Seventh Plan, commencing in July 1992.

Economic assistance from India and others continued to underpin Bhutan's efforts at self-reliance. India enhanced its payment of duty drawback from Rs 55 million (US$2.13 million) to Rs 86.3 million, starting with the 1990-91 financial year.

A new Bhutan Broadcasting Service complex in Thimphu was formally handed over to the government on 15 March. Provided as a turnkey project by India, the complex was built at a cost of Nu 80 million, with expertise provided by All-India Radio.

The government and UNDP/FAO signed into effect the first three-year phase of an integrated horticultural development project. The programme is designed to improve nutrition in rural communities and encourage more cash-crop cultivation.

The Swiss organisation Helvetas and the government agreed to extend the existing integrated livestock and fodder development programme in Bumthang, and the high altitude area development project in the Bumthang-Tongsa-Wangdi valleys. The project extension, which has received funds totalling Nu 24 million from Helvetas and Nu 13 million from the government, is designed to improve local cattle and horse breeds, fodder development and conservation and improve milk production within the project zone.

The EC agreed to grant US$3-4 million a year for the Seventh Plan. It gave about US$16 million between 1983-92, of which US$11 million went towards human resource development in agriculture and US$5 million to promoting veterinary science.

A German technical delegation discussed further cooperation. The group's present projects include support for the Royal Technical Institute in Kharbandi, improvement of seeds and equipment for the Thimphu General Hospital. The Japanese Government has agreed grant aid of ¥300 million (US$2.25 million) to be used to import agricultural machinery and vehicles. In addition, Japan and Bhutan exchanged notes in New Delhi at the end of July for an domestic telecommunications project costing ¥1.54 billion, under the aegis of the Japan International Cooperation Agency.

The project will link all Bhutan's *dzongkhags*, or administrative regions — Thimphu, Tongsa, Jakar, Mongar, Tashigang Tongsa, Shemgang, Geylegphug, Damphu, Tashigang, Pema Gatshel and Samdrup Jongkhar — through a microwave-based telecommunications network under a three-phase plan. The project is expected to extend from late 1991 to completion in 1994.

Deposits at the Bank of Bhutan, which now has 26 branches, increased to Nu 1.132 billion against loans of Nu 318.2 million at the end of 1990. Declared profit in 1990 was Nu 47.5 million. In April, the Bhutan Development Finance Corp. was incorporated under the Companies Act and delinked from the civil service.

Tremendous damage and loss have been inflicted on teak and other hardwood plantations by militants and timber smugglers since September 1990, according to the forestry department. It estimates it may lose up to Nu 500 million in revenues within the next two to three years if indiscriminate felling of trees in southern Bhutan is not checked. Bhutan has 617 timber plantations, covering 174,000 ha.

Some 15-20% of existing plantations — established in the early 1950s in the foothills across the southern part of the country — have already been lost in the worst hit areas, particularly in Samchi, Phuntsholing, Kalikhola, Nganglam and Samdrup Jongkhar. Hardwood stands of teak, sissoo and champ have most heavily affected. The authorities also have had great difficulty protecting the country's four wildlife sanctuaries and six reserved forests.

The Bhutan Tourism Corp. (BTC), privatised in mid-1990 and floated the government's Nu 20.94 million equity to the public in July at Nu 1,000 a share. BTC management forecast 2,000 arrivals in 1991 and projected an increase of between 4-5,000 in 1996. This year's figures are lower than previously forecast due to cancellations in February and March, presumably the result of the Gulf War.

Despite the privatisation of BTC, the government will continue to determine tourism policy through the Tourism Authority of Bhutan (TAB), under the Ministry of Trade and Industries (MTI). Besides the normal tax on profits, BTC will pay a royalty of 30% of revenues from foreign tourists to TAB.

Druk-Air's single BAe 146 jet needs an average 37 passengers each flight to be economically viable. At present, flights average 29 passengers aboard the 80-seat aircraft. Flights were disrupted for five days in late July because of the failure of an engine originally supplied with the aircraft. This was the second disruption for technical problems in 1991.

Penden Cement Authority Ltd in its annual report for 1990 recorded a pre-tax profit of Nu 42.595 million, down 19% on the previous year. Disturbances by militants during 1990 caused the destruction of four power transmission towers between Gomtu and Phuntsholing, disrupting production for two months. Nevertheless, almost 4,000 tonnes of cement was exported to Bangladesh in 1990.

The government continued its campaign to privatise other state-owned industrial units. Companies affected included Bhutan Board Products, which offered a large number of shares for public purchase in July, following on an earlier offer in 1990. Another was Bhutan Calcium Carbide Ltd (BCCL), which offered for sale the government's entire 36% stake. The

**Tourism: preparing for more visitors.**

remaining shares are owned by Tashi Commercial Corp. (20%) and public shareholders (44%). The company's pre-tax profit was Nu 5.81 million in 1989, but only Nu 1.87 million in 1990. The company reported production of 11,398 tonnes of calcium carbide for the period January-June 1991.

Bhutan Ferro Alloys Ltd also floated shares in August, offering 10% of its total stock. Government and BCCL shareholders each hold 25% of equity, Tashi Commercial Corp. and Marubeni Corp. of Japan 20% each with remainder offered to the public. A 12-year agreement has been signed with Marubeni for the annual export of 50% of ferro silicon (5,700 tonnes) and 80% micro silica (3,000 tonnes) to Japan and other countries.

The Chukha Hydroelectric Project was formally handed over to the MTI on 30 June. Built at cost of Nu 2.4 billion, the project had already earned Nu 1.28 billion for the government by April. Darachu hydroelectric, a 200-kW installation at Dagana, began operation in September after a two-month delay in 1990. The 200-kW power station at Chanchey Chu, begun in May 1990 and completed in June the following year, was also delayed by the disturbances in September-October 1990. Both plants were constructed by Dai Nippon Co. of Japan, at a combined cost of about ¥874 million.

# Data

**Major industries** (1988): Cement, 151,676 tonnes (147,692); distillery products; minerals; veneer/plywood; high-density polythene pipe.

**Major agriculture** (1988-89): Maize, 31,130 tonnes (n.a.); rice, 43,140 tonnes (n.a.); wheat, 4,800 tonnes (n.a.); oranges, n.a. (same); potatoes, n.a. (same).

**Oil and natural gas:** Nil.

**Mining** (1988): Dolomite, 196,689 tonnes (242,399); limestone, n.a. (3,674 tonnes); coal, n.a. (same); gypsum, n.a. (15,900 tonnes); slate, n.a. (same).

**Major imports** (1988): Aircraft, US$23.32 million (nil); rice, US$4.64 million (US$4.02 million); diesel oil, US$3.24 million (US$3.47 million); passenger motor cars, US$2.74 million (n.a.); tyres and tubes, US$2.5 million (US$2.31 million.); truck chassis, US$2.41 million (US$1.8 million); lubricants, US$1.74 million (n.a.); sugar, US$1.74 million (n.a.); beer, US$1.66 million (n.a.); petrol, US$1.53 million (US$1.56 million).

**Major exports** (1988): Electricity, US$22.26 million (US$21.22 million); timber, US$13.28 million (US$9.32 million); cement, US$7.29 million (US$7.94 million.); calcium carbide US$4.45 million (nil); oranges, US$2.92 million (US$1.52 million); cardamom, US$2.47 million (US$1.7 million); block boards, US$2.04 million (US$2.25 million); alcoholic beverage, US$1.2 million (US$1.11 million).

**Tourism and transport** (1990): Arrivals, 1,540 (1,480); departures, 1,540 (1,480); International airline, Druk-Air; no railway network; privately owned buses and minibuses link the main towns; jeep taxis available in main towns.

**Finance:** 1 joint-venture, public-sector bank, 26 branches. No stock exchange.

**Currency:** Ngultrum (100 chetrum). Nu 25.30 = US$1 (Sept. 1991).

**Public holidays** (1992): 2 Jan. (Winter Solstice), 16 Jan. (Traditional day of offering), 4-5 Feb. (Losar [Iron Monkey] year), * (Shapdrun Kuchy), 2 May (Birth anniversary of Drugyel Sumpa [HM Jigme Doriji Wangchuck]), 2 June (Day of Lord Buddha's Parinivana), 2 June (Coronation Day of IVth Druk Gyalpo [HM Jigme Singye Wangchuck]), * (Summer Solstice), * (Birth anniversary of Guru Rimpoche), * (First sermon of Lord Buddha), 21 July (Death anniversary of Drukgyel Sumpa), * (Thimphu Dubchen), * (Thimphu Tsechhu [Thimphu only]), * (Blessed Rainy Day), * (Dasai), 11-13 Nov. (Birth anniversary of IVth Druk Gyalpo [HM Jigme Singye Wangchuck]), * (Descending day of Guru Rimpoche from Heaven), * Meeting of Nine Evils: 17 Dec. (National Day).

(* Based on lunar calendar; to be decided.)

**Weather:** Minimum approximate temperatures in Bhutan range from –10°C (Paro, Thimphu) to 15°C (southern foothills); maximum from 30°C (southern foothills) to 35°C (Paro, Thimphu). Annual rainfall: from 1,200-1,500 mm (Paro, Thimphu) 2,500-5,000 mm (foothills). Average days of sunshine per year: 250 (foothills) to 310 (Paro, Thimphu). Average relative humidity: from 40-50% (Paro, Thimphu) to 85% (foothills).

**Government ministries:** Ministry of Agriculture: Thimphu, tlx (890) 221 MAGFOTPU BT, tel. (00975) 22368; Ministry of Communications, Tashichhodzong, Thimphu, tlx (975) 233 MINCOMTPU BT, tel. (00975) 22567; Ministry of Finance, Tashichhodzong, Thimphu, tlx (890) 201 MFINTPU BT, tel. (00975) 22855; Ministry of Foreign Affairs, Tashichhodzong, Thimphu, fax (975) 22459, tel. (0890) 22575 (Protocol Div.), tlx (890) 214 MFATPU BT;

Ministry of Home Affairs, Tashichhodzong, Thimphu, fax (975) 22141, tel. (00975) 22325; Ministry of Social Services, Tashichhodzong, Thimphu, fax (975) 22578, tlx (890) 203 MSSTPU BT, tel. (00975) 22893; Ministry of Trade and Industries, Tashichhodzong, Thimphu, tlx (890) 215 MITITPU BT, tel. (0890) 22665.

**Major public bodies:** Bhutan Chamber of Commerce and Industries, PO Box 147, Thimphu, tel. (00975) 22506. Bhutan Tourism Corp., PO Box 159, Thimphu, tlx (890) 217 BTCTPU BT; Druk-Air Corp., Thimphu, tel. (000975) 22215, tlx (890) 219 DRUAIR TPU BT; Helvetas (Swiss Association for Development and Cooperation), Thimphu, PO Box 157, tel. (00975) 22870, cable HELVETAS THIMPHU, tlx (890) 213 HELAS TPU BT; Planning Commission, Tashichhodzong, Thimphu, tlx (890) 204 PLANCOTPU BT, tel. (000975) 22503; UNDP Mission, Thimphu, tlx (890) 205 UNDPTPU BT, tel. (00975) 22424, 22443, 22315, 22498, 22657.

**Major banks:** Bank of Bhutan, head office, Phuntsholing, PO Box 75, tel. 300, 402, 225, 268, cable BHUTANBANK, tlx (890) 304 BANKPLG BT (Managing Director, Phuntsholing), (890) 218 BANKTPU BT (Thimphu). F. 1968, has 26 branches, one extension counter at Tashichhodzong and a foreign exchange counter at Paro airport (Sept. 1991); auth. cap. Nu 40 million, p.u. cap. Nu 10 million; res. with RMA, Nu 596.7 million, dep. (incl. foreign liabilities) Nu 1,132 million (31 Dec. 1990). 80% of shares held by Bhutan Government, 20% by State Bank of India. Chairman, Lyonpo Dorji Tshering.

**Royal Monetary Authority** (RMA): PO Box 154, Thimphu, tel. 22540, 22847, cable ROMA, tlx (890) 206 RMATPU BT, fax (975) 22847. F. 1982, it is Bhutan's highest banking authority, dealing with foreign exchange, currency and coordination of financial institutions and implementation of a unified monetary policy. Managing Director, Bap Kesang.

**Foreign investment rules:** The government's 5-point guideline for industrial development adopted in 1987 affirms that foreign capital equity investment in agro-industries is acceptable: investment proposals for all other industries (eg. forest-based) will be considered on a case-by-case basis.

**Taxation:** Taxes were reviewed and revised in early 1989 and further changes came into effect from 1 July 1990. Most existing tax rates were retained and some increased. The following rates are in effect as of late 1991. Corporate and business tax: 30% on net profits for the financial year, payable by all business operating under an industrial licence or Royal Charter. Certain enterprises exempted if turnover is below Nu 1.5 million a year: others may be substantially exempted if private capital is used in export-oriented business with retention of profits for 3 years. Salaries tax: nil up to Nu 1,599 pm base pay; 2% above Nu 1,600. Business income tax of 30% of net profits from 1 Jan. 1989. Sales tax: hotel accommodation draws 15% sales tax. Customs duty: levied on all dutiable goods imported from countries, other than India, at rates from 60-200% ad valorem. Industrial licences: for civil works contractors, registration from Nu 1,000-8,000 and annual licence fee from Nu 500-4,000, depending on category. Foreign travel tax: Nu 100 for each passenger departing Paro airport. Visa fee: Nu 510 for visas validated at Paro airport.

**Exchange control:** Indian rupees circulate at par. Hard currency allocation subject to approval by the Ministry of Finance and/or issue of import licences.

# BRUNEI

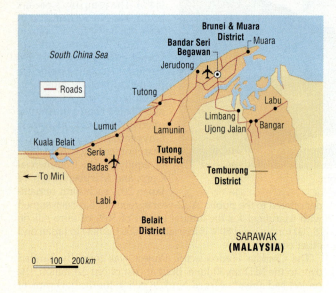

## Politics/Social Affairs

**B**runei's ruling Sultan Hassanal Bolkiah has moved steadily to reinforce a more conservative, religiously oriented dogma as the basis of his rule.

He has continued the concentrate on the principles of *Melayu Islam Beraja*, (MIB) or Malay Muslim monarchy, now the official basis of the state which he first outlined in detail in July 1990 on his 44th birthday. Announcing the creation of a national body to formulate the concept, the sultan described MIB as a "just and excellent system of governance for everyone in the country, Muslims and non-Muslims alike." The move was accompanied by a distinct shift in the sultan's style of rule towards a more direct handling of key social and economic issues.

Since then, he has introduced a total ban on the public consumption of alcohol — effective from 1 January 1991. Bruneians have been instructed to celebrate all Muslim holidays on a large scale, and the government has set up a committee to bring Brunei's civil laws into line with Islamic law. The sultan has also called for the reinforcement of an "Islamic work ethic."

Institutional reinforcement of MIB is likely to follow. There are already plans to set up an Islamic bank and a savings scheme to fund Bruneians wishing to make the pilgrimage, or

**Sultan Bolkiah: Islamic tenets.**

haj, to Mecca. As a financial institution, the Brunei Islamic Trust Fund will operate along Islamic principles, allowing Muslims not only to save towards the cost of performing the haj, but also allow Muslims to invest their money in a way acceptable to Islam.

In February, the sultan stated that Brunei "is not a secular country, even though we experience rapid development and progress." But while calling for a reassessment of a national education system, as he put it "inclined to the West," he rejected any possibility of closing the country to any foreign influences, as long as they were acceptable to the dominant local culture.

Commentators in Brunei agree that the strengthening of MIB, and its use as a dominant theme in all the sultan's pronouncements over the past year, confirms the pre-eminent influence of Education Minister Pehin Dato Abdul Aziz. Aziz is believed to bring influence to bear on the sultan through the intermediary efforts of another senior official, Pehin Baharruddin.

Even though MIB is fast becoming a fact of daily life in Brunei, many of the social problems the sultan is seeking to resolve through this more conservative approach to his rule continue to exist. Drug abuse and other forms of delinquency persist among younger Bruneians, and the problem has even affected discipline in the ranks of the armed forces.

Delivering a strong message to the officer corps in September 1991, the sultan called on senior officers to set a good example to their men. The sultan spoke of the damage caused by the influence of older leaders whose values were not in line

**T**he former empire of the Brunei sultans had shrunk to little more than a fragment of Borneo when Britain took on the sultanate as a protectorate in 1888. In 1906 Britain became more deeply involved, and it was not until Brunei had grown wealthy on oil exports that control was passed back to local hands. The British had hoped the sultanate would join the new nation of Malaysia in 1963. However, in the 1962 elections — the first and last held in Brunei — an anti-Malaysia and anti-British socialist party swept the polls. When it was prevented from taking power, its supporters staged a rebellion that was quickly crushed by British forces. Sultan Sir Omar Ali Saifuddin decided not to take Brunei into Malaysia because the federal government would have taken nearly all of the oil revenues. He abdicated in 1967 in favour of his eldest son, Sir Muda Hassanal Bolkiah but remained a strong influence in Brunei until his death. On 1 January 1984 Brunei became a sovereign independent country and subsequently joined Asean as a full member. Following independence, the colonial-era Council of Ministers was replaced by a seven-strong cabinet headed by the present sultan and including his father and two brothers. After the death of the sultan's father in 1986, the cabinet was increased to 11 ministers, and though the number of commoners was increased, the ruling family continues to retain a strong hold on government.

**Head of State** (and **Prime Minister, Minister of Defence**)
Sultan Haji Hassanal Bolkiah Mu'izzaddin Waddaulah.
**Foreign Affairs**
Prince Muda Haji Mohammed Bolkiah;
**Finance**
Prince Muda Haji Jefri Bolkiah;
**Home Affairs, Special Adviser to the Sultan**
Pehin Dato Isa;
**Education**
Pehin Dato Abdul Aziz;

**Law**
Pengiran Bahrin;
**Industry and Primary Resources**
Pehin Dato Haji Awang Abdul Rahman;
**Religious Affairs**
Pehin Dato Dr Mohammad Zain;
**Development**
Pengiran Dato Dr Ismail;
**Culture**
Pehin Dato Hussein;
**Health**
Dato Dr Johar;
**Communications**
Dato Seri Awang Zakaria.

with Islamic teachings. "To my mind," he said, "we should introduce a new leadership style, oriented towards Islam and Brunei."

The sultan also announced a restructuring of the armed forces. From 1 October 1991, they will consist of five components: land forces, air force, navy, support services and a training corps. There is speculation that this military reorganisation could be a prelude to the expansion of the armed forces and the purchase of more equipment. Brunei has plans to buy one squadron of British Aerospace Hawk fighters, maritime patrol aircraft from Indonesia and at least one corvette for the navy. But diplomats in Bandar Seri Begawan have recently detected a degree of hesitancy on the part of the government.

One factor is said to be the armed forces' limited scope for providing enough Bruneians with the technical knowledge capable of using the new equipment. This alone, a Western diplomat said, is likely to mean that foreigners will continue to serve as officers on secondment to the armed forces.

However, elsewhere in his September address to the officer corps, the sultan stressed the need to enhance Brunei's defence capability. He noted that since the adoption by countries in the region of exclusive economic zones, Brunei's maritime territorial rights have become an important component of national defence. Brunei's lucrative offshore oil fields lie close to disputed areas in the South China Sea, and overlap part of Brunei's declared economic zone. □

# Foreign Relations

In line with its fellow Asean members, Brunei has stepped up bilateral exchanges with its regional neighbours in an effort to forge closer bonds. The year saw visits to Brunei from the new Singaporean Prime Minister Goh Chok Tong, Malaysian Prime Minister Datuk Seri Mahathir Mohamad and former Japanese prime minister Toshiki Kaifu. In addition, Brunei's ruling Sultan Hassanal Bolkiah paid a state visit to the Philippines in August.

Relations with Brunei's closest neighbour, Malaysia, though excellent, were brought into sharper focus by domestic events in Malaysia. Brunei watched uneasily as the Malaysian federal government stepped up political involvement in Sabah after the 1990 general elections and the upset caused by the abortive support of the ruling Parti Bersatu Sabah for the federal opposition. The sultan also felt compelled to publicly deny that he contributed campaign funds to the Malaysian opposition leader, Tunku Razaleigh Hamzah.

Indonesia's normalisation of ties with China, followed by diplomatic ties between Singapore and Peking, paved the way for Brunei to follow suit in September. Brunei is also expected to establish diplomatic relations with the Soviet Union in the near future.

Brunei's position as a small but wealthy Asean nation without a strong military capability attracted considerable attention amidst talk of the need for new regional security arrangements in the wake of the Cold War. Members of the Five Power Defence Agreement, which groups Malaysia and Singapore with Britain, Australia and New Zealand, are waiting for Brunei to decide whether to join as the sixth member.

Meanwhile, Brunei is also being actively wooed by the US. Closer bilateral military cooperation has already been under way for some time, with the annual "Kingfisher" exercises conducted by the US in Brunei. However, in July Brunei's Foreign Minister Prince Mohammad Bolkiah ruled out speculation that the US could establish bases in the country.

Nevertheless, under a memorandum of understanding to be signed with Washington, US warships will be invited to visit Brunei and Brunei forces will train alongside US military personnel. "It is not a defence agreement as such, but an understanding to enable training," Mohammad said.

The foreign minister said an agreement with the US similar to that concluded by Singapore — which allows US warships to use Singaporean facilities for repairs — was out of the question because Brunei does not possess the technical facilities. The memorandum will result in visits by up to three US warships a year to Brunei. □

# Economy/Infrastructure

Brunei's economy contracted somewhat in the course of 1991, though new offshore oil discoveries made by the French company Elf-Aquitaine significantly boosted prospects for the long term.

Brunei's Sixth Five-Year Plan was scheduled to start at the beginning of 1991, but did not appear. Observers pointed out that the Fifth Five-Year Plan, launched in 1986, was published by March of that year. The new plan is not expected to be out before the end of 1991. But as one foreign banker put it: "It is very important for the credibility of the government that the plan is issued soon."

Most analysts suspect the plan has already been drawn up and simply awaits royal approval. One view is that overspending on government projects has forced some recalculations. However, the delay has affected the economy.

Businessmen in Bandar Seri Begawan say that expectation of the new plan, combined with the treasury's annual closure for one month at the end of 1990, held up the approval of new contracts and payment on those already implemented. The carry-over of this delay into the first few months of 1991 caused what one source described as a severe liquidity problem in the construction sector.

Another problem appears to be the refusal of the finance ministry to honour some contracts already entered into by other government departments. The fact there is no process for using the Brunei Government for compensation has alerted foreign businesses to difficulties.

Overall, the situation appears to have increased the perception of business risk in Brunei. Business sources speculate that when the Sixth Five-Year Plan does finally emerge, overseas contractors will bid for tenders more cautiously than in the past.

Brunei's stated interest in becoming an offshore banking centre came no nearer to being achieved, while the domestic banking sector itself faced difficulties. An attempt by the Brunei Association of Banks to raise interest rates by 0.5% in line with Singapore's early in the year was opposed by the finance ministry. As the Brunei

**Oil: French bid to catch up with Shell.**

HILARY ANDREWS

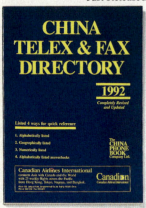
dollar is tied to the Singapore dollar, the banks' move made sense. But the treasury insisted that Brunei's sovereignty was at stake, and the finance ministry did not see the need to follow trends in Singapore's interest rates.

The government's persistent reluctance to increase wages also limited opportunities for the country's small banking sector. The government sector dominates local employment and so affects the consumer market. Government wages have not been increased since 1984, though a small cost-of-living adjustment of B$50-100 (US$30-60) was made early in 1991. As a result, all Brunei's banks are actively promoting personal-loan schemes.

The sluggish pace of growth in the non-oil sector continues, and overall GDP growth is not expected to exceed 4% in 1991-92. Apart from new investment in the oil sector, little progress has been made towards the government's stated aim of diversification.

Indeed, while the Ministry of Industry and Primary Resources has been praised for its one-stop investment agency, investors are concerned about other departments warning of the dangers of allowing too many immigrant workers into the country. An estimated 10,000 Malaysians, 7,000 Thais and a similar number of Filipinos currently work in Brunei, probably boosting the country's last official population of 264,000 to almost 300,000.

The oil sector was a major beneficiary of the Gulf War which, by some estimates, allowed production to double. Longer term, Elf-Aquitaine's attempts to become a major producer from the area following Brunei Shell, appear to be paying off. Exploration began in 1987, and by last year it was clear that the company's Maharaja Lela 1 field was proving successful. This year Elf-Aquitaine made another new discovery at Jamalulalam Barat 1 approximately 60 km northeast of Bandar Seri Begawan.

The company declines to comment on the precise commercial potential of these finds, but they are said to be significant. Part of the problem is the need for Elf-Aquitaine, operating with a 72.5% stake in association with Jasra International Petroleum and other private Brunei interests, to work out a co-operation agreement with Brunei Shell for use of offshore pipeline facilities.

Brunei Shell is also planning major new investment in the coming two years, much of it maintenance and repair work in preparation for the renewal of its natural gas contract with Japan in 1993. ☐

## Data

**Major industries:** Oil, 150,000 bpd (same); natural gas, 877 million ft³/day (867 million).
**Major agriculture:** Rice, 16,000 tonnes (720); vegetables, 16,000 tonnes (10,849); fruit, 39,000 tonnes (n.a.).
**Major imports** (1986): Machinery, B$550.8 million (B$456.3 million); manufactured goods, B$305.7 million (B$289.9 million); food, B$209.1 million (B$196.1 million).
**Major exports:** Crude petroleum, B$1.7 billion; natural gas, B$1.645 billion.
**Tourism** (1988): Total visitor arrivals, 457,400.
(Figures for 1989 unless otherwise stated.)
**Finance:** 7 commercial banks operating 10 branches of foreign banks. No central bank. No stock exchange.
**Major banks** (all in Bandar Seri Bagawan): Citibank, tel. 243983; Hongkong and Shanghai Banking Corp., tel. 242305; Malayan Banking Bhd, tel. 242494; Overseas Union Bank, tel. 25477; Standard Chartered Bank, tel. 242386; United Malaysian Banking Bhd, tel. 22516; International Bank of Brunei, tel. 21692. Few restrictions on import or export of local or foreign currency.
**Currency:** Brunei dollar (100 cents). B$1.69 = US$1 (Oct. 1991), convertible at a par with Singapore dollar.
**Public holidays** (1992): 1 Jan. (New Year's Day), 27 Jan. (Chinese New Year), 23 Feb. (National Day, Israk Mesraj), * Apr. (Idul Fitri), 31 May (Armed Forces Day), * June (Idul Adha), 15 July (His Majesty's Birthday), 25 Dec. (Christmas Day), 26 Dec. (Boxing Day). (* Based on lunar cycle, to be decided.)
**Weather:** Brunei has a tropical climate with uniformly high temperatures, humidity and rainfall. Temperatures range from 23-25°C, while rainfall varies from 2,500 mm annually on the coast to 7,500 mm annually in the interior. There is no distinct wet season.

# BURMA

Railways

0   100   200 km

B urma's political history began in the 5th century when a people called the Pyus founded a kingdom above the Irrawaddy Delta under strong Indian cultural influence. Later, the Mons ruled the whole of lower Burma until the Burmans, under King Anawrahta, arrived from the north in the 11th century.

Warfare with the Mons and Thais continued almost up to the beginning of the last century, when the Burmans came into conflict with the British. Burma was annexed in stages up to 1885 and became a province of British India. Serious rural rebellions broke out in 1931 and 1937, which led to Burma's separation from India and limited internal self-government.

The Japanese occupation of 1942-45 gave a group of young nationalists, the so-called 30 Comrades, a chance to rise to political prominence. The Union of Burma was declared an independent republic on 4 January 1948, but immediately faced rebellions launched by communist groups and various ethnic minorities.

On 2 March 1962, the military, led by Gen. Ne Win, seized power and ended a 14-year-long experiment with parliamentary democracy under prime minister U Nu. The country then went into a state of self-imposed isolation, from which it began to emerge in 1973.

It became the Socialist Republic of the Union of Burma on 3 January 1974 after a new constitution had been promulgated. Ne Win resigned as president in 1981 but remained chairman of the only legally permitted political party, the Burma Socialist Programme Party (BSPP). He was succeeded as president by San Yu.

Both Ne Win and San Yu resigned from their respective posts in July 1988, amid mounting opposition against the one-party rule of the BSPP. Sein Lwin became president and party chairman, but was forced to resign on 12 August after widespread protests. He was succeeded by Maung Maung who remained at the helm for a month until Gen. Saw Maung assumed power in September and suppressed the anti-government movement.

General elections were held on 27 May 1990 and the main opposition party, the National League for Democracy, won a landslide victory. Nevertheless, the ruling military showed no sign of stepping aside, and the 19-member State Law and Order Restoration Council junta now rules Burma by decree.

**Prime Minister** (and **Defence**)
Gen. Saw Maung.
**Foreign Affairs**
Ohn Gyaw;
**Planning and Finance** (and **Trade**)
Brig.-Gen. David Abel;
**Energy and Mines**
Vice-Adm. Maung Maung Khin;
**Transport and Communications** (and **Labour and Social Welfare**)
Lieut-Gen. Tin Tun;
**Home and Religious Affairs** (and **Information and Culture**)
Lieut-Gen. Phone Myint;
**Industry (1) and (2)**
Lieut-Gen. Sein Aung;

**Construction and Cooperatives**
Lieut-Gen. Aung Ye Kyaw;
**Livestock Breeding and Fisheries** (and **Agriculture and Forests**)
Lieut-Gen. Chit Swe;
**Health and Education**
Col Pe Thein;
**Chief Justice**
Aung Toe;
**Attorney-General**
Tha Dun;
**Auditor-General**
Khin Zaw.

# Politics/Social Affairs

B urma's uncompromising military hardliners further consolidated their grip on power during 1991, effectively muffling the opposition National League for Democracy (NLD) which scored a landslide victory in a surprisingly free and fair election in May 1990.

Following anti-government unrest among Buddhist monks and some violent clashes with the army towards the end of 1990, Gen. Saw Maung, chairman of the ruling State Law and Order Restoration Council (SLORC), ordered the dissolution of all Buddhist organisations involved in anti-government activities. A few days later, troops stormed 133 monasteries in Mandalay and scores of monks were arrested while several monasteries in Rangoon were also raided. More than 350 monks were detained. Although most of those arrested appeared to be young monks, some senior and well-respected Buddhist personalities were also detained — the most prominent being U Thumingala, head of a renowned teaching monastery in Rangoon.

In many ways, the last hope for the democratic opposition was pinned on the monks. Few Burmese thought the military would turn against the most respected segment of Burmese society, but when that happened almost all overt opponents of the SLORC lost heart.

The military's obvious determination to hold onto power at all costs raised the question as to why it agreed to the May 1990 election in the first place. Some observers speculated that it miscalculated and had not expected the NLD to win. Others, while acknowledging the magnitude of the NLD's victory — 392 out of 485 contested seats — might have surprised the SLORC, also maintained that the ruling junta, with its efficient and widespread web of informers, could not possibly have been unaware of the popular mood.

The second school of thought argued that it was more plausible that the SLORC, having arrested the main opposition leaders in 1989, a year later wanted to identify the second-rung activists and silence them as well. The election campaign, though severely restricted, provided an opportunity to do exactly that.

Whatever the case, the systematic way in which the SLORC cracked down on the NLD in late 1990 and throughout 1991 lends some credence to the latter theory. More than 1,000 NLD organisers and other grassroots opposition activists were arrested, including 45 elected candidates. Hundreds of others fled across the Thai border, where a government-in-exile was proclaimed on 18 December 1990, comprising about a dozen elected candidates who had escaped the net in the urban areas.

This jungle-based government is headed by Sein Win, a first cousin of the NLD's popular general-secretary, Aung San Suu Kyi, who was placed under house arrest in Rangoon on 20 July 1989. However, Sein Win's government has failed to win any international recognition and the move was dismissed by Rangoon-based diplomats as counter-productive as it provided the SLORC with another excuse to continue, and even increase, its campaign against the NLD.

Under intense pressure from the SLORC, the few remaining NLD officials in Rangoon were forced on 23 April to formally drop Aung San Suu Kyi and party chairman Tin U — who was also arrested on 20 July 1989 — from its leadership. Having effectively dismantled the NLD, the SLORC moved on to extend more effective control over civil servants and those candidates still at large.

As part of this process, all civil servants were in April given a list of 33 written questions, the answers to which had to be returned to the authorities. The list included such questions as: "Are you in favour of a CIA [US Central Intelligence Agency] intervention [in Burma]?"; "Do you support the [outlawed] Communist Party of Burma?"; "Do you support Sein Win's [exiled] government?"; "Do you want Burma to lose its sovereignty?"; and "Is Burma the United States of America?"

Elected candidates received a much more elaborate compilation of 301 questions which concentrated on such subjects as: "Was it right or wrong of the military, led by Gen. Ne Win, to assume state power in 1962?"; "Should a person who is married to a foreigner become the leader of Burma?" (Aung San Suu Kyi is married to a British academic.) At the same time, thousands of people were forcibly resettled in new "satellite towns" outside the old urban centres where they were placed under more effective military control. By May, the last voices of dissent inside the country had been silenced.

To consolidate its grip on power, the SLORC went shopping for arms. China obliged and became Burma's main arms supplier, and by extension its closest international ally. Between August 1990 and July 1991, China provided Burma with 12 F7 jet fighters, six Hainan-class naval patrol boats and an unspecified number of smaller naval vessels, about 100 light and medium tanks, armoured personnel carriers and infantry fighting vehicles, between 20-30 anti-aircraft guns, rocket launchers, assault rifles, mortars, ammunition and radio equipment. At least five Chinese instructors visited Burma to advise the military on how to use and maintain the new equipment, and an unknown number of Burmese naval officers and air force pilots was sent for training in China.

Observers feel that this massive build-up is intended to control and intimidate the population, rather than for fighting Burma's numerous border insurgencies. For after crushing all organised opposition inside the country, the SLORC successfully neutralised several of these border insurgencies during 1990-91. The winning over of some of the rebel groups on Burma's periphery was done with promises of development schemes and political concessions, reflecting a new approach to the country's decades-long insurgencies.

A helping hand: Saw Maung and China's premier Li Peng.

Following the collapse of the Communist Party of Burma (CPB) and the truce agreed on between the government and dissident members of the party, other resistance groups made peace with Rangoon. They included the 2,000-strong Shan State Army and 800 men from the 4th Brigade of the Kachin Independence Army (KIA), which operated in the Kachin-inhabited areas of northeastern Shan State adjacent to the former CPB territory. The third remaining ethnic rebel group in the area, the 600-strong Palaung State Liberation Army, made a truce with the SLORC on 23 April. In March, the 500-strong Pa-O National Army, active in southern Shan State but not dependent on CPB aid, also signed a peace treaty with Rangoon.

By the end of 1991, only four major insurgent groups remained in the border areas: the main KIA in Kachin State; the Karen National Union and the New Mon State Party along the Thai border; and the All-Burma Students Democratic Front, which has units along the Thai border as well as in Kachin State.

Despite these peace agreements, the Burmese armed forces nevertheless continued to grow during 1991. Before the 1988 pro-democracy uprising, Burma's armed forces totalled between 185,000-190,000 men. By mid-1991 they were believed to be closer to 280,000, including new recruits undergoing training. Simultaneously, Burma's secret police, the Directorate of the Defence Services Intelligence, expanded its network of neighbourhood informers and other agents. □

# Foreign Relations

Burma's external relations throughout 1991 were characterised by the continuing condemnation by Western democracies of the military government's human-rights abuses and an increasingly cordial relationship with China. The Asean countries maintained their "business-as-usual" relationship with Burma, with Thailand and Singapore even signalling outright support of the ruling State Law and Order Restoration Council (SLORC). Brisk trade links were also maintained with South Korea, though Japan adopted a more cautious attitude.

However, the decision to award National League for Democracy (NLD) leader Aung San Suu Kyi — who has been under house arrest in Rangoon since July 1989 — the 1991 Nobel Peace Prize in mid-October was a clear signal to the SLORC that it can expect a tougher time internationally, as Western powers in particular increase their pressure on Rangoon and its supporters or apologists. The SLORC's reaction to the award was, perhaps, predictable. "I don't think there will be any impact on Burma . . . our present government is going to solve the problems in our country according to our plan," Nyunt Swe, Burma's ambassador to Thailand, reportedly told the Thai press on 15 October.

The award symbolised the strength of growing international concern over the situation in Burma. During September 1990, 18 countries — the 12 members of the EC, the US, Canada, Australia, New Zealand, Japan and Sweden — issued coordinated statements urging the SLORC to respect the outcome of the 27 May election and to release the detained leaders of the NLD. When no response was forthcoming, these countries raised the issue in the UN general assembly. In November, Sweden, supported by all major Western democracies, tabled a resolution harshly criticising Burma's military government and demanded that it turn over power to the civilians who won the election.

However, at the request of Japan, the resolution was withdrawn for a year following fierce opposition from China, Cuba, Singapore and Mexico. Japan was reportedly concerned that a premature resolution would hinder the work then being done by a UN human-rights investigator, Japanese academic Sadako Ogata, who had been appointed by the UN Commission on Human Rights in February.

Ogata's report was submitted to the commission in Geneva in February 1991. It contained a description of various aspects of the human-rights situation in Burma and outlined the people and places she had either been allowed or denied access to during her SLORC-supervised visit to Rangoon the previous November. The outcome of the report was a resolution by the commission that expressed concern over the continued detention of a number of politicians, including leaders of the NLD. The commission also decided to appoint a new independent investigator, Yozo Yokota, a Japanese legal expert. His appointment was, however, rejected by the Burmese Government.

Despite its decades-long isolation from the rest of the world, Burma has always prided itself on having had a friction-free relationship with the UN. The SLORC was clearly taken aback by the initiatives taken by the world body, which was reflected in radio and press commentaries during and after Ogata's visit. Nevertheless, the Burmese military chose to ignore the UN's recommendations. The SLORC also paid no heed to two public appeals during the year by UN Secretary-General Javier Perez de Cuellar to release Aung San Suu Kyi. The first appeal

was issued in December 1990 and it was repeated in September 1991. The SLORC, for their part, instead decided to extend her house arrest term by another three years.

The EC countries continued to take the international lead in the diplomatic campaign against the SLORC during 1990-91. Apart from passing several resolutions condemning continuing human-rights abuses in Burma, the EC parliament also took an open stand against the SLORC on 10 July by awarding its Sakharov Prize for Freedom of Thought to Aung San Suu Kyi. The parliament's president, in an unusually strongly worded speech at the ceremony, said: "Our prize-winner is unable to be with us today, as she is being held against her will and that of the people by tyrants who imagine that with their blind attitude they can stop the course of history . . ."

Of the EC countries, only France deviated from the common Burma policy when in July it wrote off debts totalling US$82 million outstanding against Burma. The debts were incurred in the 1970s when Burma took official development loans from France. The move was not officially criticised by the other EC members, though concern over France's intentions was raised privately.

Relations between Burma and the US also remained cool. The post of US ambassador to Burma has been vacant since the 1990 elections when Burton Levin, a career diplomat, retired. His replacement, Frederick Vreeland, was rejected by

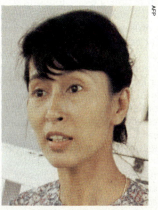

**Aung San Suu Kyi: symbol.**

Rangoon in October following statements he made at his senate confirmation hearing on economic sanctions, human-rights abuses and the possible involvement of the Burmese military in the narcotics trade. It was not until 19 July that US President George Bush announced that he would nominate Parker Borg, a state department official, as ambassador.

On the same day, however, the State Department notified Congress that Bush had decided to impose economic sanctions against Burma. The US became the first country to take such a step, though the action was seen as fairly limited: the US decided not to renew the bilateral textile agreement with Burma which lapsed on 31 December 1990. Textiles accounted for just over US$9 million of the total direct Burmese exports to the US in 1990 of US$22 million. In the first five months of 1991, Burmese textile exports to the US had decreased by 26% in volume and 21% in value compared with the same period in 1990. Although cosmetic in nature, the move was nevertheless seen as politically important.

On the other hand, observers pointed out that even if more widespread economic sanctions were to materialise, they would probably only have a limited effect on Rangoon's present policies because of the close links between the SLORC, some Asean countries and, more importantly, China. During 1991, Burma emerged as China's closest ally in the region, primarily as a buyer of Chinese arms and ammunition.

The dependence on China for military supplies has become essential for the Burmese regime. On 29 July, the EC called for an embargo on the sale of military equipment to Rangoon, confirming the blockade that most democratic nations have adhered to since the formation of the SLORC. Prior to the bloody events of 1988, Burma bought military hardware from Germany, Britain, the US, Sweden and Czechoslovakia, but all these sources of arms have now dried up.

Over the past few years, China has also emerged as Burma's most important foreign trade partner. Since an agreement was signed on 6 August 1988 to open official cross-border trade, Burma has become China's main foreign market for cheap consumer goods. Official Burmese statistics have valued two-way trade with China at Kyats 1.2 billion (US$184 million) a year, while unofficial estimates by World Bank researchers say nearly US$1.5 billion worth of goods are exchanged along the Burma-China frontier — not including a flourishing trade in narcotics from the Burmese sector of the Golden Triangle.

But analysts emphasise that Burma's dependence on China now goes far beyond arms supplies and cross-border trade. Rangoon-based diplomats reported that the Burmese also rely on the Chinese for advice on diplomacy and propaganda and that SLORC officials and Chinese Embassy staff in Rangoon meet regularly to discuss these issues.

Striking similarities in the propaganda campaigns launched by the governments of Burma and China lend credence to this suggestion. Both Burma and China have frequently referred to past colonial excesses by Western powers to justify harsh repression of political activities and other human-rights abuses in their respective countries. Both have also sought to use the drug issue, and natural calamities such as floods, to attract support and sympathy from abroad.

The importance of Burma's relations with China was underscored when the SLORC's chairman Gen. Saw Maung, in his first overseas trip since coming to power in 1988, paid an official visit to China in August accompanied by a 53-strong delegation. The immediate outcome of the visit was a badly needed boost of morale for the isolated Rangoon regime. Peking agreed to give Rangoon a Rmb 50 million (US$9.3 million) interest-free loan for unspecified "economic projects" and to build a television station. Details about further arms shipments were also believed to have been discussed.

The warming of China-Burma relations was bound to be perceived with suspicion in India, Burma's other large neighbour and China's traditional rival in the region. In what appears to be an attempt to counter growing Chinese influence in Burma, India has on several occasions expressed support for the pro-democracy movement and also sheltered a number of Burmese refugees, including some candidates who were elected in May 1990.

The most controversial of these refugees were two young Burmese students who hijacked a Rangoon-bound Thai airliner to Calcutta on 10 November 1990. The hijacking was resolved peacefully and the two students gave themselves up to the Indian authorities. They were later released on bail, which apparently infuriated the Burmese authorities. This may have been the motive behind a letter, classified as top secret, which was circulated within the Burmese military in early 1991. Dated 22 February and signed by army commander-in-chief and SLORC vice chairman, Gen. Than Shwe, the letter cited India as a country which "encourages and supports internal insurgents" and "interferes in [Burma's] internal affairs, [acts which are] not compatible with the [expected] behaviour of a friendly neighbour." Military analysts also noted a build-up of Burmese forces along the Indian border and the creation in 1990 of a new regional command area encompassing Sagaing Division and Chin State in the northwest.

Burma's relations with Asean remained friendly throughout 1991. Trade with Thailand and Singapore continued to be brisk and, in July, Asean as a whole rejected US pressure for a tougher line towards the SLORC. Singapore's Foreign Minister Wong Kan Seng said: "Asean is of the view that the development of human rights [in Asia] cannot be at the same pace as those in Europe or in the West." Thailand's Foreign Minister Arsa Sarasin said his government preferred a policy of "constructive engagement" with the SLORC rather than boycott and condemnation. Asean did, however, agree to send Philippine Foreign Minister Raul Manglapus, who assumes the chairmanship of the grouping in 1992, to Rangoon for talks with the SLORC. □

# Economy/Infrastructure

B urma's open-door economic policies, introduced after the formation of the State Law and Order Restoration Council (SLORC) in September 1988, came under fresh scrutiny in 1991.

In the face of mounting inflation, rising prices and shortages of some foodstuff in urban areas, Burma's intelligence chief, Maj.-Gen. Khin Nyunt said in an address to the nation on 21 May: "Prices have soared . . . because of the dishonest activities of some private capitalists and big traders . . . instead of cooperating in the interests of the nation [the capitalists] only import goods that have good markets, and many of the people involved show immense greed to make instant wealth."

On 8 September another prominent SLORC member, commander of the Rangoon Division Maj.-Gen. Myo Nyunt, warned the military may impose strict regulations on private trading and start its own production to counter what he branded "an economic offensive by political opponents" to the ruling junta. "We have all the necessary requisites — manpower, finance, raw materials, markets and management — to carry this out, and there is no way that we can fail."

A series of restrictions on how businessmen can spend their foreign-exchange earnings were introduced in July. Under the new ruling, exporters can allocate only 90% of their profits towards exports, of which 20% will have to be spent on items stipulated by the government. Guidelines are also expected to confine certain types of exporters to specific items.

Since the open-door economic policies were announced in late 1988, almost 4,000 private companies have registered with the authorities. The vast majority of them are trading companies dealing in such consumer goods as radios, electronics, photographic equipment, refrigerators and video players. In exchange for these items, they sell precious stones, jewellery, forestry products and Burmese antiques — the export of which is forbidden.

In effect, most of Burma's private imports and exports are carried out on a barter basis, prompted by a totally unrealistic exchange rate. This, rather than the "greed of the merchants," is the root of Burma's economic problems, analysts said. By September 1991, the black market kyat–US dollar rate shot up to more than Kyats 100 to US$1, an increase from Kyats 60-70 a year before. This compares to the official rate of Kyats 6.4 to US$1 in September 1991 and Kyats 6.5 a year before.

The government's refusal to devalue the kyat was explained by SLORC chairman Gen. Saw Maung in a speech in November 1989. He claimed that a devaluation would only increase Burma's foreign debt, which has now passed the US$5 billion mark. In October 1990, Minister of Finance and Trade Brig.-Gen. David Abel also ruled out a devaluation, saying it would fuel inflation.

Inflation soared during 1991, with average price increases climbing about 60% in the first five months of the year while real wage levels deteriorated. The military has blamed inflation on the surge of goods into Burma that fuelled GDP growth of little more than 5% in 1990. Burma's record trade deficit of US$570 million in 1990 is expected to grow 40% in 1991.

Analysts say that while inflation will be spurred by rises in import prices, it is also a result of the government's willingness to print huge amounts of its debased currency to fund a budget deficit conservatively estimated at 13.7% of GDP. The money supply was cut by 70% to Kyats 7 billion after an overnight demonetisation in September 1987. In 1991 it was estimated at a record Kyats 40 billion.

Government spending throughout 1991 appeared to be

mostly military-related. Official statistics put defence expenditure at Kyats 3.83 billion, or 32% of Burma's budget for fiscal 1990-91, up from 27.3% the year before and 12.5% in 1987-88, before the 1988 upheaval. Independent analysts, however, put total defence-related expenditure at closer to 50% of the Kyats 12 billion total.

The Ministry of Home and Religious Affairs, which controls the National Intelligence Bureau, increased its expenditure from Kyats 485 million in 1987-88 to Kyats 1.19 billion in 1990-91. The Information Ministry, which produces only military propaganda, increased its budget from Kyats 85 million in 1987-88 to Kyats 110 million in 1990-91.

What is left of Burma's heavy industry is almost entirely defence-oriented, and its expenditure increased from Kyats 18 million in 1988-89 to Kyats 32 million in 1990-91. Pensions and gratuities, mostly to retired army officers and their families, amounted to Kyats 428 million in 1990- 91. In addition, a large percentage of the health budget went to provide medical services for the army. Large amounts of money were also spent on the construction of new army camps and other installations.

The near-collapse of the country's manufacturing sector has been hastened by power shortages, which became endemic during 1991. According to statistics released by the Ministry of Planning and Finance, capacity utilisation in food industries slumped to 20% in 1990 from 83% six years earlier. Textiles' capacity usage dropped to 37% from 73% and metal industries to 17% from 60%.

Foreign investment has been limited to about 40 foreign firms, which have invested a total of US$661 million in Burma over the past three years — with 10 oil companies accounting for approximately 65% of that amount. The modest investment in manufacturing and tourism reflected a widespread belief that the safest return on capital is from small-scale trad-

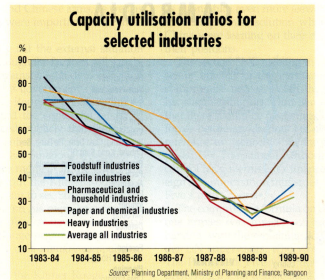

## Capacity utilisation ratios for selected industries

- Foodstuff industries
- Textile industries
- Pharmaceutical and household industries
- Paper and chemical industries
- Heavy industries
- Average all industries

1983-84   1984-85   1985-86   1986-87   1987-88   1988-89   1989-90

Source: Planning Department, Ministry of Planning and Finance, Rangoon

ing and resource extraction, particularly in forestry and fisheries. Analysts say most foreign companies are reluctant to invest in manufacturing, given the difficulty locally produced goods would have in competing with cheap Chinese consumer goods that are flooding Burma's markets.

Officially admitted non-oil investment is confined largely to companies from Singapore, Thailand and South Korea. Thai companies are primarily engaged in logging, fishing and mining, while Singapore companies operate department stores, engage in light manufacturing such as metal fabrication and wooden door assembly, and provide oil and shipping services. Tradewinds, a subsidiary of state-controlled Singapore Airlines, also flies to Rangoon.

Only South Korean companies engaged in noteworthy capital investment in 1991. Daewoo Electronics established a US$10 million joint venture with state-owned Myanmar Heavy Industries to produce television sets, stereos and refrigerators. Myanmar Daewoo International Ltd, a 50:50 joint-venture garment factory between the Daewoo Corp. and the Union of Myanmar Economic Holdings Ltd, a military-run investment company, also started up during the year. The US$1.15 million facility is expected to have an annual capacity of 126,000 dozen shirts and blouses for domestic consumption and export.

The government's hope for a solution to the country's economic crisis, however, rests primarily on the foreign oil companies — Petro-Canada; Amoco and Unocal of the US; Idemitsu Oil of Japan; Yukong of South Korea; Kirkland Resources, Premier Oil and a joint venture between Croft Exploration and Clyde Petroleum of Britain; Royal Dutch Shell and Broken Hill Pty of Australia. However, in two years since these companies signed production-sharing agreements with state-run Myanmar Oil and Gas Enterprise, no new oil has been recovered and early enthusiasm about Burma's prospects has cooled. □

## Data

**Major industries** (1990-91): Sugar, 24,990 tonnes (34,350); textiles, US$260 million (US$234 million); fertilisers, 286,800 tonnes (192,000); cement, 420,000 tonnes (454,420); paper, 15,410 tonnes (14,940).

**Major agriculture** (1990-91): Paddy, 13.96 million tonnes (13.80 million); pulses and beans, 1.26 million tonnes (1.41 million); teak, 415,000 cubic tonnes (405,000).

**Oil and gas** (1990-91): Oil, 15,890 bpd (15,068); gas, 97.7 million ft³ a day (108.8 million).

**Mining** (1990-91): Refined lead, 2,750 tonnes (2,717); zinc concentrates, 4,500 tonnes (4,350); tin concentrates, 326 tonnes (304); tungsten concentrates, 30 tonnes (17); mixed tin and tungsten, 1,446 tonnes (1,188); copper concentrates, 31,500 tonnes (16,932); refined silver, 190,000 oz (same); gems, 411,332 carats (213,871); gold, 25,200 Troy oz (1,371).

**Major imports** (1989-90): Consumer goods, US$35.15 million (US$28.4 million); raw materials and spares for industrial use, US$157.6 million (US$125.2 million); capital goods, US$164.95 million (US$216.4 million); unspecified commodities (including military equipment), US$164.58 million (US$159.77 million).

**Major exports** (1989-90): Agricultural products, US$64.17 million (US$19.63 million); animal and marine products, US$14.55 million (US$10.23 million); forest products, US$154.23 million (US$107.9 million); minerals and gems, US$31 million (US$26.6 million); others (including border trade), US$159 million (US$169.32 million).

**Tourism and transport** (1990): Arrivals, 8,968 (5,044); departures, n.a.; national airline, Myanmar Airways.

**Banks:** 1 state-owned banking system with Union of Myanmar as central bank and 4 functional banks — Myanmar Agricultural Bank, Myanmar Economic Bank, Myanmar Foreign Trade Bank and Myanmar Investment and Commercial Bank; no foreign banks, no stock exchange.

**Currency:** Burmese kyat = 100 pyas. Kyats 6.4 = US$1 (Sept. 1991 official rate) (Kyats 6.5 = US$1 Sept. 1990); blackmarket rate Kyats 100-105 = US$1 (Sept. 1991) (Kyats 65-75 = US$1, Sept. 1990).

**Public holidays** (1992): 4 Jan. (Independence Day), 12 Feb. (Union Day), 2 Mar. (Farmers' Day), 18 Mar. (Tabaungpwe Festival), 27 Mar. (Armed Forces Day), 12-16 Apr. (Thingyan, Burmese New Year and Water Festival), 1 May (May Day), 16 May (Pouring Water on the Banyan Tree Festival), 14 July (Start of Buddhist Lent), 19 July (Martyrs' Day), 11 Oct. (Tadingyut, Festival of Lights), 9 Nov. (Dasaungdai Festival), 19 Nov. (National Day), 25 Dec. (Christmas Day).

**Weather:** Burma has a mainly tropical climate with a well-defined rainy season (mid-May–mid-Oct.). The cool season is Nov.-Feb. and the hot season Mar.-May. Rainfall in the coastal regions of Arakan in the west, Tenasserim in the southeast and the mountainous areas of the north exceeds 5,000 mm a year, while the Irrawaddy Delta has 2,500-3,000 mm.

**Government ministries:** Agriculture and Forests, Bo Aung Gyaw Rd, tel. 85011 ext 19, tlx 75080; Defence, Signal Pagoda Rd, tel. 81611 ext 46, tlx 21316; Energy, 74/80 St John's Rd, tel. 86195, tlx 21307; Foreign Affairs, Prome Rd, tel. 83333 ext 8, tlx 21313; Industry (1), 191 Kaba Aye Rd, tel. 56064, tlx 21513; Industry (2), Bo Aung Gyaw Rd, tel. 81273, 83581, tlx 21500; Planning and Finance, Bo Aung Gyaw Rd, tel. 74237; Trade, tlx 21338.

**Taxation:** No corporate tax. Goods and services tax on all sales of consumer goods and services by the state provides about 60% of total tax receipts. Threshold for income tax is Kyats 8,001 a year. Income tax ranges from 2.4-50%. Foreign exchange is strictly controlled and must be channelled through the Myanmar Foreign Trade Bank or the Myanmar Investment and Commercial Bank. However, there is a flourishing black market.

Phnom Penh palace for the first time since early 1979 — analysts began to assess the political hazards involved in the UN's shaky peace programme for the country.

Shepherding the 340,000 Thai-based refugees back to Cambodia for resettlement in time for the coming election promised to be an immensely difficult operation. It also assumes the UN will be able to prevent the factions, but particularly the Khmer Rouge, from moving refugees under their sway to areas where they could be marshalled for continued political control. Even before the peace accord was signed, the Khmer Rouge had been warned by the UN after they were reportedly forcing refugees from among the 43,000 in the Site 8 camp on the Thai border back into their controlled zones in Cambodia.

There is also the prospect of a free-for-all over land once the refugees return to Cambodia, as the Hun Sen government two years ago issued land titles to those in the country, whether they had previous legal rights or not.

Registering eligible voters among the 8 million population threatens to be another headache, not only because there has been no recent census in the country, but Cambodia lacks administrative documentation and statistics of any kind.

Although Sihanouk's role promised to continue to be crucial in holding the process together — and he seemed assured of being elected president after the general election — some diplomats viewed the future political situation as a further struggle between opposing communist forces. Both the ruling party in Phnom Penh and the Khmer Rouge have officially dropped Marxist-Leninist ideology, but observers doubt whether either can be labelled non-communist.

The move by Phnom Penh's ruling communist party to change its image came just before the 23 October peace signing, and was seen as a ploy to bolster its domestic political appeal and international relations before the 1993 elections. At a 17-18 October congress, the Kampuchean People's Revolutionary Party changed its name to the Cambodian People's Party. It announced that it was abandoning Marxist-Leninist ideology to support a multi-party political system and a free market. The party also removed its ineffectual president, Heng Samrin, and replaced him with Chea Sim, formerly No. 2 in the party hierarchy and chairman of the national assembly. Hun Sen remained prime minister, but also became party vice-president.

Chea Sim, widely regarded as a party hardliner, had in 1990 gained the upper hand in a power struggle with Hun Sen, the regime's best-known politician both at home and abroad because of his crucial role in negotiating the peace agreement. But as the peace process gained momentum in 1991, diplomats said Chea Sim realised the party could not survive without major reform, and therefore moved to reach a compromise with Hun Sen. Political sources in Phnom Penh thought the newly named party would probably split into two or three smaller factions before the UN-supervised election. They say this would reflect efforts to ensure Phnom Penh's current leadership remained in power, despite the erosion of their control because of the arrival of the SNC and the fact that a large UN contingent would play a major role in the country's administration ahead of the polls.

Perhaps most concern, both internationally and among Cambodians, centred on the fact that the Khmer Rouge had gained a share in the SNC and might move on to regain power in the future. Up to 1 million people are estimated to have died through execution, disease and starvation during the Khmer Rouge reign of terror from 1975 until the Vietnamese invasion in December 1978. Yet the party will be allowed to take part in the scheduled 1993 election — perhaps 10-15% of the population can be relied on as its supporters — though some of its officials have let it be known they have no illusions the Khmer Rouge will win. Instead, leaders were looking fur-

ther ahead when the faction expected to be better organised politically nationwide.

The Khmer Rouge's most notorious leaders will probably keep a low profile, at least for the foreseeable future. For the time being the Khmer Rouge's nominal leader, Khieu Samphan, will continue to represent the faction on the SNC.

While the Khmer Rouge said in Paris that it would fully abide by the conditions of the peace agreement, many observers remain worried that it is conserving its military and political strength for a future campaign. Internal party documents are reported to reveal that the "new" Khmer Rouge political party will be clandestinely controlled by the same leaders who ruled Cambodia in 1975-78. Ieng Sary was reported in one document to have said that while the Khmer Rouge faced a new political situation under a capitalist system, "our ideals remain unchanged and we are still fighting the same fight." □

# Foreign Relations

The comprehensive peace agreement for Cambodia reached in Paris on 23 October involved many countries, without whose efforts to persuade the four warring factions to overcome their differences would almost certainly have meant the country would still have been at war in late 1991.

A total of 19 countries signed the peace agreement, an event many involved hoped marked the final session of the Paris International Conference on Cambodia, which had been jointly chaired by France and Indonesia and helped by a special representative of UN Secretary-General Javier Perez de Cuellar. Among those who signed were senior officials of the UN Security Council's Permanent Five countries (the US, Britain, France, the Soviet Union and China), Asean, the EC and Cambodia's neighbours Vietnam and Laos.

Overall, it can be said the Permanent Five had made the running in urging the four factions, grouped under the Supreme National Council (SNC), towards peace throughout the year. The factions had eventually agreed on a slightly modified peace draft drawn up by the Permanent Five in August. When the Cambodian leaders initially argued over the plan, members of the Permanent Five let it be clearly known that the world was tiring of the 12-year war.

But above all, members of the SNC were egged on to swift compromise and peace by the sideshow of moves by China and Vietnam to normalise relations. Until 1990, Vietnam had staunchly backed the Phnom Penh regime of Prime Minister Hun Sen in its fight for survival against the three resistance factions while China remained the main supporter and military-supplier of the Khmer Rouge and its two non-communist resistance partners.

Firm moves towards rapprochement between Peking and Hanoi began in late 1990, but the process gathered speed in 1991 leading to full normalisation in November. A substantial by-product of this exercise was that the Phnom Penh regime and the Khmer Rouge began to feel that their backers would no longer support their confrontational positions. Whether there was direct pressure from China and Vietnam on their respective proteges remains an open question, but the two factions knew that it was time to reach a political accommodation.

Indirectly, the process was started by Soviet President Mikhail Gorbachov. By presiding over the dismantling of much of the communist world, Gorbachov had effectively ended Cambodia's role as an ideological and literal battleground. As China and Vietnam began to feel isolated as two of the world's few remaining hardline communist states, they were compelled to at least normalise their relations — which in turn meant resolving their differences over Cambodia. Another major factor for both Vietnam and Cambodia was the withdrawal of Soviet aid, including military supplies. As Vietnam became intent on encouraging investment, trade and aid from other sources, so Phnom Penh sought to reduce its reliance on Hanoi.

The mood in Phnom Penh became more apparent during the 17-18 October congress of the ruling Kampuchean People's Revolutionary Party shortly before the Paris accord. The party decision to drop its communist image by becoming the Cambodian People's Party, effectively distanced itself from Vietnam, which had set up the party in January 1979 and supported it militarily until September 1989.

Vietnam remains unpopular among many Cambodians, despite its role in ousting the Khmer Rouge. Vietnamese sources at the time of the congress said Phnom Penh had informed Hanoi that it no longer needed Vietnamese party advisers and instructors. Further, the Cambodian party school, built by Vietnam on the outskirts of Phnom Penh, would be turned into a social science institute if the UN's peacekeeping forces were not interested in renting it.

Although Vietnam formally congratulated the Cambodian party after the congress, it became clear that Hanoi was anxious about its decision to abandon socialism and the potential erosion of Cambodia's place in the basically Vietnamese-led Indochinese fold. Vietnam had sought an invitation from Phnom Penh for its party chief Do Muoi to receive a briefing before the congress, but the Cambodian leaders informed Hanoi that they did not have the time. In the event, Gen. Le Duc Anh, who spearheaded Vietnam's 1978 invasion and has since ranked second in the Vietnamese party hierarchy, made a secret trip to Phnom Penh a few days before the congress opened.

Anh was informed about the coming political changes and consulted on the prospective military changes after the demobilisation of 70% of all four factions' forces, as laid down by

**Khmer Rouge: armed and still dangerous.**

the Paris agreement. As one Cambodian political source said at the time: "We don't know if we'll need Vietnam, again. War may break out again, so we don't want to burn our bridges."

As relations with Hanoi became more distant, Phnom Penh apparently sought to improve its ties with Washington. The US Government announced it would end its trade embargo against Cambodia shortly after the Paris accord, and there would be no inhibition on financial institutions such as the World Bank and IMF in aiding the country. The Cambodian and US governments also agreed on a programme for US teams to enter the country to look for the remains of US soldiers missing in action during the Indochina War.

Before the peace signing Cambodia had also welcomed officials from a number of countries wishing to establish embassies in Phnom Penh, notably Japan, the US, Australia, North Korea, France, Britain and some Asean countries. Meanwhile, SNC delegates took their place as Cambodia's representatives to the UN General Assembly. A delegation also travelled to Bangkok in November to resume Cambodia's membership of the Mekong Committee, rejoining Thailand, Vietnam and Laos after an absence of 15 years. Maintaining good relations with Thailand is expected to be a priority for Cambodia.

The Thais had been the most successful among the Asean members in promoting the peace process in the months immediately before the Paris agreement. Further, Bangkok has become a staging post for investors wanting to do business with Cambodia. One result of this was an agreement in late 1991 under which direct air traffic between Bangkok and Phnom Penh would be substantially increased, a move which not only drew Cambodia closer to Thailand but further eroded its links with Vietnam. □

# Economy/Infrastructure

The signing of the Paris peace agreement has given Cambodia the first glimmer of hope that foreign aid donors and investors will help rebuild the country. While its non-communist neighbours have prospered, Cambodia has slipped back since 1970 to the extent that Phnom Penh government officials surmise — in the absence of hard economic data — that the country's GDP now stands at about 75% of the level achieved in the late 1960s.

Phnom Penh representatives attending the IMF/World Bank meetings in Bangkok in October 1991 estimated that the country needs at least US$900 million in aid and loans to finance reconstruction. Japan, which is expected to pay most of the UN's peacekeeping costs in Cambodia, has announced it will organise a donors' conference in Tokyo before March 1992 to solicit funding for a major reconstruction effort.

Phnom Penh's abrupt loss of Soviet aid, coupled with widespread floods in August and September and continued international isolation prior to the peace accord, hit the Cambodian economy hard. One example is daily electricity brown-outs in the capital, caused by fuel shortages, lack of spare parts and the withdrawal of Soviet technicians. Less than 100 Soviet advisers remain in the country, down from about 1,300 two years earlier.

Before the economic crisis in the Soviet Union, Moscow had given Phnom Penh about US$100 million a year in trade credits and grant aid. Under this agreement, the Soviets supplied roughly 200,000 tonnes of oil products and 35,000 tonnes of fertiliser, as well as cement, steel, cotton and vehicles. Phnom Penh sold many of these commodities to finance its budget.

Trade with the Soviet Union, long Phnom Penh's dominant trade partner, has also collapsed. In 1990, Phnom Penh had imported Soviet goods worth Rbl 103.3 million (US$175.5 million), while its exports to the Soviet Union reached only Rbl 20.1 million, according to Mao Thora, director of the Foreign Trade Department. For the past decade, Moscow had given Phnom Penh credits to cover its massive trade imbalance.

The abrupt loss of Soviet trade forced Cambodia to look to the international market, where it had to use hard currency. Thora estimated that roughly 70% of Cambodia's official trade in the first six months of 1991 — imports totalled US$90 million while exports reached only US$40 million — was with Singapore. The other main trading partners are Thailand and Vietnam, Cambodia's two most important neighbours.

But the government's shortage of foreign currency forced trading companies to look to the free market for US dollars, sharply driving down the value of the riel, the country's currency. It fell from Riel 760 to US$1 on the free market in May to Riel 1,100 in October, a devaluation of 45% in five months. The official exchange rate was forced to follow, dropping from Riel 600 to US$1 in May to Riel 1,000 by October.

Ironically, the riel's free-fall was exacerbated by the peace prospects. "There's a rumour that when a new government is formed, it will introduce new money," Thora said. "So people with riel are rushing to the market to buy US dollars and gold." In an attempt to stabilise the value of the riel, the government in September banned the free-market trade in gold.

Inflation also soared as a result of the government's growing budget deficit, which was worsened by the loss of Soviet aid, a building boom in anticipation of an influx of foreign peacekeepers and aid workers and the country's worst floods in decades. The price of rice jumped from Riel 200 per kg in July to Riel 350 in September, while a 1 kg of pork rose from Riel 800 to Riel 1,400. Rapidly rising prices hit civil servants on fixed salaries of less than Riel 10,000 per month particularly hard.

Two serious floods in August and September damaged Routes 3 and 4 in the south and destroyed roughly 10% of the country's rice fields. Some of the losses will be made up by an expected good rice harvest in the south, which had suffered drought for the previous two years; but the country is still expected to encounter a rice shortfall in 1992, according to Try Meng, deputy director of the Agronomy Department. Cambo-

Tourism: field of opportunity.

dia faced a grain deficit of about 100,000 tonnes in 1991 as a result of drought, the end of cheap Soviet fertiliser imports and loss of production from many rice fields, particularly in the fertile northwest, because of the war.

Besides foreign aid, Phnom Penh officials are also looking to foreign investors and tourists to finance its economic recovery. The resumption of direct flights from Bangkok and Singapore in 1991 and the completion of Phnom Penh's first luxury hotel prompted a sharp increase in foreign visitors. Nearly 9,000 tourists visited the country in the first four months of the year, compared to less than 1,600 in all of 1990.

Foreign businessmen, who had previously bypassed Cambodia because of its civil war, began visiting the country in growing numbers to explore investment opportunities, even though it still lacks adequate laws to protect investors. Ouk Chay, deputy director of the Department of International Economic Cooperation, told the REVIEW in October that the government had received 250 investment applications since the country's foreign-investment code was promulgated in 1989, of which 55 have been approved.

Chay said that more than 40 of the investment licences have gone to foreign and domestic firms interested in leasing state-owned factories. Many of these had been established in the 1960s and had been losing money due to the end of cheap Soviet raw materials as well as shortages of investment capital, power and spare parts. Phnom Penh's official newsagency reported that the government had earned US$1.8 million in the first half of the year from rental fees for 10 of its largest factories, a tenfold increase from 1989 when they were still run by the state.

In early October, Phnom Penh signed its first offshore oil exploration agreement with Britain's Enterprise Oil and France's Compagnie Europenne des Petroles. Thach Xoval Say, deputy director of the Department of Geology and Mines, said three more agreements had been approved and would be signed before the end of the year with companies from Australia, Spain, Hongkong, Hungary and Japan.

Companies from Thailand, Singapore and Indonesia won concessions to extract 85,000 m³ of timber in 1992 from the country's sizeable forest reserves. However, some Cambodian forestry officials fear the country's desperate need for foreign exchange could pose a serious threat to the country's environment. In 1990, Cambodia felled some 350,000 m³ of timber — of which 110,000 m³ were exported — but only replanted about 500 ha, according to Uk Sokhon, deputy director of the forestry department. The UN's Food and Agriculture Organisation estimates that the country's forest cover fell from 74-76% in the late 1960s to 58-60% two decades later.

Companies from France, Singapore, Taiwan and Thailand have also investigated the possibility of investing in rubber. Cambodia had produced over 50,000 tonnes of crepe per year before the war, but this figure had dropped to 20,000 tonnes in 1990 because most of the rubber trees are old and the country lacks skilled workers and investment capital.

Other foreign firms were negotiating to build new hotels to cater to the expected increase in tourists and business visitors. Bangkok's Siam Commercial Bank, in a joint venture with the Cambodian National Bank, established the country's first commercial bank in mid-1991. □

## Data

**Major industries:** Timber, 350,000 m³ (280,000); electricity, 195 million kWh (200 million).

**Major agriculture:** Rice, 1.86 million tonnes (2.6 million); fisheries, 96,000 tonnes (82,000); rubber, 20,000 tonnes (31,000).

**Oil and natural gas:** Nil.

**Mining:** n.a.

**Major imports:** Official imports totalled Rbl 103.3 million and US$12 million (Rbl 110.9 million and US$24 million), including machinery, vehicles, fuel, consumer goods, raw materials, fertiliser and insecticides.

**Major exports:** Official exports totalled Rbl 20.1 million and US$14.6 million (Rbl 26.8 million and US$17.4 million); including timber, 110,000 m³ (80,000); rubber, 20,000 tonnes (35,000).

**Tourism and transport:** Arrivals, 8,989 tourists during first quarter 1991 (1,542 in all 1990). Airlines: Bangkok Airways from Bangkok; Star Airways and Phnom Penh Airlines from Singapore; Air Kampuchea and Vietnam Airlines from Ho Chi Minh City; Lao Aviation from Vientiane; Vietnam Airlines from Hanoi. Twice weekly flights to Siem Reap (Angkor Wat) and 1 flight per week to Stung Treng. Train from Phnom Penh to Battambang and Kompong Som every 4 days. Visas hard to obtain as Cambodia only has embassies in Vietnam, Laos, India, the Soviet Union and some East European countries. (Figures for 1990 unless specified, previous year in brackets.)

**Finance:** 1 state bank, though some function being hived off to planned state-owned commercial banks. The Cambodian Commercial Bank, a joint venture between Thailand's Siam Commercial Bank and the state bank, established in 1991. The country has no finance companies, building societies, credit unions or stock exchanges.

**Banks:** State Bank, Blvd Son Ngoc Minh, Phnom Penh; Cambodian Commercial Bank, 26 Achar Mean Blvd Phnom Penh, tel. 2-5664.

**Currency:** Riel 1,000 = US$1 in Oct. 1991 (Riel 560 = US$1 in Oct. 1990).

**Major ministries:** Council of Ministers, Blvd Georges Dimitrov, Phnom Penh, tel. 2-5103; Foreign Affairs, Quai Karl Marx, Phnom Penh, tel. 2-4441, 2-4641; Trade, Blvd Tou Samuth, Phnom Penh, tel. 2-2975.

**Public holidays** (1992): 7 Jan. (National Day), 13 Apr. (Khmer New Year), 17 Apr. (Victory over American Imperialism Day), 1 May (Labour Day), 22 Sept. (Feast of the Ancestors).

**Weather:** Cambodia has a tropical climate, with an annual average temperature of 27°C and average rainfall of 1,560 mm.

**Taxation:** All enterprises in principle pay taxes varying according to their activities and geographical locations. A foreign investment code was promulgated in 1989.

# CHINA

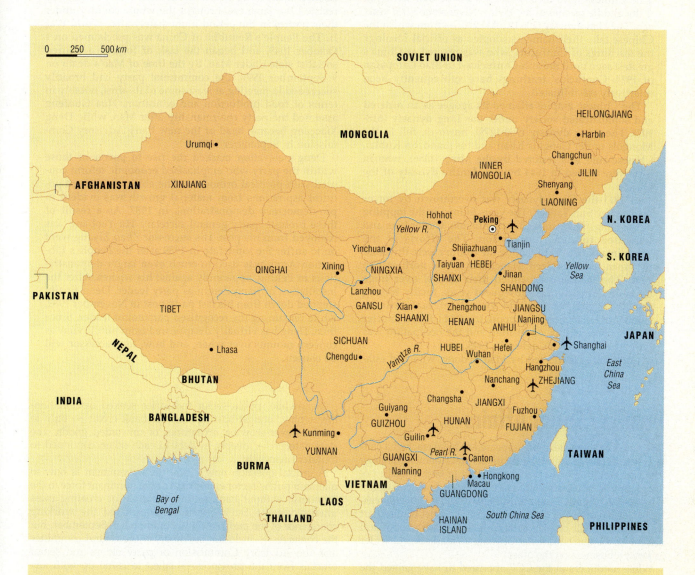

**Head of State**
President Yang Shangkun.
**Vice-President**
Wang Zhen;
**Premier**
Li Peng;
**Vice-Premiers**
Tian Jiyun, Wu Xueqian, Yao Yilin, Zhu
Rongji, Zou Jiahua;
**State Councillors**
Chen Junsheng, Chen Xitong, Li Guixian,
Li Tieying, Qian Qichen, Qin Jiwei, Song
Jian, Wang Bingqian, Wang Fang;
**Secretary-General**
Luo Gan;
**Chairman Central Military Commission**
Jiang Zemin;
**Foreign Affairs**
Qian Qichen;
**National Defence**
Qin Jiwei;
**State Planning Commission**
Zou Jiahua;
**State Restructuring of Economic System**
Chen Jinhua;

**Education**
Li Tieying;
**State Science and Technology**
Song Jian;
**Science, Technology and Industry for
Defence**
Ding Henggao;
**Nationalities Affairs**
Ismail Amat;
**Public Security**
Tao Siju;
**State Security**
Jia Chunwang;
**Supervision**
Wei Jianxing;
**Civil Affairs**
Cui Naifu;
**Justice**
Cai Cheng;
**Finance**
Wang Bingqian;
**Personnel**
Zhao Dongwan;
**Labour**
Ruan Chongwu;

**Geology and Mineral Resources**
Zhu Xun;
**Construction**
Hou Jie;
**Energy Resources**
Huang Yicheng;
**Railways**
Li Senmao;
**Communications**
Huang Zhendong;
**Machine Building and Electronics
Industry**
He Guangyuan;
**Aeronautics and Astronautics**
Lin Zongtang;
**Metallurgical Industry**
Qi Yuanjing;
**Chemical Industry**
Gu Xiulian;
**Light Industry**
Zeng Xianlin;
**Textile Industry**
Wu Wenying;
**Posts and Telecommunications**
Yang Taifang;

**Water Resources**
Yang Zhenhui;
**Agriculture**
Liu Zhongyi;
**Forestry**
Gao Dezhan;
**Commerce**
Hu Ping;
**Foreign Economic Relations and Trade**
Li Lanqing;
**Materials and Equipment**
Liu Suinlan;
**Culture**
He Jingzhi (acting);
**Radio, Cinema and Television**
Ai Zhisheng;
**Public Health**
Chen Minzhang;
**Physical Culture and Sport**
Wu Shaozu;
**Family Planning**
Peng Peiyun;
**People's Bank of China**
Li Guixian;
**Auditing Administration**
Lu Peijian.

The Chinese trace their origins to a tribe that settled in the middle reaches of the Yellow River some 5,000 years ago. The Han dynasty (206 BC-AD 220) — from which the Chinese take their name — adopted as official ideology the teachings of Confucius, who was revered as China's greatest sage until the anti-Confucius-Lin Biao Campaign of 1974. Confucius' teachings have subsequently been selectively rehabilitated.

The Chinese empire attained its apogee as an ordered and sophisticated society under the Tang dynasty (618-907). The Song dynasty (960-1279), however, fell to the Mongols under Genghis Khan and his grandson Kublai. Chinese rule was restored by the Ming (1386), who in turn were ousted in 1644 by the Manchu dynasty of the Qing.

In 1911 the Qing dynasty was overthrown by forces inspired by Sun Yat-sen. The years following the toppling of the Qings were marked by confusion, warlordism and increased foreign intervention. The efforts of the Kuomintang (KMT) to reunite the country were thwarted by Japan, which seized Manchuria in the northeast in 1931. The Japanese expanded their control over huge tracts of China during subsequent years, finally forcing the KMT government into virtual internal exile in Chongqing. Despite US support, the KMT failed to offer the Japanese serious opposition and the occupation was only lifted by Japan's defeat in 1945.

Communist forces led by Mao Zedong, who had established themselves in the north where they effectively resisted the Japanese, brought the whole country under their control in the period immediately after World War II. The People's Republic of China was proclaimed on 1 October 1949, and began the task of forging a unified socialist state under Mao. By the time of Mao's death on 9 September 1976, the communist party had broadly succeeded in meeting at least some of its aims, notably in terms of food production and education. Hua Guofeng assumed the party chairmanship after Mao, while Deng Xiaoping became head of the new Party Advisory Commission in September 1982.

Deng's elevation marked the rise to power of those within the party who emphasised economic reform coupled with political orthodoxy. The ability to divorce political aspirations from material growth was evident in pro-democracy demonstrations in 1987. As a result of these protests, party general secretary Hu Yaobang was removed from his post. His successor Zhao Ziyang went on to suffer the same fate in 1989 after the People's Liberation Army was used to crush even larger demonstrations in Peking, apparently against his wishes. After the installation of Jiang Zemin as party leader, Deng finally stepped down from his last party post in November 1989, while remaining the recognised paramount leader. Since then, Deng has virtually disappeared from public view as concern mounts over when, and how, his successor will be chosen.

# Politics/Social Affairs

China's ageing leadership appeared to have reached a consensus on the country's decennial development strategy that would allow it to have the best of both worlds: political control with economic reforms. Critics, however, doubt whether the Chinese Communist Party (CCP) — now increasingly isolated after the disintegration of its Soviet counterpart in August — will be able to keep a tight leash on political dissent on the one hand while opening its markets ever wider to foreign business on the other.

While hardliners in the CCP appeared to have gained the upper hand for the moment, the more reformist-minded were the ones with the dynamic answers to economic ills. Their influence was felt in the economic sector, notably through the biggest cutbacks in price subsidies for basic commodities sold in urban areas in more than a decade and the abolition of export subsidies.

The collapse of the communist party in the Soviet Union after a failed coup by hardliners created fresh anxieties for Peking, now the last significant communist power in the world. Military exercises in the autonomous regions of Xinjiang and Tibet, and in the key cities of Peking and Canton, underscored the CCP's nervousness. The party also attempted to consolidate its hold on the military by purging middle-ranking officers and intensifying political indoctrination.

Severe summer floods, which devastated the lower Yangtze River valley and parts of northeast China, provided a windfall opportunity for the government to show off its organisational strengths in the name of socialism. The floods also highlighted how run-down and over-burdened the country's infrastructure had become during the fast-growth era of the 1980s, and bolstered the conservatives' arguments for steadier growth in the next stage of economic development.

Meanwhile, public-sector industries soaked up inflation-threatening, budget-busting sums of bank credit — only to produce ever-growing inventories of unwanted goods. The state enterprises, deeply in debt to each other, continued to founder financially.

A crucial question now facing the government is how to maintain public-sector enterprises as the dominant force in the economy, without bankrupting the state or creating mass unemployment. Such questions dominated the working conference of the party's central committee in September. But the conferees — including members of the central committee and the Advisory Commission of party elders and senior officials from the provinces — failed to come up with any conclusive answers. Nor could they agree on the timing — much less the content — of the forthcoming eighth party plenum and the ensuing full party congress, expected to be held in early 1992.

Before the Soviet coup attempt, many political observers had forecast that the CCP congress would witness major personnel and organisational changes. It was strongly rumoured that President Yang Shangkun would retire and be replaced by Premier Li Peng, still largely disliked for his role in the 1989 crackdown on demonstrators in Peking.

Li's post would then become available to one of his two likely successors: vice-premiers Zhu Rongji and Zou Jiahua, who were both promoted to their present positions in April. Zhu, known to be the more cosmopolitan and reformist-minded of the two, is a former mayor of Shanghai. Zou, a former head of the State Planning Commission, is perhaps unsurprisingly said to favour central planning. He also has strong military links.

Yang's retirement could also swing the balance of power within the powerful Central Military Commission (CMC), where he sits as vice-chairman and his younger step-brother, Yang Baibing, serves as general-secretary. The commission is chaired by party general-secretary Jiang Zemin, a dark horse apparatchik who was catapulted to power by Deng Xiaoping as a compromise candidate after the fall of former party secretary Zhao Ziyang in 1989.

Without much of a personal power base, Jiang had been assiduously cultivating politically moderate professionals in the army through his CMC role. Yang Baibing, on the other hand, concentrated on the ideological purity of the military, in line with his position as head of the People Liberation Army's (PLA) General Political Department. Prior to August, PLA professionals seemed to have the upper hand, but the failed Soviet coup put the stress back on party loyalty above military competence, enhancing Yang's position.

Deng: unseen power.

In the aftermath of the Soviet putsch, it also looked likely that Li would hang on to his premiership at least until the 1993 meeting of the rubber-stamp National People's Congress (NPC), the nominal legislature. And the council of elders — or at least a truncated version of it — may get a new lease on life, institutionally.

The life expectancy of party elders remained a topic of intense speculation. The year was punctuated by recurrent rumours about the death or illness of one or another gerontocrat. Deng, 87, virtually gave up appearing in public, while Yang, whose political standing was enhanced by his relatively robust constitution, became ill late in the year. Other senior figures said to ailing included politburo standing committee member Yao Yilin, 73, conservative economist Chen Yun, 86, and the Chinese People's Political Consultative Conference (CPPCC) chairman Li Xiannian, 82.

The order in which they die could affect the jockeying for power within the party and the government. Zou and Zhu, for example, could vie for Yao's standing committee seat. Which of them would get it could well hinge on whether Chen outlasted Deng or vice versa.

One obvious candidate to eventually replace Li as CPPCC chairman is Ye Xuanping, 66, the energetic ex-governor of booming Guangdong province. Although recalled to Peking to serve as CPPCC vice-chairman in April, Ye made no secret of his reluctance to leave his native province, where he had served for 13 years and still wielded great influence.

Relations between the centre and the provinces remained vexed over such issues as policy accountability and tax revenue sharing. Ye reportedly served as effective tribune for the provinces in fending off a reassertion of central control at the seventh party plenum in 1990. By gathering regional strong men, such as Zhu and Ye to the capital, Peking's conservative centralists may hope yet to impose their will on the southern coastal provinces.

Whatever the machinations beneath the surface, China's media — firmly under the control of hardliners — remained blandly and uniformly sycophantic. However, a challenge to the unquestioned media domination of the hardliners came in October, when Wang Meng — a liberal former minister of culture — brought a libel action against a literary magazine. In a letter to the editor of a local daily, the magazine had alleged that a short story of Wang's had been a veiled attack on Deng. Such crypto-literary controversies often proved to be the opening salvo in bitter political campaigns and purges. Wang's case was notable as the first well-publicised, high-level attempt to use China's courts to redress a political wrong.

In recent months, the judiciary appeared to have softened its stance, possibly as a result of international pressure, to the advantage of a few pro-democracy dissidents who received "light" sentences of five to eight years in recognition of their repentant attitudes. Even Wang Juntao and Chen Zemin, convicted masterminds of the 1989 protests, got off with 13 years each — markedly shorter than the jail terms meted out following previous crackdowns. When Wang and Chen went on hunger strikes to protest their prison conditions, the authorities even made a few minor concessions — a departure from their previous intransigence.

Less fortunate were the hundreds picked up in dragnets aimed at social ills ranging from corruption to drug trafficking and prostitution. Some of them were subjected to public trials and summary execution, others were sent to labour reform camps. The move towards stricter policing partly reflected the perceived need to tighten political control and partly to suppress a rising crime wave. Many people nostalgically recalled the simpler, more honest times following the 1949 revolution when ideological zeal was still uncorrupted.

One beneficiary of this nostalgia was the late party chairman Mao Zedong, whose public image seemed brighter than at had been for a decade.

To the popular mind, Mao symbolised clean, decisive leadership, in contrast to the disillusionment and drift of the present. In an attempt to revive the party's past glory and to give current policies some ideological legitimacy, the leadership raked up long-dormant Maoist doctrines such as class struggle, national self-reliance and vigilance against foreign-instigated "peaceful evolution."

But the party was careful not to go too far with its ideological drive for fear of reviving the excesses of the Cultural Revolution. One of the demons of that era, Mao's arch–radical widow, Jiang Qing, committed suicide in mid-May at the age of 77. Jiang had never repented her Cultural Revolution role, and reportedly lived a fairly comfortable life under house arrest after her 1981 death sentence had been commuted to life imprisonment. □

# Foreign Relations

China gradually emerged from under the diplomatic cloud that had hung over the regime since 1989 through deft backstage diplomacy and a studied neutrality in the Gulf War. Political assertiveness on major Hongkong-related issues, sympathy for victims of heavy flooding and a few highly publicised human-rights concessions also paid off in 1991.

While Peking's ties with Japan, most European countries and Australia returned to a level of relative normality, relations with the US remained strained over human-rights issues, trade infractions and arms sales. The US Democratic Party, groping for a foreign issue in the 1992 US presidential elections, harped on the administration's equivocal stance towards China. President George Bush, however, managed to muster enough votes to fend off a Congressional over-ride of his veto of a bill attaching stringent conditions to the renewal of most favoured nation (MFN) trading status for China.

But, to keep Congressional critics at bay, the administration invoked earlier trade legislation to "get tough" with China on violations of US import quotas and copyrights. Bush also angered Peking by receiving the Dalai Lama, Tibet's exiled spiritual leader, at the White House.

With Sino-US ties strained, China devoted more effort to its relations with the Soviet Union. In May, the then Soviet defence minister Dmitri Yazov visited Peking — and shortly afterwards China agreed to buy 24 Soviet Su27 combat aircraft for US$700 million. In the same month, Jiang Zemin became the first Chinese Communist Party (CCP) secretary to visit Moscow in 30 years. On the largely ceremonial visit, Jiang signed a few minor border agreements and offered the Soviets a modest commodity credit.

Talks with Soviet President Mikhail Gorbachov were carefully bland, despite the virulent criticism in internal Chinese media of his apostasy to world communism. But Jiang went out of his way to snub an invitation to meet Russian President Boris Yeltsin. That decision must have haunted Peking when, just three months later, the abortive Moscow coup left Yazov ousted, Gorbachov weakened and Yeltsin strengthened. The debacle in the Soviet Union also came during a string of top-level state visits that Peking had carefully lined up to celebrate its diplomatic "coming out."

Rather than basking in the expected glow of renewed international respectability, China found itself having to listen to more hectoring on human rights from leaders like British Prime Minister John Major and Italian Prime Minister Giulio Andreotti. The only visiting luminary who refrained from reproaching Peking for its human-rights abuses was former Japanese prime minister Toshiki Kaifu, who visited China just before the Moscow coup.

For his forbearance, Kaifu was rewarded with Chinese promises to sign the nuclear non-proliferation treaty and to co-sponsor the UN arms-transfer registry. These agreements seemed to typify an emerging pattern in which the US stridently demands Chinese concessions which Peking then grants, in a belated and abridged version, to the less abrasive Japanese.

Out of consideration for Tokyo's sensibilities, Peking also cancelled the year's commemorative ceremonies for Chinese victims of the 1937 Nanjing massacre and of Japan's World War II concentration camps. As with many other Asian countries, Peking seemed in a mood to put bygone wars behind it and restore long-strained relations.

Vietnam, which tilted towards the Soviet Union during the Sino-Soviet split and fought a border war with China in 1979, seemed ready for rapprochement now that Peking was back on talking terms with the disintegrating Soviet Union. The main stumbling block remained Hanoi's continued support for Hun Sen's regime in Cambodia, which it has backed since the 1979 ouster of the China-backed Khmer Rouge. In a "Red solution" jointly brokered by Peking and Hanoi, Hun Sen and the Khmer Rouge have now agreed to join a coalition Supreme National Council in Phnom Penh.

Vietnam's former foreign minister Nguyen Co Thach, a China critic, fell from power in June at the country's communist party congress — which adopted a Peking-style platform that stressed economic development while putting political reform on hold. Thach's successor, Nguyen Man Cam, lost no time in going to Peking to pave the way for a visit by newly elected party chief Do Muoi in November, when relations between the two states were proclaimed fully "normalised."

China also seemed ready to normalise ties with South Korea. With bilateral trade already approaching US$5 billion, the two sides hurried to put the finishing touches on agreements covering trade, taxation and investment protection. A 66-member business delegation from Seoul visited China in July.

In what appeared to be a quid pro quo, Peking pressured its long-standing ally North Korea to accept separate UN membership — clearing the way for the South to simultaneously enter the world forum. In the wake of the Moscow coup, Peking ostentatiously demonstrated its socialist solidarity by according a lavish state welcome to North Korea's President Kim Il Sung, a frequent, but usually unannounced, visitor to China. Kim even met unofficially with China's paramount leader Deng Xiaoping, the only foreign dignitary so favoured during the year.

Despite the fanfare, Kim left China without securing any economic aid and arms supplies to supplant his now-defunct Soviet patrons; no explicit linkage of a Peking-Seoul normalisation to a recognition of Pyongyang by Tokyo and Washington and no public endorsement of his son, Kim Chong Il, as his legitimate successor. Instead, Chinese Premier Li Peng lectured Kim on the importance of economic reform and persuaded him to respond to Bush's tactical nuclear-arms reduction initiative by allowing international inspection of North Korea's nuclear facilities.

Peking exhibited no such fastidiousness over nuclear developments in countries farther afield. China, which has aided the nuclear programmes of 40 countries — including Algeria, Iran, Pakistan, Jordan and Brazil — maintains its support is strictly peaceful, though it continues to balk at allowing international monitoring of its nuclear exports. Foreign press reports also accused China of selling missile parts to Pakistan and negotiating the sale of missiles to Syria. Closer to home, China stepped up military sales to the Burmese military junta, a regime under increasing international pressure for its human-rights and political abuses.

**Arms sales: explosive issue.**

Nuclear assistance and missile sales were raised by two US under-secretaries of state during their visits to Peking at mid-year. The issues continue to rankle legislators in Washington, as did a host of other grievances. During the year, these centred around China's US$10 billion trade surplus with the US, the use of prison labour in export production, intellectual property violations, mis-labelling of garments to evade US import quotas and the ever-present human-rights question. One US Congressional delegation staged an "impromptu" memorial service on Tiananmen Square.

More protests came when US customs investigators raided the premises of Chinese companies in New York. Trade talks broke down and China seemed headed for inclusion on Washington's "Special 301" watch-list of retaliatory trade sanction targets.

Another old imperialist enemy, Britain, proved much more tractable due to the leverage provided by the transfer of Hongkong to Chinese sovereignty in 1997. Hongkong's plans to build a HK$127 billion (US$16.3 billion) airport and port facilities aroused Chinese fears that the colony would be crippled with debt long after its return to China. Peking's objections sparked a flurry of behind-the-scenes visits and negotiations, culminating in the British capitulation to Chinese demands for effective veto power over all pre-1997 decisions. To sign the airport agreement, Major gave Peking "face" by going to the capital, the first Western head-of-government to do so since the Tiananmen massacre.

With Hongkong in the bag, China turned its attention to Taiwan. Cross-straits relations got a boost when Taipei formally rescinded in May the decades-old "temporary provisions during the period of communist rebellion" — a long-standing barrier both to Taiwan-mainland links and to Taiwan's full democratisation.

Peking's satisfaction was not unalloyed, since democratisation of Taiwan only strengthened a popular outcry for sovereignty. Seizing on the occasion of Taiwan's 10 October Peking accordingly stepped up its rhetoric against Taiwan independence, with Chinese President Yang Shangkun warning independence advocates that "those who play with fire will perish by fire."

# Economy/Infrastructure

Rising inflation once again threatened to destabilise China's socio-economic structure. From a 1986 peak of nearly 40%, inflation had dropped to less than 3% in 1990. By August 1991, though, it was back up to an annualised 11% in major cities.

Worse could be in store as two main factors contributed to inflation: rising administered prices and an increase in the money supply due to massive credits from the government-controlled banking system to foundering state enterprises. Neither factor looks likely to go away.

With an estimated 65% of raw materials and nearly 75% of consumer goods already freed from price controls, the government needs to press on with price reform to limit its own budgetary haemorrhage and rationalise supply and demand. Living costs jumped perceptibly in May, with the removal of subsidies on key commodities ranging from grain and cooking oil to steel and cement.

Further rises in food prices can be expected when the full impact of the summer's floods makes itself felt in the autumn and winter harvest. But damage to the food supply could be less severe than feared: the projected 428 million tonne aggregate grain output for the year still ranked as the second highest in China's history, just behind 1990's record 435 million tonnes.

As for the state enterprises, the government's credit injections may have accomplished the primary objective of stimulating production after the austerity years. But retail sales remained sluggish, especially for consumer durables, so a good deal of the output has simply built up as inventory.

The result was a gridlock of inter-company debt in the public sector, as enterprises postponed their payables to suppliers while waiting on slow-to-materialise sales revenues. About a third of the 40,000 or so "backbone" state enterprises of the economy were in the red, and another third could be in financial trouble if their receivables were realistically written down.

In the short term, the only way out of this debt dilemma seemed to be more of the same. By the third quarter, the government announced that the banking system was ready with what amounted to take-out loans for fully 80% of the companies enmeshed in the debt chain. Refinancing was promised for the rest.

That begged the question of how to deal with the nearly Rmb 300 billion (US$55.76 billion) overhang of debt left over from the 1990 bank credit binge which had got the debt chain started in the first place. The loans had been an attempt to pacify the urban workforce and buy political stability in the wake of the austerity measures and the 1989 anti-democracy crackdown.

Yet, unless a way is found to defuse the inflationary impact

of such a massive monetary expansion, the credit injections could prove destabilising in the long run. China's economic policymakers, however, still have some room for manoeuvre as underlying anxieties about inflation and industrial reform occur against a background of relatively optimistic economic statistics.

Industrial output for the first three quarters was up by nearly 14%, though the two officially cosseted sectors — heavy industry and government enterprises — lagged at 12% and 9% respectively. Even allowing for the expected fourth quarter slowdown, aggregate output could end the year significantly outperforming the 8% increase predicted in the budget.

Retail sales grew by an encouraging 13% in the eight months to August, though the biggest increase (18%) was in purchases by institutions, rather than the much-courted individual consumer. In sales growth, too, state-sector firms (at 13%) and collectives (8%) far underperformed joint ventures (21%) and individual retailers (17%).

The question of how to salvage the lacklustre state enterprises was the topic of endless seminars and commentaries in the party-controlled media. Rising political star Zhu Rongji, the reformist ex-mayor of Shanghai, was handed special responsibility for the public sector turn-around shortly after his elevation to vice premier in April. Seasoned observers, however, remained divided over whether this represented a mark of confidence or a trap set by his conservative rivals.

Public enterprise defaults feed on themselves in a vicious circle. Under China's "double guarantee" system, state firms can get preferential access to inputs, transport and credit as long as they remit agreed amounts of tax and profits. Economists report that part of 1990's record 22% increase in domestic lending was to cover government firms' remittance obligations so that they could continue to be eligible for "double guarantee" benefits.

The laggard performance of the public sector is of more than ideological concern. On an immediate and practical level, a failing state sector will only aggravate the steadily worsening central-government deficit.

Having lost out in its 1990 bid to claw back a greater share of provincial tax receipts, the central government was forced to rely increasingly on revenue from public enterprises. But, instead of reaping taxes and profits, Peking found itself saddled with budget-busting subsidies to state-run firms for everything from raw materials to bank credit and concessional purchases of shoddy goods just to run down public-sector inventories.

Except for 1985, the reported central-government deficit grew consistently over the past decade. The Rmb 13.3 billion deficit included in the 1991 budget submission was so daunting that even the normally submissive National People's Congress was emboldened to require a largely symbolic Rmb 1 billion cut, half to come from tax increases and half from expenditure cuts.

The 1991 budget called for an expenditure rise of just 5%, well under the projected GNP increase — a feat the government has not even come close to achieving in practice since 1988. Major stress was to be placed on defence, education, agriculture and key construction projects. Price, export and enterprise subsidies were all due to be trimmed.

Military spending was to rise by 12%, its second successive annual increase. That did not include the significant off-budget revenues of the PLA's commercial and industrial enterprises or the military research and development spending concealed under civilian budget headings — factors which could double the actual military outlay to more than 5% of GNP.

Even so, the declared deficit grossly understated China's fiscal extremity. Unlike most countries, China includes government borrowings at home and abroad as "revenue." Otherwise, the deficit would stand at nearly Rmb 49 billion, about 3% of GNP.

Of the Rmb 30 billion in bonds and interest falling due in 1991, about half were held by individuals. Most of the remainder, held by enterprises and institutions, was rolled over. Another Rmb 12 billion worth of bonds were issued this year, a 30% increase over 1990.

Most of the expansion was accounted for by a competitively priced three-year issue through a 58-bank consortium headed by the central bank. This represented a major marketing advance over the previous practice of force-feeding government paper to state employees through their work units. Planned secondary bond markets should further increase liquidity.

Liquidity growth on China's nascent stockmarkets was steady, but less spectacular than if were it to be free from Peking's suspicion for equity trading. The Shanghai Stock Exchange, opened in late 1990, was joined in July 1991 by a similar one in the Shenzhen special economic zone (SEZ), near Hongkong. Foreign investment on both exchanges remained strictly limited.

**State enterprises: non-performing assets.**

Peking still prefers direct, rather than portfolio, investment from abroad. New investment contracts were set to top 1990's record of US$6.6 billion, though most still came from Taiwan and Hongkong, as did the visitors who bid up tourist receipts to nearly US$2.5 billion, well above pre-Tiananmen levels.

International borrowing, too, is on the mend. The World Bank lent China nearly US$1.5 billion in its latest fiscal year, while Japan — the source of nearly 75% of China's overseas credit, both official and commercial — renewed its US$5.7 billion credit package, suspended after Tiananmen. Hongkong banks are estimated to have booked nearly US$6 billion worth of China business, notwithstanding the country's still-depressed credit ratings.

Whatever their qualms about political risks, bankers had no cause to worry about China's ability to rake in foreign exchange. The country's export engine continued to perform indefatigably, despite reductions in export subsidies in a bid by Peking to forestall protectionist backlash and wheedle its way into Gatt.

Exporters were also hit by further devaluations of the renminbi under its managed float since April. Much as this may have enhanced competitive pricing of Chinese exports, it also bid up costs of capital equipment and intermediate goods for value-added exporters.

Even as US dollars became costlier at swap centres around the country, some previously privileged exporters were forced to turn over more of their hard-currency earnings to the state. Foreign-exchange retention rates were slashed from 80% to 50% in the export-oriented SEZs. Hard-hit southern coastal provinces struggled to rescue their export enterprises by allowing them to sell part of their output into the lucrative domestic market and even import consumer goods from abroad for local sale.

On the other hand, inland provinces were granted enhanced foreign-exchange retention rates. So were certain targeted industries like electronics, which is heavily concentrated around Shanghai.

The subsidy cuts, depreciation and rejigged retention rates saw China's visible trade surplus plunge to a mere US$80 million by April, less than a tenth of what it had been at the start of the year. But by August it was back up to a more normal US$900 million, and the cumulative surplus for the first eight months stood at US$5.6 billion.

Relations were particularly vexed with the US, China's third main trading partner after Hongkong and Japan. For the first eight months, two-way trade, at US$8.1 billion, stood 13% above the same period in 1990. But exports grew faster than imports by seven percentage points, prompting an angry backlash from the Bush administration which had fought to preserve China's MFN trading status. □

# Data

**Major industries:** Textiles, 18.9 billion m² (18 billion); cement, 203 million tonnes (210 million); pig iron, 61.8 million tonnes (58.2 million); steel, 66 million tonnes (61.6 million); silk, 55,200 tonnes (52,300).

**Major agriculture:** Rice, 189.3 million tonnes (180.1 million); wheat, 98.2 million tonnes (90.8 million); soybeans, 11.2 million tonnes (10.2 million); cotton, 4.5 million tonnes (3.8 million); corn, 96.8 million tonnes (78.9 million); sugar cane, 57.6 million tonnes (48.8 million); oil-bearing crops, 16.1 million tonnes (12.9 million); pork, beef and mutton, 28.6 million tonnes (26.3 million).

**Energy:** Crude oil, 138.1 million tonnes (137.2 million); gas, 15.6 billion m² (15.3 billion); electricity, 604 billion kWh (585 billion).

**Mining:** Coal, 1.08 billion tonnes (1.05 billion).

**Major exports:** Textile yarn and fabrics, US$7 billion (US$6.99 billion); clothing, US$6.85 billion (US$6.14 billion); oil, US$4.47 billion (US$3.63 billion); textile fibres and wastes, US$1.1 billion (US$1.55 billion); vegetables and fruit, US$1.76 billion (US$1.63 billion).

**Major imports:** Grains, US$2.4 billion (US$2.98 billion); food and meat, US$3.33 billion (US$4.19 billion); textile fibres and waste, US$1 billion (US$2.28 billion); mineral fuels, US$1.27 billion (US$1.65 billion); fertilisers, US$2.6 billion (US$2.36 billion); textiles, US$2.75 billion (US$2.84 billion); iron and steel, US$2.85 billion (US$5.79 billion); special industrial machinery, US$5 billion (US$5.67 billion); electrical equipment and parts, US$2 billion (US$2.39 billion); organic chemicals, US$1.13 billion (US$1.4 billion); resins, plastics and cellulose, US$1.5 billion (US$2.2 billion).

**Tourism and transport:** Arrivals, 27.5 million (24.5 million), of which Hongkong, Macau and Taiwan Chinese represent 25.6 million (23 million); Overseas Chinese, 91,000 (68,500); other foreigners, 1.7 million (1.5 million). Of foreigners, Japanese represent 26.5% (24.6), Americans represent 13.3% (14.7). Tourism revenue, US$2.2 billion (US$1.9 billion).

**Currency:** Renminbi (100 fen). Rmb 5.39 = US$1 on 6 Nov.1991 (Rmb 4.72 on 5 Nov. 1990).

**Finance:** 8 banks under People's Bank of China; some foreign bank branches plus representative offices in Peking, Shanghai, Canton and special economic zones; experimental stock exchanges in some cities. Renminbi is a non-convertible currency.

**Major banks:** People's Bank of China, Sanlihe, Xichengqu, Peking, tel. 868731, tlx 22612 PBCHO CN; Bank of China, 410 Fuchengmennei Dajie, Peking, tel. 6016688, tlx 22254 BCHO CN; China Investment Bank, Wan Shou Lu, Peking, tel. 863027, tlx 22537 CIBCN; Agricultural Bank of China, 25 Fuxing Lu, Peking, tel. 812050, tlx 22017 ABC CN; People's Construction Bank of China, 5 Wanshou Lu Xijie, Haidian Qu, Peking, tel. 8011166, tlx 222467 PCBC CN; Bank of Communications, 200 Jiangxi Zhong Lu, Shanghai, tel. 255900, tlx 33438 BOCOM CN, fax 291400; Industrial and Commercial Bank, 13 Cuiwei Lu, Haidian Qu, Peking, tel. 8217720, tlx 22770 ICBHO CN; CITIC Industrial Bank, CITIC Bldg, 19 Jianguomenwai, Peking, tel. 5002255, tlx 22987 CITIC CN, fax 5001535.

**Government ministries** (all in Peking): Agriculture, 11 Nanli Nongzhanguan, tel. 5003366, tlx 22233 MACR CN; Commerce, 45 Fuxingmen Nei Dajie, tel. 668581, tlx 20032 BFAMC CN; Finance, Sanlihe, tel. 868731, tlx 222308 MOFFD CN; Foreign Affairs, 225 Chaoyangmen Nei Dajie, tel. 553831, 558801, fax 5124661; Foreign Economic Relations and Trade, 2 Dong Changan Jie, tel. 5126644; State Economic Commission, Yuetan Nanjie, Sanlihe, tel. 862234, tlx 22552 SEC CN; Culture, A82 Donganmen Dajie, tel. 446571; Posts and Telecommunications, 13 Xi Changan Dajie, tel. 661365, fax 6011370; Education Commission, 37 Da Meicang Hutong, Xidan, tel. 658731-2275, fax 6013648, tlx 22014 SEDC CN.

**Public holidays** (1992): 1 Jan. (New Year's Day), 4-6 Feb. (Lunar New Year), 1 May (May Day), 1 Oct. (National Day).

**Weather:** The north has more seasonal variations than the south, which is subtropical, hot and humid Apr.-Oct. Temperatures in Peking range from –4.7°C in January to highs of 25.5°C in July-Aug. In the south, Canton has temperatures above 21°C for 7 months of the year. Average annual rainfall is 721 mm in Peking, 1,706 mm in Canton and 1,672 mm in Shanghai.

**Taxation:** Individual, under Rmb 800, nil; Rmb 801-1,500, 5%; Rmb 1,501-3,000, 10%; Rmb 3-6,000, 20%; Rmb 6-9,000, 30%; Rmb 9-12,000,40%; above Rmb 12,000, 45%. Foreign corporations, joint-venture income tax, 33%, with 10% levy if profits are remitted abroad. Foreign enterprise income tax, 33%.

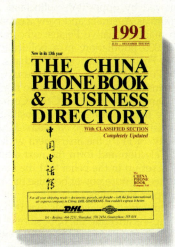

# FIJI

F iji obtained independence in 1970 after 96 years of British rule. By then, the native Fijian population was outnumbered by the descendants of plantation workers and small businessmen who arrived either as indentured labour or on their own initiative from India, plus European, Chinese and Rotuman immigrants. However, the balance of political power remains held by ethnic Fijians. In May 1987, a coup by the Fijian-dominated army removed a newly elected Indian-dominated government. By the end of that year, Fiji had left the British Commonwealth and a military government led by coup leader Col Sitiveni Rabuka had been succeeded by a semi-civilian interim government led by President Ratu Sir Penaia Ganilau and former prime minister, Ratu Sir Kamisese Mara, was restored to that office. In 1990, Fijian chiefs approved a new constitution structured to preserve Fijian political control. An election due to be held in 1992 will be for a 70-member elected House of Representatives dominated by Fijian members. A Fijian-dominated senate will be appointed by the president and non-Fijians are barred from office as president or prime minister.

**President**
Ratu Sir Penaia Ganilau.
**Prime Minister** (and **Foreign Affairs**)
Ratu Sir Kamisese Mara;
**Deputy Prime Minister, Finance and Economic Planning**
Josefata Kamikamica;
**Deputy Prime Minister, Home Affairs**
Sitiveni Rabuka;
**Attorney-General and Justice**
Sailosi Kepa;
**Education, Youth and Sport**
Filipe Bole;
**Primary Industries and Cooperatives**
Viliame Gonelevu;
**Health**
Dr Apenisa Kurusaqila;
**Indian Affairs**
Irene Jai Narayan;

**Fijian Affairs and Rural Development**
Col Vatilai Naunisaravi;
**Tourism, Civil Aviation and Energy**
David Pickering;
**Women and Social Welfare**
Adi Finau Tabakaucoro;
**Forestry**
Ratu Serupepeli Naivalu;
**Lands and Mineral Resources**
Ratu William Toganivalu;
**Infrastructure and Public Utilities**
Tomasi Vakatora;
**Housing and Urban Development**
Ratu Ovini Bokini;
**Employment and Industrial Relations**
Taniela Veitata;
**Trade and Commerce**
Berenado Vunibobo;
**Information, Broadcasting, Telecommunications**
Ratu Inoke Kubuabola.

## Politics/Social Affairs

B y the end of September 1991, just over 83% of the 386,000 people eligible to vote had registered for a twice-deferred general election that Fiji's army-installed government rescheduled for mid-1992.

The election is to be held under a disputed constitution imposed in 1990 to replace the one done away with by the Fijian-dominated army in 1987 after it toppled an elected government composed of an ethnic Indian ministerial majority.

The constitution is the product of Fijian nationalism and is viewed by opposition politicians, and such regional neighbours as Australia and New Zealand, as racist. It is designed to maintain native Fijians, who form just under 49% of the 740,000 population, in a politically dominant position over non-Fijians — particularly Indians. Fijians will occupy 37 of the 70 seats in an enlarged House of Representatives, and only Fijians can be appointed prime minister and president.

During the year, the Great Council of Fijian Chiefs, which gave final approval to the constitution, busied itself with organising the *Soqosoqo Ni Vakavulewa Ni Taukei* (Fijian Political Party, or FPP), the instrument with which they intend to win the election and form the next elected government. The FPP was set up in the belief that the new constitution would guarantee it future power because the mass of Fijian voters would support the chiefs.

But events showed this was by no means assured. A series of upsets affecting the opposition — a coalition of the smallish Fiji Labour Party (FLP) and the virtually wholly Indian-supported National Federation Party (NFP) — as well as the chiefly establishment, put the result of the election increasingly in doubt. Commentators, including army coup leader Sitiveni Rabuka, concluded the opening of new divisions in the Fijian community could produce a situation in which the chiefs' party could find itself outnumbered in parliament by a combination of Indian MPs and Fijians disinclined to accept the continuation of chiefly political authority. Such a scenario would repeat the events that prompted the 1987 coup.

But the chiefs could be saved by divisions among the opposition. In April, the opposition coalition lost its leader Adi Kuini Bavadra, widow of deposed prime minister Timoci Bavadra, who died in 1989. She left for Australia after becoming disenchanted with intra-opposition bickering.

The NFP leader Harish Sharma took over as acting leader, but was succeeded in August by Jokapeci Korroi, head of the nurses' union, who said she would occupy the post until a leadership squabble among several Fijian candidates was settled. In August, Labour and the NFP began to part forces after FLP secretary Mahendra Chaudhry, the driving force of the Fiji Trades Union Congress (FTUC), failed in an attempt to achieve a merger of the two parties.

Lawyer Jai Ram Reddy, the most influential NFP figure, persuaded his party to drop its plan to boycott the election as a protest against the constitution's anti-Indian bias. Reddy argued that a boycott by the NFP would make a gift of the seats to Indian candidates of what the opposition believes will be merely a continuation of the post-coup interim government. However, the FLP resolved to stick with the boycott.

Like the chiefs' party, the NFP seemed to observers to be over-optimistic in claiming to be sure of making a clean sweep of Indian seats. The year saw the launching of several new Indian political parties, notably the Fijian Indian Congress, who favoured a non-confrontational approach and were prepared to work with the chiefs and their FPP in restoring good race relations.

Several small ethnic Fijian groups appeared as potential thorns in the side of FPP. The launch of the All National Party (ANP) as a multi-racial, western Fiji–based party preparing to fight more than 50 constituencies, poses a particular challenge to the chiefs' party and the other opposition groups. The ANP is led by Apisai Tora, a militant politician and trade union official with a long record of switching loyalties. In July he was dismissed as works minister by Prime Minister Ratu Sir Kamisese Mara after he accepted the ANP presidency. Tora is the most vocal of the western Fijians who argue it is time to end the century of political domination of the country by the eastern Fijian chiefs, personified by Mara and President Ratu Sir Penaia Ganilau.

In June, the regime had seemed to be on a collision course with the FTUC and National Farmers' Union (NFU). The NFU, backed by the FTUC, had delayed the start of the vital 1991 sugar harvest over a dispute about the 1990 cane price and other sugar industry issues. However, Ganilau intervened to do a deal with the FTUC and NFU, supported surprisingly by Rabuka, who congratulated the FTUC and condemned the government he put in power for being out of touch with grassroot sentiments.

But Rabuka's continued verbal assaults, including criticism of his own Fijian chiefs, produced another temporary crisis. Although Ganilau is the paramount chief of Rabuka's home district and Rabuka a commoner, the then army commander said having made him president, he could also unmake him. Ganilau's response was an icy letter to Rabuka, accusing him of putting his loyalty in question and ridiculing the entire government. Rabuka later delivered a formal Fijian apology to Ganilau, but did not withdraw his criticism.

Mara: reign nearly over.

In September, after months of criticising the government — including hints at another military takeover — Rabuka left the army and accepted Mara's invitation to join the cabinet as home affairs minister and co-deputy prime minister. Rabuka said he was willing to accept the leadership of the FPP, if offered it, and become prime minister if the party won the election.

However, Mara, who has led Fiji since 1970, announced he was retiring from politics, and was expected to back his protege Josefata Kamikamica as his successor. □

# Foreign Relations

Four years of strained relations with New Zealand and Australia began to ease during 1991. But while Fiji began the year by welcoming China's President Yang Shangkun when he transitted through the country to and from a South American trip, by the end of the year Suva's relations with Peking were strained as a result of its dealings with Taipei.

Australia and New Zealand, strong critics of the 1987 military coup, continued to express reservations about a new constitution that relegated non-Fijians to a position of political inferiority. However, New Zealand's Prime Minister Jim Bolger and his deputy Don McKinnon, while agreeing the constitution was defective, said it at least represented a step towards the restoration of parliamentary government. During a visit to New Zealand in May, Fiji's Prime Minister Ratu Sir Kamisese Mara said he was "happy" about changes in New Zealand's attitude. Mara, noting foreign criticism of the constitution endorsed by him, said it was "totally erroneous" to equate it with apartheid, since there was no legislated separation of people.

Australia's Prime Minister Bob Hawke also took a less critical line during the year, as did his Foreign Minister Gareth Evans. Evans, whose denunciation of the coup and the new constitution at a UN General Assembly meeting angered the Fijian Government, mended fences when he met Mara at the South Pacific Forum meeting at Pohnpei during August. The meeting was conciliatory and Evans is due to visit Suva in early 1992.

Co-deputy Prime Minister and Finance Minister Josefata Kamikamica, tipped as the most likely candidate to take over as Fiji's prime minister in 1992, visited Canberra in July where he met Hawke and Treasurer John Kerin. He was the first Fiji minister to be officially invited to Australia since 1987, and his visit was viewed as a success.

China maintains a large embassy in Suva and has extended cheap loans and other aid to Fiji. During the year, the embassy delivered several informal protests about a revival of Fiji's links with Taiwan. In August, Mara travelled to Taiwan after attending the forum meeting where he told the Taipei government that Fiji would support their move to become associated with the forum as a "dialogue" partner. He also signed an agreement for technical assistance to Fiji's sugar industry, described as the highest-level document ever signed by Taiwan with a country it has no diplomatic ties with. In addition, Mara discussed an air rights deal to enable Air Pacific, Fiji's national carrier, to open a service to Taipei in 1993.

Malaysian Prime Minister Datuk Seri Mahathir Mohamad, who stopped over in Fiji in July on his way to and from a South American tour, mentioned a proposal for a Fiji-Malaysia business council and said Malaysia Airlines was looking at using Nadi Airport as a transit stop for a planned service to South America. Mahathir and Mara are viewed as having close ties since Malaysia supported Fiji after the 1987 coup. In October, Malaysia signed an agreement with Fiji under which the central banks of each country would guarantee payments on behalf of exporters and importers.

Fiji's Trade and Industry Minister Berenado Vunibobo headed frequent missions abroad in an effort to develop new trade and investment ties. Asia, North America and such key Pacific island markets as Papua New Guinea, New Caledonia and the Solomon Islands were explored. These missions produced new export business for manufactured products worth several million dollars, with the promise of follow-up orders worth much more.

At the regional level, Fiji suffered a few failures. Mara was unsuccessful in trying to persuade the South Pacific Forum to appoint his former foreign secretary Jioji Kotobalavu as its next secretary-general. Fiji also failed to get one of its candidates appointed as vice-chancellor of the University of the South Pacific. There is a feeling throughout the region that Fiji, in many ways the most prosperous of the Pacific island nations, is too keen to exploit its hub position by seeking to host regional institutions and offices.

While the Fijians are aware of this attitude — which they see as discrimination — they launched a campaign in October for Suva to become the site of the South Pacific Commission (SPC). This has been based in New Caledonia since the late

first by a Western leader since China became an international pariah following the violent crackdown on pro-democracy activists in June 1989. Major publicly expressed his reservations over the political price he was obliged to pay, and tried to recover some credibility by pressing China's leaders to improve human rights in the country.

One immediate consequence of the signing of the memorandum was sudden progress on a number of issues that had fallen victim to the earlier diplomatic tug-of-war. On the day of the signing, the two sides announced the Sino-British Land Commission would give early agreement to the granting of a construction site for a post-1997 British consulate.

Chinese and British representatives also immediately resumed meetings of the JLG which in early October reached agreement on another contentious issue, the relocation of British naval base. Peking had previously objected to Britain's plans to move the base from its current site in the central business district to an island in the harbour. Peking's permission for the move will relieve local anxieties over having the Chinese military set up its headquarters in the heart of the city, and will also allow the government to redevelop the prime site.

Arrangements announced at the same meeting for a Court of Final Appeal to replace Britain's Privy Council in time for the 1997 handover, proved more disappointing for local residents. The two sides agreed that the court would be composed of the chief justice, three Hongkong judges — either Chinese or expatriate — and a fifth member to be invited alternatively from two panels. Panel A would be made up of retired and serving Court of Appeal judges in Hongkong, and Panel B would include retired judges from other common law jurisdictions. Local lawyers argued that the court as described by the JLG will lack flexibility and independence. There was also concern that such terms as had been agreed had not been put into writing, nor had expressions such as "Hongkong judges" been specifically defined.

While Peking made substantial gains in acquiring influence over local affairs, Hongkong voters expressed their dissent at the ballot-box in the colony's first direct elections to the lawmaking Legislative Council (Legco) on 15 September. Out of 54 candidates contesting 18 available seats, liberal candidates made a clean sweep, with only one seat gained by a conservative candidate. Liberals also performed impressively in elections to the district boards and municipal councils earlier in the year.

In the Legco elections, 11 seats went to the United Democrats of Hongkong (UDHK), who failed to place only two of their candidates. The top vote-getters were Martin Lee, Szeto Wah and Lau Chin-shek, all critics of the government and leaders of the Hongkong Alliance in support of Patriotic Democratic Movements in China. The Alliance, set up in 1989 to support the failed protest movement in Peking, has been labelled as subversive by China. Most of the other successful candidates were either members of liberal political groups allied with the UDHK, or independents with similar strong views on democracy and human rights.

Following the polls, Chinese officials questioned whether Alliance members could be voted in again in the next elections scheduled for 1995 as they would not be considered acceptable as members of the proposed "through-train" legislature which will straddle the 1997 handover. Lee and Szeto have offered to open a friendly dialogue with the local branch of the New China News Agency (NCNA), Peking's main repre-

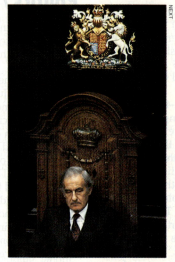

**Wilson: listening harder.**

sentative in the colony, but their advances have been coolly rebuffed.

Although local pro-Peking newspapers published editorials warning voters not to cast their ballots for candidates likely to disturb the Hongkong's prosperity and stability, no pro-Peking candidates was elected. Similarly, members of the colony's other main political party, the conservative Liberal Democratic Federation (LDF) and representing the business community, also failed to gain a single seat. If there was any comfort for Peking it was in the low turnout at the polls. Only 39% of the registered voters cast their ballots, in contrast to a 50% turnout predicted by the government and up to 70% forecast by some privately commissioned surveys.

While Lee and Szeto charged that the electoral roll was inaccurate and inflated, and therefore made the turnout a suspect indicator of public interest, other analysts attributed the lukewarm response to inadequate promotion of the elections by the government and the lack of any genuine contest in most constituencies. Another likely reason was the public's recognition that their first step towards democracy was a feeble one, with directly elected legislators making up less than one third of the 60-member council. In the indirectly elected so-called functional constituency — representing certain professions — conservatives and moderates took nearly all of the 21 available seats.

After the elections, the UDHK urged the governor to reflect the public mandate and include liberals in his further 18 direct appointments. In a controversial move, the party even supplied a list of 20 people they considered desirable for inclusion. But when the appointments were announced on 21 September, only one person on the UDHK's list was included. Most of the rest were low-key conservatives and pro-establishment moderates. However, some of the democrats' key adversaries failed to have their tenure extended.

The public vote for "subversives" notwithstanding, Peking's impending sovereignty and Hongkong's ties with the mainland were clearly expressed in a local fund-raising drive for victims of China's catastrophic summer floods. Groups and individuals of all political persuasions raised more than HK$600 million in relief funds, and while the emphasis was on patriotism, some observers saw the exercise as an effort by some to mend relations with China.

Likewise, protest marches calling for democracy and human rights in China attracted markedly fewer participants. An estimated 50,000 people turned out for a ceremony on the second anniversary of the 4 June 1989 killings in Peking, but only a fraction of that number attended protest marches that had previously filled the streets.

Around 50 activists in three different groups gathered on 30 September for a protest outside the restaurant where the NCNA was holding its annual cocktail party to celebrate China's national day on 1 October. Despite a minor clash between police and protesters, the latter succeeded in holding up banners and chanting slogans at arriving and departing guests, including the Hongkong governor. In previous years the protesters had been kept well away from the guests, and this year's relative tolerance was attributed to passage of Hongkong's Bill of Rights in June.

The bill, based closely on the UN Covenant on Civil and Political Rights, was initially criticised for excluding key rights such as a fully elected legislature and self-determination. The government has also imposed a renewable one-year freeze period on challenges to certain questionable laws that may have to be amended to bring them into compliance with the Bill of Rights.

But the bill has already made its presence felt, with key court rulings calling for the repeal of drug possession laws that contravened presumption of innocence. The bill's effect on law enforcement brought it under criticism by Chinese officials, who said it might be repealed after 1997 if it is found to clash with the Basic Law.

Some foreign governments also began to take more vocal stands on the progress of democracy and human rights in the colony. The US and Canada, in particular, eschewed their previous positions of low-key support to express concern with the Hongkong and British governments' handling of the airport issue and the slow pace of democratic reform. Some diplomats also expressed doubts that the Joint Declaration, which they regard as the key to maintaining Hongkong's capitalist system, might not be upheld in letter and spirit by the Chinese Government. Late in the year members of US Congress began drawing up a bill to outline an explicit policy towards Hongkong.

Despite such concerns, local residents showed less inclination to ensure a safe future by acquiring a foreign passport. Applications for Canadian and Australian passports tapered off from the flood occasioned by the panic following the political upheavals of 1989, while a US scheme granting delayed-entry immigration visas to key employees of US companies was unexpectedly under-subscribed.

The British Nationality Scheme, which offered full British passports to 50,000 carefully selected residents and their families, was also undersubscribed. The government had anticipated 300,000 applications for the first phase in February, but only one fifth of that number actually applied.

While the desire — or ability — of local people to leave Hongkong appeared to wane, efforts increased to deal with unwanted immigrants from China and Vietnam. In March, two major building contractors were successfully prosecuted and fined for employing illegal immigrants from China on their construction sites. The prosecutions were brought under legislation passed in November 1990 that for the first time made main contractors liable for the presence of illegal immigrants.

The long-running controversy over the handling of Vietnamese migrants appeared to reach resolution in October, with Vietnam for the first time expressing a willingness to take back people refused refugee status under a controversial screening programme introduced by the Hongkong Government three years before. Out of a total of 63,000 Vietnamese now held in Hongkong camps, 19,000 have been classified as economic migrants while another 39,000 have yet to be screened. Only one out of every five or six asylum-seekers are expected to obtain refugee status.

Local authorities have since March of 1989 been actively encouraging non-refugees to return to Vietnam voluntarily. Just over 10,000 have agreed to do so. The Vietnamese Government has been sensitive to accepting returnees classified as "non-voluntary." But in September, Hanoi for the first time agreed to the use of the term "illegal immigrants" to refer to non-refugees, putting them on a par with illegal immigrants in other parts of the world, who are routinely repatriated against their will. The first "non-voluntary" group were flown back to Vietnam on 9 November.

Hanoi's change of position was attributed to growing pressure in Hongkong to put an end to the policy of "port of first asylum," and indications that the US Government was beginning to weaken its long-standing insistence that all Vietnamese migrants be treated as political refugees. In anticipation of possible unrest in Vietnamese camps and detention centres,

the police were put on alert, putting additional pressure on thinning ranks already stretched in coping with a general breakdown in law and order in the colony.

In the course of the year, the number of major robberies increase sharply over the previous year, with an average of 53 violent crimes a day. Some of the more sensational crimes included a record-breaking HK$167 million security van robbery, an armed raid on a fur warehouse and a sweep through five jewellery shops by a single gang in one day. The growing use of automatic weapons during robberies heightened concern that criminals — many of whom entered the colony from China to carry out the raids — were becoming increasingly ruthless.

In August, the government introduced a draft Organised Crime Bill for public consultation over plans to tackle crime syndicates. Some measures in the bill have raised concern, especially those impinging on the right to privacy. The government also passed new legislation to crack down on high-powered speedboats used for smuggling between Hongkong and China. □

# Economy/Infrastructure

In a year that saw political unrest in China, war in the Middle East, deep recession in many major Western markets, domestic banking crises and financial scandals in the US and Japan, Hongkong's main concerns revolved around three years of double-digit inflation that hit 13.9% in April.

During the year, the complacency — albeit born largely out of impotency — with which the colony's administration and private-sector economists had viewed Hongkong's persistent inflation, disappeared. Even the Hongkong Government conceded that inflation, which it had persistently forecast was on the wane, was in fact rising and revised upwards their official estimate of 1991's average inflation rate to 12%.

By that time, however, the malign side-effects of persistent inflation, coupled with negative real interest rates, had already been felt. To protect the value of their savings, Hongkong residents increasingly turned to the overheated and speculative housing market, with the result that in the first half of the year values of small flats rose by some 30-50%.

The roots of Hongkong's inflation were widely discussed, and the usual suspects — high wage settlements, undervalued currency, profligate government spending — were duly paraded for increasingly unconvincing denunciations. The real reasons for Hongkong's inflation seemed, to some analysts, to lie fairly clearly in the one-way extension of the colony's manufacturing base into southern China, particularly Guangdong province.

Although the economic symbiosis between Hongkong and Guangdong has become obvious, financial integration hardly progressed. Using Hongkong as its primary port, businesses in China had built up not only large trade surpluses, but also massive holdings of Hongkong dollars. By the middle of the year, these overseas holdings totalled some HK$63 billion (US$807.7 million), or more than the Hongkong banking system's entire demand deposit base.

These Hongkong dollars were repatriated to the colony through the interbank market, but the local financial system was either unable or unwilling to lend them back to China. Instead, lending remained overwhelmingly concentrated on Hongkong-based assets, notably mortgage lending. Property linked loans grew 32% in the first half of the year, compared with a rise in overall lending of 16.7%. The resulting asset inflation duly made its way through the system, manifesting itself not only in higher residential rents but also in higher wages to pay the rents and, in turn, higher prices of consumer goods.

Hongkong's domestic trading situation could not have shown clearer signs of substantial overheating. Largely unnoticed, the colony's domestic trade position lurched sharply and deeply into the red. Stripping out an entrepot trade now worth HK$414 billion — equal to 76% of GDP — Hongkong, which prides itself on its trading expertise, went into the final quarter of the year trailing a HK$20.6 billion visible trade deficit. To put this into context, that is nearly 10 times larger than the HK$2.3 billion trade deficit Hongkong ran up at the same period in 1990. The reasons for the speeding red ink were twofold: first, domestic exports had remained effectively stagnant for two years and second, retained imports were growing at something like 15.5%, on the back of wage settlements which, in some cases, more than matched the local inflation rate.

Hongkong's transformation into a service economy continued, with the proportion of the workforce employed by service industries totalling 64%, compared with 62.4% in 1990. The rise in service-sector employment was matched almost exactly in a fall in manufacturing employment: in 1991, only 26% of the workforce actually made anything tangible, compared with 27.7% in 1990.

The conspicuous lack of concern about the colony's deteriorating trade performance is the result of the continuing spectacular growth in Hongkong-related re-exports from China. In the first seven months of the year, the value of re-exports rose 28% to HK$328.8 billion. Although there are no accurate figures for the number of people now employed in Guangdong factories by Hongkong investors, anecdotal evidence points to around 4 million.

For all the talk of increased inter-Asian trade, Hongkong's re-exports in the first eight months of the year were more than ever dependent upon Western markets, particularly in terms of textile and clothing. While re-exports to the US and Britain rose only 16% and 20%, shipments to continental Europe were booming, rising 63% to Germany and 46% to France. Meanwhile, re-exports to Taiwan and South Korea grew only 15% and 13% respectively, and Singapore took 8% fewer of Hongkong's re-exports.

But if Asian countries were taking proportionately less of the colony's re-exports, they were nonetheless the prime beneficiaries of Hongkong's appetite for imported goods. Imports from Singapore rose 34%, from Taiwan 31% and from South Korea 27%. But most stunningly, a 28% rise in imports from Japan, combined with stagnant domestic exports to Japan and only 21% rise in re-exports, produced a bilateral trade deficit which by September was running at about HK$56 billion, or roughly HK$1,000 per head of Hongkong's population.

If Hongkong's economic performance with the rest of the world looked worryingly weak, the domestic economy looked strong, with government economists expecting GDP growth for the year to reach about 4%, compared with 1990's rate of 2.4%. While unemployment rose only to an estimated 2.3% in the second quarter, per capita earnings climbed by leaps and bounds. By the second half of the year, workers in the manufacturing sector were taking home about 16% on average more than the previous year, while in construction take-home pay had risen 18%. The generally higher paid service sector fared less well, with a local oversupply in hotels coupled with a worldwide contraction in the financial-services industry leading to average per capita rises of 11%.

The higher earnings were reflected in higher spending. In January-July 1991, total retail sales were 12.9% higher in value and 5.7% higher in volume than the same period in 1990. Sales of clothing and shoes in July 1991 were 41.6% higher than in July 1990, while sales of consumer durables rose 29.9% in value and 23.4% in volume over the same period.

Under these circumstances, the large fiscal surpluses which the Hongkong Government had previously reaped from surging growth could have helped reduce the pressure on the economy by taking money, and demand, out of the economy. However, the combination of a taxation system which still relies almost exclusively on profits — highly sensitive to the rate of economic growth — and a failure of political nerve that scaled back proposed increases in indirect taxes, left the government struggling to balance its books.  □

# Data

**Major industries:** Clothing (except knitwear and footwear), US$2.46 billion (US$2.29 billion); basic metals, fabricated metal products, machinery and equipment, US$2.12 billion (US$1.97 billion); textiles (including knitting), US$1.83 billion (US$1.65 billion); electrical and electronic products, US$1.62 billion (same); plastic products, US$888 million (US$848 million).

**Major agriculture:** Vegetables, 112,000 tonnes (131,000); pigs, 413,000 head (536,000); chickens, 25,000 tonnes (26,200); eggs, 111.9 million (156.1 million).

**Mining:** Kaolin/feldspar sand, 16,587 tonnes (44,562); feldspar, 3,820 tonnes (5,152).

**Major imports:** Raw materials and semi-manufactured goods, US$31.88 billion (US$29.54 billion); consumer goods, US$31.76 billion (US$25.83 billion); capital goods, US$12.12 billion (US$10.81 billion); foodstuffs, US$4.74 billion (US$4.35 billion); mineral fuels, lubricants and related materials, US$2 billion (US$1.72 billion).

**Major exports:** Clothing, US$9.25 billion (US$9.21 billion); manufactured articles, US$3.42 billion (US$3.46 billion); photographic apparatus, equipment and supplies and optical goods, watches and clocks, US$2.75 billion (US$2.51 billion); electrical apparatus, machinery and appliances, US$2.21 billion (US$2.29 billion); telecommunications, sound recording and sound reproducing equipment, US$2.13 billion (US$2.06 billion).

**Tourism and transport:** Visitor arrivals, 5.9 million (5.46 million); visitor expenditure (est.) US$5.12 billion (US$4.59 billion).

(All figures for 1990 with 1989 figures in brackets, except major industries which for 1989 and 1988 respectively.)

**Currency:** Hongkong dollar (100 cents). HK$7.8 = US$1 (same).

**Finance:** Licensed banks, 166 (165); locally incorporated 30 (32); foreign banks representative offices, 155 (160); Stock Exchange of Hongkong, 293 companies listed (303).

**Major banks:** Hongkong and Shanghai Bank, tel. 8221111; Standard Chartered Bank, tel. 8203333; Bank of China, tel. 8266888; Hang Seng Bank, tel. 8255111; Citibank, tel. 8078211; Bank of East Asia, tel. 8423200; Bank of America, tel. 8475333; Security Pacific Asia Bank Ltd, tel. 8411811; Shanghai Commercial Bank, tel. 8415415; Overseas Trust Bank, tel. 5756657; Nanyang Commercial Bank, tel. 8520888.

**Government departments:** Major departments located in Central Government Offices, Lower Albert Rd, Hongkong. Finance, tel. 8102669; Economic Services, tel. 8102762; Banking Commission, 29/F, Queensway Government Offices, 66 Queensway, tel. 8672671, tlx 64282 COFB HX; Trade, 1-8 & 17-19/F, Trade Dept Tower, 700 Nathan Rd, Kowloon, tel. 3985333, tlx 45126 CNDI HX; Industry, 10, 14/F, Ocean Centre, 5 Canton Rd, Kowloon, tel. 7372573, tlx 50151 INDHK HX; Constitutional Affairs, tel. 8102684; Education and Manpower, tel. 8102630; Health and Welfare, tel. 8102637.

**Public holidays** (1992): 1 Jan. (New Year's Day), 4-6 Feb. (Lunar New Year), 17-20 Apr. (Easter), 4 Apr. (Ching Ming), 13-15 June (Queen's Birthday), 5 June (Tuen Ng), 29-31 Aug. (Liberation Day), 12 Sept. (Mid-Autumn Festival), 5 Oct. (Chung Yeung Festival), 25-26 Dec. (Christmas).

**Weather:** Hongkong's climate is sub-tropical, with the year broken into a hot summer and a cool, generally dry winter. Summer temperatures range from 26-32°C, with high humidity. Winter temperatures seldom fall below 10°C. Typhoons can affect Hongkong between Apr.-Dec., but are most frequent between July-Sept.

**Taxation:** Individual, 15%; corporate, 16.5%; unincorporated business, 15%.

# INDIA

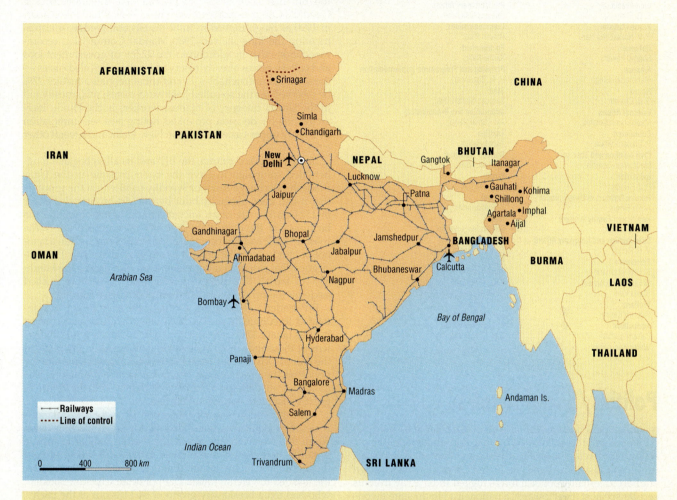

By the 1760s, Britain's East India Co. was ruler of Bengal and firmly lodged in the southern coastal region. Through conquest, the company extended its grip from Calcutta to as far as what is now northern Pakistan, while Bombay became another major centre of British trade and military power. The company's rule ended after the great revolt of 1857-58 in northern India, when it ceded power to the British crown.

The late 19th and early 20th centuries saw growing demands for independence, centred on the Indian National Congress, founded in 1885, and the All-India Muslim League, founded in 1906. The non-violent philosophy of Mahatma Gandhi provided the strategy that culminated in independence on 15 August 1947, though former British India and the native states were divided along predominantly Hindu-Muslim geographical lines into modern India and Pakistan.

The unresolved status of Kashmir became an immediate cause of war between India and Pakistan, and its end marked the start of the still-tense division of the territory along the truce line. Two other wars followed in 1965 and in 1971.

India's international stance of non-alignment was initiated by its first prime minister, Jawaharlal Nehru. However, relations with China were frozen for nearly three decades after Himalayan border disputes led to a short war in 1962.

Domestically, the Congress party has ruled for all but about four years since independence, but its monolithic grip has weakened steadily since Nehru's death in 1964. The imposition of emergency rule in 1975-77 by Nehru's daughter Indira Gandhi led to the ousting of Congress in the 1977 elections by a loose coalition under Moraji Desai. Gandhi regained power in 1980, but was murdered by Sikh bodyguards on 31 October 1984 to avenge the army storming the Sikh's Golden Shrine in Amritsar during a battle against Sikh separatists.

Her son Rajiv Gandhi succeeded her and was confirmed in a landslide election victory in December 1984. Mounting scandals, and the defection of senior Congress figures such as V. P. Singh, led to Gandhi's defeat by an anti-Congress coalition during the November 1989 elections. Singh formed a National Front-Left coalition that included the agrarian socialist Janata Dal, regional parties and leftists, with outside support from the Hindu revivalist Bharatiya Janata Party.

This administration collapsed a year later, and a Janata Dal splinter group under Chandra Shekhar formed a government with Congress support. The fall of this government in March 1991 preceded general elections in May-June. Rajiv Gandhi was assassinated on 21 May during the election campaign. Congress emerged with the most parliamentary seats, and though still short of a majority, formed a government under P. V. Narasimha Rao.

| | |
|---|---|
| **Head of State** | **Railways** |
| President R. Venkataraman. | C. K. Jaffer Sharief; |
| **Vice-President** | **Parliamentary Affairs** |
| S. D. Sharma; | Ghulam Nabi Azad; |
| **Prime Minister** | **Communications** |
| P. V. Narasimha Rao; | Rajesh Pilot; |
| **Defence** | **Environment** |
| Sharad Pawar; | Kamal Nath; |
| **Finance** | **Planning and Programme Implementation** |
| Manmohan Singh; | H. R. Bhardwaj; |
| **Home** | **Steel** |
| S. B. Chavan; | Santosh Mohan Deb; |
| **External Affairs** | **Information and Broadcasting** |
| Madhavsinh Solanki; | Ajit Kumar Panja; |
| **Commerce** | **Textiles** |
| P. Chidambaram; | Ashok Gehlot; |
| **Civil Aviation and Tourism** | **Surface Transport** |
| Madhavrao Scindia; | Jagdish Tytler; |
| **Industries** | **Power** |
| P. J. Kurien; | Kalpanth Rai; |
| **Human Resources Development** | **Labour** |
| Arjun Singh; | K. Ramamurthy; |
| **Health and Family Welfare** | **Mines** |
| M. L. Fotedar; | Balram Singh Yadav; |
| **Law, Justice and Company Affairs** | **Coal** |
| V. B. Reddy; | P. A. Sangma; |
| **Petroleum** | **Food** |
| B. Shankaranand; | Tarun Gogol; |
| **Urban Development** | **Food Processing Industries** |
| Sheila Kaul; | Giridhar Gomango; |
| **Welfare** | **Chief Justice** |
| Sitaram Kesari; | Rangnath Mishra; |
| **Agriculture** | **Chief of Army Staff** |
| Balram Jakhar; | Gen. S. F. Rodrigues. |
| **Water Resources** | |
| V. C. Shukla; | |

# Politics/Social Affairs

India experienced a year of convulsive change as many of the pillars of its political, economic and diplomatic edifices were undercut. Externally, these came through the collapse of the socialistic ideal and the Soviet Union, its chief foreign support. Internally, political forces tugged India away from its secular socialist ideal towards a nationalist Hindu state on one hand, and from its elitist reality towards a populist democracy of the lower-caste masses on the other.

The general elections called after the collapse of the minority Chandra Shekhar government on 6 March would probably not have resolved this question had they run their course without a tragic intervention. The assassination of Congress party leader and former prime minister Rajiv Gandhi on 21 May during the three days of polling abruptly changed the mood. After the solemnity of a state funeral, the electorate still to vote swung back perceptibly to Congress. The 106-year-old party increased its representation in the lower house of parliament and was called on to form a government.

In consensus leader P. V. Narasimha Rao — a former foreign minister not even in parliament and heading for retirement after a heart operation — the party found an unsuspected man of the hour. Prime Minister Narasimha Rao surprised all with his deft handling of Congress factions that left able reformists in key economic portfolios. This team turned Indian economic policy away from its post-independence autarkic trend towards market-based systems and integration with the global economy.

The period from the fall of the 11-month-old V. P. Singh government in November 1990 to the elections was marked by instability and paralysis at the centre, even as India drifted towards international bankruptcy. Singh's minority coalition of the National Front (NF, formed of Singh's own Janata Dal and various regional parties) and the Left Front of communists lost a vote of confidence in the lower house after the Hindu revivalist Bharatiya Janata Party (BJP) withdrew support.

The alliance of the intrinsically divergent NF, Left Front and the BJP had been based on mutual determination to oust Gandhi's Congress party in December 1989. It had fallen apart in 1990 as Singh moved to fulfil his election pledge of implementing the long-shelved 1980 Mandal Commission recommendations that in addition to the 22.5% of government jobs and college places already reserved for the scheduled castes — the so-called untouchables — and tribal peoples a further 27% be reserved for the so-called backward castes, who mostly fall in the *Shudra* category of manual workers in the Hindu hierarchy. Singh's decision provoked rioting and self-immolation by mostly upper-caste students in New Delhi and several other cities.

In an interlinked drama, the BJP and its allies began a long-heralded campaign to have the Babri mosque in the Uttar Pradesh pilgrimage town of Ayodhya shifted on the grounds that it had been allegedly built by the Muslim invader Babar in 1524 on the site of an ancient Hindu temple marking the birthplace of the deity Ram. The BJP raised this issue — the mosque itself had not been used for many years — into a symbol of Hindu humiliation and psychological slavery. The BJP argued that restoring a Ram temple would liberate the Hindu 83% of India's 844 million people, who were being pushed aside by the privileges of Muslims and other minorities.

BJP leader L. K. Advani's tour of the nation that was intended to culminate in Ayodhya was thwarted by his arrest by the Janata Dal state government in Bihar. Nevertheless, tens of thousands of Ram devotees converged on Ayodhya at the end of October and were beaten back from the mosque by police on the orders of the Janata Dal state government. The casualties — perhaps a score were killed, but the figure is greatly disputed — became martyrs.

With the Hindu majority inflamed by caste and religious issues, few politicians were anxious to see an election when Singh fell. Nor were the alternative parties willing to form a minority government themselves. After both Congress and the BJP refused an invitation from President R. Venkataraman, the task fell to veteran Janata Dal politician Chandra Shekhar, who had led a breakaway group of 54 MPs out of the party.

With Congress support, his Socialist Janata Party (SJP) formed an interim government that was expected to act as a puppet for Gandhi's Congress until such time as Gandhi felt confident enough to force an election. The Janata Dal state governments shifted sides to stay in power: in Uttar Pradesh, Chief Minister Mulayam Singh Yadav moved to the SJP to replace BJP backing with that of Congress, as did Chimanbai Patel in Gujarat. In Haryana, the government shifted with its patron Devi Lal, who jumped ship with Chandra Shekhar. In two other states where Janata Dal governed in its own right, Bihar's Lalloo Prasad Yadav and Orissa's Biju Patnaik stayed with Singh.

Chandra Shekhar performed the job with more aplomb and independence than Gandhi perhaps expected, while then finance minister Yashwant Sinha produced a budget that squarely tackled the runaway government deficit built up during Gandhi's 1984-89 tenure. While this was a condition of IMF balance-of-payments support, Gandhi hoped to postpone this electorally risky step by insisting instead on a 'vote-on-account' to keep the government running on existing lines for the first few months of the 1991-92 fiscal year (beginning April).

In early March, however, the situation changed after Gandhi took exception to the surveillance of Congress party headquarters by state police from SJP-controlled Haryana — ostensibly posted to watch for SJP defectors — and called a Congress boycott of the lower house. The opposition parties moved for a vote of confidence, and on 7 March Chandra

Shekhar announced he had offered his resignation and advised the president to call elections.

Although the president took a week to accept the advice, Chandra Shekhar's gambit was successful. Elections were called and Chandra Shekhar remained the head of a caretaker government. He, rather than Gandhi, had the advantage of incumbency with its control over government machinery, notably the state television and radio monopolies — the country's principal source of information.

The electorate was faced with three broad options. The BJP promised a government of discipline and unity that would reduce bureaucratic obstruction, act decisively and firmly against anti-national forces in Kashmir and other disturbed states, restore Hindu pride and push Indian interests more decisively abroad. A massive rally in New Delhi on 5 April showed that the Ram fervour was still a potent force. When several prominent civil servants, military figures and entertainers made public their support for the BJP, the party demonstrated its disciplined image had exposed dissatisfaction among the elite.

The Janata Dal camp under Singh looked at the social mathematics from a horizontal dimension, rather than the BJP's vertical view based on a divide between Hindus and Muslims. The backward castes falling under the Mandal-recommended reservations form about 52% of the population. Singh made Mandal the symbol of a long overdue recognition of the historic underlings of India, and he attempted to draw a common cause between the backward castes and the *Harijans*, or untouchables, who had traditionally looked to Congress for protection. This would be an unbeatable combination in the northern Hindi belt if it came off. Allies would clean up elsewhere: the Dravida Munnetra Kazhagam (DMK) in Tamil Nadu, the Telugu Desam Party (TDP) in Andhra Pradesh and the communists in West Bengal and Kerala.

**Narasimha Rao and Gandhi: unlikely heir to slain Congress leader.**

Congress was under attack in its traditional vote banks. Janata Dal was appealing to the Harijans, to Muslims through its defence of the Ayodhya mosque and to the backward castes usually directed to vote by pro-Congress upper caste landlords. Further, the BJP was drawing away disgruntled upper castes and sections of the Hindu urban bourgeoisie. Meanwhile, Gandhi's own image had not recovered from the various arms purchase scandals under his premiership, the party had failed to use its 18 months in opposition to weed out has-beens and opportunists, while Gandhi's indecisiveness about the election date added to questions about his competence and control of the party.

The first day of polling on 20 May showed heavy Congress losses in some of the most populous states. Its share of the vote dropped by 15% in Uttar Pradesh, by over 6% in Bihar and 8% in Andhra Pradesh. Conversely, in two states with incumbent BJP governments the Congress made gains: 2% in Rajasthan and 6% in Madhya Pradesh. Had this swing continued in the two later polling days then scheduled for 23 and 26 May, Congress would undoubtedly have seen up to 30 lower house seats shaved off the 194 it held before the elections, putting it close to parity with the BJP and the fractured Janata Dal–Left Front camp.

But on the evening of 21 May during last-minute campaigning in Tamil Nadu, a woman suicide assassin detonated a bomb hidden in a concealed belt as she presented a garland of flowers to Gandhi. He was killed instantly. That night, after meetings involving Venkataraman, Chandra Shekhar and Election Commissioner T. N. Seshan, the final rounds of voting were put off to 12 and 15 June, and New Delhi asked union and state security forces not to hesitate in clamping down on violent outbursts. The fear was that like the anti-Sikh pogrom in New Delhi after prime minister Indira Gandhi's murder by Sikh bodyguards in 1984, Congress supporters would wreak their revenge. But in Rajiv Gandhi's case, suspicion soon fell on the Liberation Tigers of Tamil Eelam (LTTE), the Sri Lankan secessionist group which was a force largely offstage in India.

Gandhi's death removed the focus of the Congress campaign, and a large coterie of personal hangers-on without a political base. The party found itself adrift after being dominated for much of its history by four generations of the Nehru-Gandhi dynasty. Gandhi's own children, son Rahul and daughter Priyanka, were too young to stand for parliament though immediate pressure came from this group for Gandhi's Italian-born widow Sonia to assume the party leadership. Although she declined, the party did not accept this decision as final. The choice then devolved on Narasimha Rao, but it was left unclear whether he would become party candidate for prime minister after the election.

Other parties now felt they had to mute the anti-Congress content of their campaign. The results of the last two days of polling showed a distinct sympathy swing towards Congress, though nothing like the sweep that had followed Indira Gandhi's assassination in 1984. In the states where polling took place both before and after Gandhi's death, the tide swung back to Congress — though in the crucial state of Uttar Pradesh the Congress vote was still down 8.4% on 1989.

In the event, Congress increased its representation from 194 of the 512 lower house seats occupied before the election, to 227 of the 510 seats filled in the election. However, the Congress' share of the vote fell by about 3.5%. The party was all but wiped out in the two biggest states of Uttar Pradesh and Bihar, where the BJP and Janata Dal respectively cleaned up. Congress improved its tally in the western state of Maharashtra, where Chief Minister Sharad Pawar emerged in control of Congress' largest state block of seats in the lower house. The sympathy factor helped Congress in the southern states of Karnataka, Tamil Nadu and Kerala, where it held the ground gained in the 1989 elections. But in Andhra Pradesh, its lower house seats fell from 38 to 24, while the TDP tally went up from two to 13. Congress gained in those seats where the BJP was in power at state level: Madhya Pradesh, Rajasthan and Himachal Pradesh.

The Congress fared well in two states where simultaneous elections were held for state assemblies. In Kerala, a Congress-backed coalition ousted a leftist state government. In Tamil Nadu, where the backlash over Gandhi's killing was strongest, the Congress-allied All-India Anna Dravida Munnetra Kazhagam (AIADMK) led by J. Jayalalitha reduced the Janata Dal ally DMK — accused of supporting the LTTE while in power — to a single seat in the state assembly.

For Janata Dal, the split in the party was extremely damaging. It lost badly in its former stronghold of Uttar Pradesh, where the BJP capitalised on the split vote and not only scooped up lower house seats but also won the simultaneous state elections. In the south, the party and its allies suffered from the pro-Congress sympathy vote — and in the case of Orissa from the usual anti-incumbent swing.

The BJP greatly increased its share of the vote and seat tally, to become the second-biggest block in the lower house with 119 seats against 84 before the elections. The achievement was all the more impressive because it had fought the campaign on its own, unlike in 1989 when it had a vote-sharing agreement with Janata Dal and other anti-Congress parties. Yet the party lost seats in those areas where it had governed — an ill omen for Uttar Pradesh, where a backlash next time could ruin its chances of forming a government in New Delhi.

Holding power in Uttar Pradesh posed an even more acute dilemma: the BJP state government of Chief Minister Kalyan Singh was sworn to defend the constitution and laws. It was now responsible for law and order at Ayodhya, and keeping the mosque intact while the Supreme Court heard a case concerning the site. While the BJP rank-and-file thought the party was now in a position to deal with Ayodhya, a wrong move could wreck the BJP's image for the next general election.

The Janata Dal was thrown into a prolonged crisis by its sharply reduced profile. Singh's leadership came under open attack by a section under Uttar Pradesh–based Ajit Singh which was clearly ready to defect to Congress once it had the requisite one third of party numbers to avoid disqualification from parliament under the anti-defection law. Narasimha Rao pointedly kept the industries portfolio in his cabinet empty as bait for Ajit Singh, who had held the job in the Singh government. Some in Janata Dal wanted Singh to abandon his stress on Mandal and caste-based equity in the Janata Dal structure itself. But Singh retained a core of party support led by the forceful young Harijan politician Ramvilas Paswan and Bihar Chief Minister Yadav.

For both the opposition groups, an emerging problem was that Congress as a political target had moved on. The tough restructuring budget and economic reform plans gave plenty of opportunities for populist agitation — though Congress went slow on the most difficult area of public-sector redundancies — but risked damaging the reputation for competence and responsibility Singh and Advani had built up as alternative prime ministers. Nor did they have anything in common any longer, except disassociation with Congress. This allowed the minority Narasimha Rao government to survive and pass its first budget in September by virtue of a walkout by both BJP and the Janata Dal–Left camp.

With this tacit truce virtually ending election threats until the end of 1991, political speculation centred on the direction of the Congress party itself. A section of the party still hoped Sonia Gandhi would contest her husband's vacant seat, and if she did, her inevitable election would create a rival power centre in the party. The most obvious alternative to Narasimha Rao was Sharad Pawar, who quit as Maharashtra chief minister and moved to New Delhi as defence minister after the election. Aviation and Tourism Minister Madhavrao Scindia, the hereditary maharaja of Gwalior — now part of Madhya Pradesh — also emerged as a potential leader. Narasimha Rao gave no sign of willingness to step aside, and gave every indication that he was chosen to complete the modernisation of

India as embarked upon by Rajiv Gandhi.

The economy was the central task of the government. But the disturbed states of Jammu and Kashmir, Punjab and Assam presented ever more intractable problems. Application of direct rule from New Delhi and heavy use of army and paramilitary forces pushed aside regional political structures and tended to widen political divisions.

Kashmir's insurgency continued, with Pakistan-backed Islamic fundamentalist groups taking a more prominent role in place of the pro-independence Jammu and Kashmir Liberation Front (JKLF). The new tactic of kidnapping prominent officials goaded New Delhi into ever fiercer security crackdowns. Although the new government talked of initiatives to revive the state's political process, it was clear that previous political forces such as the state-based National Conference party were completely discredited. The stalemate led some to suggest New Delhi's best option was to cultivate the JKLF, most of whose best-known leaders were in Indian jails.

Under pressure from the Chandra Shekhar government, election were called in Punjab for the first time since 1987. Congress and the Left parties, knowing they faced Sikh hostility, abstained. As the election date of 22 June approached, candidates contesting in the face of a boycott called by militant proponents of an independent Sikh state of Khalistan were being cut down by murder squads. A decision by New Delhi on the eve of the election to postpone the poll to 23 September led state governor O. P. Malhotra to resign in protest. But well before the new election date, it became known that legislation would be introduced to abandon the polls. President's rule was extended by another six months, and elections were promised by 15 February 1992.

In the tea and oil-rich eastern state of Assam, the general elections also ended nine months of president's rule imposed because of insurgency by the separatist United Liberation Front of Assam (ULFA). Army operations begun in November 1990 were called off in April after ULFA offered a truce. The elections saw Congress beating the local Asom Gana Parishad, which had previously ruled the state on a platform of excluding immigrants from neighbouring regions and enhancing state autonomy. The ULFA resumed its terrorist campaign by kidnapping officials, which provoked the return of the Indian army to offensive operations throughout the state. □

# Foreign Relations

Growing rapprochement between the US and the Soviet Union, the end of the Cold War and the fading of the Soviet state itself removed the familiar markers by which India had positioned itself since 1947. The Non-Aligned Movement (NAM), in which India had invested much hope, lost its relevance and New Delhi found itself increasingly on the periphery of world issues. The pre-election political atmosphere allowed little opportunity for any substantial rethinking of policies — and for much of the first half of 1991 India was without a foreign minister after the disqualification from parliament of V. C. Shukla.

India voted for and complied with the 1990 UN sanctions against Iraq, but many leaders and opinion-makers were profoundly uneasy at the concordance of Washington and Moscow in the Gulf crisis. Fears were expressed of a unipolar world in which weaker countries would be at the mercy of US arms and economic strength without a Soviet counterbalance.

The 19 August attempted coup in Moscow saw New Delhi promptly dump its often-proclaimed special friendship with President Mikhail Gorbachov. Prime Minister P. V. Narasimha Rao said it was a warning to those who pursued reform too quickly, a message some took as hinting that India should slow down its economic liberalisation. India's Foreign Ministry rebuffed Western pressure for India to join the international protest, and Minister of State for External Affairs Eduardo Faleiro said the coup was an internal affair of the Soviet Union. While the Indian Left openly rejoiced at the prospect of a hardline communist resurgence in Moscow, many government officials also saw it as beneficial to India. With Gorbachov's restoration, New Delhi quickly changed its tune, but India's standing with the new forces in the former Soviet republics was damaged.

The unravelling of the Soviet empire presented new challenges to India. The Central Asian republics were seen as open to a sweep of potentially hostile forces — Islamic fundamen-

Security: mixed signals from the Soviet Union.

talism, Pan-Turkic nationalism or competing ethnicities. The announcement in September by Washington and Moscow of a cut-off in military supplies to their Afghan clients from 1 January 1992 added to these worries about the northwest frontier and beyond. The example of a successful assertion of sovereignty was not lost on separatists in Punjab, Kashmir and Assam, and some Indians argued it required New Delhi to urgently address long-simmering questions about devolution of power to the states.

The impact of Soviet developments was felt on Indian foreign, security and economic policies. The 1971 Indo-Soviet treaty implicitly extended a Soviet umbrella against any US or Chinese nuclear threats. A parallel rupee-rouble trade agreement swapped Indian products for Soviet oil, minerals and paper, and let India's defence forces buy modern weapons with rupees. New Delhi renewed the expiring Indo-Soviet treaty for another 20 years only three weeks before the Moscow coup attempt.

Even before the coup, India was finding problems with the Soviet relationship. Military supply was the most pressing, as India's armed forces were reliant on the Soviet Union for at least 70% of their equipment — Kashin-class destroyers, Kilo-class submarines, TU142 patrol aircraft, Il76 transports, MiG29 and MiG27 fighters, T72 tanks and many types of missiles and ammunition. Soviet factories were demanding hard currency which India could not afford. Minister of State for Defence Krishna Kumar went to Moscow a few days before the coup in an effort to restore military spares to the rupee trade, and claimed to have secured agreement on 10 out of 13 crucial items. But the problem of getting factory directors to fulfil low-reward orders from India was expected to worsen as economic control shifted to the republics. India will now almost certainly have to pay hard currency for new weapons.

Civilian trade was also disrupted, to the extent that the rupee-rouble agreement might be wound up well before it is due to expire in 1995. The trade worked as long as Moscow could secure sufficient quotas of oil and other commodities for India from Soviet production units at the internal market's low official prices to match Indian shipments bought with an artificially high rouble. The increasing autonomy of Soviet republics and enterprises has now made this difficult. Oil, scrap metal, copper ore and paper shipments fell short of quota during 1991. India had a mounting bilateral surplus of Rs 27.1 billion (US$1.05 billion) in 1990-91 (April-March), for which the only use was to repay India's rouble debt for the steel mills, power plants and military equipment bought in the past, put at about Rbl 10 billion (US$17.13 billion).

Outwardly, ministers and officials alike asserted there was no basic problem with the Soviet relationship. Behind the scenes, however, cautious efforts were made to secure alternative sources of support. Although the US continued to remain the butt of popular rhetoric — and the two countries remained engaged in disputes about nuclear non-proliferation and intellectual property rights — the steady improvement of relations with Washington begun in the early 1980s continued. For example, the US adopted a low-key position on New Delhi's indecisiveness over granting then withdrawing permission for its military transport planes to refuel in India en route to the Gulf. Around the same time, US President George Bush cleared the export of a second Cray supercomputer to India for use in its space programme. Further, a vote in the US Congress to extend the Pressler amendment — which links US aid to fulfilment of nuclear non-proliferation standards — to India as well as Pakistan was later overturned.

In August, Indian Chief of Army Staff Gen. S. F. Rodrigues visited the US, and returned with a list of proposals for joint activities and cooperation with the US army. The commander-in-chief of the US Pacific Fleet, Adm. Charles Larsen, visited India in October to push for greater naval cooperation. The US also offered to sell India military equipment, including jet trainers, self-propelled artillery and heavy transport aircraft. The Indian Foreign Ministry, anxious not to compromise the country's official non-aligned stance, advised caution.

The government, meanwhile, began drafting a new foreign policy to match the more open economic strategy adopted after the elections. With the external affairs portfolio given to the low-key Madhav Sinh Solanki, economic ministers such as Finance Minister Manmohan Singh and Commerce Minister P. Chidambaram increasingly emerged as the external face of India. To avoid over-dependence on the US, India looked to Germany and Japan in particular. In his first foreign visit in office, Narasimha Rao visited Germany in September to open a Festival of India cultural exposition — intended as a prelude to closer trade and investment ties.

India's foreign relations with its regional neighbours were mixed. Tension rose and fell with Pakistan, which was perceived by New Delhi as pursuing a treacherous double-track policy based on promoting senior-level talks on various confidence-building measures, while simultaneously infiltrating separatist fighters into Kashmir and Punjab in a war by proxy. During the caretaker government's tenure in March-June, the Foreign Ministry dismissed out of hand Pakistan Prime Minister Nawaz Sharif's proposal for a five-nation discussion of a South Asia nuclear-free zone.

New Delhi struggled to keep rivalry with Pakistan from spilling across other areas of foreign policy. Preventing internationalisation of the Kashmir question was one effort, though many foreign governments believed the state's future should be settled bilaterally under the 1971 Simla agreement while a mounting chorus of Western legislators and human-rights groups argued for more creative approaches to this intractable problem.

Talks continued at the official level towards fixing the lengthy Himalayan border with China, but a decision in principle to re-open local crossing points after a nearly 30-year shutdown was not implemented by the time the mountain passes were closed by winter snows. India redressed a long-held Bangladesh grievance by agreeing to hand over the narrow Teen Bigha corridor of land, which had cut off a section of Bangladesh territory from easy access. However, accusations that Bangladesh was helping rebels in nearby eastern states showed continuing suspicion.

The assassination of Rajiv Gandhi led to a crackdown on Liberation Tigers of Tamil Eelam (LTTE) facilities in Tamil Nadu, while Indian naval forces stepped up patrols in the narrow Palk Strait between India and northern Sri Lanka where the LTTE is fighting for a separate homeland.   □

# Economy/Infrastructure

Growing fiscal and external imbalances brought India to the brink of default on foreign borrowings at the beginning of 1991. Economic management has been conducted in a state of virtual emergency in an effort to nurse along a precarious foreign-reserves balance. Nevertheless, from this dire situation emerged fresh impetus for economic restructuring, with reduction of the government's appetite for national savings the centrepiece of reform.

Economic growth slowed down in the 1990-91 (April-March) fiscal year from the boom of the late 1980s, but was still put at 5%. A third good monsoon in mid-1990 raised agricultural production by 4%, while booming domestic demand fed by increased availability of credit created an 8% jump in industrial production.

However, behind the domestic boom was mounting government domestic debt, equal to 55% of GDP by March 1991, which had been accumulated by central government deficits running over 8% of GDP during the late 1980s. Much of this deficit was monetised by the Reserve Bank of India (RBI, the central bank). Increased government spending increasingly went on maintaining establishments, consumer subsidies and financial support to loss-making public enterprises rather than into infrastructure and profitable investment. There was a massive government sequestering of bank deposits through reserve ratios totalling 53.5% and directed lending to assigned sectors of another 18.6%.

A mounting savings gap was covered by external borrowings. As at end March 1991, total long- and medium-term debt was estimated at US$51 billion as against US$16.4 billion in March 1980. Guaranteed bank deposits by non-resident Indians (NRI) added another US$10.4 billion, while short-term credits of less than one-year maturity totalled US$3.55 billion. The total debt of US$65 billion was about 23% of GDP, not large by Latin American standards but difficult to manage because of the recent reliance on NRI and short-term debt.

The crisis came with an increased oil import bill due to the Gulf War, which helped push the trade deficit out by US$667 million to US$8.44 billion in 1990-91. The Gulf conflict and domestic political violence also hit invisibles earnings, with an 8.8% drop in tourist arrivals in 1990-91, and direct foreign-investment approvals declined to less than US$100 million for the year. The flow of NRI deposits picked up initially during the crisis, but then turned to a sustained outflow. The import cover of foreign reserves fell to three weeks by the end of December 1990. Having drawn SDR 487 million from the IMF in July-September 1990 — its first resort to the IMF in nine years — India again went to the IMF in January 1991 for US$1.8 billion.

The IMF loans carried conditions. The minority Chandra Shekhar government drafted a budget which attempted to comply with deficit-cutting measures, but it fell in early March with only temporary finance arranged for the 1991-92 fiscal year. On 17 March, the RBI was empowered to take drastic measures to arrest a further decline in reserves. Savage loading of premiums on foreign exchange for imports and a raise in domestic interest rates created an instant import compression and slump in domestic consumer durables. An uneasy four months followed, with the RBI keeping India afloat by further IMF credits, Asian Development Bank and Japanese loans, a sale of confiscated smuggled gold and credit pledged against gold reserves shifted to the Bank of England.

The new Congress government formed after the May-June general elections gave economic reform top priority. The rupee was devalued by nearly 20% in two stages in early July. This slowed the outflow of NRI deposits, which had been running at about US$71 million a week over April-June, to about US$24 million a week over July and August.

In mid-July, Commerce Minister P. Chidambaram announced a sweeping simplification of the Indian foreign trade regime, which he said had led to "delays, waste, inefficiency and corruption." Essentially the new system links all but a few essential imports, such as oil, to earnings from exports. The vehicle for this was a second currency, called Exim scrip, which would be earned at the rate of 30% of export proceeds and be freely tradable. All import items would be progressively shifted to the open list. Export subsidies were withdrawn immediately, as Exim scrip — which fetches a market premium of 30% or more of face value — was deemed sufficient incentive. Chidambaram said the reform was aimed at making the rupee convertible on the trade account in three to five years.

On 24 July, the government simultaneously introduced a tough budget and a new industrial policy. Finance Minister Manmohan Singh said India had been "at the edge of a preci-

Foreign investment: ready for the real thing.

pice" for seven months, and that reform had to start in the government's own house. The budget aimed to cut the overall central government deficit from 1990-91's revised estimate of Rs 433.3 billion (US$16.8 billion) to Rs 377.3 billion, a reduction to 6.5% from 8.4% of GDP.

Measures to achieve this included a 40% increase in the subsidised fertiliser price, higher petrol and liquefied gas prices and steeper holding tax and levy rates. Total defence spending went up by only 3.8% to Rs 183.5 billion, implying a cut in real terms. Singh was forced to give some ground before the budget was passed in mid-September, but the Rs 10 billion added back was to be made up by a 5% spending cut ordered on all ministries.

Singh also announced several steps to attract NRI investment in property and bonds, and an amnesty for untaxed money lodged with the National Housing Bank. The RBI began studying proposals for a national gold bank or bond system to liquidise some of the estimated 10,000 tonnes of gold held privately.

The budget was put in context as the first step in a three-year financial reform that would reduce the government pressure on savings to a sustainable level of 3-4% of GDP in the third year. This was the level seen by a World Bank report as enabling reserve ratios on banks to be cut to 30% to restore commercial standards to a highly bureaucratic 90%-nationalised financial sector.

Industrial licensing was abolished for all sectors, save a list of 17 considered hazardous or polluting, strategic, or for elitist consumption. The Monopolies and Restrictive Trade Practices Act was stripped of provisions for all companies above a stipulated size to seek government clearance for any expansion or diversification of business. Foreign joint ventures were promised virtual automatic approval for foreign equity up to 51% in a wide range of designated priority sectors, as long as foreign equity covered the foreign-exchange requirements of start-up capital. In existing joint ventures where foreign equity was normally limited to 40%, similar approval for topping up to 51% was promised prompt approval. Submissions for foreign equity up to 100% would be considered on a case-by-case basis.

The new policy met with general approval, even from domestic industry associations. The strongest criticism was that the government failed to confront the problem of the so-called sick enterprises in the public sector. An accretion of regulations and court orders made it almost impossible for private companies to close failed operations or lay off redundant staff. Many of the 244 central government enterprises are uneconomic by commercial standards, as are hundreds of state enterprises. The government promised only that a new body similar to the Board of Industrial and Financial Reconstruction would be charged with revival/rehabilitation schemes for public enterprises, and that social-security schemes would look after affected workers.

The other widely noted problem was that India had decided to open up just as the global economy encountered a shortage of capital. In a world seemingly bent on dividing itself into regional trading blocks, India was left an economically isolated country that sought solace by arguing against the Gatt system along North-South lines.

New Delhi's policy changes received a cautious welcome from Western and East Asian business and government circles, though potential investors waited to see how the promised reduction of bureaucratic obstruction worked in practice. The IMF appeared largely satisfied with the budget reforms, though the reliance of some US$1 billion in asset sales to reduce the deficit was something not normally acceptable to the fund. Nevertheless, the IMF cleared a further US$635 million loan to India on 12 September. Negotiations started on a further US$2.2 billion stand-by credit to be released over an 18-month period starting in October.

At the annual meeting of the Aid-India Consortium, 13 countries and multilateral institutions pledged US$6.7 billion in assistance for 1991-92. This was a bare 7% increase on the previous year's level, but a significant recognition of India's foreign payment's plight was a decision that US$2.3 billion be given fast disbursement.

Just as India appeared to be out of immediate external difficulties and hoped to attract commercial loans that would allow remaining short-term debt to be refinanced with medium-term credits, the domestic economy headed for a downturn and stagflation as a result of the import and credit crunch. The finance ministry's July forecast of 4% growth for 1991-92 was followed in September by an RBI forecast of 3% growth, but even this appeared a shade optimistic despite a reasonably good 1991 monsoon. Inflation, meanwhile, jumped from around 12% in 1990-91 (by the wholesale price index) to an annual rate of 15.6% by late September.

Falling domestic oil production also brought new pressure on the trade balance. Because of mismanagement by the state-owned Oil and Natural Gas Corp. in the Bombay High offshore field and insurgency around the smaller Assam onshore fields, domestic output was expected to fall to 27 million tonnes from the 30.3 million tonnes in 1990-91 and 32.5 million tonnes in the peak year of 1989-90. Development of existing discoveries was held up for two years until late 1991 by political changes and bureaucratic hesitation. Meanwhile, Soviet deliveries of a pledged 4.5 million tonnes under the rupee-rouble trade agreement seemed likely to fall short by 700,000 tonnes in 1991-92.

Infrastructure came under strain as result of lagging investment in the late 1980s, particularly in electricity supply. The World Bank continued a moratorium on aid for new power projects, withholding some US$1.5 billion in previously sanctioned credits. It sought faster progress in commissioning new plants, tighter discipline in the collection of electricity charges from consumers and reduction of a 23% loss in power transmission. Finance Minister Singh said 13 of the 17 state electricity boards were running at a loss, with over US$2 billion in accumulated losses in March 1990. Only two returned the statutory minimum of 3% on net fixed assets. □

# Data

**Major industries:** Finished steel, 13.4 million tonnes (13 million); cloth, 20.35 billion m² (18.7 billion); cement, 48.8 million tonnes (45.8 million); nitrogenous fertilisers, 7 million tonnes (6.7 million); vehicles, 318,000 (317,200).

**Major agriculture:** Rice, 75 million tonnes (74 million); sugarcane, 233.4 million tonnes (222.6 million); raw cotton, 10.2 million bales (11.4 million); raw jute and mesta, 9 million bales (8.4 million); tea, 719 million kg (703 million).

**Oil and natural gas:** Crude, 33 million tonnes (34.1 million); gas, 18 billion m³ (17 billion).

**Mining:** Coal, 215.8 million tonnes (199 million); bauxite, 5.3 million tonnes (4.7 million); copper ore, 5.2 million tonnes (5.1 million); iron ore, 54 million tonnes (53 million); manganese, 1.4 million tonnes (1.3 million); limestone, 68 million tonnes (64 million).

**Major imports:** Gems and precious stones, US$2.35 billion (US$1.98 billion); petroleum and lubricants, US$2.24 billion (US$2.94 billion); iron and steel, US$1.28 billion (US$1.21 billion); capital goods, US$2.11 billion (US$3.65 billion); food and edible oils, US$1.17 billion (US$1.23 billion); fertiliser and fertiliser feedstock, US$986 million (US$642 million).

**Major exports:** Gems and jewellery, US$2.94 billion (US$2.98 billion); engineering goods, US$1.8 billion (US$1.6 billion); textiles and clothing, US$1.79 billion (US$1.37 billion); leather and leather goods, US$1.08 billion (US$1 billion) tea, US$502 million (US$414 million); iron ore, US$515 million (US$464 million).

(All figures for 1990-91.)

**Tourism and transport** (1990): Arrivals (excluding Bangladesh, Nepal and Sri Lanka), 1.4 million (1.2 million). Visitor spending, US$1.3 billion (US$1.5 billion).

**Currency:** Rupee (100 paise). Rs 25.81 = US$1 Nov. 1991 (Rs 18.09 = US$1 Nov. 1990).

**Finance:** 278 commercial banks, of which 24 are foreign. Public-sector bank branches 53,526 (51,004); private-sector bank branches, 4,163 (6,092); foreign bank branches, 140.

**Major banks:** State Bank of India, New Administrative Bldg, Madam Cama Rd, Bombay-400021, tel. 2022426/2045338, tlx 011-3813/3814; Central Bank of India, Chandramukhi, Nariman Pt, Bombay-400021, tel. 2026428, tlx 011-4428/2909; Bank of India, Express Tower, Nariman Pt, Bombay-400021, tel. 2026428, tlx 011-2208/2281/2983; Bank of Baroda, Baroda House, PO Box 506, Mandvi, Baroda-390006, tel. 555045, tlx 0175-204; Punjab National Bank, 7, Bikhaji Cama Place, New Delhi-110066, tel. 602303, tlx 72000/72193; Canara Bank, 112, J. C. Rd, PO Box 6648, Banglore-560002, tel. 220490/221581, tlx 0845-205/8075; New Bank of India, 1 Tolstoy Marg, New Delhi-110001, tel. 3314854/3311574, tlx 031-66867/66920.

**Government ministries:** Prime Minister's Office, South Block, New Delhi-110011, tel. 3018939, fax 3016857; Agriculture, Krishi Bhavan, New Delhi-110011, tel. 382711, tlx 31-65054; Finance, North Block, New Delhi-110011, tel. 3015510, tlx 31-66175; Industry, Udyog Bhavan, New Delhi-110011, tel. 3011589, tlx 31-66565; Commerce, Udyog Bhavan, New Delhi-110011, tel. 3014667, tlx 31-65970.

**Taxation:** Individual income tax comes into effect at Rs 20,000 a year. From Rs 22-30,000 tax is at 20%. From 30-50,000 at 30% plus Rs 1,600. From Rs 50-100,000 40% plus Rs 7,600. Above Rs 100,000, 50% plus 12% surcharge on the amount exceeding Rs 75,000 plus Rs 27,600. Corporate tax is levied at 45% for "widely held" companies, 50% for "closely held" companies. A 15% surcharge was continued in 1991-92. For foreign companies, royalties and fees from Indian concerns under an approved agreement are 30% on agreements signed after 31 Mar. 1976, 65% on agreements signed before that date.

# INDESIA

The Hindu and Buddhist kingdoms that developed in Sumatra and Java from the 7th century succumbed in the 14th century to the slow advance of Islam. European incursion began in the 16th century, led by the Portuguese who built fortresses in the Moluccas to protect their lucrative spice trade.

The Portuguese were replaced in the 17th century by the Dutch, who began the gradual subjugation of Java and other islands which they completed in the 19th century.

The Dutch did much to foster the economic development of Java, albeit mainly through the oppressive "cultural system" — the forced cultivation of cash crops. Dutch rule effectively ended when Japanese forces occupied the archipelago in early 1942.

During the subsequent three years of Japanese military rule, nationalist groups were able to organise and, on Japan's surrender, declared independence from the Netherlands on 17 August 1945. Dutch-held West New Guinea was incorporated into Indonesia as Irian Jaya in 1963 and the former Portuguese colony of East Timor followed in 1976.

Sukarno became president of the new Indonesian republic and proclaimed a unitary state on 15 August 1950 after the Dutch ended their efforts to reimpose colonial rule.

Sukarno, a flamboyant, populist leader who maintained ties with the local communists and China, pursued a military campaign of "confrontation" against Malaysia in the early 1960s.

His administration, known mainly for its extravagance and inefficiency, was toppled by military leaders led by Gen. Suharto following what was apparently an abortive communist coup in September 1965.

Suharto, inaugurated as president in 1968, has sought to diversify the economy away from dependence on primary — mainly oil — production towards greater industrialisation while keeping a firm grip on the levers of political power.

**Head of State**
President Suharto.
**Vice-President**
Sudharmono.
**Coordinating Minister for Political and Security Affairs**
Sudomo;
**Coordinating Minister for Economic, Financial and Industrial Affairs**
Radius Prawiro;
**Coordinating Minister for People's Welfare**
Soepardjo Roestam;
**Home Affairs**
Rudini;
**Foreign Affairs**
Ali Alatas;
**Defence and Security**
Gen. L. B. Murdani;
**Justice**
Ismail Saleh;
**Information**
Harmoko;
**Finance**
J. B. Sumarlin;
**Trade**
Arifin Siregar;
**Industrial Affairs**
Hartato;
**Agriculture**
Wardojo;
**Forestry**
Hasjrul Harahap;
**Mines and Energy**
Ginandjar Kartasasmita;
**Public Works**
Radinal Mochtar;
**Communications**
Azwar Anas;
**Cooperatives**
Bustanil Arifin;
**Manpower**
Cosmas Batubara;
**Transmigration**
Soegiarto;
**Tourism, Post and Telecommunications**
Soesilo Soedarman;
**Education and Culture**
Fuad Hassan;

**Health**
Adhyatma;
**Religious Affairs**
Munawir Sjadzali;
**Social Affairs**
Haryati Soebadio;
**State Secretary**
Murdiono;
**National Development Planning**
Saleh Afiff;
**Research and Technology**
B. J. Habibie;
**Population and Environment**
Emil Salim;
**Public Housing**
Siswono Yodohusodo;
**Youth and Sport Affairs**
Akbar Tandjung;
**Administrative Reforms**
Sarwono Kusumaatmadja;
**Women's Affairs**
A. S. Murpratomo;
**Cabinet Secretary**
Saadillah Mursjid;
**Attorney-General**
Singgih;
**Chief Justice**
Ali Said;
**Commander of the Armed Forces**
Gen. Try Sutrisno;
**Army Chief of Staff**
Gen. Edi Sudradjat;
**Head of State Intelligence Board**
Maj.-Gen. Sudibyo.

# Politics/Social Affairs

The run-up to general elections scheduled for June 1992 dominated Indonesia's political milieu during 1991. Groups in parliament, the bureaucracy and the armed forces jockeyed for position throughout the year, while issues ranging from economic policy and press freedom to immigration rules became, in a sense, proxy referenda on President Suharto's rule.

Nine months after the general elections, the 1,000-member People's Representative Council (MPR) will meet to select a president for the period 1993-98. Suharto, who will be 72 and have been in power for more than 25 years by the time the MPR convenes, is thought by many analysts to be keen for another term.

In any case, the base of Suharto's political support seems secure. Indonesia's two main power centres — the armed forces (Abri) and the Islamic community — remain institutionally committed to him, though elements of each are eager for change at the top.

Observers noticed Suharto's continuing efforts to install military officers close to him in top positions. Early in the year, he appointed his former adjutant, Lieut-Gen. Kunarto, as chief of police. Since 1988, two other former Suharto adjutants, Gen. Try Sutrisno and Maj.-Gen. Kentot Harseno, have risen to become armed forces commander and Jakarta military garrison chief, respectively. Maj.-Gen. Wismoyo Arismunandar, Suharto's brother-in-law who currently commands Kostrad, the strategic reserve, is tipped for further promotion before the elections.

Political activity in Indonesia's rural areas — where some two thirds of the country's 180 million population live — is mostly channelled through the bureaucracy and does not pose a threat to the Jakarta establishment.

One exception to this was found in Aceh, the northern-most province of Sumatra, where the government waged a bitter campaign against a secessionist group fighting for an independent Islamic state. Sustained military activity between the rebels and army ceased around mid-year, though before that the government was sharply criticised by human-rights activists and lawyers who accused Abri of widespread abuses, including torture. More than 1,000 people are believed to have died in the 18-month conflict.

Attention was also again focused on East Timor after Indonesian soldiers opened fire on a crowd gathered at a cemetery in the capital Dili on 11 November, killing as many as 100 people and wounding many others. Abri officially announced that 19 died in the clash, 91 were wounded and 308 detained.

The army, which described the demonstration as "brutal and violent," said soldiers opened fire on the crowd — who had gathered to call for independence — in order to protect themselves. However, foreign and Timorese eyewitnesses described the demonstration as orderly and disciplined, and said the army fired directly into the densely packed crowd without warning or provocation.

Most commentators believe the order to fire did not come from senior Indonesian army officers. Brig.-Gen. R. S. Warouw, the senior military officer in East Timor, appeared pale and shaken at a 14 November news conference and told the REVIEW he was ashamed at what had happened. There were subse-

quent reports that a second massacre had taken place on 15 November, when troops executed up to 100 people, according to East Timorese exiled in Australia. These unconfirmed killings were linked to efforts to suppress information about the earlier deaths in Dili.

While remote, predominantly Catholic East Timor largely remains a sideshow in domestic politics, events there are closely monitored by the international community and the killings are likely to reactivate pressure on Jakarta to account for its actions since it annexed the former Portuguese colony in 1976.

In late 1990, several cabinet ministers indicated a tolerance for a freer climate of expression in Indonesia, while Suharto encouraged Indonesians to become more creative and "dynamic." The season of openness, or *keterbukaan*, got off to a bad start in late 1990, when the government shut down several satirical plays, closed a newspaper and denied a well-known poet approval to read his poems. The first half of 1991, however, saw a resurgence of public debate in the press, parliament and non-governmental groups on such issues as land ownership, press freedom, the environment and government-imposed restrictions on speech and overseas travel by dissidents.

In April, 45 prominent intellectuals established the Forum of Democracy to promote discussion of democratic values and institutions. The forum was headed by Abdurrahman Wahid, the influential leader of the 35-million-strong Nahdlatul Ulama (NU), Indonesia's largest Muslim organisation. In the following months, two similar groups were established, one by veteran human-rights campaigner H. J. C. Princen and the second by former Asean secretary-general, retired lieutenant-general H. R. Dharsono.

Suharto: expected to soldier on.

Indonesia's most well-known collection of dissidents, the Group of 50, rejoined the country's public debate after a decade of being relegated to the political wilderness. In 1980, the group — which includes several prominent former military figures — complained that Suharto's autocratic style of leadership was a threat to Indonesian democracy. They were subsequently forbidden to travel abroad and the press was told not to publish their names or pictures.

In late 1990 the press was allowed to mention Group of 50 members, though the travel ban remained in place. The dissidents, unofficially led by former Jakarta mayor and retired lieutenant-general Ali Sadikin, lobbied for greater political liberalisation and made news by criticising a series of government decisions, including the extension of their own travel ban.

In July and August, Indonesia's three political parties — Golkar, the Indonesian Democratic Party and the United Development Party — finalised their candidate lists for the general elections scheduled for June 1992. Golkar's list became a subject of controversy in September when it became apparent that the Golkar leadership — reportedly under instructions from Suharto — had removed the names of some of the most outspoken members of parliament.

Also in September, Indonesia's Attorney-General Singgih banned the circulation of four books, including Yoshihara Kunio's *The Rise of Ersatz Capitalism in Southeast Asia*, which was translated into Indonesian in September 1990. Singgih said the book discredited Suharto and the armed forces.

Suharto's apparent interest in serving another term as president has focused extra attention on the vice-presidential post. Many observers believe Vice-President Sudharmono will step down in 1993, and Try is the leading candidate to fill the position. Other names often mentioned are Home Affairs Minister Rudini and Minister for Research and Technology B. J. Habibie.

Suharto also made a concerted effort to strengthen his links with the Islamic community. The most visible sign was the formation of the Association of Muslim Intellectuals (ICMI), originally established in December 1990. Members of ICMI include several high-ranking government officials and leaders of several major Islamic groups and is chaired by Habibie.

One notable absentee from ICMI was Wahid, who said he was wary of seeing Islam become too politicised. Many Indonesian Muslims, frustrated by the steady marginalisation of Islam from political power during Suharto's rule, welcomed the new association. Others, however, were more critical and voiced the fear that ICMI could be used by Suharto to co-opt Islamic-based dissent without bringing Islamic concerns any closer to the centre of Indonesia's policymaking circles.

In May, Suharto made his first pilgrimage to Mecca. In August, he announced he would contribute Rps 3 billion (US$1.53 million) as start-up capital to Bank Muamalat Indonesia, the first Indonesian Islamic bank. Suharto also said he would persuade other wealthy Muslims to contribute to the bank, which needs initial capital of Rps 10 billion to comply with banking laws.

Suharto's efforts to placate the Muslim community, however, were challenged when some 2,000 youths demonstrated in the West Java city of Bandung on 9 November against a state-sponsored lottery. While the demonstration ended peacefully and with no arrests, it highlighted the frustration felt by some elements within the Islamic community over government priorities.

Public discussion of the lottery, known as the Philanthropic Donation with Prizes, has become increasingly strident over the past six months. Islamic groups say the lottery is equivalent to gambling, which is prohibited by Indonesian as well as Islamic law. The government contends it needs the money raised by the lottery to fund sporting events, welfare programmes and disaster relief efforts.

In July, Minister for Social Affairs Haryati Soebadio overrode Islamic protests and pushed ahead with a plan to allow nine supplemental lottery drawings in the last six months of the year.

In the following months, Islamic schools, universities and student groups began returning funds received from the foundation which administers the lottery. A dispute over the propriety of accepting money from the lottery foundation had riven the NU. The foundation said an NU-sponsored school in East Java agreed to accept a donation from the lottery funds, an admission which caused one senior NU leader to resign and put NU chairman Wahid in a tight spot.

The escalation of opposition to the lottery is politically embarrassing for Suharto, and some analysts view the dispute as a test case for his relations with Indonesia's Islamic community.

Tensions between ethnic Chinese businessmen and their indigenous, or pribumi, counterparts rose during the year. At the centre of the debate was the contention by pribumi businessmen that the government in general and Suharto in particular had shown favouritism to Indonesian-Chinese businessmen in allocating government contracts. Suharto, several of the more influential pribumi businessmen claimed, had helped Chinese-run groups like Liem Sioe Liong's Salim Group grow into major conglomerates without doing the same for pribumi-run enterprises.

Among Suharto's senior ministers, Try and Minister for Mines and Energy Ginanjar Kartasasmita are said to be the most sympathetic to pribumi businessmen's concerns. An army seminar in December 1990 debated the issue at length.

A tight monetary policy introduced by the central bank in mid-1990 aggravated the situation by reducing the supply of domestic credit to the private sector. Many of the ethnic Chinese–controlled groups, who collectively dominate Indonesia's private business sector, were able to ease their funding shortages by borrowing from abroad, an alternative not available to most pribumi-owned businesses.

Consequently, the government came under pressure to restore subsidised credit programmes to help smaller businesses. In addition, the most important pribumi businessmen appealed to the government to consider implementing a variant of Malaysia's race-based wealth distribution programme known as the New Economic Policy (NEP). These businessmen were convinced that the government would have to play a stronger role in alleviating tensions between social groups.

In a speech commemorating independence day in August, Suharto affirmed the government's commitment to ensuring equitable development for all sections of society while specifically rejecting the possibility of imposing new policies which overtly distinguish between races.

"Our constitution guarantees equal status to our citizens before the law and the government," Suharto said on 16 August. "It would be erroneous if, among us, as a nation, there were still those who had the attitude of making distinctions because of narrow-minded reasons, such as ethnic origin, race, social status, religion, etc."

Ethnic Chinese businessmen are not alone as a source of resentment. Many businessmen complained that several of Suharto's children enjoy unfair advantages in securing government licences and credit from state-owned banks.

While consideration of programmes such as Malaysia's NEP has been effectively sidelined for the time being, political analysts say the subject of privileged businessmen is likely to remain a potent issue in the run-up to the elections.  ☐

# Foreign Relations

The foreign affairs highlight for Indonesia in 1991 should have been its election in September to chair the 103-nation Non-Aligned Movement (NAM) for the 1992-95 period. However, the massacre in East Timor on 11 November, and subsequent reports of a second wave of killings a few days later, overshadowed the country's relations with many countries within the region and beyond.

Reaction to the killings from Indonesia's most important trading partners was strong. Australia, the US and Japan have all expressed concern and urged a full investigation, as did the UN and the International Committee of the Red Cross. Sanctions, such as cuts in military and perhaps other forms of aid, were called for in some Western legislatures if it were found the killings were unprovoked.

International condemnation elicited a strong response from Jakarta. Indonesian armed forces (Abri) commander Gen. Try Sutrisno said that while he regretted the killings, they were an internal matter. He also rejected criticism about human-rights violations, and was reported to have said that "Indonesia is a member of the UN Human Rights Commission. There is no doubt about human rights in Indonesia."

The standing of Foreign Minister Ali Alatas, who had lobbied to have a Portuguese parliamentary team visit East Timor — a former Portuguese colony annexed by Indonesia in 1976 — has also been weakened, analysts said. The visit, scheduled for November, was cancelled after a dispute over which journalists could accompany the Portuguese party. The UN continues to treat Portugal as the administrative power in East

Timor, and most Western countries have not officially recognised Indonesia's take-over. The proposed visit and its subsequent cancellation was seen by some observers to have led to the heightened level of tension in East Timor that formed a backdrop to the killings.

Some fear that the army may again close the province and crack down on all signs of opposition. This would be a major setback for officials like Alatas who have pushed for more openness.

Political ties between Indonesia and the EC, already strained as several European nations broached the possibility of making aid and trade with Asean conditional on improved human rights and environmental protection, are likely to sour further in the wake of the killings. Insurgencies in Aceh as well as East Timor lent weight to these efforts. In May, Dutch Minister for Development Johannes Pronk, who also chairs Indonesia's multinational aid forum, caused a stir by nudging Indonesia to quicken its pace of democratisation.

Alatas, who succeeded in making Indonesia a member of the Geneva-based Human Rights Commission in January, warned that Western countries who attempted to link aid with changes to the political systems of recipient nations would fail.

"We are all for democratisation . . . but we reject the notion that there is only one form of democracy, the Westminster or American style. That flies in the face of another right — of a people to choose their own political and social systems," Alatas said in an interview in July.

The East Timor killings also removed some of the lustre attached to Indonesia's status as the new NAM chairman. Having been denied the NAM chairmanship in the movement's two previous summit meetings, Indonesia is now due to host the NAM's 10th summit in Jakarta, probably in September 1992. Alatas, who had lobbied behind the scenes for the NAM chairmanship, said he would focus the movement's attention on international economic relations and on new forms of South-South cooperation.

**East Timor: back on the agenda.**

Political analysts said Alatas is likely to try to use the NAM platform to show off several of Indonesia's development policies as models for the developing world. The two most obvious choices, they said, were Indonesia's successful food self-sufficiency effort and its widely praised family planning programme.

The NAM, founded 30 years ago with Indonesia as a founding member, existed primarily to offer countries a third alternative to the world's two superpowers. In the aftermath of the Cold War, however, members spent much of a September conference in Ghana debating the movement's new priorities. The emphasis for the future, Alatas said, was on "cooperation instead of confrontation." Indonesia's non-aligned credentials were tested in the early part of the year when it came under pressure to take sides in the Gulf War. Home to the world's largest Muslim community, Indonesia has, under President Suharto, leaned towards the West on matters of military and political cooperation. It did not join the multilateral coalition which drove Iraqi forces from Kuwait, but it also turned a deaf ear to pleas from some groups to support Baghdad.

In early June, Alatas made another attempt at bringing rival Cambodian factions together in a bid to overcome remaining obstacles to peace in Indochina. The aim of the Jakarta talks had been to find common ground between Phnom Penh Prime Minister Hun Sen and the Khmer Rouge–dominated tripartite resistance on a draft agreement for peace in Cambodia which had been hammered out earlier by the five permanent members of the UN Security Council.

Little progress was made, much to Alatas' exasperation, and Indonesia — which has expended a great deal of energy in recent years in bringing the various Cambodian factions together for talks — was largely left out of the picture later in the year when the factions reconvened first in Thailand and then in Paris, where a peace treaty was signed in October.

Indonesian diplomats tackled another regional dispute in July, when senior officials from 10 Asian nations attended a meeting in the West Java city of Bandung to discuss sovereignty of the Spratly Islands in the South China Sea. Six nations claim all or some of the islands. Little in the way of concrete action was expected or achieved from the meeting, but the delegates did agree not to use force to settle their claims.

On the broader issue of regional economic cooperation, Malaysia's Prime Minister Datuk Seri Mahathir Mohamad made news in December 1990 by putting forward a blueprint for an East Asian Economic Group (EAEG), a rival grouping to the larger and older Asia Pacific Economic Cooperation (Apec). Unlike Apec, the EAEG excludes Canada and the US and is perceived as being closer to a trade bloc.

The debate over the EAEG came to the fore in March at an Asean conference in Bali. Mahathir offered a ringing defence of his proposal while Suharto, among others, implicitly rejected the EAEG framework by renewing support for Apec and its emphasis on cooperation rather than confrontation.

Differences over regional trading arrangements was not the only point of friction between the two neighbours. Over the course of the year, Indonesian diplomats and military officials criticised what they called Malaysia's tacit support for rebels fighting for an independent, Islamic state in Aceh province on the northern tip of Sumatra.

Indonesia and Malaysia also found themselves in disagreement in mid-year over two disputed islands off the east coast of Borneo. Indonesia was offended that Malaysia had developed one of the islands into a tourist resort before territorial issues had been settled.

Finally, Indonesian leaders were unhappy with Malaysia's encouragement of indigenous Indonesian businessmen who visited Kuala Lumpur to study Malaysia's race-based wealth distribution programme known as the New Economic Policy.

Jakarta's relations with Singapore strengthened in 1991. The Indonesia-Singapore axis of the so-called growth triangle, a Singapore-devised plan to link the economies of Singapore, Malaysia's Johor state and Indonesia's Riau Islands, made solid progress during the year. Several industrial estates on Batam Island accepted their first tenants in 1991, many of them from Singapore.

Meanwhile, development of nearby Bintan Island began in earnest. In June, Indonesia signed a long-term contract to sell Singapore 60 million gallons of water a day collected from catchment areas on Bintan.

# Economy/Infrastructure

Indonesia's economic planners spent the better part of 1991 coping with stresses caused by rapid growth in 1989-90. Corrective measures were taken in response to some of the most serious problems and most businessmen said they remained bullish on Indonesia's long-term prospects.

But massive new investment in 1989-90 has seriously strained infrastructure and government services, leading many economists to forecast lower economic growth in 1991-92 than the 7.4% expansion of GDP recorded in both 1989 and 1990.

One of Indonesia's most pressing concerns is to upgrade essential infrastructure such as roads, ports, power plants and telecommunications networks. Another task is to rein in a surging inflation rate brought about by runaway growth in the money supply. To accomplish this, the government in 1991 forced up commercial lending rates to more than 30%, thereby convincing many would-be investors to postpone or cancel their investment plans.

One of Indonesia's most attractive features for investors is a lack of foreign-exchange controls. But the downside to an open capital account became apparent to policymakers as they struggled to gain control of money supply. Many of Indonesia's largest businesses were able to sidestep the government's efforts to slow down credit growth by borrowing offshore.

Bankers estimate that Indonesian companies borrowed about US$7 billion overseas in 1990 and will borrow at least that amount again in 1991. The borrowing binge pushed up Indonesia's total foreign debt to US$66 billion by the end of March, according to the IMF.

The government took firmer action to screen new foreign borrowing. A presidential decree dated 4 September established a Foreign Commercial Debt Team consisting of 10 cabinet ministers. In future, all projects connected in any way with the government or with state-owned enterprises, need approval from this team before seeking funds in the international capital markets.

Economists welcomed the move, saying it would help restore confidence in Indonesia as a credit risk. The government has a high credit rating among bankers as it has never sought to reschedule its loans, even during times of domestic austerity.

But bankers are less sure about the viability of private firms, many of which borrowed heavily for expansion plans in 1989-90. Cigarette manufacturer Bentoel threw a scare into bankers in July when it announced it was suspending payments on its US$370 million debt. Bentoel's advisers are negotiating a restructuring plan with the company's creditors.

A major concern for investors is the state of Indonesia's infrastructure. By the middle of 1991, new investors in West Java were unable to secure supplies of electricity from the government power utility, PLN. A decree easing imports of diesel generators improved the situation somewhat, but only at a higher cost to manufacturers.

To help meet demand for new power plants, the government announced it would encourage private firms to participate in the construction and operation of new power stations. A PLN official said in September that 100 private firms had expressed interest in investing in power generation facilities. The official projected private firms would account for about 45% of the 11,000 MW of new power generating capacity scheduled to be built in 1993-98.

In January the government awarded both American Telephone and Telegraph and NEC of Japan contracts to supply switching equipment for 350,000 new telephone lines. Both companies chose as local manufacturing partners firms owned by President Suharto's children.

A slowdown in non-oil export growth and an increase in imports and interest payments combined to push up Indonesia's current-account deficit. Non-oil exports in 1990 rose 6.7% against 21.5% a year earlier, while non-oil imports jumped 25.4% in 1990, following 19% the year before. The result was a doubling of the current-account deficit to US$3.7 billion for the fiscal year ending in March. Economists believe Indonesia's current-account deficit will rise sharply again to US$5-6 billion in fiscal 1992.

The government remains committed to further deregulation of the economy and to the promotion of private-sector–led growth. Reform has gone furthest in the financial sector. In addition, the government is chipping away at non-trade barriers and other restrictions on the productive sector, though many restrictions remain in such industries as plywood, rattan, automobiles and several agricultural products.

In June, Indonesia issued a new deregulation package which removed non-tariff barriers on 322 items and freed the export of palm and coconut oil. In addition, the package lowered tariff rates on 562 items and reduced the maximum import tariff on finished goods from 40% to 30%. Also in June, Indonesia agreed to allow more imports of foreign films, a point of some contention with the US.

The Inter-Governmental Group on Indonesia, a foreign donors' club that meets annually in the Netherlands, helped ease Indonesia's funding shortfall by pledging in June US$4.75 billion in aid for the current fiscal year, a 5.3% increase over the previous year's commitment. Japan and the World Bank contributed more than half of the total.

The Gulf War, in one respect, was a boon for Indonesia. Higher-than-budgeted oil and gas revenues dropped an extra US$4 billion into state coffers in fiscal 1991. Indonesia, the world's 14th-largest oil producer, signed a record number of production sharing contracts in 1987-90. At least 22 others were expected to be signed in 1991.

Exploration expenditures reached an estimated US$2.3 billion in 1991, 80% higher than the year before, according to the US Embassy's annual *Petroleum Report*. Nonetheless, at current rates of consumption and production, Indonesia is likely to become a net oil importer by the end of the century.

Natural gas, however, will be one of Indonesia's major export earners for many years to come. Production has grown an average 7.5% annually since 1981 to total 62.3 m$^3$ in 1991, the report said. Indonesia, already the world's largest exporter of liquefied natural gas, aims to reach a sustained export level of 30 million tonnes a year by 2010. That amount would be equivalent, in export revenue terms, to 90% of 1990's crude oil exports.

Non-oil investment grew strongly in 1991, according to approvals granted by the Investment Coordinating Board (BKPM). The board approved some US$6.5 billion in new investment in the first half of 1991, against US$8.7 billion in 1990. However, BKPM officials warned that many of the projects may not be implemented as scheduled because of infrastructural constraints — especially power — and high interest rates.

Nevertheless, production and export of rubber, wood products, shoes, textiles, chemicals and industrial machinery were up in 1991. One area set back by the Gulf War was tourism. 1991 was officially designated Visit Indonesia Year, but hostilities in the Middle East caused tourist traffic to plummet in the first half.

A large part of the new investment into Indonesia in the past three years has gone into labour-intensive industries such as shoes, electronics, garments and textiles. In 1991, the frequency of labour disturbances in these industries rose sharply. The worst affected areas were the industrial satellite towns which have spread around major cities such as Jakarta,

Surabaya and Semarang.

Only one labour union is recognised by the government though another, unofficial labour organisation, the Solidarity Free Trade Union, was established in late 1990. The chief complaint by workers and labour activists was that many firms continued to pay below the government-set minimum wage which, in most parts of the country, averages less than US$1 a day.

In response to a growing number of strikes, Coordinating Minister for Politics and Security Sudomo in August called on the armed forces to use troops to stop labour unrest from becoming "intolerable." Other government officials appealed for a less confrontational approach. Labour activists said employee relations would deteriorate unless the government made a greater effort to enforce laws on wages and other worker benefits.

Environmental awareness increased in 1991, helped by the formation in late 1990 of a new environmental protection agency, known as Bapedal. The Ministry for the Environment had earlier issued new national standards for water effluents in a bid to clean up Indonesia's major rivers. Bapedal is also working on new air emission standards.

Deforestation remains one of Indonesia's chief environmental concerns. The World Bank estimates Indonesia is losing about 1 million ha of tropical forest annually to loggers, fires and "slash and burn" cultivators. Huge fires in parts of Kalimantan and Sumatra, that spread a smoke-based haze over large areas of Southeast Asia in the latter part of the year, further underlined the extent of the problem. The government is considering granting a private company a contract to monitor forestry concession areas. Environmentalists hope such a move will force loggers to comply with tree-felling limits and enable the government to collect more fees for reafforestation.

The government's plans for regional development moved

**Timber: chainsaw massacre.**

forward most noticeably in the Riau Islands off Sumatra. The islands of Batam and Bintan represent the Indonesian corner of the so-called growth triangle which also includes Singapore and southern Malaysia.

In Batam, several industrial estates began accepting tenants in 1991, mostly in electronics and basic manufacturing. Nearby, in Bintan, another industrial estate began construction while planning started for a 10,000-ha tourist development project. Disputes over land clearance, however, may delay the tourism project. On both islands, Liem Sioe Liong's Salim Group is the principal private developer.

Probably the most serious hurdle facing Indonesia's economic policymakers is to ensure an equitable distribution of benefits to society. In 1990-91 the government was severely criticised for allowing conglomerates and well-off individuals to benefit disproportionately from economic reforms at the expense of the poor.

In Indonesia, this debate represents a sensitive political issue because Indonesia's private sector is dominated by Indonesian-Chinese owned businesses. Throughout the year the government, led by Industry Minister Hartarto, campaigned for big businesses to establish linkages with smaller firms. He encouraged conglomerates to engage smaller firms as suppliers, subcontractors and distributors.

Calls for more openness in economic policymaking are likely to increase, however. A major source of contention for many large and medium-sized businesses is the perception that Indonesia's largest business groups enjoy privileged access to credit and government contracts.

One well-publicised example of this treatment was the monopoly in the trade in cloves granted in January to Tommy Suharto, the president's youngest son. Cloves are a main component of Indonesia's popular *kretek* cigarette, a US$3 billion a year business. □

# Data

**Major industries** (1990-91): Textiles, 5.03 billion m (4.49 billion); steel, 1.99 million tonnes (1.58 million); vehicle assembly, 271,400 (174,800); cement, 15.78 million tonnes (14.10 million); cigarettes (kretek), 139.3 billion (130.4 billion); (regular), 34.8 billion (30.3 billion); plywood, 8.37 million m³ (7.69 million).

**Major agriculture** (1990): Rice, 45.27 million tonnes (44.73 million); copra and coconut, 2.25 million tonnes (2.2 million); rubber, 1.26 million tonnes (1.21 million); palm oil, 2.41 million tonnes (1.97 million); cassava, 15.59 million tonnes (17.12 million); cane sugar, 2.12 million tonnes (2.11 million); coffee, 424,000 tonnes (401,000).

**Oil and natural gas** (1990-91): Oil, 1.52 million bpd (1.41 million); gas, 6.05 trillion ft³/day (5.51 trillion).

**Mining** (1990-91): Coal, 11.21 million tonnes (9.48 million); tin, 30,100 tonnes (30,000); nickel ore, 2.3 million tonnes (1.65 million); bauxite, 1.33 million tonnes (994,800).

**Major imports** (1990-91): Capital equipment, US$7.66 billion (US$5.37 billion); oil and oil products, US$3.39 billion (US$2.34 billion); chemical products, US$1.41 billion (US$1.1 billion); base metal, US$2.33 billion (US$1.6 billion); food, beverages and tobacco, US$1.51 billion (US$1.34 billion).

**Major exports** (1990-91): Oil and oil products, US$8.05 billion (US$6.29 billion); LNG, US$4.71 billion (US$3.05 billion); timber, US$3.48 billion (US$3.59 billion); textiles, garments and handicrafts, US$3.08 billion (US$2.28 billion); rubber, US$900 million (US$980 million); coffee, US$366 million (US$499.2 million).

**Tourism and transport** (1991): Arrivals, 2,100,000 (1,625,965); departures, 1,521,979 (1,911,433).

**Currency:** (Nov. 1991) Rupiah. Rps 1,977 = US$1. (Rps 1,872=US$1)

**Public holidays** (1992): 1 Jan. (New Year's Day), 1 Feb. (Pilgrimage of the Prophet), 5 Mar. (Hari Raya Nyepi/Saka New Year's Day), 5-6 Apr. (Idul Fitri), 17 Apr. (Good Friday), 16 May (Vaicak Day), 28 May (Ascension Day), 11 June (Idul Adha), 2 July (Muslim New Year), 17 Aug. (Independence Day), 9 Sept. (Mohammad's Birthday), 25 Dec. (Christmas Day).

**Government ministries:** Finance, Jl. Lapangan Banteng Timur No. 4, Jakarta, tel. 373309, fax 353710, tlx 44319 DEPKEUIA; Trade, Jl. Moh. Ikwan Ridwan Rais No. 5, Jakarta, tel. 3841403, fax 374361, tlx 45725 DEPDAG IA; Industry, Jl. Jend. Gatot Subroto Kav. 52-53, Jakarta, tel. 515509, tlx 44477 DEPPIND JKT; National Development Planning Board, Jl.

Taman Suropati No. 2, Jakarta, tel. 336207, fax 3105374, tlx 61333 BAPNAS JKT; Research and Technology Board, Jl. M. H. Thamrin No. 8, Jakarta, tel. 324319, tlx 61321 BPPT IA; Population and Environment, Jl. Merdeka Barat No. 15, Jakarta, tel. 371035, 371619, fax 374371, tlx 44240 SEKNEG IA; State Secretariate, Jl. Veteran No. 17, Jakarta, tel. 3847198, 3842429, fax 352685, tlx 46143 SEKNEG IA; Foreign Affairs, Jl. Taman Pejambon No. 6, Jakarta, tel. 371508, fax 360517, tlx 45611 DEPLU IA; Agriculture, Jl. Harsono RM. No. 3, Jakarta, tel. 7804116, 7804265, tlx 44246 DEPTAN JKT; Mining and Energy, Jl. Merdeka Selatan 18, Jakarta, tel. 3804242, 360232, fax 3847671, tlx 44363.

**Major banks:** (State banks) Bank Negara Indonesia 1946 (BNI), Jl. Jend. Sudirman Kav. 1, Jakarta, tel. 5701001, 5700980, fax 5700907, 5701831, tlx 45524, 45539 KB BNI IA; Bank Bumi Daya (BBD), Jl. Imam Bonjol No. 61, Jakarta, tel. 333721, 330516, tlx 61805 BDIMB IA, 61608 BDIMS IA; Bank Dagang Negara, Jl. M. H. Thamrin No. 5, Jakarta, tel. 3800800, 321707, fax 323618, tlx 44149 BDN KT JKT; Bank Expor Impor Indonesia (Bank EXIM), Jl. Lapangan Setasiun No. 1, Jakarta, tel. 6900991, fax 670347, 674734, tlx 42030, 42032; Bank Rakyat Indonesia, Jl. Jend. Sudirman No. 44-46, Jakarta, tel. 5704313, 5704247, fax 5704154, tlx 45234, 45229 KAPEBRI IA; (National private banks) Bank Central Asia (BCA), Jl. Jend. Sudirman Kav. 22-23, Jakarta, tel. 5703711, 5710050, fax 5710869; Lippobank, Jl. Gatot Subroto Kav. 35-36, Jakarta, tel. 5201100, 5207090, fax 5201092, tlx 62007; Bank Internasional Indonesia (BII), Jl. M. H. Thamrin Kav. 22, Jakarta, tel. 3104646, fax 3104587, tlx 61160 BII TH; Bank Duta, Jl. Kebon Sirih No. 12, Jakarta, tel. 3800900, 3800901, fax 3801516, tlx 44008 DTAJK IA; Bank Danamon, Jl. Kebon Sirih No. 15, Jakarta, tel. 3804800, 3805200, fax 325601, tlx 61342 BDIKP IA; Bank Niaga, Jl. M. H. Thamrin No. 55, Jakarta, tel. 332628, 332239, fax 373723, tlx 44996, 61334 NAGAHO IA; Bank Bali, Jl. Hayam Wuruk No. 84-85, Jakarta, tel. 6498006, 6496050, fax 6296412, 6290565, tlx 63051, 63068; (Foreign banks) Citibank, Landmark Bldg, Jl. Jend. Sudirman, Jakarta, tel. 5712007, fax 5719303, tlx 62828 CITIBKJKT; Chase Manhattan Bank, Jl. Jend. Sudirman, Jakarta, tel. 5712213, tlx 62152 CMBCM IA; Standard Chartered Bank, Jl. M. H. Thamrin No. 53, Jakarta, tel. 325008, fax 323619, tlx 61651 SCBFX IA; ABN Bank, Jl. H. Juanda 23-24, Jakarta, tel. 362309, fax 372422, tlx 44124; Bank of Tokyo, Mid Plaza, Jl. Jend. Sudirman, Jakarta, tel. 5706185, tlx 62467 TOHBKIA; Hongkong and Shanghai Bank, Jl. Hayam Wuruk No. 8, Jakarta, tel. 3803306, fax 362373, tlx 44160 HSCB JKT.

# YEN AND YANK

## Has the balance of power in Asia shifted?

Japan has challenged US dominance in Asia where both governments and individuals are looking to Tokyo for a lead. But, despite their growing economic might, the Japanese seem reluctant to play this role. The rest of Asia remains unsure what Japan's ultimate intentions are.

Now comes a book which examines these important questions, as seen primarily from the viewpoint of Japan's neighbours. Compiled by correspondents of the *Far Eastern Economic Review*, Asia's most respected journal, "Japan in Asia" reveals what other Asians think of Japan.

Send now for this unique and fascinating study of the most significant Asian power-shift in decades. Essential reading for business people and, indeed, anybody with an interest in the region.

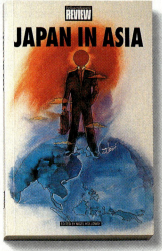

# JAPAN

## Politics/Social Affairs

The unexpected withdrawal of Toshiki Kaifu from the Liberal Democratic Party (LDP) presidential race on 5 October set the stage for Kiichi Miyazawa to become Japan's 18th post-war prime minister.

His victory in the 27 October party election over rival faction leaders Michio Watanabe and Hiroshi Mitsuzuka was a foregone conclusion once he won the open support of Shin Kanemaru and Noboru Takeshita, leaders of the largest LDP faction and still the most powerful figures in the party.

Kaifu had been little more than a puppet of the Takeshita faction during his two years as prime minister, taking his cues on major decisions from Ichiro Ozawa, a protege of Kanemaru who appears likely to emerge as the future leader of the Takeshita faction.

Ozawa, as LDP secretary-general and arguably the most powerful figure in the Kaifu administration until he resigned in April to take responsibility for the defeat of an LDP-backed candidate in the Tokyo gubernatorial election, would have been the logical Takeshita faction candidate for the party's presidency. However, Ozawa was in hospital for two months following an apparent heart attack in May, and at 49 is considered still too young to be prime minister.

The sequence of events which led to Miyazawa's assumption of office began with the illness and subsequent death of Shintaro Abe in May. Abe, Miyazawa and Takeshita had been the main contenders to succeed Yasuhiro Nakasone as prime minister in 1987. In the event, Takeshita assumed the office that year on the understanding that he would be succeeded first by Abe and then Miyazawa.

This arrangement unravelled with the Recruit bribery scandal in 1989, which forced then finance minister Miyazawa and Takeshita from office and implicated Abe. With the chain of succession broken until they were politically rehabilitated at the February 1990 Lower House parliamentary elections, the LDP hierarchy turned first to Sosuke Uno and then to Kaifu to serve as stand-in national leaders.

The revised script, which called for Abe to resume his place and replace Kaifu this October had to be abandoned after

Apart from the introduction of Chinese script, little of the outside world intruded into Japan until the Portuguese arrived in the middle of the 16th century, quickly followed by the Dutch and the British. After some 80 years of contact with Europeans, however, the Tokugawa government decided isolation had its merits and banished the foreigners.

This isolation was finally broken by Commodore Mathew Perry in 1853. As Japan modernised its administrative and social structure, for most of the next century it embarked on a series of conquests which included Korea, Manchuria, China and, finally, Southeast Asia. Following its defeat in 1945, Japan elected to take a low international profile and concentrate its energies on rebuilding its economy, to the exent that took less than 40 years to emerge as one of the richest countries in the world.

More recently, the government has grappled with ways to match its economic performance with diplomatic influence. Under Yasuhiro Nakasone, Japan tried to identify itself as a "member of the West" and showed greater interest in defence issues. Noboru Takeshita who succeeded Nakasone as prime minister in 1987 was forced to resign in 1989 because of his party's involvement in the Recruit scandal. Takeshita's successor, Sousuke Uno, lasted a mere two months, plunging the ruling Liberal Democratic Party into a crisis, culminating in its defeat in the July 1989 Upper House parliamentary election. His successor, Toshiki Kaifu, credited with improving Japan's international image but without a domestic powerbase, abandoned the prime ministership in early October 1991 and was replaced by Kiichi Miyazawa.

Abe's death, and threw open the leadership succession to claimants from all major factions. The Takeshita faction's final decision to back Miyazawa can therefore be viewed in part as a return to the original backroom agreement on sharing political spoils that was reached among the three main LDP factions in 1987.

As a result, however, Miyazawa assumed office heavily indebted to the Takeshita faction. The direction and tone of Japanese politics over the next two years will now largely turn on the tension between Miyazawa's efforts to assert himself as a leader and the power of the Takeshita faction, in particular the ambitions of Ozawa. Ozawa aspires not only to be prime minister but to become a political overlord in the mould of Kakuei Tanaka, who personally dominated Japanese politics from the early 1970s until a disabling stroke in 1985.

The first major test facing Miyazawa as prime minister will be the thorny problem of whether and how to open Japan's rice market to foreign competition, an issue of critical symbolic importance in US-Japan relations and in the Uruguay Round of the Gatt, which is due to be concluded by the end of 1991.

In May, former prime minister Kaifu indicated his willingness to resolve the dispute with the US over access to Japan's rice market by the end of the year. The Federation of Economic Organisations, or Keidanren, has publicly supported liberalising Japan's rice import policy in order to facilitate progress at the Uruguay Round.

Takeo Nishioka, chairman of the LDP's executive council, stated that Japan should partially open its rice markets "after taking alternative steps to assist domestic producers," while Kanemaru warned of intensified US protectionism if the rice dispute were not resolved. However, Mitsuzuka, campaigning against Miyazawa, expressed opposition to opening the rice market. The resignation of Seizo Yamazaki as chairman of the Keidanren's agricultural committee in September also removed a strong advocate of market liberalisation within the business community.

While the LDP faces an uncertain future in its present form, wider events have conspired to erode the ideological foundations of other Japanese political parties. The Japan Communist Party (JCP), in particular, has been rendered increasingly irrelevant by the collapse of communist parties in the Soviet Union and Eastern Europe and the marginalisation of the remaining communist and socialist regimes. The communists currently hold only 16 out of the Lower House's 512 seats against the LDP's 280 seats, the Social Democratic Party of Japan's (SDPJ, formerly the Japan Socialist Party) 139, and the Komei Party's 46.

The SDJP, the country's largest opposition party, appears headed for a split between its traditional Marxist leftwing, who dominate party headquarters, and the more centrist-oriented leaders, who hold most of the socialist seats in parliament. Riven by ideological disputes, the socialists failed to live up to the high expectations generated by their victory in the July 1989 Upper House elections, when for a time it appeared that genuine two-party politics might be possible in Japan. The SDPJ was hit hard during the April 1991 local elections when its share of contested seats fell from 16.6% to 12.8%, the party's worst showing ever.

**Miyazawa: the chosen one.**

SDPJ chairman Takako Doi, the first woman to lead a major Japanese political party, resigned in June and was replaced by Makoto Tanabe. As leader of the party's centrist Suiyo-kai faction, Tanabe has moved the SDPJ towards recognition of the constitutional legitimacy of the Self Defence Forces (SDF) and the US-Japan Security Treaty — both long anathema to the Left.

Support for the Komei, Japan's second-largest opposition party, was seriously weakened by the struggle between the clergy of the Nichiren Shoshu Buddhist faith and Daisaku Ikeda, the charismatic leader of the Soka Gakkai organisation of lay Nichiren Shoshu believers. The Komei was originally established as the political arm of the Soka Gakkai, but its "clean government" image was seriously damaged by the involvement of party leaders in the Recruit scandal.

As a result, the Komei has increasingly operated as part of a tacit coalition with the LDP and the Democratic Socialist Party (DSP, a small left-centre party which broke away from the Japan Socialist Party in the 1960s), making it possible for the LDP to pass legislation through the Upper House which it no longer controls.

The Komei and DSP, for example, both supported the LDP's plan to allow the SDF to participate in UN peacekeeping operations overseas, a proposal opposed by the SDPJ and the JCP, who claimed it would violate the anti-war provisions of Japan's constitution.

But even as the political base of the opposition parties deteriorates, mounting public cynicism has also raised questions about the prospects for permanent political dominance by the LDP. Kaifu's transparent status as a popular but powerless puppet prime minister, selected and operated by the LDP bosses, has been an important factor in eroding public confidence in the party.

The LDP's pre-eminent role in Japan's post-war political arrangements has also been challenged by a continuing series of political and financial scandals. The most recent scandals involved the failure of the Ministry of Finance (MOF) to adequately supervise stockbrokers. Nomura Securities, Nikko Securities and other major brokerages made secret payments to compensate major clients for stock trading losses. The MOF's securities bureau had apparently known about the payments, but failed to alert the public or take effective steps to bring the practice to a halt.

In addition to the Nomura and Nikko cases, other recent securities and finance-related scandals have brought about the resignations of the chairmen or presidents of Sumitomo Bank, Itoman Corp., Kyowa-Saitama Bank, Fuji Bank and the Industrial Bank of Japan. Several of these cases also involved alleged links to organised crime figures.

While there have so far been no serious allegations directly linking political leaders to any of the more recent financial scandals, both the LDP and the government image have been tainted by the disclosures. These events have also given a heightened urgency to the movement for political reform, ostensibly the issue over which Kaifu withdrew his candidacy in the LDP presidential race.

Kaifu issued what was in effect an intention to dissolve parliament and hold new elections after a package of three political reform bills he sponsored were killed in committee on 30 September. Four days later, however, leaders of the LDP's dominant Takeshita faction made it known they had withdrawn their support for Kaifu, who promptly announced that he would not stand as a candidate for another term as LDP president.

The bills would have tightened controls on campaign funding and redrawn the map of Japan's electoral districts, replacing the present multiple-member constituency electoral system in the Lower House with a dual system combining single-member "first-past-the-post" constituency elections and nationwide, proportional party-based balloting. Under the multiple constituency system, both the LDP and opposition parties can usually count on "safe seats" in each district. The most hard-fought electoral contests are between candidates from rival LDP factions, rather than candidates from different parties.

The single-seat constituency system would force politicians to compete with candidates from different parties, rather than rival factions, a change which proponents of reform believe would transform the election process into a true referendum on government policy rather than the popularity contest it largely is at present. ☐

# Foreign Relations

Japan spent much of 1991 trying to balance its role as a global economic superpower with its image as a lightweight player in international affairs. Sharply exposed to this dilemma during the Gulf War, Tokyo moved to assume a higher profile in issues where it had previously chosen to remain largely detached, including arms control and seeking a political settlement in Cambodia. However, Japan's efforts failed to significantly alter the fact that it remains — for the time being at least — a close follower of US policies, lacking its own vision of a radically changed world order.

Tokyo's foreign policy agenda between late 1990 and the first few months of 1991 was dominated by a heated debate over what role Japan should play in the Gulf crisis. The United Nations Peace Cooperation Corps Bill submitted in October 1990 was dropped a month later after opposition parties strongly argued that it was unconstitutional. The proposal would have enabled Japan to provide non-combat assistance in UN-sanctioned military and peacekeeping operations.

On 17 January, the Gulf War broke out and Japan was hard pressed to provide some sort of physical presence in the region, however symbolic, to show support for the efforts of its Western allies. On 24 January, Tokyo decided to contribute an additional US$9 billion to the US$4 billion committed in September 1990 for the coalition war effort, and send aircraft to the Gulf to help evacuate refugees.

While the second contribution won generally popular support, the electorate could not accept the idea of sending Japanese personnel, under whatever arrangement and for whatever purpose, to the war zone. In the end, Japan could only despatch a handful of doctors to the Gulf as even its proposed refugee airlift was dropped in the face of widespread opposition.

**Gulf contribution: too little, too late.**

The timing and nature of Tokyo's response to the crisis was criticised overseas, reinforcing Japan's image as a self-absorbed country seeking a free ride. In an effort to contain the damage, the government moved quickly after the war in an effort to demonstrate its political responsibility.

On 25 April, a day before Kaifu began an official tour of Asean, Tokyo sent four navy minesweepers and two support vessels to the Gulf. Their departure marked the first time Japanese military personnel had been sent overseas on an operational mission since the end of World War II.

However monumental the despatch of the flotilla may have appeared to Tokyo, it pleased few parties. In the US, where criticism of Japan's inaction during the Gulf War was the strongest, the damage had already been done. In many Asian countries, on the other hand, there were fears that the minesweepers represented the beginning of a resurgence in Japanese militarism.

US-Japanese relations were also tested in April when local agricultural officials forcibly removed a small quantity of rice displayed by the US Rice Council at an exhibition in Chiba, near Tokyo. Japanese officials said the display violated the ban on rice imports. However, the overall economic atmosphere was an improvement on 1990, when the Structural Impediment Initiative aimed at improving mutual market access cast a pall over ties between Tokyo and Washington. The reduction of Japan's merchandise trade surplus, at least in early 1991, helped to keep US trade critics at bay.

Negotiations on US access to Japan's construction and semiconductor markets were completed during the year after Tokyo made last-minute concessions. On rice — despite the fracas in Chiba — Tokyo was slowly moving towards a consensus to allow some imports, but its plan was derailed by Washington's insistence on using tariffs rather than quotas to regulate market liberalisation. Tokyo was expected to be under greater pressure to import rice once the US and the EC finally agree to reduce agricultural aid.

The 16-19 April visit to Japan by Soviet President Mikhail Gorbachov, the first by a Soviet leader and seen by Tokyo as of enormous significance, however failed to resolve the Kurile Islands dispute. Hopes had been high that Gorbachov would indicate Soviet willingness to end the strain in Moscow-Tokyo relations that the islands continue to engender. These were boosted when Ichiro Ozawa, then secretary-general of the ruling Liberal Democratic Party, travelled to Moscow in late March to pave the way for Gorbachov's visit and reportedly spoke of providing up to US$28 billion in economic aid in return for Moscow's recognition of Japanese sovereignty over the islands. In the event, Tokyo failed to get Moscow to even reaffirm an offer made in a 1956 Japan-Soviet joint declaration to hand over the two smaller islands of Shikotan and Habomai.

Following August's abortive Soviet coup attempt and the subsequent removal of the hardliners, however, there are indications that Moscow may now be ready to make a deal with Japan over the Kuriles. The first sign of flexibility came from Ruslan Khasbulatov, acting chairman of the Russian parliament and the first senior Russian republic official to visit Japan since the failed putsch.

Khasbulatov told Ozawa in a meeting during September that

Russia was "ready to realise the long-cherished dream of the Japanese people" and was willing to settle the issue. In response to the new signals, Tokyo announced a US$2.5 billion aid package for the Soviet Union in early October, comprising government credits, trade insurance to encourage Japanese exports and humanitarian aid. The package, the biggest of its kind from Japan to the Soviet Union, paved the way for the visit of then foreign minister Taro Nakayama to the Soviet Union on 12 October.

Sino-Japanese relations had a quiet year, as Tokyo moved slowly towards full normalisation after ties were suspended between mid-1989 and mid-1990 following the Peking massacre. In January, then finance minister Ryutaro Hashimoto went to Peking to finalise a ¥810 billion (US$6.23 billion) economic assistance package for 1990-95. This was the first visit by a Japanese cabinet minister to China since the Peking massacre in June 1989, and paved the way for higher-level contacts.

On 10-13 August, Kaifu visited Peking, the first by a leader of a major industrialised nation since June 1989. He pledged US$1.5 million worth of assistance to flood victims, and also made available ¥130 billion in loans for Chinese infrastructure projects as part of the 1990-95 package. As an obvious gift for Japan's help in bringing China back to the world's diplomatic community, Peking announced its acceptance of the nuclear non-proliferation treaty during Kaifu's visit. On the sensitive topic of human rights, Kaifu explained that Japan shared Western countries' hopes that China would make changes to its human-rights policies. Peking listened politely, but made no commitment.

Japan's relations with South Korea were cordial, despite a growing trade surplus in Tokyo's favour. President Roh Tae Woo made a two-day visit to Tokyo on 10-11 January and secured a promise that finger-printing of all ethnic Koreans in Japan would soon end. Emperor Akihito and Kaifu both apologised to Roh for Japan's wartime atrocities towards the Koreans.

Normalisation talks between North Korea and Japan, however, hit a snag when Pyongyang demanded compensation for Japan's colonial rule over the Korean peninsula in 1910-45, as well as for post-war damages. Tokyo only acknowledged Pyongyang's right to seek property damages linked to colonial rule, but not those incurred afterwards. Another sticking point was Japan's insistence that North Korea sign a nuclear safeguards agreement to provide inspection of its nuclear facilities by the International Atomic Energy Agency. The Pyongyang-Tokyo dialogue finally ground to a halt after North Korea backtracked on an earlier pledge to sign the non-profileration treaty in Vienna in mid-September.

Japan's relations with Asean received a major boost with Akihito's 11-day visit to Thailand, Malaysia and Indonesia in late September, the first by a head of the Japanese royal family. Tokyo carefully chose destinations where public hostility towards the emperor and empress were unlikely. Nevertheless, the visit failed to satisfy many in the region who had expected the emperor to formally apologise for Japan's war-time behaviour. Instead, some observers noted that the tone of Akihito's speeches during the tour were even more lukewarm than his previous comments on the war.

Aside from Japanese expressions of regret, what some Southeast Asian countries wanted from Tokyo was its support for a regional trading bloc, the East Asian Economic Group proposed by Malaysian Prime Minister Mahathir Mohamad. Despite repeated invitations, Japan remained cool to the idea for fear of upsetting the US. By contrast, and to the surprise of many observers, Japan showed its interest in playing a greater regional political role by suggesting at the Asean annual meeting on 22 July that an informal forum for "political discussions to improve the sense of security among us" be established. The idea was immediately rejected by suspicious Asean members.

Parties seeking a political settlement of the Cambodia civil war, however, welcomed Tokyo's involvement, not least because they recognised Japan's economic assistance was essential to make the peace settlement workable. □

# Economy/Infrastructure

In 1991 Japan presented the remarkable and possibly unique spectacle of a country where the so-called real economy appeared to function independently of the financial economy — the former characterised by boom and the latter by bust.

By August, as the economy entered its 57th month of consecutive growth, it was obvious that the *Heisei* economic boom would exceed in duration the former record *Izanagi* boom of the late 1960s. The roaring consumption and investment underpinning this latest boom appeared heedless of high interest rates in Japan, an unprecedented stockmarket crash and considerable turmoil in the financial markets.

However, it seems inevitable that in 1992 both economies will converge in what at best will be a "growth" recession and at worst an absolute recession. The real economy will be seen to be lagging rather than defying the trend in the financial economy.

The seeds of destruction for the financial boom which boosted Japan's asset values — stock and land prices in particular — to absurd levels during the late 1980s were scattered at the end of that decade when Yasushi Mieno became head of the central bank, Bank of Japan (BOJ).

Mieno viewed with alarm the monetary profligacy which for five years had kept official interest rates at remarkably low levels in Japan, thereby fuelling a liquidity bubble which threatened to spill over into runaway inflation. Nevertheless, consumer price inflation averaged a modest 2-3% annually during the years when Japan's bubble economy was at its height from the late 1980s to the early 1990s, albeit largely due to a stronger yen, lower energy costs and wage restraint.

However, rising housing prices that climbed beyond the level where new home buyers could afford more than the most modest accommodation — along with perceived inequalities of wealth between workers and speculators — threatened to provoke wage and general cost pressures.

While the origins of Japan's easy money policy cannot easily be pinned down, they emerged against a background of conflicting external pressures during the mid-1980s to reduce the protection-inducing thrust of Japanese exports and to boost domestic demand. However, the 1985 Plaza agreement to revalue the yen in order to reduce Japan's export competitiveness ought in theory to have dictated higher interest rates — though this would have conflicted with the need to offset reduced exports by increasing domestic demand. A relatively tight fiscal policy designed to cut the government's budget deficit also dictated an emphasis on easier money.

There is also speculation that the Japanese Government compensated exporters for having to cope with a much higher yen after Plaza by keeping interest rates low, thereby making borrowing cheap and boosting the stockmarket to the point where capital-raising also became inexpensive.

Whatever the cause — or combination of causes — for the low interest rate policy, it was clear by the time Mieno assumed the governorship of the BOJ that matters had been allowed to go to the point where they risked running out of control.

Japanese businessmen had quite naturally taken advantage of low interest rates and cheap capital-raisings through the stockmarket. However, they were not using the super-abundance of funds to simply finance productive investments but also to indulge in an orgy of stockmarket and property speculation. The result was that stock prices soared — even by Japanese standards — to levels where they bore no relation to companies' earning power, while land and property values reached astronomic heights well beyond the purchasing power of most individuals.

The land-price bubble, in particular, threatened to foster social discontent in Japan while the money-making ethos that had arisen out of stockmarket speculation, or *zaiteku*, promised to undermine Japanese industry's dedication to more productive activities.

Against public opposition from then finance minister Ryutaro Hashimoto, who wanted to ensure the continuance of Japan's politically popular economic boom, Mieno forced through a series of increases in the official discount rate (ODR) which took it from the late 1980s level of 2.5% to a new high plateau of 6%.

The stockmarkets were the first to see the significance of such moves. An end to cheap money meant an end to ever-

Stockmarket: waving or drowning?

rising share prices. By the beginning of 1990 the Tokyo Stock Exchange began a nine-month plunge which took the Nikkei-225 average down by almost 50% from its 1989 all-time high of nearly 40,000 points.

Although the market steadied somewhat in early 1991, it soon entered a second bear stage once it became obvious that the BOJ was not going to relent in its tight money policy. Then, around the middle of the year, came a series of scandals at Japanese securities houses and banks which dealt investor confidence another serious blow.

The market went into what looked like a free fall until July when the BOJ edged the discount rate a half-point lower — apparently in response to Finance Ministry anxiety about the health of the overall economy. By this time it was becoming obvious that consumer demand — one of the principal legs of the Heisei economic boom — was faltering and that capital investment by Japanese business — the other major leg — was looking more problematic.

Official concern about the continuing descent in stock values was based on more than consideration for investors. Japanese commercial banks count on unrealised gains from their heavy investment in stocks to boost their capital base. With values badly eroded, the banks appeared in danger of not being able to meet capital:asset ratios mandated by the Bank for International Settlements (BIS). The Nikkei average has to climb at least back into the mid-20,000 range before the banks can again feel comfortable on this score.

There were thus numerous grounds for reducing interest rates. Japan's bubble economy had burst — certainly as far as stock prices were concerned, even if the fall in land and property values had been more muted overall than the BOJ would have liked.

What is remarkable is that Japan's economic activity was maintained at such high levels in 1991, despite the persistence

# Data

**Major industries:** Iron and steel, 110.3 million tonnes (107.9 million); motor vehicles, 13.5 million units (13 million); colour TV sets, 13.2 million units (12.6 million); industrial electronic equipment, US$78.1 billion (US$78.6 billion); machine tools, US$10 billion (US$8.7 billion).

**Major agriculture:** Rice, 10.5 million tonnes (10.4 million); fisheries, 5.7 million tonnes (6.2 million); beef and pork, 2.1 million tonnes (same); logs, 29.8 million m³ (30.5 million); vegetables, 13.7 million tonnes (14.1 million).

**Oil and natural gas:** Oil, 632,000 kl (641,000); gas, 2.1 billion m³ (2 billion).

**Mining:** Coal, 8.3 million tonnes (10.2 million).

**Major imports:** Petroleum, US$41.3 billion (US$29.8 billion); machinery and equipment, US$40.9 billion (US$32.4 billion); foodstuffs, US$31.6 billion (US$31 billion); fish and shellfish, US$10.5 billion (US$10 billion); timber and wood products, US$7.5 billion (US$8.2 billion); coal, US$6.2 billion (US$5.9 billion).

**Major exports:** Machinery and equipment, US$215.1 billion (US$205.5 billion); motor vehicles, US$51 billion (US$48.5 billion); chemicals, US$15.9 billion (US$14.8 billion); iron and steel, US$12.5 billion (US$14.8 billion); textiles, US$7.2 billion (US$6.9 billion); ships, US$5.6 billion (US$4.4 billion).

**Tourism and transport:** Arrivals, 35.1 million (29.9 million); departures, 110 million (96.6 million); total visitor expenditure, US$3.6 billion (US$3.1 billion).

(All figures for 1990, previous year in brackets.)

**Currency:** Yen. Y129.35 = US$1 in Nov.1991 (Y126.5 = US$1).

**Finance:** 11 city banks, 64 regional banks, 68 member banks of the Second Association of Regional Banks (including Sogo banks), 7 trust banks, 3 long-term credit banks, 87 foreign banks and 11 government financial institutions. Stock exchanges in Tokyo, Osaka, Nagoya, Kyoto, Niigata, Sapporo, Fukuoka, Hiroshima. 1,633 companies quoted on Tokyo stock exchanges.

**Major banks:** Dai-Ichi Kangyo Bank, 1-1-5 Uchisaiwai-cho, Chiyoda-ku, Tokyo 100, tel. 03-3596-1111, fax 03-3596-2179; Mitsui Taiyo Kobe Bank, 1-3-1 Kudan-Minami, Chiyoda-ku, Tokyo 100-91, tel. 03-3230-3111, fax 03-3221-1084; Sumitomo Bank, 1-3-2 Marunouchi, Chiyoda-ku, Tokyo 100, tel. 03-3282-5111, fax 03-3282-8480; Fuji Bank, 1-5-5 Otemachi, Chiyoda-ku, Tokyo 100, tel. 03-3216-2211, fax 03-3216-6055; Mitsubishi Bank, 2-7-1 Marunouchi, Chiyoda-ku, Tokyo 100, tel. 03-3240-1111, fax 03-3240-2567; Sanwa Bank, 1-1-1 Otemachi, Chiyoda-ku, Tokyo 100, tel. 03-3216-3111, fax 03-3215-1776; Tokai Bank, 2-6-1 Otemachi, Chiyoda-ku, Tokyo 100, tel. 03-3242-2111, fax 03-3243-0969; Daiwa Bank, 2-1-1 Otemachi, Chiyoda-ku, Tokyo 100, tel. 03-3231-1231, fax 03-3231-1262; Bank of Tokyo, 1-3-2 Nihonbashi Hongoku-cho, Chuo-ku, Tokyo 103, tel. 03-3245-1111, fax 03-3241-9377; Kyowa Saitama Bank, 1-1-2 Otemachi, Chiyoda-ku, Tokyo 100, tel. 03-3287-2111, fax 03-3212-3663; Hokkaido Takushoku Bank, 1-3-13 Nihonbashi, Chuo-ku, Tokyo 103, tel. 03-3272-6611, fax 03-3281-6057.

**Public holidays** (1992): 1 Jan. (New Year's Day), 15 Jan. (Coming of Age Day), 11 Feb. (National Foundation Day), 21 Mar. (Vernal Equinox Day), 29 Apr. (Green Day), 3 May (Constitution Day), 4 May (public holiday), 5 May (Children's Day), 15 Sept. (Respect for the Aged Day), 23 Sept. (Autumnal Equinox Day), 10 Oct. (Health-Sports Day), 3 Nov. (Culture Day), 23 Nov. (Labour Thanksgiving Day), 23 Dec. (Emperor's Birthday).

**Government ministries:** (All ministries in Kasumigaseki — either 1, 2 or 3-chome — Chiyoda-ku, Tokyo 100). Foreign Affairs, tel. 03-3580-3311, fax 03-3581-9675; Justice, tel. 03-3592-7004, fax 03-3592-7011; Finance, tel. 03-3581-4111, fax 03-3592-1025; Education, tel. 03-3581-4211, fax 033591-8072; Health and Welfare, tel. 03-3503-1711, fax 03-3501-4853; Agriculture, Forestry and Fisheries, tel. 03-3502-8111, fax 03-3592-7697; International Trade and Industry, tel. 03-3501-1657, fax 03-3501-2081; Transport, tel. 03-3580-3111, fax 03-3580-7982; Posts and Telecommunications, tel. 03-3504-4411, fax 03-3504-0265; Labour, tel. 03-3593-1211, fax 03-3502-6711; Construction, tel. 03-3580-4311, fax 03-5251-1922; Home Affairs, tel. 03-3581-5311.

of relatively high interest rates. The reasons for this have to do partly with the nature of Japanese society, but more to do with what is known as lagged reaction.

Japanese household savings are high by international standards, and for the past few years families have chosen to run down at least part of these savings to finance consumption. Personal consumption now represents something like 60% of GNP. To the extent that it is not financed by credit, such consumption is not directly dependent on the cost of money.

Another major factor behind Japan's economic boom has been the huge surge in Japanese capital investment by Japanese business, both at home and overseas. Such investment now accounts for more than one fifth of GNP and contributes a similar proportion of annual economic growth.

The reason why the investment boom could continue unabated in the face of rising interest rates was that it was financed largely out of huge cash reserves built up by Japanese companies during the late 1980s. These came partly from export surpluses, but also from the fact that corporates are major stockmarket players.

Japanese companies raised something like ¥85 trillion (US$62 billion) through the stockmarket during the second half of the 1980s, at a remarkably low cost. They were able to do this through financial innovation which brought the effective cost of borrowing down to virtually nil in many cases. The stockmarket crash brought a sudden end to this orgy of cheap capital-raising, pushing the cost of borrowing and obtaining money through equity-derivatives such as warrant-bonds back up to 6-7% or even higher.

Although the rate of increase in capital investment eased from double-digit to single-digit rates between fiscal 1990 and 1991, the fact that the capital investment boom was able to

continue at all in the face of dearer money was due largely to the fat cash-cushion Japanese business was sitting on. The size of this cushion was estimated at around ¥170 trillion at the start of 1990, and during that year Japanese business invested some ¥90 trillion in plant and equipment. A similar, or higher, rate of spending in 1991 was expected to leave the cash reserve just about depleted.

While leading Japanese companies had insisted at the beginning of 1991 that their capital spending programmes would not be damaged by the stockmarket crash or dearer money, few were quite so sanguine towards the end of the year.

If the increase in capital spending falls, as expected, to around 6% for the fiscal year ending 30 March 1992 compared with 13% in the previous year, one of the major props of economic expansion will have gone.

With recent figures for various components of personal consumption — ranging from retail sales to housing starts — also showing a much weaker trend, the prospects for the continuance of the Heisei boom appear doubtful.

Nevertheless, a 2.7% jump in Japan's real GNP growth during the first quarter of 1991 — which translates into a startling 11.2% on an annualised basis — appeared to confound widespread predictions of an economic slowdown. However, the picture of robust growth masked a continuing slowdown in underlying domestic demand and a resurgence of Japan's external surpluses. In the second quarter of the year growth slumped to just 0.5%, slowing the annualised increase to just 2%.

The first quarter growth meant the official Economic Planning Agency (EPA) had to revise the figure for real (inflation-adjusted) economic growth for the fiscal year ended 31 March 1991 from 5.2% to 5.7%. The EPA forecast for fiscal year end-

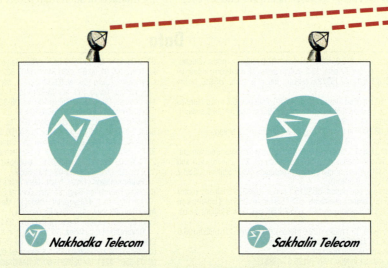

ing in March 1992 remains unchanged at 3.8%, though the actual outcome could fall short of this.

An earlier than expected end to the Gulf War and the subsequent softness in oil prices had been expected to benefit Japan's energy-hungry economy. But over half the first-quarter GNP rise was accounted for by an increase in Japan's net export earnings. This was all the more remarkable as net exports now account for less than 10% of Japan's GNP. Recent trade surpluses — rising strongly in August for the eighth consecutive month — have been signalling a dramatic turnaround in the nation's trade account.

Special factors, such as Japanese companies' repatriation of overseas profits to offset tighter credit conditions at home, played some part. But the clear message is that Japan's export competitiveness has fully recovered from post–Plaza agreement yen strength, mainly due to heavy capital investment at home and huge investments in overseas production.

Japan's trade surplus appears set to return to the record levels achieved five years ago, rising from US$63.5 billion in calendar 1990 to at least US$75 billion in 1991, and to around US$88 billion in 1992.

This reflects the strength of the 100 or so major companies that account for around 72% of Japan's total exports, and which are believed to be competitive even if the yen strengthens to around ¥120 to US$1. The US and half a dozen Asian countries absorb the bulk of these exports, though Japan's surplus with Europe has also been rising dramatically.

A return to export-led growth in Japan might neatly offset the prospects for declining personal consumption and capital investment, but it would almost certainly excite fresh trade tensions with the country's major trade partners.

So far, the export surge has occurred mainly in Europe where German companies, engaged in rebuilding the reunited eastern part of the country, have ceded some markets to Japan. By the second half of the year there were signs the surplus with the US was also rising again. Meanwhile, France and other European countries were growing restive about their deficits with Japan.

However comfortable the trade and current-account picture looks for Japan — especially now that remitted profits from overseas investments are becoming such a major item — the contribution to GNP growth from the external sector is marginal compared with domestic consumption and investment.

This points to a need for more reductions in official interest rates — probably taking the ODR down by at least one percentage point by the end of 1991 — and even further in 1992 as the pace of economic growth continues to slacken. The scope for such moves is enhanced by the dramatic plunge in Japanese annual money-supply growth during 1991.

However far interest rates fall, it is unlikely that this could trigger a rise in capital spending or in personal consumption large enough to push Japan's economy back onto the growth path it entered in the mid-1980s. This raises the question of how much fiscal stimulus the government will be prepared to apply to the economy. The Finance Ministry has made it clear in recent years that its priority is to reduce the national debt rather than boost spending.

The ministry will probably be forced to relent somewhat with a major supplementary budget around the end of the year. Nevertheless — allowing for the fact that Japan has pledged under the Structural Impediments Initiative with the US to raise public spending substantially over the next 10 years — it is clear this will not be enough to maintain the country's economic boom. □

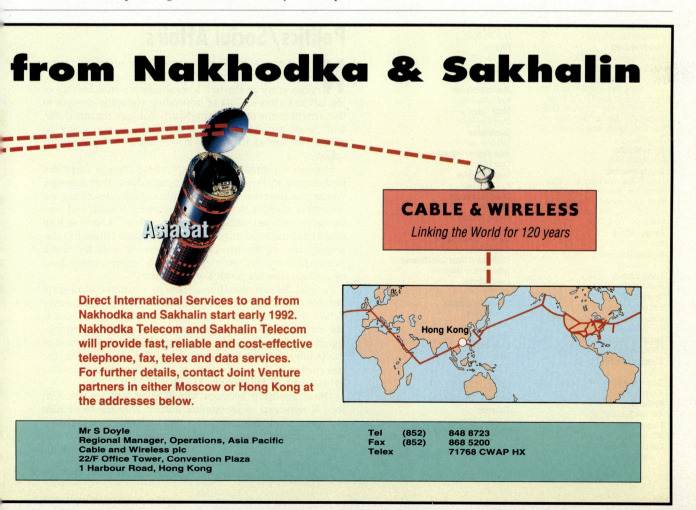

# KOREA — NORTH

At the end of World War II, US and Soviet forces entered Korea and, by prior agreement, two occupation zones were set up: the Soviets in the industrialised North and the US in the agrarian South, with rival Korean governments established in Pyongyang and Seoul.

The Soviet-backed resistance leader Kim Il Sung became head of North Korea in September 1948. In June 1950 the communist regime attempted to reunite the peninsula by force, but the fighting — in which China intervened to oppose US-led UN forces, — left the border largely unchanged and mutual distrust deeply ingrained. An armistice was signed at Panmunjom in July 1953 and still remains in force.

Purges of opponents, a repressive system of internal control and the deft neutralisation of Chinese and Soviet influence on his country's internal politics enabled Kim to remain in power for 43 years. However, the collapse of communism in the Soviet Union and growing Chinese wariness has forced his regime on to the defensive and led to a more conciliatory tone in its dealings with the South. Nevertheless, Kim has entrenched his position, largely through the creation of a personality cult that has elevated him to a semi-deity. The hallmarks of this cult have now been transferred to his son, Kim Jong Il, with the intention that Jong Il should succeed his father and rule in essentially the same manner.

## Politics/Social Affairs

North Korea's international position suffered unprecedented blows during 1991, culminating in the simultaneous entry of the two Koreas into full membership of the UN in October. Talk of impending sweeping changes to the current terms of the South-North dialogue remained rife, with Seoul persistently hinting that far more was going on beneath the surface than above it — especially in the economic sphere.

However, intimations of impending change were not forthcoming in President Kim Il Sung's New Year message, which was dismissive of worldwide detente, describing the international order in terms of "continuing tension and confrontation between socialism and imperialism." Likewise, Kim underlined the imperative of maintaining class struggle in dismissing the significance of official contacts with the South Korean Government, referring to them as "efforts monopolised by a single class [of South Korean society]."

At least the determination to hew to a hardline ideological position held the advantage of forestalling any possibly messy debate within the Korean Workers' Party (KWP), and so it is not surprising that the party should have evinced no signs of significant change in 1991. All full and candidate members of the politburo maintained their status and their ranking, the one change to the composition of the politburo being caused by the death of full member Ho Dam in May.

The relationship between Kim Il Sung and his son Kim Jong Il remained in its familiar mould, with the older Kim stating openly to foreign visitors that his son is now in charge of all party and economic affairs. However, the elder Kim, in his 80th year, remains the public face of the regime, with his frequent public appearances and on-the-spot guidance tours. His son, by contrast, remains almost reclusive, though pre-

**Head of State**
President Kim Il Sung.

**Vice Presidents**
Pak Sung Chol, Li Jong Ok;

**Politburo** (full members in order of hierarchy at May 1990)
Kim Il Sung, Kim Jong Il, O Jin U, Yon Hyong Muk, Li Jong Ok, Pak Sung Chol, So Chol, Kim Yong Nam, Choe Gwang, Kye Ung Tae, Chon Byong Ho, Han Song Ryong, Kang Song San, So Yun Sok;

**Prime Minister**
Yon Hyong Muk;

**Deputy Premiers**
Hong Si Hak, Kim Yong Nam, Choe Yongg Rim, Kim Hwan, Hong Song Nam, Kang Hui Won, Kim Bok Shin, Kim Dal Hyon, Kim Yun Hyok, Kim Chang Ju, Chang Chol;

**Foreign Affairs**
Kim Yong Nam;

**Building Materials**
Chu Yong Hun;

**Public Security**
Peak Hak Rim;

**Coal Industry**
Kim Gi Ryong;

**Natural Resources Development**
Kim Se Yong;

**Nuclear Power Industries**
Choe Hak Gun;

**Shipping Industries**
Li Sok;

**Communications**
Kim Hak Sop;

**Railways**
Pak Yon Sok;

**Foreign Trade**
Kim Dal Hyon;

**External Economic Affairs**
Chong Song Nam;

**Forestry**
Kim Jae Ryul;

**Finance**
Yun Gi Jong;

**Commerce**
Hang Jang Run;

**Machine Industry**
Kye Hong Sun;

**Metal Industry**
Choe Man Hyon;

**Construction**
Cho Chol Junx;

**Joint Venture Industries**
Chae Hi Jong;

**Local Industries**
Kim Song Gu;

**Chemical Industry**
Kim Hwan;

**Mining Industry**
Kim Pil Hwan;

**Marine Transportation**
O Song Ryul;

**Chairmen of State Commissions**
(equivalent to Ministers)

**Light Industry**
Kim Bok Shin;

**External Economics**
Kim Dal Hyon;

**Agriculture**
Kim Won Jin;

**State Planning**
Choe Yong Rim;

**Transport**
Li Gil Song;

**Power Industry**
Li Ji Chan;

**Fisheries**
Choe Bok Yon;

**State Science and Technology**
Li Ja Bang;

**Electronics and Automated Industries**
Kim Chang Ho.

sumably exercising wide powers behind the scenes.

During inter-Korean talks in 1991, the most senior public level of formal South-North contact remained the inter-Korean premiers' discussions, no observable progress was made. As always, the bone of contention was the South's proposal for a gradualist agenda of confidence-building measures vs the North's proposal that the two sides proceed immediately to a non-aggression pact. In a series of commentaries throughout the year, the North Korean media rejected the validity of confidence-building measures, maintaining that promotion of people-to-people contacts and economic relations constituted efforts by external forces to "blow into the North winds of liberalism."

Conforming to the ritual pattern of previous years, the premiers' talks entered their customary winter freeze after a third unproductive session on 12-15 December 1990, and in February the talks were suspended unilaterally by the North on the eve of the annual South Korean–US "Team Spirit" military exercises. After a five-month hiatus, marked by uncompromising North Korean policy statements, on 11 July the North proposed a resumption for 27 August. In a quintessential Pyongyang move, this meeting was postponed in the wake of the attempted Soviet coup, with the North citing a current "cholera epidemic" in the South as the reason. The fourth session of the premiers' talks convened on 23 October in Pyongyang, and found the North Koreans willing to negotiate a document that combined features of Seoul's agenda with their own. This was hailed as a breakthrough of sorts, but where it might lead remains dependent on yet another tortuous negotiating process. While the absence of any signs of a broader change in Pyongyang's strategy suggested the move was tactical, as the talks were held 10 days after Kim Il Sung returned from Peking it also bore the hallmarks of yet another grudging Pyongyang response to Chinese pressure.

Elsewhere, various non-government initiatives such as the formation of joint sporting teams and some direct barter trade were duly cited by observers as evidence of progress in inter-Korean relations. It was equally clear to observers, however, that such non-official contacts are viewed by Pyongyang as strategies intended to undermine the Seoul government by emphasising the North's willingness to deal with non-government bodies.

**Kim: little help from friends.**

bowed to the inevitable with an announcement on 27 May that it would also seek separate UN admission. This was duly accomplished on 8 July.

The nuclear issue attracted considerable international attention. There seems little doubt that a nuclear weapons programme is well advanced in the North. Numerous reports that North Korea would be able to produce between three and six nuclear weapons by 1995 have not been contradicted by official sources. It has also become clear that Pyongyang intended to play on its nuclear potential for maximum strategic advantage.

The North's basic tactic appeared to be to link its acquisition of nuclear capability to the presence of US tactical nuclear weapons in South Korea, and thus force the US into direct negotiations over the head of the South Korean Government with a view to moderating the mutual threat.

Given its reputation for brinkmanship and outright provocation, North Korea's refusal to sign a nuclear safeguards agreement was widely viewed as ominous. As a result, international pressure built up steadily during the year, to the extent that any future economic and diplomatic gains the North might hope to make with industrialised nations — in particular Japan and the US — emerged as unambiguously dependent on its signing the safeguards agreement and allowing inspection.

Confronted with this powerful check, North Korea spent much of the year in a contradictory mood. On 15 July it appeared to moderate its demand that US nuclear weapons in the South also be subject to inspection when it informed the International Atomic Energy Agency (IAEA) that it would unconditionally sign a safeguards agreement in September. However, a day later, a spokesman reconfirmed the link with US inspection and the agreement. On 12 September the IAEA passed a resolution demanding North Korean action.

In the wake of President George Bush's nuclear weapons reduction announcement in September, which included the planned withdrawal of US tactical nuclear weapons from the Korean peninsula, the North maintained a wait-and-see attitude.

Relations with the Soviet Union deteriorated sharply following the announcement on 1 October 1990 that Moscow and Seoul would establish formal diplomatic relations, an act Pyongyang immediately described as a "betrayal." It was therefore not surprising that Pyongyang could scarcely conceal its delight during the brief period when it appeared that August's abortive Soviet coup might succeed, nor that the restored Soviet authorities should have made known their deep displeasure at this attitude.

By contrast, relations with China remained friendly during the year, despite the 20 October 1990 announcement that China and South Korea would exchange semi-official trade offices with consular functions.

The pace of Pyongyang-Peking exchanges remained brisk as the North sought to define how much China was prepared to assume the economic and political burden discarded by the Soviet Union. Accordingly, Korean Workers' Party (KWP) secretary Hwang Jang Yop visited Peking in November 1990 for talks with Chinese Communist Party general secretary Jiang Zemin, and was followed by Prime Minister Yon Hyon Muk and a team of economic portfolio ministers. The tenor of the Chinese response appears to have been that the level of political support would remain essentially unchanged and

# Foreign Relations

**N**orth Korea's international position continued to erode sharply during 1991. With the Soviet Union and China both moving perceptibly closer to South Korea, its long-standing objections to simultaneous entry of the two Koreas to the UN were disregarded, forcing Pyongyang into an abrupt about-face. Meanwhile, talks with Japan stalled, and widespread international pressure continued to be brought to bear on Pyongyang over its apparent intention to acquire a nuclear weapons capacity by 1995.

As the year wore on, it became clear that South Korea would achieve its policy objective of separate full UN membership for the two Koreas after the threat of Soviet and/or Chinese veto had been removed. After waging a vigorous campaign, in which it warned of unspecified consequences if simultaneous UN entry were to go ahead, North Korea ultimately some limited economic assistance would be forthcoming to compensate for reduced Soviet deliveries.

Chinese Premier Li Peng reciprocated with a visit to Pyongyang in May, where he apparently reaffirmed Peking's support for the North's "confederal republic" formula for reunification. He also reportedly advised the North Koreans that China would not veto the South's application for full UN membership. Kim Il Sung finally visited China between 4-13 October in what was widely seen as the culmination of a year-long effort to readjust in the wake of crumbling ties with the Soviet Union. While Kim would no doubt have been grateful for economic assistance from China, he appears to have got much the same measured response that Yon received, along with some advice from Peking on the need to make some gesture to reduce political tensions on the peninsula.

Any basis for improving North Korea–Japan relations proved harder to find. Following the non-government joint Liberal Democratic Party–Japan Socialist Party mission to Pyongyang in September 1990 and subsequent government level discussions, formal talks at the vice-ministerial level were convened in Pyongyang in January. However, they resulted in little more than a reiteration of long-standing and long-known differences. From the Japanese side, the sticking points remain the North's demand for pre-1945 reparations, and the North's refusal to permit IAEA inspection of its nuclear facilities.

This pattern of insubstantial contacts continued with a return KWP visit to Japan in February and a second round of talks in Tokyo on 11-12 March. These talks collapsed after a third session in Peking on 20-22 May amid North Korean objections to the Japanese raising the issue of the possible North Korean abduction of a Japanese national in 1978. They were later revived with an inconclusive session on 2 September, when the Japanese reported that the nuclear inspection issue remained the key stumbling block.

Although observers tended to see the North's decision to enter into this dialogue as motivated primarily by economic considerations, the unwillingness of Pyongyang to depart from its hardline position suggested the potential for it acquiring substantial benefits has been subsumed — for the present at least — by the desire to maintain more fundamental ideological positions.

Contact with US officials continued at the counsellor level in Peking, while a noticeable shift in diplomatic priority from Africa to Southeast Asia was evident. A number of North Korean missions in African countries were closed or downgraded, while relations with the Philippines were established and contacts resumed with Thailand. □

## Data

**Major industries:** Steel, 4.2 million tonnes (4.4 million); cement, 8 million tonnes (8.5 million); textiles, 500 million m² (560 million).

**Major agriculture:** Rice, 4 million tonnes (same); maize, 500,000 tonnes (same); potatoes, 1 million (same); wheat, barley and millet, 750,000 tonnes (800,000).

**Mining:** Coal, 43.3 million tonnes (40.7 million); iron ore, 12.9 million tonnes (same); non-ferrous metals, 290,000 tonnes (same).

**Finance:** Korean Central Bank controls all domestic banking. All foreign transactions are conducted through the subordinate Foreign Trade Bank (Muyok Unhaeng), and there are at least 2 other specialist foreign trade banks — Kumgang Bank and Daesong Bank.

**Currency:** Won (100 jon). Won 0.97 = US$1 (Won 0.94 = US1).

**Public holidays** (1992): 1 Jan. (New Year's Day), 16 Feb. (Kim Jong Il's birthday), 15 Apr. (Kim Il Sung's birthday), 25 Apr. (Armed Forces Day), 1 May (May Day), 9 Sept. (National Foundation Day), 10 Oct. (Korean Workers' Party Foundation Day).

**Weather:** North Korea has 4 distinct seasons. Winter last from early Nov.–late Mar. and are cold (average –5°C) but usually clear and sunny, though the chill factor can be extreme. Spring extends from late Mar.–early June and is dry and mild. Summer spans early June–late Aug. and is hot, humid and oppressive. Autumn, from early Sept.–late Oct. is dry, clear and mild.

**Government ministries:** External Economic Commission (Foreign Trade Ministry), Central District, Pyongyang, tel. 36684, tlx 5354 KP; Foreign Affairs, Central District, Pyongyang.

# Economy/Infrastructure

There were no marked improvements in North Korea's economic performance during 1991, with food production remaining a serious problem. The North is estimated to be suffering a shortfall of around 1 million tonnes of rice after a succession of poor harvests, and Pyongyang actively bought rice during the year — including an unprecedented deal for 100,000 tonnes from South Korea. In addition, serious energy shortages reportedly caused industry to operate at about 50% of capacity.

South Korea's National Unification Board estimated North Korea 1990 growth rate at –3.7%, a turnabout of unlikely suddenness from its 2.6% growth estimate for 1989. While the declining trend no doubt accelerated during 1990, it was generally accepted that such figures as these partly reflected efforts to compensate for past over-estimates.

Further, such estimates are made in the continuing near-total absence of meaningful data from the North. In a country where the media routinely blacks out or reverses unfavourable sports scores involving North Korean teams, doubts must surround the few figures presented in the 1991 budget to the Supreme People's Assembly in April.

As presented, revenue and expenditure would rise 4% and 4.5% respectively in a total budget of US$7.34 billion. In strictly comparative terms, however, these figures are slightly below the 5-6.3% range established in the years since the mid-1980s slump, and represent the closest to an acknowledgment of renewed economic difficulty as could be expected through the North Korean media.

The economy also received a setback with an agreement in November 1990 with the Soviet Union to settle trade accounts in hard currency from January 1991. Since the Soviet Union accounts for about 50% of total North Korean trade, this move might seem potentially disastrous to Pyongyang. However, with trade already being conducted against the background of US$3-4 billion in North Korean debts to the Soviet Union, and amid a maze of commodity delivery agreements, Moscow remains committed to protecting its past investments. While North Korea will obviously suffer — not least through the additional effects of the disintegrating Soviet economy — the immediate result of the hard-currency measures will be little more than to further increase the size of this debt.

Some compensation was offered by a sharp rise in inter-Korean trade during the year. As recently as 1988, this trade — carried on almost entirely through third parties — totalled barely US$1 million. However, in the first eight months of 1991 it reached US$124 million, to make South Korea one of the North's major trading partners. As in South Korea's trade with China and the Soviet Union, the trade pattern is chiefly determined by political factors and is tantamount to disguised aid. South Korean firms often find themselves under direct pressure from Seoul to accept North Korean commodities and products of dubious quality, and are unable to export to the North unless they do so under barter arrangements because of Pyongyang's lack of foreign exchange. As a result, the trade ratio runs at about 10:1 in the North's favour.

Seoul also showed particular interest in hints that Pyongyang might adopt the Chinese strategy of creating special economic zones. On 13 September, Kim Yong Sun — a leading Korean Workers' Party international relations specialist — expressed interest in the joint development of the Tumen River basin in concert with "neighbouring countries." There has been a good deal of initial survey work done on this concept, but it is understood that the three principal parties concerned — North Korea, the Soviet Union and China — still have basic disagreements about how best to proceed. □

# KOREA — SOUTH

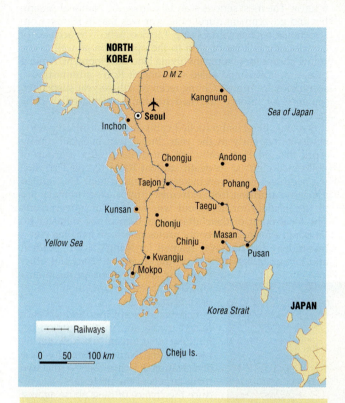

**Head of State**
President Roh Tae Woo.
**Prime Minister**
Chung Won Shik;
**Deputy Prime Minister (and Economic Planning)**
Choi Gak Kyu;
**National Unification**
Choi Ho Joong;
**Foreign Affairs**
Lee Sang Ock;
**Home Affairs**
Lee Sahng Yeon;
**Finance**
Rhee Yong Man;
**Justice**
Kim Ki Choon;
**National Defence**
Lee Jong Koo;
**Education**
Yoon Hyoung Sup;
**Culture**
Lee O Young;
**Information**
Choi Chang Yoon;
**Youth & Sports**
Park Chul Un;
**Agriculture, Forestry & Fisheries**
Cho Kyung Shik;
**Trade & Industry**
Lee Bong Suh;

**Energy & Resources**
Jin Nyum;
**Construction**
Lee Jin Seol;
**Health & Social Affairs**
Ahn Pil Joon;
**Environment**
Kwon E Hyock;
**Labour**
Choe Byung Yul;
**Transportation**
Lim In Taik;
**Communications**
Song Eon Jong;
**Government Administration**
Lee Yun Taek;
**Science & Technology**
Kim Jin Hyun;
**First State Minister for Political Affairs**
Choi Hyong Woo;
**Second State Minister for Political Affairs**
Lee Kye Soon;
**Office of Legislation**
Choi Sang Yup;
**Patriots & Veterans Affairs Agency**
Min Kyung Bae;
**Emergency Planning Committee**
Chung Jin Tae;
**Attorney-General**
Jeong Ku Young;
**Chief Justice**
Kim Deok Ju.

The 35-year-long Japanese rule in Korea ended after World War II when the country was divided, with the US holding the South and the Soviets the North.

In 1948, Syngman Rhee became president of South Korea and Kim Il Sung became head of North Korea. In June 1950 war broke out between the two newly created states. The UN mandated a US-led expeditionary force to aid South Korea, while China eventually aided the North. An estimated 500,000 people died in the three-year conflict, which also wrecked much of what was then a largely agrarian economy. In April 1960, Rhee was toppled following student riots, and the nation changed its form of government from a presidential to a cabinet system. John Chang was subsequently elected as prime minister, but his government was ousted in a military coup in May 1961 led by Gen. Park Chung Kee.

President Park ruled South Korea until 26 October 1979, when he was assassinated. He was replaced by Choi Kyu Hah, who released political detainees and promised to introduce political reforms. However, following violent student demonstrations that culminated in a major insurrection in Kwangju, Choi resigned on 16 August 1980. This cleared the way to power for Gen. Chun Doo Hwan, who was elected president on 27 August. After seven years in power, Chun stepped aside for military classmate Roh Tae Woo, who won the presidential elections on 17 December 1987 by more than 2 million votes after the opposition failed to unite and ran two rival candidates.

Unification of the divided peninsula moved closer to reality following the collapse of communism in Eastern Europe and the Soviet Union in the late 1980s and early 1990s, as the North — beset by economic problems and the loss of its major patrons — slowly began to adopt a more conciliatory attitude towards the South.

## Politics/Social Affairs

Although anti-government riots and demonstrations shook the country from April to June, South Korea continued to move steadily towards democratic politics and open government. Despite repeated challenges from leftist extremists on university campuses and in the labour movement, the country as a whole held firmly to a centrist, moderate course. In a climate of improved economic opportunities and political consciousness, South Korea looked increasingly like a society based on stable middle-class values. The radical forces of the Left were slowly being marginalised.

Campus unrest and inflation did not deter President Roh Tae Woo from holding two local elections in the first serious revival of local autonomy in three decades. Voters going to the polls in March elected 4,304 local district councillors in a campaign notable for its orderliness and frugal spending. Under the law, political parties were kept out of this most elementary stage of autonomous administration.

However, contests in June to elect 866 members of municipal and provincial assemblies in the eight provinces and Seoul were a different story. Here, the ruling Democratic Liberal Party (DLP) faced an array of opponents headed by the main opposition New Democratic Party (NDP) under Kim Dae Jung. A lot of mud-slinging accompanied the campaign, and several parties — including those in the opposition — were accused of selling nominations to candidates prepared to buy public office.

In addition, South Korean society was having to face many problems — ranging from the environment to housing and improved education — associated with the emergence of rising expectations. A series of political corruption scandals involving members of the National Assembly early in the year also undermined the public's confidence in Roh's leadership, which Kim sought to make a key issue in the local elections.

Kim's efforts backfired as the prolonged student riots —

137

and particularly the physical attack on newly appointed Prime Minister Chung Won Shik — turned the tide against the opposition. The DLP won 40% of the vote, taking a majority in most local assemblies including Seoul. Kim's NDP, perceived to be the vehicle of radical forces, performed poorly with just 22%. The tiny opposition Democratic Party hit both the NDP and the DLP to take 14% of the vote, with support spread evenly across the country.

The results raised faint but visible danger signals for the government. The combined opposition vote of 36% came close to the 40% won by the DLP, and a mid-year popularity poll indicated that the governing party could face a serious challenge in the March 1993 general election. One of the most trustworthy opinion polls showed the combined opposition popularity rate at 23.2% — dangerously close to the DLP's 26.1%.

But the low voter turnout for these elections — June's poll drew less than 60% of the electorate — demonstrated what appeared to be a growing crisis of public confidence in the existing political parties. Support for government was tepid, reflecting the lack of a better alternative than solid popularity. Further, Roh faced increasing criticism for his administration's insufficient attention to economic management, including its failure to tackle an inflation rate running at more than 10% during the year. Nor did the main opposition inspire much hope. At the end of two local elections, Kim's chances of becoming a future president appeared to have been seriously damaged.

Nevertheless, Roh's commitment to a more democratic political system remained firm. With about two years left before his retirement from office in February 1993, he began to depoliticise a military establishment that has overshadowed the country's political process for the past three decades. In December 1990, the government enforced a new code of conduct for armed forces personnel, laying down detailed regulations that barred them from political activities. In March 1991, Roh publicly warned his politically active relatives not to get involved in the succession issue. "The next president should come neither from the army nor from my family circle," he declared.

Roh: paving the way for his successor.

Specifically, that warning was directed against his brother-in-law, retired general Kim Bok Dong, who was hoping for the DLP nomination as the next presidential candidate. It also meant taking out political powerbrokers like former trade minister Kum Jin Ho and former state minister of political affairs Park Chul On. Kum is related to Roh by marriage and Park is a distant nephew. The removal of Park from a position of power seemed an important step in giving Roh's official team of advisers greater influence at the expense of his private team of aides.

Roh also moved quietly and methodically to take the military out of politics by retiring politically ambitious senior officers and appointing generals with professional reputations to key posts in the armed forces. The number of generals identified with Roh's home city of Taegu or with his alma mater Kyungbuk High School dropped markedly in the list of top 15 armed forces commanders. Given South Korea's economic maturity and requisite political development, the trend seemed to be as inevitable as it was desirable.

But the long-festering problem of political corruption dismayed the country as six legislators were either convicted or detained on charges of extorting funds from the business community. The most serious scandal to rock the National Assembly and government during the year was that of Hanbo Construction Co. chairman Chung Tae Soo, who was accused of contributing billions of won to the opposition as well as the ruling parties for favours involving land development. Among those implicated and jailed was one of Roh's administrative secretaries. In August, Chung received a three-year suspended sentence for bribery and had his company placed in bank receivership.

Scandals like Hanbo fuelled campus radicalism, triggering student riots early in the year. But it was in Seoul during April that the riots really got out of hand after a group of policemen clubbed to death student Kang Kyong Dae during a protest against an increase in tuition fees. This ignited a massive uprising from extremist groups eager to make use of the incident for an all-out war on the Roh government. The focal point of their attack was then prime minister Ro Jai Bong, a former university professor whose hardline views on student activities was blamed for Kang's death. Student and labour radicals rioted on the streets of Seoul and other cities for weeks, their protests sustained by the self-immolation of eight of their number.

This wave of suicides and violence rallied media and public opinion behind the government, and Roh quickly modified the National Security Law and National Police Act — the two main targets of the protesters — to reduce the chance of their abuse against demonstrators. He also replaced the unpopular prime minister with former education minister Chung Won Shik. But as the year drew to a close, the government had still failed to enact more liberal legislation governing demonstrations and other forms of street protest.

In September, when several hundred students from Seoul National University fire-bombed a nearby police station, the police opened fire and killed a student who was not part of the demonstration. With public outrage directed against the students as much as the police for using their guns, various radical groups disavowed the use of fire-bombs.

The media and public opinion condemned both the government and the political parties for failing to effectively deal with this type of incident. Under rising criticism, opposition figures Kim Dae Jung and Lee Ki Taek merged their parties on 10 September to become the Democratic Party. This represented the creation of the first integrated opposition camp since 1987, when Kim Dae Jung abandoned his opposition rival Kim Young Sam to run for president on a separate ticket.

In the past, neither Kim nor Lee has come anywhere near meeting halfway on political issues, so it was far from clear if their alliance would hold. Nevertheless, their unity restored the tradition of bipartisan politics in South Korea. Also, with Kim's power base in the southwestern region of Cholla and Lee's significant support in the rival Kyongsang area, the new grouping was expected to help blunt the combative nature of the country's regional relationships. The emergence of this stronger opposition foreshadows a closely fought campaign in the 1993 general election.

# Foreign Relations

The collapse of Soviet communism and the end of the Cold War raised hopes on the Korean peninsula that confrontation between North and South Korea could at last be laid to rest. This process came a step nearer when both North and South Korea simultaneously joined the UN in September. Their mutual recognition and implicit peaceful coexistence within the UN framework has profound implications for the future of the two Koreas.

Pyongyang's announcement in May that it was abandoning its long-held policy of an indivisible Korea and would join Seoul in the UN represented a triumphant success for South Korea's Northward diplomacy based on rapid reunification. The core of that policy has been the need for President Kim Il Sung's North Korean Government to accept the peninsula's status quo.

For decades Kim has refused to deal with the UN — let alone join it — on the grounds that it would perpetuate division. Instead, the Korean peninsula was left with the impractical position of holding a single membership, with the two sides alternately holding the seat.

Kim's purpose was to keep the Korean agenda beyond the UN's domain, conceivably so that North Korea could work out a revolutionary takeover by supporting a "people's democratic revolution" in the South, a policy enshrined in the charter of the ruling Korean Workers' Party. Having attempted to put this policy into action in 1950, triggering a three-year internecine war, Kim's decision to join the UN signalled the North's first official change in its previously overt hostile outlook.

The new realism in the North occurred against the backdrop of what may be judged the terminal phase of world communism following the demise of the Soviet system and reinforced by China's isolation after the 1989 Peking massacre. The failure of the hardliners' coup in the Soviet Union in August effectively ended whatever hopes Pyongyang may have held for superpower support for its position. In this respect, Kim's visit to Peking in October looked more like an effort to boost Northern morale than a demonstration of strong solidarity. In Peking, Kim got a clear message that he could expect no more economic aid from China. Chinese leaders also conveyed the world's concern over Pyongyang's secret nuclear weapons programme.

That China was now playing a different game on the whole Korean question was evident. At the UN in early October, China's Foreign Minister Qian Qichen officially met South Korean Foreign Minister Lee Sang Ock for the first time. This was in response to Lee's praise for Peking's role in helping to get Pyongyang into the UN and complimenting Seoul's efforts in resolving the difficult issue of Taiwan's representation at the Asia Pacific Economic Cooperation (Apec) meeting held in Seoul during November. Qian was pleased by Seoul's behind-the-scenes diplomacy persuading Taiwan to accept the name of Chinese Taipei rather than Republic of China.

Peking's fundamental position of recognising both Koreas seemed beyond doubt. Not only was Qian going to Seoul for the Apec conference despite strong objections from Pyongyang, but Seoul and Peking also began talks on a series of agreements covering trade and protection of investments. China is eager for South Korean investment in the development of the northeastern region bordering North Korea and the Soviet Union.

The North's rapidly worsening economy also raised the ominous spectre of a sudden collapse of Kim's government. Given Kim's rigid Stalinism, few analysts thought such a calamity could occur, but for the South it was the sort of nightmare scenario President Roh Tae Woo wanted to avoid, not least because it would have required billions of dollars worth of aid.

In order to shore up the North's sagging economy, Seoul continued trading directly or otherwise with Pyongyang, importing US$100 million worth of raw materials such as coal, and providing emergency rice shipments to alleviate food shortages. The one-way trade clearly amounted to economic aid as Seoul was exporting virtually nothing in return. Roh has suggested this kind of trade could rise to US$2 billion a year if the North desisted from nuclear weapons development and opened up communications, trade and visits with the South.

China was gently pushing Kim to accept these proposals, and the North responded alternately with a mixture of reason and prevarication. It agreed on the resumption of talks by the premiers in Pyongyang, while in New York North Korean Foreign Minister Kim Yong Nam courted US officials by publicly welcoming US President George Bush's initiative on elimination of tactical nuclear weapons. However, Kim essentially maintained that the North would not accept international inspection of its nuclear facilities unless the US agreed to remove its tactical nuclear weapons deployed in South Korea.

The US and South Korea have clearly rejected such a quid pro quo, insisting on separating the two issues. The US position has been to encourage reconciliation in direct dialogue, while the US would deal with its own nuclear issue under a global strategic framework with superpowers like China and the Soviet Union.

Seoul brought increasing pressure to bear on the North over the nuclear issue by mobilising every economic and diplomatic resource available, including a threat to have the UN Security Council adopt a resolution for mandatory inspection, such as the one imposed on Iraq. Moscow's new friendship with Seoul, reinforced by a large amount of economic aid, allows no complacency on the part of the North on the probable success of such an action. Pyongyang's position appeared vulnerable with only Peking theoretically capable of vetoing such a move.

These implications underscored the growing diplomatic position of South Korea in the international community, especially in the Asia-Pacific region as demonstrated by its hosting the Apec conference. Roh also made state visits to Canada and Mexico during the year, discussing trade and investment.

The new relationship with Moscow gained in depth and breadth despite that country's political and economic turmoil. Roh backed Soviet President Mikhail Gorbachov and Russian President Boris Yeltsin during the abortive August coup. As soon as Gorbachov resurfaced, Seoul released the disbursement of US$500 million in commercial loans — the remainder of US$1 billion originally pledged — and exports of consumer goods under additional trade credits resumed. This was the price Seoul was prepared to pay for opening relations in 1990 and Gorbachov's historic visit to South Korea in April 1991, which resulted in his promise to endorse South Korea's entry into the UN. Seoul also recognised the three Baltic republics, and prepared to open consulates in 1992 — two in Russia and one in the Kazakhstan republic where a large number of ethnic Koreans live.

With the US — Seoul's chief military and economic partner — the two meetings Roh and Bush held during the year narrowed differences on many contentious areas, including the trade deficit and the opening of South Korean markets to US goods. Despite the continuing reduction of US troops and concern over Bush's initiative on tactical nuclear weapons, the US reiterated that South Korea would remain under the US

# LAOS

CHINA

VIETNAM

BURMA

• Phong Saly

• Muong Sing

• Ban Houei Sai

Sam Neua •

Mekong R.

• Luang Prabang

Gulf of Tonkin

• Paksane

Vientiane ⊙

• Thakhek

• Savannakhet

THAILAND

• Pakse

Attopeu •

0   50   100 km

CAMBODIA

**State President and Party President**
Kaysone Phomvihan.
**Premier**
Khamtai Siphandon;
**Vice-Premiers**
Phoun Sipaseut, Khamphoui Keoboualapha;
**Defence**
Lieut-Gen. Choummaly Sayasone;
**Foreign Affairs**
Phoun Sipaseut;
**Interior**
Asang Laoli;
**Economy, Planning and Finance**
Khamphoui Keoboualapha;
**Commerce and Foreign Economic Relations Committee**
Phao Bounnaphon;
**Agriculture, Forestry, Irrigation and Cooperatives**
Inkong Mahavong;
**Industry and Handicrafts**
Soulivong Daravong (acting);
**Transport, Communications and Posts**
Oudom Khattiya;
**Education, Sports, Physical Education and Fine Arts**
Samane Vignaket;

**Public Health and Social Welfare**
Khambou Sounixay;
**Culture**
Thongsing Thammavong;
**Justice**
Kou Souvannamethi;
**State Bank**
Pani Vangkhamtou (Mrs);
**State Control Committee**
Maychantane Sengmany;
**Science and Technology Committee**
Souli Nanthavong;
**Social Sciences Committee**
Sisana Sisane;
**Head, Office of Council of Ministers**
Maisouk Saysompheng;
**Chairman, Supreme People's Assembly**
Nouhak Phoumsavan;
**Military Chief of General Staff**
Sisavat Keobounphan;
**Politburo**
Kaysone Phomvihan, Nouhak Phoumsavan, Khamtai Siphandon, Phoun Sipaseut, Maychantan Sengmani, Samane Vignaket, Oudom Khattigna, Choummali Sayason, Somlat Chathamath, Khamphoui Keoboualapha, Thongsing Thammavong.

**L**aos was first unified in 1353 by Fa Ngum, who brought several scattered Lao fiefdoms together into the powerful Kingdom of Lan Xang, or Kingdom of a Million Elephants. However, Lan Xang quickly succumbed to its expansionist Thai and Vietnamese neighbours, and Laos was little more than a Thai vassal state when the French made it a protectorate in the 1890s.

France granted Laos independence in 1953, but fighting soon broke out between the US-backed Royal Lao Government and the pro-communist Pathet Lao. The civil war ended two decades later, when the two sides signed a ceasefire in February 1973 and established a coalition government in April 1974.

In the wake of the communist victories in neighbouring Vietnam and Cambodia in early 1975, the Pathet Lao gradually seized control of the government. On 2 December 1975 they declared the establishment of the People's Democratic Republic of Laos. The new communist rulers allied themselves with Vietnam and the Soviet Union and moved quickly to collectivise agriculture and shut down private traders.

However, these policies brought Laos' already backward economy to the brink of collapse, forcing the communists to introduce market-style reforms in the mid-1980s and take steps to improve their relations with Thailand, China and the US.

In August 1991, the Supreme National Assembly, elected in 1989 during the country's first national elections since the communist takeover, approved Laos' first constitution since the previous one was abolished in 1975. The constitution formalised the party's monopoly over Lao political life, while reaffirming the goal of moving the country towards a free-market economy.

# Politics/Social Affairs

**I**n August 1991, Laos' Supreme National Assembly (SNA) — or nominal parliament — passed the country's first constitution since the communists seized power in 1975 and elected Lao People's Revolutionary Party leader Kaysone Phomvihan as state president. Kaysone was replaced as prime minister by defence minister, Khamtai Siphandone, but is expected to remain the most dominant figure in Lao politics.

Earlier, the country's communist leadership reaffirmed at the party's fifth congress, held between 27-29 March, the goal of moving the country towards a free-market economy while ruling out sharing power with other political groups. The party also took its first steps in preparation for a generational change by retiring three veteran leaders and appointing five new members to the ruling politburo.

At its meeting in August, the SNA appointed Khamphoui Keoboualapha, a newly elected politburo member and former minister of trade, as deputy prime minister and minister of economy, planning and finance, replacing Sali Vongkhamsao, who had died in January. Lieut-Gen. Choummali Sayasone, a deputy minister of defence, was elected to head the ministry following Khamtai's promotion.

The new, 80-article constitution declared the communist party as the "leading organ" of the country's political system, apparently ruling out any political reform similar to that sweeping much of the former communist world. Reflecting the country's recent economic reforms, the constitution affirmed "equality" between all economic sectors and pledged to protect and promote "private ownership by domestic capitalists and foreigners who make investments" in Laos.

The new constitution also reorganised the government's administrative structure. The role of the state presidency, until now largely a ceremonial office, was upgraded to become the most powerful government position with the right to issue decrees and appoint or dismiss the prime minister, government ministers and provincial governors. The president was also named head of the armed forces.

The once cumbersome council of ministers, which has long made most decisions and overseen the activities of individual ministries, was abolished in the new constitution. Although the council continued to function at the end of the year, the gradual phasing out of the body would — at least in theory — streamline government decision-making and dramatically increase the power and responsibilities of the prime minister and individual ministers.

The constitution also gave an increased political role — again in theory — to the country's legislature, which was renamed the National Assembly. The August session of the Supreme People's Assembly (SPA) also adopted a new law on elections, under which a new National Assembly will be elected in late 1991 or early 1992 for a five-year term.

The new constitution spelled out in some detail the rights of citizens in an apparent attempt to stop frequent abuse and arbitrary treatment by officials. It declared that "all acts of bureaucratism and harassment that can be physically harmful to the people and detrimental to their honour, lives, consciences and property are prohibited," adding that "Lao citizens cannot be arrested or searched without a warrant or approval of authorised organisations, except in cases stipulated by law."

But human-rights groups, which have frequently criticised the government for practising long-term detention of individuals without charge or trial, are concerned that references to "cases stipulated by law" do not provide adequate guarantees against arbitrary arrest and detention. Amnesty International reported in March that Laos still held 33 political prisoners in re-education camps established following the communist victory in 1975.

In apparent recognition that legal abuses were not uncommon, Nouhak Phoumsavan, who ranks second in the politburo and serves as chairman of the SPA, told the legislature that many of the country's law-enforcement officials are "only neophytes whose standards are low . . . some of them may even lack a sense of impartiality, thereby leading courts to give out unjust verdicts against the accused."

**Kaysone: survivor.**

After the new constitution was ratified, Nouhak called on the delegates to take steps to upgrade the country's legal system. "We must gradually and systematically transform this constitution into many laws and regulations with a view to protecting our citizens' rights to mastery and democratic freedom," he said.

The three senior statesmen retired from the politburo at the party congress in March were Souphanouvong, who served as state president until August, Phoumi Vongvichit, who had been acting president since Souphanouvong suffered a stroke five years ago, and Sisomphon Lovansai, a former vice-chairman of the SPA.

A fourth man dropped from the politburo was armed forces chief of staff Sisavat Keobounphan. Sisavat, who is also mayor of Vientiane, is best known for his role in negotiating a ceasefire four years ago with Thai military leaders to end a bloody border war between the two countries. Lao sources say Sisavat's active business dealings with the Thai military and private Thai companies had offended many party officials.

Two former alternate members of the politburo and three new members were elected to the 11-man politburo. The new members are Somlat Chanthamath, head of the central committee's propaganda and training committee, Khamphoui, the newly elected vice–prime minister, and Thongsing Thammavong, vice-president of the SPA.

All three are believed to be supporters of the economic reform policies of Kaysone, who was re-elected party chief, a job he has held since the party was founded in 1955. Despite his failing health, Kaysone remains the driving force behind the party's attempts to establish a free-market economy and improve its relations with the outside world.

The congress changed Kaysone's title from "general secretary" to "president of the party." This new title — along with the congress' decision to abolish the nine-man secretariat which had previously run party affairs on a day-to-day basis — will give the party chief even greater powers.

Foreign observers believe the secretariat was abolished in an attempt to streamline decision-making and recentralise some of the political power lost to the provinces as a result of the economic reforms. In recent years, provincial party committees had often been able to ignore central government orders — like the ban on logging to protect the country's dwindling forests — by appealing directly to the secretariat.

The congress also elected 15 new members, including four alternates, to the 59-member central committee, while dropping 14 former members. Most of those ousted were ageing or sick, while many of the new members were provincial party officials and younger technocrats.

The most surprising removal from the central committee was Kaysone's wife Thongvinh, who is in her 50s and heads the country's youth association. Observers believe she was removed because party leaders viewed her trading, logging and construction activities as inappropriate for a central committee member.

Lao sources said the reorganisation of the party will also be followed by efforts to streamline the bureaucracy by reducing the number of ministries and vice-ministers in individual ministries, which often have four or more deputies with overlapping duties.

Preparation for the fifth congress involved greater participation of party members than previous congresses, which did little more than rubber stamp decisions already made by the politburo. On several occasions before the congress, private businessmen, intellectuals and Buddhist monks were invited to meetings to discuss the party's economic policies.

Although the congress remained a subdued, formal affair, foreign diplomats report that a secret plenum held just before it opened witnessed heated debates and forced three votes before agreeing on the final central committee line-up.

Many people in the capital appeared relieved that the congress had reaffirmed the party's economic reform policies, though some intellectuals and mid-level officials privately complained about the lack of political liberalisation. However, few people appear to support calls for a multi-party democracy by three former senior government officials who were arrested in October 1990.

"People want to live better, but they don't want to see what happened in Eastern Europe happening here," a Soviet diplomat told the REVIEW. "With 30% of the population illiterate, only a few people are involved in politics. The rest are struggling to find enough food to survive."

The third plenum of the central committee, meeting in early August, concluded that the party had been slow in implementing the new policies set forth by the March congress. "The correct line set forth by the fifth party congress has not yet been profoundly comprehended while its implementation is still rather slow," official Vientiane radio reported after the meeting.

"The difficult livelihood and economic, social and cultural problems and other negative phenomena have not been solved in a timely manner, thus resulting in considerable repercussions on the development of our country." □

# Foreign Relations

Laos' communist leaders, apparently recognising that the geopolitical map of the world had been redrawn with the collapse of communism in Eastern Europe and the Soviet Union, focused most of their diplomatic energy in 1991 on China and Thailand. Vientiane's relations with these two neighbours had soured after the communist victory in 1975, when Laos had aligned itself with the Soviet Union and Vietnam.

The visit to Laos in March by Thai army commander Gen. Suchinda Kraprayoon — his first foreign trip after the February military coup in Thailand — demonstrated how much ties between Vientiane and Bangkok have improved in recent years. During his talks with Lao armed forces chief of staff Gen. Sisavat Keobounphan, the two generals agreed to withdraw their troops from a disputed border area where their armies had fought a brief but bloody campaign in late 1987, early 1988. Since the fighting ended, technical experts from Laos and Thailand have surveyed the disputed area and held several rounds of talks, but so far they have failed to resolve their differences.

Suchinda, who is deputy chairman of the National Peacekeeping Council which toppled Thailand's civilian government, and his Lao counterpart agreed to exchange military attaches and discussed the possibility of future joint military exercises. They also agreed to work together to stem the activities of Lao anti-government insurgents using sanctuaries in Thailand to mount raids on Laos and Thai communist guerillas using Lao territory to launch attacks into Thailand.

A few months later, the Thai Government announced that Laos would receive nearly half of a new Baht 200 million (US$7.8 million) development aid fund established to help poor countries. Thai officials said most of the money would be used to provide technical training for Laotian officials and students. Some observers viewed Thailand's stepped-up

friendship campaign as an attempt to reduce Laos' dependence on Vietnam.

Laos demonstrated its enthusiasm for Thailand's overtures when, during a visit to Bangkok in April, Deputy Prime Minister and Foreign Minister Phoun Sipaseut awarded Thai Princess Maha Chakri Sirindorn the Decoration of Honour, the highest award the Lao communist government has ever granted a foreigner. The princess had visited Laos in March 1990.

During Phoun's visit to Bangkok, he and Thai Foreign Minister Arsa Sarasin agreed to establish two separate high-level committees to oversee border security and economic cooperation between the two countries. When Arsa visited Laos in May on his first foreign trip after the coup, Thailand agreed to reduce tariffs on Lao agricultural exports and help increase Laos' hydroelectric power output. The two sides also agreed to set up a joint-venture company to replace the organisation that has long had a monopoly on transporting transit goods to landlocked Laos.

Lao-Thai trade and Thai investment in Laos have increased sharply since the border clash ended in early 1988. But Lao officials are concerned that Thai businessmen, who have already depleted their own country's forest and mineral resources, will over-exploit their neighbour's still largely untapped natural wealth.

Diplomacy: looking for new allies.

In an attempt to resolve another problem which has long plagued relations between Vientiane and Bangkok, Laos, Thailand and the UN High Commissioner for Refugees (UNHCR) agreed in June on a plan under which all 60,000 Lao refugees now in camps in Thailand would be repatriated or resettled in third countries by the end of 1994. Vientiane, recognising that it needs to reassure refugees that they will not be mistreated when they return home, agreed in August for the first time to let refugee representatives visit proposed resettlement sites in Laos. About 8,000 Lao refugees, many of them minority highland peoples, have returned to Laos since 1980 under a voluntary repatriation programme organised by the UNHCR.

Vientiane and Peking took further steps to improve their ties following the fence-mending visit to China by party chief Kaysone Phomvihan in late 1989. China had supported the Lao communists in their war against the US, but relations soured when Laos sided with Vietnam following its 1978 invasion of Cambodia that ousted the Chinese-backed Khmer Rouge.

Chinese Premier Li Peng travelled to Laos in December 1990. During his visit, the first by a Chinese premier to its tiny southern neighbour, the two sides signed three economic agreements. One of these included a Rmb 50 million (US$9.3 million) credit for economic and technical cooperation over the next five years. Peking also provided Vientiane aid to build a satellite television relay station.

Li's trip was followed by a surge of party, state, military and provincial delegations between the two countries. Even Kaysone, who for more than a decade had gone to the Soviet Union or Vietnam to relax, took a holiday in China in September. Technical teams held several rounds of talks to resolve their border disputes, and the two countries agreed in August that China Southern Airlines would begin flights in late 1991 between the Lao capital and Canton.

The two sides also took steps to repatriate the nearly 4,000 Lao refugees living in China since relations between the two sides deteriorated in the late 1970s. The first known group of refugees, totalling some 130 people, returned in March, and Laos agreed in August to begin receiving 100 to 200 refugees each month from China, Vientiane Radio reported.

Laos also continued its attempts to improve relations with the US by stepping up its work to resolve the problem of some 528 American servicemen missing since the end of the Indochina War. Laos agreed in 1991 to several joint searches for the remains of the missing, mainly aircrew whose aircraft crashed on bombing raids. The search areas were extended into the provinces of Houa Phan and Xieng Khouang in the north and Khammouane in the south, where the US military had not been allowed to work before.

Following high-level bilateral talks in April, Vientiane agreed for the first time to work on "discrepancy cases," or those which Washington says it has evidence that servicemen may have survived and become prisoners of war.

Laos also continued to cooperate with the UN and the US on the suppression of narcotics, an issue which has strained relations between Vientiane and Washington in recent years. An official US report on narcotics released in March 1991 no longer charged Laos with being the world's third-largest opium producer.

"The past two years have seen a dramatic turnaround in Lao willingness to discuss narcotics issues realistically and to ask for and receive assistance in the narcotics area," the report said. It said opium production in Laos had fallen 27% to about 275 tonnes, mainly due to the introduction of tougher laws against trafficking and government cooperation on training and crop substitution projects. Many Lao officials and foreign diplomats in Vientiane believe the US had long over-estimated Laos' actual opium production.

In late 1990, Vientiane agreed to accept the first US Peace Corps volunteers to work in Laos. The volunteers were to provide assistance in small business development and in teaching English, particularly in government ministries. In February, Laos sent its first ever trade mission to the US. Vientiane's policy of cooperating with Washington finally paid off in mid-November, when US President George Bush announced that full diplomatic ties had been restored between the two countries.

Despite Vientiane's improving ties with the rest of the world, Laos' communist leadership did not appear willing to abandon its longstanding "special relations" with Vietnam. When Vietnam dropped these words from a draft political report prepared for its seventh party congress in June, Laos and Cambodia protested. Hanoi, which apparently had wanted to signal that it was downgrading its relations with its two smaller neighbours following its 1989 troop withdrawal from Cambodia, obliged and returned the words "special friendship and solidarity" to describe relations among the three countries.

# Economy/Infrastructure

Serious floods in Laos' fertile southern provinces in September — following drought and pest infestations in the north earlier in the planting season — threatened the country's rice crop and the recent modest economic gains that stemmed from the communist party's five-year reform programme. Despite the loss of massive amounts of aid from the Soviet Union, Laos' inflation rate had fallen since early 1990, its exchange rate had stabilised and its businessmen had become more confident in the country's economic future.

Inflation fell from 68% two years ago to 18% in 1990 and to an estimated 15% in 1991. Foreign observers attribute this improvement to the government's banking reforms, which included establishing several new commercial banks and introducing tighter fiscal and monetary policies. Credit to money-losing state enterprises has been cut, while excess cash in the market had been absorbed by the banks which began offering savings-account interest rates higher than inflation.

The Lao kip, the national currency, which had lost nearly half of its value in 1989, has stabilised at around Kip 700 to US$1 for the past two years. The government's decision to allow the free exchange of hard currency and gold helped stop runs on the local currency.

Rice: shortages loom after floods.

Much of this success was threatened, at least in the short term, by the floods and droughts which ravaged the 1991 rice crop, on which 75% of the population depends for its livelihood. Vientiane's official newsagency said nearly 93,000 ha, almost 25% of the country's lowland rice growing area, had been damaged. As a result, the report said, the rice harvest was expected to reach only 1.08 million tonnes, leaving Laos with a 185,000-tonne shortfall. Good rice harvests during the previous two years had stabilised the price of food and helped slow inflation. Favourable weather and the communist party's decision to de-collectivise agriculture had boosted rice production to 1.5 million tonnes in 1990, up from just over 1 million tonnes two years earlier. Laos' GDP increased about 9% that year, up from only 2.1% two years earlier.

In April, the IMF gave the country a US$12 million loan to support the government's reform programme, improve its economic growth prospects and strengthen its balance of payments.

But Laos' modest economic successes could not hide the country's overwhelming problems. A weak infrastructure, poorly trained workforce, lack of skilled managers and a shortage of capital and foreign exchange continue to hobble economic growth. The failure of many officials to implement the party's economic reforms further slowed development, Deputy Minister of Economy, Planning and Finance Khamsai Souphanouvong told the party congress in March. Khamsai also said the government's bureaucracy is "too bloated and large" and "the system of management is still confusing and overlapping."

The government's budget deficit has averaged around 60% in recent years, even though new tax policies have increased tax revenue eight-fold. Because this deficit was largely financed by foreign aid, the sharp Soviet aid cuts that started in

January 1991 will make it harder for the government to cover its expenses and will force it to cut capital investment. Already many civil servants, particularly in the countryside, have not been paid for up to two years and, according to the Asian Development Bank (ADB), gross investment fell from 25.1% of GDP in 1989 to 19.5% in 1990.

Vientiane had received grant aid and credits worth Rbl 571.7 million (US$957 million at the September 1991 rate) from socialist countries, primarily from the Soviet Union, between 1986-90, according to Lao estimates. Although Moscow suspended its aid in January 1991, it will continue dispensing roughly Rbl 50 million left unspent from the previous five-year plan, Soviet officials said. Most of these funds will be spent on education and health projects. The Lao military will be required to begin paying for its equipment, spare parts and training from the Soviet Union.

The Soviet Union has also suspended credits to Laos, which over the past 15 years have reached Rbl 750 million, or about 75% of the country's foreign debt. Moscow has not, however, insisted that Vientiane begin repaying these loans before the end of the decade.

But Laos, unlike Vietnam and Cambodia, can depend on help from Japan and the West to make up some of this loss in Soviet aid and credits. Non-Soviet assistance to Laos has grown in recent years, with Japan, Sweden and Australia being the three largest donors. Official capital inflows from non-communist sources reached US$68.4 million in 1990, up from US$54.4 million the year before, according to the ADB.

Soviet diplomats estimate that trade between Laos and the Soviet Union would be cut to roughly US$40 million in 1991, about half the level of the previous year, and will be calculated in hard currency at world market prices. Soviet exports of oil, cement, vehicles and medicines totalled about Rbl 350 million between 1986-90, while Lao exports of agricultural and for-

estry products, tin ore and coffee reached less than Rbl 60 million, according to Soviet figures. Lao officials said Moscow had pledged to supply Vientiane with only about 50% its 100,000-tonne oil requirements in 1991, against about 90% in the past.

The political and economic chaos in the Soviet Union forced Laos to explore new markets in the capitalist world. Laos' foreign trade has increased since the economic reforms were introduced five years ago, but its exports in 1989 totalled only US$97 million, well under half the cost of its US$230 million import bill.

Vientiane faces enormous difficulties in reducing this trade deficit. Although the country's exports of electricity and wood products — each of which make up about nearly a third of the country's export income — grew by 42% and 25% respectively in 1990, export earnings still only covered about one third of Laos' imports, according to ADB estimates. Laos' 1990 current-account deficit reached nearly US$140 million, or about 20% of GDP, the ADB said.

Laos' landlocked status has further hampered export development. The cost of trans-shipment through Thailand or Vietnam increases the price of Lao goods by as much as 60%, making them less competitive on the international market, Lao officials say.

Laos' trade with Thailand reached Baht 3.8 billion (US$148 million) in 1990, up sharply from only Baht 566 million five years earlier. Lao officials hope Bangkok's agreement in August to cut import tariffs on Lao products to a maximum of 20% will help Vientiane increase its exports further. Previously, Thailand had charged taxes of 40-80% on most Lao products. The first bridge linking Laos and Thailand — construction of which was due to begin in November 1991 with funding from Australia — should also help increase trade across the Mekong River.

The Lao Government has also been looking for foreign companies to help the country expand its exports. Some 109 foreign-investment contracts, worth US$231 million, have been approved since the country's liberal foreign-investment code was promulgated in 1988, according to officials from the Ministry of Commerce and External Economic Relations.

Most of these contracts are worth less than US$5 million each, and almost 50% have been signed with Thai companies interested in logging and developing hotels and tourism. About a dozen European and Asian garment manufacturers have begun producing jeans and T-shirts in Laos, which is not subject to EC quotas. In addition, Lao Aviation, the country's flag carrier, has formed a joint venture with three firms from the US, Thailand and Australia to increase and upgrade its international flights.

Several US and Australian companies have begun prospecting for minerals. In April, the government — with assistance from Australia — organised a conference for foreign mining companies to publicise Laos' mineral potential, which includes iron and tin ore, coal, gypsum, limestone, potash, precious stones and gold. Enterprise Oil of Britain and Hunt Oil of the US are exploring for oil and natural gas in the far south.

Some foreign companies have also taken over unprofitable enterprises privatised by the Lao Government. A Thai company has leased a cigarette factory, while others from Japan and Thailand have joined forces to run a factory producing tin-roofing sheets.

Khamsai told the party congress that 400 of the state's former 600 enterprises have been transferred to "other forms of ownership," meaning that they have been partially privatised or leased to domestic capitalists or foreign companies. □

## Data

**Major industries:** Electric power (1989), 698 million kWh (552 million); timber (1989), 250-300,000 m³ (est.); textiles (1987), 830,000 m (967,000).

**Major agriculture:** Rice (1990), 1.5 million tonnes (1.4 million); sugarcane (1986), 112,000 tonnes; maize (1987), 35,725 tonnes (41,680); tobacco (1987), 24,727 tonnes (13,999); coffee (1987), 5,312 tonnes (5,011); cotton (1987), 4,010 tonnes (2,645).

**Mining:** Gypsum (1989), 104,000 tonnes (80,000); coal (1987), 1,505 tonnes; tin (1987), 501.2 tonnes (559).

**Oil and gas:** Nil.

**Major imports** (1989): US$230 million (US$155.4 million).

**Major exports:** Total 1989, US$98 million (US$71.5 million). Logs and wood products (1988), US$45 million (US$32.8 million); electricity (1989), US$14.9 million (US$11 million); coffee (1987), US$9 million (US$2.9 million); tin and gypsum (1987), US$3.5 million (US$4.2 million).

**Tourism and transport** (1989): Tourist arrivals, 2,631, (470). Vientiane can be reached by air from Bangkok on Lao Aviation and Thai International flights. Lao Aviation and Air Vietnam connect Vientiane to Hanoi and Ho Chi Minh City. Lao Aviation also flies to Phnom Penh. Aeroflot connects Vientiane to Moscow. Lao Aviation operates a number of domestic routes, including services to Luang Prabang, Phonesavan, Pakse and Savannakhet. There is no railway system in Laos. Car hire is available, but foreigners need permission to travel by road outside Vientiane.

**Major banks:** State Bank, Pangham Rd, Vientiane, tel. 2000; Banque Pour le Commerce Exterieur, Pangham Rd, Vientiane, tel. 2646, 3646, tlx 4301 BCEVTELS; Joint Development Bank, Lane Xang St, a joint venture with a Thai company.

**Finance:** Laos has no finance companies, building societies or stock exchanges.

**Currency:** Kip 705 = US$1 in Nov. 1991 (Kip 697 = US$1 in Nov. 1990).

**Major ministries:** Council of Ministers, Nong Bone Rd, Vientiane, tel. 3171; Foreign Affairs, Nong Bone Rd, Vientiane, tel. 2107; Commerce and Foreign Economic Relations, Nong Bone Rd, Vientiane, tel. 2331; State Planning Committee, Luang Prabang Rd, Vientiane, tel. 3770, 3815.

**Public holidays** (1992): 1 Jan. (New Year), 13-14 Apr. (Lao New Year), 1 May (Labour Day), 2 Dec. (National Day).

**Weather:** Laos has a tropical climate, with about 5 months of heavy rainfall from May-Sept. Average temperature in Vientiane between Apr.-May 38°C; Dec.-Jan. 21°C. Average rainfall in Vientiane, 1,720 mm.

**Taxation:** All state and private enterprises pay taxes varying according to their activities and geographical locations. The Foreign Investmemt Code passed in 1988 allows 100% foreign ownership of companies, with tax rates ranging from 20-35%, depending on the investment sector.

# MACAU

Map labels: CHINA · Areia Preta · Reservoir · Inner Harbour · CHINA · Outer Harbour · Casino · Proposed bridge · Bridge · Proposed reclamation area · TAIPA ISLAND · Trotting Track · Town · Causeway · Xiaohengqin Is. · Proposed Cargo Port · COLOANE ISLAND · Town · Hac Sa Van · Dahengqin Is. · Roads · 0  1  2 km

Macau was settled by the Portuguese in 1557 to provide a base for their trade with China. Annual tribute was paid for the territory until the Portuguese declared it separate from China in 1849. China only recognised the annexation in 1887, when Portugal undertook "never to alienate Macau and its dependencies without agreement with China."

During the height of the 1966-67 Cultural Revolution in China, Macau experienced one of the worst crises of its 400-year history that permanently altered its relationship with China. The incident, sparked after officials refused a building permit to a communist school, saw leftists launch massive anti-government protests.

Badly shaken, the governor was reported to have offered to abandon the enclave within one month. Peking turned down the offer, but settled for a pledge to eliminate Kuomintang influence from Macau. Since then, Peking's influence has been predominant and the colonial administration little more than a facade.

Following the 1974 military coup in Portugal, the new leftist government reportedly tried to return Macau to China. When Peking again declined, Lisbon redefined Macau as a Chinese territory under Portuguese administration. In 1979, when Peking and Lisbon were discussing establishing diplomatic relation, Portugal again raised the question of the status of Macau. Again, China was prepared to accept the status quo.

Macau's future status was finally resolved in April 1987 with the signing of the Sino-Portuguese joint declaration. This bound both parties to an agreement under which Macau would become a special administrative region of China in 1999, to be run by Macau people enjoying "a high degree of autonomy."

## Politics/Social Affairs

Following Carlos Melancia's resignation as governor of Macau in September 1990, Portuguese President Mario Soares announced he would not name a successor until after Portugal's January 1991 elections, and appointed Under-Secretary for Economic Affairs Francisco Nabo as acting governor.

After being re-elected president, Soares — apparently after consultations with centralist Prime Minister Anibal Cavaco Silva — appointed Gen. Vasco Rocha Vieira, then minister with special responsibility for the Azores Islands, as Macau's new governor. It was reported in Portugal that Soares — constitutionally responsible for selecting the governor — wanted a government consensus over the appointment following the resignations of two previous Macau governors, Pinto Machado and Melancia.

Six by-elections were called in Macau in March to increase the Legislative Assembly from 17 to 23 deputies. Two of the seats were directly elected by universal suffrage, two through community associations registered as "functional constituencies," and the remaining two were appointed by the new governor.

The so-called 2-2-2 increase was enshrined in 1990's reform of the Macau Organic Statute, which constitutes the enclave's mini-constitution until 20 December 1999, when it will be replaced by the Basic Law of the future Macau special administrative region (SAR) when sovereignty reverts to China. However, the two-week election campaign for the two new direct seats attracted little interest among Macau's 97,648 registered voters, only 18.68% of whom cast their ballots. During the 1988 October general election 29.71% of the then 67,492 registered electorate voted.

Liberal candidates concentrated their efforts on demands for greater democracy and social justice, while the pro-Peking traditionalists stuck to their litany of "stability and prosperity" for the enclave in the run-up to the Chinese takeover. Nevertheless, liberals and traditionalists both demanded that Chinese be made the enclave's official language in order to speed up localisation of the 12,000-strong civil service and to build up a locally based judicial system.

Unlike in neighbouring Hongkong, the elections were a disaster for the liberals, who were divided into several camps. They failed to win either of the directly elected seats, both of which went to the well-organised pro-Peking "Union of Promotion of Progress," which took almost 50% of the votes cast. This result contrast strongly with the October 1988 general elections, when liberals won 44% of the votes cast against 34% for the pro-Peking groups.

Some pro-democracy activists said the record low turnout partly represented a protest against the Legislative Assembly itself, which is dominated by conservatives concerned mainly with protecting their own interests.

The enlarged assembly leaves intact the old balance of 35% directly and 35% indirectly elected seats, and 30% of the seats for government appointees. In this respect, the Macau assembly can pride itself on having a more democratic assembly than Hongkong's Legislative Council, which after 1991's first direct elections, has only 30% elected members. The new assembly is made up of seven Macanese, 13 ethnic Chinese and three Portuguese.

Macanese lawyer Carlos Assumpcao has chaired the assembly since its inception in 1976, while banker Edmund Ho, a pro-Peking community leader widely tipped to become the first chief executive of the Macau SAR in December 1999, has been vice-chairman since October 1988. Of the 23 legislators, nine may be considered pro-government, nine pro-Peking, three liberal and two politically independent.

Presumably to quell any resentment over the issue, Soares decided the Legislative Assembly should vote on confirmation of Vieira as the new governor. The vote was held behind closed doors, and a spokesman said it unanimously favoured the appointment.

Vieira's appointment was also broadly welcomed by community leaders, many of whom remembered him from when he served as chief-of-staff of the Portuguese garrison between 1973-74 and as director of public works and communications between 1974-75.

When Vieira was sworn in as governor in Lisbon on 23 April, he pledged to maintain the "financial equilibrium" of Macau's budget during the transition and continue the development programme — which includes an ambitious airport project — started by his predecessors.

Even before his arrival, on 10 May, the new governor made his first two cabinet changes. He appointed the popular Jorge Rangel as under-secretary for education, youth and administration, and Ana Maria Perez to the social affairs and health portfolio. On 16 May a new cabinet of seven under-secretaries — five of them Portuguese and two Macau-born — was sworn in. In his subsequent address, Vieira made it clear who was in charge, declaring that under-secretaries "do not have powers of their own, but only those that are purposely delegated to them by the governor."

This was in marked contrast to Melancia's administration, when the under-secretaries built up their own spheres of influence, much to the detriment of political cohesion.

A week after his arrival, Vieira received a petition from the Macau Union for the Development of Democracy asking for the immediate appointment of a commissioner against corruption. On 10 July he replied — albeit somewhat obliquely — when he said "the fight against corruption has already started, namely through the fight against bureaucracy, holding civil servants responsible for what they do." He then announced he would appoint a High Commissioner Against Corruption and Administrative Illegality, a post created by the Legislative Assembly in July 1990.

A three-day official visit by Zhuhai special economic zone mayor Liang Guangda to Macau in July was the first official contact between a senior mainland China official and the new governor. The visit apparently led to the easing of relations between the two neighbours, severely strained by competition for Peking's blessing for their rival airport projects during the mid-1980s. Both sides agreed on joint efforts in fighting smuggling between the two territories and to hold joint cultural events.

Relations with Peking remained generally cordial. In August, during Vieira's first visit to Portugal since becoming governor, Soares announced the establishment of a Chinese visa office in Macau, with quasi-diplomatic status. At the end of August, the director of the New China News Agency's Macau bureau announced a new "division of labour" at vice-directorate level — often viewed as China's de facto "shadow" government in the enclave — to deal with Macau's "three big issues." These are the localisation of the civil service, making Chinese an official language on a par with Portuguese — which was agreed at a Sino-Portuguese Joint Liaison Group meeting in Peking during September — and localising the legal and judicial systems, including translating Portuguese laws into Chinese. China had pledged in the Sino-Portuguese Joint Declaration that the existing Portuguese legal system would remain basically unchanged for 50 years after 1999.

Vieira announced a "triangular approach" to resolving the main issues during the transition period on his return from Portugal on 25 August. He said the array of problems facing the enclave in the run-up to 1999 had "outgrown the decision-making capacity of the Macau Government," and it was therefore necessary for all major issues regarding Macau to pass through Lisbon and Peking in order to reach solutions based on consensus. As a consequence of this new approach, the governor announced trilateral talks on the Macau airport project would be held in Peking. This approach was in stark contrast to Melancia's, who had repeatedly criticised Peking and Lisbon for their alleged "interference" in Macau's internal

**Vieira: in step with the times.**

affairs.

The Macau Basic Law drafting process created little interest among the enclave's 500,000 inhabitants, despite the fact that it will determine their lives for 50 years after the change-over to China. When the 145-article Basic Law provisional draft was opened for four months of public consultation ending in mid-November, it stirred little debate among the majority of Macau's residents save for the enclave's small but vocal pro-democracy movement and representatives of the Portuguese-speaking Macanese minority.

Representatives of the 7,000-strong Macanese community complained that their political rights after 1999 had been severely curtailed by such proposals that called for the Legislative Assembly to have a 20% limit for non-Chinese. They also complained that most top positions in the future Macau SAR, such as chief executive, all members of the Executive Council, and the chairman and vice-chairman of the Legislative Assembly, were reserved for those of Chinese origin. The final draft of the Macau Basic Law is scheduled to be approved by the Drafting Committee's eighth plenary meeting in March 1992.

It was also announced that a Supreme Court of Justice would be set up in the enclave by the end of the first half of 1992 to serve as Macau's highest court of appeal. The court would give Macau complete autonomy in judicial affairs, subject neither to Lisbon nor Peking for the first time in its history.

While Macau's political life was dominated by the departure of Melancia and arrival of Vieira, most residents were concerned about the rising rate of violent crime. Late 1990 and the first nine months of 1991 witnessed a dramatic surge in armed robberies, murders and bloody territorial fights among rival triads. Smuggling between Macau and Zhuhai also increased.

On 9 May, on the eve of Vieira's arrival, chief inspector of the Macau fire brigade was shot dead outside his flat in front of his wife and two young children. The murder turned out to be connected to a criminal organisation run by firemen and policemen of the Macau Security Forces. In early July, eight suspects believed to be responsible for the murder were arrested — among them two policemen, three firemen and one self-confessed professional killer from China. The gang was reportedly involved in blackmail, armed bank robberies, theft and kidnapping.

In May, the powerful gambling syndicate run by Stanley Ho — which operates the Lisboa Casino among other money-spinners — was hit by three armed robberies. Police sources admitted in May that an increasing number of rival triad gangs from Macau, Hongkong, Taiwan, China and Thailand had stepped up territorial fights over loansharking, trafficking in illegal immigrants, control of gambling tours, prostitution and protection rackets.

Police sources put down the increase in violence partly to the ease in smuggling firearms from Zhuhai into Macau and to hired gunmen from neighbouring Guangdong province who carried out raids or killings in the enclave. Portuguese military officers seconded to the Macau Security Forces admitted there was a "severe lack of discipline in the police force."

In June, a senior police officer was detained after he had attacked a nightclub manager who had failed to pay him protection money. In August, a police intelligence officer was detained after he had allegedly tried to blackmail an illegal immigrant prostitute. Police officers said the 5,000 or so Chinese, Thai, Filipino and European prostitutes working in Macau were easy prey for protection rackets.

Macau Security Forces were also confronted with a sharp rise in smuggling between Macau and Zhuhai. Macau Marine and Customs Police officers said in July that professional smugglers had apparently moved some of their operations from Hongkong to Macau in the wake of a crackdown on smuggling in the British colony earlier in the year. Anti-smuggling operations by both Zhuhai and Macau in July and August led to a number of confrontations between their respective marine police forces in disputes over jurisdiction when chasing smugglers.

The influx of illegal immigrants from China through Zhuhai into Macau continued unabated during the year. On average, 100 illegal immigrants, most of them caught in routine identity card checks in the streets, were sent back over the border each week. □

# Economy/Infrastructure

A series of economic problems plagued the enclave's administration over the past 12 months. They ranged from falling exports, a negative trade balance and related budgetary austerity measures, trouble over its international airport project, a row over alleged illegal transhipments of knitwear made in China, bickering with China over land-lease policy and property speculation by investors from China and Hongkong.

The airport project off Taipa Island, where site clearance started in September 1989, is now at least two years behind schedule and has almost doubled its original projected price.

The major problems have been protracted complaints over noise pollution raised by the adjoining Zhuhai special economic zone (SEZ) and delays in the supply of sand from China, which has delayed the reclamation necessary to build the 3,350-m runway.

Talks between Macau and China on the noise issue were held in Macau at the end of November 1990. The Macau Government insisted the airport would not cause any noise pollution to Zhuhai because aircraft would not fly over China's coastal areas. The controversy petered out in March, presumably after Peking made it clear to the Zhuhai authorities that the airport was a fait accompli. The row over sand was taken up by the Portuguese delegation to the Sino-Portuguese Joint Liaison Group a routine meeting in Lisbon during early December 1990, though no resolution was publicly announced.

In mid-January 1991, the Macau Government announced the establishment of a civil aviation authority that would be empowered to directly negotiate landing and other air traffic rights. The civil aviation authority's main problem will be how to deal with the fact that Macau has no airspace of its own. At present, Macau has to consult China on all aspects of landing and airspace rights.

Given these problems, by mid-February there were serious doubts about whether the airport would be scrapped altogether. However, senior Macau Government officials maintained that it was too late to abandon the project as this would politically damage Sino-Portuguese relations. On 22 February, Chinese Foreign Minister Qian Qichen said the project had Peking's "unequivocal political support" during a visit to Portugal.

Santon Ferreira resigned as chairman of the Macau Airport Franchise Co. (CAM), but not before he accused Chinese companies of virtually sabotaging the project through overcharging for sand and other materials. Local magnate Stanley Ho took over as CAM's acting chairman in his capacity as its largest single private shareholder. Ho holds 42% of the company's stock through his Sociedade de Turismo e Diversoes de Macau gambling empire and other subsidiary companies. Shortly after the arrival of newly appointed Governor Vasco Rocha Vieira, Ho suggested selling off 55% of CAM to the Hongkong Government. Macau Government officials rejected Ho's idea as "absolutely unacceptable," while the New China News Agency described it as "politically impossible."

At the end of September it was announced CAM would issue bonds, initially up to the value of Patacas 1 billion (US$125 million), in early 1992 and redeemable before Macau reverts to Chinese sovereignty in 1999. It was also announced the airport would not be operational until the first half of 1995 and would cost Patacas 6.5 billion, rather than the projected Patacas 3 billion. Ho and other CAM investors, however, estimated it would cost just over Patacas 7.1 billion. CAM shareholders also stressed that the airport had to be ready by 1995, or its operational feasibility would be jeopardised by the opening of the new Hongkong airport a year or so later.

According to Macau Government estimates, the new airport will handle 2 million passengers and 150,000 tonnes of cargo in its first year of operations. By 1999, it is forecast to handle 6 million passengers and 600,000 tonnes of freight, though some analysts think these figures are too optimistic.

The airport overshadowed Macau's other large projects, most of which were also experiencing delays. Work on the 130-ha, Patacas 1.3 billion Praia Grande Bay land reclamation project was delayed until early 1992, reportedly over trouble between investors and the government land-lease conditions.

The Patacas 200 million Ka Ho container terminal, officially inaugurated in June 1990, remains idle — apparently because local shippers are reluctant to move their operations from the Inner Harbour to Coloane Island. Officials of franchise holder

Macauport — chaired by Ho — said they were prepared to offer favourable rates in order to lure shipping away from the Inner Harbour docks.

In October, Macauport signed a joint-venture agreement with Peking's Nam Kwong Petroleum and Chemicals Co. Ltd to build an oil terminal next to the container port. Total investment in the oil terminal is expected to be about Patacas 300 million, with construction due to start in July 1992. Macauport will take 5% of the venture, while Nam Kwong holds the rest. The terminal is intended to serve the future airport.

The second Macau-Taipa bridge is due to be completed before the end of 1991. The 3,900-m long, four-lane bridge — which will link the new airport through a connecting highway to Gong Bei in Zhuhai SEZ — was commissioned by the Macau Government and built by a Portuguese consortium in cooperation with mainland Chinese sub-contractors for Patacas 390 million.

Completion of the new Outer Harbour passenger terminal was further delayed to early 1993 due to piling problems. The Patacas 450 million project is expected to have a top capacity of 13 million passengers a year, and 3,600 passengers an hour at peak times. It will replace the existing, and notoriously cramped, passenger wharf. In October the government also announced two sewage treatment plants would be built. At present, untreated sewage is disposed of at sea.

The US cut certain types of garment quotas from Macau in late 1990 after alleging that large quantities of clothing were being made in China and only labelled as made in Macau. The

quota cuts were restored after Macau instituted stricter checks on goods coming across the border. Despite the temporary quota cuts, the share of knitwear products in Macau's overall export value increased from 63% in 1989 to 65% in 1990, mainly due to the increase in the export unit price index to the US and Europe and because of the growth of knitwear exports to the EC.

Overall, however, exports recorded their first fall during the year since the 1950s. In addition, and for the first time in a decade, Macau braced itself for a negative trade balance. According to government figures, total exports showed an 11.1% drop in the first half of 1991, as against the same six-month period in 1990. Macau's trade balance recorded a deficit of Patacas 1.2 billion over the first half of 1991.

From January through June, export revenue reached Patacas 5.7 billion, or Patacas 717 million less than in the first half of 1990. Meanwhile, imports reached Patacas 6.9 billion over the first half of 1991 — a 17.1% increase over the same six-month period in 1990.

Officials said the increase in imports over the first half was mainly due to Macau's infrastructure projects and the booming housing construction sector, which called for the import of large amounts of raw materials and semi-manufactured items. But Vieira admitted the slide in exports signalled a worrying trend for Macau.

Economic analysts pointed out that falling exports indicated Macau's manufacturing sector was in the throes of a structural crisis. "There has been very little reinvestment by local businessmen in new production facilities in Macau, [they] simply rely on the cheap labour of tens of thousands of immigrants from China," one banker said.

The gambling and tourism sector, however, grew steadily in the first half of 1991. A total of 2.9 million visitors arrived in Macau from Hongkong in the first six months, or 1.3% more than in the same six-month period in 1990. Hongkong residents — most of whom headed for the enclave's casinos — comprised 2.4 million, or 83%, of the visitors, or 4.1% more than during the first half of 1990. The average hotel occupancy rate reached 79.12% in July 1991, as against the whole-year average of 78% in 1990 and compared to 64% in 1986.

The Macau Government collected gambling franchise taxation totalling Patacas 1.95 billion over the first nine months of the year, or more than the Patacas 1.936 billion collected in the whole of 1990. The total 1991 receipts are expected to exceed the 1990 figure by about one third.

Inflation approached the two-digit threshold in July when the consumer-price index recorded an increase of 10.02% against the same month in 1990. The inflation rate over the first seven months of 1991 reached 9.8% over the same period in 1990. The GDP deflator (1982 = 100) stood at 196.75 in 1990, as against 159.64 in 1988. The GDP growth rate in real terms reached 9.1% in 1990, compared to only 2.2% in 1989. Per capita GDP at current market prices tipped Patacas 65,200 in 1990, as against Patacas 55,300 in 1989, or nearly double Portugal's level.

Net foreign assets grew to Patacas 19.5 billion in July, which represented a 26% year-to-year increase. As in the years before, the pataca remained pegged to the Hongkong dollar, and thereby indirectly linked to the US dollar.

Macau's property sector experienced a boom in 1991, mainly due to speculative interest from Hongkong — much of it on Taipa in anticipation of a boom linked to the eventual completion of the airport. The surge in buying interest unnerved many Macau residents, who earn an average of 50% less than the monthly salaries paid in Hongkong, and there is now widespread local concern they could be driven out of the property market if the speculation were allowed to continue.  □

## Data

**Major exports:** Textiles and garments, US$1.24 billion (US$1.18 billion); toys, US$172.4 million (US$166.4 million); artificial flowers, US$31.3 million (US$44.34 million); footwear, US$18.1 million (US$12.1 million); electronics, US$12.3 million (US$14.65 million); luggage, US$13.4 million (US$16 million); optical goods, US$10.3 million (US$11 million); ceramics, US$7.33 million (US$13 million).

**Major imports:** Industrial materials, US$961 million (US$989 million); capital goods, US$183 million (US$152 million); consumer goods, US$165.7 million (US$146.6 million); foodstuffs, beverages, tobacco, US$152.2 million (US$125.6 million); fuels and lubricants, US$71.5 million (US$62.5 million).

**Tourism and transport:** Visitor arrivals, 5.942 million (5.619 million). (All figures for 1990, previous year in brackets.)

**Currency:** Pataca (100 avos). Pataca 8.05 = US$1 (same).

**Finance:** Licensed banks, 21; locally incorporated, 6; foreign, 15. No stock exchange.

**Major banks:** Banco Nacional Ultramarino, tel. 376644; Banco Fonecas & Burnay, tel. 550254; Banco Luso, tel. 378977; Banco Pinto & Sotto Mayor, tel. 550022; Banco Portugues do Atlantico, tel. 378089; Banco Hang Seng, tel. 555222; Banco Totta & Acores, tel. 573299; Banco Weng Heng, tel. 335678; Banco Comercial de Macau, tel. 569622; Bank of China, tel. 371077; Banque Indosuez, tel. 550378; Banque Nationale de Paris, tel. 562777; Citibank, tel. 378188; Deutsche Bank, tel. 378440; Hongkong & Shanghai Bank, tel. 553669; Standard Chartered Bank, tel. 378372; Security Pacific Asian Bank, tel. 568821.

**Government departments:** Government Palace (Governor's office), Rua da Praia Grande, tel. 565555, fax 563377, tlx 88201 GOVMA OM; Economic Services, Edificio Luso Intl., Rua Dr Pedro Jose Lobo, tel. 562622, fax 590310; Statistics and Census, Rua Inacio Baptista, 4-6, tel. 550935, fax 307825; Finance, Rua da Praia Grande 69-A/B, tel. 571600, fax 300133; Tourism, Largo do Senado, Edificio Ritz, tel. 315566, fax 374321; Labour and Employment, Rotunda Carlos Maia, tel. 564109, fax 550477; Lands, Public Works and Transport, Estrada Dona Maria I, 32-36, Edificio da CEM, tel. 589666, fax 313047; Security Forces, Quartel General, tel. 559999, fax 317633; Immigration, Rua de Xangai, Outer Harbour, Macau Chamber of Commerce Bldg, tel. 577338, fax 780826, Civil Aviation Authority, Rua Dr Pedro Jose Lobo, 1-3, Edificio Luso Intl, 26/F, tel. 5113213, fax 338089; Government Information Services, Rua Sao Domingos, 1A-1B, tel. 332886, fax 336372; Monetary and Foreign Exchange Authority, Rua Pedro Nolasco da Silva, 44, tel. 325425, fax 317633.

**Public holidays** (1992): 1 Jan. (New Year), 4-6 Feb. (Lunar New Year), 4 Apr. (Ching Ming), 17-18 Apr. (Easter), 25 Apr. (Portuguese Revolution Day), 1 May (Labour Day), 5 June (Dragon Boat Festival), 10 June (Portuguese National Day), 24 June (St John the Baptist Day, peninsular Macau only), 13 July (Municipal Holiday, Coloane and Taipa Islands only), 1 Sept. (Mooncake Festival), 1 Oct. (China's National Day), 5 Oct. (Portuguese Republic Day), 2 Nov. (All Souls' Day), 1 Dec. (Portuguese Restoration of Independence Day), 8 Dec. (Feast of the Immaculate Conception), 24-25 Dec. (Christmas).

**Weather:** Macau's sub-tropical climate ranges from a relatively cool autumn and winter to a hot and humid summer. Winter temperatures seldom fall below 10°C, while summer temperatures range between 26-33°C, with an average humidity of 85%. Typhoons can affect the enclave between May-Oct.

**Taxation:** Individual 15%, corporate 15%.

# MALAYSIA

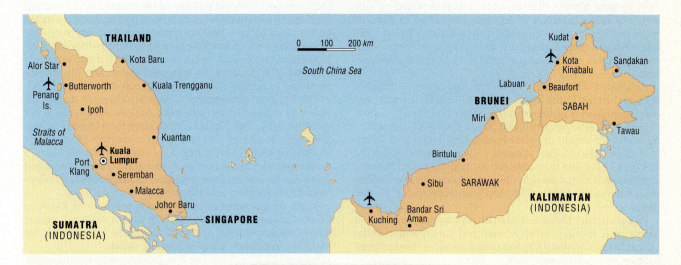

A fter experiencing centuries of cultural influences from India and China, the Malay peninsula underwent an extended period of Western domination following the Portuguese capture of Malacca in 1511. The Dutch, in turn, won control of Malacca in 1641, and were followed by the British who acquired Penang in 1786. In 1795 Britain had taken over most of the peninsula's west coast after wresting Malacca from the Dutch.

British interest in the Malay peninsula rapidly switched from regarding it a strategic asset protecting sealanes to China to a valuable source of commodities in its own right. Tin mining and later rubber plantations formed the basis of Malaya's wealth and therefore significance to Britain.

British control was shattered by the 1941 Japanese invasion, which exposed many of the pretensions of colonial rule and spurred local nationalist sentiments. The post-war period was dominated by a 12-year communist insurgency, which successfully contained led directly to Britain granting independence to Malaya's 11 states in 1957. Malaysia was formed with Sabah, Sarawak and Singapore in 1963, though Singapore pulled out in 1965 to become an independent republic.

The present 13 states, plus the Federal Territory of Kuala Lumpur and Labuan, are ruled by a constitutional monarch elected for a five-year term by the nine hereditary sultans of the traditional Malay states from among themselves on a rotational basis.

Malaysia is governed by a bicameral parliament, an executive and a three-tier judiciary. The present prime minister is the fourth since 1957. Elections are held every five years and since independence the three-party multiracial Alliance and its successor, the 12-party National Front, have retained political power.

Malaysia's population now stands at around 17.7 million, broken down along ethnic lines as 61.9% bumiputra (mostly Malays), 29.5% Chinese and 8.6% Indians. Its social problems stem from the rural-urban drift, undercurrents of racial sensitivities and the presence of as many as 1 million illegal migrant plantation workers in peninsular Malaysia and in Sabah. Since the 1980s, Malaysia has slowly shifted from a commodity-based economy to light industry.

**Head of State**
King (Yang di-Pertuan Agong) Sultan Azlan Muhibuddin Shah ibni al-Marhum Sultan Yussuf Izzuddin Ghafarullahu-lahu Shah.
**Prime Minister** (and **Home Affairs**)
Datuk Seri Mahathir Mohamad;
**Deputy Prime Minister** (and **Rural Development**)
Abdul Ghafar Baba;
**Ministers in the Prime Minister's Department**
Datuk Abang Abu Bakar Mustapha, Syed Hamid Jaafar Albar (and **Justice**);
**Transport**
Datuk Seri Ling Liong Sik;
**Energy, Telecommunications and Posts**
Datuk Seri S. Samy Vellu;
**Primary Industries**
Datuk Seri Lim Keng Yaik;
**Defence**
Datuk Seri Najib Tun Abdul Razak;
**Works**
Datuk Leo Moggie anak Irok;
**International Trade and Industry**
Datuk Seri Rafidah Aziz;
**Domestic Trade and Consumer Affairs**
Datuk Abu Hassan Omar;
**Agriculture**
Datuk Seri Sanusi Junid;
**Science, Technology and Environment**
Law Hieng Ding;

**Education**
Datuk Sulaiman Daud;
**Foreign Affairs**
Datuk Abdullah Ahmad Badawi;
**Finance**
Datuk Seri Anwar Ibrahim;
**Housing and Local Government**
Dr Ting Chew Peh;
**Youth and Sports**
Annuar Musa;
**Land and Cooperative Development**
Tan Sri Sakaran Dandai;
**Health**
Datuk Lee Kim Sai;
**Information**
Datuk Mohamed Rahmat;
**Culture, Arts and Tourism**
Datuk Sabbaruddin Chik;
**Public Enterprises**
Datuk Mohammad Yusof Nor;
**National Unity and Community Development**
Datuk Napsiah Omar;
**Human Resources**
Datuk Lim Ah Lek;
**Lord President**
Tun Abdul Hamid Omar;
**Attorney-General**
Tan Sri Abu Talib Othman;
**Chief of Defence Forces**
Gen. Tan Sri Hashim Mohamed Ali.

# Politics/Social Affairs

R elations between the federal government and Malaysia's component states dominated politics during 1991, as some of the latter tried to assert greater administrative control. Sabah and Kelantan — the only two states run by parties opposed to the country's ruling National Front coalition — attracted the most attention, though political manoeuvres ahead of elections in Sarawak, water shortages in Malacca and Johor's assertive economic plans also vied for Kuala Lumpur's time.

On 5 January, Sabah Chief Minister Datuk Seri Joseph Pairin Kitingan was arrested on three graft charges, 36 hours after his aide Maximus Ongkili was detained under the Internal Security Act (ISA) in Kuala Lumpur. Kitingan was charged with three counts of corruption involving M$12 million (US$4.37 million) worth of construction contracts in his home town of Tambunan and a 2,000-ha timber concession, in which his relatives were among the beneficiaries. The case is due to be heard in Sabah's High Court in January 1992.

Ongkili, the deputy chief executive of Sabah's Institute of Development Studies (IDS) think-tank, was detained on suspicion of being involved in activities prejudicial to national security. The IDS had come under federal scrutiny in late 1990, when Kuala Lumpur accused it of inciting anti-federal sentiments. Ongkili was released after 59 days of police interrogation.

As a senior IDS official, Ongkili was also close to Kitingan's younger brother Datuk Jeffrey Kitingan, the IDS chairman and executive director of the powerful Sabah Foundation. Jeffrey Kitingan — who already faced seven counts of corruption involving the export of Sabah Foundation timber and failure to declare M$40 million in assets — was arrested under the ISA on 13 May and later detained for two years for allegedly threatening national security. His arrest was the first linking the Parti Bersatu Sabah (PBS) top leadership to the alleged plot.

Prime Minister Datuk Seri Mahathir Mohamad, speaking in Sabah on 21 February when he launched the expansion of the United Malays National Organisation (Umno) — the dominant partner in the National Front — into the state, said: "There is some connection with a third country. I don't know which. But there is a definite plot to take Sabah out of the federation."

The arrests of the Kitingan brothers and Ongkili — all leading names among Sabah's ethnic Kadazans — further strained relations between Kuala Lumpur and the state. The timing of the arrests, less than three months after the PBS defected to the opposition Semangat '46 coalition midway through the 1990 general election campaign, led many Sabahans to think the arrests were politically motivated, whatever the merits of the government's case.

To counteract ethnic Kadazan political dominance, Umno decided to launch itself in Sabah, using its United Sabah National Organisation (Usno) ally as a vehicle. Usno was all but dissolved in February when party president Tun Mustapha Datu Harun led several thousand members into Umno Sabah. Political expediency, however, demanded that Usno remained a nominal political party in order to enable Usno's then 12 assemblymen to retain their seats. On 11 May, Mustapha won the Usukan by-election on an Umno Sabah ticket, securing the party's first foothold in Sabah.

Since then, the PBS has re-examined its defection. At its annual assembly in August, Pairin Kitingan urged delegates not to search for scapegoats for what some now consider an ill-advised move. He reiterated the PBS' commitment to standing up for state interests, though he conceded that it was vital that all parties come to terms with Umno.

States in peninsular Malaysia also felt the weight of the centre's hand. Changing rainfall patterns and inefficient water management had led to an acute shortage in Malacca state in March. While the quick remedy was to buy water from neighbouring states, the central government also decided to set up a national water authority to consolidate Malaysia's water resources and ensure an even supply throughout the country. However, land and water come under state jurisdiction, and the individual states jealously guard their few remaining rights. Mahathir's decision to place water under federal control upset even Johor, the cradle of Umno.

Land concerns, this time in the context of private ownership, emerged with the passage of the controversial Land Acquisition (Amendment) Act on 30 July. The law empowers the government to buy land for public purpose and economic development which can later be sold to third parties for development not necessarily of the kind for which it was originally acquired. The anxieties pre-supposed abuse, and the government had to declare that it would not rob the people of land.

The Kelantan government's main achievement during the year was marked by its outwardly smooth coexistence, if not quite cordially, with Kuala Lumpur since Parti Islam (Pas) and Semangat '46 gained power in the conservative Muslim state in October 1990. Despite Pas' long-standing role as Umno's main rival, after initial problems over agricultural licences and subsidies, its leaders have managed to keep federal development funds trickling into the state.

Much of this administrative finesse stems from Kelantan Chief Minister Nik Abdul Aziz Nik Mat, a religious teacher whose mild-mannered approach has made it impossible for Mahathir to publicly adopt a hardline stand.

BACARIA

**Mahathir: addressing a wider audience.**

The Pas government's main agenda, apart from maintaining a reasonable level of economic development, is the Islamisation of Kelantan — though steps in this direction have been halting. In October, the state government issued a ruling — albeit without the force of a government decree — encouraging women to adopt the Islamic dress code by 1 January 1992. Non-Muslims were also urged to wear "decent dress."

The most serious of Pas' attempted innovations centred around plans to introduce *hukum huddud*, a legal code which makes the offences of adultery, accusing a woman of good character of adultery, theft, apostasy and drinking alcohol automatically punishable under Islamic jurisprudence. Pas' main problem with establishing hukum huddud is its non-application to other communities. The federal constitution expressly states that such laws apply only to Muslims; with that assurance, Kelantan's small Chinese community was largely content to let Pas do as it pleased.

Initial friction within the unlikely Pas–Semangat '46 partnership has been smoothed over with time. Semangat '46 leaders refrain from publicly commenting on Pas' Islamic pronouncements, while Pas learnt to live with the occasional defections within Semangat '46 ranks back to Umno. The viability of the partnership was proven during two by-elections on 24 August, when Semangat '46 candidates were returned with comfortable though reduced margins, thereby depriving Umno of even a foothold in the state legislative assembly.

Yet, it also became obvious in 1991 that with the National Front's sweep of two thirds of the 177 parliamentary seats in October 1990, Semangat '46 has been reduced to just a Kelantan-based party. Even in independent-minded Penang state, a July by-election favoured the National Front. Voters in Prai, a predominantly working-class Chinese community, swung away from the opposition Democratic Action Party (DAP) — their traditional champion — leaving it with only 13 out of 33 state seats in the DAP's frontline state.

The question of Mahathir's successor was also the subject of a fresh round of speculation during the year. Following the long-anticipated resignation of Tun Daim Zainuddin as finance minister in February, the portfolio was given to Datuk Seri Anwar Ibrahim. Anwar first emerged as Mahathir's protege in 1982 but has since come into his own, holding various portfolios supposedly designed to prepare him for the prime minister's office.

Since Anwar is now one of three Umno vice-presidents — a traditional stepping stone to the prime minister's job — his performance as finance minister is being watched closely. His appointment has been seen as a tacit endorsement from Mahathir, despite rumours of a certain level of friction between them. Umno Vice-President Datuk Abdullah Ahmad Badawi was appointed foreign minister at the same time, while Anwar's other rival, Agriculture Minister Datuk Seri Sanusi Junid, was unaffected by the cabinet changes. But as a member of Mahathir's inner circle, Anwar remains the front-runner.

Following the 1990 general election, race relations in the peninsula generally took a backseat. Ethnocentric anxieties were perhaps most strongly enunciated by Malaysian Indian Congress (MIC) president Datuk Seri S. Samy Vellu. Amid fears that the Indian community was in danger of becoming politically marginalised, Vellu urged Indian couples to have five children each in order to maintain the ethnic Indian presence at around its current 8% of the population.

Racial hackles were also raised after the Malaysian Chinese Association (MCA) mooted the idea of a M$5 million Chinese cultural centre and depository for Chinese literature and artifacts. But Umno — as the guardian of Malay pre-eminence in a country where the indigenous bumiputras, most of whom are Malays, make up 61% to the Chinese 30% of the 17.7 million population — took it as a challenge to Malay dominance. The MCA quickly backed off, but the issue again highlighted the racial sensitivities lying just below the surface.

Environmental issues became more overtly political during the year, as the government was put on the defensive by overseas criticism of logging in Sarawak and the threat to hinterland minorities. On 5 July, eight foreign environmental activists chained themselves to log barges at Kuala Baram in Sarawak to protest against Sarawak's export of tropical timber. They were later jailed for two months each.

Timber was one of the main issues in the 27 September Sarawak state elections, with the opposition accusing Chief Minister Tan Sri Abdul Taib Mahmud's ruling coalition of profiting from indiscriminate logging. In the event, the ruling Barisan Tiga — a tripartite, multiracial coalition — won a victory that surprised even some of its own leaders and ensured Taib another five-year term. Of the 56 seats contested, Taib's own Parti Pesaka Bersatu Bumiputra won 27, the Dayak-based Sarawak National Action Party took six and the Sarawak United People's Party delivered the Chinese vote in 16.

The anticipated assertion of Dayak ethnic rights came to nothing, to the surprise of many Sarawak politicians of all stripes. The Dayaks — the umbrella term for the 33% Iban, 9% Bidayuh and 3% Orang Ulu ethnic communities — have never been so united, yet the Parti Bansa Dayak Sarawak (PBDS) was reduced to half its former strength with only seven state assembly seats. Within a day of the results, PBDS president Datuk Leo Moggie announced his party would apply to join the ruling state coalition, to the relief of the federal government.

Federal leaders were in a difficult position during the campaign because though the PBDS is an opposition party in Sarawak, it is a member of the National Front in Kuala Lumpur. Nevertheless, Mahathir and several members of his cabinet had clearly endorsed Taib — lending legitimacy to the kind of state-federal ties so markedly absent in Kuala Lumpur's dealings with neighbouring Sabah. □

# Foreign Relations

**M**alaysia expended considerable energy on boosting its international profile during 1991. However, not all its efforts were rewarded with recognition, and some generated friction with Malaysia's trading partners and regional neighbours.

One initiative that dominated Malaysia's diplomatic efforts for most of the year was Prime Minister Datuk Seri Mahathir Mohamad's proposal for an East Asian Economic Grouping (EAEG), which he first enunciated at a banquet for visiting Chinese Premier Li Peng on 10 December 1990.

Mahathir argued that to counter growing economic blocs in the West, Asia-Pacific countries should "form a bloc to countervail the others. If not, we will not be able to protect our trade share, as individually we don't have the strength," he said.

Mahathir also said that if no other country was willing to do so, Malaysia would take the lead in the formation of the new trade bloc, which would include China and Japan.

The proposal immediately drew fire from Malaysia's Asean partners, East Asian investors and Western trading partners — all of whom objected to its definition as a trade bloc. Despite widespread disappointment over the stalled Uruguay Round trade negotiations, the region remained opposed to the erection of more trade barriers. Perhaps, most damaging of all, neither Japan nor China embraced the idea.

To rescue the proposal, Malaysian officials hurriedly recast EAEG in a less hostile mould by backing away from the notion of a trade bloc. They declared that the EAEG was consistent with free-trade principles and would work towards removing or reducing trade barriers in the international trading system. This adjustment won EAEG Singapore's backing, but Indonesia and the Philippines remained strongly opposed.

Malaysia — using its advantage of chairing the Asean Standing Committee — then moved to have the idea adopted by Asean, but needed to forge a consensus.

In October, Asean economic ministers met in Kuala Lumpur and finally settled on a compromise which redefined the EAEG in less concrete terms as an East Asian Economic Caucus.

Malaysia may have tested the limits of Asean cooperation by pushing hard to have the EAEG accepted, but the proposal won Mahathir a great deal of international attention. At home he won praise for acting as a world leader, while in other forums — notably the Commonwealth — his activist approach was rewarded with consultative positions. In October, Mahathir became chairman of the Commonwealth's Group of 11 on South Africa.

With the 1990 election behind him and threats to his mandate laid to rest, Mahathir seemed set on polishing his credentials as an international statesman. In March, he delivered a speech at an Asean conference in Bali that touched on many aspects of regional affairs, in particular for other Southeast Asian states to be considered as future members of Asean.

Mahathir also introduced a theme at the Bali conference that was to dominate his public utterances for the rest of the year. Commenting on the spread of democracy in Eastern Europe, he warned that democratic tendencies were not necessarily a panacea for economic and development ills. "The proponents of democracy are not averse to international dictatorship," he said.

In subsequent speeches, Mahathir dwelt at length on human-rights and environmental issues. The main thrust of his argument was that the West sought to impose its own human-rights and democratic values on the region, and used these issues to undermine Asean's economic success. Addressing the UN General Assembly in September, Mahathir delivered his strongest anti-Western critique when he said that "hegemony by democratic powers is no less oppressive than hegemony by totalitarian states."

The theme was not without its supporters in Asean, but many of Malaysia's regional partners felt that Mahathir's tone was too strident. Many suspect Mahathir is seeking the intellectual leadership of Asean now that Singapore's Lee Kuan Yew has left the stage. Not all Malaysians necessarily agreed with their prime minister's arguments, but they were pleased to see him put their country on the diplomatic map.

Malaysia's efforts to seek ways of marking its economic ascendancy in the region on occasion also strained bilateral relations with its neighbours. Perennial intrusions by Indonesian and Thai fishermen into Malaysian territorial waters were dealt with more harshly. The Thais reacted by arresting Malaysian forestry officials who had allegedly strayed into Thailand, and in an incident which prompted an official protest from Kuala Lumpur, armed Thai police raided a border market at Padang Besar in Perlis state at the end of June.

Relations with Indonesia also came under pressure. Kuala Lumpur's initial reluctance to return a group of some 200 villagers fleeing from the violence associated with a separatist campaign in the north Sumatran province of Aceh prompted a strong reaction from Jakarta. Malaysia's concern was that their immediate deportation might be construed as inhumane by the international community.

Malaysia's development of two islands off the East Malaysian state of Sabah also claimed by Indonesia increased bilateral tension, though it remains unclear why Jakarta decided to revive its claim over Sipadan and Ligitan islands — a dispute which has remained dormant for 22 years.

On both these issues, tension was defused after both sides agreed to the creation of new bilateral consultation mechanisms. During the first meeting of the Malaysian-Indonesian Joint Commission — held at a ministerial level in Kuala Lumpur in mid-October — Malaysia agreed to return those Acehnese who were willing to be voluntarily repatriated, while a committee was set up to discuss overlapping claims on the two islands off Sabah.

Relations with Singapore, traditionally prone to varying degrees of tension, actually seemed to improve during the year. Singapore's Prime Minister Goh Chok Tong made a state visit to Malaysia in January, his first formal overseas trip after assuming office in November 1990. Goh's early qualified endorsement of the EAEG also helped cement ties between the two countries.

However, there were also moments of tension more typical of relations between the two neighbours. In the most serious, Singapore expressed concern when Malaysia and Indonesia held joint military exercises in the southern state of Johor during July. The Singapore press accused Malaysia of not informing Singapore when the exercises would be held and of staging them close to Singapore's national day.

The affair tripped off a chain of more or less typical accusations of interference from the Malaysian side after two Singapore air force aircraft crashed in Johor, and the allegation that Singapore army mortar rounds landed within Johor waters. In addition, local politicians revived an outstanding territorial dispute towards the end of the year over the ownership of Batu Putih island — known as Pedra Branca by Singapore — on which Singapore maintains a lighthouse.

In a further dispute over islands, Malaysia's development of an island in the Spratly chain added to the build-up of tension in the South China Sea. China, Taiwan and Vietnam lodged protests with Malaysia over the development of Terumbu Layang Layang as a deep-sea fishing resort with an airstrip which could be potentially used for military purposes.

While Kuala Lumpur sparred with its neighbours over islands and fishermen, relations with Canberra suffered a setback over an Australian television drama series portraying life in an Australian embassy in a fictitious Asian country.

Subsequent remarks by senior Malaysian officials, including Mahathir, focused on Australia's "unfriendly attitude" towards Malaysia. Amid fears that the rift was on the verge of upsetting bilateral trade and investment ties, Australian Foreign Minister Gareth Evans sought to resolve the problem while in Kuala Lumpur for the Asean Post-Ministerial Conference in July. Finally, after talks between Mahathir and Australian Prime Minister Bob Hawke at the October Commonwealth meeting in Zimbabwe, relations were declared to be back on an even keel. □

# Economy/Infrastructure

**M**alaysia's economy got off to an unsettled start in 1991 as imminent war in the Middle East made it difficult to gauge the impact of oil-price swings on export earnings and other key barometers. While the quick end to the fighting in February yielded an improvement in some areas, other factors combined to reveal fresh problems.

On the favourable side were Bank Negara, the country's central bank, estimates that real GDP growth would still weigh in at 8-8.3% for the year — after posting near-record expansion of 10% in 1990. Foreign investments in the manufacturing sector — especially from Taiwan and Japan — continued to pour in after doubling to a record M$17.7 billion (US$6.5 billion) in 1990. Approved domestic investments tripled from the previous year to M$10.5 billion in 1990.

These investments are expected to ripple through the economy for at least a year — providing an impetus that will offset further economic slowdowns. Even the modest cool-off was greeted with relief by some planners who said it would provide the economy, which was in danger of over-heating, a much-needed breathing space to cope with inflationary pressure and infrastructural bottlenecks. As it was, industrial activity eased only moderately, with the Manufacturing Production Index declining by about 2% to 15% in January-July 1991, compared to the 17.48% recorded for the same period in 1990.

A much-feared slowdown in demand from Western trading partners had also not reached dramatic proportions by late 1991, despite residual concern about the US recession and a sluggish Japanese economy. Nevertheless, Malaysia's still prodigious growth rate continued to produce some undesirable side-effects. Inflation, as measured by the consumer price index (CPI) is expected to top 4% in 1991 after hovering at a revised 3.1% in 1990. Some independent forecasters fear the CPI could increase by more than 5% in 1991.

Malaysia's weak balance-of-payments position also slipped further, with some analysts forecasting that the current-account deficit could surge from M$4.7 billion in 1990 to nearly M$8 billion in 1991. Sharp increases in consumer spending and foreign investment also continued to wreak havoc with the country's merchandise trade deficit.

The cumulative trade deficit during the first seven months of 1991 totalled M$5.6 billion, compared with a trade surplus of M$460 million for the same period a year earlier. This was largely due to increasing purchases of foreign manufacturing equipment and luxury goods.

Although some planners said the imbalance was a small price to pay for the boost to Malaysia's productive capacity that would accrue from such investment and spending, 1991 clearly showed that inflation and other weaknesses could no longer be tolerated as passing irritants.

Malaysia's worsening labour shortage is an example of one

of the most serious side-effects of the huge foreign and domestic investment inflows since the 1985-86 recession. The Federation of Malaysian Manufacturers claims its sector is short by about 80,000 workers, with industrial areas such as Penang the most badly affected.

Shortages in all categories has led to across-the-board wage increases as companies step up competition for the shrinking number of workers in the country's labour pool. This, in turn, is fuelling inflation. The official wage bill per employee in manufacturing — an index maintained by the Department of Statistics — surged by 9.4% to M$802 in June 1991 from M$733 for the same month in 1990.

The labour shortage also became much more apparent in the non-manufacturing and non-agricultural sectors during the year. Once confined to factories and plantations, the shortage is now one of the most pressing problems facing the financial, tourism and retail sectors. Bankers complain they cannot find competent administrators or even clerks, while electronics manufacturers said there were fewer technicians and workers to run their assembly lines. The crunch is so serious that Japanese manufacturers — Malaysia's second-largest source of foreign investment — have said they are having second thoughts about investing more money in the country.

Other soft spots in the economy were continuing inadequacies in the nation's infrastructure of roads, ports, energy and telecommunications systems as demand for such services continued to outstrip supply. Telephone and power supply breakdowns are increasingly common even in the well-developed urban areas. Kuala Lumpur was chocked by traffic jams as road construction failed to keep pace with a sharp increase in the number of private cars and commercial vehicles. Ports were hard-pressed to service exporters, while limited airport facilities at popular resorts discouraged higher tourist arrivals after the official Visit Malaysia Year 1990 programme was extended into 1991.

There were also signs of trouble in the property market — which has served as one of the economy's main engines of growth — in 1991. By mid-year, Kuala Lumpur and other urban areas were feeling the first repercussions of a condominium glut fanned by over-building in the past two years. The overhang was most serious in the lower end of the condominium sector, but also showed signs of spreading to luxury units.

Demand for new office and commercial space, on the other hand, remained high with 100% occupancy rates being reported for many office buildings in Kuala Lumpur's prestigious Golden Triangle business area throughout the year.

The Malaysian Government appeared to react swiftly to these new challenges confronting the economy, though some analysts questioned whether its measures were far-reaching enough. To combat inflation, Bank Negara took pre-emptive steps to restrain excess liquidity by abruptly raising reserve requirements for the country's financial institutions on 16 August. This led to increases in most lending rates. As of 16 September, one-, three- and six-month Kuala Lumpur Interbank Offered Rates rose to 8.15%, 8.35% and 8.55% respectively, compared to 7.2%, 7.3% and 7.5% in July.

The central bank also took steps to control inflation through repeated and active intervention in the money market. Con-

**Imports: expensive tastes.**

trols on some consumer goods were implemented, notably during the Gulf War, to prevent price-gouging while Bank Negara also imposed stricter guidelines on housing and other loans to dampen consumption and encourage savings.

To counter the labour shortage, the authorities launched a raft of training programmes to supplement the existing education system. It is also exploring a plan to require companies to pay a fixed percentage of their annual earnings into a national manpower training fund.

A key step to boost Malaysia's power-generating capacity was also taken in early 1991, when Tenaga Nasional, the semi-privatised national electricity provider, pushed ahead with plans to buy seven gas-powered turbines from a foreign supplier at a total cost of nearly M$1 billion. This will boost the country's combined generating capacity by about 793 MW to 5,850 MW.

The federal government announced in September its intention to build Southeast Asia's largest international airport at Sepang, Selangor, about 40 km south of Kuala Lumpur. The proposed facility, which will eventually replace the capital's existing international airport at Subang, will be built at a projected cost of M$20 billion.

Further additions to the nation's physical plant will be made under the Sixth Malaysia Plan, which was announced on 10 July. A total of M$104 billion was earmarked for infrastructural, social development and defence expenditure over the next five years. The government also sent a strong signal that it will accelerate its programme of privatising state industries and reducing total public allocations to the private sector.

The Sixth Plan also supplements the New Development Policy (NDP) — a long-awaited successor to the 20-year-old New Economic Policy (NEP) — and a Second Outline Perspective Plan (OPP2) for 1991-2000, which was tabled by Prime Minister Datuk Seri Mahathir Mohamad on 17 June.

The NDP furnishes an ideological framework for the OPP2 and the Sixth Plan — memorialising the government's thinking on the sensitive issue of racial quotas and the micro-management of the economy into the next century. In a key change from the NEP, planners noted the government will de-emphasise its long-espoused goal of redistributing 30% of the nation's wealth to Malaysia's bumiputra, or mainly Malay, majority by a specified date. This will increase the government's flexibility in making reforms which benefit all segments of the country's multiracial population.

The government also noted that the NEP, which expired in December 1990, had gone a long way in fulfilling the 30% bumiputra mandate. Between 20% and 23% of the nation's assets had already been transferred into bumiputra hands by 1991, paving the way for a more liberalised approach to national priorities.

One of the revised goals will be the elimination of "hardcore" poverty — especially among palm oil and rubber-plantation workers and the aboriginal population. There is also much emphasis on boosting the management expertise of the bumiputra business community to make it less reliant on special incentives. Mahathir made it clear the government will be less inclined to provide a free ride to a class of politically tied but incompetent bumiputra businessmen who prospered under the aegis of the NEP.

The NDP, OPP2 and the Sixth Plan also form the cornerstones of a popular 20/20 policy mooted by Mahathir in March to transform Malaysia into an advanced nation by 2020, a theme celebrated with much fanfare in the annual National Day festivities in August 1991.

However, footing the bill for such nationalist aspirations posed a greater challenge than ever in 1991. New Finance Minister Datuk Seri Anwar Ibrahim, who replaced Tun Daim Zainuddin on 15 March, noted the need to diversify sources of federal revenue. Government revenue grew by only 0.6% for every 1% growth in the economy during the 1980s — half the rate of the previous decade. There was growing talk about introducing value-added tax on goods and services, and imposing a separate head tax on the large number of foreign workers from Indonesia and other countries.

Anwar's move to the finance ministry followed Daim's 1991 national budget that included a number of tax cuts, including reductions in the income-tax rate for individuals in certain brackets and cuts in the so-called development tax on corporations. Reversing such ingrained fiscal trends will be difficult, and Anwar showed no signs of diverging significantly from the policy course set by Daim. But Anwar, a former education minister with roots in the Islamic student movement, has already displayed a tendency to place more weight on social and political factors than his predecessor.

Anwar's main weakness appears to be his lack of training in economic affairs, and he has had to rely heavily on the advice of senior finance ministry bureaucrats. Nevertheless, he has warned the heads of government agencies that he will not tolerate them abusing their position for financial gain, and has publicly stated that the United Malays National Organisation (Umno) — the dominant party in the ruling National Front coalition — should withdraw from all business activities.

Whether the party actually severed its ties from the business world was no clearer in 1991 than it was in 1990. Umno contends it cut all links with party-owned businesses after its corporate assets were turned over to an official assignee in the wake of its 1988 court battle with party dissidents. Those assets have since been transferred to a group of private businessmen with ties to Umno.

In any event, Renong — the corporate umbrella for a group of companies formerly controlled by Umno — continued to engage in corporate manoeuvres throughout the year intended to rationalise its structure and increase earnings. The company, which controls units such as the giant civil-engineering firm, United Engineers Malaysia, and Fleet, a diversified media group, announced a second complex restructuring on 2 February which increased Renong's issued capital from 1.34 billion to 2.13 billion shares.

The move also places Faber Group — a once ailing hotel and property concern left out of the first reorganisation of the party's assets in April 1990 — squarely in Renong's orbit through a convoluted series of share swaps.

Other events left their mark on Malaysia's corporate scene throughout 1991. The most protracted was a threatened, and as yet unresolved, takeover of Malayan United Industries (MUI) by a group of companies headed by Malaysian tycoon Vincent Tan Chee Yioun. The struggle, which began in August, was sparked after IGB (a former business ally of MUI) sold off its crossholding in the company to hostile parties.

The major business scandal of the year was revealed on 3 July when state-owned Bank Bumiputra said its securities unit, BBMB Securities, lost M$72 million in several "irregular" transactions between September 1989 and March 1990 involving shares of Sungei Besi Mines (Malaysia), a defunct tin miner which attracted public attention in April 1990 by acquiring a nearly 30% stake in a major sugar refining firm. The disclosures, which were part of a prolonged government investigation of insider-trading activities, eventually led to the indictment of a former top BBMB official in August.

The incident focused attention on the issue of insider trading, and drew charges that the government was doing little to combat the problem. Although Mahathir said in late August that the government had found no evidence of insider trading on the Kuala Lumpur Stock Exchange, most analysts said it was clear the authorities would have to take sterner measures to police Malaysia's financial markets. □

# Data

**Major industries** (gross revenue, 1990): Electrical products, US$3.14 billion (US$2.16 billion); food, US$2.49 billion (US$2.11 billion); petroleum refining, US$1.63 billion (US$885.5 million); transport equipment, US$1.02 billion (US$439.4 million); textiles, US$186.18 million (US$172.8 million).

**Major agriculture** (Jan.-July 1991): Rubber, 690,100 tonnes (1.29 million); crude palm oil, 3.21 million tonnes (6.1 million); cocoa, 250,000 tonnes est. for 1991 (247,000); rice, n.a. (1.764 million tonnes).

**Timber** (1990): Sawlogs, 40.146 million m³ (39.709 million); sawn timber, 8.63 million m³ (8.441 million).

**Oil and natural gas** (1990): Crude petroleum, 29.55 million tonnes (27.95 million); LNG, 6.7 million tonnes (6.61 million).

**Mining** (1991 est): Tin-in-concentrates, 23,000 tonnes (28,468).

**Major imports** (Jan.-Aug. 1990): Machinery and transport equipment, US$3.26 billion; manufactured goods, US$8.97 billion; food, US$693.7 million; crude petroleum, US$97.62 million.

**Major exports** (1990): Manufactured goods, including petroleum and rubber products, US$17.25 billion; crude petroleum, US$3.77 billion; sawlogs, US$1.55 billion; rubber, US$1.16 billion; crude and processed palm oil, US$1.59 billion; tin, US$295.8 million.

**Tourism and transport** (1990): Arrivals, 7.5 million (3.9 million est.); departures, 3.577 million. Airlines: International and domestic airline, Malaysia Airlines and Pelangi Airways; railway network (Peninsular Malaysia only); extensive road network in Peninsular Malaysia and parts of East Malaysia; bus services; taxis and car-hire widely available.

**Currency:** Ringgit (100 sens). M$2.7435 = US$1 in Nov. 1991 (M$2.699 = US$1 in Nov. 1990).

**Finance:** 38 commercial banks, 16 foreign. Stock exchange, Kuala Lumpur, 312 companies listed on 6 Nov. 1991.

**Major banks:** Malayan Banking Bhd, 100, Jalan Tun Perak, 50050 Kuala Lumpur, tel. 2308833, tlx MA 30438 MBBREM, fax 2304027; Bank Bumiputra Malaysia, Menara Bumiputra, Jalan Melaka, 50100 Kuala Lumpur, tel. 2981011/2988011, tlx MA 30445 PUTRA, fax 2987135; United Malayan Banking Corp., Bangunan UMBC, Jalan Sultan Sulaiman, 50000 Kuala Lumpur, tel. 2309866/2305833, tlx MA 30484 UMBC, fax 2322627; Public Bank, Bangunan Public Bank, 6, Jalan Sultan Sulaiman, 50000 Kuala Lumpur, tel. 2741766, tlx MA 32371 PUBLIC, fax 2742179; Hongkong and Shanghai Banking Corp., 2 Leboh Ampang, 50100 Kuala Lumpur, tel. 2300744, tlx MA 30381 HSBCKL; Standard Chartered Bank, 2 Jalan Ampang, 50450 Kuala Lumpur, tel. 2326555, tlx MA 30266 SCBKUL, fax 2383295.

**Public bodies:** Federation of Malaysian Manufacturers, 17/F, West Wing, Wisma Sime Darby, Jalan Raja Laut, 50350 Kuala Lumpur, tel. 2931244, tlx MA 32437 FMM, fax 2935105; Associated Chinese Chambers of Commerce and Industry of Malaysia, G/F, Selangor Chinese Assembly Hall, 1, Jalan Maharajalela, 50150 Kuala Lumpur, tel. 2380278, tlx MA 32995 KLSCC, fax 2320473; Associated Indian Chambers of Commerce and Industry of Malaysia, 116, 1/F, Jalan Tuanku Abdul Rahman, 50100 Kuala Lumpur, tel. 2924817, fax 2911670; Malay Chamber of Commerce and Industry of Malaysia, 17/F, Tower Block, Plaza Pekeliling, 2, Jalan Tun Razak, 50400 Kuala Lumpur, tel. 4427664, fax 4414502; Malaysian International Chamber of Commerce and Industry, 10/F, Wisma Damansara, Jalan Semantan, 50490 Kuala Lumpur, tel. 2542677, tlx MA 32120 COMER, fax 2554946; National Chamber of Commerce and Industry of Malaysia, 17/F, Plaza Pekeliling, Jalan Tun Razak, 50400 Kuala Lumpur, tel. 4429871, tlx MA 33642 NACCI, fax 4416043.

**Public holidays** (1992): 1 Jan. (New Year [all states except Johor, Kedah, Kelantan, Perlis and Trengganu]), 4-5 Feb. (Lunar New Year [Kelantan and Trengganu, 4 Feb. only]), 4-5 Apr. (Hari Raya Puasa), 1 May (Labour Day), 17 May (Wesak Day), 6 June (King's birthday), 11 June (Hari Raya Haji), 2 July (Awal Muharram), 31 Aug. (National Day), 9 Sept. (Prophet Muhammad's birthday), 26 Oct. (Deepavali [except Sabah, Sarawak and Federal Territory of Labuan]), 25 Dec. (Christmas).

**Weather:** Malaysia has uniformly high temperature throughout the year, ranging 23-31°C. Coastal areas are humid, while temperatures in the highlands are lower, especially at night. Northeast monsoon from Nov.-Apr., southwest monsoon from May-Oct., with heavy rainfall during changeover periods.

**Taxation:** Compulsory monthly deductions for employees and companies. Individuals up to maximum 40%, corporations 35%. Development tax will be reduced from 3% to 2% for 1992 assessment year and abolished from the 1993 assessment year. Import duties on cigarettes will be increased by 54-56% per kg. Excise duty of 10% per kg will also be increased on these items. Import duties on alcoholic beverages will be increased by 50-185%. Excise duty of 10% will also be increased on these items. Reduction in the import duty on textile and garment materials from a range of 5-55% to 2-20%. Import duty for goods in the chemical, housing and printing industries will also be reduced.

# MALDIVES

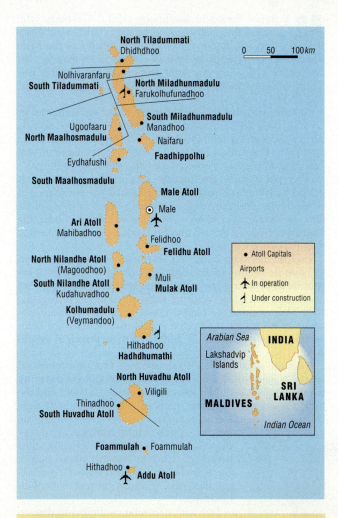

Map labels:

North Tiladummati
Dhidhdhoo
Nolhivaranfaru
South Tiladummati
North Miladhunmadulu
Farukolhufunadhoo
Ugoofaaru
North Maalhosmadulu
South Miladhunmadulu
Manadhoo
Naifaru
Eydhafushi
Faadhippolhu
South Maalhosmadulu
Male Atoll
Male
Ari Atoll
Mahibadhoo
Felidhoo
Felidhu Atoll
North Nilandhe Atoll
(Magoodhoo)
Muli
South Nilandhe Atoll
Mulak Atoll
Kudahuvadhoo
Kolhumadulu
(Veymandoo)
Hithadhoo
Hadhdhumathi
North Huvadhu Atoll
Viligili
Thinadhoo
South Huvadhu Atoll
Foammulah    Foammulah
Hithadhoo
Addu Atoll

0    50    100 km

Atoll Capitals
Airports
✈ In operation
✈ Under construction

Arabian Sea
Lakshadvip Islands
INDIA
SRI LANKA
MALDIVES
Indian Ocean

---

**President** (and **Commander-in-Chief Armed Forces, Minister of Defence, National Security** and **Finance**)
Maumoon Abdul Gayoom.
**Foreign Affairs**
Fatholla Jameel;
**Atolls Administration**
Iliyas Ibrahim;
**Tourism**
Abdulla Jameel;
**Fisheries and Agriculture**
Abbas Ibrahim;
**Health and Welfare**
Abdul Sattar Moosa Didi;
**Education**
Abdulla Hameed;
**Home Affairs and Sports**
Umar Zahir;
**Planning and Environment**
Ismail Shafeehu;

**Transport and Shipping**
Ahmed Zahir;
**Justice**
Mohamed Rasheed Ibrahim;
**Public Works and Labour**
Abdulla Kamalodeen;
**Minister of State for Finance**
Ismail Fathy;
**Minister at President's Office**
(and acting **Attorney-General**)
Mohamed Zahir Hussain;
**Minister of State for Presidential Affairs**
Abdul Rasheed Hussain;
**Chief Justice**
Moona Fathy;
**Speaker of Citizens Majlis** Ahmed Zaki.

# Politics/Social Affairs

President Maumoon Abdul Gayoom entered the fourth year of his third five-year term without indicating whether he would stand again. However, there is no obvious successor to Gayoom, 54, who has served as head of state and government of the Maldives for the past 18 years — nor does he seem to be actively grooming an eventual replacement.

Under the Maldivian constitution, parliament must choose a single candidate for the presidency, who must in turn obtain the endorsement of the electorate at a national referendum. Gayoom obtained more than 90% of the votes polled at the past two elections, and with his current term due to continue till 11 November 1993, still has plenty of time to decide whether he wishes to continue in office.

However, local observers do not see Gayoom as a politician who would wish to extend his tenure indefinitely. They point out that his predecessor Ibrahim Nasir was one of the few modern dictators who knew his time was up, and left the country after arranging an orderly succession.

Nasir was accorded all state honours when he left the country for exile in Singapore in 1968, where he still lives. It was only after Nasir had left that allegations of corruption were made against him and unsuccessful attempts made to obtain his extradition. In July 1990, during celebrations marking the Maldives' 25th independence anniversary, Gayoom made the surprise announcement that Nasir was being pardoned in recognition of his role in winning independence from Britain. Nasir, however, has not chosen to return to the Maldives.

Gayoom is cast in a completely different mould from his predecessor. A democrat, sensitive to the need to liberalise a traditional society, the former university lecturer has accorded high priority to education — particularly in the distant atolls far from the capital island of Male where most of the Maldivian elite lives. Young Maldivians are being educated abroad in increasingly large numbers, both on scholarships and at the expense of families grown prosperous from tourism and other business enterprise.

Greater access to education and other opportunities has led to a mounting desire for change among many of these young people. While Gayoom is believed to be personally sympathetic to many of these calls, he also has to accommodate the interests and sentiments of the more traditional elite and steer a careful course between the competing groups.

---

The Maldives became a British protectorate in 1887, though in practice Britain largely left the Maldives alone and did not install a governor or representative there. The islands' sultans ruled as autocrats until 1932, when their powers were restricted under the country's first written constitution. A short-lived republic was founded in 1953, with Amin Didi as the country's first president. His rule lasted less than a year, when a coup returned the Maldives to a sultanate. However, the last sultan, Mohamed Farhid Didi, ruled in name only from 1957 as the prime minister and later president Ibrahim Nasi gradually consolidated control over the country.

From 1957-65, the Maldives were locked in a dispute with the British over the terms of leasing Gan Island in Addu Atoll as an air force staging base. The matter was resolved on 26 July 1965, when the Maldives became an independent nation and Britain was granted leasing rights to Gan. In 1976, the British prematurely terminated their lease and closed the airbase. Nasir resigned in 1978 and Maumoon Abdul Gayoom was elected to replace him, taking power on 11 November 1978. In November 1988, an abortive coup attempt mounted by a mixed group of Maldivians and Sri Lankans was crushed after India rushed troops and warships to support Gayoom's government.

With Gayoom's own plans for a possible fourth term still unclear, there is cautious speculation in Male about a possible successor. Among those mentioned are Foreign Minister Fatholla Jameel, Education Minister Abdulla Hameed and Atolls Administration Minister Iliyas Ibrahim, the president's brother-in-law. Long regarded as his country's strongman, Ibrahim has held the Ministry of Trade and Industry portfolio and served as deputy defence minister with Gayoom as defence minister.

In May 1990, Ibrahim — who has many critics and detractors in Male — left the country while a case of embezzlement and misappropriation of government funds was under investigation that the authorities said could only proceed after Ibrahim had been questioned. Ibrahim and his family left the country after Gayoom had apparently told him he was being dismissed from government to enable inquiries to proceed.

Ibrahim returned to Male within three months, and by March 1991 was back in government as Minister of Atolls Administration. According to reports from Male, his return to the cabinet indicated he had been cleared of any charges, while local observers noted that his latest portfolio provided excellent opportunities to build a future political base. Gayoom, however, has distanced Ibrahim from the Maldives' security apparatus.

In early 1991, reports from the Maldives spoke of a wave of unprecedented arrests and detentions that were said to indicate simmering dissent. There were also reports of a series of arson attacks and an attempt to bomb the conference hall built for the South Asian Association for Regional Cooperation summit held in Male during 1990. In May 1991, Amnesty International published a report on the Maldives that expressed concern over the arrests and human-rights abuses.

The report alleged that those arrested since March 1990 included a member of parliament, newspaper owners, editors and journalists. It said there had been allegations of ill treatment of prisoners, harassment of their families and, in some cases, that confessions were extracted under duress.

Gayoom's address at the opening of parliament in March 1991 provided some clues to the possibility that the government had cracked down on dissent. Stressing that stability was essential for the development process, he said "any difference of opinion and thought that may occur among the people should not be allowed to affect the stability of the country."

In August 1991, the Maldives Government announced that 17 Tamil rebels jailed for attempting to overthrow the country's administration in 1988 would be repatriated to Sri Lanka. The Sri Lankan Tamils, members of the People's Liberation Organisation of Tamil Eelam guerilla group, were among 68 mercenaries hired by a Maldivian businessman to overthrow the government. The attempt was crushed after India rushed paratroops and naval units to the islands. A government statement said the men were being sent away on the condition "they never return to the Maldives."

Since the 1988 coup attempt, Male boosted its security forces from about 350 personnel to more than 1,500 and acquired new weapons and sophisticated surveillance equipment. Gayoom keeps a tight hold on the security apparatus, and has frequently spoken about the need for a UN mechanism to guarantee the sovereignty, territorial integrity and independence of small nations from acts of aggression by mercenaries and similar security threats. □

# Foreign Relations

**M**aldivian President Maumoon Abdul Gayoom, who assumed the chairmanship of the South Asian Association for Regional Cooperation (Saarc) at the Male summit in November 1990, was called on to exercise his diplomatic skills one year later to prevent the possible collapse of the association following a row between Sri Lanka and India.

Gayoom was due to hand over the Saarc leadership to Sri Lankan President Ranasinghe Premadasa at the Colombo summit scheduled for November 1991. However, the event for which Premadasa had made elaborate preparation was cancelled at the last moment following the king of Bhutan's decision not to attend the summit's finale. India chose to adopt the position that the Saarc charter required the attendance of either the head of state or government of each of the association's seven member states — Bangladesh, Bhutan, India, the Maldives, Nepal, Pakistan and Sri Lanka — and the meeting was accordingly cancelled.

The row between India and Sri Lanka — which appeared to have its origins in Premadasa's refusal to host the 1989 summit in Colombo due to the then presence of Indian troops in northern Sri Lanka and his subsequent absence from the 1990 Male summit — placed Gayoom in an awkward position as he sought to steer a course that would not compromise relations with the Maldives' two principal neighbours.

After the collapse of the Saarc summit, Premadasa pushed to get at least some association leaders to Colombo during the meeting's scheduled dates. In the event, Gayoom and the Indian and Pakistan prime ministers attended, though New Delhi — which in 1988 sent paratroops and warships to Male

Gayoom: no obvious successor.

to crush an attempt by mercenaries to topple Gayoom — would clearly had preferred that he remained at home. Gayoom, however, did not wish to endanger the good relations he had built with Colombo.

Ties with Colombo continued to deepen during the year. During a state visit to Sri Lanka in November — the second in 1991 — Gayoom discussed bilateral trade and economic cooperation issues with Premadasa, and the two leaders also agreed to improve coordination between each other's immigration authorities.

Two days after the November visit, Male announced that visa procedures for Sri Lankans visiting the Maldives — enforced since the 1988 coup attempt — would be lifted for bona fide workers and tourists. Male noted that Sri Lankans were the largest group of foreigners employed in the Maldives, many working as teachers and in the booming tourist industry.

Gayoom and Premadasa also agreed that Maldivian and Sri Lankan authorities involved in the suppression of terrorism would liaise more closely, and that an early meeting of the relevant authorities would be held. The Sri Lankan Tamil mercenaries who unsuccessfully attempted to overthrow the Gayoom administration in 1988 were seeking, among other objectives, an island based in the Maldives to wage their separatist war against Colombo.

During the year, Male also agreed to give special consideration to Sri Lankan fishing trawlers detected poaching in Maldivian waters. Male first released the crews of 18 seized trawlers, and following Premadasa's intercession on behalf of the boat captains during Gayoom's visit to Sri Lanka in August, Gayoom ordered a waiver of 75% of the heavy fines imposed on them. Maldivian Foreign Minister Fatholla Jameel, who conveyed this decision to his Sri Lankan counterpart, said the decision had been taken in view of the friendly ties between the two countries.

Due to lack of land on the capital island, Male does not encourage foreign countries to establish resident diplomatic missions in the Maldives. Only India, Pakistan and Sri Lanka maintain resident missions in the Maldivian capital. Libya has a representative in Male, but not a full-fledged People's Bureau (Embassy), while only the UN Development Programme among international organisations maintains a resident mission. All other envoys accredited to Male are either resident in Colombo or New Delhi.

**Income: fish and trippers.**

early 1970s. By 1990, more than 20,000 tonnes of fresh fish were being exported a year and a thriving canning industry developed. A new tuna processing plant at Felivaru is said by government officials to be unable to cope with rising overseas demand, and another cannery is planned for Laamu Atoll.

While physical and climatic limitations in the Maldives have always meant that agriculture has played a secondary role in the economy, it nevertheless contributed nearly 9% of GDP in 1990. Although coconut products remain a traditional secondary source of income for many families, other crops grown primarily for local consumption include bananas, onions, chillies, millet, cassava and breadfruit. However, most of the fruit and vegetables intended for the tourism sector still have to be imported.

Foreign investment is encouraged in a number of areas — notably tourism, fisheries and manufacturing — with 100% foreign-owned enterprises permitted. In recent years, the availability of European and North American textile quotas for the Maldives has encouraged the establishment and growth of garment factories on Addu Atoll, site of Britain's former Gan airbase, and elsewhere. The manufacturing sector — which in addition to export oriented garment production, ranges from printing and brick making to aerated water bottling — is second only to fishing as a source of employment, engaging 20% of the Maldivian workforce.

# Economy/Infrastructure

The past 25 years have seen the traditional subsistence economy of the Maldives undergo rapid modernisation, with tourism outpacing fishing as the country's mainstay. Tourism now contributes over 18% of GDP against the fisheries' 15.2%.

In addition, exports of sun-dried and smoked Maldive fish — highly prized in neighbouring Sri Lanka — have now been overtaken by frozen and canned tuna. Exports of copra — dried coconut kernels used for producing edible oil and animal feed — are now insignificant, though agriculture still contributes 8.9% of GDP.

The stated objectives of the Maldives' three-year development plan that ended in 1990 were to improve living standards, balance population density and development between the capital island of Male and the small atolls and to attain a measure of self-reliance. Its relative success can be measured in that per capita income now stands at around US$650 against US$480 in the mid-1980s, while the annual economic growth rate rose an estimated 15% during 1990.

Tourism, which began in the Maldives during the early 1970s, now earns most of the country's hard currency and over 25% of government revenue. The first tourist resorts were developed in the uninhabited islands of the Male Atoll in 1972 and offered around 350 beds. In 1992, the number of resorts are projected to reach 72, offering around 10,000 beds to handle more than 200,000 expected arrivals. Over 195,000 tourists visited the Maldives in 1990, while arrivals between January and August 1991 neared 125,000 — with the important winter season yet to be assessed. The country's Hulhule international airport, which can already accommodate wide-bodied jets, is currently being expanded to meet the growing demand.

While tourism produces the bulk of the Maldives' hard currency, fishing remains the main source of employment. Long reliant on the local *dhoni* sailing craft, moves to mechanise the Maldives' fishery began in 1974. By 1987 some 1,340 dhonis had been fitted with engines which, together with the introduction of custom-built modern fishing boats, have significantly increased the size of the national fish catch.

The first exports of frozen tuna and skipjack began in the

## Data

**Major industries:** Fisheries, total catch, 76,400 tonnes (71,500).

**Major agriculture:** Coconuts, n.a. (12.5 million).

**Major imports** (Jan.-Aug. 1991): Consumer goods, US$74 million (US$39.6 million); intermediate and capital goods, US$42.6 million (US$25.6 million); petroleum products, US$21.78 million (US$13.78 million).

**Major exports** (Jan.-Aug. 1991): Marine products, US$30.5 million (US$21.36 million); apparel and clothing accessories, US$14.63 million (US$12.52 million).

**Tourism:** Arrivals (Jan.-Aug 1991), 124,591 (195,156 for all 1990); Air Maldives operates domestic flights; no public transport.

**Currency:** Rufiyaa. Rf 9.5094 = US$, end-Oct. 1991 (Rf 9.2 = US$1). (Previous year's figures in brackets).

**Finance:** Central bank; Maldives Monetary Authority (MMA), Majeedee Bldg, Marine Drive, Male, tel. 322290, tlx 66055, fax 323862. The MMA issues currency, supervises foreign-exchange dealing and advises the government on banking and monetary matters. No stock exchange.

**Major banks:** Bank of Maldives Ltd, 11 Marine Drive, Male, tel. 323091, tlx 77030, fax 328233; State Bank of India, tlx 66015; Bank of Ceylon, tlx 66080; Habib Bank Ltd, tlx 66016.

**Government ministries** (all in Male): President's Office, Marine Drive, tel. 323701, tlx 66013, fax 325500; Attorney-General, Huravee Bldg, Ameer Ahmed Magu, tel. 323809; Atolls Administration, Faashanaa Bldg, tel. 322826; Defence and National Security, Ban'deyrige, tel. 322118, tlx 66056, fax 325525; Education, Ghaazee Bldg, Ameer Ahmed Magu, tel. 323262, tlx 66032, fax 321201; Finance, Ghaazee Bldg, Ameer Ahmed Magu, tel. 324345, tlx 66032, fax 324432; Foreign Affairs, Marino Drive (North), tel. 323405, tlx 66008, fax 323841; Fisheries and Agriculture, Ghaazee Bldg, Ameer Ahmed Magu, tel. 322625, tlx 77033, fax 326558; Health and Welfare, Ghaazee Bldg, Ameer Ahmed Magu, tel. 323216, tlx 66181, fax 328869; Home Affairs and Sport, Huravee Bldg, Ameer Ahmed Magu, tel. 323821, tlx 77039, fax 324739; Justice, Ghaazee Bldg, Ameer Ahmed Magu, tel. 322301, fax 324103; Planning and Environment, Ghaazee Bldg, Ameer Ahmed Magu, tel. 322965, tlx 66110, fax 327351; Tourism, Ghaazee Bldg, Ameer Ahmed Magu, tel. 323224, tlx 66019, fax 322512; Trade and Industries, Ghaazee Bldg, Ameer Ahmed Magu, tel. 323668, tlx 77076, fax 323756; Transport and Shipping, Huravee Bldg, Ameer Ahmed Magu, tel. 32818, tlx 77066, fax 323994.

**Public holidays** (1992): 1 Jan. (New Year), 5 Feb. (Martyrs' Day), 6-7 Mar. (Beginning of Ramadan), 4-6 Apr. (Fith'r Eid), 10 June (Haj Day), 11-15 June (Al'h'aa Eid), 2 July (Islamic New Year), 26-27 July (Independence Day), 29-30 Aug. (National Day), 9 Sept. (Prophet Mohammed's Birthday), 3 Nov. (Victory Day), 11-12 Nov. (Republic Day), 28 Nov. (Huravee Day).

**Weather:** The climate is generally warm and humid with sunshine throughout the year. Average daily temperature varies between 31°C and 26°C. Average annual rainfall is 1,610 mm.

# MONGOLIA

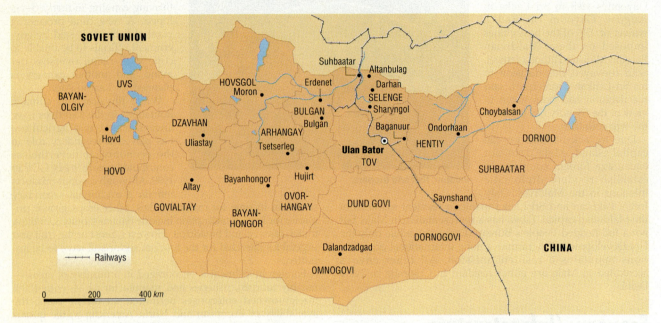

The northern Mongol princes, long feudatories of China's Qing emperors, declared independence under Russian protection when the dynasty fell in 1911. A revolutionary government came to power in 1921 with Soviet help and the Mongolian People's Republic was proclaimed in 1924, the world's second communist state.

Mongolia is still essentially a pastoral country, its main wealth lying in its vast herds of sheep, goats, cows, camels and horses. Arable farming, industrialisation and mining of mineral deposits were developed with Soviet and Eastern bloc help, but the general collapse of communist economies in the late 1980s left Mongolia with a legacy of imbalances, shortages, pollution and inefficiency.

Calls for reform and the formation of non-communist political parties in 1990 brought about the resignation in March of the Mongolian People's Revolutionary Party leadership and the government it had dominated. The country's first multi-party elections to the People's Great Hural (national assembly) in July led to a degree of power-sharing in the State Little Hural or standing legislature, which formed a new government. A new constitution is likely to replace the Great and Small Hurals with a 75-member directly elected single-chamber assembly to be empowered after elections in mid-1992.

**President**
Punsalmaagiyn Ochirbat.
**Vice-President**
Radnaasumbereliyn Gonchigdorj;
**Majority Party General Secretary**
Budragchaagiyn Dash-Yondon;
**Prime Minister**
Dashiyn Byambasuren;
**Chief Deputy Prime Minister**
Davaadorjiyn Ganbold;
**Deputy Prime Ministers**
Dambiyn Dorligjav, Choyjilsurengiyn Purevdorj;
**Agriculture**
Dandzangiyn Radnaaragchaa;

**Defence**
Lieut.-Gen. Shagalyn Jadambaa;
**Foreign Relations**
Tserenpiliyn Gombosuren;
**National Development**
Jamyangiyn Batsuur;
**Trade and Industry**
S. Bayarbaatar;
**Chairman of the Supreme Court**
Dashdorjiyn Dembereltseren;
**State Procurator**
Gombodorjiyn Bahdal;
**Armed Forces Chief of Staff**
Maj.-Gen. Rashmaagiyn Gavaa.

## Politics/Social Affairs

Mongolian politics were dominated for much of the year by a public debate over the draft of the country's new constitution. The version approved by a committee of the State Little Hural, or standing legislature, in May 1991 and published on 5 June, differed slightly from an earlier version that had been circulated for scrutiny by international lawyers.

The debate tended to focus on symbols — whether the country was to continue to be called the Mongolian People's Republic or simply Mongolia; whether the name of the capital would change; whether the national emblem should include a five-pointed star or lotus leaves, or whether the title of the constitution should reflect that of the Great Law of the 13th-century leader Genghis Khan.

However, the most contentious issue remained whether Mongolia would adopt a presidential or parliamentary system of government. The former was favoured by the majority communist Mongolian People's Revolutionary Party (MPRP), which has strong support in the countryside, and the latter by the opposition democratic parties and their allies who draw their support from the towns. A directly elected State Great Hural of 75 members, as proposed, might replace the bicameral, indirectly elected legislature formed after the July 1990 elections in which the People's Great Hural had 430 members and a disproportionate MPRP majority.

After three months' of national debate, the Constitution Drafting Commission chaired by President Punsalmaagiyn Ochirbat made 8,000 further amendments to the draft for consideration by the Little Hural in October 1991 and by the next session of the People's Great Hural in November. Once the new constitution is adopted, a general election is expected be called in mid-1992.

Under a presidential decree in September, Mongolia's president, vice-president and other leaders of the government and judiciary, including officials in the defence and security services, diplomats and journalists in the official media, were banned from membership of any political party. The decree particularly affected the MPRP's 100,000 members, forcing the resignation from the party of such prominent central committee members as Ochirbat, Foreign Relations Minister Tserenpiliyn Gombosuren and the chiefs of staff of the armed forces and border troops.

The collapse of communist power in the Soviet Union following August's attempted coup, the banning of the Soviet Communist Party and the confiscation of its property led to similar calls in Mongolia and renewed the crisis inside the MPRP. It seemed likely that in order to survive, the MPRP — for 69 years the country's ruling and only political party — would have to excise its communist past and become the Mongolian People's Party once more.

While they remain generally uncontaminated by direct links with Yumjaagiyn Tsedenbal — the former MPRP leader, premier and president ousted in 1984, who died in Moscow on 21 April — the party's leadership was attacked for being slow in introducing the market economy and other reforms. Although the MPRP's political base in the countryside was still largely unchallenged, inflation and shortages were seen by politically more sophisticated townspeople as proof of the bankruptcy of the party's policies.

The party's former unity was threatened by factional opposition to the conservatives, which centred on the "party renewal" section headed by Kinayatyn Dzardyhan, vice-chairman of the Little Hural and an MPRP reformer who had launched a campaign for political change long before the national democracy movement got under way.

Another faction promoted restoration of the traditions of the MPRP's predecessor, the Mongolian People's Party. The MPRP's own democratic group, based in Erdenet, Mongolia's third-largest city, called for the MPRP to be disbanded. The party's Mongolian Revolutionary Youth Union was replaced by a non-sectarian National Youth Federation in December 1990, but reconstituted along its former lines in February 1991.

**Ochirbat and Bush: a wider world.**

The MPRP's supposedly reformist chairman Gombojavyn Ochirbat, elected in March 1990, said in his report to the party's 20th Congress in February that Mongolia had taken the wrong path since the 1921 revolution, with the result that "state socialism" had been founded on coercion. This must now be discarded in favour of building democratic scientific socialism under Mongolian conditions, he said. However, the new 99-member central committee responded by choosing a new chairman, Budragchaagiyn Dash-Yondon. It also promoted Choyjilsurengiyn Purevdorj, a deputy–prime minister responsible for power and technology issues, and President Ochirbat's aide Budsurengiyn Tumen to presidium membership.

Celebrations held in Ulan Bator during July to commemorate the 70th anniversary of the Mongolian revolution were, for the first time, conducted without political slogans or demonstrations. The troops in the military parade wore new uniforms with Mongolian *oldxziy* (endless knot) symbols instead of five-pointed stars on their epaulets.

The Mongolian Democratic Union (MDU), the country's largest opposition group, at its June congress elected its chief coordinator Sanjaasurengiyn Dzorig to the post of president. It also adopted a new constitution declaring that it adhered to the "universal truth of mankind and Mongolia's historic and cultural traditions." Coordinating council member Elbegdorj was appointed chief coordinator in September, following the adoption of new rules vesting the party's supreme authority in the council rather than the congress.

The attempted coup against Soviet President Mikhail Gorbachov shook the MPRP's fragile coalition with the MDU, Social Democrats and New Progress Party. Ochirbat, responding to the Soviet emergency committee's takeover, appealed for national unity and stated that Mongolia hoped good relations and cooperation with the Soviet Union would continue. However, the government paper *Ardyn Erh*, as well as the MPRP's *Unen*, printed the statements of the emergency committee in full for two issues.

On the other hand, MDU leader Dzorig expressed deep anxiety about the state of emergency in the Soviet Union, describing it as a conservative attempt to halt perestroika. The Social Democrats in the Little Hural also voiced regret at the action. When the coup failed, Ochirbat sent Russian President Boris Yeltsin a message expressing his "deep satisfaction" at the outcome. The MPRP also said it was glad that Gorbachov was back.

But thousands of people demonstrated in Ulan Bator to protest the Mongolian leaders' handling of the situation, with the democratic forces being joined by MPRP radicals. Damdinsurengiyn Batsuh, leader of the New Progressive Union, demanded the banning of the MPRP on the grounds that it might stage a similar coup in Mongolia. The armed forces' general staff later admitted that some Mongolian army units had been put on alert during the putsch, but denied any "political forces" had been planning a military coup.

The public procurator announced on 20 August that 12 former members of the MPRP politburo who had resigned in March 1990 or before would be tried for corruption and abuse of office. He also sought the removal of parliamentary immunity from former premier and director of the Mongol State Oil Co., Dumaagiyn Sodnom. The State Rehabilitation Commission, chaired by Vice-President Randnaasumbereliyn Gonchigdorj, reported at the beginning of October that over the past two-and-a-half years the Supreme Court had rehabilitated 2,436 "victims of repression" falsely charged with espionage, nationalism and anti-party activities during the dictatorship years, 1930-50s. The foundation stone of a monument to the victims was laid in Ulan Bator by Gonchigdorj in July.

In December 1990, Ochirbat held a meeting with the country's religious leaders at which he noted that the laws and regulations concerning religion were in conflict with state policy. Hajj Sayraan, head of the Mongolian Muslim Society, emphasised the dangers of religion being used as a political weapon — a reference to the founding of the Buddhist Democratic Party in July 1990.

Divisions among the country's Buddhists were highlighted when the abbot of Armbayasgalant monastery rejected the abbot of Gandantegchinlen monastery in Ulan Bator as the country's Buddhist leader. The establishment of a Presidential Council for Religious Affairs was agreed, and a new law regulating relations between the church and state was adopted the same month. Ochirbat attended Mongolia's first official celebrations of Buddha's Conception Day on 28 May.

The Dalai Lama's visit to Mongolia in September as the guest of Gandantegchinlen monastery — earlier postponed following pressure from Peking — included an address to believers in the Ulan Bator stadium where he said Tibet was encouraged in its struggle for independence by Mongolia's experience in throwing off communism. The Ministry of Foreign Relations emphasised the Dalai Lama's visit was at the invitation of religious organisations, not the government. □

# Foreign Relations

President Punsalmaagiyn Ochirbat travelled to Washington at the end of January 1991 to discuss Mongolian-US relations with President George Bush. During the visit, the US agreed to help Mongolia's transition to a market economy, train personnel and provide science and technology equipment. Science and technology and trade agreements were also signed.

In New York, Ochirbat met UN Secretary-General Javier Perez de Cuellar and US business leaders, while Deputy Prime Minister Choyjilsurengiyn Purevdorj held talks with officials of the UN Development Programme.

Prime Minister Dashiyn Byambasuren visited the US in June, when Mongolia was accorded most-favoured nation status following its adoption of a new emigration law. In July, US Secretary of State James Baker returned to Mongolia, having had to cut short his first visit a year before because of Iraq's invasion of Kuwait.

Ochirbat flew home from Washington through Moscow, where he and Soviet President Mikhail Gorbachov emphasised the need to strengthen Mongolian-Soviet relations. They concluded that the work done since their last meeting in May 1990 had been unsatisfactory and agreed their prime ministers would meet to stimulate action on trade, joint ventures, construction projects and geological prospecting.

At a meeting with Soviet Premier Valentin Pavlov in February, Byambasuren called for greater efficiency and the "balancing" of economic ties. They agreed to revise and update the contractual and legal basis of economic cooperation, but the problem of Mongolia's Rbl 9.5 billion (US$16.24 billion) debt repayment was not resolved. Byambasuren also had talks with Russian Premier Ivan Silayev and signed the first intergovernmental agreement with Russia on economic cooperation, trade and joint ventures.

High unemployment in Mongolia's westernmost province of Bayan-Slgiy, inhabited mostly by Kazakhs, encouraged migration to neighbouring Soviet Kazakhstan where as many as 30,000 farmers and construction workers sought work. President Nursultan Nazarbayev of Kazakhstan met the Mongolian ambassador in Moscow in July to discuss a trade and economic agreement and the easing of travel restrictions, including opening a new border crossing at Tashanta. A labour market agreement with Kazakhstan was signed in Ulan Bator in September.

The withdrawal of Soviet troops from the country continued, with the large garrison town of Choyrr on the Trans-Mongolian Railway returned to the gov-

**Livestock: the nation's wealth.**

ernment. About 3,000 Soviet soldiers are due to remain in Mongolia until 1992 to complete the despatch of equipment.

Estonian, Latvian and Lithuanian independence were quickly recognised by Mongolia and diplomatic relations established in August. Mongolia's full membership of the Non-Aligned Movement was confirmed in September, while diplomatic relations were established with Israel in October.

Mongolian People's Revolutionary Party chairman Gombojavyn Ochirbat met Chinese Communist Party general-secretary Jiang Zemin in Peking during February — the first meeting between leaders of the two parties for 30 years. Mongolian Defence Minister Lieut-Gen. Shagalyn Jadambaa visited Peking in April, where he met Premier Li Peng. During Vice-President Radnaasumbereliyn Gonchigdorj's visit to Peking in June, Mongolian and Chinese officials signed agreements on the opening of eight new border crossing points. The first of these, in Xinjiang's Qinghe county, opened in July.

In August, Chinese President Yang Shangkun paid a state visit to Mongolia — the first by a Chinese head of state. Ochirbat said that they shared "identical" views on expanding cooperation between the two countries. He made special mention of new agreements signed on the transit of Mongolian goods through China via Tianjin, and on postponing Mongolia's debt repayments to China.

Following the visit of a Taiwanese Mongolian and Tibetan Affairs Commission official to Mongolia in August, it was reported from Taipei that Mongolia welcomed Taiwan investment in agriculture, manufacturing and tourism. The Mainland Affairs Council approved rules permitting Mongolians to visit Taiwan by invitation of organisations. However, Taiwan continued its policy of not recognising Mongolia. □

# Economy/Infrastructure

Mongolia was granted around US$155 million in aid at a conference in Tokyo during September 1991, signalling the prospect of large-scale international relief for the faltering economy during the country's transition to a market system. The conference, co-sponsored by Japan and the World Bank, was the culmination of a series of international contacts that began with an appeal for emergency aid by National Development Minister Jamyangiyn Batsuur in May, included Foreign Minister Tserenpiliyn Gombosuren's European aid-seeking tour in June, and the visits to Ulan Bator by US Secretary of State James Baker and former Japanese prime minister Toshiki Kaifu.

Both the US and Japan agreed to provide urgently needed food aid immediately. The US offered credits worth US$10.6 million and promised further help, while Japan gave a cash grant of US$15 million in development aid and US$7 million for improved communications.

The guiding principles for Mongolia's switch to a market economy were contained in a government resolution adopted by the State Little Hural on 28 December 1990. It encouraged privatisation of state property and the leasing of land, with state control of prices of consumer goods and wages, and promised to protect the interests of foreign investors.

Reporting to the Little Hural on the first half-year of the government's economic activity,

Prime Minister Dashiyn Byambasuren said the government would halve planned capital investment in 1991, cut budgetary expenditure by Tugriks 1.7 billion — the national currency — and cancel 10 major construction projects. Tugriks 20 million would be put into the development of small industries and the creation of 5,500 jobs. However, unemployment rose from 31,000 in December 1990 to 83,000 in August 1991, including some 38,000 technical and vocational-school leavers.

At the beginning of 1991, the government doubled wages and savings accounts to meet the expected doubling of retail prices as controls were lifted. By July, the budget deficit was estimated at Tugriks 1.4 billion for the full year, though it was planned to offset it by auctioning the US$20 million reserves held at the beginning of 1991.

Byambasuren commented that Mongolia's economic decline would continue for two or three years "until we learn how to live within the limits of our own potential." Government five- and 10-year interest-bearing loan bonds were due to go on sale in October, with 20% of the face value to be paid in US dollars.

A massive devaluation of the Tugrik in June changed the official exchange rate from Tugriks 7.1 to US$1 to Tugriks 40 to US$1. The government freed wholesale prices on some 60% of goods in circulation in early September, but retained control over the prices of coal, petrol, diesel, timber, medicines, children's clothing and some foods and utilities. At the end of September, President Punsalmaagiyan Ochirbat re-imposed price controls and called for measures to boost production.

The transition to foreign trade settlements in hard currency from 1 January cut foreign trade to one third of the 1990 level due to economic disruption and the shortage of hard currency in Mongolia and the Soviet Union — Mongolia's main trading partner. The country remained acutely short of petrol, spare parts and imported foods and medicines. There were frequent power cuts and industrial stoppages, road transport was disrupted and local air services grounded. To save hard currency, more than half the Soviet technicians working in industry — who were due to be cut to 3,000 personnel by the end of 1991 — had to be sent home.

Further, to make up for the 1990 harvest — which was delayed by fuel shortages and spoiled by bad weather — Mongolia needed to import some 65,000 tonnes of wheat during the year. According to mid-year estimates, Mongolia's foreign trade deficit would reach US$40 million by the end of 1991.

Following shortages due to panic buying and hoarding, rationing of basic foodstuffs and consumer goods was imposed in some Mongolian provinces in December 1990 and introduced in Ulan Bator and other main towns in January.

The urban population is generally without livestock and its food requirements, including a large proportion of imported and processed foods, are met by local shops. The ration per head of the urban population per month averaged 3 kg of flour, 550 g each of rice and granulated sugar, 350 g of butter, and one bottle of vegetable oil and four bottles of arhi (local vodka) per family. Green tea from the Soviet Union, soap and detergent were also rationed. Candles and matches were in short supply because of domestic production shortfalls.

A meat ration for townspeople of 2.7 kg per head per month was introduced in May. Meat rationing was due to 30% under-fulfilment of the autumn 1990 meat procurement plan and was preceded by shortages in the major towns. The government called for two meatless days a week, but did not plan to import meat since it expected supplies to pick up in July — however, meat rationing was still in force in October. To supplement urban milk supplies, 2,600 tonnes of dried milk were ordered from abroad.

For the 50% or so of the Mongolian population living in the countryside, the food shortages were less acute since their needs are largely met by their own livestock. Mongolia's total head of cattle, sheep, goats, horses and camels reached the record figure of 25.7 million by the end of 1990. Surviving newborn stock in 1991 reached 9.3 million by mid-year, but heavy livestock losses were reported in some areas.

About 25% of the country's livestock is privately owned, the number slowly increasing as herdsmen started to take their animals out of the *negdels* (herding cooperatives) after privatisation of negdel property was approved in June. The pastures remained state-owned under a law on land privatisation adopted in October.

A government Privatisation Commission was set up in January under the chairmanship of Chief Deputy Prime Minister Davaadorjiyn Ganbold to plan and implement a programme for denationalising state property. As of May, 58.4% of the country's industrial and economic units (91.2% of assets in money terms) belonged to the state, 27.3% to public cooperatives (7.4% of assets) and 8.8% (0.2% of assets) to private individuals.

In June, it was decided that each citizen would be issued with share certificates worth Tugriks 10,000. Foreigners and foreign companies were permitted to buy shares or complete properties. So-called "little" privatisation began the same month with the auctioning of several Ulan Bator shops and restaurants to private individuals and was due to be completed by the year's end.

The "big" privatisation of large state industrial enterprises was due to begin towards the end of the year and take up to 30 months. However, the government retained full control of strategic sectors, such as railways and the national airline, and a 51% interest in power stations, coal and metal ore mines, communications links and some large food and building industry enterprises. □

## Data

**Major industries:** Electric power, 2.83 billion kWh (3.01 billion); cement, 440,800 tonnes (515,300); woollen cloth, 1.06 million m (1.95 million); carpets, 2 million m² (2.1 million); leather footwear, 4.8 million pairs (4.3 million); flour, 187,000 tonnes (201,900).

**Major agriculture:** Grain, 718,300 tonnes (798,600); potatoes, 131,100 tonnes (146,700); green vegetables, 41,700 tonnes (46,800); hay, 893,600 tonnes (1.05 million); livestock, 25.4 million head (24.6 million).

**Oil and natural gas:** Nil.

**Major imports** (1989): Petrol, diesel and paraffin, 798,000 tonnes (868,000); sheet metal, 67,000 tonnes (70,800); trucks, 1,069 (1,490); buses, 249 (343); tractors, 624 (615); fertiliser, 36,000 tonnes (36,200); paper, 7,800 tonnes (9,200); cotton cloth, 59.1 million m (59.5 million); woollen cloth, 1.4 million m (same); TV sets, 7,800 (20,200); washing machines, 2,800 (8,200); refined sugar, 43,800 tonnes (42,700).

**Major exports** (1989): Cement, 175,000 tonnes (157,000); sawn timber, 71,100 m³ (93,600); wool, 3,500 tonnes (4,900); hides (large), 218,000 (189,000); hides (small), 542,000 (771,000); meat, 30,800 tonnes (29,800); wheat, n.a. (31,000 tonnes); copper concentrate, 352,900 tonnes (n.a.).

**Tourism and transport** (1989): Visitors, 10,000 (same); Mongolian National Tourism organisation, Ulan Bator, tel. 20163; Juulchin Foreign Travel Co., Hu'sgalchdyn Gudamj, Ulan Bator, tel. 202246, tlx 232. National airlines, MIAT, external routes through Peking and Moscow. Railway line from Soviet to Chinese border through Ulan Bator with branches to Erdenet, Sharyn Gol, Baganuur and Bor-ondor and Dzuunbayan, and line from Soviet border to Choybalsan with branch to Marday. Some long-distance inter-urban bus services, including one to the Soviet Union; trolley bus line in Ulan Bator; urban bus and taxi services; no car hire.

**Finance:** 5 commercial banks with overall financial control through the state Mongol Bank, no credit unions, building societies or consumer finance companies. Individual foreign-exchange facilities at main hotels, which have duty-free shops. Visa credit card agreement concluded 1991.

**Stock Exchanges:** Mongolian Stock Exchange, Suhbaataryn Talbay, Ulan Bator, Agricultural Exchange and Trade Information Exchange, all founded in 1991.

**Major Banks:** Mongol Bank, Hudaldaany Gudamj 6, Ulan Bator, tel. 22847; Bank for Capital Investment and Technological Innovation; Trade and Industry Bank; Industrial Shares Bank; Mongolian Insurance Bank and Mongolian Cooperative Bank.

**Currency:** Tugrik (Togrog) (100 mongo). Mongolian official rate (June 1991), Tugrik 40 = US$1 (1990, Tugrik 5.62 = US$1).

**Public holidays** (1992): 1 Jan. (New Year), 3-4 Feb. (Lunar New Year, or *Tsagaan Sar*), 11-13 July (National Day or *Naadam*).

**Taxation:** Personal taxation raises only 0.7% of budgetary revenue, most of which comes from turnover tax.

**Weather:** Mongolia has a harsh climate, with Jan. average temperature of −26.1°C, and a July average of 17°C. There are many sunny days a year, with the highest rainfall in July.

# NEPAL

CHINA

Lapche Pass
Mahakali R. Humla
Namja Pass
Darchula
Seti R. Jumla Dolpa Mustang
Mahendra Bheri R.
Nagar Rolpa Kali Pokhara
Gandaki R. Gorkha
Nepalgunj Lumbini Chitawan
Butawal Kathmandu Sun Kosi R.
Narayani R. Bhojpur Tamur R.
Birgunj Bagmati R. Ilam
INDIA Raxaul
Janakpur Biratnagar
Sapta Chandragadhi
Kosi R.
0    100    200 km

**F**rom 1846 to 1951, Nepal was in effect ruled by a family of hereditary Rana prime ministers, who pursued a policy of close cooperation with the British power in India. Agitation by the Nepali Congress Party in the late 1940s for a more democratic government led to a revolution, through which the royal line — represented by King Tribhuvan — returned to power.

A general election, on the style of Western democracies, held in June 1959 delivered an overwhelming victory to the Congress Party headed by Bisweswore Prasad Koirala. However, towards the end of 1960, King Mahendra, who had succeeded his father King Tribhuvan, dismissed the country's first parliamentary government and inaugurated personal rule through the medium of the partyless *Panchayat* system.

Mahendra died on 31 January 1972 and was succeeded by his Western-educated son, Birendra, who was officially crowned in February 1975. A national referendum was held on 2 May 1980, resulting in a narrow mandate for the continuation of the Panchayat system.

In 1990, Congress and the Left stepped up pressure on the king. After clashes in which 500 people died, the king conceded sovereignty and Nepal became a constitutional monarchy with a multi-party parliament.

**Head of State**
King Birendra Bir Bikram Shah Dev.
**Prime Minister** (and **Defence, Foreign and Royal Palace Affairs**)
Girija Prasad Koirala;
**Water Resources and Communications**
Basu Dev Risal;
**Housing and Physical Planning**
Bal Bahadur Rai;
**Land Reform Management**
Jagan Nath Acharya;
**Social Welfare, Labour and Cooperation**
Sheikh Idris;
**Education and Culture**
Ram Hari Joshi;
**Forestry, Environment and Agriculture**
Sailja Acharya;
**Home**
Sher Bahadur Deupa;
**Local Development**
Ram Chandra Paudyel;
**Industry**
Dhundi Raj Shastri;

**General Administration**
Maheswore Prasad Singh;
**Local Supply**
Chiranjibi Wagle;
**Law, Justice and Parliamentary Affairs**
Tara Nath Bhatt;
**Public Works and Transport**
Khum Bahadur Khadka;
**Commerce**
Gopal Man Shrestha;
**Health**
Ram Baddan Yadav;
**Finance**
Mahesh Acharya;
**Armed Forces Commander-in-Chief**
Gen. Gadul Shamshere Rana;
**Inspector-General of Police**
Ratna Shamshere Rana;
**Chief Justice**
Biswa Nath Upadhyay;
**Attorney-General**
Moti Kazi Sthapith.

## Politics/Social Affairs

**N**epal held its first free general election for 32 years on 12 May 1991 following the collapse of the partyless, autocratic *Panchayat* system the previous year. The Nepali Congress Party, which had been in power when the country had previously tasted Western-style democracy in 1959-60, won 110 of the 205 parliamentary seats and formed a majority government. The Nepal Communist Party–United Marxist Leninist (NCP-UML), a coalition partner of the Congress Party in the movement for the restoration of democracy and in the interim government that presided over the transfer of power, emerged as a strong opposition party with 69 seats.

The population's resentment over 30 years of Panchayat rule was illustrated by the disastrous performance of two ex-Panchayat parties. The National Democratic Party (Chand) and National Democratic Party (Thapa), won a combined total of just four seats. Outstanding as losers were politicians who supported the discredited system, including ex-premiers Lokendra Bahadur Chand, Surya Bahadur Thapa and Marich Man Singh Shrestha.

Other parties to win seats included the United People's Party (nine), the pro-Indian Sadbhawana Party, or Goodwill Party (six) and the Nepal Peasants' and Workers' Party (two). Three successful independent candidates later joined Congress, bringing its strength up to 113.

Around 7.3 million of Nepal's 11.2 million eligible voters went to the polls, a turnout of 65%. The election was watched by 46 international observers from 23 countries and was deemed to have been peaceful, free and fair.

Although Congress emerged as the most powerful force in parliament, its victory was clouded by the defeat of former prime minister Krishna Prasad Bhattarai at the polls. His loss was blamed on his government's failure to take action against corrupt members of the previous Panchayat administration.

Bhattarai was succeeded as prime minister by Congress general secretary Girija Prasad Koirala. The third member of his family to become prime minister, Koirala is known as a staunch anti-communist. He formed a 15-member cabinet on 29 May, initially taking the portfolios of foreign relations, defence, palace affairs, finance and health for himself. Later he handed the finance and health portfolios to two junior ministers.

While NCP-UML president and opposition leader Man Mohan Adhikari pledged the communists would be a constructive opposition, this promise was soon put to the test. The NCP-UML supported Nepalese civil servants' agitation for more pay and ignored the government's call for a one-year wage moratorium it said was necessary because Panchayat rule had drained government funds. However, the failure of the hardline communist coup in the Soviet Union in August led to internal turmoil for the NCP-UML. Six of its central committee members resigned and many leftist activists joined Congress.

Ideological conflicts within the NCP-UML were brought to a head as the result of a meeting between King Birendra and NCP-UML general secretary Madan Bhandari on 13 August, partly to discuss growing violence in some areas of the country. Four people were killed when police opened fire in the mountain districts of Khotang, Agrakhachi and Jumla. While the NCP-UML and other opposition parties criticised the government for its failure to maintain law and order, the ruling party blamed the opposition for inciting a mob to set government offices on fire.

After the talks Bhandari praised the king as a "key force" in the balance of power between Congress and the communists. This remark led to a barrage of criticism against Bhandari from both Congress and his own party. A month later Bhandari changed his stance, saying that he regarded the monarch as only one component in the balance of forces. But the damage had already been done. Prominent central committee members Ekraj Pandey, Lok Narayan Subedi and Sharan Bikram Malia left the NCP-UML in September, saying the party had become "right-oriented" by issuing, among other things, a statement in favour of the king.

The NCP-UML infighting grew more intense after some members announced they were planning to launch a new party and another faction decided to merge with Congress. Government officials said the result of the communists' internal feuding was to neutralise the power of the opposition, giving Congress a free hand in running the country.

However, just as events appeared to be running smoothly for the government it threatened to shoot itself in the foot. Congress leader Ganesh Man Singh stunned the ruling party by expressing a desire to retire from the political scene and by demanding Koirala's resignation. He accused Koirala of nepotism and favouritism in his appointment of ambassadors and other officials.

But the crisis, which could have torn the government apart, was resolved at a meeting of Congress' central committee when the party announced that Singh would remain its leader and Koirala would stay prime minister. Analysts said resolution of the crisis meant that Koirala would probably remain prime minister until the next general election in May 1996, as no obvious successors had yet emerged in the ruling party.

The government has been frustrated in its attempts to prosecute members of the Panchayat administration over human-rights abuses. The government tabled a report in the House of Representatives submitted by Justice Janardan Lal Mullick on the alleged atrocities and excesses committed by civil servants and the police during the movement for the restoration of democracy in February-April 1990. The security forces killed 90 people when they opened fire during celebrations marking the end of the Panchayat system in Kathmandu on 16 April 1990.

The Mullick Commission recommended that action be taken against the police, the civil service and ministers in the then government and the members of the Central Resistance, Security and Coordination Committee for suppressing the pro-democracy movement. The main flaw of the commission's report, however, was that it did not outline specific charges against individuals over particular incidents, and as a result the government did not take any action against those implicated.

Foreign observers noted a significant improvement in Nepal's human-rights record under the democratic system. In its 1991 report, Amnesty International cited Nepal's increased protection of human rights and the country's plans for future legislation prohibiting torture and removing the death penalty. It noted that most political prisoners had been released and all charges against them dropped. Amnesty said widespread torture and ill-treatment ceased after mid-April, though isolated reports of torture of suspects in police custody continued

throughout the year. As a result of recommendations submitted by Amnesty to the government, Nepal acceded to a number of international human-rights conventions and covenants.

Birendra prorogued the first session of the parliament on 29 September. During the session 24 bills were passed, 18 originating in the House of Representatives and six in the National Assembly. With the parliamentary session over, political interest shifted to the question of when and how elections to 4,022 village development committees and 33 municipalities were to be held. Minister for Local Development Ram Chandra Poudel plans to table the bills in parliament to allow the elections to be held in April-May 1992. □

# Foreign Relations

Continuing the improvement in relations with India was the cornerstone of Nepal's foreign policy in 1991. The two countries held three rounds of talks about areas of cooperation under the umbrella of the Joint Task Force, while Nepal's Prime Minister Girija Prasad Koirala paid a four-day state visit to India in November. During the trip, separate agreements on trade, transit and control of smuggling were signed.

Koirala held talks with his counterpart P. V. Narasimha Rao and also met Indian opposition leaders. He assured New Delhi that Nepal would not do anything against India's national interests. India pledged Rs 1 billion (US$39 million) in aid to Nepal for a number of development projects, including the construction of the Sunsari-Jhapa road.

The Task Force also discussed cooperation in the use of Nepal's water resources, joint industrial ventures and prospects for wider economic agreements. Hydroelectric joint ventures, expansion of trade and the production of goods in demand in both countries were also on the agenda. However, a proposed Raxaul-Kathmandu rail-link was cancelled due to its projected high costs.

Koirala, who also holds the foreign affairs portfolio, outlined Nepal's policy towards neighbouring India and China soon after taking office. Maintaining good relations with Peking and New Delhi were Kathmandu's priorities, he said.

Nepal's foreign policy has, however, been heavily criticised by the communist opposition. Nepal Communist Party–United Marxist Leninist (NCP-UML) leader Man Mohan Adhikari said that under the rule of King Birendra, the country's foreign policy had been influenced by the US and now it tilted too much towards India. While it was important to be on friendly terms with India, the relationship should get no closer than that, he argued. Adhikari also called for a review of the 1950 peace and friendship treaty with India.

The NCP-UML has also proposed that Nepal signs non-aggression treaties with both India and China and called for a national consensus on foreign policy. Adhikari warned that an international conspiracy was being hatched to dismember India and China by using Nepal as a base. Koirala replied by saying that the government would never try to play off one neighbour against another.

However, relations with another of Nepal's neighbours became increasingly tense during the year. More than 6,000 Bhutanese of Nepalese origin sought refuge in Nepal during 1991. This exodus followed actions

Koirala: substitute.

by Bhutan's King Jigme Singye Wangchuk to assert Bhutanese culture and deny the expression of Nepalese Hindu culture. Although Nepal has no border with Bhutan, the open frontier with India made it possible for the refugees to reach Nepal.

Among the refugees were six senior Bhutanese Government officials of Nepalese descent who sought political asylum in June. They were followed by five members of parliament from southern Bhutan in October. Many of the refugees were activists of the Bhutanese People's Party and human-rights groups. The resurgence of democracy in Nepal and the challenge to its monarchy have given a fillip to the democratic forces in Bhutan. The ruling Nepali Congress Party and various leftist parties have strongly backed pro-democracy dissidents of Nepalese origin in Bhutan.

Koirala told parliament that Nepal extends its moral support to the people of Bhutan who are struggling for multiparty democracy and human rights. However, Bhutanese Foreign Minister Lyonpo Dawa Tsering accused Kathmandu of aiming to form a "Greater Nepal," that would include ethnic Nepalese across northeastern India and southern Bhutan.

Nepal strengthened its ties with Japan and the EC during the year. Japan's then finance minister Ryutaro Hashimoto visited Nepal in July and pledged aid worth US$40 million for various development projects. Nepal is planning to open a separate embassy in Brussels as a mark of the importance with which it regards its relations to the EC.

The Nepal Ex-Servicemen's Association, a powerful national lobby group, met Koirala over Britain's decision to reduce the size of the Gurkha contingent in the British army to 2,500 men from 8,000 over the next five years. The association asked the prime minister to attempt to persuade the British Government to keep the Brigade of Gurkhas at current levels if possible, or at least not cut it so drastically. The issue was discussed during visits to Nepal by Britain's Under-Secretary of State for Foreign and Commonwealth Affairs Mark Lennox-Boyd and Minister of State for Armed Forces Archibald Hamilton in October and November, respectively.

Koirala's conduct was brought into question over the appointment of ambassadors to Germany, Japan, the US, China, Thailand, the Soviet Union and the UN. Out of the seven, six belonged to the Brahmin caste. The appointment of Chakra Banstola as ambassador to India also caused controversy. Banstola had been charged with masterminding the hijacking of a Nepalese aircraft in 1972, and India's delay in accepting his credentials led to speculation that the appointment could damage Kathmandu–New Delhi relations. □

# Economy/Infrastructure

**N**epal's new government faces a daunting task as it attempts to grapple with the country's largely agricultural and aid-based economy. Its problems were exacerbated a few months after taking office, when India's decision to devalue its currency in July 1991 was matched — out of commercial necessity — by Nepal's central bank.

India's 22% devaluation of its currency preceded the unveiling of the Congress Party government's fiscal 1991-92 budget — the first by an elected government in nearly three decades.

As India remains Nepal's major trading partner — accounting for some 30% of its exports — Kathmandu had little alternative than to follow suit, and the Nepal Rastra Bank, the country's central bank, devalued the local currency by 21.2% against the US dollar in two separate moves over a 48-hour period. Nepal's devaluation lifted market prices by 25-35%, mainly due to higher prices for imports from third countries, though the inflation rate had been officially calculated at 21% on a month-to-month basis.

Nepal's broader economic problems stem in part from a marked decline in agricultural production due to a poor monsoon and the government's failure to check the illegal export of food grains, which forced the authorities to import 65,000 tonnes of rice and wheat from India during the year. The 1990-91 weak 3% annual agricultural growth rate produced a farm output of 5.8 million tonnes, while land productivity recorded a growth of only 0.5%.

Problems also abound in Nepal's 125,000 or so small-scale industrial concerns, only 25% of which are currently functioning. The remainder have either closed or are on the verge of closing. The sector is under pressure due to a shortage of affordable financing, lack of raw materials and high transport costs. Cottage and small industries contribute 7.5% of GDP, 66% of total exports and generate employment for over 450,000 people.

Mahesh Acharya was appointed as Minister of State for Finance a week before the public exchequer's budget for 1991-92 was tabled before parliament. While German-trained

GERHARD JÖREN

**Gurkhas: contemplating a bleak future.**

economist Acharya, 36, pledged to reform Nepal's distorted economy, ensure a consistent supply of consumer goods, develop free and competitive markets and encourage domestic entrepreneurs, critics said none of these programmes showed any sign of being implemented.

Acharya's Rs 26.64 billion (US$623.8 million) 1991-92 budget — the largest ever presented in Nepal — allocated Rs 18.89 billion to development expenditure, some Rs 12 million of which he hoped will be met from foreign bilateral and multilateral assistance and loans. Of this sum, 70% was earmarked for rural areas in an effort to generate employment and develop cottage industries and traditional crafts.

A further Rs 9.74 billion was allocated for regular expenditure — which includes public-sector, military and police salaries — and repayment of principal and interest of the public exchequer's foreign loans. Of this total, 32% went to national security and the police.

Education received Rs 3.2 billion, and schooling up to the sixth year was declared free from 17 July, the start of the financial year. Transportation will get Rs 2.88 billion for the development of national highways, bridges, rural feeder roads and mule tracks, Rs 1.9 billion was allocated for electricity power generation and Rs 1.7 billion for agriculture.

Acharya hopes to meet an anticipated Rs 2.08 billion deficit through internal bank lending, the sale of treasury bills and development time bonds bearing more than 13% tax-free interest. Hotel and airport taxes were also increased.

He also announced a 25% cut in customs tariffs on imports of industrial raw materials to help domestic industries compete with India in overseas markets. Further, a 50% customs rebate was announced on additional duties on Chinese imports through Tibet to make them cheaper than other overseas imports, though more expensive than Indian products.

The public exchequer collected revenue worth Rs 10.71 billion during fiscal 1990-91, of which Rs 3.11 billion was from tax and Rs 2.6 billion was from non-tax collection, or about 15.4% more than in 1989-90. Internal borrowing totalled Rs 4.15 billion, of which about 90.5% went to help state-run corporations pay off commercial bank loans drawn on government financial guarantees.

During the 1988-90 period, Nepal participated in a World Bank/IMF–backed structural adjustment programme (SAP) in an effort to meet its shortage of foreign exchange through increased exports. The SAP helped remove distortions in the economy by introducing policies intended to stimulate economic activity and provide a more fertile environment for the private sector. The government is now planning to launch an extended structural adjustment fund (ESAF) to help bolster the industrial sector. An IMF team which visited Nepal in November assured the government of about US$62 million soft loans for ESAF for fiscal 1991-92, a finance ministry said.

Nepal's exports totalled Rs 7.6 billion by value during 1990-91, Rs 1.7 billion of which were shipments to India. The bulk of the exports comprised hand-knitted woollen carpets (Rs 4 billion), ready-made cotton garments (Rs 1.75 billion) and handicrafts. In the current year, woollen-carpet exports are expected to earn Rs 4.5 billion and ready-made garments the equivalent of Rs 2 billion, according to a finance ministry official.

Over the same period, however, Nepal's import bill reached a high record of Rs 24.21 billion, of which imports from India totalled Rs 7.86 billion. The finance ministry official said while the trade deficit had been put at Rs 16.01 billion, the balance-of-payments shortfall was Rs 4.08 billion because of such "invisibles" as tourism and remittances from British and Indian Gurkha soldiers. British-enlisted Gurkhas provided Rs 2.66 billion during 1990-91 and those serving in the Indian army Rs 1.32 billion in the form of salaries, gratuities and pensions.

Nepal also received Rs 1.01 billion in the form of cash grants and Rs 6.65 billion in the form of bilateral, multilateral grants and loans from international financial institutions.

As of November 1991, Nepal's foreign-exchange reserves totalled just over Rs 18.35 billion — a record for the country. The government has yet to announce how it intends to utilise the reserves, which are sufficient to meet the country's import bills for eight months.

Japan tops the list of aid donors, followed by the US, Germany, Britain, France, Finland, Denmark, Switzerland, China and India. Japan has provided an average of US$80 million in grants annually for the past few years, much of which have been directed at small-scale hydroelectric-power projects, improved drinking-water supply and bridge building. In addition, Japan is underwriting the construction of an 800-tonne-per-day cement plant in Udayapur under a soft-loan scheme which is expected to be converted into grants once it becomes operational in late 1992. When completed, the plant would increase national cement supplies by around 30%.

Among other aid donors, Germany has provided Rs 732 million to cover such areas as commodity aid, solid-waste management and help in developing the tourism industry. Britain, which normally provides some Rs 1.24 billion in financial aid each year, granted additional Rs 74.8 million for 1991-92 to help implement administrative reforms. France converted a Rs 749.7 million loan into unconditional grants for communications, transportation, manpower training and public health service projects, while Paris also provided Rs 394.32 million for the Nepalgunj-Mahendranagar high-power transmission line and a number of other projects. China continues to work

on the Pokhara-Mugling highway in western Nepal and the construction of a conference hall in Kathmandu, while India has pledged over Rs 1 billion for a medical college and a hospital, a rural telephone exchange and a road.

The International Development Agency has extended Rs 2.75 billion worth of soft-loan assistance to Nepal to improve sanitation and the supply of potable water, while the UN Capital Development Fund will provide loans totalling Rs 272 million for the second phase of the Marchwar Lift Irrigation Project in Rupandehi which will provide irrigation facilities to 5,600 ha of agricultural land.

Problems have continued to plague some major infrastructure projects, notably the 404 MW Arun Three hydroelectric-power station. Planned in 1988-89 to cost US$650 million and be on line by the second half of 1990, the project is now estimated to cost US$1 billion and be operational no earlier than 1993-94. If Arun Three is delayed much longer, Nepal will face electricity shortages from 1992 onwards which may seriously affect its already fragile economy.

The final preparations for Nepal's eighth Five-Year Plan, delayed in 1989-90 by the trade and transit row with India, are under way. The new plan is expected to allocate Rs 200 billion with the aim of increasing GDP by 5-8% a year, raising educational standards, boosting private-sector industries and continuing the development of Nepal's physical infrastructure. □

## Data

**Major industries:** Cement, 184,000 tonnes (101,179); steel rods, 56,704 tonnes (36,339); jute, 20,064 tonnes (15,600); sugar, 41,399 tonnes (31,927); cotton textiles, 6.4 million m (5.2 million); synthetic textiles, 21.3 million m (13.6 million); beer, 13.3 million litres (6.8 million); soap, 28,553 tonnes (11,943); vegetable ghee, 11,499 tonnes (11,810); tea, 1,930 tonnes (1,393); cigarettes, 8.78 billion sticks (6.31 billion).

**Major agriculture:** Paddy, 3.5 million tonnes (3.4 million); maize, 1.23 million tonnes (1.2 million); wheat, 836,000 tonnes (855,000); millet, 232,000 tonnes (225,000); barley, 29,000 tonnes (27,000); oilseeds, 99,250 tonnes (98,150); sugarcane, 1.1 million tonnes (988,000); potatoes, 738,000 tonnes (671,000); citrus fruits, 98,450 tonnes (79,560); non-citrus fruits, 568,099 tonnes (406,680); tobacco, 7,000 tonnes (7,100).

**Major imports:** Manufactured goods, US$197.28 million (US$177.84 million); machinery and transport equipment, US$190.35 million (US$133.08 million); chemicals and pharmaceuticals, US$94.77 million (US$99.15 million); mineral fuel and lubricants, US$71.52 million (US$47.44 million); food and live animals, US$64.92 million (US$56.45 million); basic materials, US$64.24 million (US$55.16 million); animal, vegetable oils and fats, US$22.51 million (US$16.72 million).

**Major exports:** Manufactured goods and articles, US$184.94 million (US$139.55 million); basic materials, US$10.3 million (US$8.37 million); animal, vegetable oils and fats, US$5.81 million (US$705,758); chemicals and pharmaceuticals, US$1.07 million (US$382,724); food and live animals, US$832,811 (US$128,365).

(All figures for 1991, with previous year in brackets unless otherwise stated.)

**Tourism and transport** (1990): Arrivals, 254,885 (239,945). Tourists spent US$109.59 million in 1990 (US$91.17 million). Airlines: international and domestic services by Royal Nepal Airlines; Kathmandu also served by Singapore Airlines, Dragonair, Thai International, CAAC (via Lhasa), Aeroflot, Lufthansa, India Airlines, Druk Airways of Bhutan, Bangladesh Biman.

**Currency:** Rupees (100 paisa), Rs 42.6 = US$1 in Nov. 1991 (Rs 24 = US$1 in Nov. 1990).

**Finance:** 5 private banks, 3 joint-venture banks and 3 public-sector banks. Stock exchange in Kathmandu with 49 registered companies.

**Major banks:** Nepal Rastra Bank (central bank), Baluwatar Kathmandu, tel. 410158, fax 227378, tlx 2207 RABA NP; Nepal Bank Ltd, Dharma Path, Kathmandu, tel. 223790/221337, tlx 2220 LUXMI NP, fax 222383; Rastriya Banijya Bank, Tangal, Kathmandu, tel. 413884, tlx 2247; Nepal Arab Bank, Kantipath, Kathmandu, tel. 227181/226585, tlx 2431 NABIL NP/2385 NABIL NP, fax 226905; Nepal Indosuez Bank, Durbar Marga, Kathmandu, tel. 228229/227228, tlx 2435, fax 226349; Nepal Grindlay Bank, tel. 212683, tlx 2531, fax 226762.

**Prime Minister's office:** Central Secretariat, Singha Durbar, Kathmandu, tel. 411356/228555, fax 227286. Prime Minister's residence, Baluwatar, Kathmandu, tel. 411356/212490, fax 419680.

**Public holidays** (1992): 30 Jan. (Martyrs Day), 19 Feb. (National Democracy Day), 2 Mar. (Lord Shiva's Day), 8 Mar. (Women's Day [half-day holiday for women]), 18 Mar. (Fagu Purnima [Colour Festival]), 10-11 Apr. (Lord Ram's birthday), 13 Apr. (Nepalese New Year), 17 Apr. (Mother's Day), 8 May (Lord Buddha's birthday), 10 July (Teachers Day), 26 July (Raksha Bandhan [Sacred Thread]), 13 Aug. (Lord Krishna's birthday), 20 Aug. (Fathers Day), 23 Aug. (Teej [women only]), 25 Aug. (Tishi Panchami), 4 Sept. (Indra Jatra Festival), 20 and 26 Sept. to 3 Oct. (Dasain-Durga Puja Festival), 18-20 Oct. (Deepawali [Festival of Lights]), 24 Oct. (UN Day), 8 Nov. (Queen's birthday), 9 Nov. (Nepal Constitution Day), 28 Dec. (King's birthday).

**Taxation:** Wage earners pay maximum 50%, additional 12% income tax for non-residents.

# NEW ZEALAND

North Cape

NORTH ISLAND

Tasman Sea

Auckland

East Cape

Hamilton

New Plymouth

Gisborne

Napier

Wanganui

Lower Hutt

Nelson

Wellington

Greymouth

Cook Straits

Hokitika

SOUTH ISLAND

Christchurch

Pacific Ocean

Dunedin

Invercargill

Stewart Is.

Foveaux Straits

0    100    200 km

**Head of State**
Queen Elizabeth II.
**Governor-General**
Dame Catherine Tizard;
**Prime Minister**
Jim Bolger;
**Deputy Prime Minister, Foreign Affairs, External Relations and Trade**
Don McKinnon;
**Employment, Labour, Immigration, State Services**
Bill Birch;
**Finance**
Ruth Richardson;
**Attorney-General and Crown Health Enterprises**
Paul East;
**Agriculture and Forestry**
John Falloon;
**Maori Affairs, Fisheries**
Doug Kidd;
**Commerce, Industry, Trade Negotiations**
Philip Burdon;
**Health, Science**
Simon Upton;
**Police, Tourism**
John Banks;

**Social Welfare**
Jenny Shipley;
**Defence, Local Government**
Warren Cooper;
**Justice, Disarmament and Arms Control**
Doug Graham;
**Education**
Lockwood Smith;
**State-owned Enterprises**
Maurice McTigue;
**Transport, Lands, Environment**
Rob Storey;
**Conservation**
Denis Marshall;
**Housing, Energy**
John Luxton;
**Revenue, Customs, Senior Citizens**
Wyatt Creech;
**Broadcasting, Statistics**
Maurice Williamson;
**Chief Justice**
Sir Thomas Eichelbaum;
**Chief of Defence Staff**
Maj.-Gen. Bruce Meldrum.

# Politics/Social Affairs

**P**rime Minister Jim Bolger's new government was elected in October 1990 with 40% of the registered voters and 37 seats in the 97-member parliament. Within 11 months, Bolger's governing National Party popularity rating had slumped to just 13% in the respected monthly Heylen poll.

This collapse of support reflected the frustration in an electorate entering the seventh year of an economic restructuring programme that has yet to deliver promised growth. It also represented the voters' exasperation at the failure of Bolger's administration to switch economic policy and thereby fulfil his party's election mandate.

Bolger chose instead to side with his hardline, rightwing Finance Minister Ruth Richardson. He imposed severe cuts in welfare benefits and sharply raised existing user-charges for public social services, introducing new ones for people with above-average weekly earnings. When Bolger also broke an explicit election promise to remove a tax surcharge from state pensions, and instead imposed a harsh means-test in the July budget, his own back bench rebelled.

Two MPs, Hamish MacIntyre and Gilbert Myles, resigned from the party in August to form the Liberal Party. On 2 October, the division's reached the cabinet when Bolger dismissed Maori Affairs Minister Winston Peters for disloyalty. Peters had openly opposed Richardson's economic theories well before the election, calling the deregulatory, liberalising policies of the previous Labour government — which were intensified by Richardson — a dangerous experiment. He continued his opposition in office, arguing that as minister of Maori affairs he could not stand by while Maori unemployment climbed to nearly three times the general rate.

On 17 November, Sir Robert Muldoon, National Party prime minister from 1975-84, announced his intention to resign from parliament. Muldoon has been in poor health since a heart operation in 1990, but gave his primary reason as intense dissatisfaction with Bolger's deregulatory policies.

Meanwhile, the Labour Party — led by its former trade minister Mike Moore — has seen its support hold close to the

**N**ew Zealand became a British colony in 1840 under the Treaty of Waitangi, signed with all but a few of the indigenous Maori tribes. It has been self-governing since 1852, and fully independent since 1947, while acknowledging titular allegiance to the British crown as a member of the Commonwealth. A full free-trade agreement signed with Australia in 1983 has closely integrated those two economies.

The country is divided into North Island and South Island, separated by a narrow strait. Pastoral agriculture occupies a central place in the economy, accounting for about 50% of all exports. Forest-based industries, fish and tourism are other major contributors.

The population is made up of two main races: the Maori, a Polynesian people who first arrived in the country during the 9th or 10th centuries, now form about 12% of the 3.1 million population. The remainder are mainly of European stock, either the descendants of those who colonised the country from the early 19th century or subsequent migrants. They have the same status before the law except that four parliamentary seats are reserved for Maoris voting on a special roll. Immigrant Polynesians from South Pacific islands form about 3% of the population.

The democratic socialist Labour Party led by David Lange won power in 1984 and was re-elected in 1987, presiding over a massive programme of economic restructuring and deregulation. Lange resigned, handing over to his deputy, Geoffrey Palmer, in August 1989. He in turn was displaced by then trade minister Mike Moore, who was unable to prevent the election in October 1990 of a conservative National Party government, led by the present Prime Minister Jim Bolger.

29% of the registered vote it got in the 1990 polls. This partly reflected the lingering effects of its own unpopularity while in power, partly because dissent by Peters and other National MPs overshadowed Labour criticisms of the government and partly because the process of reconstruction required a period of introspection.

Voters, for their part, either switched their attention to minor parties or switched off. After getting a total of 14% of the registered electorate in 1990, minor parties' combined poll rating climbed to 20% in September-October.

In early December 1990, four of them decided to form an alliance with a common platform and an agreed slate of candidates. Observers — and even participants — doubted the durability of the alliance, which pulls together the old-style social democratic

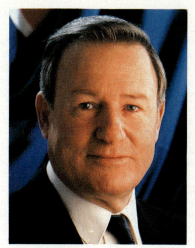

**Bolger: flagging support.**

New Labour Party (a splinter from Labour), the environmentalist Greens, the Maori ethnocentric Mana Motuhake Party and the Democrats, founded in 1953 originally to gain acceptance of monetary reform. But, in agreeing on their opposition to economic deregulation, they did strike a chord with the electorate which holds out the possibility of a serious challenge to both Labour and National.

Bolger's dismissal of Peters drew attention to the broader problems of the Maori community, not least that there were no other Maori in his parliamentary party of sufficient stature to appoint in Peters' place. As a result, for the first time since 1981 a non-Maori was appointed. For many Maori, this raised the spectre of a return to the paternalism which the previous government's reforming policies had begun to redress.

Even before Peters' sacking, Bolger had handed the sensitive issue of settlement of land grievances over to Justice Minister Doug Graham. Graham must find solutions that are affordable, do not unduly offend New Zealanders of European descent and can serve as final settlements to Maori claims. The last attempt at "final" compensation in the 1940s was never considered a full settlement by Maori.

Graham demonstrated a sensitivity to Maori aspirations that Maori negotiators said promised real progress on the major, and in effect determinant, claims. These are claims by the Ngai Tahu tribe in respect of large tracts of South Island, and by the Tainui and Taranaki tribes for compensation for vast areas confiscated by the colonial government in the 1860s in reprisal for Maori armed resistance to forced sales to colonists of their land.

It is widely agreed by most Maori leaders that progress on improving their community's education, health and economic performance depends partly on the recognition of Maori worth that meeting these claims would entail. However, many involved in education and the social services see a bleak long-term future for the Maori, as poorly educated and low-income parents fail to encourage their children and further entrench a cycle of poverty and its attendant ills.

This despairing attitude contrasts sharply, for example, with fellow–Polynesian Samoan immigrants, who prize education. However, they and European New Zealanders are eclipsed by the performance of Asian children — both those born of New Zealand ethnic Asians from the small Chinese community established since the 1860s gold rushes and a smaller, more recent, Indian community and those born of recent immigrants.

This sort of performance has encouraged both main political parties to back greater immigration in order to attract those with either entrepreneurial or technical skills on the assumption they will create employment. Changes to the immigration

laws introduced during 1991 aim to generate net immigration of around 20,000 a year. This contrasts with a net emigration of around 16,000 a year in the 1980s.

Bolger's government is keen to attract more migrants from Europe — particularly from the well-educated but economically poor former Eastern bloc countries — partly to offset Asian immigration, which tripled as a percentage of the total during the 1980s to near European levels. That was partly because Asians, particularly Taiwanese, have dominated the business migrants scheme under which people with business experience and NZ$250,000 (US$140,000) in capital (recently raised to NZ$500,000) could obtain New Zealand residence qualifications in return for investing in the country.

The scheme was abused. Many Asians invested only the minimum of time and money necessary to obtain residence and returned home. Little track was kept of whether they did in fact invest in job-creating businesses in New Zealand.

New Zealand is slowly adjusting to the reality of its geography on the fringe of Asia, an adjustment made harder by a growing recognition by the current generation of European-descended New Zealanders of the value of deepening their own cultural heritage. Politically, this complicates matters in a country that has enough to deal with trying to get its economy in order, after having lived far beyond its means since the mid-1970s in an effort to hold on to its 1950s' status as one of the 10 richest societies in the world. ☐

# Foreign Relations

The nuclear issue returned to centre-stage in 1991 when Prime Minister Jim Bolger met US President George Bush on 24 September, the first between leaders of the two countries since 1984.

The meeting came a few days before Bush's decision to remove nuclear weapons from US navy surface warships. This meant that the presence of surface warships in New Zealand harbours would no longer offend legislation banning vessels carrying nuclear weapons, or that could or would not declare whether they were so armed. US policy has long been to neither confirm nor deny the presence of nuclear weapons aboard its warships.

Bolger was therefore able to stick to a pre-1990 election promise not to overturn the anti-nuclear legislation — a pledge that reversed the National Party's previous stance in favour of full membership of the Anzus treaty that linked Australia, New Zealand and the US, irregardless of the nuclear issue. Washington had effectively frozen Wellington out of Anzus after New Zealand had rejected a ship visit in early 1985.

However, there still remains the problem of nuclear propulsion, which is also covered by the legislation. In a country which has banned nuclear power generation, polls revealed opinion against nuclear-powered ships was as strong as the opposition to nuclear weapons. Not surprisingly, there was uproar when Bolger announced he would review that clause to enable US nuclear-powered warships to enter New Zealand ports.

The prime minister was caught in a dilemma. The US made it clear the price of ship visits, and therefore a full restoration of ties, depended on the legislation banning nuclear-powered vessels being revoked or amended. The National Party rank and file wanted the visits to resume as part of a stronger defence arrangement. Bolger himself had made normalisation of relations with the US a central foreign policy plank of his government, and had appointed a pro-Anzus advocate, Don McKinnon, as foreign minister.

But for a government already desperately unpopular, defying public opinion — which though generally pro-US was more against nuclear power than for visits — seemed foolhardy. All other significant political parties remained implacably against any change in the legislation, which in turn led to the US indicating that it did not want a "light-switch" policy over the issue, with ship visits being allowed or banned depending on the result of each election.

Defence policy priorities also reflected the new government's differing views from the previous administration, which had narrowed defence interests into the south and southwest Pacific, including Australia. Bolger's government issued a policy paper which refocused attention beyond these areas, and based on a concept it called "self-reliance in partnership."

The paper said self-reliance was "not self-sufficiency," which was impossible for a country as small as New Zealand. It identified the need for partnership with countries which can keep the peace — with New Zealand willing to play a global role with those partners. This approach was reflected in Bolger decision's to commit forces to the Iraq-Kuwait conflict.

While the US remains the exemplar of the overall strategic partner, at an operational level ties are obviously strongest with neighbouring Australia, with whom New Zealand has long shared a belief that any threat to one represents a threat to the other. Beyond that, the objective is "to maintain and develop defence cooperation with Asean countries."

This global approach, with an emphasis on Southeast Asia, meshes with the government's policy towards trade. During the year, Wellington's primary trade concern was to help get some movement in Gatt's Uruguay Round in order to reduce trade barriers, in particular those on agricultural commodities which form around half of New Zealand's exports.

While New Zealand expressed its wish to be associated with developing regionalism in Asia, work also began a study to mesh the Australia–New Zealand free trade agreement with that between Canada and the US. In general, however, the government tended towards willingness to trade freely with anyone who would reciprocate. □

# Economy/Infrastructure

As New Zealand headed into its eighth year of economic restructuring there was increasing evidence that while fundamentals were coming right, sustained growth continued to be elusive. The heavily indebted, commodity-dependent economy, isolated from the main trading blocs or areas, still has some distance to go before an upturn can be achieved.

The main new policy ingredients introduced by the National Party government were heavy cuts in social-welfare spending and near-total deregulation of the labour market. There were positive spinoffs from both: steep interest-rate falls from the fiscal squeeze and lower wages and more flexible work practices from the labour reforms. However, high social costs put the political sustainability of the changes — an important ingredient of their success — into doubt.

The good news was that imports dropped 9.3% by value in the year to September against the same period a year earlier, while exports — partly lifted by domestic suppliers having to find alternative outlets — rose 2.8% over the same period. The merchandise trade surplus swung from a deficit of NZ$419 million (US$234.3 million) to NZ$1.12 billion over the same period.

Helped by the recession, inflation dropped like a stone, reaching 2.2% in the year to September — among one of the lowest in the world. With inflation down, interest rates also fell. Benchmark five-year government bonds dropped from a monthly average of 12.3% in December 1990 to 8.6% in October, while 90-day bank bills fell from 13% to 8% over the same period. The slide was not just in nominal rates, but in real rates, which by October were at the bottom end of rates for heavily indebted small countries.

In addition, labour productivity continued to rise: by 2.1% in the year to June in manufacturing, compared with the year to June 1990. The resultant higher competitiveness was aided by a slight fall in the exchange rate, from a monthly average of 58.8 on the trade-weighted index in December 1990 to 56 in October. Corresponding falls were from 59.5 US cents to 56.7 US cents and from ¥79.6 to ¥74.1.

Given the restraint on factor costs, the real exchange rate fall was around 6% in the 11 months to November. While manufacturers continued to complain that it was still too high — and were joined by agricultural commodity producers suffering a 13% downswing in prices for dairy products and wool — at least the movement was in their favour after the local _ — dollar's rollercoaster ride since it was floated in 1985.

By late 1991, the Reserve Bank — the country's central bank — at last seemed to have weathered a long controversy over its competence as an independent controller of inflation. During 1990, it was accused by exporters and rightwing economists of holding interest rates and the exchange rate too high. They charged that the bank was overcautious in its drive for 0-2% inflation by end-1993, and was in danger of reaching that target early and overshooting it in 1993, causing unnecessary damage to the real economy.

While the bank never conceded the point, in September it nevertheless based a slight loosening of the money supply on its assessment that domestic demand was so low that there was no danger of an inflationary blowout in either lower interest or exchange rates.

Most economists agreed with the bank, but they also agreed that nominal inflation is set to climb in 1992 as government charges bite and as one-off downward pressures — such as declining oil prices — that cut inflation in 1991 wear off. In October, the respected independent New Zealand Institute of Economic Research (NZIER) forecast a peak of 3.7% during 1992. The bank may not find its 1993 target easy to achieve.

The same may go for a second major policy target: a balanced budget by 1993-94. Finance Minister Ruth Richardson inherited a worsening fiscal situation in which the Treasury was forecasting a deficit of NZ$1 billion in fiscal (July-June) 1990-91, NZ$3.7 billion for 1991-92 and NZ$5.2 billion by 1993-94 on unchanged policies.

True to her belief that state spending, at 43% of GDP, was too high for an efficient economy, Richardson set about trimming spending. In a late December 1990 mini budget, she made cuts totalling NZ$2.4 billion on a full-year basis, more than half in welfare benefits.

The welfare cuts depressed already weakening domestic demand. Retail sales dropped 6% in real terms in the year to June, compared with the same period a year earlier. Unemployment, which ended 1990 at under 9%, climbed to over 10% by June. Real GDP fell 2% in the year to June. Falling demand cut business profits and employment and so income-tax revenue. Higher unemployment pushed up spending, despite cuts in the level of unemployment benefits. The budget balance receded and 1990-91 saw a deficit of NZ$1.3 billion.

Undeterred, Richardson cut heavily again in the 30 July budget, with some NZ$600 million slashed from existing departmental budgets outside the social spending areas. Hardest hit was defence, losing NZ$260 million from an allocation already heavily pruned in previous years. Richardson also continued to cut social spending. The generous state pension scheme was subjected to a severe means test, while health spending was cut by 6% in real terms.

On budget night, Richardson projected a deficit of NZ$1.7 billion, NZ$200 million below most financial market forecasts. The hoped for interest-rate payoff, however, took seven weeks to emerge. Financial analysts believed — accurately as it turned out — that the scheme would not deliver the NZ$670 million full-year savings credited to it because of evasion, and that it would have to be modified to accommodate political pressure from pensioners and the government's own parliamentary backbench. In early October Bolger announced a return to a modified version of the existing scheme, accepting a much more modest savings target.

Richardson made good a promise in the mini budget to impose user-part-charges for a range of social services, notably in health where they were supposed to raise NZ$250 million in revenue in a full year. These, too, were cut (by NZ$25 million) in October, to make them practical and more politically acceptable.

By this time, economists were estimating the 1991-92 deficit at between NZ$500 million and NZ$1.5 billion above the projected figure, with flow-on implications for future years. This was partly due to direct shortfalls in expected savings, but also to the continuing impact of welfare and pension cuts and the dual impact on middle-income people of user-charges of cuts in disposable income and uncertainty about future risks.

On top of this were piled cuts in wage rates forced through by employers in the wake of labour market deregulation in May. A system of national or regional "awards" upheld by the state through a special labour court since 1894 was replaced by one resting on individual contracts, with bans on unions using coercion to obtain collective agreements. The negotiating balance shifted heavily in favour of employers, many of whom took advantage of it to enforce effective or actual wage cuts or replace high-wage employees with lower-wage labour.

At the household level, real disposable income fell by 0.5% in the year to June compared with the same period in 1990, with the greatest fall in the middle and low-income groups. At the business level, the picture was correspondingly grim. Permits for commercial buildings of all types dropped 25% from an already low level. Manufacturing output fell 7% and new investment by 21% in real terms in the year to June, in each case to the lowest levels in more than a decade. Machinery imports in the June quarter were 22% below the same 1990 quarter. Total real GDP growth in the five years to June amounted to 0.5%; in the four years from 1987 there was a cumulative drop of 1.8%.

Business confidence correspondingly reversed an upward climb since the election. The NZIER reported in October that "firms report that they have been through yet another very poor quarter, especially in the domestic market. The average level of capacity use has hit a new record low [in nearly 30 years of institute surveys]." While costs were held to a zero increase, prices were cut — and along with prices went a "very hard" cut in profitability.

Compounding this gloomy domestic picture, terms of trade worsened 5.6% in the year to June, compared with the year to June 1990. However, in its October report on business confidence, the NZIER said that "by contrast [with the domestic economy], the export sector stands out as strongly performing yet again. Prospects remain good."

This was especially so with respect to the main market for manufactured goods, Australia. After nearly a decade of microeconomic reform, New Zealand business by late 1991

had labour cost advantages over Australia of up to 50% in some sectors. Not only did that encourage New Zealand exports to Australia, and so help build a larger and growing domestic market for exports farther afield, but it also encouraged foreign companies to consider New Zealand as a business base for the southwest Pacific and to some extent as an English-speaking base for exports to Southeast Asia.

The microeconomic reform is to continue. The government decided in September to cut tariffs over the four years up to 1996 by one third from the average 17-17.5% level applying by the end of the current reduction programme in mid-1992. Tariffs, though still high for textiles, clothing and cars, were levied on only 7% of imports by value and there was almost no other assistance. That may change, however, for though the government continued to eschew direct subsidies, it intensified its search for other assistance measures to promote business.

The problem remains the twin deficits of the budget and the external accounts. The deficit on the current account in the year to March was NZ$2.3 billion, due to deficits of NZ$1.9 billion on services and NZ$3.8 billion on invisibles.

For New Zealand, 1992 represents its 19th consecutive year of balance-of-payments deficits that has left it with foreign debt of NZ$50.4 billion, representing 71% of GDP and making it the second-most indebted country in the OECD and one of the most indebted on a per capita basis in the world. □

## Data

**Major industries:** Pulp and paper to Mar. 1991, 2.16 million tonnes (1.99 million); fertiliser to Dec. 1990, 1.25 million tonnes (1.02 million tonnes); cement to June 1991, 620,000 tonnes (718,000); crude steel to Mar. 1991, 770,000 tonnes (790,000); aluminium to Dec. 1990, 261,939 tonnes (259,200).

**Major agriculture:** Meat to Sept. 1991, 1.13 million tonnes (1.12 million); dairy products to May 1991, 342.1 million kg of milkfat processed (330.1 million); wool to June 1991, 227,000 tonnes clean (231,000); timber to Mar. 1991, 2.16 million m³ (2.12 million); barley to Dec. 1990, 434,900 tonnes (326,800).

**Oil and natural gas** (1990): Oil and condensate, 1.77 million tonnes (1.71 million); natural gas, 6 billion m³ (6.07 billion).

**Mining** (1990): Coal, 2.59 million tonnes (2.4 million); ironsand, 2.3 million tonnes (2.37 million); limestone for agriculture, 1.05 million tonnes (983,285); gold, 4,620 kg (2,400); silver, 4,914 kg (4,837).

**Major imports** (year to June 1991): Electrical machinery and equipment, US$1.01 billion (US$895.7 million); motor vehicles, US$769.37 million (US$1 billion); oil and petroleum products, US$687.3 million (US$555.3 million); aircraft, US$371.1 million (US$543.5 million); optical, photographic, technical and surgical equipment, US$272.3 million (US$289.1 million).

**Major exports** (year to June 1990): Meat, US$1.52 billion (US$1.43 billion); dairy products, US$1.18 billion (US$1.27 billion); forest products, US$887.9 million (US$810.2 million); wool, US$565.9 million (US$810.2 million); fruit and vegetables, US$513.3 million (US$615 million).

**Tourism and transport** (to Mar. 1991): Arrivals, 974,042 (932,711); departures, 738,434 (713,959); airlines: Air New Zealand (international and domestic), Ansett New Zealand (domestic); two networks of commuter airlines, each linked with major airline. Rail network is mainly freight; coach services widespread; hire car service widely available.

**Finance:** 21 registered banks, 5 local and 16 foreign-owned; 1 part-government-owned, 2 community-owned, rest private; 3 merchant banks, 14 significant consumer finance companies and 10 building societies; national stock exchange with branches in Auckland, Wellington and Christchurch with 135 companies listed; futures exchange; full cross-trading foreign-exchange market with no foreign exchange controls.

**Currency:** New Zealand dollar (100 cents). NZ$1.8064 = US$1 (28 Oct. 1991). NZ$1.6255 = US$1 (29 Oct. 1990).

**Public holidays** (1992): 1-2 Jan. (New Year), 6 Feb. (Waitangi Day), 17-20 Apr. (Easter), 25 Apr. (Anzac Day), 1 June (Queen's Birthday), 26 Oct. (Labour Day), 25-26 Dec. (Christmas).

**Government ministries:** External Relations and Overseas Trade, Private Bag, Wellington, tel. (04) 4728877; Commerce, PO Box 1473, Wellington, tel. (04) 4720030; Treasury, Private Bag, Wellington, tel. (04) 4722733.

**Major banks:** Australia and New Zealand Bank, PO Box 1492, Wellington, tel. (04) 4738622, tlx 3385; Bank of New Zealand, PO Box 2392, Wellington, tel. (04) 4746999, tlx 3344; National Bank of New Zealand, PO Box 1791, Wellington, tel. (04) 4729549, tlx 3388; Westpac Banking Corp., PO Box 691, Wellington, tel. (04) 4747499, tlx 3365.

**Taxation:** Corporate, 33% (38% for non-resident companies), personal, 15% to NZ$9,500, 28% NZ$9,500-30,875, 33% above NZ$30,875. Fringe benefits tax 49% (deductible), goods and services tax 12.5% (except financial transactions), no land or capital gains taxes. Overseas Investment Commission must approve foreign purchases of companies and land for commercial use; Minister of Lands may veto land purchases.

**Weather:** Mainly temperate with 4 distinct seasons, subtropical in north; rainfall varies from 400 mm a year to 2,000 mm; mean annual daytime temperature ranges from 8°C to 15°C; prevailing winds westerly.

# PAKISTAN

Map labels:
SOVIET UNION · CHINA · Boundary claimed by India · NWFP · Line of control · AFGHANISTAN · Peshawar · Islamabad · Rawalpindi · Indus R. · PUNJAB · Lahore · IRAN · Quetta · Multan · Kalat · Sutlej R. · BALUCHISTAN · INDIA · Bela · SINDH · Gwadar · Arabian Sea · Karachi · 0 100 200km

**Head of State**
President Ghulam Ishaq Khan.
**Prime Minister** (and **Foreign Affairs**)
Mian Muhammed Nawaz Sharif;
**Defence**
Ghaus Ali Shah;
**Commerce**
Malik Mohammed Naeem Khan;
**Finance**
Sartaj Aziz;
**Food and Agriculture**
Lieut-Gen. Majeed Malik;
**Health**
Tasneem Nawaz Gardezi;
**Housing and Works**
Tariq Mahmood;
**Interior**
Chaudhry Shujaat Hussein;
**Kashmir Affairs and Northern Areas**
Mehtab Ahmad Khan Abbasi;
**Labour**
Mohammed Ijazul Haq;
**Narcotics**
Rana Chandar Singh;
**Petroleum and Natural Resources**
Chaudhry Nisar Ali Khan;
**Planning and Development**
Chaudhry Hamid Nasir Chatha;

**Production**
Islam Nabi;
**Defence Production**
Hazar Khan Bijrani;
**Communications**
Ghulam Murtaza Jatoi;
**Parliamentary Affairs**
Chaudhry Ameer Hussein;
**Industries**
Sheikh Rasheed Ahmad;
**Religious Affairs**
Abdus Sattar Niazi;
**Rural Development**
Ghulam Dastgir Khan;
**Information**
Abdus Satter Lalika;
**Law and Justice**
Chaudhry Abdul Ghafoor;
**Railways**
Ghulam Ahmed Bilour;
**Water and Power**
Mohammed Yusuf;
**Provincial Coordination**
Aslam Khattak;
**Science and Technology**
Ilahi Baksh Soomro;
**Environment and Urban Affairs**
Anwar Saifullah Khan.

P oet-philosopher Muhammad Iqbal articulated the concept of Pakistan in its basic form in 1931, when he proposed a separate state comprising Muslim majority areas in northwestern India. The All-India Muslim League led by Muhammad Ali Jinnah adopted the concept in 1940, and the name "Pakistan" came into immediate use. The Muslim state that emerged from the partition of British India on 14 August 1947 included an eastern wing, comprising mainly the eastern half of Bengal province and parts of Assam.

Pakistan was proclaimed an Islamic republic on 23 March 1956. A federal parliamentary system functioned until Field Marshal Muhammad Ayub Khan seized power in a coup in October 1958. Ayub proclaimed a presidential system in the constitution of 1962 and ruled until March 1969, when he was deposed by Gen. Yahya Khan.

In the country's first free elections, held in December 1970, Zulfikar Ali Bhutto's Pakistan People's Party (PPP) dominated the west, while Sheikh Mujibur Rahman's Awami League swept the board in the east. Mujib's call for autonomy was rejected by Bhutto and Yahya, leading the Bengali leader to proclaim the People's Republic of Bangladesh on 26 March 1971. Civil war followed after Yahya, supported by Bhutto, ordered troops to arrest Mujib and put down the uprising. The war ended in December 1971 following Indian intervention with the formation of Bangladesh in the east. Yahya handed over power to Bhutto, who ruled until July 1977.

Gen. Zia-ul Haq took over initially to hold elections and transfer power to a civilian regime, but the elections were postponed. Bhutto was later tried for the murder of a political opponent and executed. Zia died in a mysterious aircraft crash in August 1988. After the November 1988 elections, Bhutto's daughter Benazir and leader of the PPP became prime minister. Her government was dismissed by President Ghulam Ishaq Khan in 1990 and, after new elections, Nawaz Sharif formed a coalition with the PPP in opposition.

## Politics/Social Affairs

F ears of a reversion to military rule remained widespread during 1991, despite the effort of the army chiefs to project the other two components of the ruling troika — the president and the prime minister — as running the country in accordance with Pakistan's constitution.

The fears receded somewhat with the smooth induction of the low profile Gen. Asif Nawaz Janjua as new army chief in August in place of the retiring incumbent Gen. Mirza Aslam Beg. Towards the end of the year, both President Ghulam Ishaq Khan and Prime Minister Nawaz Sharif confidently declared that the elected representatives would complete the remaining four years of their term. But the opposition, and even some of the ruling Islamic Democratic Alliance's (IDA) allies, were equally confident that the government would not see out 1992.

The main source of anxiety was the constant infighting among members of the ruling coalition and between leaders of the Muslim League, which provides the bulk of the seven-party IDA. The alliance ruled at the federal level in various coalitions, with the Awami National Party in the North-West Frontier Province (NWFP) and the Muhajir Qaumi Movement (MQM) — the ethnic party of immigrant Indian Muslims — in Sindh. Punjab, which Sharif ran as chief minister before becoming premier, was ruled by the IDA alone, while it led a coalition with five other parties in Baluchistan.

Equally disturbing was the growing lawlessness throughout most of the country, but particularly in Sindh, where the leaders pivotal to the IDA's survival were widely seen as patrons of the law-breakers. The ethnic Sindhi areas seemed to have been abandoned to armed gangs who kidnapped people for ransom, including foreign workers and visitors, and looted villages. The Sindh government remained largely ineffective and reacted mainly by arresting opposition activists on charges of terrorism, while protecting the armed gangs. The MQM was accused of violent attacks on critics — especially journalists. The opposition argued that since the arrests did not improve the situation, the action was mere political intimidation, an argument that gained some credence when arrested opposition members who changed political sides were subsequently freed.

The third pressure on the IDA government was the collapse of the cooperative societies in Punjab in the wake of the Bank of Credit and Commerce International (BCCI) failure. The societies were set up by a number of business interests and politicians that had, by offering higher than average interest rates, attracted vast deposits. The government stated that the cooperatives had collected Rs 16 billion (US$666 million) from some 2.5 million depositors in Punjab, with the three largest collecting more than Rs 9 billion. The opposition placed the figure much higher.

However, the interest rates proved unsustainable and the cooperatives — which were generally badly managed and often run for the benefit of their principal owners rather than the smaller members — began to crumble. Among those named for withdrawing money and contributing to their collapse was Sharif's family business group Ittefaq, as well as Interior Minister Chaudhry Shujaat Hussein's family concern, the Chaudhry Group.

Although the two groups announced that they would fully repay all the cooperative loans they had taken, the damage had been done to their own credibility and that of some other IDA politicians.

The opposition published bank records which assessed Ittefaq's net worth in 1977 at Rs 220 million, and then produced a government agency's 1990 record that showed the value of its assets had subsequently risen to Rs 6 billion. It was also argued that Ittefaq's phenomenal growth had accelerated in 1991, as public-sector financing agencies had loaned the group Rs 2 billion. Replying to the accusations in the National Assembly, the interior minister added fuel to the fire by saying borrowing for legitimate business was no crime, and that Ittefaq had paid Rs 1.5 billion in taxes in the previous fiscal year alone.

**Sharif: embattled.**

Despite the government's argument that the largest number of cooperatives was registered under the Pakistan People's Party (PPP) ousted by Ishaq Khan in 1990, the opposition continued to pursue its campaign. It argued that when the central bank had attempted to circumscribe the cooperatives' activities, Punjab — then ruled by Sharif — had thwarted this by accusing it of interference in provincial rights. Ittefaq countered by saying it had been forced to borrow from the cooperatives as it had been denied loans by public-sector banks then under federal control exercised by PPP chief Benazir Bhutto.

A further BCCI-linked uproar erupted over the allegation that the cooperatives scandal was linked with the bank's collapse. Local BCCI branches had made loans against overseas deposits maintained by some Pakistanis. Under local law, Pakistanis cannot keep more than US$1,000 abroad. The BCCI branches accepted nominal local collateral to circumvent the central bank's regulations, but the closure of BCCI abroad forced the local branches to ask debtors to repay before the central bank began going through their records. It was alleged that money was borrowed from the cooperatives to settle accounts with the local BCCI. Ittefaq, however, refuted the allegation that it had borrowed from the Muslim Commercial Bank to repay its loans from the cooperatives. The bank had been denationalised just before the scandal, amid allegations

by Bhutto that its new owners were really fronting for powerful political interests.

Apart from the opposition's accusations, Sharif faced growing criticism from the country's religious establishment, including some of his far-right partners in the IDA. This, coupled with the alarming rise in crime, forced him to amend the constitution to allow the creation of quick trial courts, enhance punishments for various crimes, threaten to revive public hangings and adopt a bill to bring all laws and practices in line with Islam. The Shariat Act created commissions to Islamicise the country's economy and educational system, and while this failed to satisfy his critics it saved the IDA from an imminent break up.

To stabilise the IDA, Sharif expanded his cabinet to a record level — 28 full ministers, three advisers of full ministerial rank and 18 ministers of state. The large number of parliamentary secretaries, in addition to the 50-strong cabinet, invited the derisive comment that it was a rare and unlucky IDA legislator who was not an office-holder.

The bloated cabinet was part of the price Sharif had to pay as a result of his efforts to secretly secure opposition support for amending the constitution. Under the earlier Eighth Amendment to the constitution pushed through by Zia, the president had assumed sweeping powers, including the exclusive right to select chiefs of the three services, appoint governors of the provinces and nominate judges of the superior courts. It also gave the president the right to dismiss the cabinet and the National Assembly — as Ishaq Khan did with the Bhutto government.

The opposition disclosed that Sharif had secretly sought its backing for annulling the amendment — something it fully supports — which would have reduced Ishaq Khan to a mere figurehead and effectively end his influence with the army. But the leak forced Sharif to retreat in the face of opponents within the IDA, who all but pulled him down with the aid of a large number of dissenters.

Mounting criticism from his partners also forced Sharif to call his first IDA leadership meeting since taking over as the premier. Despite the opposition from two IDA components, he expelled Hizbe Jehad from the alliance after Jehad leader Naveed Malik called for the Sharif government's dismissal on the grounds of corruption and incompetence and because he said the 1990 elections were rigged. Malik, who was Sharif's adviser when he was leading the IDA's election campaign, had announced in August that he regretted his role in rigging the polls for the IDA.

These factors prevented Sharif from capitalising on his achievements, notably his appointment of a National Finance Commission and the implementation of its report on the division of revenue between the federal and provincial governments. The findings largely satisfied the provinces, which had long been complaining of the previous unfair allocation of funds. He also convened the first meeting of the Council of Common Interests — a statutory body for resolving all inter-provinces issues — which was able to settle an old dispute over sharing river waters. Under the council's agreement, all the provinces declared their satisfaction with the allocation of its share of waters, though a dispute still persists over Punjab's plan to build a dam on the Indus River. The NWFP and Sindh consider the plan would damage their interests, while Punjab maintained it was free to do what it wished within its allotted share.

Given the scandals and the IDA infighting, Sharif made little headway in implementing his catchy slogans that called for national self-reliance and running the government by national consensus. Towards the end of the year calls for his government's dismissal were becoming louder, though Ishaq Khan continued to insist that the law and order situation was not abnormal and charges against Sharif and his own family were a smear campaign. This prompted the opposition to warn that by not providing redress within the constitution the president was risking extra-constitutional intervention. □

# Foreign Relations

Islamabad's foreign relations in the wake of the Gulf War were dominated by US pressure against its nuclear programme, US-Soviet pressure for a political settlement of the Afghan War, a likely reduction in foreign aid and the perceived evolution of an Indian-US strategic relationship. The result was a steady increase in local anti-US sentiment and a possible strategic relationship that links Pakistan, Iran and China.

The outcome of the Gulf War also disturbed Pakistan. While Islamabad sent a token force to Saudi Arabia to guard the Saudi-Yemeni frontier — more than 1,000 km away from the scene of action — Pakistan's army commander referred to Iraq's military as a Muslim asset. The hawk's gloom deepened with the US-Soviet decision to wind down the Afghan War by ending their respective support to the guerillas and the Kabul regime in order to force both sides to negotiate a settlement. The hawks had hoped for a military victory by the rebel mujahideen and the installation of a friendly set of rulers in Kabul.

**US arms embargo: a riposte.**

Nevertheless, Pakistani diplomats continued to maintain their links with guerilla leaders, and persuaded most of the factions to visit Moscow ahead of a UN-sponsored, intra-Afghan dialogue aimed at establishing an interim national government.

Foreign relations were also not helped by Prime Minister Nawaz Sharif's frequent declarations that he did not need US assistance if it limited his policy options. Since the US, Germany and Japan had already reduced their economic assistance and the US embargo on supplies of military equipment remained firmly in place, the prime minister's critics accused him of merely seeking to turn his lack of options into a virtue through rhetoric. Washington's tough stance was based on Pakistan's refusal to comply with its nuclear non-proliferation regime.

Islamabad's search for an alternative to its previous dependence upon the US made the idea of some form of trilateral arrangement that would link Pakistan, China and Iran appear attractive. Both Teheran and Peking supported Islamabad on the nuclear issue; China had been Pakistan's most dependable arms supplier since 1966 and Iran's US$18 billion average annual oil revenue made a strong economic argument for improving ties.

Perhaps the most significant factor, however, stemmed from a remark made by Iran's army chief Mohsin Rezai when he declared his country had a strategic relationship with Pakistan. This represented a radical change in Iranian thinking. Ac-

cording to some analysts, Pakistan now has little option other than to become close to Iran having been deprived of US support. The China dimension was further deepened during Chinese President Yang Shangkun's state visit to Pakistan at the end of October, when he described Sino-Pakistan relations as an all-weather friendship. However, there was a clear understanding in Islamabad that no formal military alliance was possible, not least because both Teheran and Peking opposed it.

Yang's visit was also significant as it closely followed that of China's air force commander to Pakistan and coincided with Pakistan army chief Gen. Asif Nawaz Janjua's visit to China. After his Peking visit, Janjua visited Teheran. Chinese Premier Li Peng had visited Teheran earlier, and Yang followed his visit to Pakistan with a tour of Iran. In late September, Pakistan's President Ishaq Khan visited Iran and, in his address to the Iranian parliament, condemned any form of hegemonistic world order. Almost simultaneously, China announced its view of a world order based on total equality between all nations and non-interference in internal affairs.

From Pakistan's perspective, such a declaration was reinforced when a visiting US envoy warned Islamabad during October that it could join a list drawn up in Washington of countries — Iran, Iraq, Syria and Libya — considered to support terrorism on the basis of its support of Kashmiri separatists.

Pakistan argued throughout 1991 that as a UN-recognised party to the Kashmir dispute, it was justified in extending moral and political support to the struggle. But it denied Indian charges that it was training, arming and infiltrating Kashmiri militants across the so-called Line of Actual Control in Kashmir.

Pakistani diplomats also expressed understanding for Teheran's desire to develop economic relations with New Delhi, and China's reluctance to support Islamabad's emphasis on the human-rights aspect of the Kashmir struggle, given its own experience in Tibet. Pakistan's position was based on the belief that its allies' quest for relations with India would not be at its own expense.

Indeed, Pakistan emulated the Iranian and Chinese example. After meeting Indian Prime Minister P. V. Narasimha Rao at the Commonwealth Heads of Government Conference held in Zimbabwe during October, Sharif stated that they had both agreed to discuss all outstanding issues. This attitude contrasted sharply with the frequent military clashes between the two countries' armed forces in Kashmir, Pakistan's complaints over the concentration of Indian troops in Rajasthan — opposite Pakistan's Sindh province — as well as allegations that India was sending terrorists into Pakistan. □

# Economy/Infrastructure

Fiscal 1990-91 was a hard one for Pakistan. Increased crude oil and finished petroleum product prices followed the Gulf War, while Pakistan's virtual pre-war dependence on Kuwait meant a serious disruption of supplies. These factors combined with a decline in remittances from workers in the Middle East, the loss of Gulf export markets and the cost of repatriating nationals from Kuwait and Iraq to bring total balance-of-payments losses to around US$700 million.

An additional problem was the decision by the World Bank and IMF to withhold various loans due to Pakistan's failure to meet a number of conditions. The last tranche of a structural adjustment facility loan was withheld, primarily because of Pakistan's failure to reduce the budget deficit to 4.2% of GDP by the end of fiscal 1990-91. The US$140 million tranche was finally released in October following a visit by a World Bank team, which accepted Pakistan's assurance that the deficit would be reduced to 4.2% by June 1992. Agreement was also reached to hold talks in early 1992 over the release of US$1.16 billion from the World Bank and Japan to compensate for Gulf War–related financial losses.

The most important economic event, certainly in the longer term, was the government's package of reforms based on increasing the rate of privatisation and deregulation. Plans were unveiled during the year to disinvest over 200 public-sector enterprises worth around US$11 billion, including the Telecommunications Corp. of Pakistan, variously valued at US$5.5-6 billion. A start was made with the transfer of management and sale of 26% of the Muslim Commercial Bank and the Allied Bank to the employees of the banks and private investors respectively. The new owners were guaranteed 25% more shares at the same price they had bought in.

Next on the auction block were 101 companies, ranging from vehicle parts manufacturers to producers of chemicals, pesticides, fertilisers, cement, engineering goods, bakery products and edible oils. By the end of October, bids had been received for 30 companies. No offers came for another 12, while negotiations were in progress with bidders for the remaining 59 to raise their offers to within 90% of the government valuation.

Soon after inviting the bids for the 101 firms, the government asked investors to bid for the National Development Finance Corp., the Industrial Development Bank of Pakistan — both investment banks — and the United Bank of Pakistan, Habib Bank and the National Bank of Pakistan. The National Bank was withdrawn from the sale following pressure from politicians and bureaucrats, who pointed out that it functioned

both as a treasury and a central government agency in regions where the central bank had no branches. The government's original plans were to sell off all the companies identified for privatisation by the end of 1991, despite the World Bank's advice to privatise in phases. Although the government fell behind its own timetable, the completed sales were the fastest of public enterprises anywhere in the world.

A major step was also taken towards the goal of eventually making the local currency fully convertible. All restrictions were removed from the export and import of foreign currency and the banks were permitted to open accounts for residents and foreigners in US dollars, deutschemarks, yen and sterling.

The restriction requiring government approval for setting up an industrial enterprise was withdrawn, except for cases involving arms and ammunition, high explosives, radioactive substances, security printing and currency. Foreigners were given permission to invest in any business, retain 100% control and allowed unrestricted repatriation of capital and profits without any official agency's prior approval.

The stock exchange was also opened to foreign investors, while the restriction on foreign companies borrowing capital from local banks was abolished. The government further declared that unless it was asked to guarantee a loan repayment, local and foreign companies and individuals were free to contract foreign loans on any terms.

Import licences were abolished for a long list of items, and foreign companies which had earlier been barred from trading were allowed to export on the same basis as the locals. Designated export zones are totally tax-free, but tariffs on production in the rest of the country was reduced to 90% in 1991-92, and will be cut to 50% by July 1994.

Towards the end of the year, pressure was rising from banks and other businesses for a downward adjustment in the par value of the local currency — the consensus was for around 15%. This was due to the devaluation of the Indian rupee and the improved quality of its textile and yarn products, which are providing tough competition to Pakistan's exports. However, the central bank continued to resist any abrupt change in its policy of gradual downward adjustment. □

# Data

**Major industries** (July 1989–June 1990): Cloth, 294.9 million m² (269.9 million); yarn, 911.6 million kg (757.9 million); fertilisers, 3.03 million tonnes (2.92 million); cement, 7.5 million tonnes (7.12 million); sugar, 1.8 million tonnes (1.86 million); hydrogenated edible oil, 683,000 tonnes (624,000).

**Major agriculture** (provisional 1990-91 estimates): Wheat, 14.5 million tonnes (14.3 million); rice, 3.3 million tonnes (3.2 million); cotton, 9.6 million bales (8.6 million); sugarcane, 35.9 million tonnes (35.5 million); tobacco, 68,000 tonnes (same).

**Oil and natural gas** (official 1990-91 estimates): Crude oil, 23.5 million barrels (19.47 million); natural gas, 15 billion m³ (14.1 billion).

**Mining** (official 1990-91 estimates): Coal, 2.7 million tonnes (same); limestone, 91 million tonnes (7.7 million); magnesite, 4.1 million tonnes (7.2 million); bauxite, 24.6 million tonnes (16.3 million); ochre, 1.3 million tonnes (2.3 million); gypsum anhydrite, 468,000 tonnes (491,000); sulphur, 295,000 tonnes (342,000).

**Major imports** (fiscal 1990-91): Petroleum and products, US$1.53 billion (US$1 billion); non-electrical machinery, US$1.22 billion (US$1.03 billion); chemicals, US$627 million (US$617.7 million); transport equipment, US$463.33 million (US$409.6 million); edible oil, US$365 million (US$334.5 million); iron, steel and manufacturers thereof, US$287.4 million (US$283 million); chemical fertilisers, US$239 million (US$179.6 million); pharmaceuticals, US$178.4 million (US$150.7 million); electrical goods, US$199.5 million (US$172.4 million); tea, US$151 million (US$157 million); grains and flours, US$156 million (US$374 million); sugar, US$145.5 million (US$77.7 million); paper, board and stationery, US$130.2 million (US$116.4 million), dyes and colours, US$86.5 million (US$75.6 million); non-ferrous metals, US$85.4 million (US$105 million).

**Major exports** (fiscal 1990-91): Cotton yarn, US$1.08 billion (US$725 million); garments, US$755 million (US$580 million); cotton cloth, US$615.3 million (US$485.8 million); raw cotton, US$386.7 million (US$386.6 million); rice, US$317.6 million (US$208 million); synthetic textiles, US$316 million (US$184.4 million); leather, US$250.4 million (US$243 million); carpets, US$202.4 million (US$199.3 million); sports goods, US$125.5 million (US$94.4 million); fish, US$104.3 million (US$81.9 million); surgical instruments, US$76.9 million (US$60.8 million); petroleum and products, US$35.9 million (US$9.5 million); footwear, US$29.3 million (US$20.4 million).

(Previous period in brackets.)

**Tourism and transport:** Arrivals, n.a.; departures, n.a.

**Finance:** 7 local merchant banks with 6,827 branches in the country and 176 overseas; 20 foreign banks with 53 branches. Of the local banks, 2 are in private sector and 10 newly licensed banks are due to open in 1992. Of the remaining 5 all but 2 are due to be privatised during 1992. There are stock exchanges in Karachi and Lahore listing all public limited companies. Another has been licensed to open in early 1992 in Islamabad. Companies listed on stock exchanges are open to local and foreign investors without any upper limit to foreign holding.

**Major banks:** National Bank of Pakistan, I. I. Chundrigar Rd, Karachi, tel. 227011; Habib Bank, Habib Bank Plaza, Karachi, tel. 219111; Muslim Commercial Bank, Adamji House, I. I. Chundrigar Rd, Karachi, tel. 224091.

**Currency:** Pakistani Rupee (100 paisas). Rs 24.59 = US$1 Nov. 1991 (Rs 21.77 = US$1 Nov. 1990).

**Public holidays** (1992): 23 Mar. (Pakistan Day), 15-17 Apr.* (Eidul Fitra), 1 May (May Day), 25 June* (Eidul Azha), 1 July (bank holiday), 22 July* (Ashura), 24 Aug. (Independence Day), 6 Sept. (Defence of Pakistan Day), 11 Sept. (anniversary of Jinnah's death), 23 Sept.* (Eid Miladun Nabi), 25 Dec. (Christmas).

(*Approximate dates; actual dates subject to lunar cycle.)

**Government ministries:** Foreign, Constitution Avenue, Islamabad, tel. 812470, tlx 5800 FARBD PK; Finance, Block Q, Pakistan Secretariat, Islamabad, tel. 822164, tlx 5774 MIND PK; Commerce, Block A, Pakistan Secretariat, Islamabad, tel. 822164, tlx 5774 MIND PK; Industries, Block A, Pakistan Secretariat, Islamabad, tel. 825708, tlx 5859 COMDN PK; Production, Block D, Pakistan Secretariat, Islamabad, tel. 822175, tlx 5579 MNPRO PK.

**Weather:** Hottest season on plains is June-Aug., with dry heat followed by hot and humid weather with temperatures up to 48°C. Winter Nov.-Mar., varying from cool to extremely cold, with sub-zero temperatures in some parts in Dec.-Jan. Annual average rainfall is 440 mm in the plains and up to 1,750 mm in the northern mountain ranges.

**Taxation:** Agreement with several countries for avoiding double taxation; expatriates can declare income in their home countries; foreign currency bank accounts not taxed. No income tax on industries established away from specified areas up to June 1995; imported machinery for these industries exempt from customs duty, sales tax and import surcharge leaving only 2% ad valorem to be paid as import licence fee; income tax reduction for export industries. Designated export zones tax free, but tariff on production in rest of the country up to 90%, due to be reduced to 50% by July 1994.

# PAPUA NEW GUINEA

Map: 0 150 300km

MANUS · Lorengau
Pacific Ocean
Vanimo
WEST SEPIK
ENGA
WESTERN HIGHLANDS
Wewak
EAST SEPIK
MADANG
NEW IRELAND
Kavieng
Rabaul
Bismarck Sea
EAST NEW BRITAIN
Kieta
Madang
Wabag
Kundiawa
Mount Hagen
Mendi
Goroka · Lae
Kimbe
WEST NEW BRITAIN
BOUGAINVILLE
SOUTHERN HIGHLANDS
GULF
MOROBE
Kerema
Daru
CHIMBU
NORTHERN
Popondetta
Solomon Sea
EASTERN HIGHLANDS
WESTERN
CENTRAL
Alotau
IRIAN JAYA (INDONESIA)
Port Moresby
Milne Bay
Coral Sea

**Governor-General**
Sir Wiwa Korowi.
**Prime Minister** (and **Resources Development**)
Rabbie Namaliu;
**Deputy Prime Minister** (and **Fisheries and Marine Resources**)
Akoka Doi;
**Foreign Affairs**
Sir Michael Somare;
**Finance**
Paul Pora;
**Justice and Attorney-General**
Bernard Narokobi;
**Defence**
Benais Sabumei;
**Home Affairs and Youth**
Matthew Bendumb;
**Police**
Mathias Ijape;
**Correctional Services**
Tenda Lau;
**Provincial Affairs**
Fr John Momis;
**Labour and Employment**
Tony Ila;
**Public Service**
Jacob Lemeki;
**Works**
Lukas Waka;
**Minerals and Energy**
Patterson Lowa;

**Communication**
Brown Sinamoi;
**Culture and Tourism**
Gerald Beona;
**Civil Aviation**
John Wauwia;
**Transport**
Anthony Temo;
**Land and Physical Planing**
Sir Hugo Berghuser;
**Trade and Industry**
John Giheno;
**Agriculture and Livestock**
Tom Pais;
**Education**
Utula Samana;
**Interior**
Karl Stack;
**Housing**
Bob Bubek;
**Health**
Galeva Kwarara;
**Forests**
Jack Genia;
**Environment and Conservation**
Michael Singan;
**Chief Justice**
Sir Buri Kidu;
**Defence Force Commander**
Brig.-Gen. Rochus Lokinap.

PNG was granted internal self-government on 1 December 1973 and became an independent nation on 16 September 1975. However, independence also brought separatist pressures from some of the regions that had nothing more in common with each other than having been ruled by a mixture of British, German and Australian colonial administrators.

In 1976, separatists on Bougainville Island threatened to secede from PNG, but were mollified — at least temporarily — by being granted internal self-government. The island's huge copper mine remained the mainstay of the national economy until 1988, when landowners on Bougainville, who had been claiming compensation from the mine's Australian operator, turned to sporadic guerilla warfare when their claims were not met.

Bougainville Copper Ltd, which had been operating the mine since 1972, closed the facility indefinitely in 1989 after sabotage attacks and raids intensified. Some 2,000 members of PNG's security forces were sent to the island, but were unable to contain the violence or seize the rebel leadership. Following negotiations, PNG withdrew its forces from Bougainville in early 1990, while maintaining a blockade of the island.

The island now remains under the internal control of the self-styled Bougainville Liberation Army. Various efforts to break the stalemate through negotiations have failed, and the island remains cut off from all but the most rudimentary humanitarian aid and whatever supplies that can be smuggled in from the nearby Solomon Islands.

Michael Somare and his Pangu Party ruled from independence to early 1980, when he was ousted and replaced by his former deputy Sir Julius Chan. Somare returned to power in mid-1982, but was replaced in November 1985 by Paias Wingti, who lost power in July 1988 to Rabbie Namaliu. Somare currently serves as foreign minister.

By the end of 1991, Namaliu had become the second-longest serving premier and had managed to introduce a number of legislative reforms which provided a measure of political stability. The country remains heavily dependent on its mining and commodities sectors, especially gold, coffee and — until the closure of the Bougainville mine — copper. In addition, PNG's first oil field is due to start production in mid-1992.

## Politics/Social Affairs

Papua New Guinea (PNG) started to see something new in 1991, as reformist Prime Minister Rabbie Namaliu pushed long-postponed legislative change through parliament.

This set the stage for elections in mid-1992, and the start of the next parliament's five-year rule that coincides with the peak of the country's gold, copper and oil receipts. Revenue in 1993-94 is estimated to be about US$2.5 billion, compared with 1990 resources revenues of US$630 million and an annual budget of only US$1.3 billion.

This might lead, with judicious and self-disciplined leadership, to the broad-based take-off that the country has been desperately awaiting — or to PNG's further sundering into two nations, the wealthy Port Moresby–based elite and the rural majority, whose cash incomes collapsed in 1991.

During the year, Namaliu became the second longest-serving prime minister after PNG's founding father, Sir Michael Somare — now foreign minister and still ambitious. Despite being pressed by rampant crime, the continuing bloody rebellion on Bougainville Island, anti-corruption riots that forced the closure of the country's two universities and a political crisis that saw the forced resignations of both the deputy prime minister Ted Diro and the governor-general Sir Serei Eri, Namaliu still managed to press on with an ambitious reform programme.

This included giving future governments 18 months' grace from no-confidence votes to provide greater stability, raising the electoral nomination fee from US$100 to US$1,000 to reduce the lottery element when dozens of candidates stand for a seat, and closing the gap between an election and the first parliamentary session to seven days in order to reduce the customary bribery and threats that accompany the formation of a PNG government. He also outlawed compensation threats — principally over land — and limited the sums payable, tackled crime by reintroducing the death penalty, set up a national youth service, passed an act that enabled unemployed young people to be sent back to their home villages and changed the onus of proof in tribal fighting cases from prosecution to defence.

Namaliu's government also enacted a range of structural economic reforms urged by both the private sector and the World Bank — arguably the greatest external influence on PNG in the 1990s.

Many of these measures, as constitutional changes, required 75% support in parliament — rarely obtained in the past. Namaliu demonstrated considerable persistence, and a political acumen with which the quietly spoken former academic and public service chief had not previously been credited.

Throughout the year he retained the crucial support of the historically fissiparous bloc of Papuan MPs, despite the travails of their leader Diro. A judicial tribunal in September found Diro guilty of 81 counts of corruption — many related to his association with Singaporean and Malaysian interests while he was forests minister in 1985-86 — and to his receipt of US$140,000 in cash from Indonesian Defence Minister L. B. Murdani.

The tribunal ordered Diro to pay a modest fine, but more crucially barred him from all public office for three years — ruling him out of the 1992 election race when he was expected to have mounted a strong challenge against Namaliu. The focus of attention then shifted to former governor-general Eri, who had been founding president of Diro's People's Action Party (PAP). Eri, a former senior public servant and ambassador, refused to formally sign the tribunal's verdict.

However, the outrush of support that had been predicted in Port Moresby — heartland of the Papuan region — if the two leaders were found guilty never emerged. After a few days' stand-off, they resigned and Akoka Doi — previously dismissed as a political lightweight — took over the party's leadership and the deputy premiership and kept the PAP in government. In November, Wiwa Korowi, a genial Southern Highlander and former diplomat, was chosen by parliament as the new governor-general.

Events on Bougainville Island began to impinge less on the rest of PNG during 1991 as hopes for a peaceful settlement were dashed and the conflict assumed the nature of a prolonged siege. Although government and rebel leaders had signed the Honiara Accord on 23 January in the capital of the Solomon Islands, that at least had offered the prospect of a return to a form of normalcy, mutual suspicion and soon eroded whatever understanding that had been reached.

Through the year PNG consolidated its hold on the northern island of Buka, just off Bougainville, and re-established links with traditional leaders on the north and south of the main island. But the Bougainville Revolutionary Army retained its firm grip of its heartland — the central area embracing the copper mine, shut since mid-1989, and the devastated towns of Arawa and Kieta.

The nature of the fighting was revealed when a PNG army colonel admitted to an Australian television team that his troops had killed civilians and dumped their bodies at sea from a helicopter. The officer was swiftly sacked from the army by Defence Minister Ben Sabumei.

**Namaliu: reformer.**

One of Namaliu's failures was to complete his reform agenda by re-establishing the country's 19 costly provincial governments as part-time, honorary structures whose members are chosen from and by unpaid local government leaders. Many provincial governments have been suspended from time to time for misappropriation since their establishment in 1977 — with the ironic exception of Bougainville, always cited as an example of the system working at its best. This year, after the East Sepik government was suspended, its premier, Bruce Samban, was charged with burning down the offices in revenge.

Following a major anti-crime meeting in February, curfews were introduced across much of the country, temporarily staunching the fast-rising crime rate and halving insurance claims. However, as the economic recession drove up beer prices, the market for home-grown marijuana boomed. Police reported a 500% rise in associated court cases over the past four years.

Education Minister Utula Samana embraced a massive restructuring of the education system, originally tailored to train clerks to replace expatriate public servants but long proven inappropriate for PNG's changed needs. Only 70% of children start primary education, and of these only one third can find places in secondary schools. The new scheme guarantees an extra two years' schooling for all, and thereafter will offer a practical stream as well as a more academic option. □

# Foreign Relations

Having established formal treaty relationships with all its neighbours, Papua New Guinea (PNG) spent much of 1991 fine-tuning its foreign ties. Gabriel Dusava, a career diplomat, was appointed new foreign affairs permanent secretary to replace Bill Dihm on his promotion to head of the public service department.

Nevertheless, two points of tension emerged. The most potentially serious was relations with neighbouring Solomon Islands, as Honiara gradually began to dissociate itself from its firm alliance with Port Moresby over the Bougainville rebellion.

The Solomon's ambivalence was not unexpected. In 1977 Bougainville's provincial government had opted for the name North Solomons, while many Bougainvilleans retain links with Solomon Islanders to whom they are more closely geographically and culturally linked than they are to the rest of PNG. As the rebellion dragged on into its fourth year, Solomon Islands' sympathies wavered.

The Bougainville rebels were able to establish a semi-permanent office in Honiara, despite a formal PNG Government request that the rebels be banned. In addition, most of the rebels' supplies and contacts with the outside world came through the Solomons, only a canoe journey away. It was through Honiara that rebel representative Joe Kabui left Bougainville to address a UN sub-commission in Geneva on discrimination against minorities. Nevertheless, a Solomons court jailed 10 armed rebels who had been caught in the Solomon Islands.

The Commonwealth Secretariat became involved in fruitless attempts during the year to seek a negotiated settlement between the PNG Government and the

Bougainville rebels. However, its emissary to the rebels — a Nigerian general — abandoned his efforts when rebel leaders insisted on retaining their arms even after the agreed advent of a multinational supervisory group. New Zealand's offer of the services of its former governor-general Sir Paul Reeves were also ultimately rejected.

The second, albeit much less serious, point of tension in international affairs emerged with Washington, and stemmed from the creation of a considerable — if unrealistic — popular expectations of a major investment drive from the US. In addition, the government had been confident that its nominee for the 1991-92 presidency of the UN General Assembly, Foreign Minister Sir Michael Somare, would be elected in New York in September. However, the country's long and expensive campaign failed by 83-47 votes when a last-minute Saudi candidate emerged, strongly backed by the US.

Prime Minister Rabbie Namaliu, who immediately cancelled a planned visit to the US to launch a PNG trade and investment exhibition, said: "It is a pity because the United States passed up a unique opportunity to demonstrate its interest in the Pacific island nations in a tangible way. When island leaders met President Bush in Hawaii a year ago, we all hoped there would be a greater and more positive US interest in our region. Given today's opportunity which the US obviously did not take up, the Pacific islands have reason for disappointment."

The incident now enabled PNG to assess where it stood and who its friends were, Namaliu said. Relations with Australia, PNG's oldest ally, remained cordial through the year. Eight Australian and six PNG ministers attended the third ministerial forum in Canberra, during which a revised version of the PNG-Australia Trade and Commercial Relations Agreement, first introduced in 1977, was signed. The revised accord granted PNG duty free and concessional access to Australian markets and offered PNG assistance in quality control, market research and small business development. However, PNG was also warned of the diminishing value of its concessions, as Australia gradually dismantles its general protective framework.

In response to Australian concerns over the use of four military helicopters given to the PNG armed forces by Canberra were being put to in Bougainville, Port Moresby withdrew the aircraft to Madang on the PNG mainland. A review of PNG's security priorities during the year led Australia — PNG's major military supplier and trainer — to reorientate its support towards the police and away from the armed forces.

PNG remained sidelined in the Asia Pacific Economic Cooperation (Apec) process, thanks in part to an Australian oversight when the original invitations went out. But it emphasised, as an observer at the November Apec meeting in South Korea, its desire to join and may do so in 1992.

Relations with Indonesia remained harmonious through 1991, helped early in the year with a formal Indonesian apology for earlier incursions by troops chasing Irian Jayan rebels across the PNG border. The death of Irian Jayan rebel leader Mecky Salosa, who was arrested in PNG in December 1989 and sent back to Indonesia in July 1990 — reportedly of natural causes after escaping from jail in Jayapura where he was serving a life sentence — had no visible impact on relations.

In April, Namaliu made an official visit to China, where he signed an investment promotion and protection agreement. China provided a US$15 million interest-free loan, plus the design and much of the labour to build the major stadium in Port Moresby for the South Pacific Games that PNG hosted in September. Given this support, China's newly appointed Ambassador Wang Nonsheng was clearly shocked to discover Taiwan's trade representative at a reception in September and succeeded in having him asked to leave. The perennial and global struggle between the "two Chinas" is far from over in PNG, however, as Taiwan is building Somare's Pangu Party's new 14-storey headquarters directly opposite the Chinese Embassy.

Japan also provided considerable assistance for the South Pacific Games infrastructure, with its Eximbank loaning the funds for the Lae stadium and swimming pool. Japanese construction company Kumagai Gumi carried out the work, as it did for the Japanese aided US$22 million Port Moresby hospital upgrading project, and the US$20 million new headquarters for PNG's postal and telecommunications corporation, again facilitated by Eximbank. □

# Economy/Infrastructure

So far, the 1990s have been boomtime for Papua New Guinea's (PNG) capital Port Moresby, with construction companies hard pressed to keep pace with the new offices, apartments, stores, hospitals, stadiums and roads. The city's population is growing faster than any other area of the country, as wealth from gold and the imminent prospect of oil acts as a magnet.

Placer Pacific's Porgera gold mine exceeded expectations to produce more than 1 million ounces in 1991, while the smaller Misima gold mine — also operated by Placer — is running smoothly. The Ok Tedi copper mine is now operating profitably and will reduce debt sufficiently to pay company tax in 1993 or 1994. The US$1 billion Chevron-led Kutubu joint venture is set to produce 128,000 barrels per day in July 1992, just after the scheduled national election, while by 1 April 1992, Kennecott Ltd — now owned by Rio Tinto Zinc — must indicate whether it intends to develop the world's largest gold find this century at Lihir island in New Ireland province.

As resource revenues rise, so direct aid and concessional funding are likely to diminish. Oil and gold, then, will provide PNG with a temporary buffer period during which it can adjust towards greater self-reliance through broad-based — which means rural-based — economic growth.

Prime Minister Rabbie Namaliu believes the structural economic reforms his government put in place in 1991 will provide the right platform to attract non-mining investment. He claims the government's own public investment programme will help build the climate required for such investment decisions by providing 30,000 jobs over the next three years. These will chiefly be in infrastructure projects contracted out by government to private companies.

The 1991 restructuring included reshuffling the bureaucracy responsible for investment, simplifying work permit and visa applications for expatriate staff, replacing an onerous training and localisation requirement with a 2% training levy and permitting 50-50 joint ventures to be registered as local companies.

A further liberalisation, however, was provoked by more pressing needs. Export taxes on primary produce and import duties on agricultural, manufacturing, fisheries and tourism inputs were suspended due to the collapse of the prices for most of PNG's main commodities. In the 1991 June quarter, coffee prices were down 8.5% on the corresponding period of 1990, cocoa was down 4.2%, copra down 11.2% and tea down 19.4%. While palm oil and logs bucked the trend, the terms of trade had fallen 6% in 1990, following a 16.1% decline in 1989.

Mainly as a result of poor prices, PNG's increasingly

smallholder-based rural industries recorded even greater drops in export volumes. Coffee exports in the June quarter fell 66.2% against the matching 1990 period, while cocoa dropped 50%, copra 83.2%, palm oil 30.1%, tea 92% and logs 7.4%.

Despite the circumstances, Namaliu refused to follow World Bank/Asian Development Bank advice and abolish PNG's stabilisation fund for its leading commodities. These funds, obtained from the now suspended export levy, provide a subsidy to producers when prices are low through diverting a premium when they are high. The government itself had to step in during 1991 to keep the funds liquid.

The country's precarious dependence on mining was underlined by a slump in the share of non-mineral exports in total exports, recorded in the 1991 June quarter, to 14.7% against 42% in the same period of 1990. Attempts to reshuffle programmes of capital support for the agriculture sector continued in 1991, but in a country where land titles are rarely registered and often held in common, bankable collateral is minimal.

The government did, however, succeed in merging its own support agencies for the key coffee sector into a Coffee Industry Corp., which it aims to use as a model for other commodities. A Spice Industry Board was also established to foster agricultural diversification into this promising new field. In addition, the government allocated US$8 million to subsidising interest rates on agricultural loans, pegging them at 8%.

The 1992 budget, delivered by Finance Minister Pual Pora on 12 November, resisted the usual pre-election temptations while also avoiding overdue spending cuts or pushing along the still largely theoretical privatisation process. It assumed instead substantially similar conditions to those of 1991 — 5.5% inflation; real growth of 5-6%; no increase in real wages; a stable kina, the national currency and almost on par with the US dollar; lower interest rates and 4% private-sector employment growth, or about 7,000 jobs.

It introduced no new taxes, cut the business withholding tax from 17% to 10%; set up a new first home–ownership scheme; provided tax exemptions on interest to encourage savings and introduced a new credit facility for infrastructure development associated with resource projects.

A tax summit in October focused on the effects of introducing a broad-based value added tax — in line with the general World Bank prescription — though most of the PNG decision-makers present remained unconvinced. This partly reflected the challenge in implementation of such a policy, given the disarray of PNG's public service — which is split between a national government and 19 provincial governments that have adopted increasingly inventive ways to raise their own revenues.

In the first half of 1991, PNG's balance of payments shifted into a US$95 million deficit, against a US$59 million surplus in the same period of 1990. The public-sector debt service figure reached 17.25% in 1991, high enough to cause the World Bank to recommend continuing abstinence from commercial borrowing for the budget. The overall debt service ratio was expected to decline from 1990's massive 45.7% to 34.1% — chiefly driven by borrowings for the

**Port Moresby: paving the streets with gold.**

country's huge new resources projects.

A constitutional challenge by lawyer Peter Donigi, that would have had the effect of replacing the British common law vesting of minerals ownership with the state by the US principle of vesting with the landowner, ultimately failed — to the collective relief of the mining and oil majors producing or exploring in the country.

Exploratory talks were held between Foreign Minister Sir Michael Somare and Chicago-based investor Jay Pritzker about replacing the non-operational Bougainville copper mine's owners — led by Australia's CRA Ltd — with another structure. But little real progress was made. The continuing isolation and despoliation of rebel-controlled Bougainville led the commercial banks to write off loans in their 1990 returns. The overall return to PNG bank shareholders' funds fell from 12.3% in 1989 to a negative 4.2% in 1990.

The heavily controlled transport sector received a fillip, with the government's announcement of total deregulation — except for strategic air routes, which remain monopolies of the state airline Air Niugini. And the major third level operator Talai — whose owner, Australian Dennis Buchanan, had said in 1990 he was about to leave PNG — continued flying.

The government's conversion under Namaliu to an open, rationalist economic stance was questioned by its entering a US$40 million joint venture with South Korea's Halla group to import and grind clinker at Lae in order to produce cement protected by a total import ban of indefinite duration.

In February the US$50 million Yoki hydroelectric project in the Eastern Highlands — built by South Korea's Hyundai group — was opened and will produce power for the Highlands and PNG's second city, Lae.

The country's biggest 1991 project, the construction by Bechtel Corp. of a 265-km pipeline for the US$1 billion Kutubu oilfield — the country's first — was on schedule and within budget, with oil set to flow in the second week of July 1992.

## Data

**Major agriculture** (1990): Coffee, 54,600 tonnes (85,000); cocoa, 33,900 tonnes (46,600); copra, 55,000 tonnes (60,700); copra oil, 34,800 tonnes (34,600); palm oil, 142,700 tonnes (131,700); rubber, 2,300 tonnes (3,600); logs, 923,000 m³ (1.35 million).
**Oil and natural gas:** n.a.
**Mining** (1990): Copper, 196,500 tonnes (208,800); gold, 32.8 tonnes (31.3).
**Major exports** (1990): Gold, US$384 million (US$317 million); copper, US$349 million (US$345 million); tree crops, US$190 million (US$270 million); timber, US$62 million (US$90 million).
**Currency:** Kina (100 toea). Kina 1 = US$1.05, Nov. 1991 (Kina 1 = US$1.06, Nov. 1990).
**Major banks:** ANZ Banking Group, tel. 211666; Bank of South Pacific, tel. 212444; Indosuez Niugini Bank, tel. 213533; Papua New Guinea Banking Corp., tel. 229700; Papua New Guinea Agricultural Bank, tel. 256900; Westpac Bank, tel. 220700.
**Public holidays** (1992): 1 Jan. (New Year), 17-20 Apr. (Easter), 15 June (Queen's Birthday), 23 July (Remembrance Day), 16 Sept. (Independence Day), 25-26 Dec. (Christmas).
**Weather:** Temperatures in Papua New Guinea vary little during the year, with coastal areas averaging 21-32°C. In the highlands, temperatures vary with altitude and nights can be cold. Average rainfall is some 2,500 mm, but can be double that in some areas.
**Tax:** personal tax 15-45%, company tax 35% (48% non-resident). Company taxes; mining 35% (48), petroleum 50% (same), others 30% (48). No restrictions on import of foreign currency, but export of kina is restricted. Non-residents may take out the amount of foreign currency they brought in.

# PHILIPPINES

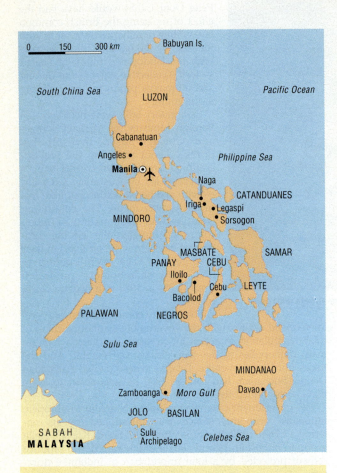

**President**
Corazon Aquino.
**Vice-President**
Salvador Laurel;
**Executive Secretary**
Franklin Drilon;
**National Economic and Development Authority**
Director-General Cayeatno Paderanga Jr;
**Press Secretary**
Tomas Gomez III;
**Agrarian Reform Secretary**
Benjamin Leong;
**Foreign Affairs**
Raul Manglapus;
**Agriculture**
Senen Bacani;
**Finance**
Jesus Estanislao;
**Budget and Management**
Guillermo Carague;
**Education, Culture and Sports**
Isidro Carino;
**Environment and Natural Resources**
Fulgencio Factoran Jr;

**Health**
Alfredo Bengzon;
**National Defence**
Renato de Villa;
**Trade and Industry**
Peter Garrucho;
**Labour and Employment**
Ruben Torres;
**Interior and Local Government**
Luis Santos;
**Public Works and Highways**
Jose de Jesus;
**Science and Technology**
Ceferino Follosco;
**Social Welfare and Development**
Mita Pardo de Tavera;
**Tourism**
Rafael Alunan;
**Transportation and Communications**
Nicomedes Pete Prado;
**Justice**
Silvestre Bello III;
**Armed Forces Chief of Staff**
Gen. Lisandro Abadia.

The Philippines initially won independence on 12 June 1898 after centuries of Spanish domination, only to fall quickly into the hands of the US. The Republic of the Philippines was proclaimed on 4 July 1946 with Manuel Roxas as the first president.

A communist-inspired rebellion in central Luzon raged between the 1940s and the early 1950s, but was successfully crushed with the help of the US. Ferdinand Marcos was elected president on 9 November 1965, under the Nacionalista Party banner and won a second term four years later.

The assassination on 21 August 1983 of Marcos' main political rival Benigno Aquino on his return from self-exile in the US precipitated a clamour for political change. Mass anti-Marcos rallies led to the May 1984 National Assembly elections in which opposition candidates won in 60 of the 183 seats contested.

In February 1986, a popularly supported military revolt in Manila started a chain of events that led to Marcos' departure from the Philippines to exile in the US, where he died in September 1989. A new government led by Aquino's widow Corazon, and including many members of the former opposition, took office in March. Despite this "People's Power" revolution, dissatisfied factions within the military and traditional oligarchy, rural and urban communist guerillas and a faltering economy have combined to create a volatile political culture that has yet to evolve the institutional mechanism needed to ensure stability.

## Politics/Social Affairs

After being hit by one misfortune after another during the previous two years, Filipinos could hardly be blamed for wondering what else could go wrong as they faced 1991. The 15 June eruption of Mt Pinatubo, and the way the Central Luzon volcano would come to dominate much of the year's events, provided the tragic answer. Further jolts came with the US bases issue, the return of former first lady Imelda Marcos in the latter half of the year and a flood disaster that killed up to 8,000 people.

In what was one of the world's biggest volcanic eruptions this century, Pinatubo effectively destroyed Clark air force base as it dumped up to 2 m of sandy ash in a 20-km radius of its crater. By year-end, the three central provinces of Pampanga, Zambales and Tarlac were still struggling to come to grips with a disaster that seems to have no end.

About 200 people died as a direct result of the eruption, most of them in the ruins of buildings which collapsed under the weight of rain-sodden ash. But the death toll climbed steadily to more than 500 as disease and sickness spread through hastily built evacuation centres. Many of the victims were among the estimated 50,000 Aeta tribespeople, who had carried out subsistence farming around Pinatubo's slopes for centuries.

Filipino and US vulcanologists had predicted the eruption about a month earlier, but as Pinatubo had remained dormant for 600 years they could not assess how violent it would be. When the volcano did erupt, at the height of a tropical cyclone, it spewed out an initial 330-km plume that rose to an altitude of more than 25 km. Over the next few weeks, repeated but less violent eruptions sent superheated flows down the mountain's river valleys and blanketed the surrounding landscape with ash as thick as heavy snow.

More than half a million people were deprived of their livelihoods and, though volcanic activity slowly subsided, mudflows threatened villages and towns and added to a relief bill that could eventually exceed US$1 billion. With an estimated 3-8 km³ of debris filling ravines and generally transforming the topography of the mountain, experts said mudflows could be a danger for the next five years, particularly during the wet season.

The Philippines' reputation as "the unlucky country" was further enhanced on 5 November when flash floods and landslides triggered by a tropical cyclone killed as many as 8,000 people in the eastern Visayan islands of Leyte and Negros. In terms of human loss, it was the worst disaster to hit the country in more than a century. The government initiated an inquiry into allegations by local officials that deforestation caused by illegal logging was responsible for the heavy death toll.

Most of the deaths were among the western Leyte city of Ormoc's population of 130,000. Hundreds of the victims were carried out to sea or buried under mud that cascaded down mountain slopes behind the city during a day-long cloudburst.

President Corazon Aquino — by now a seasoned veteran of both natural and man-made disasters — muddled into the sixth and final year of her presidency wrestling with numerous problems, but without having to confront any serious challenge to her leadership. Indeed, she even felt sufficiently confident to allow Imelda Marcos to return. Marcos and her entourage returned to Manila aboard a chartered jet on 4 November — four days after the surprise arrival of her son, Ferdinand "Bongbong" Marcos Jr.

Unrepentant as ever, the self-styled "mother of the nation" gave her usual performance as the aggrieved widow before crowds which clearly fell below her expectations. For the moment at least, the remains of the ousted late president Ferdinand Marcos rest in a mausoleum in Hawaii while the family debated whether to accept the government's decree that it be flown directly to Marcos' northwestern province of Ilocos Norte for final burial.

There was widespread speculation whether Imelda Marcos' return would affect the outcome of the general elections scheduled for 11 May 1992 — an event whose shadow fell ever more deeply over the Philippines as the year wore on. Although most of the party conventions were not scheduled to be held until December-January, it was already clear that the presidential race will be the biggest — and certainly the most fiercely contested — in Philippine electoral history.

House of Representatives Speaker Ramon Mitra and former defence secretary Fidel Ramos remained in a two-way struggle for the nomination of the ruling Lakas ng Demokratikong Pilipino (LDP), despite efforts by Aquino's relatives to promote the idea that she might seek a second term. Although the president persistently denied her intention to stand again, the rumours only seem to have harmed the LDP's cause and conveyed the impression that Mitra and Ramos did not have the confidence of influential party members.

Among the other presidential runners, disaffected Vice-President Salvador Laurel, Sen. Juan Ponce Enrile and former Marcos associate Eduardo "Danding" Cojuangco were engaged in a bitter fight for the opposition Nacionalista Party (NP) slot. The struggle came to a head in early November when Laurel, as NP president, expelled Enrile and Cojuangco for infringing party rules.

Cojuangco and Enrile each called separate sessions of what they claimed was the party's national directorate, on 12 and 15 November, during which they engineered the ejection of Laurel — and each other — from the NP. There are now three claimants to the divided party's name, all of whom think they can win next May's election.

Other possible candidates included senator and former film actor Joseph Estrada and former agrarian reform secretary Miriam Defensor-Santiago, both of whom consistently topped the popularity polls during the year. While neither have the money nor a recognisable party machine, in the sort of tight contest that is expected they could still have a major impact on the outcome.

For the Commission on Elections — the body responsible for running the polls — the prospect of electoral chaos loomed following the failure of efforts to "desynchronise" the presidential, congressional and local elections. Political wrangling ended efforts to stagger polling in all three elections, and now the country's 31 million voters will have to write down as many as 51 names on a blank ballot paper.

For many, the prospect of anarchic elections have revived widely held fears of a return to the "guns, goons and gold" syndrome that previously dominated Philippine politics. Election officials have already identified the northern Luzon provinces, Nueva Ecija in central Luzon, Masbate in southern Luzon and Muslim-dominated western Mindanao as the worst potential trouble-spots, but they warned there could also be violence in other areas where some of the old-established families are making a comeback after the setbacks of 1986-88.

Aquino: end of term.

The Aquino cabinet remained basically intact for much of the year, though there was one important exception. After replacing executive secretary Catalino Macaraig in late December 1990 in an effort to galvanise the presidential Malacanang Palace, 40-year-old former congressman Oscar Orbos lasted barely seven months before he was replaced by justice secretary Franklin Drilon. The president is said to have become irritated at Orbos' frequent absences from the palace and at a series of news leaks, which she seemed to blame on him.

Perhaps Aquino's most important — and controversial — decision during the year was to overlook seniority as the main factor in the selection process and appoint Gen. Lisandro Abadia as the new Armed Forces of the Philippines (AFP) chief of staff and Maj.-Gen. Arturo Enrile as army commander. The mid-April promotions, which leapfrogged Abadia over 46 other more senior generals, marked the ascendancy of the Philippine Military Academy's class of 1962 — a group of 55 alumni that is now expected to dominate key positions in the AFP until the mid- or late 1990s.

Significantly, Abadia and Enrile quickly set about trying to establish a bridge to the rebel Reform the Armed Forces Movement (RAM) and the Young Officers' Union (YOU), which had already suffered a major setback on 2 February with the capture of chief RAM strategist Lieut-Col Victor Batac and YOU leader Maj. Abraham Purugganan within hours of each other. The arrests seemed the clearest sign so far that the rebels were in no position to carry out their threat of another coup, despite the bombing of Drilon's house and foiled attacks on Basa airbase and a Manila oil refinery.

Although indirect contacts between the two sides began some time after Abadia's appointment, it was not until late August or early September that he had a face-to-face meeting with fugitive RAM leader Gregorio Honasan. Over the next month, an increasing number of hold-outs began giving themselves up, culminating on 1 November with the announced surrender of Eduardo "Red" Kapunan, who along with Batac and Honasan had formed the core group of RAM, and 14 other rebel officers.

All this does not necessarily mean the end of the threat.

Instead, it seemed to reflect recognition that with a more enlightened military leadership in power and the country looking ahead to the 1992 elections, there was little to gain from remaining underground. The rebels may also have been encouraged by a new sense of confidence and assertiveness being shown by Abadia, which many observers believe the notoriously short-sighted civilian political structure would be wise not to ignore.

Apart from the apparent conciliatory moves towards the military rebels, talks were also initiated in September with the National Democratic Front (NDF), the front organisation for the Communist Party of the Philippines (CPP) and its military arm, the New People's Army (NPA). At least two meetings were held in Hongkong within weeks of each other involving Netherlands-based NDF leader Luis Jalandoni, Philippine National Police chief-of-staff Maj.-Gen. Gerardo Flores and AFP intelligence chief Brig.-Gen. Alfredo Filler.

The talks came only a month after agents caught NPA chief Romulo Kintanar and his wife, CPP finance commission secretary Gloria Jopson. The pair, who had recently undergone cosmetic surgery, were among 13 key functionaries captured in Metro-Manila during a week-long period. Government agents also uncovered the NPA's main Manila communications centre and seized an intelligence treasure trove of more than 400 computer disks from a string of newly identified NPA safehouses.

Overall, the communist movement continued to decline in strength and organisation as the army concentrated its attention on two of the NPA's strongest base areas — the Marag Valley in northern Kalinga-Apayao province and Mindanao's northeastern coastal province of Surigao del Sur. But though military leaders were predicting a so-called strategic victory by the end of 1992, senate armed services committee chairman Ernesto Maceda remained sceptical that the AFP's vaunted "seize-hold-consolidate" strategy was working as well as advertised.

# Foreign Relations

Filipino students in future will have another landmark date to memorise when they open their history books — 16 September 1991. On that day, 12 members of the 23-strong Philippine Senate, four more than were actually needed, voted to reject a controversial proposed treaty which would have allowed the US navy to remain at its Subic Bay base for another 10 years.

Clark airbase and the nearby Crow Valley combat practice range had ceased to be part of the bases equation on 15 June when they were effectively destroyed by the eruption of the Mt Pinatubo volcano. But that disaster, and the resulting widespread unemployment across Central Luzon, failed to sway those senators who wanted the US military out of the Philippines.

As the year drew to a close, the US and Philippine governments were negotiating a withdrawal agreement which could give the US navy up to three years to pull out of Subic. US officials, however, still hold out the hope that the next Philippine administration may want to consider a limited access arrangement, similar to that which the US has with Singapore.

In the interim the US will begin to slim down its military presence, which has been a major factor in Philippine life for the best part of a century. Under current planning, Subic's replenishment capabilities will be moved to Guam, while the base's ship-repair work will be parcelled out to yards in Singapore, Japan, Hawaii and possibly Malaysia. The Philippine Government has plans to turn Subic over to commercial work, but the US navy says this will depend on its ability to maintain the present level of expertise and whether it can offer competitive prices.

The senators who voted against the treaty — Jovito Salonga, Agapito Aquino, Juan Ponce Enrile, Joseph Estrada, Teofista Guingona, Sotero Laurel, Ernesto Maceda, Orlando Mercado, Aquilino Pimentel, Rene Saguisag, Wigberto Tanada and Victor Ziga — did so for a multitude of reasons, ranging from an unacceptable level of compensation to a constitutional ban on nuclear weapons.

Those senators who voted for the treaty were Herherson Alverez, Edgardo Angara, Neptali Gonzales, Ernesto Herrera, Jose Lina, John Osmena, Vicente Paterno, Santanina Rasul, Alberto Romulo, Leticia Shahani and Mamintal Tomano. Although dissatisfied with the monetary terms, most based their "yes" vote on the country's sagging economy and on the effect the base closures would have on employment — particularly in Angeles City and Olongapo.

Efforts to resolve the bases issue went back to May 1990, when US and Philippine negotiators first met to decide whether they had anything to talk about. While the US initially assumed the Philippine Government was at least willing to grant a new lease extension, it quickly became clear that Foreign Secretary Raul Manglapus and his team were seeking not only to extract as many concessions as possible but also to impress a critical domestic audience.

In a process which US special negotiator Richard Armitage was later to describe as "intense, acerbic, abrasive, yet cathartic," the two panels skirted the key issues of duration and compensation until the fourth round of talks in early January. Then Manila suddenly called for a five-year phase out of the bases and an end to all US military activity in the Philippines beyond 16 September 1996.

Armitage, who had annoyed Manglapus months before by accusing him of pursuing "cash-register diplomacy," responded angrily, saying "as Americans prepare to fight and die in the Middle East, Filipinos define their own victory in terms of how many and how quickly US forces can be removed from their country."

During the fifth round of talks in February, Washington unveiled an annual US$360 million compensation package while holding out the prospect of a range of other benefits depending on how long US forces could stay. Manila, for its part, demanded US$825 million a year for a seven-year lease — US$400 million in cash and US$425 million in the form of an unspecified debt-reduction package and greater trade concessions. Once again, US negotiators pointed out that budgetary constraints and events in Eastern Europe had changed the rules of the game.

The two sides remained deadlocked through a sixth negotiating session in early May. Then, on 15 June, Mt Pinatubo intervened. With Clark and Crow Valley out of the picture, the US negotiators dropped their offer to US$360 million for the first year of a new 10-year accord and US$203 million for the remaining nine years, along with other non-related assistance, in a package amounting to an estimated US$4.5 billion over the total period. On 17 July, the Philippine Government decided it was better than nothing and accepted.

The Senate's position, however, had hardened and by the time it voted on 16 September — only hours before the expiration of the Military Bases Agreement — it was already clear the treaty would be killed. President Corazon Aquino quickly announced that she would hold a national referendum on the issue, but barely 10 days later she had backed away from the idea in the face of an expected legal challenge in the Supreme Court. At the same time, the Senate sought to lessen the impact of its decision by agreeing to a longer withdrawal period.

Although the Philippines has long been little more than a sleeping partner in Asean, it did begin to take a more constructive interest in the regional grouping during the year. At the Asean foreign ministers' meeting in Kuala Lumpur in July, Manglapus called for a treaty on economic cooperation, in essence seeking to revitalise one aspect of the alliance that has been neglected for the past decade. The idea was broadly accepted at the Asean economic ministers' meeting in Kuala Lumpur in October and seems destined once again to become a live issue.

In early June, while Washington and Manila continued to haggle over the bases issue, the Philippine Department of Foreign Affairs and the Thai Foreign Ministry co-hosted a conference in Manila to discuss the way events in Eastern Europe and the Soviet Union had affected security perceptions in the region. Although there seems to be little interest in a defence cooperation pact, the discussions indicated that security is still likely to remain a priority item on the association's agenda.

Newly appointed Philippine military leaders also made a point of calling on their Asean counterparts, in what appeared to be the beginning of an unprecedented new approach for a country which had traditionally relied on the US to underwrite its security. The visit by Armed Forces of the Philippines chief of staff Gen. Lisandro Abadia to Malaysia, in particular, went at least part of the way towards smoothing over past differences between Manila and Kuala Lumpur.

Ties between the Philippines and Taiwan, linked by an informal though nevertheless fruitful relationship, were less smooth. A serious row broke out early in the year after the Philippine navy impounded eight Taiwanese fishing boats for operating on the Philippine side of the Luzon Strait — a disputed area since the 1970s when both countries declared overlapping 320-km maritime economic zones.

Subsequent negotiations — first in Manila in June and then in Taipei the following month — ended in an agreement designating a specific sealane through which Taiwanese fishing boats would be allowed to pass into the Pacific Ocean. All this talk, however, did nothing to placate Peking, which felt impelled to remind Manila of its stated one-China policy on a number of occasions.

Probably the most important visitor during the year was then Japanese prime minister Toshiki Kaifu, who visited Manila in early May during a Southeast Asian tour. Kaifu arrived a day after delivering a major policy speech in Singapore that had signalled a greater political role for Japan in Asia. His visit coincided with that of a Japanese navy minesweeping flotilla which stopped over at Subic Bay on its way to the Gulf.

For Manglapus, however, 1991 was not a year he will look back on with any relish. First there was the failed bases treaty. Then there was moment when he forgot that the man he still thought was the Philippine ambassador to Moscow had left the post months before. Finally, it was alleged by self-styled US mercenary Jack Terrell that he had been hired by Manglapus to kill military rebel leader Gregorio Honasan and other political opponents of President Corazon Aquino. While Manglapus strongly denied the charges, he did acknowledge having several meetings with Terrell. To most observers, the entire affair seemed highly implausible, but the Senate armed services committee decided to investigate in order to resolve the matter. □

# Economy/Infrastructure

By the close of 1991, the Philippine economy had returned to nearly the same parlous state it had been 12 months earlier, despite some promising flickers of life during the year.

The IMF's decision not to renew the extension of its "seal of good-housekeeping" meant that US$2.5 billion in approved official loans would not be disbursed until Manila undertook effective measures to correct its budget deficits. The IMF move also prevented implementation of the country's third major debt-restructuring package, which would have converted about US$5.3 billion in commercial bank loans to the Philippine public sector into long-term loans or have retired it through a buy-back operation.

Nevertheless, there has been some improvement in debt-service ratios on the country's US$28.85 billion foreign liabilities over the past few years. While still a drag on the economy, the debt-to-GNP ratio has fallen from its 1985 peak of 82% to 61% for 1991 and the debt-service ratio has decreased to 28% from 36% in 1985.

Apart from growth in GNP, this reduction was due to two factors. First, the debt-for-equity swap scheme, reopened in 1991, had retired foreign loans amounting to US$2.8 billion since the programme's launching in 1987. Second, a major debt-buyback operation which retired US$1.34 billion in foreign loans was completed in January 1990.

Economic recovery seemed to be imminent during the first months of the year. The swift end of the Gulf War brought down oil prices, interest rates were drifting lower, the IMF had given the go-ahead for the disbursement of about US$715 million in foreign loans, and the stockmarket surged to become Asia's best performing bourse.

But GNP declined 0.23% in the first half of the year, and towards the end of 1991 the economy seemed likely to post a gain of no more than 1%. This represented a steep downturn for an administration which had presided over an annual average growth rate of 4.6% over the 1986-90 period.

In January, a 9% additional import levy had been imposed as an emergency measure to raise government revenues to help cover a budget deficit estimated to hit P36 billion (US$1.35 billion) during the year. The levy led unsurprisingly to a contraction of imports, which in turn threw the import-dependent economy into recession. In the face of sustained public

JOHN McBETH

**Mt Pinatubo: force majeure.**

pressure against the levy, the government reduced it to 5% in September and exempted capital and raw material imports by industries registered with the Board of Investments.

A further problem during the year was the unexpected strengthening of the peso to P27 to US$1, after the local currency was effectively devalued from P24 to P28 in November 1990. This was the first time since the country adopted a floating-rate foreign-exchange system that the peso had appreciated. Its rise was due to a combination of factors: the contraction in imports as a result of the 9% levy, a new central bank regulation restricting the amount of US dollars commercial banks could hold and the sudden inflow of foreign credits after the IMF reopened the loan tap on 21 February.

The peso's upward shift put the central bank in a quandary, for in order to prevent the currency from appreciating further — which would dampen Philippine exports — it had to purchase US$1.3 billion from the foreign-exchange market. This meant that the central bank had to release roughly P35 billion into the system, while at the same time siphoning of money by issuing Treasury bills at a rate of P5 billion a week as a means of controlling inflation.

Inflation was being stoked by such factors as increased tariffs by privately owned power distribution companies and rising petroleum product prices, in addition to the peso's appreciation and the expansion of the money supply. Annualised inflation was logged at 19.6% at end-June, though the tightening of monetary policy seemed to bring rising consumer prices under control in the last quarter of the year, with the October rate posted at 17.3%.

The silver lining, though, was that the central bank's purchases beefed up the country's international reserves to an end-September level of US$3.6 billion, the highest ever recorded in the Philippines. These reserves have also given the central bank enough resources to prevent speculation on the US dollar when it decides to allow a depreciation of the peso as a means of injecting vigour into the lacklustre export sector.

The issuance of Treasury bills to cover budget deficits kept Philippine interest rates up, which at over 20% were among the highest in Asia. Some modest gains were made in 1991 towards solving the problem the bills had created, with the conversion of about P30 billion in 90-day bills held by the social security system into three-year Treasury notes.

Overall though, pressure from budget deficits is unlikely to ease soon. Rehabilitation costs to cope with the aftermath of the Mt Pinatubo eruption reached P5 billion, with more to come. In addition, a Supreme Court restraining order in late 1990 that prevented the National Power Corp. (Napocor) from raising its electricity tariffs led to an estimated P4-7 billion in losses — most of which the government has to cover.

The Napocor issue threatened the country's economic stabilisation programme with the IMF, which was holding back standby credit tranches until it is convinced Manila can untangle the Napocor problem — mainly through increased power rates. The state-owned company's financial mess also means it is unlikely Napocor will be able to undertake the rapid construction of new power plants in order to alleviate the country's chronic electricity shortages.

The 1991 budget deficit was estimated at P18.7 billion, and is forecast to nearly double to P32.1 billion in 1992. To raise revenues in the face of Congressional recalcitrance over imposing new tax measures, the government is rushing to sell off government holdings in Philippine Airlines, Philippine National Bank, the Manila Hotel, the Philippine Associated Smelting and Refining Corp., the Philippines Phosphate and Fertiliser Corp. and the National Steel Corp. The government expects to generate at least P4.7 billion from the sale of these assets.

Against that, the Treasury bills' interest payments have worsened the deficit. For the year to end-September, interest payments on government domestic debt reached P41 billion, three times the equivalent P14 billion paid for foreign debt.

The country's agricultural sector, which accounts for 22% of GDP, propped up the economy. For the first half of the year, the sector grew 3.5%, while manufacturing declined 0.7%. But the industry which really pulled down GDP growth was construction, which fell 27.2% during the period. This stemmed from a plateauing in condominium and shopping mall–oriented private construction and a slowdown in government infrastructure projects. The service sector, accounting for 42% of GDP, expanded by only 1.1%.

The decline in economic output would have been steeper if not for overseas workers' remittances, estimated to have amounted to US$680 million in the first half of the year. This represented a 20% increase from the level during the second

## Data

**Major industries** (Jan.-Aug. 1991): Food processing, US$1.43 billion (US$1.19 billion); electronics, US$486.9 million (US$348.3 million); chemicals, fertilisers, US$187.2 million (US$146 million); sugar, US$63.6 million (US$52.4 million).

**Major imports** (1990): Raw materials and intermediate goods, US$5.8 billion (US$5.38 billion); capital goods, US$3.12 billion (US$2.42 billion); mineral fuels and lubricants, US$1.84 billion (US$1.39 billion); consumer goods, US$1.06 billion (US$898 million).

**Major exports** (1990): Manufactured goods, US$5.7 billion (US$5.19 billion); mineral products, US$723 million (US$829 million); coconut products, US$503 million (US$541 million); other agro-based products, US$431 million (US$454 million); fruits and vegetables, US$326 million (US$319 million); petroleum, US$155 million (US$95 million); sugar products, US$133 million (US$113 million); forest products, US$94 million (US$197 million).

**Crude oil** (Jan.-Aug. 1991): 50.7 million barrels (63.2 million Jan.-Sept. 1990).

**Tourism and transport:** Arrivals (Jan.-Aug. 1991): 600,938 (715,698 all 1990). Total visitor expenditure (Jan.-June 1991): US$587.8 million (US$709.33 million all 1990).

**Finance:** 32 commercial banks; 26 private domestic banks, 4 foreign banks branches and 2 government banks. 160 companies listed at both exchanges at Manila and Makati.

**Major banks:** Philippine National Bank, PNB Bldg, Escolta, Manila, tel. 402051, fax 496091; Bank of the Philippine Islands, BPI Bldg, Paseo de Roxas, Makati, Metro-Manila, tel. 8177936; Metropolitan Bank and Trust Co., Metrobank Plaza Bldg, Sen. Gil Puyat Av., Makati, Metro-Manila, tel. 8103311; Far East Bank and Trust Co., Muralla St, Intramuros, Manila, tel. 401021, fax 479263; Citibank, 8741 Paseo de Roxas, Makati, Metro-Manila, tel. 8139333, fax 8157703; Philippine Commercial International Bank, PCIBANK Towers, Makati Av., Makati, Metro-Manila, tel. 8171021; United Coconut Planters Bank, UCPB Bldg, Makati Av., Makati, Metro-Manila, tel. 8188361, fax 8151179; Land Bank of the Philippines, 319 Sen. Gil Puyat Av. Extension, Makati, Metro-Manila, tel. 874204, fax 8161350; Rizal Commercial Banking Corp., 333 Sen. Gil Puyat Av. Extension, Makati, Metro-Manila, tel. 8193061; Equitable Banking Corp., 262 Juan Luna St, Binondo, Manila, tel. 407011; Allied Banking Corp., Allied Bank Centre, corner Makati/ Ayala Av., Makati, Metro-Manila, tel. 8163311, fax 8160047. Solidbank Corp., Solidbank Bldg, Dasmarinas St, Binondo, Manila, tel. 49431119; Prudential Bank, Prudential Bank Bldg, 6787 Ayala Av., Makati, Metro-Manila, tel. 8178981; China Banking Corp., Paseo de Roxas, Makati, Metro-Manila, tel. 8177981; Citytrust Banking Corp., 379 Gil Puyat Av., Makati, Metro-Manila, tel. 8180411.

**Currency:** Philippine peso. P26.7 = US$1 Nov. 1991 (P27.944 = US$1 Nov. 1990).

**Chambers of Commerce:** Makati Business Club, 2/F, Princess Bldg, 104 Esteban St, Legaspi Village, Makati, Metro-Manila, tel. 8162660/861608; Philippine Chamber of Commerce and Industry, ODC International Plaza, Makati, Metro-Manila, tel. 8176981; Japanese Chamber of Commerce and Industry, 6/F, Jaycem Bldg, 104 Rada St, Legaspi Village, Makati, Metro-Manila; American Chamber of Commerce, 2/F, Corinthian Plaza, Paseo de Roxas St, Makati, Metro-Manila, tel. 8187911; European Chamber of Commerce, 5/F, Kings Court 2 Bldg, 2129 Pasong Tamo corner dela Rosa Sts, Makati, Metro-Manila, tel. 866995; Federation of Filipino-Chinese Chambers of Industry and Commerce, Federation Centre Bldg, Muelle de Binondo, corner Dasmarinas Sts, Binondo, Manila, tel. 474921; Taiwan Chamber of Commerce and Industry, 8/F, Sagittarius Bldg, dela Costa St, Salcedo Village, Makati, Metro-Manila, tel. 8190068/8190323; Indian Chamber of Commerce, 5/F, Campos Rueda & Sons Bldg, 101, Urban Av., Makati, Metro-Manila, tel. 867222.

**Public holidays** (1992): 1 Jan. (New Year), 9 Apr. (Araw ng Kagitingan), 16 Apr. (Holy Thursday), 17 Apr. (Good Friday), 1 May (Labour Day), 12 June (Independence Day), 30 Nov. (Bonifacio Day), 25 Dec. (Christmas), 30 Dec. (Rizal Day).

**Weather:** The Philippine climate is tropical, with a wet season between June-Nov. and a dry season between Dec.-May. Hottest time of year between Mar.-June. Typhoon season between May-Nov.

**Taxation:** Individual, progressive taxation; corporate, 35%; value-added tax of 10% on goods and services. All inward and outward remittances of foreign exchange need to be registered with the Central Bank of the Philippines. Foreign investments must be registered with the Central Bank and the Board of Investments. Foreign equity participation in certain vital industries is limited to 30-40%.

half of 1990, a rebound largely due to the rapid end of the Gulf War. Towards the end of the year, more encouraging signs for the economy became evident. The country seemed to have overcome its fear of the potential impact on business confidence resulting from the withdrawal of US military bases, though this is at least partially rooted in the three-year withdrawal period.

Surprisingly, and despite the recession, direct foreign investment from January to August grew 44% to US$285.9 million, bringing total investment from 1970 — when the government first started monitoring these inflows — to US$3.3 billion. Although the pace of their investments has slowed, US firms accounted for the major slice at US$1.8 billion, with Japan investments totalling US$502.4 million.

One improvement in the Philippine investment climate was the passage into law of the Foreign Investments Act, which corrects discretionary and vague aspects in the regulatory framework by specifying a "negative list" of industries in which foreign capital is restricted. Manila's success in enacting the law signals a significant shift in the country's anti-foreign capital sentiment, itself a reaction to the oligopolistic position of US firms from the pre-war period up to the 1960s. The momentum could lead to a revision of the 1948 banking law that would open the financial system to foreign banks.

Another development was the consensus reached for a tariff-reform package. Although it also reflected the power of entrenched groups in the country, as it stretched the original one-step lowering of tariff rates over a five-year period, the passage of Executive Order No. 470 is considered significant as it will eventually change the decades-old tariff system and reduce the country's effective protection rate from 25% to 19% by 1995.

The stockmarket index, after dipping to a low of 902 on 12 September from its pre-Pinatubo high of 1,178 points, rebounded to reach the 1,000-mark three weeks later. Most players are expecting the stockmarket to rise towards the May 1992 elections, since the first year of a new administration could mean a surge in optimism over the country's economic prospects. The economy continues to be propped up by official development assistance (ODA) loans. ODA inflows in the first half totalled US$1.7 billion, which together with the accounting procedure of treating rescheduled loans as new inflows allowed the country to post a balance-of-payments surplus of US$1.1 billion despite a trade deficit of US$1.8 billion.

Despite budget deficits, several high-visibility infrastructure projects in Metro Manila were launched in 1991. These included two major interchange construction projects costing P679 million: one at the rapidly expanding commercial-financial centre at the Ortigas–Epifanio de los Santos (Edsa) intersection and the second at the Ramon Magsaysay Avenue–Nagtahan bridge crossing, both of which have been major chokepoints in Manila's traffic system.

Also started were the 10-lane extension of Edsa to Roxas Boulevard, which will mean easier access between the Makati financial district and Manila's bay-front area, and the six-lane Araneta Avenue that will interconnect with Rizal Avenue by the end of the year.

Major infrastructure projects elsewhere in the country started in 1991 included improvement of the coastal road from Manila to Cavite, which has proved to be a key factor for the area's rapid growth as a site for foreign-oriented industrial estates. A P938 million road project was also started to link Laguna and Quezon provinces and stimulate business activity within the so-called Calabarzon area (Cavite, Laguna, Batangas, Rizal and Quezon), which the government hopes will become the leading growth area in Luzon.  □

# SINGAPORE

JOHOR (MALAYSIA)

Johor Straits · Woodlands New Town
Nee Soon
Bukit Mandai
Yio Chu Kang
Bukit Panjang
Choa Chu Kang · Bulim
Ang Mo Kio New Town
Serangoon
Paya Lebar
Ubin Is.
Johor Straits
Tekong Is.
Changi
Jurong Industrial Estate
Tuas
Bukit Timah
Toa Payoh New Town
Bedok New Town
Queenstown
Buona Vista
Southern Is.
Telok Blangah New Town
Sentosa
Singapore Straits
0    2    4 km

S ingapore is believed to have been a thriving port in the 7th century, but when the British arrived under Sir Stamford Raffles in 1819 it was inhabited only by a small Malay community.

Under Raffles the island developed rapidly from 1819, and in 1832 it became the centre of government for the newly created Straits Settlements and later a thriving entrepot for the Malayan hinterland and much of the region.

Despite the construction of a massive naval base and extensive fortifications after World War I, Singapore fell to the advancing Japanese in 1942, an event that helped undermine the British colonial mandate throughout its pre-war empire.

Singapore became internally self-governing in 1959 and formed part of Malaysia from 1963-65. Following deep differences with Kuala Lumpur, however, Singapore separated from Malaysia on 9 August 1965 to become fully independent.

On 22 December 1965, Singapore was declared a republic headed by a president. Since 1959, the island has been ruled by the People's Action Party headed by Lee Kuan Yew.

Lee handed over the prime ministership to Goh Chok Tong on 29 November 1990, but continues to remain in the cabinet as a senior minister.

**Head of State**
President Wee Kim Wee.
**Prime Minister**
Goh Chok Tong;
**Senior Minister**
Lee Kuan Yew;
**Deputy Prime Minister**
Ong Teng Cheong;
**Deputy Prime Minister, Trade and Industry**
Lee Hsien Loong;
**National Development**
S. Dhanabalan;
**Education**
Tony Tan;
**Environment, Muslim Affairs**
Ahmad Mattar;
**Defence**
Yeo Ning Hong;

**Law, Home Affairs**
S. Jayakumar;
**Finance**
Richard Hu Tsu Tau;
**Labour, Education**
Lee Yock Suan;
**Foreign Affairs**
Wong Kan Seng;
**Health, Community Development**
Yeo Cheow Tong;
**Information, Arts**
George Yeo Yong Boon;
**Communications**
Mah Bow Tan;
**Attorney-General**
Tan Boon Teik;
**Chief Justice**
Yong Pung How;
**Armed Forces Chief-of-Staff**
Maj.-Gen. Winston Choo.

## Politics/Social Affairs

S ome nine months into his premiership, Goh Chok Tong felt "the ground was sweet" and called a snap election on 31 August 1991 to seek endorsement for his consultative style of government. The results, however, represented a clear setback for both Goh personally and his young cabinet. Four members of the opposition parties were elected, two junior ministers lost their seats and the ruling People's Action Party's (PAP) share of votes cast fell to 59.7%.

The opposition's strong showing vindicated the electoral strategy of Chiam See Tong, leader of the Singapore Democratic Party, which won three of the four opposition seats and 47.5% of the votes cast in the nine constituencies his party contested. Chiam had previously been the lone opposition voice in parliament.

Chiam campaigned on the need for a strong opposition, and said the polls should be treated as a by-election because Goh had already received the mandate he sought when 41 of the 81 seats held by the PAP were returned unopposed on nomination day.

After the elections, Goh warned that the PAP would close ranks in parliament and said there would be no more government parliamentary committees headed by back-benchers who questioned ministers closely on policy. He later softened his stance and said the committees would continue — being the public's only vehicle for expressing views directly to the government — but PAP MPs would no longer play their past critical roles since there was now a strong opposition.

The poll results showed the electorate's rejection of the PAP's decade-long campaign to persuade them that there was no need for an opposition in Singapore. The government had created an opening for non-PAP voices in parliament by allowing the entry of up to six non-constituency MPs (NCMP, in effect, runners-up in vote counts) and nominated MPs (NMP). But following the poll, the seats left for NCMPs were occupied by the four elected opposition MPs in the new parliament, leaving the two NMPs caught between a ruling party sensitive about its fall in popularity and opposition MPs conscious of their growing strength. The PAP's victory was virtually assured by the redrawing of constituency boundaries and the re-classification of several into new and larger group representation constituencies (GRC), wherein the four seats in each had to be contested on a party ticket and one of the seats had to be occupied by either a Malay or a non-Chinese candidate. There were 21 single-constituency seats and the remaining 60 seats were in 15 GRCs. Twenty single constituencies and five GRCs were contested. Only the opposition Workers' Party had non-Chinese candidates and was able to contest the GRCs, though Low Thia Khiang won a seat in a Teochew-dialect dominated housing estate — one of the three PAP heartlands that crossed over to the opposition.

Local commentators attributed the PAP losses, and Chiam's larger margin of victory, to dissatisfaction among the lower-income groups with rising costs stemming from changes in education, transport and health-care policies that many saw as benefiting the elite more than the working classes. Goh's predecessor, Senior Minister Lee Kuan Yew saw the election result as a message of resentment from the Chinese-educated population about policies seen to benefit the minorities — Malays, Indians and the English-educated Chinese.

"It is important to read the signals correctly," Lee said. "The mainly Chinese-educated lower-middle and lower-income groups feel they have been neglected . . . Neither the Malays nor the English-educated are the centre of Singapore society. The Chinese mass base has reminded the government of their weight." Lee extended this interpretation into a comment that some ministers — including Goh — were unable to read Chinese newspapers or speak Mandarin and therefore unable to represent a larger segment of the population.

With the focus on ill-defined dissatisfaction among the Chinese-educated, the emphasis then shifted — with Lee's help — to the issue of Chinese language in schools. The Mandarin lobby — which had persistently called on the government to force more ethnic Chinese schoolchildren to study Mandarin as a first language — was unhappy with new streaming arrangements that proposed offering ethnic Chinese children who are weak in languages the easier option of taking only oral tests in Mandarin. Lee called on the Chinese clan associations to run Mandarin schools, in effect asking them to take over responsibility for maintaining the Chinese language in Singapore. Although Goh said he supported the idea, the clans baulked.

But the lobby won a concession in early November, when Goh's Chinese-educated deputy Ong Teng Cheong announced the scrapping of the untried oral option and its replacement by a system requiring reading knowledge of either Mandarin, English, Malay or Tamil in addition to oral tests. At the same time, the government announced that either Mandarin, Malay or Tamil could be the first language of instruction if parents desired. Lee cautioned the lobby against repeating the government's mistake with language in schools for future generations. English, he said, was the language of technology and business and many children could not cope with the pressure of learning two first languages.

**Goh: tested at the polls.**

Meanwhile, Goh, after nearly six weeks of silence on the implications of the election results, said during a visit to the Commonwealth Heads of Government meeting in Zimbabwe that his government would try to "balance" the interests of all groups. Goh bemoaned the fact that Singaporeans were using the ballot box to pressure the government on issues, including a highly unpopular switch to usage-based telephone charges. The prime minister was seen as particularly sensitive to such pressures, not least because of his pledge during and after the election campaign to again test his government's popularity through by-elections some 12-18 months after the August polls.

Goh made the undertaking when critics suggested the elections had been timed to prevent Workers' Party leader J. B. Jeyaretnam from taking part. Jeyaretnam's five-year ban from contesting a parliamentary seat expired on 10 November. Goh did not clarify how he would ensure that by-elections would take place.

Earlier in the year, parliament finally passed legislation converting the present ceremonial post of president into a directly elected executive position with wide-ranging powers over financial affairs and senior government, statutory board and military appointments. Candidates cannot be members of political parties, though parties can campaign for candidates. The incumbent, President Wee Kim Wee, assumed the powers provided by the bill and the first presidential elections will be held when his term expires in 1993.

After the bill's passage on 3 January, Goh turned his

attention to the creation of a national ideology called "shared values" based on Confucian or Asian traditions. The five shared values were itemised as: nation before community and society above self, the family as the basic unit of society, respect and community support for the individual, consensus instead of conflict and racial and religious harmony. Enthusiasm for the bill was largely confined to the cabinet — with the notable exception of Lee, who questioned its practicality — and the campaign to promote this ideology soon ran out of steam.

Early into his premiership, Goh said the then newly created Ministry of Information and the Arts would review the country's rigid censorship laws. In February, the government granted a month-long temporary licence enabling financial institutions to receive US-owned Cable News Network satellite-transmitted broadcasts so they would have timely information on potential market-moving events such as the Gulf War.

Goh's administration also lifted the more than two decades long ban on former leftwing politicians active in the 1950-60s. These included such founding members of the PAP as Abdul Samad Ismail — banned in 1976 — and James Puthucheary, who had been exiled to Malaysia.

But despite much talk of openness since Goh became prime minister, the only specific relaxation applied to film censorship. On 1 June, Singapore's cinemas showed a flood of soft-porn movies under a new film classification. Malay opposition candidates campaigned against the relaxation, and Goh admitted that older conservatives had also expressed unhappiness. The government, upset that it became an election issue, decided after the ballot to replace the system and only allow R-rated movies with "artistic merit."

Legislation to control the press and restrict political activity remained on the books. However, from 1 October, the government allowed the *Asian Wall Street Journal* (AWSJ) to circulate 2,500 copies following a stormy relationship over three years in which the newspaper's circulation had been restricted to 400 copies after being accused of engaging in domestic politics. On 11 January, the AWSJ, its editor and publisher were found to be in contempt of Singapore's courts and fined a total of S$9,000 (US$5,360) for comments made by Peter Kann, president of Dow Jones Inc. — which publishes the newspaper and the *Far Eastern Economic Review* — on the verdict of an earlier libel case brought by Lee against the RE-VIEW which the magazine had lost.

In May, the results of the 1990 population census were released. They put Singapore's total population at 3,002,800, of whom 2,690,100 were Singaporeans and foreign citizens with permanent residence permits. The census showed that the Chinese majority had slipped slightly from 78.3% in 1980 to 77.7% in 1990, while the Indian percentage had risen from 6.3% to 7.1% in that same decade. The number of Malays had declined slightly from 14.4% a decade ago to 14.1%.

The declining fertility rate among the Chinese population seems to have been halted since 1987, when new policies encouraging people to have more children were introduced. However, the proportion of Chinese women in the 25-39 age group who remained unmarried rose from 35.2% to 42.3% in 1990, while the number of unmarried Malay women in the same age group declined from 25.6% to 24.9%.

The percentage of Christians increased from 10% in 1980 to 13% in 1990 — the majority religion being Buddhism or Taoism at 68%. Nearly 20% of all households now use English at home, a sharp increase from 12% in 1980. The use of Mandarin rose even more sharply to 26%, compared with 10.2% in 1980, with a corresponding decline in the use of Chinese dialects from 59.5% in 1980 to 36.7% in 1990. In Chinese households, the use of English rose from 11% to 21% and the use of Mandarin from 13% to 33%. □

# Foreign Relations

The year was chiefly significant for events that tested the new leadership's ability to deal with difficulties involving Malaysia. The most serious of these developed as Singapore celebrated its 26th year as an independent republic in August, and was sparked by a joint Malaysian-Indonesian military exercise held around the same time in Malaysia's southern Johor state — separated from Singapore by a narrow strait.

However, all sides quickly sought to defuse the tension. Shortly after the exercise, Malaysia's armed forces commander-in-chief Lieut-Gen. Datuk Abdul Rahmad Hamid announced that Malaysia and Singapore would resume joint army exercises in 1992 after a two-year lapse.

Meanwhile, Singapore's President Wee Kim Wee presented Indonesian armed forces commander-in-chief Gen. Try Sutrisno with the country's highest military honour in recognition of his role in facilitating joint army exercises between the two countries and the development of training facilities for the Singapore and Indonesian air forces. A few days before, Singapore and Indonesia had signed an agreement to jointly develop an air-combat range near the east Sumatran town of Pekan Baru.

A potentially more serious dispute surfaced when Johor reasserted its claim to a small island off its coast where Singapore — which calls the island Pedra Branca while the Malaysians refer to it as Pulau Batu Putih — maintains a lighthouse. In October, Malaysia's Deputy Prime Minister Ghafar Babar told Malay leaders in Johor that while Singapore had said it would refer the Pedra Branca/Pulau Batu Putih dispute to the International Court of Justice in The Hague if consultations between the two countries' foreign ministries failed, Malaysia would nevertheless continue to claim ownership of the island.

Singapore's relations with Malaysia had been on edge since four Pakistanis hijacked a Singapore Airlines Airbus on a flight from Kuala Lumpur on 26 March. Singapore commandos stormed the aircraft after the hijackers — who demanded the release of several prisoners in Pakistan, including the husband of former prime minister Benazir Bhutto — threatened to start killing their hostages. All the hijackers were killed by the commandos and the 114 passengers released unharmed. There were accusations of slack security at Kuala Lumpur's Subang airport, though the matter faded when it was revealed that the hijackers' weapons consisted of a penknife and in-flight cutlery.

It was a high-profile year for the Singapore armed forces, which until recently had rarely sent its personnel overseas for anything other than training. A medical team was sent to assist the coalition forces in Saudi Arabia during the Gulf War, followed by a team that joined the UN-Iraq-Kuwait Observer Mission, another to the UN Angola Verification Mission and a third for a six-month mission in the Western Sahara, also under UN auspices.

In May, Minister for Information and the Arts George Yeo visited Hongkong, where he maintained that Singapore's position outside the relationship that linked the British colony with China and Taiwan could offer it a role as an intermediary in helping to settle disputes. Wee made a state visit to China in September, which further strengthened Singapore's relationship with Peking.

On 31 October, Vietnam's Prime Minister Vo Van Kiet visited Singapore with the aim of normalising diplomatic relations that had been suspended since Vietnam's invasion of Cambodia in 1978. Minister of Trade and Industry Lee Hsien Loong said Singapore's ban on investment in Vietnam would be lifted shortly after the signing of the Cambodian peace treaty in Paris on 23 October. □

# Economy/Infrastructure

Confidence stemming from Singapore's protracted burst of strong economic growth and the short duration of the Gulf War in early 1991, gave way to a surprisingly strong note of pessimism by the year's third quarter.

This change in sentiment, however, was partly accounted for by previous excessive optimism rather than the mild — and some analysts maintained necessary — slowdown in an economy still expected to grow by 6.5% in 1991, against 8.3% in 1990 and slightly off the early 1991 forecast of 7.5%. But within Singapore, what stood out is that the growth rate will be the lowest since 1986, when GDP grew by just 1.8%.

After growth rates of 11.1% in 1988 and 9.2% in 1989, many analysts argued that the current slowdown was beneficial, in that continued high growth could overheat the economy whereas it will now have a chance to cool off and consolidate for the next upswing. The 1992 growth rate has been officially forecast at 5-7%.

Singapore's economy remains excessively dependent on trade. The value of its total trade is about three times that of GDP, and therefore the slowdown in the US — Singapore's largest trading partner — has had an effect. Nevertheless, the current slowdown also reflects such supply side constraints in the domestic economy as labour, which has traditionally been tight. Singapore's unemployment in the third quarter was 2.7%, which in practical terms means that the economy is operating at more than full employment.

This means that Singapore, with no labour to spare, will be unable to take advantage of any future external economic stimulus unless it imports more workers. The government, however, is reluctant to do this because it believes such a move could spark social problems, and also because it thinks cheap labour would discourage local industries from moving on to more automated and higher value-added activities.

The topic of imported labour is so sensitive in Singapore that the government does not release statistics on the number of foreign workers employed in the country. Analysts estimate, however, that Singapore must now have about 250,000 foreigners working in its industries, with the largest concentrations in the construction and ship-repair sectors. If accurate,

this would make the Singapore economy one of the most dependent on foreign labour in Asia, with overseas workers accounting for about 20% of the 1.3-million-strong local workforce.

Against this background, it is unsurprising that labour costs rose sharply in Singapore this year. Unit labour cost rose 6.4% in the second quarter while indirect taxes and levies rose an estimated 18%, both contributing heavily to rising business costs. The Singapore dollar, which in the third quarter was trading at a record level of S$1.69 to US$1, also helped slow the export-dependent economy.

First quarter GDP growth was 7.5%, which slipped to 7% in the second and to 6.5% in the third. A small open economy like Singapore cannot expect much help from domestic consumption, even if it were robust. However, in the event, private consumption — which grew by 5.4% in the first quarter — had dropped to 3.7% in the second quarter.

It was therefore left to external demand, mostly in the form of trade, to give the economy whatever momentum it had during the year. During the first seven months of 1991, export growth was 14.7% in nominal terms and import growth 11%, again in nominal terms. External demand growth was 9.1% in the second quarter, up from 7.7% in the first quarter.

With the US economy in recession in the first two quarters of the year, trade with the EC and Japan — Singapore's other two main trading partners — contributed to the total growth in trade. But as the EC and Japanese economies entered what is being viewed by many analysts as a slow growth period that will stretch from the second half of 1991 into early 1992, external stimulus from these sources will no longer be available to Singapore.

Growth was already moderating in such star sectors of the economy as manufacturing and the financial and business services in the second half of the year. The manufacturing growth rate had fallen to 6% in the second quarter compared with 10.3% in the first, while financial services had slowed in the same period to 9% compared with 10.2%. The construction sector was the exception, and grew by 17.1% in the second quarter, up from 12.7% in the first. But construction accounts for only about 5% of the total economy, and therefore this sector's strength was not enough to offset weakness elsewhere.

Singapore traditionally runs a deficit in its merchandise trade and 1990 — the last full year with available figures — was no exception. The deficit ran to S$9.3 billion, nearly twice as high as 1989's S$4.8 billion. However, massive foreign capital inflows more than made up for the trade deficit, and the 1990 current account ended with a surplus of S$4.3 billion. The overall balance of payments registered a massive surplus of S$9.9 billion, nearly twice as high as the S$5.3 billion achieved in 1989.

The Singapore Government's official foreign reserves — the sum total of the state's own surplus, the surpluses from government investments and the compulsory savings scheme operated for the entire workforce — totalled S$52 billion in September 1991. Almost all of this is now said to be invested abroad in the treasuries of the major developed countries and

**Growth of external trade**
(at current prices)

S$ billion — Left scale
%  — Right scale

| | 3Q 1989 | 4Q | 1Q 1990 | 2Q | 3Q | 4Q | 1Q 1991 | 2Q |

Import (Left scale) · Export (Left scale)
Total trade (Right scale) · Import (Right scale) · Export (Right scale)

Source: Singapore Economic Statistics

blue-chip corporate bonds. However, the government has announced it plans to convert more of its cash hoard into direct investments.

Another problem facing the Singapore economy was rising consumer price inflation, which climbed to 4% in June and July this year, and to 3.8% for the first half of 1991. While this may appear low, Singapore had not recorded an inflation rate of above 3% since 1983. One of the reasons the authorities allowed the Singapore dollar to run up to record levels, despite the negative impact it may have on exports, was to contain imported inflation.

Interest rates moved little during 1991. The prime rate started at 7% in the first quarter, rose to 7.5% in the second before slipping back to 7.25% in the third. Since Singapore's interest rates generally track those in the US — which have been easing — and since the government wants to keep rates low to boost the economy, they are not expected to rise sharply in the near future. □

# Data

**Major industries:** Electronic products and components, US$16.44 billion (US$14.7 billion); petroleum refineries and petroleum products, US$6.9 billion (US$5.22 billion); fabricated metal products excluding machinery and equipment, US$2.14 billion (US$2.11 billion); industrial chemicals and gases, US$1.92 billion (US$1.82 billion); electrical machinery and appliances, US$1.4 billion (US$1.49 billion).

**Major imports:** Machinery and transport equipment, US$29.2 billion (US$25.5 billion); mineral fuels, US$10.35 billion (US$8 billion); manufactured goods, US$8.43 billion (US$8.2 billion); chemicals, US$4.84 billion (US$4.41 billion).

**Major exports:** Machinery and transport equipment, US$28.41 billion (US$25.67 billion); mineral fuels, US$10.29 billion (US$8 billion); manufactured goods, US$3.96 billion (US$4.17 billion).

**Tourism and transport:** Arrivals, 5.32 million (4.83 million); Singapore Airlines national carrier; underground urban railway; extensive bus network and 11,000 taxis; car hire is widely available and cars can be driven into Malaysia.

(All figures for 1990 unless otherwise stated. Previous year in brackets.)

**Currency:** Singapore dollar (100 cents). S$1.6805 = US$1 in Nov. 1991 (S$1.7015 = US$1 Nov. 1990).

**Finance:** 13 local banks, 124 foreign banks, including 88 offshore. 180 companies listed on main board of the Stock Exchange of Singapore. A further 14 companies listed in the SESDAQ over-the-counter market and another 129 regional stocks quoted in the CLOB market, including 118 Malaysian.

**Major banks:** Bank of Singapore, Tong Eng Bldg, 101 Cecil St 01-02, 0106, tel. 2255577; DBS Bank, DBS Bldg, 6 Shenton Way, 0106, tel. 2201111; Far Eastern Bank, 156 Cecil St, 0106, tel. 2210955; Industrial and Commercial Bank, ICB Bldg, 2 Shenton Way, 0106, tel. 2211711; International Bank of Singapore, 02-01 Overseas Union Hse, 50 Collyer Quay, 0104, tel. 2234488; Oversea Chinese Banking Corp., OCBC Centre, 65 Chulia St, 0104, tel. 5357222; United Overseas Bank, 01-00 UOB Bldg, 1 Bonham St, Raffles Place, 0104, tel. 5339898.

**Government ministries:** Communications and Information, PSA Bldg, 36-00, 460 Alexandra Rd, 0511, tel. 270-7988; Community Development, 512 Thomson Rd, 1129, tel. 258-9595; Defence, Gombak Drive, 2366, tel. 760-8188; Education, Kay Siang Rd, 1024, tel. 473-9111; Environment, 40 Scotts Rd, 0922, tel. 732-7733; Finance, 8 Shenton Way, Treasury Bldg, 0106, tel. 225-9911; Foreign Affairs, 250 North Bridge Rd, 07-00, 0617, tel. 336-1177; Health, 16 College Rd, 0316, tel. 223-7777; Home Affairs, Phoenix Park, Tanglin Rd, 1024, tel. 235-9111; Labour, Havelock Rd, 0105, tel. 533-6141; Law, 250 North Bridge Rd, 21-00, 0617, tel. 336-1177; National Development, 7 Maxwell Rd, 5th Storey, tel. 222-1211; Trade and Industry, 8 Shenton Way, 48-01, Treasury Bldg, tel. 225-9911.

**Public holidays** (1992): 1 Jan. (New Year), 4-5 Feb. (Lunar New Year), 5 Apr. (Hari Raya Puasa), 17 Apr. (Easter), 1 May (Labour Day), 17 May (Vesak Day*), 11 June (Hari Raya Haji), 9 Aug. (National Day*), 24 Oct. (Deepavali), 25 Dec. (Christmas).

(* Following Monday a public holiday.)

**Weather:** Singapore has a tropical climate, with regular high daytime temperatures and high relative humidity. Average maximum daily temperature is 30.7°C and average minimum 23°C. There are no distinct seasons, but the northeast monsoon brings heavy showers in Nov.-Jan. Brief showers are frequent throughout the rest of the year.

# SOVIET ASIA

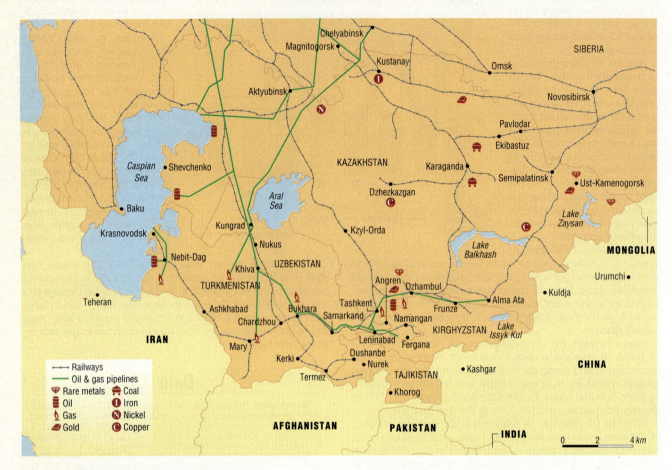

Railways
Oil & gas pipelines
Rare metals — Coal
Oil — Iron
Gas — Nickel
Gold — Copper

## Politics/Foreign Relations

The 19 August coup attempt by a disorganised group of Soviet hardliners was the blow that demolished the shaky foundations of Soviet communism and paved the way for a radical restructuring of the sprawling and disparate union.

When the eight ringleaders' collective nerves failed, they left the Russian republic's President Boris Yeltsin effectively in charge of the rapidly fragmenting union when the putsch fell apart on 21 August.

Yeltsin's rapid moves to ban Communist Party of the Soviet Union activities in Russia and nationalise its property sealed the fate of the once all-powerful party. With the collapse of the party's apparatus, the Union of Soviet Socialist Republics effectively ceased to exist — leaving Mikhail Gorbachov caretaker president of the remnants of a union whose future status is deeply uncertain.

The break-up of the Soviet Union will have a profound effect on Asia. While most of the sovereign states which replace the Soviet Union may form a loose political association or commonwealth, they will also have diverging foreign policy interests. The Russian republic, inheritor of the key levers of Soviet power, has already announced that it will end all aid and credits to other countries. Further, the Soviet Union's Ministry of Foreign Affairs will be cut back to two thirds or less of its former size, depending on how much money Russia is willing to pay for its upkeep.

With the disintegration of Soviet power, the once feared

military threat has all but dissolved, though control over the armed forces remains centralised in the union's Ministry of Defence. However, 1992's defence budget will be drastically reduced and the armed forces cut by up to 50% from their present 3 million personnel in the next few years. Nevertheless, there remains a danger that elements of the Soviet nuclear arsenal could fall into the wrong hands.

Even this "worst-case scenario" is losing its credibility as the US and the Soviet Union initiate nuclear cuts, notably the removal of all land- and sea-based tactical nuclear missile systems. Strategic nuclear weapons based in the Ukraine and Kazakhstan are due to remain in place under central control until they are dismantled, while both Kazakhstan and Russia have declared an end to nuclear testing in their territories.

The republics, including all those in Asia, which have agreed to retain at least an economic community, have now entered a transitional phase. During this transition they have agreed to maintain four main central structures: the defence, foreign affairs and interior ministries and a transformed KGB. The railways also remain under central administrative control. Administration is being handled by a government council and an inter-republic economic council.

The duration of this transition period will depend on how willing the republics are to compromise. Shorn of the Baltics and Moldavia — and perhaps the Ukraine, Azerbaijan and Georgia — they may eventually coalesce into a working political confederation. However, differences over the extent of power to be delegated to central bodies may equally well drive the republics apart. Yeltsin, for example, has already threatened to create a Russian army if the other republics carry out their threats to develop independent armed forces in addition to the militias they are already raising.

The economic agreement signed on 2 October by eight republics in Alma Ata may also be less solid than initially hoped, with predictions it will not survive its three-year span. The agreement is less than precise on such key issues as whether republics can independently join international financial institutions and on the coordination of financial policy. Yeltsin's 16 November decrees that Russia would effectively assume control over most of the Soviet Union's key exports — including oil, gold, precious metals and diamonds — while also repudiating the authority of the Soviet central bank, can only deepen the rifts between the de facto Russian centre and the republics.

In East Asia, the structuring of post-communist foreign relations will be mainly Russia's responsibility. In general, analysts expect continuity of the policies set out by Gorbachov at Vladivostok in 1986 and Krasnoyarsk in 1988. Relations with China are expected to remain cordial and correct, despite the Chinese leadership's obvious concern over events throughout the Soviet Union. For the immediate future, the relationship will depend largely on its economic dimensions. The head of the sub-committee for Asia in the Russian parliament forecast that arms sales to China will continue, both because they are economically advantageous and they show Moscow's good intentions towards Peking.

Relations with Japan are expected to produce more dramatic changes. The dispute over Shikotan and the Habomai Island groups in the Kurile Islands chain — occupied by the Soviets at the end of World War II and the pivot upon which Soviet-Japanese relations balances — may soon be resolved due to a warmer political climate.

The major obstacle to the fulfilment of the 1956 declaration, which stipulated the return to Japan of Shikotan and the Habomai group on the signing of a peace treaty, is now the public opposition being organised in the Far East by Sakhalin's nationalist governor.

**Yeltsin and Gorbachov: unequal partners.**

The two sides had begun to work on ways of improving the climate between them during Gorbachov's April visit to Tokyo. To facilitate this process, the Soviets ended restrictions on visits to Japanese graves in the disputed islands and provided lists of Japanese prisoners of war who died on Soviet soil. The Japanese reciprocated by announcing a programme to train Soviet specialists on implementing economic reforms.

Former Japanese foreign minister Taro Nakayama's mid-October talks in Moscow resulted in the creation of two new working groups to negotiate a long-delayed World War II peace treaty. The group dealing with the territorial dispute will be led by a Russian deputy foreign minister, while other questions will be handled by an official of the Soviet Union's foreign ministry. During the Nakayama visit, Soviet Foreign Minister Boris Pankin also announced that the number of Soviet military personnel based on the islands claimed by Japan would be cut by 30% and that visa-free travel to the Kuriles for former Japanese residents will start at the beginning of 1992.

Japan then announced it would offer US$2.5 billion in economic aid to the Soviet Union, US$1.8 billion of which was to be earmarked for government guarantees for Japanese firms doing business there. Another US$500 million of the aid was provided as credits for purchase of Japanese medicine or food products. The Soviet Union still owes around US$500 million to Japanese companies.

Relations with South Korea has already radically improved following the normalisation of ties in 1990. Trade soared to US$1.5 billion during 1991 and could reach US$10 billion in four or five years, South Korea's ambassador to the Soviet Union predicted. Gorbachov's brief stopover in South Korea following his Japan visit underscored both sides' intention to maintain the momentum in their growing relationship, though the cooperation treaty discussed at that time seemed to have been a political rather than a well–thought out economic idea. While Seoul offered US$3 billion in credit for 1991-93 to maintain trade with the cash-short Soviet Union, Moscow had originally hoped for a much larger sum.

The Soviet Union's relations with North Korea have, not surprisingly, cooled since diplomatic relations were opened with the South. One example of the extent of how frosty ties have become was the reported annulment of an agreement to let Pyongyang take 200,000 tonnes of fish a year without payment from Soviet waters. The accord ended after Pyongyang was accused of selling part of their quota to Japan and allowing Japanese vessels to fly North Korean flags.

North Korean timber concession in the Khabarovsk region also came in for strong criticism from local people, though the agreement was renewed with a provision for reforestation. North Koreans are now working off their Rbl 2.7 billion (US$4.58 billion) debt by building housing and other facilities in the region. Moscow has also sought to convince North Korea's President Kim Il Sung that he should open the country's nuclear installations for international inspection.

Relations with former allies Vietnam and Afghanistan now seem to be fading fast. Vietnam may retain a trading role with Russia and some of the other resource-rich republics such as Uzbekistan, but its strategic value to Russia has largely been overtaken by Northeast Asian countries. However, Vietnam still owes something close to Rbl 12 billion to the Soviet Union, so well-established trade links will not simply be abandoned.

Afghanistan — which has long been dependent on Soviet fuel and grain supplies — will see much of its aid cut at the beginning of 1992 when arms deliveries to Kabul are due to be terminated under a US-Soviet initiative to end the country's civil war.

Moreover, a number of Russian politicians have made no secret of their belief that some mujahideen chieftains were the legitimate leaders of Afghanistan, rather than President Mohammad Najibullah's Soviet-installed government. □

# The Republics

The path August's failed coup against President Mikhail Gorbachov opened to the post-communist world for all Soviet republics may prove particularly rugged for Kazakhstan and the four republics of Central Asia.

The Central Asian republics are surrounded by examples they may or may not wish to follow, or that may simply spill over whatever their leaders want. Among their immediate neighbours, Islamic fundamentalism still dominates across the border in Iran, Afghanistan's future seems to lie in localised fiefdoms, while Turkey — variants of whose language is spoken by Azeris, Turkmens, Uzbeks, Kirghiz and Kazakhs — moves steadily closer to Europe as a modernising, secular state.

To the north, the Russian republic — stretching from Europe to Vladivostok and Kamchatka — is also moving towards Western-style democracy, while further to the east the economic success of the free markets of South Korea, Singapore and Taiwan offer powerful role models. On the other hand, China's disciplined approach to economic reform appeals to some former communist leaders searching for new sources of legitimacy now that Moscow's patronage network has gone.

With the erosion of ideological boundaries, Central Asia has an opportunity to again become a centre of commerce and culture, as it was in the days of Bukhara and Samarkand. As Kazakhstan's President Nursultan Nazarbayev has pointed out, the opening of markets and borders could do much to end inter-ethnic disputes and bring prosperity to this once-remote hinterland of Soviet power.

In the post-coup chaos, leaders in each republic moved to assert their nationalism. Premature declarations from Russian President Boris Yeltsin's entourage about Russia's legal right to Soviet property and right to re-examine borders with neighbouring republics may have accelerated the rush to declare sovereignty. Uzbekistan, Tajikistan and Kirghyzstan have all declared themselves independent states, while the people of Turkmenia voted 94% in favour of independence in an October referendum.

Further, the communist parties of Uzbekistan and Kazakhstan changed their names — Uzbek communists are now the People's Democratic Party, while in Kazakhstan the new name is "Socialist." In Tajikistan, even the renamed communist party — also "Socialist" — has been banned following its attempt in September to declare a state of emergency.

For the present, the political paths of these republics are diverging. The coup quickened the pace of democratisation in Kirghyzstan and Kazakhstan, while Tajikistan hovers on the edge of changes that seem likely to take it closer to the Islamic world. Most analysts agree a mujahideen victory in Afghanistan would have a powerful effect in the republic, given the large Tajik population on the Afghan side of the border. However, the presidential election in November was won by former Communist Party boss Rakhmon Nabiyev. He won 57% of the vote, while his closest rival, film director Davlat Khudonazarev, got 31%. Khudonazarev, supported by a coalition of democratic and Islamic forces, contested the result on the grounds of widespread cheating.

Turkmenistan has moved more slowly into the post-communist era. President Saparmurad Niyazov first nationalised the Soviet Communist Party's property, then — following an October vote for independence — pronounced himself to be against "formal democracy," which he said would be a burden for the people. He has advocated leasing and family contracts in farming, as against private ownership of property, and also opposed privatisation of the republic's trade sector, which he said had been a major source of inter-ethnic conflict.

At their party congress the republic's communists were expected to divide into two or three smaller parties. An independent Democratic Party, formed in October and claims to be the only true opposition party, supports economic liberalisation and dealing with pollution caused by extensive cotton cultivation.

One of the dramas of the August attempted coup occurred in tiny Kirghyzstan, formerly known as Kirghizia. Here the scholarly President Askar Akayev, elected by parliament in late 1990, surprised the local party apparatus by staging his own fight against the putsch. On 24 August Akayev issued a decree confiscating party property and excluding the party from its traditional role in public organisations. With no one approaching his stature in the republic, he ran unopposed in the 12 October presidential election.

Nothing so dramatic occurred in Kazakhstan during the August upheavals. President Nursultan Nazarbayev did not immediately condemn the coup, though he did call for an extraordinary session of the Congress of People's Deputies. He also claimed some credit for helping prevent troop movements into the Kirghyz capital of Bishkek (formerly Frunze).

The coup's aftermath in Alma Ata is likewise not so clearcut as the anti-communist sweep that took place in Kirghyzstan. The communists have transformed themselves into a socialist party, whose leadership is substantially different from the former inner circle. But press reports say the former party leaders are being given ministerial posts in the new government. Opinions are divided as to whether the new party will emerge as the same old apparatus with a new name, or whether the socialists will restrict themselves to the role of a genuine parliamentary party. Nevertheless, a public opinion poll has registered only 19% popular support for the transformed party. Other parties now officially registered include a republican, a social democratic and an independence party.

Nazarbayev will seek a mandate for his programme of privatisation in presidential elections on 1 December. His major rival, leader of the nationalist Zheltoksan (December) movement Hasen Kozhametov, was prevented from collecting enough signatures to register his candidacy. Zheltoksan has criticised some of the president's economic programmes, including plans to develop the Tengiz oilfield with the US Chevron company.

In Uzbekistan, the line has been firmly drawn against the spread of democracy. President Islam Karimov kept a low profile during the coup and has since emerged speaking the language of sovereignty. But his 31 August declaration of independence to the republic's parliament was unpopular and few people in Uzbekistan are taking it seriously. The leader of the Birlik (Unity) movement, Abdurahim Pulatov, reacted by calling it the "replacement of one system of slavery by another." Karimov, who has stated that ending the communist party's role in the republic would throw the economy into chaos, prefers the Chinese model of limited economic reform within a disciplined political environment.

Since the attempted coup, Karimov has allowed one party to register, the Democratic Party (Erkh), which claims around 3,000 members and plays the role of "loyal opposition." But he has taken no steps to loosen his grip on the press, and has broken up demonstrations to mark the victory of the Yeltsin forces in Russia with arrests and fines. Presidential elections will be held on 29 December, but Karimov shows no sign of allowing Birlik, the largest opposition group, to register their candidates.

Although each republic is now following its own path, there

are forces which may eventually unite them and, in the eyes of some Central Asians, could speed their rebirth. Islam is destined to play an important role in both Uzbekistan and Tajikistan, observers believe, as it is still deeply interwoven with the local culture. Moreover, both republics have only small Slav minorities.

Islamic leaders played a decisive role when they forced the communists to back down during a protracted standoff between party stalwarts and a democratic opposition coalition in Tajikistan's capital Dushanbe. The Islamic Rebirth Party, which has begun to operate openly since the coup, is believed to have strong rural support. Dushanbe's Islamic challenge to the communist leadership was echoed by demonstrations in Uzbekistan's Fergana Valley at the end of September, when Muslims called on Karimov to resign or take an oath on the Koran that he would serve the people. Turkmenia may also be deeply influenced by its growing contacts with Iran.

The Pan-Turkic idea, which strongly appeal to some Uzbek and Kazakh intellectuals, could unite a large percentage of the region's people in a common cause. Rumours have circulated that some hardline leaders have agreed to join their republics in a communist "Turkestan," but for the moment none of the regional political forces seems to have decided that such a union is in their interest. However, most agree that they should build economic links to their southern neighbours. □

# Economy/Infrastructure

While the Soviet Central Asian republics may have declared political independence, economic independence remains a long way off. However, though the region's immediate future now appears likely to be based on some form of economic union among the republics, trading links with other countries are being rapidly expanded and investors willing to develop industry and infrastructure courted.

In addition, due to uncertain world prices for raw materials and the difficulty of developing new markets, immediate self-sufficiency is not something they can count on. Even Uzbekistan's and Kazakhstan's gold reserves will not guarantee self-reliance, as Russian President Boris Yeltsin's 16 November decree appears to have effectively sequestered all gold production throughout the union.

Turkmenistan's dilemma is fairly typical. While richly endowed with natural gas and high-quality cotton, it remains one of the Soviet Union's poorest republics. Its economists claim that they were underpaid by the Soviet government for their resources. So far they have beaten a hard-currency payment of US$70 million a year out of the union government for their gas sales, but given Russia's apparent intention to control exports of strategic or valuable commodities, the republic's plans to construct a gas pipeline to the Gulf through Iran now seem stillborn.

Having asserted their right to handle their own affairs, the Central Asian republics have agreed to join an economic union, which Kazakhstan President Nursultan Nazarbayev helped to nurse into existence. Fiscal policy will be coordinated by a banking union backed by a reserve system and members will coordinate policies on hard currency, foreign trade and the free movement of labour. There will be no customs barriers, and a fixed tax from national income will be paid to the central administration. Parallel to this agreement, the republics have signed bilateral trade agreements.

Nazarbayev moved fast to strengthen his republic's economic sovereignty, decreeing that all Kazakhstan's union industries will become the property of the republic before the end of 1991. From 1992, all import-export activities will be carried out exclusively by the republic, and two special economic zones will be developed to concentrate on minerals processing. Kazakhstan will also seek to create its own gold and diamond reserves. However, a controversial deal with the Chevron Co. to develop the Tengiz oilfield by the Caspian Sea has been put on hold. Critics say the deal is far too generous to Chevron, giving it equal rights with the republic. The success of Nazarbayev's efforts are now contingent on how far Russia is willing to push for control over Kazakhstan's key resources.

Uzbekistan's economy has faltered along with the rest of the unions' this year, with disrupted economic links causing a steep fall in income. After the budget shortfall reached Rbl 1.1 billion (US$1.96 billion) in the first half of the year, the republic's cabinet reduced spending by 25% in August and started to draw up plans to transfer loss-making state and collective farms to leasing or cooperative ownership. By the end of October, however, the cotton harvest was forecast at around 4.64 million tonnes, or 200,000 tonnes above plan. For the first time, farms will be able to sell 5% of their cotton on the free market, as well as any produced above their quota.

Kirgyzstan's 1992 budget projects a Rbl 2.4 billion income, with outlays of Rbl 8.7 billion. Yeltsin helped cover this year's deficit with a Rbl 600 million subsidy to fellow democrat President Askar Akayev's administration, but a gaping deficit remains. Observers believe hostility from neighbouring Uzbekistan conservatives could combine with economic austerity to cause trouble for Kirgyzstan, which also adopted a liberal foreign-investment code in October. □

# Siberia/Soviet Far East

Siberia and the Soviet Far East will be less politically and economically dependent on directives from Moscow, and more dependent on the region's ability to attract foreign investment, now that decentralisation is becoming a reality.

The transition could be chaotic, local leaders admit. The region is dependent on outside food and fuel supplies, which under the old Soviet system were heavily subsidised. As prices are increasingly decontrolled, the cost of living in the Far East could soar and the relatively high wages paid to the labour force may not be enough to prevent a movement of workers back to the west. Some officials advocate the retention of government subsidies for 70% of essential supplies to prevent a popular revolt, while unemployment resulting from the closure of unprofitable plants and military industries will be another possible cause of unrest.

Local plans for special economic zones (SEZ) are under way, and could speed up the region's integration into the broader Pacific economy. Following the unsuccessful putsch in August, Vladivostok has finally declared its intention to become an open city at the start of 1992. The neighbouring port of Nakhodka is preparing to build an industrial park, is developing communication facilities with Britain's Cable and Wireless Co. and is building three hotels in cooperation with China to promote its own SEZ.

Major enterprises in the region have also set up a consortium called the Far Eastern Union to promote economic and social development in the area. Foreign shareholders include US, South and North Korean investors. The group will develop transport and infrastructure, largely in order to extract natural resources in Siberia and the Far East.

# SRI LANKA

**INDIA**

Palk Strait

Bay of Bengal

Jaffna

Railways
Main roads

Gulf of Mannar

Medawachchiya

Trincomalee

Puttalam

Sigiriya

Batticaloa

Kurunegala

Kandy

Negombo

Kegalla

Badulla

Pottuvil

Colombo

Dehiwala
Panadura
Kalutara

Ratnapura

Wellawaya

Okanda

Indian Ocean

Hambantota

Galle
Matara

Tangalla

0    50    100 km

Ceylon became independent on 4 February 1948. In September 1959, prime minister Solomon Bandaranaike, leader of the Sri Lanka Freedom Party, was assassinated by a Buddhist monk. An insurrection by mainly unemployed youths in April 1971 was crushed by the United Front (UF) government of Sirimavo Bandaranaike, widow of the former prime minister. On 22 May 1972 the country was renamed the Republic of Sri Lanka. The UF lost power in the 1977 general election and the United National Party (UNP) administration of prime minister J. R. Jayewardene took over.

Jayewardene replaced the 1972 constitution and assumed unprecedented power as executive president, becoming both head of state and head of government. He was elected to a second six-year term in October 1982, and in a referendum won a mandate to extend parliament to 1989. In late 1988, former prime minister Ranasinghe Premadasa was elected executive president and in 1989 the UNP won a large majority in parliamentary elections.

In July 1983, communal violence directed mainly at the country's Tamil community broke out, sparking a separatist war in northern and eastern provinces that still continues. Under a peace agreement signed in 1987, India sent its troops into the northern Jaffna peninsula, where they sought to quell the Tamil uprising. Indian forces were withdrawn in early 1990 after an inconclusive campaign. Fighting between Tamil separatists and the Sri Lankan armed forces reached a height in mid-1991 with a series of set-piece battles around Jaffna, but has since tailed off as both sides consider their options for reaching a peace settlement.

**President,** (and **Minister of Buddha Sasana, Policy Planning and Implementation, Defence, Education and Higher Education**)
Ranasinghe Premadasa.
**Prime Minister** (and **Finance, Labour and Vocational Sevices**)
D. B. Wijetunge;
**Foreign Affairs**
Harold Herat;
**Trade and Commerce**
A. R. M. Munsoor;
**Public Administration, Provincial Councils and Home Affairs**
Festus Perera;
**Environment** (and **Parliamentary Affairs**)
M. Vincent Perera;
**Industries, Science and Technology**
Ranil Wickremesinghe;
**Lands, Irrigation and Mahaweli Development**
Gamini Atukorale;
**Fisheries and Aquatic Resources**
Joseph Michael Perera;
**Tourism** (and **Rural Industrial Development**)
S. Thendaman;
**Posts and Telecommunications**
A. M. S. Adikari;

**Justice**
A. C. S. Hameed;
**Plantation Industries**
Rupasena Karunstillake;
**Handlooms and Textile Industries**
U. B. Wijekoon;
**Reconstruction, Rehabilitation and Social Welfare**
P. Dayaratne;
**Housing and Construction**
B. Sirisona Cooray;
**Power and Energy**
K. D. M. O. Bandara;
**Transport and Highways**
T. Wijayapala Mendis;
**Food and Cooperatives**
Weerasinghe Mallimarachchi;
**Ports and Shipping**
Alick Aluvihare;
**Agricultural Development and Research**
Dharmadasa Banda;
**Health and Women's Affairs**
Renuka Herath;
**Cultural Affairs and Information**
W. J. M. Lokubandara;
**Youth Affairs and Sport**
C. Nanda Mathew.

# Politics/Social Affairs

President Ranasinghe Premadasa faced one of the toughest tests in his long political career during the year when he overcame an impeachment threat challenging his tenure.

The resolution to impeach Premadasa came on 28 August as he chaired the weekly cabinet meeting. He received a letter from speaker M. H. Mohamed during the meeting saying he had "entertained" a resolution to impeach Premadasa under Article 38 of the constitution, which lays out the grounds under which a president may be impeached. They are mental or physical infirmity, intentional violation of the constitution, acts of treason or bribery or any offence under the law involving moral turpitude.

Premadasa called the impeachment attempt a "conspiracy" between the opposition led by former prime minister Sirima Bandaranaike's Sri Lanka Freedom Party (SLFP) and a group of dissidents from his ruling United National Party (UNP). With his party commanding a comfortable majority in parliament and the SLFP in tatters with Bandaranaike and her son, Anura, publicly quarrelling over the party leadership, few would have considered even a feeble effort to topple Premadasa was possible.

The president acted swiftly to meet the impeachment threat. He first prorogued parliament for 25 days, giving himself time to group his forces. Intensive activity began to identify those UNP MPs who had signed the resolution. When confronted, some said their signatures had been obtained by misrepresentation and one claimed his signature may have been forged.

However, it soon became clear that the impeachment strategists had played on the fears of many UNP MPs that Premadasa could dissolve parliament prematurely and call an election to exploit the divided opposition's weakness, and some feared their seats may be at risk. The president's aides were able to persuade these MPs to write to the speaker retracting their signatures.

Lalith Athulathmudali and Gamini Dissanayake, two powerful ministers in the J. R. Jayewardene administration in which Premadasa was prime minister, were found to be leading the UNP dissidents. Both men had vied with Premadasa for the UNP ticket to succeed Jayewardene, and competed fiercely with each other to become prime minister when he was elected. However, when elected Premadasa chose an outsider, D. B. Wijetunge, as his prime minister, a post with no real power.

Although he gave the two men senior cabinet ministries following his election, Athulathmudali's portfolio was changed and Dissanayake dropped from the cabinet within a year. Premadasa was also harder on his ministers and MPs than his predecessor, which helped fuel the impeachment effort more out of personal dislike for him than anything else.

The UNP dissidents, however, claimed their motives were based on replacing the executive presidency with the Westminster-style parliamentary system that prevailed before the 1978 constitution. Premadasa countered by saying the electorate had accepted the executive presidential system and endorsed it at several successive elections since 1978 because they were convinced of its efficacy.

As the dissidents intensified their campaign, Premadasa marshalled his own forces. Following the letters that some of those who had signed the resolution sent the speaker retracting their signatures, the government parliamentary group met and adopted a resolution expressing confidence in the president and rejecting the "purported clandestine move to remove from office the president who was elected by the people." Of the 225-member parliament, 116 MPs signed this resolution.

**Premadasa: impeachment fails.**

Premadasa also quelled the fears of his MPs that he would dissolve parliament, and made it clear there would be no disciplinary action against those who had signed the impeachment resolution if they agreed to be bound by common decisions then being taken. However, when efforts to bring the dissident leaders back into the party failed, the UNP's working committee decided to expel them. This was adopted by the party's executive committee, but challenged by the rebel leaders who went to court arguing that they had merely exercised their constitutional rights which superseded party rules.

Despite strong demands in the media and elsewhere, Mohamed did not place the impeachment motion on the parliamentary agenda. While photocopies were widely circulated, no national newspaper published it because the parliamentary privileges law prevented publication of any matter before parliament until it was in an order paper.

When the three-week prorogation of parliament ended in late September, the opposition insisted that Premadasa should not come before parliament to open the new session while the impeachment motion against him remained pending. Nevertheless, Premadasa made his opening address in the face of an opposition engineered uproar. Further, the attorney-general advised the speaker that because of its non-inclusion in an order paper, the impeachment motion had lapsed.

On 7 October, the speaker finally rejected the impeachment resolution on the grounds that it "did not have the required number of valid signatures." Mohamed gave no explanation of his action, did not indicate whose signatures were invalid or even how many had signed the resolution. He stayed away from parliament until an opposition inspired no-confidence motion against him was debated and defeated with a government majority.

With the attempt to impeach Premadasa over, the SLFP —

which had closed ranks in order to concentrate on ejecting the president from office, or at least causing him grave embarrassment — resumed its internal feuding, while the legality of the UNP dissidents' expulsion from the party remains before the Supreme Court.

Potentially even more damaging allegations over the government's conduct emerged during the impeachment imbroglio, when Premadasa's administration was accused of supplying arms to the Liberation Tigers of Tamil Eelam (LTTE) separatist guerillas in 1989-90 while Indian troops were still operating in the country's northeast. At the time Premadasa and the LTTE shared a common aim in wanting the Indian army out of Sri Lanka. The defence ministry eventually admitted that there had been some "sharing of equipment" with the Tigers in order to fight the Indian-backed Tamil National Army, which was being raised at the time. In the event, the issue was buried when Premadasa prevailed over his opponents in their impeachment attempt.

During local government elections held in May across the country — except for the war-torn north and east — the UNP won 193 of the 237 municipalities, urban councils and *Pradeshiya Sabhas*, which replaced the previous village committees, that went to the polls. Its local election victory was the seventh consecutive poll of various kinds the UNP has won since its 1977 general election success.

The war in the northern and eastern provinces continued, though new peace efforts were under way at the end of 1991. LTTE guerillas suffered some reverses in the latter part of the year, including in their northern stronghold on the Jaffna peninsula. However, the LTTE also demonstrated its ability to fight a conventional war during the battle for Elephant Pass, the area around a causeway that links Jaffna with the rest of Sri Lanka.

While LTTE forces were eventually forced to withdraw, they succeeded in exacting a high casualty toll from the Sri Lankan armed forces, who mounted their largest and most ambitious operation of the war to dislodge the guerillas. While there appears to be a strong realisation on both sides on the need for peace, whether a just and durable solution is possible remained unclear as the year ended.

On 2 March, defence minister Ranjan Wijeratne — the man credited with crushing the Singhalese JVP Marxist guerila group in 1989 — was killed instantly when a bomb exploded next to his motorcade in Colombo. Although the LTTE denied planting the bomb, which also killed 25 civilians and five police escorts, they remain the prime suspects. Less than three months later, a car bomb destroyed the operational headquarters of the defence ministry in Colombo. The LTTE claimed responsibility for the attack. ☐

# Foreign Relations

Relations between Sri Lanka and India, which had steadily improved during much of 1991, took a sharp downturn due to Colombo's belief that New Delhi had sabotaged the scheduled November summit of the South Asian Association for Regional Cooperation (Saarc) at which President Ranasinghe Premadasa was due to assume the chairmanship of the regional grouping for the coming year.

Sri Lanka, which had made elaborate preparations for the summit, discovered that it would turn out to be a non-event only after the conference process leading to the summit had begun. India raised an objection to the summit being held because of King Jigme Singye Wangchuk of Bhutan's absence, just before a meeting of the Saarc council of ministers that preceded the main conference was due to begin. Despite the king's willingness that the summit should proceed in his absence with a special envoy representing Bhutan, India insisted that the Saarc charter demanded that either the head of state or head of government of all seven member states must be present at a formal meeting.

In a statement to parliament on why the summit had not been held, Sri Lanka's Foreign Minister Harold Herat said that "India's decision at the eleventh hour that the summit could not proceed until all seven leaders were personally present was not borne out by past practice." He pointed out that Pakistan's former prime minister Mohammed Khan Junejo had represented then president Mohammad Zia-ul Haq at both the Bangalore and Kathmandu Saarc summits, adding that Sri Lanka's own Prime Minister D. B. Wijetunge had represented Premadasa at the 1990 Male summit.

"This was the first time that a head of government had taken a position that the personal presence of all seven heads of state/government must be a prerequisite for the holding of a summit. This attitude of India, taken at the last minute, left no time for consultation," Herat said.

In a letter to Premadasa setting out New Delhi's position, Indian Prime Minister P. V. Narasimha Rao said that accepting Bhutan's foreign secretary, already in Colombo, as deputising for the king would imply a discourtesy. "Nor should we ignore the implications such a readiness to accept substitutes would have on our association, which has been . . . mandated to arrive at unanimous decisions at the highest level of our political leadership. Any dilution of this unanimity and the process of personal consultation through which it had been reached can only weaken the association which all of us, together, had built and nurtured over the years," the Indian prime minister wrote.

Maldivian President Maumoon Abdul Gayoom, as serving chairman of Saarc, quickly initiated measures to try and organise another summit before the end of the year. There were indications in late November that a one or two day meeting would be held in Colombo either in December or January.

New Delhi had reason to administer a diplomatic snub to Premadasa, who had refused to host the 1989 summit while Indian troops were in Sri Lanka and did not attend the Male summit the following year.

However, Colombo sought to improve relations with New Delhi when Premadasa sent Narasimha Rao a congratulatory message after the Indian prime minister's Congress Party won a series of by-elections on 16 November for the lower house. Narasimha Rao responded by reaffirming his "sincere desire to build a relationship of friendship and mutual trust between our two countries," and also said that he looked forward "to working closely with you to promote regional cooperation through the vehicle of Saarc."

With domestic critics accusing New Delhi of clumsy diplomacy that had cast doubts on India's ability to provide leadership in the region, it was clear that lost ground had to be recovered.

Good relations with India remain crucial for Sri Lanka. Mounting evidence that the Liberation Tigers of Tamil Eelam (LTTE) — the Sri Lankan Tamil separatist group that had once enjoyed Indian patronage — had been responsible for Rajiv Gandhi's assassination in May saw concerted action against the LTTE in India. This was of great assistance to Sri Lankan forces fighting LTTE in the country's northern and eastern provinces, particularly in sealing off the group's southern Indian logistical bases.

Relations between Sri Lanka, Britain and the EC deteriorated in the middle of 1991 following Colombo's decision to expel British High Commissioner David Gladstone after accusing him of interfering in local elections. Gladstone was not a popular figure with the Sri Lankan Government, where his interest in human rights was seen as an interference in the country's internal affairs. In addition, his social contacts with alleged drug dealers — including one who had jumped bail in Britain — had earlier resulted in what was believed to be an orchestrated attack on the high commissioner in parliament. Gladstone chose the electorate of the backbencher who had attacked him in parliament to observe the working of the local elections.

Efforts by Sri Lanka's foreign ministry to have Gladstone recalled failed and he was subsequently expelled. Britain reacted sharply, though stopped short of a reciprocal expulsion of Sri Lanka's high commissioner in London. Drawing attention to a statement by the EC "deploring the Sri Lankan Government's decision," London announced the suspension of high-level visits between the two countries, no new major aid commitments until a new high commissioner was in place "and then to review any such proposals in the light of the human-rights situation" and a more restrictive policy on arms sales. Although London said it intended to appoint a new high commissioner quickly, no replacement had arrived by the end of November.

Echoes of Colombo's decision to close the Israeli interest section at the US Embassy in 1990 continued to reverberate during the year. Premadasa ordered an enquiry into claims made by a former intelligence agent that the Israelis had simultaneously trained members of the government's security forces and Tamil separatist guerillas before Colombo expelled them. Although the enquiry by a Sri Lankan Supreme Court judge ruled the allegations to be untrue, the highly publicised affair nevertheless embarrassed the government by once again exposing the role played by foreign intelligence services in the country's counter-insurgency campaign. □

**Defence expenditure: economy takes a pounding.**

# Economy/Infrastructure

The Sri Lankan economy continues to suffer from the seemingly endless separatist war being waged by the Liberation Tigers of Tamil Eelam in the country's northern and eastern provinces. The country's armed forces have tripled in size since 1983, with the army alone now standing at some 77,000 men, representing a serious drain on revenue.

However, despite the war, Sri Lanka completed the implementation of an eight-year programme supported by the IMF's second structural adjustment facility during 1991, and was able to demonstrate a marked improvement in economic performance.

Production began to pick up in late 1989 and the economic recovery continued through 1990 when real GNP grew by over 6%. This trend continued through the first half of 1991, and while tea prices — on which the economy is highly dependent — declined sharply in July. Nevertheless, Prime Minister and Finance Minister D. H. Wijetunge forecast in November that the 1991 growth rate could be sustained at 5%.

In September, the IMF approved Colombo's application for loans totalling SDR 886 million (US$455 million) to be disbursed over a three-year period under the fund's enhanced structural adjustment facility (ESAF) to support the government's economic and financial programme covering the 1991-94 period. The IMF said Sri Lanka may borrow a total of SDR 112 million in two semi-annual disbursements during the first year of the ESAF-supported programme.

Presenting his 1992 budget, Wijetunge credited the "resilience" of the private sector to the country's ability to register economic growth, even during the height of the terror campaign launched by the Singhalese JVP Marxist group that brought the country to the brink of anarchy.

However, while the domestic environment had improved, the economy had to contend with the fallout from the Gulf crisis. Export earnings from tea slumped when Iraq, a major buyer, pulled out of the Colombo tea sales. Overseas workers' remittances were also lost as many Sri Lankans returned home from Kuwait and elsewhere in the Middle East during the crisis.

In addition, defence expenditure remained high as a result of the continuing war in the northern and eastern provinces. The maintenance of hundreds of thousands of refugees from the war-torn areas, as well as an unforeseen commitment for drought relief, continued to drain government revenue. This was partly ameliorated by foreign aid, with the international donors pledging US$1 billion in 1990 — the highest amount ever received by Sri Lanka.

A privatisation process, that President Ranasinghe Premadasa prefers to describe as "peoplisation," gathered momentum in 1991. Employees of state-owned enterprises being divested are being given a 10% share in the concerns free of charge. In the case of the nationalised bus service, the entire operation is being handed over to its workers. The privatisation programme generally involves offering a majority controlling interest to a single buyer to establish management control and offering the balance through the Colombo stock exchange.

Wijetunge also noted that the government has devised a new industrial strategy and is relaxing and rationalising exchange and investment controls. He said "the liberalisation of exchange control will continue, depending on the capacity to build up an adequate buffer of foreign-exchange reserves."

The Colombo stock exchange continued to boom in 1991, with surging turnover and prices. The exchange, with 174 listings, has attracted the attention of several regional and country funds which have been investing substantially in Colombo, boosting the upward movement of share prices. The equities boom enabled fast growing listed companies to float rights issues at high premiums. While twice above par was considered unrealistic at the start of 1991, by the end of the year a development bank that floated an issue at five times par was heavily oversubscribed and had to resort to a lottery to make allotments.

Tourism, which virtually collapsed after communal unrest in 1988, began to pick up in 1990. The recovery continued through 1991, with arrivals expected to top 350,000 during the year. The government's tourist board is confident arrivals will exceed 400,000 in 1992. The south and west coast beach resorts remain the chief attractions for most Western European tourists, and there is growing pressure on available room capacity as well as airline seats to Colombo during the high winter season. However, Colombo's leading hotels — which offered rooms for as little as US$25 a night during the height of the tourist slump — while recording operational profits, are finding interest on loans incurred during the bad times a drag on their balance sheets.

National carrier Airlanka — long a burden on the economy — has finally turned a profit, while many foreign airlines that had cut back or even cancelled their services to Colombo have resumed old schedules and added new flights.

The government is pumping substantial resources into infrastructure development, particularly the badly neglected road system. Work on the main Colombo-Kandy road has been completed and rehabilitation of the Colombo-Galle road along the south coast is under way. The port of Colombo has developed into a regional trans-shipment centre and container throughput continues to grow rapidly. □

## Data

**Major industries:** Textiles, wearing apparel and leather products, US$698 million (US$550 million); food, beverages and tobacco, US$550 million (US$460 million); chemicals, petroleum, rubber and plastics, US$530 million (US$300 million); non-metallic minerals (except petroleum and coal), US$188 million (US$150 million); fabricated metal products, machinery and transport equipment, US$105 million (US$80 million).

**Major agriculture:** Tea, 233.2 million kg (207 million); rubber, 114 million kg (110.7 million); coconut, 2.52 billion nuts (2.48 billion); rice (unmilled), 2.54 million tonnes (2.06 million).

**Major imports:** Consumer goods, US$700 million (US$524 million); intermediate goods, US$1.47 billion (US$1.13 billion); investment goods, US$478 million (US$300 million).

**Major exports:** Textiles and garments, US$629 million (US$440 million); tea, US$495 million (US$341 million); petroleum products, US$99 million (US$56 million); minor agricultural crops, US$79 million (US$60 million); rubber, US$77 million (same); gems, US$73 million (US$55 million); coconuts, US$69 million (US$71 million).

**Tourism:** Arrivals, 297,888 (184,732); revenue, US$1.2 billion (US$684 million). (All figures for 1990, previous year in brackets.)

**Currency:** Sri Lanka Rupee (100 cents). Rs 41.58 = US$1 Nov. 1991 (Rs 40.028 Nov. 1990).

**Major banks:** Bank of Ceylon, tel. 546790-9; Commercial Bank of Ceylon, tel. 545010-18; Hatton National Bank, tel. 21466-9; People's Bank, tel. 27841; Sampath Bank, tel. 548084; Seylan Trust Bank, tel. 29509; ABN, tel. 20205; American Express, tel. 31288; Amro Bank, tel. 540636; Banque Indosuez, tel. 36181; Deutsche Bank, tel. 547062; ANZ Grindlays, tel. 546150; Habib Bank, tel. 26565; Indian Bank, tel. 23402; Indian Overseas Bank, tel. 24422; Middle East Overseas Trust Bank, tel. 547655; Standard Chartered Bank, tel. 26671; State Bank of India, tel. 26133; Hongkong and Shanghai Bank, tel. 25435.

**Public holidays** (1992): 15 Jan. (Tamil Thai Pongal Day), 4 Feb. (National Day), 17 Feb. (Navam Full Moon Poya Day), 18 Mar. (Medin Full Moon Poya Day), 13 Apr. (Sinhala and Tamil New Year), 16 Apr. (Bak Full Moon Poya Day), 1 May (May Day), 16 May (Vesak Full Moon Poya Day), 22 May (National Heroes' Day), 14 June (Poson Full Moon Poya Day), 30 June (Special Bank Holiday), 26 July (Esala Full Moon Poya Day), 12 Aug. (Nikini Full Moon Poya Day), 10 Sept. (Milad-un-nabi [Holy Prophet's birthday]), 11 Sept. (Binara Full Moon Poya Day), 11 Oct. (Wap Full Moon Poya Day), 9 Nov. (Ill Full Moon Poya Day), 9 Dec. (Unduwap Full Moon Poya Day), 25 Dec. (Christmas Day), 31 Dec. (Special Bank Holiday).

**Weather:** Sri Lanka has a warm to hot and usually humid climate. The southwest monsoon from May-Sept. brings rain to the west coast including Colombo, while the northeast monsoon from Dec.-Feb. brings rain to the east coast. Temperatures in Colombo range from 30.4-24°C. It is cooler in the hill capital, Kandy (28.7-20.2°C) and can become cold around Nuwara Eliya (20.2-11.4°C).

**Tax levels:** Corporate companies not closely held 40%; closely held 50%; small companies 33.33%, personal rising to 40%.

# TAIWAN

**CHINA**

Keelung

Taipei ✈ ⊙

TAIWAN STRAIT
(Formosa Strait)

Hsinchu

Quemoy

Changhua • Taichung

Hualien

• Nantou

Makung

• Touliu

South China Sea

• Hsinying

Tainan

Pingtung

Kaohsiung • Taitung

Fangliao

━━━ Railways

0    50    100 km

• Kenting

**Head of State**
Lee Teng-hui.
**Vice-President**
Li Yuan-tzu;
**Prime Minister**
Hau Pei-tsun;
**Deputy Prime Minister**
Shi Chi-yang;
**Defence**
Chen Li-an;
**Justice**
Lu You-wen;
**Interior**
Wu Po-hsiung;
**Foreign Affairs**
Chien Fu;
**Finance**
Wang Chien-shien;
**Economic Affairs**
Hsiao Wan-chang;
**Education**
Mao Kuo-wen;
**Transportation and Communications**
Chien Yu-hsin;

**Ministers Without Portfolio**
Wang Chou-ming, Kuo Wan-jung,
Kuo Nan-hung, Huang Kun-huei,
Chang Chien-hen, Huang Shih-cheng,
Kao Ming-hui;
**Legislative Yuan President**
Liang Su-jung;
**Judicial Yuan President**
Lin Yang-kang;
**Examination Yuan President**
Kung Teh-cheng;
**Control Yuan President**
Huang Tzuen-chiou;
**Cultural Planning and Development Chairman**
Kuo Wei-fan;
**Council for Economic Planning and Development Chairman**
Kuo Wan-jung;
**Overseas Chinese Affairs Commission Minister**
Tseng Kwang-shun;
**Chief Justice**
Chu Chien-hung.

# Politics/Social Affairs

The gradual erosion of the traditional power structure of the ruling Kuomintang (KMT) and the rise of democratic politics raised many questions about Taiwan's future in 1991. The uncertainties, however, did not deter President Lee Teng-hui from pushing ahead with planned constitutional changes and the first full legislative elections on the island, scheduled for December.

Among the many taboos that were broken during the year were the explicit advocacy of independence by the opposition Democratic Progressive Party (DPP) and the tentative opening towards Peking via the semi-official Straits Exchange Foundation. These events showed how the island was being pulled in two directions at once. For some observers, they also illustrated the need for what one presidential adviser has called "creative ambiguity" in policymaking.

The year saw numerous public demonstrations by students and opposition groups protesting against senior parliamentarians amending the constitution in April, the arrest of four people accused of sedition in May and a vaguely worded sedition law in August. Large numbers also turned out to support an application for UN membership in peaceful marches later in the year that implicitly supported calls for Taiwan's independence.

Despite the frequency of street protests and occasional fights in the legislature, Lee stuck to his timetable for political reform. In retrospect, it appeared that by engineering consensus for his programme among discredited old guards in the National Assembly in April — a decision which sent students back to the streets and inspired a two-month boycott by the opposition of the island's elected bodies — Lee made it almost impossible for KMT conservatives to obstruct his promise to lift the "period of communist rebellion" and hold new elections.

Fulfilling his inaugural pledge of a year earlier, Lee declared on 1 May that Taiwan's civil war with China was ended and that there was no longer any justification for imposing emergency provisions that had "temporarily" suspended parts of the constitution since the late 1940s. Lee's decision also eliminated such language as "communist bandits" to describe the

In 1885, Taiwan was made a province of China. The island was ceded to Japan after the Sino-Japanese war of 1894. After its defeat in 1945, Japan turned Taiwan over to Chiang Kai-shek and his Kuomintang (KMT).

A revolt against KMT rule broke out on 28 February 1947, but was firmly suppressed. Chiang and around 1 million of his followers took refuge on Taiwan in 1949 after being defeated by the communists in the civil war. The outbreak of the Korean War brought a change in US policy and renewed military support for Chiang and the KMT.

Chiang served as president almost continuously from 1948 until his death in 1975. Chiang's son, Chiang Ching-kuo, assumed the premiership in 1972 and the presidency in 1978.

As premier, the younger Chiang began the Taiwanisation of the KMT by expanding the party to include more Taiwan-born members. He lifted martial law in July 1987 and in November the same year removed restrictions on travel to China. Chiang died in January 1988 and was succeeded by Vice-President Lee Teng-hui, who became Taiwan's first native-born president.

Lee accelerated the political reforms of his predecessor and legalised new political parties in 1989. After a struggle with the KMT's traditional power-brokers, Lee was selected for a full six-year term beginning in May 1990.

One year later, Lee declared an end to the "period of communist rebellion" and lifted the "temporary provisions" under which the presidency had enjoyed extra-constitutional powers since 1948.

Lee's decree restored constitutional rule and cleared the way for full elections to Taiwan's legislative bodies, including a constitutional convention set for 1992.

Chinese Government and unofficially recognised the existence of the Peking regime.

While the decree helped to further relax relations with China, it was primarily aimed at clearing the way for more democratic government at home. Ending the period of "rebellion" removed the rationale for the provisions which had given the president extra-constitutional powers since 1948. It also opened the way for Taiwan's first full elections for the National Assembly in December 1991 and polls for the legislature in 1992.

Lee's control of the political agenda was underscored by the retirement at the end of the year of hundreds of senior parliamentarians in the National Assembly, Legislative Yuan and Control Yuan who had held office since the late 1940s without re-election.

The assembly will meet in early 1992 to consider further proposals for constitutional reforms. How far those changes will go in accommodating demands by the opposition for more than a tinkering with the existing document will be determined by the elections and the allocation of seats at the convention.

In a rare television address during the political crisis in April, Lee asked the DPP to abandon a street march protesting against the old guard and told the country that "constitutional reform is not a revolution." He held out the promise that the 1992 constitutional convention would address the opposition's concerns.

The DPP has proposed an entirely new constitution which aims to build a "Republic of Taiwan" and permit the direct election of the president. KMT officials have said that such proposals are out of the question, but what changes they will eventually accept remains subject to bargaining both within and without the ruling party.

With the removal of the emergency provisions and the restoration of full constitutional rule, the awkwardness of Taiwan's two-track system of government became obvious — especially the ambiguous distribution of power between the president and cabinet. The conflict between the Taiwan-born Lee and his premier, former chief of military staff Hau Pei-tsun, has been largely ideological, since each leader represents different wings of the KMT. But it also raised constitutional questions about what kind of government is suitable for Taiwan — the presidential system, parliamentary rule or the present combination of the two.

With the boisterous opposition movement breaking the proscription on advocating independence, Lee's role in domestic affairs was strengthened since he kept open his lines of communication with the DPP. At the end of the year, Lee appeared more confident and less reticent to speak out on important issues than at the beginning. Still, some sympathetic critics continued to question why he did not follow more closely the example of his predecessor and mentor, former president Chiang Ching-kuo, in spending less time on ceremonial functions and more time making his views known among the people.

An embattled Hau was the president's chief lightening rod. While his decisiveness and no-nonsense style of leadership were welcomed by many businessmen and middle-class sup-

porters as a refreshing change from recent reforms, his sometimes combative politics — ranging from cancelling a multi-billion-dollar highway in order to teach a lesson to an opposition-led local government, to cracking down on an increasingly bold independence movement — often had to be softened to maintain social peace.

In one notable demonstration of his lack of restraint in February, Hau signalled his cabinet to walk out of the opening session of the legislature when opposition tactics delayed the delivery of government reports. Hau was also drowned out by protests in September when he delivered his report to the autumn session. The opening of the session was so unruly that the speaker, Liang Su-yung, postponed — for the first time ever — the question-and-answer session of cabinet members which is required by the constitution.

Hau subsequently held talks with opposition members for the first time outside the legislative chamber, which helped ease the tension. Nevertheless, the opposition continued to question his commitment to democracy and called for his resignation.

Government officials were embarrassed that Taiwan's international image has been shaped by the televised parliamentary brawls and fist fights aired overseas — including China, where the communist party tried to use the scenes to score propaganda points.

Lee: orchestrating events.

In the biggest political scandal of the year, then communications minister Clement Chang was forced to resign over revelations that his immediate family had benefited from an insider stock deal. The event pitted two of Taiwan's most influential families against each other after a long and apparently mutually beneficial friendship. The scandal, which broke in March, involved the Hualon Group of companies and the well-connected Weng family, especially the oldest of the four brothers who run the companies, Weng Da-ming.

The case highlighted the close connections between businessmen and government officials that observers said was rife throughout the country. The woman prosecutor in the case, Hsu Ah-kuei, was later indicted by the Control Yuan — one of the five government councils — for pursuing the investigation too vigorously. The prosecution of the prosecutor surprised the legal profession and opposition MPs vowed to come to her defence.

Like the KMT, the DPP had a difficult time keeping its internal disputes from paralysing the party while soliciting funds for a national political campaign for the December elections. On several occasions during the year, the DPP's moderate Formosa faction and the pro-independence New Tide faction united in taking to the streets and openly declaring their party's separatist goals. But factionalism continued to pull the party in several directions.

One advance warning of the party's radicalisation was the resignation in June of popular lawmaker Lin Cheng-chieh. Among the opposition, Lin is a rare believer in the unification of Taiwan with China and he charged that the DPP had become intolerant of such views. He accused the party he helped to establish of becoming more interested in promoting independence than democracy. Lin's resignation preceded by two months the DPP's adoption of an independence constitution and the subsequent amendment to its charter which called for a "Republic of Taiwan."

As the campaign for a new party chairman heated up in August and September, the DPP lurched towards a more radical, pro-independence line. Hsu Hsin-liang was elected as the new DPP chairman in October, narrowly defeating a hero of the New Tide wing for the post. But he faced a central committee dominated by members of the pro-independence faction.

A leader of the Formosa faction, Hsu is a former KMT member who had been blacklisted when he turned against the government in the late 1970s. He returned to Taiwan illegally in 1989 after spending more than 10 years in exile in the US. Like his rival for the party leadership post, Shi Ming-teh, he was released from prison under a presidential amnesty in 1990. DPP leaders said the party had been forced to adopt a more radical independence line because of the KMT's continuing attempts to suppress pro-independence views, as well as Peking's intransigence towards Taiwan and its refusal to renounce the use of force against the island. Under such circumstances, oppositionists claimed the DPP's open advocacy of independence could not make matters worse and also offered the voters a clear-cut alternative to the KMT's unification doctrine.

In an apparent attempt by the government to prove that it had not gone soft on political dissent, police in May arrested four people said to have had contact with an obscure Taiwanese independence activist and former communist living in Japan. The arrests sent several thousand university students and teachers on to the streets to demand Hau's resignation as well as the abolition of Taiwan's sedition laws.

In an attempt to defuse the crisis, the KMT directed the legislature to abolish the harsher sedition laws which imposed a mandatory death sentence on those convicted. But there were further arrests later in the year under the ambiguous provisions of Article 100 of the Criminal Code. Most of those arrested were returned dissidents who had been blacklisted for their support of Taiwan independence. These included officials of the banned World United Formosans for Independence, a pro-independence group that attempted to set up branches in Taiwan for the first time.

One pro-independence group, the Organisation for Taiwan Nation Building, founded by returned dissident Stella Chen, threatened to use violence in confrontations with police. Chen's radicalism made the DPP look moderate by comparison and extended the spectrum of seditious activities under government review. While Chen remained at large, a dozen other independence activists were detained or deported if they showed a US passport. DPP leaders said the return of these activists and the reaction against their arrests had added to the pressures on the party to adopt a stronger pro-independence line.

Although the DPP ignored warnings not to violate the sedition law, the KMT appeared to back away from direct confrontation over the independence issue and postponed a decision on whether to ban the DPP outright. The inaction was partly caused by indecision over how to revise Article 100 and partly dictated by the need to keep democratic reforms on track and not mar the December elections.

Despite the impression of two steps forward and one step back in loosening restrictions on political dissent, one event showed that Taiwan has put at least part of its history behind it. In September, Chiang Kai-shek's widow, now in her 90s, left Taiwan indefinitely to live in her US home. Family acquaintances said she wanted to be closer to friends and relatives since she had few close associates left in Taiwan.

One piece of history which the KMT has tried but failed to put behind it is the massacre by KMT troops of a large number of Taiwanese during an uprising in 1947. Known as the 2-28 incident from the date it began, the event has been a taboo subject during most of the past four decades. Families of victims have campaigned for full disclosure on the killings, which extended over many weeks across the island. In addition to random killings of civilians by troops, the massacre included the execution of intellectuals and Taiwanese officials whom the KMT considered disloyal.

In a gesture to relieve the bitterness still felt among Taiwanese towards the KMT, Lee received relatives of victims and both he and Hau attended memorial services. The cabinet has commissioned a new investigation of the massacre and a public report of their findings, though Taiwanese historians are doubtful that an objective account of the events is now possible. □

# Foreign Relations

Some of Taiwan's pessimism about its indeterminate status in the international community was allayed during 1991. The modest gains did little, however, to relieve popular frustration about Taiwan's political status, while the government's conduct of foreign policy became a domestic issue.

Although Taiwan's formal diplomatic prospects remain bleak, "substantive" relations with major trading partners improved steadily with the first visits by cabinet-level officials from Western Europe in more than 20 years and a steady stream of visitors from the Soviet Union and Eastern Europe.

The improved prospects resulted partly from international accommodation to Taiwan's commercial prowess and partly from changed international opinion towards China in the wake of the crackdown on the student democracy movement and the collapse of communism in Europe. President Lee Teng-hui's "pragmatic diplomacy" took advantage of the changing international environment, though he continued to struggle against rigid, one-China thinking among the old guard in the ruling Kuomintang (KMT).

Relations with France set the pace. In January, France's Minister of Industry Roger Fauroux visited Taipei, opening the way for ministerial-level visits from other Western European countries. Europe's economic ministries were impressed with Taiwan's foreign-exchange holdings, its sizeable trade surplus and prospects for participating in multi-billion-dollar infrastructure projects.

Cabinet ministers from Italy, Ireland and Sweden, and central bank governors from Bulgaria and the Soviet Union, helped to cement unofficial ties with countries that have no diplomatic representation in Taipei. Hundreds of visits by lesser officials, including former US president Gerald Ford and several former US cabinet members, were also a substitute for formal channels of diplomacy. Even Britain, which has traditionally maintained a cool attitude towards Taiwan, dispatched an under-secretary for the first substantive trade talks since the 1950s.

Despite establishing formal ties with Peking in their efforts to gain access to the UN, the newly independent Baltic republics signed agreements to open trade offices in Taipei after visits by Taiwan's Vice–Foreign Minister John Chang in November.

Taiwan also signed air rights agreements with Australia, Austria, Canada, France, New Zealand and Vietnam, and fishing pacts with the Philippines and the Soviet Union

# T

## A I

## P E I

## W O R L D

## T R A D E

## C E N T E R

**TO IMPROVE YOUR BUSINESS VISION, SEE US FIRST**

TWTC puts Asian opportunities in focus for you. With International Trade Shows.

Information services. And over 300,000 export items on permanent display.

So if you want a clear perspective on your Asian operations, we have the right prescription.

Come to TWTC, and improve your business vision. *See us first.*  TAIPEI WORLD TRADE CENTER

*Operated by* CETRA CHINA EXTERNAL TRADE DEVELOPMENT COUNCIL  *Address:* 5 Hsinyi Rd., Sec. 5, Taipei, Taiwan, R.O.C./ *Fax:* (886-2)725-1314/ *Tel:* (02)725-1111

| Line | Value |
|---|---|
| 1 | 20/200 |
| 2 | 20/150 |
| 3 | 20/100 |
| 4 | 20/80 |
| 5 | 20/60 |
| 6 | 20/40 |
| 7 | 20/30 |
| 8 | 20/25 |
| 9 | 20/20 |
| 10 | 20/15 |
| 11 | 20/10 |
| 12 | 20/5 |

during the past year. Taiwan joined the Central American Bank for Economic Integration under its official title, the Republic of China, and was admitted to the Asia Pacific Economic Cooperation (Apec) forum under the name of Chinese Taipei at the same time Peking and Hongkong joined.

Admission to Apec was a major boost for Taiwan's participation in regional economic affairs. The economics ministry estimated Taiwanese investment in the Asian region at more than US$10 billion, and still growing rapidly.

In June, Taipei received encouragement for its application to join Gatt when US President George Bush wrote to a member of the US Congress that Washington would promote Taiwan's bid. Bush's support was welcome, even though it was a concession granted during a White House campaign to renew most favoured nation status for China. Foreign Minister Fredrick Chien had asked that Taiwan's Gatt membership be considered on its merits, and separate from the political rivalry with Peking.

Foreign policy became a major domestic issue with a movement for Taiwan to apply to rejoin the UN — which it left rather than being expelled when the "China" seat was awarded to Peking. The legislature, with bipartisan support, passed a resolution in June asking the government to re-apply "at an appropriate time." The opposition Democratic Progressive Party (DPP) adopted the issue as their main foreign policy proposal. Public demonstrations in Taipei and Kaohsiung in favour of UN membership were held in September and October sponsored by the Association for a Plebiscite on Taiwan, a pro-independence group.

The biggest foreign policy setback of the year was the cancellation of Lee's long-planned trip to Central America in August. The official reason for sending Vice-President Li Yuan-tzu in Lee's place was unspecified domestic affairs. But insiders said the last-minute change of plan was caused by the collapse of an over-ambitious agenda. Lee had wanted to make informal stopovers in Japan and the US, but Peking blocked the Tokyo visit and meetings in the US with senior officials could not be arranged.

The government's potentially large foreign aid programme continued to be bogged down with inadequate funding and bureaucratic red tape. Aid has been a decisive factor in enticing some smaller countries into a diplomatic relationship with Taipei in the past three years, and in strengthening commercial ties with countries that have official relations with China.

However, the government has so far only distributed about US$114 million from its well-publicised International Economic Cooperation and Development Fund controlled by the economics ministry. When it was set up in 1988, the fund's goal was to allocate US$1.1 billion in aid over five years in the form of soft loans and technical assistance grants to "friendly" developing countries.

In addition to some US$30 million in special humanitarian aid to two dozen countries distributed by the foreign ministry, Taiwan also contributed to countries affected by the Gulf War. Jordan accepted US$20 million and US$10 million was given to help Kurdish refugees in Iraq. Under pressure from China, Egypt did not accept a US$5 million aid offer and Turkey accepted only US$2 million of a similar offer.

The lack of coordination and accountability of Taiwan's various aid programmes prompted lawmakers to propose a bill that would centralise development assistance and make it accountable to the legislature. Meanwhile, Chien pushed for more generous funding of assistance programmes aimed at developing countries in Asia and Latin America.

Chien also argued that China's attempts to isolate Taiwan not only denied the country its rightful role in international affairs, but also fuelled the island's independence movement. He credited Lee's flexible diplomacy with opening up new opportunities for Taiwan's foreign policy since 1988, though the lack of domestic consensus over relations towards China have hampered agreement on foreign policy goals.

Relations with China were prickly at mid-year, when the independence issue sparked an exchange of Chinese proverbs between leaders of the KMT and the Chinese Communist Party. China's President Yang Shangkun said Taiwan's opposition movement was playing with fire by openly advocating independence, while Taiwan's Prime Minister Hau Pei-tsun gave a similar warning to Peking if it tried to intervene in the island's domestic politics.

Generally, however, relations were relaxed and business ties between the two became increasingly routine. Trade and investment remained on an indirect basis according to Taipei's policy, though the distinction between direct and indirect dealings was often blurred. Taiwan relaxed banking rules on permitting direct remittances to China, essentially endorsing for some local banks a widespread practice among foreign banks in Taiwan. The government also published a list of service industries in China in which indirect investment would be allowed.

In April, some 2,500 small and medium-sized companies voluntarily registered their investments in China — officially estimated at more than US$700 million — with the economics ministry. Unofficial sources and the Chinese Government maintain the actual figure is several times that amount. Some large corporations — including President Enterprises, Wei Chuan Foods and Chung Shing Textiles — also received official approval for their China investments for the first time.

During the year, the semi-official Straits Exchange Foundation sent two delegations to Peking and a third to meet provincial officials in southeastern China. The visits, while lacking concrete results, may have broken the ice for some form of institutionalised ties and quasi-official cooperation on non-political issues. Peking also indicated it would set up a counterpart organisation to handle functional relations with Taiwan, and two-way exchanges appeared likely to accelerate in the future. One priority issue for cooperation was fighting piracy and smuggling in the Taiwan Straits.

Observers noted the mildness of Peking's reaction to France's decision to sell Taiwan warships in August, perhaps in recognition that there was little China could do to restrain such arms deals. A building programme for Perry-class frigates under licence from the US saw the launch at a Kaohsiung shipyard of the first in a series of the warships to be completed during the 1990s. Plans to purchase Kfir C7 fighters from Israel, however, were abandoned in the perennial hope that the US would allow the sale of F16 combat aircraft to Taiwan.

The country's indigenous defence fighter programme, which also relies on US technology, received a setback when a prototype aircraft crashed during a crucial test flight in July. One of Taiwan's top test pilots was killed in the accident, though the defence ministry claimed the failure would not delay the aircraft's production schedule.

Taiwan's relations with the US were the subject of debate among independence activists and KMT stalwarts, as both sides tried to invoke US policy to support their conflicting views on the island's future. While Hau expressed the view that Washington would not support Taiwanese independence, former US ambassador to Peking and now Deputy Assistant Secretary for Defence for International Security Affairs James Lilley encouraged pro-independence groups with his frank commentaries on Peking's "outdated" ideas of sovereignty over Taiwan. □

# Economy/Infrastructure

The government's projected 7% annual economic growth rate was met by widespread scepticism early in the year on doubts that Taiwan's manufacturers could achieve much while the US was in recession.

Nevertheless, Taiwan's economy picked up momentum during 1991 from expanding domestic markets and exports to China. By November, economists estimated that the year's annual growth rate would be 2 percentage points above the 5.2% recorded for 1990. The stockmarket also recovered somewhat from its Gulf War induced nerves, to breach the 6,000-mark several times at mid-year before settling into a trough as investors withdrew ahead of the December elections.

Other positive economic indicators included a modest increase in private domestic investment, a sharp slowdown in outward capital flows and a current-account surplus estimated at US$4 billion. Exports rose 14% and imports climbed 16% during the year's first three quarters for a total two-way trade of roughly US$103 billion to the end of September.

Taiwan's main trade problem continued to be its deficit with Japan, which surpassed its trade surplus with the US for the first time. The Japanese deficit exceeded US$9 billion due to a heavy dependence on high-technology industrial components and heavy machinery for local factories. Japan dispatched its first large buying mission in a decade in May in an effort to placate Taiwan's concerns.

The surplus with the US fell from a high of US$16 billion in 1987 to about US$8 billion in 1991, more than fulfilling President Lee Teng-hui's pledge of three years ago to reduce the trade surplus with the US by 10% a year. While the US remains Taiwan's main trading partner, it now accounts for less than one third of its exports. At mid-year, Hongkong became Taiwan's trading partner with the largest surplus, mainly due to exports through Hongkong to China. Officials were concerned that trade with China was

**Infrastructure: concrete measures.**

growing too fast and that Taiwan could become too dependent on the China market in the next few years.

The government's NT$8.2 trillion (US$310 billion) six-year infrastructure development plan announced in late 1990 became the centrepiece of national economic policy and was expected to dominate national planning through the mid-1990s. Spending on the projects began to rise during the year, though not as rapidly as expected because of planning delays as well as a labour shortage and other construction problems.

Criticism of the government's plan to finance at least 50% of the cost of the plan's 779 projects by public bond issues focused on its negative effects on private investment. Critics also said the government had badly underestimated costs. For example, estimates for one of the largest transportation projects — the high-speed rail between Keelung and Kaohsiung — increased from US$12 billion to US$18 billion before the design phase of the project had been contracted out to a French consulting company.

The debate receded late in the year when government revenue collections were higher than expected and the initial bond

auction went smoothly. The government announced in July it would float a record NT$316 billion bonds in the 1992 financial year, but the amount was soon scaled back and many observers assumed that the six-year plan would not be completed before the end of the decade.

Shirley Kuo, head of the Council on Economic Planning and Development which drafted the plan, pointed out that 60% of the plan's projects were already approved and that Taiwan's high savings rate and low debt ratio presented no difficulties for raising the needed funds.

Expenditure for the plan's projects had top priority in the government budget, which showed a record growth of 52% in public expenditure for the 1992 financial year beginning in July. This marked the first time public investment spending exceeded private investment. The government's total budget of NT$992 billion was up almost 20% over the previous year, while defence spending fell by 3% to about 25% of the total.

The Central Bank of China, the country's central bank, kept interest rates high for the second year in a row in order to retain funds at home to finance infrastructure spending and encourage more domestic investment after a sharp drop of 8.8% in 1990. The strategy appeared to work, though one side-effect was that the NT dollar appreciated strongly during the second half of the year to a two-year high against the US currency. Under pressure from local business interests, the central bank cut the discount rate modestly in July and September, but local rates remained 3% or more above those of Japan and the US.

Its strong export performance left Taiwan vying for first place with Japan for the distinction of having the world's largest hoard of foreign-exchange reserves. Holdings ranged from US$73 billion to US$76 billion during the year, excluding gold reserves of US$5.6 billion and seed money of US$7 billion for the newly established Taipei interbank money market.

With roughly 60% of foreign-exchange holdings in US dollars, the central bank reacted angrily to an inaccurate report that it had moved a large cache of funds out of US banks because of nervousness about the stability of the US banking system. Taipei bankers said the central bank had been actively shifting funds among foreign banks to be sure they were deposited with reliable institutions, but central bank governor Samuel Hsieh vehemently denied a report that large funds had been shifted out of the US to Western Europe and Japan.

Not everyone felt so sure about Taiwan's banking system, however, after the finance ministry announced in June that it was licensing 15 new private banks. The long-awaited announcement was the boldest move yet in liberalising the country's financial system and breaking the oligopoly of the state-run commercial banks. Some bankers were doubtful that so many new banks could survive the competition. Premier Hau Pei-tsun commented publicly that some of the banks were speculative ventures by big business groups.

The new banks were expected to open in early 1992 after raising a minimum of NT$10 billion each in capital. Only four of the original 19 applicants were denied a licence, mainly because of over-concentration of ownership and inadequate business plans. The new bank executives claimed it would be easy to compete with the hidebound and inefficient state banks, and expected their strong financial backing from large corporations would give them an instant deposit base from which to build a retail clientele.

Other liberalisation measures during the year included the opening of the Taiwan stockmarket to foreign institutional investors, the reform of the bond issuing system and the reopening of a forward foreign-exchange market. By November, 16 foreign securities companies had received approval for almost US$750 million for the equity and bond markets, though some fund managers were having difficulty winning over subscribers within the time allotted for bringing the funds into the country.

The bond issuing system shifted to an auction format in November for the first time and the number of primary dealers was expanded from a handful of state banks to 23 banks and trust companies and seven security firms. The more open distribution was expected to enliven the secondary market and make trading of bonds easier for the small investor, while also aiding the government in financing its massive public spending programme.

Foreign investment in Taiwan decreased by 14% during the first eight months over the same period in 1990 while outbound investment rose by nearly 20%.

Outward investment continued to flow to China and Southeast Asia as well as Europe in 1991, with official data showing a total of US$1.3 billion for the first three quarters. Private economists estimate that the actual figure is several times that amount. Malaysia was the leading destination, accounting for one third of total registered outbound investment excluding China, while Eastern Europe and the Soviet Union were the latest targets for Taiwanese business ventures.

Economics ministry officials were surprised in April when more than 2,500 companies registered their investments in China, declaring a total value of more than US$660 million. Although the investment amounts were almost certainly understated, the number of companies was double what officials had expected. Most of the Taiwanese companies had located themselves in Guangdong province or the Shenzhen special economic zone near Hongkong rather than in Fujian, which is geographically and culturally closer to Taiwan.

Direct trade and investment in China is still banned, but the government increased the number of commodities and industries permitted on an indirect basis — though the distinction continued to remain unclear. In an attempt to control commercial ties with China, the Mainland Affairs Council published a list of proposed punitive measures the government would take against companies violating national policy. However, the rules had still not received formal approval by the end of the year.

Meanwhile, the chairman of the Formosa Plastics Group, Wang Yung-ching, returned to Taiwan after a two-year absence and continued to fight for government approval of a multi-billion petrochemical complex in the Xiamen special economic zone opposite Taiwan. Wang also agreed to build a sixth naphtha cracker at a site on Taiwan's west coast, but final details delayed construction on what analysts said was essentially a confidence-building project.

Among the major new ventures of the year were Eva Airlines, a subsidiary of the Evergreen Group of companies, and Taiwan Aerospace, a joint venture between the government and private-sector corporations. Eva was launched on 1 July after a bruising political fight in the legislature over licensing and other related issues.

The national carrier, China Airlines (CAL), also launched its own subsidiary, Mandarin Airlines, to fly routes not accessible for the flag carrier, beginning with a direct service to Australia.

Taiwan's bid to build an aerospace industry at home and enter the international aerospace market was even more ambitious. The government offered its strong backing for the idea, but private corporations were reluctant to pay up their majority share of the subscribed capital of NT$10 billion until there were concrete projects which offered a return on their investment.

A plan was duly delivered in November, with a proposed equity partnership between the commercial aviation division of McDonnell Douglas Corp. (MDC) of the US and a company associated with Taiwan Aerospace Corp. (TAC). MDC persuaded TAC to offer US$2 billion for 40% of MDC's commercial aircraft section, to be spun off as a separate company. If the deal is consummated as scheduled during January 1992, and against strong US Congressional objections, it would give Taiwan an instant civil aircraft industry.

In the labour market, the government changed policies on importing foreign workers after experiencing severe manpower shortages in key industries including construction, textiles and metal working. After the voluntary repatriation of more than 25,000 foreign workers in January and February, the cabinet ruled that certain labour-short industries could import foreign workers, as well as construction companies operating on key infrastructure projects. □

## Data

**Major industries:** Steel bars, 5.12 million tonnes (10.32 million); synthetic fibres, 1.77 million tonnes (2.28 million); PVC, 920,954 tonnes (805,428); pig iron, 59,750 tonnes (29,904); TV sets, 2.1 million (5.17 million); shipbuilding, 1,211,607 grt (1,201,549).

**Major agriculture:** Rice, 1.81 million tonnes (1.86 million); fisheries products, 1.46 million tonnes (1.37 million); sugarcane, 5.58 million tonnes (6.63 million); vegetables, 2.71 million tonnes (2.95 million); timber, 113,830 m³ (157,289).

**Oil and natural gas:** Crude petroleum, 182,400 kl (135,100); natural gas, 1.3 million kl (1.4 million).

**Mining:** Coal, 470,000 tonnes (780,000); salt, 315,900 tonnes (169,982); sulphur, 99,000 tonnes (76,060); marble, 11.24 million tonnes (12.12 million); limestone, 13.92 million tonnes (14.07 million).

**Major exports:** Electrical machinery and equipment, US$17.89 billion (US$18 billion); textiles, leather, wood, paper and related products, US$13.84 billion (US$14.74 billion); metal products, US$4.05 billion (US$3.96 billion); machinery, US$3.19 billion (US$4.23 billion); food, beverages and tobacco products, US$2.27 billion (US$2.4 billion).

**Major imports:** Chemicals and pharmaceuticals, US$8.17 billion (US$7.65 billion); electrical machinery and apparatus, US$7.65 billion (US$8.61 billion); basic metals, US$6.23 billion (US$8.14 billion); machinery, US$5.39 billion (US$5.26 billion); minerals, US$4.91 billion (US$4.16 billion); textiles, leather, wood, paper and related products, US$3.56 billion (US$3.41 billion); agricultural, forestry and fishery products, US$3.02 billion (US$3.32 billion); crude oil, US$2.57 billion (US$2.61 billion).

**Tourism and transport:** Arrivals, 1.93 million (2 million); departures, 2.94 million (860,207); total visitor expenditure, US$1.74 billion (US$2.7 billion); airlines, China Airlines, Eva Air.

**Finance:** 59 banks operating, 35 branches or representative office of foreign banks, 24 local banks (including 8 medium business banks), 13 public and 11 private; Taiwan Stock Exchange, Taipei, 212 listed company.

**Currency:** New Taiwan dollar. NT$26.16 = US$1 Nov. 1991 (NT$27.26 = US$1 Nov. 1990).

**Public holidays** (1992): 1-2 Jan. (New Year), 3-6 Feb. (Lunar New Year), 29 Mar. (Youth Day), 5 Apr. (Tomb Sweeping Day), 16 June (Dragon Boat Festival), 28 Sept. (Teacher's Day), 22 Sept. (Mid-Autumn Festival), 10 Oct. (National Day), 25 Oct. (Taiwan Retrocession Day), 31 Oct. (Chiang Kai-shek's Birthday), 12 Nov. (Sun Yat-sen's Birthday), 25 Dec. (Constitution Day).

**Government ministries:** Interior, 107 Roosevelt Rd, Sec. 4, Taipei, tel. 362 5241; Foreign Affairs, 2 Chienshou Rd, Taipei, tel. 311 9292; National Defence, Chiehshou Hall, Chungkong S. Rd, Taipei, tel. 311 6117; Finance, 2 Aikuo W. Rd, Taipei, tel. 322 8000; Education, 5 Chungshan S. Rd, Taipei, tel. 351 3111; Justice, 130 Chungking S. Rd, Sec. 1, Taipei, tel. 314 6871; Economic Affairs, 15 Foochow St, Taipei, tel. 321 2200; Transportation and Communications, 2 Changsha St, Sec. 1, Taipei, tel. 311 2661.

**Major banks:** Bank of America, 205 Tunhua N. Rd, Taipei, tel. 715 4111, fax 713 2850, tlx 11339, 22378; Bank of Taiwan, 120 Chungkong S. Rd, Sec. 1, Taipei, tel. 314 7377, fax 361 3203, tlx 27500, 27501, 11201, 11202; Chase Manhattan Bank, 8-9 Fl, 673 Minsheng E. Rd, Taipei, tel. 514 1234, fax 514 1299, tlx 21823 CHAMANBK; Citibank, 742 Minsheng E. Rd, Taipei, tel. 715 5931, fax 712 7388, tlx 11722, 25604, 16744; First Commercial Bank, 30 Chungking S. Rd, Sec. 1, Taipei, tel. 311 1111, fax 361 0036, tlx 11310, 11729; International Commercial Bank of China, 100 Chilin Rd, Taipei, tel. 563 3156, fax 561 1216, tlx 11300 INCOBK.

**Weather:** Taiwan has a subtropical climate with average temperatures in the north of 22℃ and 24.5℃ in the south. Summer (May-July) is hot and humid. Winter is relatively short, with some snow in mountainous areas in Jan.-Feb. May-Nov. is typhoon season. Annual average rainfall in the north is 2,500 mm.

**Taxation:** Corporate tax, 15-25%; personal tax, 6-50%; VAT, 5%.

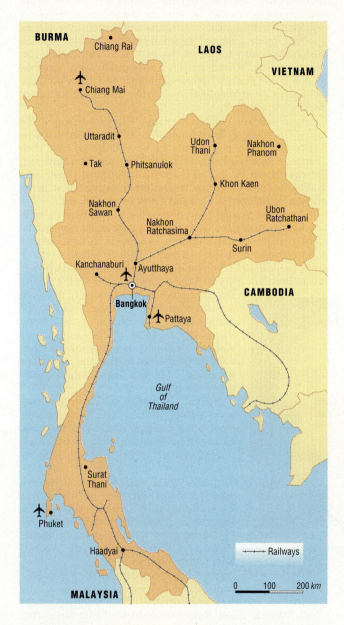

# THAILAND

The Thai monarchy's absolute power ended in a 1932 coup by a group of Western-educated civilians and army officers. The resulting government evolved into a parliamentary structure, though the monarch remains head of state.

Army officer Plaek Phibunsongkhram emerged as the power in the 1932 group, serving as prime minister from 1938-44. During World War II he led the country into an alliance with Japan, but an active Thai resistance ensured Western sympathy when the war ended. Phibunsongkhram held power between 1947-57, when he was overthrown in a coup. A succession of military strongmen, Sarit Thanarat, Thanom Kittikachorn and Prapas Charusathien, ruled in an increasingly dictatorial and repressive manner until the military government was overthrown in a popular uprising in 1973. Three years of democratic, civilian-led politics ended as the military returned to power in a bloody coup in October 1976.

In 1978 prime minister Kriangsak Chomanand was able to soften the gulf between the rightwing soldiers who ascended in 1976 and liberals and intellectuals. Kriangsak reintroduced parliamentary elections in 1979, but growing military unease over the Vietnamese invasion of Cambodia left him weak and under pressure. He resigned in 1980 to be replaced by army chief Gen. Prem Tinsulanond.

Prem remained popular during his eight years in office, surviving three democratic elections and two failed coup attempts. However, pressure for an elected leader forced Prem out in 1988, when he was replaced by Chart Thai Party leader Chatichai Choonhavan.

Chatichai's formation of a civilian coalition appeared to signal that Thailand had finally past the era of military domination. However, coalition instability and high-level corruption gave ammunition to the army, which overthrew Chatichai in a bloodless coup on 23 February 1991.

# Politics/Social Affairs

Thai politics were dominated for much of 1991 by the aftermath of the 23 February coup and the run-up to general elections promised by the military junta for early 1992.

The coup which toppled former prime minister Chatichai Choonhavan's elected government was a bloodless affair plotted by all the armed forces' chiefs. The driving force was powerful army commander Gen. Suchinda Kraprayoon who, despite his official title as vice-chairman of the military's National Peacekeeping Council (NPC), served as political strongman throughout the succeeding months. In October, Suchinda became concurrent supreme commander in addition to his other titles.

Suchinda — who initially said he had no ambition of becoming prime minister and was intent on returning the country to civilian-led democracy within a year — was less adamant on the issue towards the end of 1991, and became widely regarded as the figure most likely to become Thailand's next premier.

The issue came to a head on 19 November, when a coalition of most political parties, academic and student groups staged a 50,000-strong protest in Bangkok against the country's proposed new constitution and the junta's alleged intention to

**Head of State**
King Bhumipol Adulyadej (Rama IX).
**Prime Minister**
Anand Panyarachun;
**Deputy Prime Ministers**
Snoh Unakul, Pow Sarasin,
Meechai Ruchupan;
**Foreign**
Arsa Sarasin;
**Finance**
Sutthee Singhasaneh;
**Commerce**
Amaret Sila-on;
**Interior**
Gen. Issarapong Noonpakdee;
**Transport and Communications**
Nukul Prachuabmoh;
**Agriculture and Cooperatives**
Anat Arbhabhirama;
**Defence**
Adm. Prapas Krisnachani;

**Justice**
Prapasna Uaychai;
**Science, Technology and Energy**
Sanga Sabhasri;
**Education**
Kaw Sawasdipanich;
**Public Health**
Phairote Ningsanonda;
**Industry**
Sippanonda Ketudat;
**University Affairs**
Kasem Suwanagul;
**Armed Forces Supreme Commander**
Gen. Suchinda Kraprayoon;
**National Peacekeeping Council Chairman**
Gen. Sunthorn Kongsompong.

retain political power after elections slated for March 1992.

Suchinda later told a news conference that neither he nor any other members of the NPC would become prime minister, while the draft constitution was amended to appease its critics. Articles eliminated included one that allowed acting civil servants and military personnel to serve as cabinet officials or prime minister, and another that increased the size of the non-elected senate to give it greater power than the elected house of representatives.

A widespread mood of hostility towards the ruling military junta may now have moderated as the generals displayed an uncharacteristic willingness to compromise. Nevertheless, some politicians, academics and students at the forefront of the "democratic forces" opposed to what they view as the military's bid to retain substantial political power after the next election have vowed to fight on.

While the constitution remained the focus for the opposition campaign, the issue continues to be an apparent widespread distrust of the junta. When the military toppled Chatichai's government, they vowed to end corruption in high places, dismantle Chatichai's "parliamentary dictatorship" and return the country to democracy through an election.

Thais generally gave the military the benefit of the doubt in their distaste for the rampant corruption which characterised Chatichai's government. But now a growing number of critics claim the NPC has not kept its promises and, on the contrary, aims to perpetuate its undemocratic power by manipulating the new constitution through its tame national assembly, with little to show so far in the drive against corruption.

The February coup caught most Thais off-guard as such putschs were generally believed to be redundant given the country's political development and because two previous coup attempts in 1981 and 1985 failed. The 1991 coup, however, differed from other military takeovers. Unlike previous putschs — mainly vehicles for military figures to seize power for themselves or their surrogates — the armed forces chiefs who toppled Chatichai were widely perceived, at least initially, as having reasonable cause because many people had become exasperated by the corruption and blatant pursuit of vested interests at all levels of government.

The coup-makers also accused Chatichai — whose coalition government had an overwhelming parliamentary majority — of seeking to establish a "parliamentary dictatorship" and subvert the role of the traditionally powerful bureaucracy and military. Further, Chatichai and his powerful coterie of young advisers were accused of interfering with the police force by ousting the national police chief and moving senior police officers in order to gain effective control.

The next step in Chatichai's political programme, according to the military, was a possible attempt to try and control the army. When Chatichai was arrested as he was about to fly to the northern city of Chiang Mai for an audience with King Bhumibol Adulyadej, he was widely thought to be planning the removal of the then supreme commander Gen. Sunthorn Kongsompong — now figurehead chairman of the NPC — and perhaps even Suchinda.

On 26 November, a military-appointed anti-corruption committee set up investigate charges that Chatichai and some of his senior party colleagues were "unusually rich," announced it had ordered the seizure of assets valued at more than Baht 266.5 million (US$10.5 million) from the former prime minister. It was not immediately clear whether Chatichai would be arrested or charged as a result of the panel's findings.

The one move by the generals shortly after the coup which received broad domestic and international acclaim was to appoint an interim civilian government comprising a number of respected businessmen, technocrats and former bureaucrats. The NPC made a shrewd choice in selecting widely regarded businessman and former diplomat Anand Panyarachun as prime minister. Anand and his team quickly set to work on economic and financial reforms, running the country's administration at a working-level basis while leaving major policy decisions to the junta.

Anand had fallen foul of the then military leadership in the mid-1970s when, as foreign ministry permanent secretary, he had been active in engineering the US withdrawal from their Thai bases shortly after the end of the Vietnam War. However, he was chosen by the NPC for his subsequent career as a leading business executive in an effort to restore international investor confidence in Thailand's post-coup economy.

In the event, Anand proved to be less pliable than the military leaders may have wanted. In September, he managed to stave off requests from Sunthorn — acting in his then capacity as supreme commander-to agree to Baht 50 billion worth of arms, including a French-built air defence system and up to 40 Italian-Brazilian AMX jet fighters. Political analysts felt Anand was acting not merely prudently but from a position of power, on the basis that the junta needed him more than he needed them. Any move by the NPC to dismiss Anand would have seriously eroded international confidence in Thailand, as well as removing a popular figure from the government's helm.

**Anand: shrewd choice.**

Suchinda's immediate predecessor as army chief, Chaovalit Yongchaiyut, emerged as a leading opponent of the junta. Chaovalit has been nurturing his own New Aspiration Party (NAP) with a view to becoming prime minister himself. Although Suchinda and Chaovalit referred to each other as military brothers after the coup, Chaovalit's veiled criticism of the NPC shortcomings and Suchinda's retorts that his former chief was only trying to kindle his own political ambitions, set the two men on a collision course.

What seemed to upset Chaovalit most was the appearance of a new political party, Samakkhi Tham, organised mainly by a retired air force officer close to air force commander Air Chief Marshal Kaset Rojananin, which openly supported Suchinda as the next prime minister. While the party attracted a number of leading former MPs to its ranks, it was also apparently poised to form a formal alliance with Chatichai's old Chart Thai party.

Political analysts viewed these manoeuvres as Machiavellian even by the standards of Thai politics. In October, senior Chart Thai members elected retired air chief marshal and present Airports Authority of Thailand governor Somboon Rahong as their new leader to replace Chatichai. Somboon was not only known to be close to Kaset, but had previously been active in setting up the Samakkhi Tham party. It was thought that the two parties would work together to form the core of the next government and support Suchinda as the next prime minister.

The political arena is now polarised between those politicians supporting the military leadership, particularly Suchinda, and those surrounding Chaovalit and his NAP. While Samakkhi Tham, Chart Thai and perhaps some other parties coalesced with the Suchinda-for-prime-minister theme, others

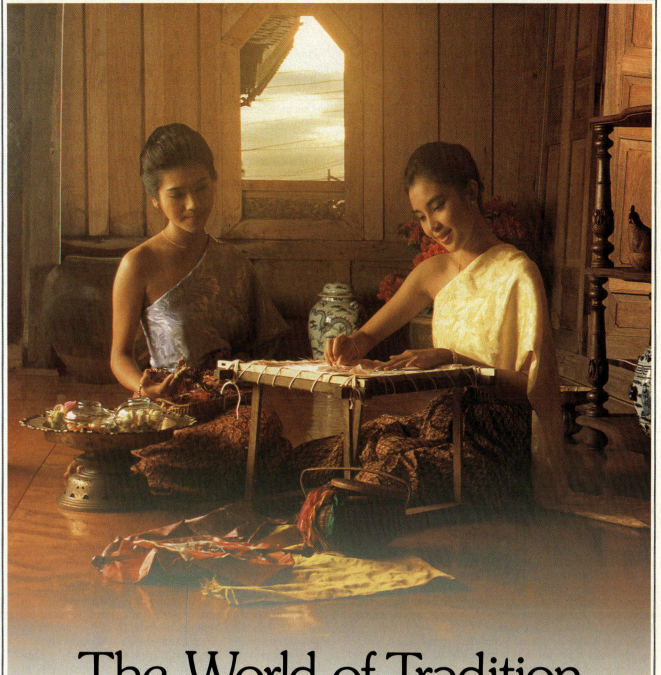

# The World of Tradition

Refinement of mind leads to fine working skills.
As it was in the past, so it is today.
Bangkok Bank Ltd., Thailand's foremost,
keeps the tradition alive to provide the finest financial services.

**Bangkok Bank Limited**
Thailand's Largest Bank

saw Chaovalit as their main hope. Despite being a former army commander — a position in Thailand which tends to breed political arrogance — Chaovalit is now seen as a politician who abides by the rules. In contrast to his former proteges now leading the armed forces, he is viewed as a champion of democracy.

At an early November forum, Chaovalit joined with Palang Dharma leader Chamlong Srimuang and Democrat Party deputy leader Banyat Bantadtan to oppose Suchinda becoming an unelected prime minister. Chamlong, a retired army major-general, is the popular Bangkok governor and his party has long been wooed by others because of its entrenched position in the capital. The Democrat Party, Thailand's oldest, has remained the most intact of all the pre-coup parties, drawing its strength mainly from the country's south.

Of the other major parties, the Social Action Party — Chatichai's ruling coalition partner until December 1990 — is now in disarray. Its former leader, respected elder statesman Kukrit Pramoj, has withdrawn from the party leadership while its current leading figure, former communications minister Montri Pongpanich, is being investigated by the NPC's assets committee for unexplained wealth.

The Solidarity Party, the second-largest parliamentary party after Chart Thai during the Chatichai era, has virtually disintegrated as its leaders have moved to NAP or Samakkhi Tham. Its leader Narong Wongwan — agriculture minister at the time of the coup — has since become the figurehead leader of Samakkhi Tham, reflecting the party's campaign to enlist well-known political names to capitalise on what it hoped the new constitution would change to a party-slate, rather than an individual candidate, method of voting.

It is clear that the coup has prompted a total revamp of Thailand's traditional party politics. Indeed, some observers believe this was one of the main intentions of the military leaders who carried out the putsch.

The NPC's secretary-general, army deputy commander Gen. Issarapong Noonpakdi, was appointed to the interim-government's powerful position as interior minister. In this capacity he made a show of organising a campaign to educate the majority of Thais who live in rural areas not to accept bribes from candidates during elections. However, most political commentators saw this effort as unlikely to have much effect on villagers, among whom the vote-buying system during elections has become ingrained.

Issarapong also announced a crackdown on organised crime and the mafia-type warlords it has spawned. The *jao poh*, or criminal warlords, were ordered to report to their local police chiefs for questioning. Some jao poh decided to leave the country for a while, while others reinforced their connections with powerful military and political figures. Overall, the campaign was not viewed as a success if its intention was to rid the country of criminal powerbrokers and the violence they perpetrated. □

# Foreign Relations

Thailand's relations with much of the industrialised world suffered as a result of the 23 February coup, as the US and other Western countries condemned the overthrow of then prime minister Chatichai Choonhavan's democratically elected government by a military junta.

The US subsequently withdrew its economic and military aid to Thailand, estimated to be worth around US$100 million a year, while Western European countries confined themselves to verbal criticism. Japan, Thailand's major foreign investor, reserved its judgment though the inflow of Japanese investment took a marked dip.

However, the military junta and its appointed interim civilian government managed to weather Western opprobrium without much difficulty. While the West viewed the military junta — formalised by the National Peacekeeping Council (NPC) — as a retrograde step on the road to a more democratic style of government, there was general acclaim when a civilian interim government led by respected businessman Anand Panyarachun was appointed. Nevertheless, Anand was not invited to visit any Western countries during his term, though he was expected to visit Tokyo at year-end.

Bangkok's primary foreign policy concerns were, in any event, concentrated on relations with its Southeast Asian neighbours and — to a lesser extent — its Asean partners. Under military-appointed Foreign Minister Arsa Sarasin, Thailand pursued a policy of trying to set itself up as a base for those countries wanting to do business with Indochina and Burma, as well as playing an important role in the process to hammer out a Cambodian peace agreement.

However, Thailand's attitude towards Burma — where many companies owned by or linked to the military have obtained lucrative contracts to exploit that country's forest, marine and mineral wealth — also aroused concern in the West, given the international condemnation of the Rangoon military regime's human-rights and political record.

Bangkok's efforts to improve its relations with, and influence on, events in Indochina proved less contentious and were generally more successful in diplomatic terms. This view was bolstered by the visit to Thailand by Vietnamese Prime Minister Vo Van Kiet in October.

Thailand and Vietnam have been long-standing adversaries in the sub-region, particularly since the Vietnamese invasion of Cambodia in December 1978 when many analysts saw non-communist Thailand as the next potential victim were Vietnam to continue its expansionist policies. Radical changes in the Soviet-led communist world have since reduced such speculation, particularly as Vietnam began to suffer from the withdrawal of Soviet economic and military aid.

Kiet and Anand signed a communique during the Vietnamese prime minister's visit that declared neither country posed a security threat to the other. In addition, the two leaders signed an investment promotion and protection arrangement, reflecting the Thai business community's desire to invest in Vietnam. There were further deals that ensured Thailand access to Vietnam's offshore gas reserves, though an accord on mutually acceptable fishing arrangements was postponed.

In this regard, the Thai interim government merely continued to follow the line laid down by its ousted predecessor in regarding Indochina as a marketplace rather than a battlefield. Bangkok also played a significant role in urging the four warring Cambodian factions into signing the 23 October peace agreement, having hosted two meetings of the Cambodian Supreme National Council in Pattaya during June and August.

Under Chatichai, Thailand was considered by other Asean countries as overly keen to forge closer contacts with Vietnam and Cambodian Prime Minister Hun Sen's Hanoi-backed regime. Arsa made it plain on taking office that Thailand's relations with its immediate neighbours were a priority, while paying lip-service to enhancing links with its Asean partners.

Arsa has had to perform a balancing act with Vietnam, given the Thai military's lingering suspicions over Hanoi's adventurist tendencies. Shortly before Kiet's arrival in Bangkok, Thai army commander and vice-chairman of the NPC Gen. Suchinda Kraprayoon publically said that Vietnam still remained a potential threat to Thailand. On the eve of Kiet's arrival, Suchinda also criticised the Vietnamese Embassy in Bangkok for maintaining contacts with Vietnamese settlers in Thailand's northeastern region. However, Anand and Arsa managed to smooth over Thai military suspicions, while also boosting Thai businessmen's chances of gaining access to Indochina's natural resources and emerging markets.

Arsa also made relations with neighbouring Laos a priority. Laos will be the main beneficiary of a newly launched Baht 200 million (US$7.8 million) a year programme intended to aid Thailand's poorer neighbours, notably through education and technology transfers. Bangkok's policy, given close Thai-Lao cultural and linguistic links, appears intended to draw its landlocked neighbour away from its ideological and economic dependence on Vietnam.

Thailand's neighbours appear to have a prevailing sense that the country sees itself as something of a neo-colonial power. While Thailand's manufacturing sector is booming, largely due to foreign investment from Japan, Taiwan, Hongkong the US and the EC, its natural resources — particularly its forests — have been severely depleted.

Indochinese countries and Burma are well aware that the Thais are looking across their borders with a view to fuelling their industry with supplies of primary products that have become increasingly difficult to secure at home. Vietnam has already warned that it is not interested in being exploited by Thais, while the Burmese are increasingly turning to other regional sources of investment — notably Singapore — to off-set the threat of Thai commercial hegemony. □

# Economy/Infrastructure

In a year marked by economic and political turbulence, Thailand managed an even deceleration of its overheated economy to come in for a soft landing by the end of the third quarter. However, while the slowdown brought an end to the post-1986 boom — during which annual growth rates averaged 10% — the 1992-96 Five-Year Plan issued during the year still forecast an average growth of 8.2% over the period.

Neither the Gulf War nor Thailand's 23 February coup had any lasting detrimental effect on the economy — indeed, the country probably benefited from both. The Gulf War brought down oil prices, which were posing a serious threat to Thailand's energy-hungry and import-dependent economy. The heavy cost of imported oil exacerbated a growing current-account imbalance, and generated overseas concerns that Thailand would be forced to either control imports or devalue the baht. In the event, neither occurred.

While the coup startled many foreign investors, the junta's swift installation of an impressive group of technocrats, led by Prime Minister Anand Panyarachun — a former president of the Federation of Thai Industries — calmed early fears. The military-appointed interim government quickly asserted its independence, and began processing scores of structural reform measures which had been stalled by political infighting over the previous three years. Meanwhile, the Bank of Thailand (BOT, the central bank), was left alone to bring the economy down to a more manageable speed.

The slowdown was sharp. At the beginning of the year commercial bank lending was growing at an annual rate of 33.5%, while deposits were lagging at 27.5%. Despite maintaining a high in-

**Property market: distorting the economy.**

terest-rate regime through June — prime was 16% — lending remained strong and money supply kept growing at over 19%. This was caused primarily by commercial banks obtaining funds offshore for their clients — corporate entities borrowing directly offshore have to pay a 15% withholding tax on interest payments, while banks do not. Further, many locals borrowed offshore to arbitrage the 4% gap between foreign and domestic interest rates, which BOT could not raise for essentially political reasons.

This rapid growth in money threatened to drive inflation up towards 7%, while at the same time the country's current-account deficit began to provoke official concern. In December 1990, imports grew at 29% against 14.4% for exports. The current-account deficit then was already US$7 billion, or nearly 9% of GDP.

By June the gap had closed, though imports were still growing at 23% against 20% for exports. With tourism depressed due to the Gulf War and recession in many Western economies, the current account was still above 8% of GDP and some projections saw it topping 10% by year end. In the April-June period, many foreign analysts believed the only way out of this situation was for the Thai authorities to impose strict import controls or devalue the baht.

The BOT chose to wait, while telling the commercial banks to stop borrowing offshore, and by September its patience bore fruit. The post–Gulf War fall in oil prices fed into Thailand's import bill in the third quarter, speculative fever in the property and stockmarkets had been broken and strong growth in manufactured exports began eroding the trade deficit. Trade estimates for the nine months through September had both imports and exports rising by 23%.

The main reasons for the quick turnaround was the fall in the price of forward-bought oil imports and manufactured exports rising at over 26% annually — led by textiles, processed foods, gems and jewellery, footwear and electrical and electronic goods. While the US remained the country's major export market, East Asia — led by Japan — was clearly growing in importance. As unexpected orders for large amounts of rice came in from Indonesia in the fourth quarter, export growth appeared sure to surpass import growth by year-end.

Nevertheless, the economy was clearly slowing. Despite cheaper prices due to tax cuts, vehicle sales declined sharply and growth in consumer sales was off. By September, bank loans were growing at only 21.7% and deposits at 20.6%. The economy appeared to be expanding at an overall rate of 7.5-8%, with growth balanced between exports and domestic consumption. Confronted with such a precipitous slowdown, BOT loosened up money supply to ensure a soft landing and interest rates began to drop — with prime at about 14.5% in November. The overall inflation rate slowed from the 7.7% average of 1989-90 to around 6% in September, though the built-in effects of the past four years of rapid growth means this rate will probably be sustained for at least two more years.

With no political interference to slow them, Anand's team of technocrats was pushing through dozens of crucial reforms, many of which had been stalled by the previous government. These included:

▶ a value-added tax, to replace the onerous business tax system;

▶ a new superstructure for the securities sector, including the establishment of a powerful oversight agency similar to the US Securities and Exchange Commission;

▶ reducing import duties, notably in the automotive and computer sectors, to force a boost in competitiveness and end implied subsidies;

▶ establishing an environmental law to police industrial polluters;

▶ easing bureaucratic obstacles on foreigners working in the country and streamlining investment procedures;

▶ freeing up foreign-exchange controls and revising taxes on financial sector instruments to set the groundwork for the establishment of a local debt market.

Investment numbers were off by about 35% at midyear compared with a year earlier, according to Board of Investment (BOI) statistics. Nevertheless, investment applications were well ahead of 1987, when the economy began its takeoff. Some analysts, however, felt there was a likely rise in investment not passing through the BOI as official incentives based on the board's approval had been diluted by various financial and tax-related liberalisations during the year.

Of those companies that did apply through the BOI, many planned to start manufacturing operations that would provide the parts, components and materials for much of the assembly industries that have arrived since 1987. They appeared to slightly outnumber applicants who want to build hotels, hospitals and other service industry operations — many of which never get off the ground.

Infrastructure remained a major problem during the year — as it will for many years to come — with Bangkok's traffic maintaining its rank at the top of the list. With Bangkok's numerous mass-transit schemes still at the haggling or blueprint stage, city road and flyover projects were hastened with enhanced budgets in an effort to squeeze a little more space out of the capital's clogged streets.

During the year the government began studies on a new airport at Nong Ngu Hao southeast of the city, slated for opening in 2000. The new eastern seaboard port at Laem Chabang was officially opened at the beginning of the year. However, usage was low as container berths were still under construction and handling equipment not yet in place. Moreover, road and rail links to the port were far behind schedule.

Telecommunications had a more positive year. Early in the year, the government awarded a concession to Charoen Pokphand Telecommunications to install 2 million muchneeded telephone lines in Bangkok by 1997. At the end of the year bids for a concession to install another 1 million lines in rural areas were being accepted. In addition, the Shinawatra group was awarded a concession to launch and operate Thailand's first telecommunications satellite.

As the year progressed local interest turned to neighbouring Indochina, not least because Thai industry began to take seriously Vietnam's potential for becoming a competitor. During the year Laos was given special help with lower duties, and Bangkok eliminated a transport monopoly which controlled Thai-Laos trade. In Cambodia, Thai organisations were helping to develop tourism and trade links. Further, Thai banks established a presence in all three Indochinese countries.

By the end of 1991 two main questions remained unanswered. The first is an imminent oversupply in the property market, which few analysts have ventured to predict how severe it will be or how it will effect the finance sector and the overall economy. The second is slower world economic growth. Some analysts are concerned this will dampen incoming investment, tourism income, export growth and leave the country with an unmanageable current-account deficit.

As a cushion, BOT has boosted official reserves to about US$18 billion during the year, and the government has been running a strong current surplus. But some observers believe the renewed emphasis on government spending over the next three years — mostly infrastructure-related — will weaken that cushion and by extension erode the economic achievements of the past four years.  □

# Data

**Major industry:** Cement, 18.1 million tonnes (15 million); integrated circuits, 1.3 billion pieces (963 million); tin metal, 15,859 tonnes (14,571); vehicle assembly, commercial and passenger, 305,145 units (213,536); sugar, 3.38 million tonnes (3.84 million); liquor, 624.1 million litres (615.7 million); synthetic fibre, 225,017 tonnes (202,347); woven cotton fabrics (1989), 1.626 billion yd² (1.478 billion); petroleum products, 13.98 billion litres (13.05 billion).

**Major agriculture:** Rice (unmilled), 17 million tonnes (21.2 million); rubber, 1.2 million tonnes (1.18 million); maize, 3.8 million tonnes (4.1 million); cassava (tapioca), 20.6 million tonnes (20.7 million); sugar cane, 40.5 million tonnes (33.6 million); soybean, 500,000 tonnes (610,000); coconut, 900,000 tonnes (1.15 million); marine fish and shrimp (1989), 2.6 million tonnes (2.4 million).

**Mining:** Tin concentrate, 19,979 tonnes (20,372); lead ore, 52,309 tonnes (58,079); gypsum, 5.75 million tonnes (5.48 million); lignite, 12.4 million tonnes (8.9 million); zinc ore, 272,488 tonnes (412,620).

**Oil and natural gas:** Natural gas production, 230.3 billion ft³ (211.4 billion); condensate, 7.2 million barrels (6.7 million); crude oil, 8.3 million barrels (7.4 million).

**Major imports:** Non-electrical machinery and parts, US$6.02 billion (US$4.7 billion); electrical machinery and parts, US$3.94 billion (US$2.66 billion); fuel and lubricants, US$3.07 billion (US$2.34 billion); iron and steel, US$2.56 billion (US$2.14 billion); vehicles and parts, US$2.18 billion (US$1.57 billion); consumer durables, US$1.72 billion (US$1.18 billion); fertilisers and pesticides, US$563 million (US$511 million).

**Major exports:** Textile products, US$3.31 billion (US$2.9 billion); rice, US$1.1 billion (US$1.78 billion); precious stones and jewellery, US$1.37 billion (US$1.11 billion); rubber, US$924 million (US$1.07 billion); tapioca products, US$908 million (US$940 million); integrated circuits, US$846 million (US$723 million); prawns, US$802 million (US$630 million); footwear, US$793 million (US$530 million); sugar, US$694 million (US$755 million); canned fish, US$617 million (US$625 million).

**Tourism:** Arrivals, 5.3 million (4.8 million); expenditure, US$4.54 billion (US$3.78 billion). All major airlines serve Bangkok and several also fly to Chiang Mai and Phuket. Flag carrier Thai Airways International serves domestic and foreign routes, while Bangkok Airways serves smaller domestic destinations and plans to serve cities in Burma and Indochina. Rail network covers major cities; bus services between Bangkok and the provinces; car hire widely available.

(All figures for 1990 unless otherwise stated. Previous year in brackets.)

**Finance:** 15 commercial banks, 1 semi–long term bank, 14 foreign banks have single branches in Bangkok and several dozen have representative offices. Nearly 100 finance and securities firms, some with offices in the provinces as well as Bangkok. Stock Exchange of Thailand has 270 companies listed.

**Currency:** Baht (100 satang). Baht 25.47 = US$1, Nov. 1991 (Baht 25.03 = US$1, Nov. 1990).

**Government ministries:** Foreign, Wang Saranrom, Bangkok 10200, tel. 2257900; Commerce, Thanon Sanam Chai, Bangkok 10200, tel. 2220827/2210877; Foreign Trade, Thanon Sanam Chai, Bangkok 10200, tel. 2244887, fax 2247269; Agriculture and Cooperatives, Thanon Rathcadamnoen Nok, Bangkok 10200, tel. 2815955; Finance, Thanon Rama VI, Bangkok 10400, tel. 2739021, fax 2739408; Industry, Thanon Rama VI, Bangkok 10400, tel. 2461137-43; Defence, Thanon Sanam Chai, Bangkok 10200, tel. 2250098/2221121; Transport and Communications, Thanon Ratchadamnoen Nok, Bangkok 10100, tel. 2813422; Bank of Thailand, 273 Thanon Sam Sen, Bangkok 10200, tel. 2823322, fax 2800449.

**Major banks:** Bangkok Bank, 333 Silom Rd, Bangkok 10500, tel. 2343333, tlx 82638 BK BANK TH; Krung Thai Bank, 35 Sukhumvit Rd, Bangkok 10110, tel. 2512111, tlx 81179 KT BANK TH; Siam Commercial Bank, 1060 New Petchburi Rd, Bangkok 10400, tel. 2513114, tlx 72008 SIAMBNK TH; Thai Farmers Bank, 400 Phaholyothin Rd, Bangkok 10400, tel. 2701122, tlx 81159 FARMERS TH; Thai Military Bank, 34 Phayathai Rd, Bangkok 10400, tel. 2460020, tlx 82324 TMBK TH; Bank of Ayudhaya, 550 Ploenchit Rd, Bangkok 10500, tel. 2538601, tlx 82334 AYUDYA TH.

**Public holidays** (1992): 1 Jan. (New Year), 18 Feb. (Makha Bucha Day), 6 Apr. (Chakri Day), 13-14 Apr. (Songkran [Water Festival]), 1 May (Labour Day), 5 May (Coronation Day), 14 May (Ploughing Day), 16 May (Visakha Bucha Day), 14 July (Asalha Bucha), 15 July (Buddhist Lent), 12 Aug. (Queen's Birthday), 23 Oct. (Chulalongkorn Day), 5 Dec. (King's Birthday), 10 Dec. (Constitution Day), 31 Dec. (New Year's Eve).

**Weather:** Thailand has a hot and humid climate with 3 seasons: Mar.-May, the hot season when temperatures can reach 38°C in Bangkok; June-Oct., the rainy season when maximum temperatures are in the low 30s and sporadic flooding can occur; and the cool, dry weather of Nov.-Feb. Average annual rainfall 1,475 mm.

**Taxation:** Personal taxes range from 5-50%; business tax 35% on profits (30% for companies traded on the Stock Exchange of Thailand). Many Board of Investment–approved companies get significant tax holidays and reductions. A 7% value-added tax due to be implemented on 1 Jan. 1992; individual and corporate tax rates due to be reduced at the same time.

# VIETNAM

CHINA
Ha Giang
Lai Chau • Lao Cai
Cao Bang
Vinh Yen
Dien Bien Phu
Hanoi ⊙ ✈
Nam Dinh • — Haiphong
LAOS
Thanh Hoa
Gulf of Tonkin
Hainan Is.
Vinh
South China Sea
Quang Tri
Hue
THAILAND
Da Nang
Quang Ngai
Kontum
Pleiku
Qui Nhon
CAMBODIA
Mekong
Ban Me Thout
Nha Trang
Da Lat
Cam Ranh
Ho Chi Minh City
Phan Thiet
Vinh Loi
Paracel Islands
Spratly Islands
0   100   200 km

**Communist Party Secretary-General**
Do Muoi.
**President**
Vo Chi Cong;
**Vice-Presidents**
Dam Quang Trung, Le Quang Dao, Nguyen Huu Tho, Nguyen Quyet, Nguyen Thi Dinh;
**Premier**
Vo Van Kiet;
**Vice-Premiers**
Phan Van Khai, Nguyen Khanh, Tran Duc Luong;
**Politburo**
Do Muoi, Le Duc Anh, Vo Van Kiet, Dao Duy Tung, Doan Khue, Vu Oanh, Le Phuoc Tho, Phan Van Khai, Bui Thien Ngo, Nong Duc Manh, Pham The Duyet, Nguyen Duc Binh, Vo Tran Chi;
**Defence**
Doan Khue;
**Foreign**
Nguyen Manh Cam;
**Interior**
Bui Thien Ngo;
**State Planning Commission**
Dao Quoc Sam;
**State Commission for Cooperation and Investment**
Dau Ngoc Xuan;
**Agriculture and Food Industry**
Nguyen Cong Tan;
**Communications, Transport, Posts and Telegraph**
Bui Danh Luu;

**Construction**
Ngo Xuan Loc;
**Commerce and Tourism**
Le Van Triet;
**Culture, Information and Sports**
Tran Hoan;
**Education and Training**
Tran Hong Quan;
**Energy**
Vu Ngoc Hai;
**Finance**
Hoang Quy;
**Forestry**
Phan Xuan Dot;
**Justice**
Phan Hien;
**Labour, War Invalids and Social Welfare**
Tran Dinh Hoan;
**Light Industry**
Dang Vu Chu;
**Heavy Industry**
Tran Lum;
**Marine Industry**
Nguyen Tan Trinh;
**Public Health**
Pham Song;
**Water Resources**
Nguyen Canh Dinh;
**Chief Justice**
Pham Hung;
**Military Chief-of-Staff**
Gen. Dao Dinh Luyen.

# Politics/Social Affairs

Vietnam's communist party, meeting for its seventh congress from 24-27 June, renewed its call for further moves towards a free-market economy and introduced widespread leadership changes, but continued to reject political pluralism. The collapse of communism two months later in the Soviet Union, long Vietnam's most important ally, stunned Hanoi — which feared it would face growing calls for greater political liberalisation.

The congress was followed in August by a National Assembly session which named new government ministers to replace those ousted from the central committee and began debating revisions to the constitution, including a radical overhaul of the state's administrative structure.

During the congress, seven members of the 12-man polit-

Ho Chi Minh declared Vietnam independent of French colonial rule on 2 September 1945 after Japan's surrender in World War II, but the French returned to rule Vietnam until their defeat at Dien Bien Phu in 1954. The Geneva Agreement temporarily divided Vietnam into north and south, pending nationwide elections.

For the next nine years, fighting between the Soviet- and Chinese-supported communist north and the US-backed south intensified. In 1965, the US committed its armed forces to the war on a massive scale, where they remained until the 1973 Paris peace agreement ended direct US involvement. Fighting between Vietnamese forces continued, and on 30 April 1975 communist troops captured Saigon and reunified the country.

In December 1978, following two years of Khmer Rouge attacks across the border, Vietnam invaded Cambodia and ousted the Chinese-backed regime. China retaliated by launching an attack against northern Vietnam, sparking a short border war.

Facing a deteriorating economic situation and international isolation, Vietnam's communist party introduced free-market reforms in 1986 and stepped up its drive to improve relations with the country's non-communist neighbours and the West. Hanoi withdrew its remaining troops from Cambodia in 1989. The collapse of communism in Eastern Europe and the Soviet Union pushed Vietnam and China closer, and the two countries normalised relations in November 1991.

buro were retired — lowering the average age of the politburo from 71 to 64. Party chief Nguyen Van Linh, 75, asked to step down and was replaced by Do Muoi, 74. Muoi, who was treated with suspicion in the south when he was elected premier in 1988 because of his role in abolishing capitalism in the late 1970s, has won the confidence of many technocrats for his recent efforts to loosen the party's control on the economy.

Documents approved by the congress, however, provided few details on how the party planned to speed up economic reform. Speeches focused mostly on hammering out the party's ideology following the disintegration of the Soviet bloc.

The newly elected central committee will be responsible for formulating policies to rescue the economy from its present state of crisis. Many Vietnamese economists believed decisions regarding the money-losing state sector, which continues to drive up the state budget deficit and fuel inflation, would be a key indicator as to how quickly the party planned to move towards a market economy.

The congress also foreshadowed changes in foreign policy, with the removal of foreign minister Nguyen Co Thach from the politburo. Although he insisted he had stepped down voluntarily, Thach's independent style had in recent years put him at odds with Hanoi's collective-style leadership.

Prior to his removal, Thach had increasingly lost control over the resolution of the Cambodian conflict and normalisation of ties with China to former defence minister Gen. Le Duc Anh, 71, who was promoted to No. 2 in the politburo.

Thach was replaced at the foreign ministry by Nguyen Manh Cam, 62, a former ambassador to the Soviet Union. The party's first candidate for the job turned it down, reportedly because he feared the ministry would be weak without a representative on either the politburo or the secretariat, which runs the party on a daily basis. The new foreign minister is responsible to Anh and Hong Ha, a member of the secretariat and former editor of the party daily, who will be in charge of foreign policy for the party.

Anh is expected to replace Vo Chi Cong as president, a post that many sources believe will be upgraded in the revised constitution. The newly defined presidential post is seen to include the chairmanship of a national security council, which will set security, defence and foreign policies.

Along with Muoi and Anh, only three other members of the former politburo survived. Vo Van Kiet, 69, replaced Muoi as premier. Kiet is a southerner and one of the most liberal members of the politburo, but he is often criticised for his limited understanding of economic issues. Dao Duy Tung, 67, who was in charge of ideology in the outgoing politburo, was named permanent secretary of the secretariat. Former military chief-of-staff Doan Khue, 68, was elected to replace Anh as defence minister.

Four of the seven new politburo members come from the south, increasing the number of southerners in the ruling body to five compared to only one previously. However, most of the new appointees are long-serving party functionaries who are expected to stress continuity rather than dramatic change.

They include Phan Van Khai, 58, a Soviet-trained economist and former chairman of the State Planning Commission, who was elected first vice-premier in August. Bui Thien Ngo, 62, was appointed interior minister, replacing Mai Chi Tho. Ngo is considered by many officials as one of the more open-minded leaders of the country's often xenophobic security apparatus. Another newcomer, Nong Duc Manh, 51, a member of the Tay ethnic group, was the first minority leader ever elected to the party's politburo.

The changes in the party secretariat were even more sweeping than in the politburo, with only three former members remaining in the body. The six newly elected members included Muoi, Anh and Truong My Hoa — the first woman to reach the party's upper echelons.

Changes in the new central committee were less wide-ranging, with only 42 new members added to the 146-strong body. Most of the new members are party, government or military officials from the central or provincial levels. Many technocrats were disappointed that few intellectuals or company directors were chosen.

Most of the congress results were predictable, but many often-critical party members felt the meeting was "more democratic" than previous congresses, which did little more than rubber-stamp decisions already made by the outgoing politburo. For example, of the 148 central committee candidates presented by the party leadership, three — including the ministers of finance and trade — were rejected by congress delegates. Another 68 candidates were nominated from the floor, but only one — the health minister — was elected.

Prior to the congress, the party's leadership had invited public debate on several key draft documents prepared for ratification by the delegates, but it faced a stiffer challenge than it anticipated from its normally placid intellectuals. Even the party's theoretical journal *Communist Review* joined the debate by publishing for the first time the views of intellectuals challenging the validity of socialism itself.

"The reason for existing shortcomings stem from our dogmatic application of socialism . . . over the past 15 years," Ha, a veteran economist at the Ministry of Labour, War Invalids and Social Affairs, reportedly told a seminar organised by the magazine. "If someone carries out the original doctrine of Marxism-Leninism, they will fail."

Several seminar participants also called on the party to study political philosophies other than those developed by Marx and Lenin. "In order to find the best way for Vietnam to develop, we have to study many doctrines which we have not studied so far," said Phan Dinh Dieu, a prominent Soviet-trained mathematician and computer scientist.

The party received even harsher criticism from Nguyen Khac Vien, 78, a retired doctor and long-time propagandist for the government. In an open letter to the leadership in January, Vien declared that the people "have lost all faith in the upper echelons." He said party organisations were "composed of comrades who are either too old, ill . . . or whose thinking and working styles are too outmoded to be able to catch up with the advances of the times."

The party was so angered by these criticisms that it ordered increased surveillance of dissidents and requested other state-controlled media to launch a campaign slamming its critics. *Nhan Dan*, the party's daily newspaper, published dozens of articles charging the critics with "arrogance" because they had been exposed to foreign ideas. The newspaper declared that "coping [with Vietnam's current difficulties] does not mean changing the colour of our flag, as has been suggested by some people who have lost their identity."

But with the collapse of communism in the Soviet Union in August, the party seemed to adopt a softer line in an apparent

Muoi: lighter touch.

attempt to avoid further alienating the country's intellectuals. Muoi had unpublicised meetings with Vien and Dieu and met with large groups of intellectuals in both Hanoi and Hô Chi Minh City.

"The party and state will listen attentively to every one of your suggestions," Muoi was quoted as telling intellectuals in the capital. "We don't fear divergence of views during discussions."

In an apparent signal to intellectuals not to push their demands too far, Hanoi arrested well-known writer Duong Thu Huong in April and planned to try her for harming national security. In November, however, the government released her on "humanitarian" grounds, while saying it stood by its original charges. When Huong was arrested, police seized documents detailing Hanoi's alleged abuses of writers and intellectuals which she had gathered to send to a human-rights conference in France. Her release was announced three days before the arrival of French Foreign Minister Roland Dumas.

The August session of the National Assembly, which has played a more active political role in recent years, reviewed more than 100 amendments to the 147-article constitution adopted in 1980 before the party began its current reforms. Many of the proposed changes detailed guiding principles for Vietnam's moves towards a free-market economy.

Other revisions focused on reorganising the government apparatus. According to the draft, the powerful but cumbersome Council of Ministers, which includes ministers and heads of a host of government agencies that duplicate and oversee the ministries, would be abolished. This proposal would streamline government decision-making and dramatically increase the power and responsibilities of the premier and ministers. The proposed constitutional changes were scheduled to be circulated for public comment before being voted on at December's National Assembly session. ☐

# Foreign Relations

Vietnam arrived at one of the most important foreign relations' watersheds in its recent history during 1991. With the fall of communism in the Soviet Union, Hanoi lost both a long-time ideological patron and its main source of foreign aid.

On the other hand, the end of the Cold War and the signing of the Cambodian peace accord on 23 October helped Vietnam patch up ties with China and Thailand, its two most important neighbours. It also paved the way for normalisation talks with the US, which holds the key to international aid and Vietnam's reintegration into the world community.

US and Vietnamese diplomats met at the UN in mid-November to begin negotiations on normalising ties, the first such talks since 1954 when North Vietnam declared independence. US President George Bush and administration officials also softened their rhetoric on Vietnam, while sticking to its reconciliation "road map." Washington unveiled the four-point plan in April following mounting congressional pressure to lift the US trade embargo on Vietnam.

The plan called for normalising ties with Hanoi only after a UN peace plan for Cambodia has been implemented, the four warring Cambodian factions disarmed and elections held to form a new national assembly. The proposal also said Vietnam must cooperate fully in resolving "discrepancy cases" and "live-sighting reports" of US servicemen still missing in action (MIA) since the Vietnam War.

Hanoi did not formally respond to the plan, though Vietnamese officials said Washington was wrong in making a Cambodia settlement a precondition for renewing US-Vietnam ties. They argued that prompt normalisation would be the best way to end the conflict in Cambodia, bring stability to Southeast Asia and help resolve outstanding bilateral issues. At the time, diplomats in Hanoi interpreted this response as Vietnam's rejection of the road map concept.

But as the Cambodian peace talks gained momentum, Hanoi and Washington stepped up cooperation on resolving the fate of some 2,273 MIAs from the war. During a visit to Hanoi in April by presidential envoy John Vessey, the US agreed to open an office in Hanoi to facilitate the search.

In regional affairs, Vietnamese party chief Do Muoi and Prime Minister Vo Van Kiet visited Peking in November for a summit with their Chinese counterparts, Jiang Zemin and Li Peng, formally ending more than a decade of enmity between the two former communist allies. Anxiety over the collapse of communism and ensuing political chaos in Eastern Europe drove Peking and Hanoi to heal a rift that began when Vietnam allied itself with Moscow in the 1970s.

Cambodia provided another bridge. Vietnam drove out the Chinese-backed Khmer Rouge government there in 1978 and then held off a Chinese retaliatory attack in 1979. But despite their differences during the 13-year Cambodian war, the two communist states were drawn closer by the peace plan which joined the warring Cambodian factions in a fragile interim coalition.

The groundwork for the Vietnamese-Chinese summit was laid during a series of meetings that started in September 1990, when former party chief Nguyen Van Linh led a delegation on a secret visit to Chengdu in southern China. In late July 1991, Gen. Le Duc Anh, now No. 2 in the Vietnamese politburo, made a covert trip to China after a surprise invitation for Hanoi to send an envoy to report on Vietnam's June party congress.

Chinese leaders told Anh that Peking "agrees completely" with the results of the congress, which reaffirmed the party's monopoly on political power and commitment to economic reform. These moves, coupled with the replacement of anti-Chinese Nguyen Co Thach as foreign minister, shifted Hanoi nearer its erstwhile Chinese adversary while distancing itself from Moscow — which has stressed political reform.

In September, Vietnam's new Foreign Minister Nguyen Manh Cam visited China, when the two countries set up technical working groups to prepare a series of documents to be signed at the summit. In the event, the four-day summit failed to meet all of Hanoi's objectives. While the leaders signed trade and provisional border agreements, they stopped short of sealing pacts restoring transport and telecommunications links severed in 1979. Vietnamese officials speculated that China was dragging its feet in order to gain concessions in other areas.

One such dispute is over ownership of the Spratly and Paracel island groups, which are claimed by China and Vietnam as well as by Taiwan, Malaysia and the Philippines. Vietnamese officials said Peking wanted Hanoi to accept the status quo, meaning China would keep the Paracels it seized in 1974 and some of the Spratlys occupied in 1988.

Along with political support from China, Hanoi hopes renewed friendship will provide an economic boost to fill the gap left by the Soviet Union. According to Vietnamese sources, Chinese officials told Cam before the Peking summit that China was willing to sell Vietnam strategic commodities such as fertiliser, steel and cotton — previously supplied by the Soviets — at preferential prices and using the barter system common among communist countries. Peking also reportedly asked Hanoi for permission to open a trade office in Haiphong. China hopes to use the port to ship exports from its land-locked southern provinces. It also wants to buy coal from northeastern Vietnam.

Unofficial trade between the two countries has soared since the border was reopened in late 1988. *Quan Doi Nhan Dan*, the army daily, estimated that two-way trade totalled US$110 million in 1990 and forecast a threefold increase in 1991.

The Cambodian peace accord also led to dramatic improvements in Hanoi's relations with its non-communist neighbours. A September visit to Vietnam by Thai Foreign Minister Arsa Sarasin prepared a late October summit in Thailand between Kiet and Thai Prime Minister Anand Panyarachun.

Arsa's visit, during which the two sides for the first time began discussing substantive bilateral issues, marked a milestone towards ending four decades of hostility. Relations had been strained since Thailand supported the US' war in Indochina by sending troops to fight in Vietnam and by providing airbases for US bombers. Post-war rapprochement efforts unravelled with Vietnam's 1978 invasion of Cambodia.

As a gesture of goodwill, Vietnam agreed to release 344 of the 846 Thai fishermen jailed in the southern Mekong Delta, while Thailand promised to free 157 Vietnamese fishermen. Arsa also promised Vietnam technical assistance in 1992 valued at Baht 220 million (US$8 million).

Despite the recent warming of relations, however, several major hurdles remain. One problem concerns the establishment of consulates. Thailand wants to open a consulate in Ho Chi Minh City to serve its businessmen working there, while Vietnam hoped to establish a consulate in Udon Thani in northeastern Thailand. The Thai military has refused to allow this because it remains wary of the loyalties of some 50,000 Vietnamese refugees who have lived in the region since the 1950s.

Thailand is looking to Vietnam as a new outlet for trade and as a source of natural gas and fish, while Vietnam is seeking to diversify its economic relations. But the behaviour of some unscrupulous Thai businessmen have left Hanoi uneasy about Bangkok's intentions. To boost economic cooperation, Arsa proposed umbrella agreements on fishing and natural gas exploitation in time for signing during the summit. But Vietnamese officials said they were only interested in fishing cooperation if Thai companies agreed to process the fish in Vietnam. They also expressed reservation about selling their natural gas to Thailand, saying Vietnam needed its gas reserves to increase domestic energy and fertiliser production.

Although Hanoi welcomed the warming of relations with Bangkok, Vietnamese officials insisted that Thailand would not get priority over other Asean countries. Kiet visited Indonesia before Thailand and signed economic cooperation agreements. Indonesian President Suharto was the first Asean leader to break the decade-long isolation of Vietnam when he signed an economic agreement with his Vietnamese counterpart during a visit to Hanoi in November 1990.

Malaysia also stepped up its contacts with Vietnam and became the first Asean country to open a consulate in Ho Chi Minh City. Hanoi has repeatedly said in recent years that it wishes to join Asean and, in its first formal step towards that goal, sent a letter to the grouping's standing committee expressing interest in acceding to its 1976 Bali treaty on amity and cooperation.

Japan, which in 1991 replaced the Soviet Union as Vietnam's largest foreign trading partner, also stepped up diplomatic contacts with Hanoi. In June, then foreign minister Taro Nakayama became the first Japanese cabinet-level minister to visit the country since the end of the Vietnam War. Nakayama promised that Japanese aid to Vietnam would resume if Hanoi influenced its Cambodian allies to settle the conflict.

Hanoi reached agreement with Britain in October on the repatriation of asylum-seekers in Hongkong that will lead to the return of an estimated 50,000 Vietnamese over three years. The forced repatriation programme began on 9 November, when 59 boat people who had re-entered Hongkong after returning voluntarily to Vietnam were flown home.  □

# Economy/Infrastructure

The abrupt loss of Soviet aid and trade at the beginning of 1991 delivered a serious blow to Hanoi's five-year economic reform programme, but the impact appears not to have been as devastating as many observers initially thought. Although trade with the Soviet Union in the first six months of 1991 reached only 15% of its 1990 level, Vietnamese exports totalled US$715 million and Rbl 69 million (US$120 million), compared with US$1.17 billion and Rbl 1 billion during the same period in 1990. But much of the resilience shown by Vietnam's export sector was due to sharply increasing sales of crude oil to Japan as well as rising exports of seafood, rubber and coffee. The export of light industrial products such as garments, textiles and handicrafts dropped abruptly due to the loss of Soviet and East European markets.

The fall in trade with Moscow resulted from both the chaos in the Soviet Union and a January 1991 agreement that stipulated future trade between the two countries would be calculated at international market prices and paid for in hard currency. Previously, the Soviet Union had supplied Vietnam with most of its strategic goods — oil products, fertiliser, steel and cotton — at concessionary prices calculated in roubles.

Rice exports also fell dramatically, threatening to dislodge Vietnam from its position as the world's third-largest rice exporter. By the end of June, the country had exported only about 300,000 tonnes of rice, down 70% from the same period in 1990. Unusually cold weather in the northern provinces caused the spring rice harvest to fall 1.1 million tonnes below the 1990 level, even though output in the south increased by 270,000 tonnes. The reduced production forced southern provinces to ship much of their surplus to the north, leaving them with less grain to export.

The north expected a good autumn harvest, but the fertile Mekong Delta was hit by severe September floods — the region's worst in 13 years — which inundated more than 80,000 ha of rice fields. The floods raised doubts about whether Vietnam could even reach its revised target of exporting 800,000 tonnes of rice in 1991, down from an estimated 1.8 million tonnes the year before.

The growing demand for foreign exchange to pay for imports forced a serious weakening of Vietnam's currency in the first eight months of the year, raising fears that the economy could be

KỶ NIỆM MƯỜI NĂM

HIỆP ƯỚC
HỮU NGHỊ HỢP TÁC
VIỆT-XÔ

1978
1988

JOHN SPRAGENS, JR

**Soviet patronage: end of an affair.**

hit by another round of hyper-inflation. The dong free-market exchange rate fell 63% between January and August, from Dong 7,200 to Dong 11,700 to US$1. The dong's free fall was halted — at least temporarily — by the State Bank of Vietnam's decision in late August to set up the country's first foreign-exchange transactions centre in Ho Chi Minh City. The dong stabilised at around Dong 11,000 in September after foreign-exchange trading began.

Economists feared the dong's continuing fall could force the government to raise its controlled prices for imported oil products and fertiliser, which would drive up the cost of local products, particularly food. Rising food costs have a sharp impact on inflation because even medium-income families spend over 60% of their income on food.

Inflation hit a monthly rate of 13.2% in January, but fell below 3% a month in the second quarter, thanks to the large shipment of rice from the south to the north. Overall prices rose 32% between January and June, much lower than the annualised rate of 200% feared by many economists early in the year.

Much of the inflationary pressure resulted from the government's budget deficit, which the central bank estimated at Dong 800 billion for the first half of the year. Foreign aid cuts were partly to blame. Premier Vo Van Kiet told the National Assembly in July that foreign aid in 1991 would provide only 6-7% of the government's revenue, down from 25-30% the year before and mainly reflecting Soviet aid cuts. In 1991, Moscow promised Vietnam credits worth US$100 million and grants totalling US$10 million. In Vietnam's 1986-90 five-year plan, the Soviet Union had offered credits worth Rbl 8.7 billion and grants totalling Rbl 150 million.

Kiem also attributed much of the deficit to state-owned companies that were Dong 200 billion behind in tax payments and cost the state another Dong 500 billion a year in loan subsidies. In addition, state companies are hobbled by huge debts, estimated at more than Dong 10 trillion. Some 15,000 state companies are believed to be around Dong 3-4 trillion behind in loan repayments to state-owned banks and face another Dong 6-7 trillion in overdue debts to each other. This massive debt resulted in a serious shortage of operating capital among companies unable to turn to banks for credit because large amounts of their funds were tied up in overdue loans to other enterprises.

Government economists estimated that 35% of the country's state enterprises were financially inoperative, while another 20% were performing better — but still not well enough to be able to pay their taxes. That left 45% which operated profitably, though many of these companies faced difficulties because they owed huge amounts of debt.

Government officials have been reluctant to close money-losing enterprises for fear that it would simply exacerbate unemployment, already estimated by the Asian Development Bank at over 10%.

Kiet told the National Assembly that industrial production rose 2% during the first half of the year, but much of this growth was due to a 26% increase in crude oil production.

This camouflaged a 3% decline in output by local state-owned industries and a 4.3% drop by private factories.

Industry in the south was also hit by up to four days of electricity brown-outs for several months prior to the resumption of the monsoon rains in July. Power consumption in the south had soared from about 1.5 million MWh in 1980 to 4 million MWh a decade later, overtaxing the Soviet-built Tri An dam, which faces critical shortages of water in its reservoir during the dry season.

Foreign investment increased in 1991, despite continuing complaints by foreign businessmen about the country's stifling bureaucracy, incompetent or corrupt officials and frequent regulation changes. Officials said investment approvals during the first half of the year equalled the total for all of 1990, when 109 projects worth US$600 million were licensed. The average size of projects increased to more than US$10 million, up from US$1 million in 1988-89.

Between mid-1988 and June 1991, the State Committee for Investment and Cooperation licensed 273 foreign-investment projects, of which roughly US$400 million had been implemented. Many of the recent licences have been for projects in agriculture, forestry and fisheries as well as in industry.

Petronas of Malaysia in September signed a 25-year product sharing contract to explore for oil and gas off the coast of southern Vietnam; Hanoi's 11th agreement with a foreign oil company since mid-1988. Meanwhile, a Soviet-Vietnamese joint-venture oil project was expected to produce 3.8-4 million tonnes of crude oil in 1991, up from 2.5 million tonnes the year before.

In June, the government issued a decree authorising foreign banks to apply to offer full banking services in Vietnam. Although the decree was vague and left many questions unanswered, at least a dozen foreign banks — including most of the seven that have representative offices in the country — submitted applications.

## Data

**Major industries:** Steel, 101,500 tonnes (84,500); cement, 2.54 million tonnes (2.09 million); chemical fertiliser, 326,600 tonnes (373,000); timber, 3.25 million m³ (3.26 million); fabrics, 310.9 million m (336.3 million); paper, 77,700 tonnes (65,700).

**Major agriculture:** Rice, 19.1 million tonnes (19 million); vegetables, 3.2 million tonnes (3.1 million); seafood, 691,000 tonnes (683,000); rubber, 52,000 tonnes (50,600); coffee, 45,200 (40,800); tea, 30,900 tonnes (30,200); sugar cane, 5.4 million tonnes (5.3 million).

**Oil and natural gas:** 3.8-4 million tonnes of crude oil projected for 1991 (2.5 million).

**Mining:** Coal, 4.2 million tonnes (3.8 million).

**Major imports (1989):** Fertiliser, US$46 million and Rbl 380 million (US$72 million and Rbl 328 million); oil products, Rbl 449 million (Rbl 556 million); steel, Rbl 104 million (Rbl 88 million); raw cotton, Rbl 75 million (Rbl 65 million).

**Major exports (1989):** Rice, US$317 million (n.a.); crude oil, US$200 million (US$77 million); agricultural and forestry products, US$211 million and Rbl 260 million (US$197 million and Rbl 205 million); handicrafts and light industrial goods, US$20 million and Rbl 432 million (US$18 million and Rbl 345 million); marine products, US$133 million (US$124 million); rubber, US$14 million and Rbl 30 million (US$6 million and Rbl 26 million); coffee, US$31 million and Rbl 43 million (US$25 million and Rbl 7 million); coal, US$21 million and Rbl 2 million (US$13 million and Rbl 2 million).

(Rouble unconverted to US$ in order to indicate level of Soviet-Vietnam trade.)

**Tourism:** Arrivals, 250,000 (60,000); revenue, US$29 million. **Airlines:** Air Vietnam serves domestic and international routes; Air France, Malaysia Airlines, Philippine Airlines, Garuda Indonesia, Lufthansa, Air Cambodia and Lao Aviation link Ho Chi Minh City to neighbouring cities in Southeast Asia. Air Vietnam, Thai International and Aeroflot serve Hanoi. Railway between Hanoi and Ho Chi Minh City; buses link most parts of the country; state-owned car hire available in major cities, but foreigners need permission to leave Hanoi and Ho Chi Minh City.

(All figures for 1990 unless otherwise specified, previous year in brackets.)

**Currency:** Dong (10 hao). Dong 12,880 = US$1, Nov. 1991 (Dong 6,350 = US$1, Nov. 1990).

**Finance:** State Bank of Vietnam functions as the country's central bank and oversees the 4 specialised state banks — the Bank for Foreign Trade, Bank for Investment and Construction, Bank for Agricultural Development and Bank for Industry and Trade — and several small, experimental private banks and credit cooperatives. There are no 100%-foreign owned banks in Vietnam, but 5 French banks along with 1 British and 1 Thai bank have opened representative offices. No consumer finance companies, building societies or stock exchanges.

**Major banks:** Vietnam State Bank, 47-49 Ly Thai To St, Hanoi, tel. 425-2831, and 79 Ham Nghi St, Ho Chi Minh City, tel. 90491; Bank for Foreign Trade, 47-49 Ly Thai To St, Hanoi, tel. 425-2831.

**Government ministries:** Council of Ministers, Hoang Hoa Tham St, Hanoi, tel. 425-8261/425-8241; Foreign Affairs, 1 Ton That Dan St, Hanoi, tel. 425-8201; Commerce, 31 Tran Tien St, Hanoi, tel. 426-2523/426-2521; State Committee for Investment and Cooperation, 56 Quoc Tu Giam, Hanoi, tel. 425-7238/425-3666, and 178 Nguyen Dinh Chieu, Dist. 3, Ho Chi Minh City, tel. 94674/30145.

**Public holidays (1992):** 1 Jan. (New Year), 1-3 Feb. (Tet [Lunar New Year]), 30 Apr. (Reunification Day), 1 May (May Day), 2-3 Sept. (National Day).

**Weather:** Vietnam has a varied climate. The north is cool, sometimes cold, from Oct.-Mar., while the south is warm to hot throughout the year. May-Nov. is rainy season in the south, while the northern rainy season is from Oct.-Mar. Average rainfall in Ho Chi Minh City is 1,910 mm; Hanoi has 1,760 mm.

**Taxation:** All state and private enterprises in principle pay taxes based on their activities and geographical location. Foreign investment law allows foreign investment up to 100%, with tax rates varying from 15-25%.

# 1991 NEWS DIARY

**5 JANUARY** — MALAYSIA
Sabah's chief minister, Datuk Seri Joseph Pairin Kitingan, arrested on corruption charges.

**14 JANUARY** — HONGKONG
China demands a veto over most of the colony's major policies.

**9 FEBRUARY** — MALAYSIA
Datuk Daim Zainuddin resigns as finance minister and is replaced by Datuk Seri Anwar Ibrahim.

**23 FEBRUARY** — THAILAND
Prime Minister Chatichai Choonhavan toppled by a military coup.

**27 FEBRUARY** — BANGLADESH
Begum Khaleda Zia becomes the country's first woman prime minister.

**2 MARCH** — THAILAND
Businessman Anand Panyarachun appointed prime minister by ruling military junta.

**2 MARCH** — SRI LANKA
Minister of State for Defence Ranjan Wijeratne killed instantly when a bomb explodes next to his motorcade in Colombo.

**6 MARCH** — INDIA
Prime Minister Chandra Shekhar resigns as the country prepares to go to the polls.

**6 MARCH** — HONGKONG
China demands that Hongkong set aside as much as HK$50 billion (US$6.4 billion) from its reserves for the post-1997 special administrative region.

**26 MARCH** — SOUTH KOREA
First local council elections in 30 years held.

**27 MARCH** — SINGAPORE
Army commandos kill four Pakistanis who hijacked a Singapore Airlines jet.

**31 MARCH** — AFGHANISTAN
Key government garrison at Khost falls to mujahideen.

**8 APRIL** — HONGKONG
British Foreign Secretary Douglas Hurd fails to win Chinese support for Hongkong airport project during Peking visit.

**16 APRIL** — JAPAN
Soviet President Mikhail Gorbachov arrives in Tokyo for an official visit — the first to Japan by a Soviet head of state — though hopes for an early settlement to territorial disputes are dashed.

**20 APRIL** — VIETNAM
In a move seen as marking a new stage in improved US-Vietnamese relations, Washington will establish an office in Hanoi to coordinate the search for US servicemen missing in action during the Vietnam War.

**26 APRIL** — JAPAN
A flotilla of six Japanese navy minesweepers leaves for the Gulf, representing the first operational deployment of the country's armed forces since the end of World War II.

**30 APRIL** — BANGLADESH
A cyclone devastates the country's southeast region, killing at least 140,000 people.

**1 MAY** — TAIWAN
President Lee Teng-hui officially ends the "period of communist rebellion" in China, signalling Taipei's desire to further improve links with Peking.

**1 MAY** — CAMBODIA
A ceasefire between all four warring factions goes into effect.

**12 MAY** — NEPAL
Prime Minister K. P. Bhattarai defeated in general elections, in which the country's communist party makes unexpected gains.

**16 MAY** — CHINA
Mao Zedong's imprisoned widow, Jiang Qing, commits suicide.

**20 MAY** — NORTH KOREA
Pyongyang rejects Tokyo's demands that it allow international inspection of its nuclear facilities.

**21 MAY** — INDIA
Congress party leader and former prime minister Rajiv Gandhi assassinated by a suicide bomber during the country's election campaign.

**28 MAY** — NORTH KOREA
Pyongyang applies for UN membership after failing to prevent Seoul's application.

**28 MAY** — CHINA
Asian Development Bank lends China US$70 million, the first such loan since the June 1989 Tiananmen massacre.

**29 MAY** — NEPAL
G. P. Koirala appointed prime minister.

**3 JUNE** — AUSTRALIA
Treasurer Paul Keating resigns after failing to topple Prime Minister Bob Hawke in a struggle for the Labor Party's leadership.

**13 JUNE** — BANGLADESH
Former president H. M. Ershad sentenced to 10 years' imprisonment after being convicted of illegal possession of firearms.

**15 JUNE** — PHILIPPINES
Mt Pinatubo erupts, throwing negotiations over US bases into further disarray.

**22 JUNE** — INDIA
The Congress party, led by P. V. Narasimha Rao, forms a minority government.

**24 JUNE** — JAPAN
Presidents of Nomura and Nikko securities houses resign over deals to compensate favoured clients for stock-exchange loses.

**26 JUNE** — CAMBODIA
The country's warring factions agree to a permanent ceasefire.

**27 JUNE** — VIETNAM
Prime Minister Do Muoi takes over as communist party party chief from ailing Nguyen Van Linh.

**30 JUNE** — HONGKONG
Bank of Credit and Commerce Hongkong accounts show HK$431 million attributable loss. Parent Bank of Credit and Commerce International collapses on 8 July after assets are frozen virtually worldwide.

**30 JUNE** — US
House of Representatives votes to extend China's most favoured nation status for one year, but will impose stringent conditions for renewal in 1992.

**4 JULY** — HONGKONG
Britain and China sign accord on colony's new airport that enshrines Peking's right to intervene in Hongkong affairs.

**3 AUGUST** — SRI LANKA
Government troops take control of Elephant Pass linking Jaffna with the rest of island after a protracted and bloody battle with Tamil Tiger guerilas.

**5 AUGUST** — JAPAN
Prime Minister Toshiki Kaifu unveils plans for far-reaching political reforms.

**10 AUGUST** — CHINA-VIETNAM
Both countries release statements announcing plans to normalise relations, marking the end of nearly two decades of hostility.

**31 AUGUST** — SINGAPORE
The ruling People's Action Party

wins general election, but with reduced majority and by a narrower margin than any previous polls.

**15 SEPTEMBER** — HONGKONG
Pro-democracy candidates triumph in colony's first direct elections for the Legislative Council.

**16 SEPTEMBER** — PHILIPPINES
Country's Senate votes to reject a new US bases agreement.

**4 OCTOBER** — JAPAN
Prime Minister Toshiki Kaifu announces he will not stand for re-election of the ruling Liberal Democratic Party.

**13 OCTOBER** — TAIWAN
The Democratic Progressive Party, Taiwan's leading opposition party, says it will seek independence for the island.

**14 OCTOBER** — BURMA
Dissident leader Aung San Suu Kyi awarded the Nobel Peace Prize.

**23 OCTOBER** — CAMBODIA
A peace agreement officially ending the country's 13-year civil war signed in Paris.

**27 OCTOBER** — JAPAN
Kiichi Miyazawa elected president of the Liberal Democratic Party and becomes the country's prime minister.

**4 NOVEMBER** — PHILIPPINES
Imelda Marcos returns to the country, and faces seven counts of tax evasion.

**5 NOVEMBER** — PHILIPPINES
Up to 8,000 die during flash floods in Ormoc City, Leyte Island, in one of the worst natural disasters to hit the country this century.

**9 NOVEMBER** — HONGKONG
Colony resumes the mandatory repatriation of Vietnamese boat people.

**12 NOVEMBER** — INDONESIA
More than 100 people said to have been killed when troops fire at demonstrators in the East Timor capital Dili. Jakarta put the death toll at 19.

**17 NOVEMBER** — CHINA
US Secretary of State James Baker fails to get any human-rights concessions from Peking during a visit.

**27 NOVEMBER** — CAMBODIA
A mob nearly kills Khmer Rouge leader Khieu Samphan within hours of his arrival in Phnom Penh.

Union Insurance Society of Canton
Hong Kong, Philippines

P.T. Maskapai Asuransi – Union
Far East, Indonesia

Guardian Assurance
Hong Kong (Life)

Guardian Royal Exchange (Asia)
Hong Kong

Royal Exchange Assurance
Pakistan, Japan

Guardian Royal Exchange Assurance
(Malaysia) Sendirian Berhad

Guardian Royal Exchange Assurance
Singapore, Taiwan

Union Insurance Society
of Hong Kong

Guardian Assurance Company
Thailand

# We've been called many names in our time.

The history of the Guardian Royal Exchange Assurance Group dates back more than two centuries.

It began in London in 1720 with the formation of Royal Exchange Assurance, and then in 1821 came the Guardian Assurance Company.

In 1835 the Union Insurance Society of Canton was formed in China and it also went on to establish a world-wide insurance network.

The merger of these three companies in the 1960's resulted in what is today one of the world's largest insurance groups.

Arising out of these international interests GRE (Asia) was formed. Today the Group in Asia offers experience, stability and commitment to some of the world's most rapidly expanding economies.

**Guardian
Royal Exchange
Assurance**

A good name to insure with.